The Individual Investor's Guide to No-Load Mutual Funds
Eighth Edition

The Individual Investor's Guide to No-Load Mutual Funds

Eighth Edition

American Association of Individual Investors

International Publishing Corporation
Chicago

The American Association of Individual Investors is an independent, non-profit corporation formed for the purpose of assisting individuals in becoming effective managers of their own assets through programs of education, information and research.

ISBN 0-942641-21-3
Library of Congress Catalog Card Number: 89-83749

Published by: International Publishing Corporation

Data in this guide were gathered from company releases. Factual material is not guaranteed but has been obtained from sources believed to be reliable.

Preface

Important additions—some major, some minor—mark the eighth edition of the *No-Load Fund Guide*. The markets are ever-changing, and the mutual fund industry is rapidly evolving in an environment of product and regulatory innovation. The *Guide* should be as dynamic as the investment opportunities it describes and responsive to the individual investors it serves.

Here are the additions:

- This year's *Guide* includes low-load funds that have a load of 1% or less and do not have annual 12b-1 plan charges. Some funds have elected to charge a small one-time load rather than an annual 12b-1 charge, and these funds may cost the investor less than no-load funds with high annual 12b-1 charges.
- Within the full-page fund data section, we now give full coverage to closed funds. This will allow investors in those funds to more easily follow the performance of the fund. It also allows potential investors to make an informed investment decision if the fund reopens, an increasingly common event.
- On the individual fund data pages, we now include the "ratio of net income to average net assets." This statistic is similar to a dividend yield, and informs investors about the relative amount of income generated by the fund.
- On the individual fund data pages, we now include the name of the portfolio manager and when the manager started with the fund. This provides more information for investors to judge the relevance of historical performance.
- The individual fund data pages include the ticker symbol of the fund. This will be helpful for investors who want to access data from various on-line computer services.

In order to make room for this new information, we have eliminated two statistics from the data pages: net investment income and net gains (losses) on investments. Under the new tax laws, the first data item is virtually equivalent to dividends from net investment income. In addition, the net gains are not as important as the distributions from net realized capital gains; net gains can be closely approximated by the difference between the beginning and ending net asset values plus the capital gains distribution.

One other change is our coverage of beta, a measure of risk. Beta has always been less meaningful and may be misleading for bond and precious metals funds. Therefore, we no longer calculate beta for these funds. Beta is most useful for diversified common stock mutual funds, and we continue to supply this statistic for them.

In this eighth edition of the *Guide* we cover 436 mutual funds. There are 47 more funds covered this year, and 423 have comprehensive share data, performance figures, and fund descriptions. Thirteen funds were new and made the NASD listings in 1988 but did not have a full year of operations; they are described in the New Funds section.

Looking back at 1988, you will no doubt recall the feelings of uncertainty about financial markets as well as the economy. Market analysts, the media, newsletter writers, economists, and money managers often expressed divergent views; market pessimism was commonplace. The market, however ignored this—as it often does—and performed exceptionally well. The experiences of 1987 and 1988 highlight the value of diversification among and within asset categories, and support the usefulness of long-term investment plans. Not only is picking individual funds important, but putting together a portfolio of funds that matches your risk tolerance, tax status, liquidity, income, and investment horizon is paramount.

The *Guide* has gathered for you the information you will need to make well-informed decisions on your mutual fund investments. Our goal, as always, is to provide pertinent information, organized to minimize the time spent collecting and comparing information on the ever-increasing number of mutual fund investment opportunities. Your time can be well spent on selecting and monitoring individual funds and building an appropriate and successful investment portfolio.

The data for this *Guide* is gathered from each fund's prospectus, annual report, and from direct contact with each fund. We calculate all performance and risk statistics, and then ask each fund to verify our information. Our standard is full, accurate disclosure of investment alternatives. The ultimate investment choice remains with you, the individual investor.

All the data collection activities and the risk and performance statistics were the responsibility of William H. Anderson Jr., financial analyst for AAII. Marie Anderson, research assistant, contacted funds and collected data. Maria Crawford Scott, editor of the *AAII Journal,* along with Jean Henrich, assistant editor, and Martha Crawford, editorial assistant, provided editorial guidance and support.

Chicago
June 1989

John Markese, Ph.D.
Vice President
Director of Research

Table of Contents

Introduction

A mutual fund is an open-end investment company that pools investors' money to invest in securities. It is open-end because it continuously issues new shares when investors want to invest in the fund, and it redeems shares when investors want to sell. A mutual fund trades directly with its shareholders, and the share price of the fund represents the market value of the securities that the fund holds.

There are several advantages that mutual funds offer individual investors. They provide:

- Professional investment management at a low cost,
- A diversified group of securities that only a large portfolio can provide,
- Information through prospectuses and annual reports that facilitates comparisons among funds,
- Special services such as checkwriting, dividend reinvestment plans, telephone switching and periodic withdrawal and investment plans.
- Recordkeeping statements that make it easy to track the value of one's own holdings and that ease the paperwork at tax time.

Many individuals feel that they can achieve better results by investing their money directly in stocks rather than in mutual funds. Whether or not this is true for you is a question only you can answer. If you can do better than the average mutual fund over a relatively long time period, then individual stock selection makes financial sense. The next question is, can you do it as efficiently? Successful investing takes time and effort. Investors must spend a considerable amount of energy searching for opportunities and monitoring each investment.

Professional investment management is relatively cheap with mutual funds. The typical advisor charges about 0.5% annually for managing a fund's assets. For an individual making a $10,000 investment, that comes to only $50 a year. If you value your time highly, your money might be well spent by paying someone else to do the work.

Of course, mutual fund investing does not preclude investing in securities on your own. One useful strategy would be to invest in mutual funds and individual securities. The mutual funds would ensure your participation in overall market moves and lend diversification to your portfolio, while the individual securities would provide you with the opportunity to beat the market by applying your investment analysis skills.

Diversification

If there is one ingredient to successful investing that is universally agreed upon, it is the benefit of diversification. The concept is so commonsensical that it is a piece of folk wisdom: "Don't put all your eggs in one basket." It is also a concept that is backed by a great deal of research and market experience.

The benefit that diversification provides is risk reduction. Risk to investors is frequently defined as volatility of return—in other words, by how much each year an investment's returns might vary. Investors prefer returns that are relatively predictable, and thus less volatile. On the other hand, they want returns that are high. Diversification eliminates some of the risk, without reducing potential returns.

Mutual funds, because of their size and the laws governing their operation, provide investors with a significant amount of diversification that might be difficult for an individual to duplicate. This is true not only for common stock funds, but also for bond funds, municipal bond funds, gold funds, international funds—in fact, for almost all mutual funds. Even the sector funds offer diversification within an industry. The degree of diversification will vary among funds, but most will provide investors with some amount of diversification.

Why No-Loads?

This book is dedicated primarily to no-load mutual funds. Investors should realize that:

- A load is a sales commission that goes to whoever sells fund shares to an investor;
- A load does not go to anyone responsible for managing the fund's assets, and does not serve as an incentive for the fund manager to perform better;

- Funds with loads, on average, consistently underperform no-load funds when the load is taken into consideration in performance calculations;
- For every high-performing load fund, there exists a similar no-load fund that can be purchased instead;
- Loads understate the real commission charged because they reduce the total amount being invested: $10,000 invested in an 8.5% front-end load fund results in an $850 sales charge and only a $9,150 investment in the fund. The load actually represents 9.3% of the net funds invested;
- If a load fund is held over a long time period, the effect of the load, if paid up front, is not diminished as quickly as many people believe; had that money been working for you, as in a no-load fund, it would have been compounding over the whole time period.

The bottom line in any investment is how it performs for you, the investor, and that performance includes consideration of all loads, fees, and expenses. There may be some load funds that will do better even factoring in the load, but you have no way of finding that fund in advance. The only guide you have is historical performance, which is not necessarily an indication of future performance. With a heavily loaded fund, you are starting your investment with a significant loss—the load. Minimize any unnecessary charges whenever possible.

Sorting Out Charges

Although it is best to stick with no-load funds, they are becoming more difficult to distinguish from load funds. Full front-end load funds have declined in popularity, and some are now turning to other kinds of charges. Some mutual funds sold by brokerage firms, for example, have lowered their loads to 4%, and others have introduced back-end loads—sales commissions paid when exiting the fund. In both instances, the load is often accompanied by 12b-1 annual charges.

On the other hand, some no-load funds have found that to compete, they must market themselves much more aggressively. To do so, they have introduced charges of their own.

The result has been the introduction of low loads, redemption fees and 12b-1 plan annual charges. Very low loads—1%—are sometimes added rather than the annual charges. In addition, some funds have instituted a charge for investing or withdrawing money, but the charge reverts to the fund and its shareholders.

Redemption fees work just like back-end loads: You pay when you get out. Some funds have sliding scale redemption fees, so that the longer you remain invested, the lower the charge when you leave. Some funds use redemption fees to discourage short-term trading, a policy that is designed to protect longer-term investors. These funds, by and large, have redemption fees that disappear after six months.

The most confusing charge involves the 12b-1 plan. The adoption of a 12b-1 plan by a fund permits the advisor to use fund assets to pay for distribution costs, including advertising, distribution of fund literature such as prospectuses and annual reports, and sales commissions paid to brokers. Some funds use 12b-1 plans as masked load charges: They levy very high rates on the fund, and use the money to pay brokers to sell the fund. Since the charge is annual and based on the value of the investment, this can result in a total cost to a long-term investor that exceeds the old 8.5% up-front sales load, yet it allows the fund to be classified as a no-load. Other funds use money from 12b-1 plans to pay only distribution costs, and still others have 12b-1 plans but don't use them to levy charges against fund assets. In some instances, the fund advisor may use the 12b-1 plan to pay distribution expenses from his own pocket. The new fee table now required in all prospectuses clarifies the impact of a 12b-1 plan.

In this guide, we include mutual funds that have 12b-1 plans if there is no front-end or back-end load or any redemption fee that continues beyond six months. We also include a few funds that have no more than a 1% load but have no 12b-1 charge. For some of the funds with 12b-1 plans, however, the charges may be equivalent to substantial loads. How can you analyze this?

One solution is to convert the annual percentage 12b-1 charge into an approximately equivalent front-end load. Figure 1 allows you to do that. For instance, a 0.25% annual 12b-1 charge is equivalent to a 1% front-end load, if you remain invested in the fund for four years; a 1.25% annual 12b-1 charge is equivalent to an astronomical 12.50% front-end load if you remain invested in the fund for 10 years. The comparison depends upon an assumed investment time horizon and investment growth rate, since 12b-1 charges are levied annually on the total value of the mutual fund. We have included

Figure 1
Front-End Equivalent of 12b-1 Charges

Holding Period (Years)	If the annual 12b-1 charge is:					
	0.10%	0.25%	0.50%	0.75%	1.00%	1.25%
	The front-end load equivalent would be:					
1	0.10%	0.25%	0.50%	0.75%	1.00%	1.25%
2	0.20	0.50	1.00	1.50	2.00	2.50
3	0.30	0.75	1.50	2.25	3.00	3.75
4	0.40	1.00	2.00	3.00	4.00	5.00
5	0.50	1.25	2.50	3.75	5.00	6.25
10	1.00	2.50	5.00	7.50	10.00	12.50
20	2.00	5.00	10.00	15.00	20.00	25.00
30	3.00	7.50	15.00	22.50	30.00	37.50

a variety of time horizons in the table, and investors must make their own assumptions.

Remember, too, that the bottom line in analyzing charges is total expenses. The 12b-1 charge is included in the "ratio of expenses to net assets" figure; a fund with a 12b-1 charge may have a lower expense ratio than a fund without a 12b-1 charge.

The introduction of fee tables, required by the SEC in all mutual fund prospectuses, makes the comparison of total expenses among funds easier. Chapter 2 describes this table in detail. Selecting a fund based solely on expenses, including loads and charges, will not give you optimal results, but avoiding funds with high expenses is important for long-term performance.

The decision as to what constitutes a significant load is difficult, but we took this approach in the guide:

- All funds with front-end or back-end loads were excluded, unless the load was less than 1%, and funds with significant redemption fees were excluded if the fee did not disappear after six months.
- Funds with 12b-1 plans were included in the guide; we note, however, if the fund has a 12b-1 plan and what the maximum annual charge is. Investors should assess these plans individually and carefully.

Investing in Mutual Funds

Selecting a mutual fund, while less time-consuming than investing in individual securities, does require some homework. No individual should put money into an investment that he does not understand. This does not require a detailed investigation of the fund's investments, but it does require some understanding of the possible risks involved along with the possible returns.

This guide is designed to provide you with that understanding. We have kept the chapters brief and to the point, so that individuals new to mutual fund investing will not be overwhelmed with unnecessary details. Those who are familiar with mutual funds may want to skip directly to Chapters 4 and 5, which describe how to use this guide most effectively.

In **Chapter 1,** we provide you with an overview of the kinds of mutual funds that are available. We have divided them into categories based on shared characteristics, primarily investment objective. The category will provide a generalized guide to the kinds of investments the fund will make, and the riskiness of the fund.

In **Chapter 2,** we describe the information that is provided by the mutual fund. Much of this information is "must reading" for the mutual fund investor, and you need to have an idea of what to look for, where to look for it and what it means.

Chapter 3 gives recordkeeping hints, as well as some things to keep in mind regarding the tax treatment of mutual funds.

Chapter 4 provides a framework for establishing a mutual fund portfolio. It is really the heart of your investment decisions, and it describes an approach that will allow you to construct a portfolio of mutual funds that will fit your investment needs. It is an approach that takes into consideration your risk tolerance, and it is what we have structured the statistical section around.

Finally, **Chapter 5** presents an explanation of the performance data and the information on the individual fund data pages. It also provides a key to the statistical section of the data pages, including a guide to the abbreviations used.

Once you are familiar with mutual funds and the systematic approach to analyzing and forming a mutual fund portfolio that we have suggested, you will want to take a look at the summaries of historical performance in **Chapter 6.** While past performance is no indication of the future, it may indicate the quality and consistency of fund management. From this section, you should pick out several mutual funds that meet your investment objectives and risk tolerance. These funds can be examined more closely in the full-page fund data pages in **Chapter 7.** Call or write the funds to get a copy of the prospectus and annual report, and make sure you read the prospectus carefully before investing in any mutual fund. Information on tax-exempt bond funds can be found in the half-page data pages in **Chapter 8.**

No-load mutual funds that started in 1988 are listed in the New Funds section at the back of this guide. Also at the back is a list of funds that are reported as "no-loads" by the financial press but that did not meet our criteria and are thus not included in this book. And, we have provided a list at the back of the guide of fund families that are primarily no-load and have two or more funds. We have listed all of the funds in each family in this section, including any load funds.

1

Mutual Fund Categories

Mutual funds come in all shapes and sizes; there are well over 400 funds covered in this book alone, each with its own characteristics. Many mutual funds have similar investment objectives, however. These shared investment objectives generally lead to other characteristics that are similar, particularly as measured by long-term returns and risk in terms of volatility of return.

These shared characteristics allow us to divide mutual funds into several broad categories. This chapter defines the mutual fund categories we used for this book. Figure 1-1 indicates the financial characteristics of the different fund categories. In this book, the individual fund data pages appear alphabetically; however, the fund's category is indicated beneath the fund's name.

Aggressive Growth Funds

The investment objective of aggressive growth funds is maximum capital gains. They invest aggressively in common stocks and tend

Figure 1-1
Characteristics of Mutual Funds by Investment Objective*

Fund Objective	1987 Return (%)	5-Year Return (%)	Bear Market Return† (%)	Bull Market Return‡ (%)	Risk (Beta)
Aggressive Growth.....	(2.3)	47.1	(26.0)	56.7	1.11
Growth........................	1.0	67.6	(22.1)	64.5	0.93
Growth & Income......	(0.4)	80.2	(20.1)	60.5	0.80
Balanced....................	(0.3)	98.7	(14.7)	54.9	0.61
Bond..........................	1.1	68.5	1.9	26.7	0.08
Tax-Exempt Bond......	(0.9)	63.4	0.2	20.0	0.13
International..............	10.8	167.8	(15.3)	125.7	0.67
Precious Metals..........	28.5	28.9	(25.2)	171.9	0.48
S&P 500.....................	5.2	113.2	(24.3)	144.7	1.00

*For all funds covered in this guide for time period ending December 31, 1987. Returns include reinvestment of distributions.
†September 1, 1987 through December 31, 1987.
‡August 1, 1984 through August 31, 1987.

Aggressive Growth Funds

The investment objective of aggressive growth funds is maximum capital gains. They invest aggressively in common stocks and tend to stay fully invested over the market cycle. Sometimes, these funds will use leverage (borrowed funds), and some may engage in trading stock options or take positions in stock index futures.

Aggressive growth funds typically provide low income distributions. This is because they tend to be fully invested in common stocks and do not earn a significant amount of interest income. In addition, the common stocks they invest in are generally growth-oriented stocks that pay low or no cash dividends.

Many aggressive growth funds concentrate their assets in particular industries or segments of the market, and their degree of diversification may not be as great as other types of funds. These investment strategies result in increased risk. Thus, they tend to perform better than the overall market during bull markets, but fare worse during bear markets.

In general, long-term investors who need not be concerned with monthly or yearly variation in investment return will find investment in this class of funds rewarding. Because of the extreme volatility of return, however, risk-averse investors with a short-term investment horizon may find that these funds lie well outside their comfort zones. The riskiness of these funds can be offset by a greater allocation of an investor's total assets to a relatively risk-free investment, such as a money market fund (this portfolio strategy is further described in Chapter 4 in the section on risk). During prolonged market declines, aggressive growth funds can sustain severe declines in net asset value.

Market timing is not a strategy we recommend, particularly over the short term. Although the transaction costs of switching in and out of no-load mutual funds are near zero, it can create significant tax liabilities. In addition, the ability to consistently time the market correctly in the short term, after adjusting for risk, costs and taxes, has not been demonstrated. However, aggressive growth funds, with their high volatility and fully invested position, do make ideal vehicles for those who believe they possess the insight to guess the next market move. The investment strategy would be to invest in aggressive growth funds during up markets, and to switch to money market funds during down markets.

Growth Funds

The investment objective of growth funds is to obtain long-term growth of invested capital. They generally do not engage in speculative tactics such as using financial leverage. On occasion, these funds will use stock or index options to reduce risk by hedging their portfolio positions.

Growth funds typically are more stable than aggressive growth funds. Generally, they invest in growth-oriented firms that are older, larger, and that pay cash dividends. You are likely to find companies such as IBM, Pepsico and McDonald's in the portfolios of growth funds. The degree of concentration of assets is not as severe as with aggressive growth funds. Additionally, these funds tend to move from fully invested to partially invested positions over the market cycle. They build up cash positions during uncertain market environments.

In general, growth fund performance tends to mirror the market during bull and bear markets. Some growth funds have been able to perform relatively well during recent bear markets because their managers were able to change portfolio composition by a much greater degree or to maintain much higher cash positions than aggressive growth fund managers. However, higher cash positions can also cause the funds to underperform aggressive growth funds during bull markets.

Aggressive investors should consider holding both growth fund shares and aggressive growth fund shares in their overall portfolios. This is an especially appealing strategy for investors who hold aggressive growth mutual funds that invest in small stock growth firms. The portfolios of these funds complement the portfolios of growth funds, leading to greater overall diversification. The combination produces overall returns that will tend to be less volatile than an investment in only aggressive growth funds.

As with the aggressive growth funds, these funds can sustain severe declines during prolonged bear markets. Since some portfolio managers of growth funds attempt to time the market over the longer market cycle, using these funds to move in and out of the market for timing purposes may be counterproductive.

Growth and Income Funds

Growth and income funds generally invest in the common stocks and convertible securities of seasoned, well-established, cash-dividend-paying companies. The funds attempt to provide shareholders with significant income along with long-term growth. They generally attempt to avoid excessive fluctuations in return. One tends to find a high concentration of public utility common stocks and sometimes corporate convertible bonds in the portfolios of growth and income funds. The funds also provide higher income distributions, less variability in return, and greater diversification than growth and aggressive growth funds. Names such as equity-income, income, and total return have been attached to funds that have characteristics of growth and income funds.

Because of the high current income offered by these kinds of funds, potential investors should keep the tax consequences in mind. Remember that, although capital gains are now taxed at the same rate as income, it is always an effective tax strategy to defer paying taxes whenever possible. The distributions from these funds are frequent and are fully taxable in the year paid. High tax bracket individuals should consider investing in these kinds of funds by using IRAs, Keoghs, 401(k)s and other pension plans.

Balanced Funds

The balanced fund category has become less distinct in recent years, and a significant overlap in fund objectives exists between growth and income funds and balanced funds. In general, the portfolios of balanced funds consist of investments in common stocks and substantial investments in bonds and convertible bonds. The proportion of stocks and bonds that will be held is usually stated in the investment objective, but it may vary over time. Balanced funds are generally less volatile than aggressive growth, growth, and growth and income funds.

As with growth and income funds, balanced funds provide a high dividend yield. Similarly, high tax bracket investors who want to invest in these funds should consider using tax-sheltered money.

Bond Funds and Tax-Exempt Bond Funds

Bond mutual funds, not surprisingly, invest in bonds. They are attractive to bond investors because they provide diversification and liquidity, which is not as readily available in direct bond investments.

Bond funds hold various kinds of fixed-income securities in their portfolios. Some specialize in municipal bond issues; others invest in only U.S. government bonds or agency issues, such as Ginnie Maes. Still others invest in corporate bonds. "High yield" bond funds invest in lower-rated corporate and municipal bonds that have a higher default risk and that must offer higher yields to compensate for the greater risk. These funds are commonly referred to as "junk" bond funds.

Bond funds have portfolios with a wide range of average maturities. Many funds use their names to characterize their maturity structure. Generally, short term means that the portfolio has a weighted average maturity of less than three years. Intermediate implies an average maturity of three to 10 years, and long term is over 10 years. The longer the maturity, the greater the change in fund value when interest rates change. Longer-term bond funds are riskier than shorter-term funds, and they tend to offer higher yields.

Since bond funds can (and do) provide investors with diversification, investors should invest in funds that are large. Large bond funds hold many more bond issues than do smaller funds, and as a result of sliding scale management fees, they tend to charge a lower percentage fee. Additionally, the expenses of large bond funds are low on a relative basis.

Bond funds that hold principally corporate or U.S. government debt obligations appear among the regular fund data listings in this book. Tax-exempt bond funds, which invest in municipal bonds, are in a separate section following the regular fund listings. Tax-exempt bond funds are similar in structure to other bond funds, but are sometimes very specialized tax shelter vehicles—state-specific tax-exempt funds are an example.

Precious Metals Funds

Precious metals mutual funds specialize in investments in both foreign and domestic companies that mine gold and other precious metals. Some funds also hold gold directly through investments in gold coins or bullion. Gold options are another method used to invest in the industry. Mutual fund investments in precious metals range from the conservative to the highly speculative.

Gold and precious metals mutual funds offer advantages similar to bond funds: They allow investors interested in this area to invest in a more liquid and diversified vehicle than would be available through a direct purchase.

The appeal of gold and precious metals is that they have performed well during extreme inflationary periods. Over the short term, the price of gold moves in response to a variety of political, economic and psychological forces. As world tension and anxiety rise, so does the price of gold. In periods of peace and stability, the price of gold declines. Because gold tends to perform in an inverse relationship to stocks, bonds, and cash, it can be used as a stabilizing component in one's portfolio. Silver and platinum react in a fashion similar to gold. Precious metals funds, like the metals themselves, are very volatile, often shooting from the bottom to the top and back to the bottom in fund rankings over the years. Investors should understand, however, that because most gold funds invest in the stock of gold mining companies, they are still subject to some stock market risk.

International Funds

International funds invest in securities of firms located in different countries. Some funds specialize in regions, such as the Pacific or Europe, and others invest worldwide. In addition, some funds—usually termed "global funds"—invest in both foreign and U.S. stocks.

International funds provide investors with added diversification. The most important factor when diversifying a portfolio is selecting assets that do not behave similarly to each other under similar economic scenarios. Within the U.S., investors can diversify by selecting securities of firms in different industries. In the international realm, investors take the diversification process one step further by holding securities of firms in different countries. The more independently these foreign markets move in relation to the U.S. market, the greater will be the diversification potential for the U.S. investor, and ultimately, the lower his risk.

In addition, international funds overcome some of the difficulties investors would face in making foreign investments directly. For instance, individuals would have to thoroughly understand the foreign brokerage process, be familiar with the various foreign marketplaces and their economies, be aware of currency fluctuation trends, and have access to reliable financial information. This can be a monumental task for the individual investor.

There are some risks to investing internationally. In addition to the risk inherent in investing in any security, there is an additional exchange rate risk. The return to a U.S. investor from a foreign security depends on both the security's return in its own currency and the rate at which that currency can be exchanged for U.S. dollars. Another uncertainty is political risk, which includes government restriction, taxation, or even total prohibition of the exchange of one currency into another. Of course, the more the mutual fund is diversified among various countries, the less the risk involved.

Other Funds

There are many specialized mutual funds that do not have their own categories. Instead, they will be found in one of the various categories mentioned above. These funds are classified here by their investment objectives rather than by their investment strategies. For instance, several funds specialize in specific industries, but one industry-specific fund does not necessarily appear in the same category as another industry-specific fund. Other specialized funds that may appear in various categories include the option-income funds, the "socially conscious" funds, funds designed solely for tax-sheltered plans, and geographically specific funds.

Asset allocation funds are relatively new and have garnered media attention lately. The term asset allocation, however, has two distinct meanings for fund management. Some allocation funds are designed to provide diversification among the various categories of investments and within each category. For example, an asset allocation fund may hold minimum percentages in stocks, bonds, cash and international investments. The second meaning given to asset allocation by some funds is that money will be moved around according to what the fund managers believe to be optimal proportions given expectations for the economy, interest rates and other market factors. These latter asset allocation funds are market timing funds, distinctly different and with greater risk than the asset allocation funds striving for diversification.

One other fund category deserves a special mention—the index fund. An example of an index fund is Vanguard's Index Trust 500, categorized as a growth and income fund. This fund was designed to match the Standard & Poor's 500 stock index, and does so by investing in all 500 stocks in the S&P 500; the amounts invested in each stock are proportional to the firm's market value representation in the S&P 500. Statistics on this fund are quite useful for comparison with other funds, since it is a representation of the market.

2

Understanding
Mutual Fund Statements

One of the advantages of mutual fund investing is the wealth of information that must be provided to fund investors and prospective investors. Taken together, the various reports provide investors with vital information concerning financial matters and how the fund is managed, both key elements in the selection process. In fact, mutual fund prospectuses, along with performance statistics, are the only sources of information most investors will need in the selection process.

To new mutual fund investors, the information may seem overwhelming. However, regulations governing the industry have standardized the reports: Once you know where to look for information, the location will hold true for almost all funds.

There are basically five types of statements produced by the mutual fund: the prospectus; the Statement of Additional Information; annual, semiannual and quarterly reports; marketing brochures; and account statements. Actually, the second report—the Statement of Additional Information—is part of the prospectus. However, the Securities and Exchange Commission has allowed mutual funds to simplify and streamline the prospectus, if they choose, by dividing it into two parts: Part A, which all prospective investors must receive, and Part B—the Statement of Additional Information—which the fund must send investors if they specifically request it. In practice, when most people (including the funds) refer to the prospectus, they are referring to Part A. For simplicity, that is what we will do here, as well.

The Prospectus

The prospectus is the single most important document produced by the mutual fund, and it is must reading for investors before investing. By law, prospective investors must receive a prospectus before the fund can accept initial share purchases. In addition, current shareholders must receive new prospectuses when they are updated, at least once every fourteen months.

The prospectus is generally organized into sections, and although it must cover specific topics, the overall structure may differ somewhat among funds. The cover usually gives a quick synopsis of the fund: investment objective, sales or redemption charges, minimum investment, retirement plans available, address, and telephone number. More detailed descriptions are in the body of the prospectus.

Fee Table: Under a recent Securities and Exchange Commission ruling, all mutual fund prospectuses must include a table near the front that delineates all fees and charges to the investor. The table contains three sections: The first section lists all transaction charges to the investor, including all front-end and back-end loads and redemption fees; the second section lists all annual fund operating expenses, including management fees and any 12b-1 charges, as a percentage of net assets; and the third section is an illustration of the total cost of these fees and charges to an investor over time. The illustration assumes an initial investment of $1,000 and a 5% growth rate for the fund, and states the total dollar cost to an investor if he were to redeem his shares at the end of one year, three years, five years and 10 years. An example of a fee table is shown in Figure 2-1.

Condensed Financial Information: One of the most important sections of the prospectus contains the condensed financial information, which provides statistics on income and capital changes per share of the fund (an example is shown in Figure 2-2). The per-share figures are given for the life of the fund or 10 years, whichever is less. Also included are important statistical summaries of investment activities throughout each period. Occasionally these financial statements are only referred to in the prospectus and are actually contained in the annual report, which in this instance would accompany the prospectus.

The per-share section summarizes the financial activity over the year to arrive at the end-of-year net asset value for the fund. The financial activity summarized includes increases in net asset value due to dividend and interest payments received and capital gains from investment activity. Decreases in net asset value are due to

Figure 2-1
The Prospectus Fee Table: An Example

Fund Expenses

The following table illustrates **all** expenses and fees that a shareholder of the Fund will incur and is intended to assist you in understanding the various costs and expenses that an investor in the Fund will bear, directly or indirectly. The expenses and fees set forth in the table are for the 1987 fiscal year.

Shareholder Transaction Expenses

Sales Load Imposed on Purchases	None
Sales Load Imposed on Reinvested Dividends	None
Redemption Fees(a)	None
Exchange Fees	None

Annual Fund Operating Expenses

Management Fees	0.67%
12b-1 Fees	None
Other Expenses	0.15%
Total Fund Operating Expenses	0.82%

(a) A redemption fee of 2% of the redemption price is imposed on shares held less than 60 days.

The following example illustrates the expenses that you would pay on a $1,000 investment over various time periods assuming (1) a 5% annual rate of return, (2) the same operating expense percentage that the Fund experienced in the past fiscal year, (3) reinvestment of all dividends and capital gain distributions and (4) redemption at the end of each time period.

1 year	3 years	5 years	10 years
$8	$26	$46	$101

This example should not be considered a representation of past or future expenses or performance. Actual expenses may be greater or less than those shown.

Source: Acorn Fund prospectus; April 30, 1988.

capital losses from investment activity, investment expenses and payouts to fund shareholders in the form of distributions.

Potential investors may want to note the line items in this section. *Investment income* represents the dividends and interest earned by the fund during its fiscal year. *Expenses* reflect such fund costs as the management fee, legal fees, transfer agent fees and the like. These expenses are given in detail in the statement of operations section of the annual report. *Net investment income* is investment income less expenses. This line is important for investors to note because it reflects the level and stability of net income over the time period. A high net investment income would most likely be found in funds that have income rather than growth as their investment objective. Since net investment income must be distributed to shareholders to avoid direct taxation of the fund, a high net investment income has the potential of translating into a high tax liability for the investor.

Net realized and unrealized gain (loss) on investments is the change in the value of investments that have been sold during the year or that continue to be held by the fund.

Distributions to fund shareholders are also detailed. These distributions will include dividends from net investment income from

Figure 2-2
The Condensed Financial Information Statement: An Example

	Year Ended December 31,									
	1978	1979	1980	1981	1982	1983	1984	1985	1986	1987
Net Asset Value, Beginning of Period	$13.01	$13.11	$14.64	$17.84	$15.52	$17.56	$19.70	$19.52	$22.99	$24.27
Investment Activities										
Income	.69	.79	.89	.90	.89	.93	.93	.97	.96	.95
Expenses	(.04)	(.04)	(.06)	(.07)	(.06)	(.06)	(.05)	(.06)	(.07)	(.07)
Net Investment Income	.65	.75	.83	.83	.83	.87	.88	.91	.89	.88
Net Realized and Unrealized Gain (Loss) on Investments	.10	1.59	3.73	(1.76)	2.29	2.85	.30	5.08	3.30	.36
Total from Investment Activities	.75	2.34	4.56	(.93)	3.12	3.72	1.18	5.99	4.19	1.24
Distributions										
Net Investment Income	(.65)	(.75)	(.83)	(.83)	(.83)	(.87)	(.88)	(.91)	(.89)	(.69)
Realized Net Gain	—	(.06)	(.53)	(.56)	(.25)	(.71)	(.48)	(1.61)	(2.02)	(.17)
Total Distributions	(.65)	(.81)	(1.36)	(1.39)	(1.08)	(1.58)	(1.36)	(2.52)	(2.91)	(.86)
Net Asset Value, End of Period	$13.11	$14.64	$17.84	$15.52	$17.56	$19.70	$19.52	$22.99	$24.27	$24.65
Ratio of Expenses to Average Net Assets	.36%[1]	.30%[1]	.35%	.42%	.39%	.28%	.27%	.28%	.28%	.26%
Ratio of Net Investment Income to Average Net Assets	5.43%	5.28%	5.05%	4.91%	5.38%	4.22%	4.53%	4.09%	3.40%	3.15%
Portfolio Turnover Rate	8%	29%	18%	12%	11%	35%	14%	36%	29%	15%
Shares Outstanding, End of Period (thousands)	5,046	5,395	5,535	5,879	6,266	11,861	14,841	17,148	19,984	33,527

[1] Includes .06% and .04% representing amortization of deferred organization and offering expenses for the years ended December 31, 1978 and 1979, respectively.

Source: Vanguard Index Trust 500 prospectus; May 1, 1988.

the current fiscal period. The new tax law requires that all income earned must be distributed in the calendar year earned. Also included in distributions will be any realized net capital gains.

The last line in the per-share section will be the *net asset value* at the end of the year, which reflects the value of one share of the fund. It is calculated by determining the total assets of the fund and dividing by the number of mutual fund shares outstanding. The figure will change for a variety of reasons, including changes in investment income, expenses, gains, losses and distributions. Depending upon the source of change, a decline in net asset value may or may not be due to poor performance. For instance, a decline in net asset value may be due to a significant distribution of realized gains on securities.

The selected financial ratios at the bottom of the per-share financial data are important indicators of fund performance and strategy. The *expense ratio* relates expenses incurred by the fund to average net assets. These expenses include the investment advisory fee, legal and accounting fees, and 12b-1 charges to the fund; they do not include brokerage fees, loads, or redemption fees. A high expense ratio detracts from your investment return. In general, common stock funds have higher expense ratios than bond funds, and smaller funds have higher expense ratios than larger funds. The average for common stock funds is 1.4%, and for bond funds about 1.1%. An expense ratio above 1.5% is high, and funds with expense ratios above 2.0% should be carefully scrutinized.

The *ratio of net investment income to average net assets* is very similar to a dividend yield. This, too, should reflect the investment objective of the fund. Common stock funds with income as part of their investment objective would be expected to have a ratio of about 3% under current market conditions, and aggressive growth funds would have a ratio closer to 0%. Bond funds would have ratios normally more than twice those of common stock funds.

The *portfolio turnover rate* is the lower of purchases or sales divided by average net assets. It reflects how frequently securities are bought and sold by the fund. For purposes of determining the turnover rate for common stock funds, fixed-income securities with a maturity of less than a year are excluded, as are all government securities, short- and long-term. For bond funds, however, long-term U.S. government bonds are included.

Investors should take note of the portfolio turnover rate, because the higher the turnover, the greater the brokerage costs incurred by the fund. Brokerage costs are not reflected in the expense ratio but instead are directly reflected in a decrease in net asset value. In addition, funds with high turnover rates generally have higher capital gains distributions, which are taxed in the year of distribution. Aggressive growth mutual funds are most likely to have high turnover rates. Some bond funds also have very high portfolio turnover rates. A 100% portfolio turnover rate indicates that securities in the portfolio have been held for one year on average; a 200% portfolio turnover indicates that securities on average have been traded every six months. The portfolio turnover rate for the average mutual fund is around 100%, but varies with market conditions.

Investment Objective/Policy: The investment objective section of the prospectus elaborates on the brief sentence or two on the cover. In this section, the fund describes the types of investments it will make—whether it is bonds, stocks, convertible securities, options, etc.—along with some general guidelines as to the proportions these securities will represent in the fund's portfolio. In common stock funds, a statement usually indicates whether it will be oriented toward capital gains or income. In this section, the management will also briefly discuss approaches to market timing, risk assumption, and the anticipated level of portfolio turnover. Some prospectuses may indicate any investment restrictions they have placed on the fund, such as purchasing securities on margin, selling short, concentrating in firms or industries, trading foreign securities, and lending securities; this section may also state the allowable proportions in certain investment categories. The restrictions section is usually given in more detail in the Statement of Additional Information.

Fund Management: The fund management section names the investment advisor and gives the advisory fee schedule. Most advisors charge a management fee on a sliding scale that decreases as assets under management increase. Occasionally, some portion of the fund advisor's fees are subject to the fund's performance relative to the market.

Some prospectuses will describe the fund's officers and directors, with a short biography of affiliations and relevant experience. For most funds, however, this information is provided in more detail in the Statement of Additional Information. The board of directors is elected by fund shareholders; the fund advisor is selected by the board of directors. The advisor is usually a firm operated by or affiliated with officers of the fund. Information on fund officers and directors is not critical to fund selection. Rarely mentioned in either the prospectus or the Statement of Additional Information, however, is the portfolio manager for the fund. The portfolio manager is responsible for the day-to-day investment decisions of the fund, and is employed by the fund advisor. Finding out who the portfolio manager is and how long he has been in the position usually requires a telephone call to the fund.

Other Important Sections: There are several other sections in a mutual fund prospectus that investors should be aware of. They will appear under various headings, depending upon the prospectus, but they are not difficult to find.

Mutual funds that have 12b-1 plans must have a description of them in the prospectus. Under new SEC rules, a description of these plans—also known as distribution plans—must be prominently and clearly placed in the prospectus. The distribution plan details the marketing aspects of the fund and how it relates to fund expenses. For instance, advertising, distribution of fund literature, and any arrangements with brokers would be included in the marketing plan; the 12b-1 plan pays for these distribution expenses. Sometimes, these plans do not charge the fund for the expenses but rather allow the advisor to pay for them. The actual cost to the fund of a 12b-1 plan will also be listed at the front of the prospectus in the fee table.

The capital stock, or fund share characteristics section, provides shareholders with a summary of their voting rights, participation in dividends and distributions, and the number of authorized and issued shares of the fund. Often, a separate section will discuss the tax treatment that will apply to fund distributions, which may include dividends, interest and capital gains.

The how-to-buy-shares section gives the minimum initial investment and any subsequent minimums; it will also list load charges or fees. In addition, information on mail, wire, and telephone purchases is provided, along with distribution reinvestment options, and any automatic withdrawal or retirement options.

The how-to-redeem-shares section discusses telephone, written and wire redemption options, with a special section on signature guarantees and other documents that may be needed. Also detailed are any fees for reinvestment or redemption. Shareholder services are usually outlined here, with emphasis on switching among funds in a family of funds. This will include any fees for switching and any limits on the number of switches allowed.

Statement of Additional Information

This document elaborates on the prospectus. The investment objectives section is more in-depth, with a list and description of investment restrictions. The management section gives brief biographies of directors and officers, and provides the number of fund shares owned beneficially by the officers and directors named. The investment advisor section, while reiterating the major points made in the prospectus, gives all the expense items and contract provisions of the agreement between the advisor and the fund. If the fund has a 12b-1 plan, further details will likely be in the Statement of Additional Information.

Many times, the Statement of Additional Information will include much more information on the tax consequences of mutual fund distributions and investment. Conditions under which withholding for federal income tax will take place are also provided. The fund's financial statements are incorporated by reference to the annual report to shareholders, and generally do not appear in the Statement of Additional Information. Finally, the independent auditors give their opinion on the representativeness of the fund's financial statements.

Annual, Semiannual and Quarterly Reports

All funds must send their shareholders audited annual and semi-annual reports. Mutual funds are allowed to combine their prospectus and annual report; some do this, but many do not.

The annual report describes the fund activities over the past year, and provides a listing of all investments of the fund at market value as of the end of the fiscal year. Sometimes, the cost basis of the investment is also given for each. Looking in-depth at individual securities held by the fund is probably a waste of time. However, it is helpful to be aware of the overall investment categories. For instance, investors should look at the percentage invested in common stocks, bonds, convertible bonds, and any other holdings. In addition, a look at the types of common stocks held and the percentage of fund assets by industry classification gives the investor some indication of how the portfolio will fare in various market environments.

The annual report will also have a balance sheet, which lists all assets and liabilities of the fund by general category. This holds little interest for investors.

The statement of operations, similar to an income statement, is of interest only in that the fund expenses are broken down. For most funds, the management fee is by far the largest expense; the expense ratio in the prospectus conveys much more useful information. The statement of changes in net assets is very close to the financial information provided in the prospectus, but the information is not on a per-share basis. Per-share information will, however, frequently be detailed in the annual report in a separate section. Footnotes to the financial statements elaborate on the entries, but other than any pending litigation against the fund, they are most often routine.

The quarterly or semiannual reports are current accounts of the investment portfolio, and provide more timely views of the fund's investments than does the annual report.

Marketing Brochures and Advertisements

These will generally provide a brief description of the fund. However, the most important bit of information will be the telephone number to call to receive the fund prospectus and annual report, if you have not received them already.

A new SEC ruling has tightened and standardized the rules regarding mutual fund advertising. All mutual funds that use performance figures in their ads must now include one-, three-, five- and 10-year total return figures. Bond funds that quote yields must use a standardized method for computing yield, and they must include total return figures, as well. Finally, any applicable sales commissions must be mentioned in the advertisement.

Account Statements

Mutual funds send out periodic account statements detailing reinvestment of dividend and capital gains distributions, new purchases or redemptions, and any other account activity such as service fees. This statement provides a running account balance by date with share accumulations, account value to date and a total of distributions made to date. These statements are invaluable for tax purposes and should be saved. The fund will also send out, in January, a Form 1099-Div for any distributions made the previous year, and a Form 1099-B if any mutual fund shares were sold.

3

Mutual Fund Recordkeeping and Taxes

Mutual funds can be advantageous in that they minimize some of the more mundane details involved in investing. Of course, these details are not eliminated entirely, and those left to the mutual fund investor primarily relate to recordkeeping and taxes.

Recordkeeping

Mutual fund investing, as with any other investment, demands some amount of recordkeeping. This is made easier by the statements sent out by the funds.

Purchases and redemptions are acknowledged by mutual funds through a confirmation statement sent to the investor. These statements should be retained both for tax purposes, and in case any dispute with the fund arises. Many mutual funds send shareholders periodic statements of their account activity, including any investments and distributions received over a certain time period. At year-end, the fund will send a summary of the yearly account activity. In addition, the fund will send separate forms (1099-Div and 1099-B) noting all the activity in the shareholder's account that will be reported to the IRS for tax purposes. These statements should be saved, both for your own information and as backup documentation that may be necessary for income tax filings.

Investors should also make it a habit to save the latest prospectus issued by the fund, so that future purchases, exchanges, and/or redemptions can be made in accordance with the fund's latest business procedures.

Taxes

It is the unfortunate fate of investors that, eventually, they all must face IRS regulations. Mutual fund investors are no different, but mutual funds do have certain tax consequences that are not readily apparent.

Investors incur two distinct types of tax liabilities from mutual funds. The first results from distributions a shareholder receives from the mutual fund, and the second results from the sale of mutual fund shares. The tax implications are quite different, and are discussed below.

Distributions From Mutual Funds: The IRS treats mutual funds as conduits between their shareholders and the corporations whose securities the fund holds. This means that the mutual fund itself is not taxed. In addition, the mutual fund itself does not pay dividends; it merely passes on income from dividends, interest and capital gains to shareholders.

Mutual funds earn income from cash dividends and interest received from the fund's investments. The fund earns capital gains resulting from price changes of the securities it holds. Capital gains and losses can be realized through the sale of the securities during the tax year, or unrealized if the securities continue to be held by the fund at the end of the tax year. All income earned by the fund, and any capital gains and losses (realized or unrealized), cause the value of the fund's assets to increase or decrease. This is reflected in the fund's per-share net asset value.

Mutual funds distribute net investment income and net realized capital gains received during the calendar year. They do so in the form of distributions to shareholders. Mutual funds are allowed to net out any investment expenses before dividend distributions, and are not required to make a distribution if investment expenses are greater than net investment income. Under the tax laws, mutual funds are required to make these distributions by the end of the calendar year, regardless of when the fund's fiscal year ends. The result is that many funds must make distributions late in the year to assure that they have distributed all income and gains through year-end.

Fund distributions are simply a transferal of assets from the fund to the shareholder. This means that when a distribution is made, the net total assets of the fund drop, and so, too, does the per-share net asset value. In fact, it drops by exactly the amount of the distribution.

Once the distribution is paid to the shareholder it is taxable, regardless of whether or not the shareholder reinvests the distribution. The tax depends on the source of the income to the fund. The kinds of distributions that a mutual fund shareholder may receive include ordinary dividends, capital gains, exempt-interest dividends and return of capital (non-taxable) distributions. Mutual funds notify shareholders of the underlying sources of the distribution when it is made.

In addition, mutual funds are required to send their shareholders at the end of each year a form for tax purposes, known as Form 1099-DIV (Statement for Recipients of Dividends and Distributions). This form indicates what a shareholder must report or take into consideration on his federal income tax return concerning all fund distributions for the taxable year; an example of the 1988 version is presented in Figure 3-1. This form contains the following information:

- The amount that you must report as ordinary dividends,
- The capital gains distributions that you must report,
- The non-taxable distributions (return of capital) that usually will reduce your stock basis,
- The foreign tax paid that you may claim as a deduction or credit,
- Any federal income tax withheld, such as the 20% tax on reportable payments under backup withholding.

Capital losses realized by the fund are not passed on to shareholders, but are used by the fund to offset capital gains. The fund

Figure 3-1
Form 1099-DIV

PAYER'S name, street address, city, state, and ZIP code		1 Gross dividends and other distributions on stock $	OMB No. 1545-0110	
		2 Investment expenses included in Box 1 $	19**88** Statement for Recipients of	Dividends and Distributions
PAYER'S Federal identification number	RECIPIENT'S identification number	3 Capital gain distributions $		Copy B For Recipient
RECIPIENT'S name (first, middle, last)		4 Federal income tax withheld $	5 Nontaxable distributions (if determinable) $	This is important tax information and is being furnished to the Internal Revenue Service. If you are required to file a return, a negligence penalty or other sanction will be imposed on you if this dividend income is taxable and the IRS determines that it has not been reported.
Street address		6 Foreign tax paid $	7 Foreign country or U.S. possession	
City, state, and ZIP code		Liquidation Distributions		
Account number (optional)		8 Cash $	9 Noncash (Fair market value) $	

Form **1099-DIV**   Department of the Treasury - Internal Revenue Service

is allowed to carry the loss forward to net against future gains for up to eight years.

There is one important tax implication of mutual fund distributions that prospective investors should consider. Since mutual fund cash distributions result in an immediate decline in per-share net asset value equal to the per-share distribution, individuals who purchase mutual fund shares before the ex-distribution date effectively have a portion of their investment capital returned to them upon distribution. Since the distribution is taxable unless the fund is held in a tax-sheltered account (IRA, Keogh, etc.), the investor is left worse off by the amount of the tax he must pay on the distribution. Therefore, under normal circumstances, taxpaying investors should wait and make significant fund purchases after the ex-distribution date. The income and capital gains distribution months are given when available in the one-page fund summaries in this guide and can also be determined by calling the fund.

Mutual Fund Sales: The other type of tax liability mutual fund investors are likely to incur are gains and losses that result from the purchase and subsequent sale, exchange or redemption of mutual fund shares themselves. As an important note, investors should remember that switching mutual fund investments from one fund to another even while staying in the same mutual fund family constitutes a sale for tax purposes. The amount of the gain or loss on a sale is the difference between the amount realized from the sale, exchange or redemption, and the adjusted cost basis of the shares.

Mutual fund investors should keep detailed records of prior purchases in order to determine and substantiate the magnitude of gain or loss once the shares are sold.

It is equally important for investors to understand the various identification methods for determining which shares were sold if the entire holdings are not liquidated.

For income tax purposes, the cost basis of mutual fund shares that have been sold can be determined by the "first in, first out" (FIFO) method, by the identifiable cost method, or by an averaging method.

The FIFO method assumes that the shares sold were the first ones acquired. Using the FIFO method when shares have appreciated over time may result in a substantial capital gain and tax due. The most productive strategy would be to sell those shares with the highest cost and thereby minimize the tax liability or generate a loss that can be used to offset other gains. The identifiable cost method is the most efficient for minimizing tax liabilities.

The identifiable cost method requires that the shares sold be specifically identified as the ones acquired on a specific date at a specific acquisition cost. The IRS states: "If you can definitely identify within the fund the shares of stock you sold, the basis is the cost or other basis of those shares of stock. However, when a number of shares are acquired and sold at various times in different quantities and the shares you sell cannot be identified with certainty, the basis of the shares you sell is the basis of the securities acquired first." When using the identifiable cost method of accounting for share costs, the IRS places the burden of proof on the taxpayer. That is, the taxpayer must be able to trace a sale to a specific block of shares. One method for doing this is to periodically request that the fund send stock certificates that represent the investor's holdings. When a sale is made, the investor should record the certificate number(s) and the date of acquisition, along with the original cost and proceeds received. This method, however, is time-consuming and cumbersome, and requires safeguarding of the certificates.

If the shares are left on deposit with the fund, as most fund investors do, shareholders should retain the records of each purchase. When a sale is desired, the shareholder would write to the fund (or telephone and follow up with a letter) and instruct the fund to sell specific shares acquired on specific dates; these shares identified for sale should have the highest cost basis in order to minimize any tax liability. Request that the fund confirm the sale in writing and save a copy of the original letter and the confirmation letter for your tax records.

Other methods allowed by the tax code provide investors with averaging techniques to compute the basis of shares sold, as long as certain requirements are met. These approaches are somewhat complex and are explained in IRS Publication 564.

Taxpayers who are determining their cost basis for tax purposes should remember that, when liquidating holdings, some of the shares may have been acquired through automatic reinvestment of distributions. Thus, the cost basis for these shares is the per-share net asset value at the time of reinvestment. The taxpayer will have already partially satisfied the income tax liability on these shares, since taxes were paid on the distribution. Ignoring the cost of shares acquired this way could result in an overpayment of income taxes. For example, suppose an individual invested $2,000 in a mutual fund two years ago. The per-share net asset value at that time was $10, and he acquired 200 shares. Recently, he sold his holdings in this fund and his proceeds were $3,000. It might appear in this instance that taxes must be paid on $1,000 of capital gains. However, suppose that the fund made two distributions during this period totaling $600, and suppose that those distributions were reinvested. Income tax on the distributions were paid; in essence, the taxpayer used the distribution to purchase new shares totaling $600. The shareholder's cost basis in the fund is really $2,600, and the investment gain subject to taxation at the time of liquidation is only $400 ($3,000 − $2,600). This illustrates the need to maintain and understand mutual fund account records.

Taxpayers should be aware that brokers, including mutual funds, underwriters of the fund or agents of the fund, are required to report to the IRS the proceeds from sales, exchanges or redemptions. They will send shareholders a written statement, Form 1099-B, detailing the transactions by January 31 of the year following the calendar year in which the transaction occurred. This is not required, though, for transactions in money market mutual funds.

Since the tax aspects of investing and mutual fund trading are among the greatest causes of investor confusion, it is a good idea for all mutual fund investors to familiarize themselves with federal tax reporting requirements. The fund prospectus gives some information on the taxation of distributions and the reporting of account activity. An excellent source of information is prepared by the IRS itself, Publication 564. In addition to listing the tax rules, the booklet gives numerous examples to illustrate how the rules apply in different situations.

A Framework for Your Fund Portfolio

Financial data and summaries of mutual fund services are presented in Chapters 7 and 8 for over 400 no-load mutual funds. Without an efficient approach and a firm idea of your financial goals and needs, searching through these funds for appropriate investments may consume a substantial amount of your time and energy. This chapter provides a framework for your mutual fund portfolio, and the information we supply in the data pages will enable you to select individual funds.

Important Considerations

Mutual fund investments should reflect a number of variables that are defined by the individual investor. These are:

- Risk tolerance,
- Anticipated holding period,
- Liquidity needs,
- Income requirements, and
- Tax exposure.

Risk tolerance refers to the potential volatility of an investment—fluctuations in return—that an investor finds acceptable. The anticipated holding period is important for the investor to define, because it affects the investor's risk tolerance. Time is a form of diversification; longer holding periods provide greater diversification across different market environments. The returns on investments held for longer periods are less volatile than returns for shorter holding periods. Thus, investors who anticipate longer holding periods can take on more risk.

The liquidity needs of an investor similarly help define the types of funds investors should consider and also impact holding period and therefore risk. Liquidity implies preservation of capital, and if liquidity is important and the amount of liquidity needed is uncertain, then mutual funds with smaller variations in value should be considered. A liquid mutual fund is one in which withdrawals from the fund can be made at any time with a reasonable certainty that the per-share value will not have dropped sharply. Highly volatile aggressive growth funds are the least liquid, and short-term fixed-income funds are the most liquid.

Income requirements are a concern if the mutual fund investment must generate some consistent level of income for the investor on a periodic basis. Bond funds produce much more reliable income flows than common stock mutual funds. However, no matter what the investment objective of a fund, there are usually periodic withdrawal programs available if certain cash flows are required.

Tax exposure presents an important decision point for investors. High tax bracket investors should seek mutual funds that are unlikely to make large distributions. The tax initiative ideally should be up to the investor, who can make the decision by timing the sale of mutual fund shares. Conversely, high tax bracket investors can advantageously relegate high distribution funds to their tax-sheltered accounts such as IRAs or Keoghs.

Life Cycles

These investment considerations change for investors over time and can be viewed as a function of the point in your life cycle. Table 4-1 below gives some generalized investment circumstances.

Many individuals, of course, do not fit neatly into life cycle categories, but they may still have similar circumstances. For instance, individuals in their early career phase may be intermediate-term, medium-risk investors, rather than long-term, high-risk investors. The important considerations are the investment circumstances themselves, because they will affect the kinds of funds chosen. Polar

Figure 4-1
The Life Cycle: Risk Tolerance, Holding Period and Tax Exposure

	Early Career	*Mid Career*	*Late Career*	*Retirement*
Risk Tolerance	High	High	Medium	Low
Holding Period	Long	Long	Intermediate	Intermediate
Tax Exposure	Low	High	High	Low

examples of mutual fund choices that reflect the different sets of circumstances are:

- The high-risk, long-term, high-tax-exposure individual, who would tend to hold aggressive growth and growth common stock mutual funds that have growth potential but low dividend yields, and who would tend to use shorter-term municipal bond funds to meet minimal liquidity needs; versus
- The low-risk, shorter-term, low-tax-exposure individual, who would tend to hold growth and income and balanced common stock mutual funds that have some growth potential but that also pay a significant dividend, and who would tend to use shorter-term bond funds or money market funds to meet liquidity needs.

Of course, these circumstances continually change, sometimes dramatically; the mutual fund portfolio should be viewed dynamically.

Beta: A Closer Look at Risk

Of the circumstances we discussed above, risk is the most difficult concept for many investors to define, and yet much of the selection question depends on this definition. For instance, the amount of money invested in money market or bond funds is a function of your anticipated liquidity needs, and your tax bracket dictates whether mutual fund investments should generate high or low levels of income. Which funds to choose, then, and how much to invest in each, becomes a function primarily of your risk tolerance.

The measure for risk that we use in this guide is beta. It is an important concept to understand, because beta can be used as a measure of risk for a single fund and for your entire portfolio. If you define your risk in terms of beta, you can select funds with betas that, taken in combination, reflect your own risk tolerance.

Beta is a measure of the relative volatility inherent in a mutual fund investment. This volatility is measured relative to the market, which is usually defined as the Standard & Poor's index of 500 common stocks. The market's beta is always 1.0, and a money market fund's beta is always 0. If you hold a mutual fund with a beta of 1.0, it will move on average in tandem with the market: If the market is up 10%, the fund will be up on average 10%, and if the market drops 10%, the fund will drop on average 10%. A mutual fund with a beta of 1.5 is 50% more volatile than the market: If the market is up 10%, the fund will be up on average 50% more or 15%, and conversely, if the market is down 10%, the fund on average will be down 15%. A negative beta, a rare occurrence, implies that the mutual fund moves inversely in some magnitude to the market.

The higher the fund's beta, the greater the volatility of the investment in the fund and the less appropriate the fund would be for shorter holding periods or to meet liquidity needs. Remember that beta is a relative measure: A low beta only implies that the fund's movement is not volatile relative to the market. Its return, however may be quite variable. For instance, industry-specific sector fund moves may not be related to market volatility, but changes in the industry may cause their returns to fluctuate widely. For a well-diversified stock fund, beta is a very useful measure of risk, but for concentrated funds, beta only captures a portion of the variability that the fund may experience. Beta is also less useful for measuring the risk inherent in bond funds or mutual funds with large bond holdings, since these funds may move relatively independent of the stock market. Betas for precious metals funds can be even more misleading. Precious metals funds often have relatively low betas, but these funds are extremely volatile. Their volatility stems from factors that do not affect the common stock market as much. In addition, the betas of precious metals funds sometimes change significantly from year to year. For these reasons, betas are not reported in this guide for bond funds and precious metals funds.

Although betas can be misleading risk measures for some mutual funds, they can be helpful in determining the stock market risk of an investor's overall portfolio.

The beta of a mutual fund portfolio is the weighted sum of the betas of the individual mutual fund investments, based on their percentage representation (at market value) in the portfolio. For example, if a portfolio is divided among three mutual funds, with equal investments (based on the current market value of the funds) in each, the portfolio beta would be:

(0.33 × beta Fund A) + (0.33 × beta Fund B) + (0.33 × beta Fund C)

The following examples illustrate the approach. However, they only represent four of the infinite combinations of mutual funds and proportions invested in each. The betas used in the examples are averages for the class of mutual fund suggested (See Figure 1-1 in Chapter 1); if you were determining your own portfolio's beta, you would use individual mutual fund betas.

The higher-risk, longer-term holding period, higher-tax-exposure individual with minimum liquidity needs: One portfolio combination might be 90% in aggressive common stock mutual funds (high capital gains potential, low dividend yield; average beta of 1.09), and 10% in tax-exempt money market funds (beta of 0). The portfolio beta is:

$$(0.90 \times 1.09) + (0.10 \times 0) = 0.98$$

The lower-risk, shorter-term holding period, lower-tax-exposure individual with higher liquidity needs: One portfolio might have 40% in growth common stock mutual funds (average beta of 0.90), 40% in growth and income common stock mutual funds (with an average beta of 0.78), and 20% in taxable money market funds (beta of 0). The portfolio beta is:

$$(0.40 \times 0.90) + (0.40 \times 0.78) + (0.20 \times 0) = 0.67$$

Alternatively, this same risk level can be achieved with a different mix: 86% in growth and income common stock mutual funds, and 14% in a money market fund (average beta of 0). The portfolio beta remains the same:

$$(0.86 \times 0.78) + (0.14 \times 0) = 0.67$$

The lower-risk, higher-tax-exposure individual: One possible portfolio would use the same funds as the first example, but would increase the investment in money market funds so that the risk is the same as the second example. Under this scenario, 62% is in aggressive growth common stocks, and 38% is in tax-exempt money market funds. The portfolio beta is:

$$(0.62 \times 1.09) + (0.38 \times 0) = 0.67$$

Defining your risk tolerance level is a crucial step in building a portfolio of mutual funds. Even if you do not go through the calculations described above, you should have some idea of how the riskiness of the fund you choose will affect your overall portfolio. The individual fund beta figures, provided in the data section, will help you do this. Once you have determined your own risk tolerance, you will have a better idea of which category to choose from in selecting a mutual fund. After considering your investment parameters (taxes, liquidity, holding period, income, and risk) you are ready to look at the individual mutual funds themselves.

5

An Explanation of the Mutual Fund Statistics

When choosing among mutual funds, most investors start with performance statistics: How well have the various mutual funds performed in the past? If past performance could only perfectly predict future performance, the selection would be easy. But, of course, it can't.

What past performance can tell you is how well the fund's management has handled different market environments, how consistent the fund has been, and how well the fund has done relative to its risk level, relative to other similar funds and relative to the market. We present performance statistics in Chapter 6 in several different forms. First, we provide an overall picture, with the average performance of each mutual fund category for the last five years, along with stock market, bond market and Treasury bill benchmarks. The top 20 and bottom 20 mutual fund performers for 1988 are given for a recent reference. The list changes each year and reflects the cyclical nature of financial markets and the changing success of individual mutual fund managers. A list of the top 50 mutual funds ranked by five-year total return is given for a long-term perspective on investment performance.

Since the performance of a fund must be judged relative to similar funds, we have also grouped the funds by category and ranked the funds according to their total return performance for 1988. To make the comparison easier, we have also provided other data in this chapter. The fund's five-year total return figure gives a longer-term perspective on the performance of the fund; the letter (superscript) indicates the fund's performance relative to all other funds that have five years of data—an "A" indicates the fund was in the top 20% in terms of performance, and an "E" indicates the fund was in the bottom 20%. Consistency of performance is indicated by the actual returns during bull and bear markets, and the accompanying letter designates the relative bull and bear market performance ranking for the period compared to all other funds. We also included the fund's beta as a measure of risk. Betas were not determined for bond funds and precious metals funds.

Individual Funds

After reviewing the performance rankings, you can find more in-depth information on the individual funds in the one-page financial summaries for each fund in Chapter 7 and in the half-page summaries for tax-exempt funds in Chapter 8. The funds here are presented alphabetically, not by category. Their categories, however, are indicated at the top of the page, under the fund's name. These pages provide six years of per-share data, performance and risk statistics, a summary of investment objectives, portfolio composition, services, and the telephone number and address of the fund.

Some of this information is taken directly from mutual fund reports (the prospectus and annual and quarterly reports), while other statistics, such as fund performance and risk, were calculated by us.

The following provides definitions and explanations of the terms we have used in the summaries of the individual funds. The explanations are listed in the order in which the data appear on the fund summary pages.

Years Ending: This indicates over what time period the per-share data applies, and varies with the fiscal year of the fund. Funds with fiscal years ending in June, in particular, have year-old data. Most funds have more recent data, since the fiscal year usually ends near or at the end of the calendar year. The fiscal year-end is when the fund's per-share data is made available to the shareholders. The performance statistics are always calculated on a calendar-year basis no matter what fiscal year the fund uses.

Dividends from Net Investment Income: Per-share income distributions reported in the fiscal year.

Distributions from Net Realized Capital Gains: Per-share distributions from realized capital gains after netting out realized losses. These distributions vary each year with both the investment success of the fund and the amount of securities sold.

Net Asset Value End of Year: Net asset value is the sum of all securities held, based on their market value, divided by the number of mutual fund shares outstanding at the end of the fiscal year.

Ratio of Expenses to Net Assets: The sum of administrative fees plus advisor management fees and 12b-1 fees divided by the average net asset value of the fund, stated as a percentage. Brokerage costs incurred by the fund are not included in the expense ratio but are instead reflected directly in net asset value.

Ratio of Net Income to Average Net Assets: The income of the fund from dividends and interest less fund expenses, divided by the average net asset value of the fund. This ratio is similar to a dividend yield and would be higher for income-oriented funds and lower for growth-oriented funds. The figure only reflects income and does not reflect capital gains or losses. It is not a total return.

Portfolio Turnover Rate: A measure of the trading activity of the fund, which is computed by dividing the lesser of purchases or sales for the fiscal year by the monthly average value of the securities owned by the fund during the year. Securities with maturities of less than one year are excluded from the calculation. The result is expressed as a percentage, with 100% implying a complete portfolio turnover within one year.

Total Assets End of Year: Aggregate year-end fund value in millions of dollars.

Annual Rate of Return: This is a total return figure, expressed as a percentage increase (decrease), and was computed using monthly net asset values per share and shareholder distributions during the year. Distributions were assumed to be reinvested when they were paid. The annual rate of return is calculated on the basis of the calendar year, regardless of the fund's fiscal year.

Five-Year Total Return: Assuming investment on January 1, 1984, the total percentage increase (decrease) in investment value if held through December 31, 1988. All distributions are assumed to have been reinvested when they were paid. The superscript letter indicates the fund's five-year ranking among all funds: An "A" indicates the fund was among the top 20%, an "E" indicates the fund was among the bottom 20%, with "B," "C" and "D" falling in between.

Degree of Diversification: Diversification is a relative concept. We have measured fund diversification relative to the S&P 500, an index of large stocks composed of industrials, transportation, financial and utility stocks, under the assumption that this proxy for the market represents a well-diversified portfolio. The diversification rankings were assigned after statistically determining how closely the returns of the fund matched the market during the three-year period starting January 1, 1986, and ending December 31, 1988. The more closely the returns matched the market during that period, the higher the diversification ranking. Common stock funds that did not track the market well, and therefore had lower diversification rankings, many times had industry or special concentrations, such as sector, gold, and international funds. Some funds, however, had lower diversification rankings due to high cash positions, even though they were not sector or specialty funds. Diversification should be thought of as market-tracking ability rather than the number or type of investments made by a fund. We ranked all of the funds based on market-tracking ability and divided them into five groups. An "A" represents the group that most closely tracked the market; "E" represents the group that tracked the market the least. The others fall into the remaining groups. The lower the degree of diversification ranking, the greater the chance that the fund's return will not follow the market. This figure was not calculated for bond funds, due to their investments in fixed-income securities.

Beta: A risk measure that relates the fund's volatility of returns to the market. The higher the beta of a fund, the higher the risk of the fund. The figure is based on monthly returns for the 36 months from the beginning of 1986 through the end of 1988. A beta of 1.0 indicates that the fund's returns will on average be as volatile as the market and move in the same direction; a beta higher than 1.0 indicates that if the market rises or falls, the fund will rise or fall respectively but to a greater degree; a beta of less than 1.0 indicates that if the market rises or falls, the fund will rise or fall to a lesser degree. The S&P 500 index always has a beta of 1.0 because it is the measure we selected to represent the overall stock market; money market funds will always have a beta of zero because their returns do not vary particularly, nor do their returns vary with the returns of the stock market. This figure was not calculated for bond funds and precious metals funds. Beta is a meaningful figure of risk only for well-diversified common stock portfolios. The majority of risk in precious metal funds is caused by factors other than the movement of the stock market. Bond funds do react in some ways to the factors that affect the stock market but the maturity of the portfolio is more indicative of risk than beta.

Bull: This rating reflects the fund's performance in the most recent bull (up) market, starting August 1, 1984, and continuing through August 31, 1987. The funds were ranked relative to all other funds according to their total return for the period. They were then divided into five groups. Group A reflects the top 20%, Group B the next 20%, and Group E reflects the bottom 20%. Funds ranked A and B performed better than average during the bull market, funds ranked C performed average, and funds ranked D and E performed worse than average during the bull market.

Bear: This rating reflects the fund's performance in the most recent bear (down) market, from September 1, 1987, through December 31, 1987. The funds were ranked relative to all other funds according to their total return for the period. They were then divided into five groups. Group A reflects the top 20%, Group B the next 20%, and Group E reflects the bottom 20%. Funds ranked A and B performed better than average during the bear market, funds ranked C performed average, and funds ranked D and E performed worse than average during the bear market.

NA: Indicates that the statistic was not available. For the five-year total return figure, the statistic would not be available for funds that have been operating for less than five years. For the beta and degree of diversification figures, funds operating for less than 36 months would not have the statistics available. Bond funds and precious metal funds do not have beta statistics. Bond funds do not have diversification statistics. For the bull and bear ratings, funds not operating during the entire bull or bear market period would not have these statistics available.

Portfolio Composition: This information was obtained directly from the fund's annual and quarterly reports, and we have indicated the date on which the information is based. Please note that some funds employ leverage, borrowing to buy securities, and this may result in the portfolio composition exceeding 100%.

Portfolio Manager: The name of the portfolio manager and the year when the manager began managing the fund are noted, providing additional information useful in evaluating past performance. A recent change in the portfolio manager may indicate that five-year performance figures are less meaningful.

Distributions: The months in which **income** and **capital gains** distributions to shareholders are made is indicated, when available.

12b-1: If a fund has a 12b-1 plan, the maximum amount that can be charged is given; remember, though, that while no fund can be charged more than the maximum, some funds are charged less than the maximum, and some are not charged at all. If the fund's advisor pays the charge, it is so noted.

Minimum Investment: The minimum initial and subsequent investments in the fund are also detailed. Often, funds will have lower minimums for IRAs; this is also indicated.

Services: Investor services provided by the fund are detailed. These include the availability for IRA, Keogh, corporate pension and profit-sharing plans, simplified employee pension plans and non-profit group retirement plans (indicated by **IRA**, **Keogh**, **Corp**, **SEP**, and **403(b)**, respectively); if the fund allows the automatic and systematic withdrawal of money from the fund (indicated by **Withdraw**); and if the fund allows for automatic investments through an investor's checking account (**Deduct**). Since all funds have automatic reinvestment of distributions options, this service was not specifically noted.

Telephone Exchange: Telephone exchanges with other funds in the family are also listed. If exchange privileges are allowed, we have indicated whether the family includes a money market fund.

Registration: The states in which the fund is registered are listed. If the fund is not registered in the state in which you reside, you will not be able to open an account in the fund.

Ticker: The ticker symbol for each fund is given for those investors that may want to access on-line data with their computer. The ticker is always four letters followed by an "X," indicating that it is a mutual fund. For example, the Acorn fund ticker symbol is ACRNX.

Other Lists

We have also included a list of new funds at the end of the mutual fund summaries. These funds appear in NASD newspaper listings but were less than one year old as of December 31, 1988, and therefore financial data or analysis was either not useful or not possible.

Mutual funds that are indicated as no-load in the financial press but that do not appear in this book are listed after the new fund section. Examples would be funds for institutional or corporate customers only and funds limited to employees or members of a particular organization.

Our last list is of fund families that contain primarily no-load funds. All of the funds within a family, including load funds, are listed.

6

Mutual Fund Performance Rankings

On the following pages, we have ranked all of the mutual funds listed in this guide by their investment performance. The funds were ranked according to several different criteria. These are:

The performance statistics also include information on bull and bear market performance, and risk as measured by beta for stock funds. **Chapter 5 presents a detailed explanation of the performance statistics**; a summary key is presented on the following page.

A summary of total return performance is presented below, along with stock, bond, and money market indexes for comparison.

Mutual Fund Categories and Total Return Performance Summary

Category	Total Return (%)						
	1983	1984	1985	1986	1987	1988	5-Year
Aggressive Growth	19.0	(11.5)	26.9	10.7	(2.3)	16.1	43.0
Growth	19.7	(2.3)	25.9	11.7	1.0	14.7	66.5
Growth & Income	21.1	4.1	25.8	13.9	(0.4)	16.2	79.8
Balanced	20.9	9.1	25.3	17.5	(0.3)	14.4	86.9
Bond	9.6	11.5	20.5	14.4	1.1	8.1	67.0
Tax-Exempt	9.5	8.5	17.5	16.6	(0.9)	10.2	62.8
International	30.4	(5.0)	33.4	51.1	10.8	14.2	156.9
Precious Metals	(1.5)	(26.2)	(7.3)	39.3	28.5	(19.2)	41.0
S&P 500	22.4	6.1	31.6	18.6	5.2	16.6	103.1
Salomon Bond Index	6.3	16.9	30.1	19.9	2.6	7.9	101.9
T-Bills	8.8	9.9	7.7	6.2	5.9	6.8	42.2

Key to Performance Rankings

Annual & Five-Year Total Return: Includes the change in net asset value and all distributions, and assumes reinvestment of distributions when paid. Five-year total returns are ranked A through E. "A" indicates the fund was in the top performance group and "E" indicates the fund was in the bottom group. "B," "C" and "D" indicate the fund was in the 2nd, 3rd or 4th performance group.

Bull: Fund performance and ranking (A through E) over the most recent bull market, from August 1984 through August 1987. For the rankings, "A" indicates the fund was in the top group and "E" indicates the fund was in the bottom group; "B," "C" and "D" indicate the fund was in the 2nd, 3rd or 4th performance group.

Bear: Fund performance and ranking (A through E) over the most recent bear market, from September 1987 through December 1987. For the rankings, "A" indicates the fund was in the top group and "E" indicates the fund was in the bottom group; "B," "C" and "D" indicate the fund was in the 2nd, 3rd or 4th performance group.

Beta: A measure of risk relative to the stock market. The market's beta is always 1.0; a beta higher than 1.0 indicates fund returns were more volatile than the market and a beta lower than 1.0 indicates fund returns were less volatile than the market. Beta is not calculated for bond or precious metals funds.

For more complete descriptions, see Chapter 5.

Key to Fund Types

A	— Aggressive Growth	**GI**	— Growth & Income
Bal	— Balanced	**Intl**	— International
Bd	— Bond	**M**	— Precious Metals
G	— Growth	**TE**	— Tax-Exempt

The Top 20 Performers: 1988

Type	Fund	Return (%)
A	Kaufmann Fund	58.6
A	Columbia Special	42.5
A	Gintel Capital Appreciation	35.6
A	Babson Enterprise	32.5
Bal	Mutual Shares	30.7
Bal	Mutual Qualified	30.2
Intl	Ivy International	29.7
G	Scudder Capital Growth	29.7
A	Neuwirth	29.6
A	Founders Frontier	29.2
G	Fidelity Value	29.0
GI	Vanguard Windsor	28.7
A	Financial Strategic Portfolio—Leisure	28.5
G	Vanguard Specialized—Health Care	28.4
GI	Guardian Mutual	28.0
GI	T. Rowe Price Equity Income	27.6
G	AARP Capital Growth	27.3
G	Nicholas Limited Edition	27.3
GI	Bartlett Basic Value	26.3
GI	Vanguard High Yield Stock	26.2

The Bottom 20 Performers: 1988

Type	Fund	Return (%)
M	US Gold Shares	(35.7)
M	Financial Strategic Portfolio—Gold	(20.0)
M	US New Prospector	(18.8)
M	USAA Gold	(17.1)
M	Lexington Goldfund	(15.0)
M	Vanguard Specialized—Gold & Precious Metals	(14.2)
M	Bull & Bear Gold Investors Ltd.	(13.5)
G	Flex Retirement Growth	(9.7)
G	Flex Growth	(5.8)
A	SteinRoe Capital Opportunities	(3.9)
G	US Good and Bad Times	(3.1)
Intl	Transatlantic Income	(2.0)
G	Gateway Growth Plus	(2.0)
G	Rightime	(1.3)
Intl	T. Rowe Price International Bond	(1.2)
A	Loomis-Sayles Capital Development	(0.3)
A	Axe-Houghton Stock	(0.2)
A	SteinRoe Stock	0.7
G	Permanent Portfolio	1.3
Bd	Treasury First	1.6

Top 50 Funds: Five-Year Total Return
(1984 through 1988)

Type	Fund	Return (%)
Intl	Vanguard Trustees' Commingled—Int'l. Port....	205.8
Intl	T. Rowe Price International Stock	180.1
Intl	Scudder International	167.1
Intl	Transatlantic Growth	164.6
GI	Vanguard Windsor	139.9
GI	Vanguard High Yield Stock	138.7
Bal	Mutual Qualified	135.6
Bal	Mutual Shares	135.0
GI	Dodge & Cox Stock	119.9
GI	Selected American Shares	117.0
G	Nicholas II	116.9
G	Gradison Established Growth	112.6
G	Boston Co. Capital Appreciation	112.3
Bal	Loomis-Sayles Mutual	109.4
G	Acorn	108.5
G	IAI Regional	107.0
A	20th Century Giftrust	105.9
A	GIT Equity Special Growth	105.8
G	Scudder Capital Growth	105.2
G	Manhattan	104.0
G	Mathers	103.8
GI	Strong Total Return	103.8
G	Sequoia	103.1
Bal	Lehman Opportunity	102.4
G	Lindner	101.4
GI	Vanguard Index 500	100.5
G	Copley Fund	100.0
A	Loomis-Sayles Capital Development	99.8
Bal	Vanguard Wellington	99.6
Bal	Financial Industrial Income	98.9
Bal	Dodge & Cox Balanced	98.5
GI	Neuberger Berman Partners	98.1
Bd	Northeast Investors Trust	96.6
Bal	Dreyfus Convertible Securities	96.3
Bal	Vanguard Wellesley Income	96.0
Bal	SAFECO Income	95.3
Bal	Lindner Dividend	93.2
G	Century Shares Trust	91.8
G	T. Rowe Price New Era	91.6
GI	Guardian Mutual	91.0
Bal	Evergreen Total Return	90.7
G	Northeast Investors Growth	90.6
A	Fidelity Freedom	90.0
G	Legg Mason Value Trust	88.4
Bd	Axe-Houghton Income	87.3
GI	Gintel ERISA	86.7
Bd	Fidelity High Income	86.6
G	Nicholas	85.5
G	Babson Growth	85.0
A	SteinRoe Special	84.8

Aggressive Growth Funds
Ranked by 1988 Total Return

Fund	Total Return (%)		Market Cycle Performance (%)		Beta
	1988	5-Year*	Bear*	Bull*	
Kaufmann Fund	58.6	NA	(37.7)E	NA	NA
Columbia Special	42.5	NA	(30.0)E	NA	1.25
Gintel Cap. Apprec.	35.6	NA	(21.4)D	NA	0.86
Babson Enterprise	32.5	72.1B	(28.0)E	110.5B	0.95
Neuwirth	29.6	60.9D	(29.4)E	110.8B	1.09
Founders Frontier	29.2	NA	(17.8)C	NA	NA
FSP—Leisure	28.5	NA	(25.0)E	127.7A	1.10
Vanguard Explorer	25.8	5.4E	(25.4)E	38.4E	0.89
Sherman, Dean	25.7	(7.5)E	(37.9)E	47.3E	0.56
GIT Equity—Special Growth ...	24.7	105.8A	(20.0)D	119.6B	0.88
Naess & Thomas Special	24.6	5.5E	(31.6)E	60.5D	1.16
Gradison Opp. Growth	23.6	63.8C	(22.0)D	93.4C	0.86
Dreyfus New Leaders	23.3	NA	(28.5)E	NA	1.10
Evergreen	23.0	81.2B	(24.7)E	116.7B	0.90
Reich & Tang Equity	22.9	NA	(9.6)D	NA	0.88
Bull & Bear Special Eq.	22.7	NA	(23.9)D	NA	NA
Shadow Stock Fund	22.5	NA	NA	NA	NA
Vanguard Explorer II	22.0	NA	(27.5)E	NA	1.11
T. Rowe Price Cap. App.	21.2	NA	(10.8)C	NA	NA
SteinRoe Special	20.2	84.8B	(21.6)D	122.8B	0.97
Legg Mason Special Inv. Tr.	19.7	NA	(29.8)E	NA	1.05
Janus Venture	19.6	NA	(17.3)C	NA	0.67
44 Wall Street	19.3	(78.4)E	(42.1)E	(37.1)E	1.48
Fiduciary Capital Growth	18.8	33.9E	(27.0)E	70.4D	1.00
FSP—Health Sciences	16.0	NA	(24.9)E	166.4A	1.21
Fidelity Freedom	15.5	90.0B	(25.5)E	143.9A	1.09
Tudor	15.3	59.5D	(27.7)E	126.8A	1.18
FSP—Energy	15.0	NA	(28.2)E	102.5C	0.88
USAA Aggressive Growth	14.3	20.4E	(26.1)E	85.4C	1.12
FSP—Technology	14.2	NA	(30.4)E	114.9B	1.28
T. Rowe Price New Horizons ..	14.0	15.1E	(28.4)E	65.5D	1.14
Bull & Bear Capital Growth	13.9	37.9E	(28.4)E	93.7C	1.09
20th Century Ultra	13.3	35.7E	(27.6)E	115.7B	1.39
T. Rowe Price Sci. & Tech.	13.3	NA	NA	NA	NA
Founders Special	13.2	43.3E	(24.2)D	102.4C	1.08
Bruce Fund	12.9	74.5B	(17.6)C	108.1B	0.73
Prudent Speculator Lev.	12.7	NA	NA	NA	NA
SteinRoe Discovery	11.8	30.7E	(28.1)E	100.9C	1.27
20th Century Giftrust	11.1	105.9A	(23.2)D	205.9A	1.36
Scudder Development	11.1	26.4E	(26.5)E	80.1D	1.15
Lexington Growth	10.5	48.5D	(25.9)E	135.1A	1.00
US Growth	10.5	(1.6)E	(27.2)E	57.6D	1.02
New Beginning Growth	9.8	78.1B	(24.6)D	132.9A	1.10
Vanguard Specialized—Tech. ...	9.5	NA	(32.6)E	64.2D	1.26
Leverage Fund of Boston	9.4	19.7E	(34.9)E	126.8A	1.33
Financial Dynamics	9.1	34.1E	(30.3)E	116.5B	1.28

Continued on next page

Aggressive Growth Funds
Ranked by 1988 Total Return

Fund	Total Return (%)		Market Cycle Performance (%)		Beta
	1988	5-Year*	Bear*	Bull*	
Continued from previous page					
20th Century Select	5.6	66.6[C]	(23.9)[D]	147.3[A]	1.09
Medical Technology	4.6	44.0[E]	(25.2)[E]	126.1[B]	1.10
US LoCap	3.4	NA	(33.6)[E]	NA	0.85
Value Line Special Sit.	3.3	(11.7)[E]	(29.1)[E]	65.3[D]	1.22
The Fairmont	3.1	59.1[D]	(26.2)[E]	117.4[B]	1.04
20th Century Growth	2.7	66.6[C]	(26.8)[E]	168.3[A]	1.26
20th Century Vista	2.4	40.7[E]	(25.4)[E]	129.7[A]	1.44
100 Fund	1.7	41.8[E]	(10.7)[C]	88.1[C]	0.86
SteinRoe Stock	0.7	41.7[E]	(26.1)[E]	127.3[A]	1.10
Axe-Houghton Stock	(0.2)	15.1[E]	(35.8)[E]	141.6[A]	1.29
Loomis-Sayles Cap. Dev.	(0.3)	99.8[A]	(18.8)[D]	188.2[A]	1.28
SteinRoe Cap. Opp.	(3.9)	26.5[E]	(27.0)[E]	119.7[B]	1.16
Average	**16.1**	**43.0**	**(26.4)**	**108.0**	**1.09**

Superscripts indicate the fund's relative ranking—see key at beginning of this chapter and Chapter 5 for a more complete description.

Growth Funds
Ranked by 1988 Total Return

Fund	Total Return (%) 1988	5-Year*	Market Cycle Performance (%) Bear*	Bull*	Beta
Scudder Capital Growth	29.7	105.2[A]	(25.4)[E]	133.0[A]	1.07
Fidelity Value	29.0	51.4[D]	(26.2)[E]	95.4[C]	0.92
Vanguard Spec.—Health Care ..	28.4	NA	(26.5)[E]	169.7[A]	0.98
AARP Capital Growth	27.3	NA	(24.7)[E]	NA	1.06
Nicholas Limited Edition	27.3	NA	(13.8)[C]	NA	NA
American Pen. Inv.—Growth ...	26.0	NA	(28.9)[E]	NA	1.11
Legg Mason Value Trust	25.8	88.4[B]	(26.4)[E]	116.2[B]	0.95
Acorn	24.7	108.5[A]	(20.6)[D]	129.4[A]	0.83
Pennsylvania Mutual	24.6	83.6[B]	(17.3)[C]	90.0[C]	0.66
IAI Apollo	24.3	NA	(20.3)[D]	NA	0.93
Fidelity Trend	24.3	69.4[C]	(28.4)[E]	119.4[B]	1.13
Stratton Growth	22.6	57.6[D]	(22.7)[D]	89.9[C]	0.88
Vanguard W.L. Morgan Gr.	22.3	69.8[C]	(25.2)[E]	117.0[B]	1.03
SAFECO Growth	22.1	48.0[D]	(19.8)[D]	80.4[D]	0.91
Boston Co. Spec. Growth	22.0	50.9[D]	(25.4)[E]	96.8[C]	1.02
Counsellors Cap. App.	21.4	NA	(19.2)[D]	NA	NA
Sound Shore	21.1	NA	(21.6)[D]	NA	0.81
Fidelity Contrafund	21.0	55.7[D]	(30.3)[E]	132.8[A]	1.08
US Real Estate	20.8	NA	(19.5)[D]	NA	NA
Lindner	20.4	101.4[A]	(14.9)[C]	91.5[C]	0.57
Salem Growth	20.2	NA	(21.6)[D]	NA	0.83
Calvert—Equity Portfolio	20.0	42.5[E]	(28.9)[E]	92.3[C]	1.00
Copley Fund	19.9	100.0[A]	(13.2)[C]	86.7[C]	0.48
Vanguard Index Tr.—Ext.	19.7	NA	NA	NA	NA
Boston Co. Cap. App.	19.6	112.3[A]	(20.1)[D]	136.6[A]	0.90
Selected Special Shares	19.6	52.6[D]	(26.7)[E]	102.4[C]	1.02
Vanguard Spec.—Service Econ.	19.1	NA	(31.8)[E]	130.6[A]	1.11
Janus Value	19.1	NA	(26.1)[E]	NA	0.91
Vanguard STAR	19.0	NA	(13.4)[C]	NA	0.55
IAI Regional	18.6	107.0[A]	(18.1)[C]	139.2[A]	0.86
T. Rowe Price New Am. Gr. ...	18.5	NA	(26.4)[E]	NA	1.15
Manhattan	18.3	104.0[A]	(27.5)[E]	153.8[A]	1.10
Unified Growth	18.2	60.7[D]	(26.7)[E]	99.1[C]	0.98
Rainbow	18.1	50.6[D]	(24.7)[E]	88.4[C]	0.91
Nicholas	18.0	85.5[B]	(19.1)[D]	101.5[C]	0.67
Dreyfus Growth Opp.	17.9	65.6[C]	(22.0)[D]	108.2[B]	0.84
Brandywine Fund	17.7	NA	(29.9)[E]	NA	1.32
Nicholas II	17.3	116.9[A]	(19.1)[D]	124.2[B]	0.81
SBSF Growth Fund	17.2	76.1[B]	(20.6)[D]	92.0[C]	0.70
FSP—Financial Services	17.1	NA	(18.4)[C]	NA	NA
Janus Fund	16.6	67.7[C]	(17.1)[C]	85.1[C]	0.66
20th Century Heritage	16.4	NA	NA	NA	NA
Babson Growth	16.0	85.0[B]	(24.9)[E]	138.2[A]	0.99
Century Shares Trust	15.7	91.8[A]	(20.2)[D]	127.6[A]	0.74
Armstrong Associates	15.5	37.8[E]	(23.9)[D]	84.4[C]	0.88
Gradison Est. Growth	15.1	112.6[A]	(13.1)[C]	134.9[A]	0.82

Continued on next page

Growth Funds
Ranked by 1988 Total Return

Fund	Total Return (%)		Market Cycle Performance (%)		Beta
	1988	5-Year*	Bear*	Bull*	
Continued from previous page					
Vanguard Primecap	14.7	NA	(24.3)[D]	NA	1.04
Harbor Growth	14.3	NA	(25.2)[E]	NA	NA
Mathers	13.7	103.8[A]	(3.7)[C]	117.3[B]	0.71
Northeast Investors Gr.	12.8	90.6[A]	(27.2)[E]	149.7[A]	0.96
Newton Growth	12.8	40.0[E]	(31.2)[E]	105.7[B]	1.07
National Industries	12.6	37.0[E]	(22.0)[D]	70.9[D]	0.92
Schroder U.S. Equity	12.2	53.6[D]	(26.5)[E]	111.5[B]	1.02
Cumberland Growth	11.6	21.1[E]	(25.9)[E]	67.8[D]	0.82
Sequoia	11.0	103.1[A]	(11.7)[C]	97.4[C]	0.50
Columbia Growth	10.8	70.1[C]	(17.0)[C]	121.0[B]	0.91
T. Rowe Price New Era	10.3	91.6[A]	(19.1)[D]	131.3[A]	0.93
M.S.B. Fund	9.8	68.2[C]	(24.9)[E]	121.8[B]	1.08
Value Line Fund	9.7	53.8[D]	(20.2)[D]	126.7[A]	1.04
Lexington Research	9.5	59.0[D]	(22.9)[D]	120.7[B]	0.88
WPG	9.3	66.7[C]	(22.9)[D]	123.8[B]	1.06
Rushmore OTC Index Plus	9.2	NA	(26.3)[E]	NA	1.20
Vanguard World—U.S. Growth	8.8	NA	(23.9)[D]	NA	0.92
IAI Stock	8.4	80.6[B]	(18.3)[C]	121.0[B]	0.87
Growth Industry Shares	7.1	47.5[D]	(18.5)[D]	85.4[C]	0.92
Wealth Monitors	7.0	NA	(37.2)[E]	NA	NA
USAA Growth	6.6	37.4[E]	(21.9)[D]	97.2[C]	0.98
Value Line Leveraged Growth	6.4	56.8[D]	(23.4)[D]	136.2[A]	1.11
T. Rowe Price Growth Stock	6.1	78.8[B]	(22.1)[D]	142.5[A]	0.92
Financial Industrial	5.9	45.3[D]	(25.9)[E]	112.3[B]	1.04
101 Fund	5.3	51.9[D]	(19.2)[D]	84.8[C]	0.77
Founders Growth	4.8	57.9[D]	(21.4)[D]	131.7[A]	0.99
Beacon Hill Mutual	4.3	61.4[D]	(21.8)[D]	114.0[B]	0.92
SteinRoe Universe	2.1	18.5[E]	(26.7)[E]	100.3[C]	1.08
Afuture	1.9	(16.2)[E]	(24.1)[D]	39.0[E]	0.90
Permanent Portfolio	1.3	27.2[E]	(3.5[C]	48.1[E]	0.22
Rightime	(1.3)	NA	2.5[A]	NA	0.50
Gateway Growth Plus	(2.0)	NA	(22.8)[D]	NA	NA
US Good and Bad Times	(3.1)	38.0[E]	(23.6)[D]	100.3[C]	0.93
Flex Growth	(5.8)	NA	(13.4)[C]	NA	0.70
Flex Retirement Growth	(9.7)	23.6[E]	(14.0)[C]	59.3[D]	0.65
Average	**14.7**	**66.5**	**(21.8)**	**109.0**	**0.90**

*Superscripts indicate the fund's relative ranking—see key at beginning of this chapter and Chapter 5 for a more complete description.

Growth & Income Funds
Ranked by 1988 Total Return

Fund	Total Return (%)		Market Cycle Performance (%)		Beta
	1988	5-Year*	Bear*	Bull*	
Vanguard Windsor	28.7	139.9[A]	(22.3)[D]	143.6[A]	0.82
Guardian Mutual	28.0	91.0[A]	(26.2)[E]	121.0[B]	0.96
T. Rowe Price Eq. Inc.	27.6	NA	(15.8)[C]	NA	0.67
Bartlett Basic Value	26.3	NA	(20.9)[D]	NA	0.66
Vanguard High Yield Stock	26.2	138.7[A]	(18.7)[D]	132.5[A]	0.54
SAFECO Equity	25.3	83.2[B]	(29.2)[E]	130.2[A]	1.05
T. Rowe Price Gr. & Inc.	25.1	57.7[D]	(23.2)[D]	86.3[C]	0.87
Vanguard Windsor II	24.7	NA	(23.4)[D]	NA	0.90
Vanguard Trustees' U.S.	24.6	71.2[C]	(27.3)[E]	122.3[B]	1.03
Evergreen Value Timing	24.6	NA	(20.2)[D]	NA	NA
Dreyfus Third Century	23.2	73.7[B]	(20.1)[D]	95.8[C]	0.77
Selected American Shares	22.0	117.0[A]	(21.4)[D]	126.3[B]	0.81
Gintel ERISA	22.0	86.7[B]	(18.4)[C]	97.7[C]	0.82
Vanguard Special—Energy	21.4	NA	(26.4)[E]	117.6[B]	0.85
Gateway Option Index	19.8	53.3[D]	(16.5)[C]	61.1[D]	0.53
USAA Income Stock	19.4	NA	(15.5)[C]	NA	NA
Babson Value	19.0	NA	(25.4)[E]	NA	1.01
LMH	18.0	69.1[C]	(14.5)[C]	71.2[D]	0.48
Fidelity Fund	17.9	82.1[B]	(23.2)[D]	124.5[B]	0.97
U.S. Boston Gr. & Inc.	17.0	NA	(23.7)[D]	NA	0.97
Vanguard Quantitative	16.6	NA	(24.4)[D]	NA	NA
Neuberger Selected Sec. + En.	16.5	65.8[C]	(23.8)[D]	97.2[C]	0.83
Pine Street	16.2	72.0[C]	(24.8)[E]	112.5[B]	0.92
Vanguard Index Trust—500	16.2	100.5[A]	(24.5)[D]	143.5[A]	1.00
Fidelity Convertible Sec.	15.9	NA	(17.4)[C]	NA	NA
Vanguard Convertible Sec.	15.7	NA	(19.2)[D]	NA	NA
Analytic Optioned Equity	15.6	65.2[C]	(11.6)[C]	67.7[D]	0.54
Strong Total Return	15.6	103.8[A]	(14.8)[C]	101.1[C]	0.67
Neuberger Berman Partners	15.5	98.1[A]	(19.5)[D]	122.3[B]	0.77
Harbor U.S. Equities	15.4	NA	NA	NA	NA
FSP—Utilities	14.2	NA	(11.0)[C]	NA	NA
Unified Mutual Shares	14.2	76.8[B]	(19.3)[D]	106.9[B]	0.75
General Securities	14.0	74.2[B]	(9.0)[C]	87.9[C]	0.47
UMB Stock	13.9	75.2[B]	(19.4)[D]	102.8[C]	0.86
Dodge & Cox Stock	13.8	119.9[A]	(20.2)[D]	165.1[A]	0.95
Eclipse Equity	12.7	NA	(6.0)[C]	NA	NA
AMA Growth & Income	12.5	NA	(21.2)[D]	NA	NA
Ivy Growth	12.4	79.9[B]	(21.7)[D]	117.4[B]	0.74
Scudder Growth & Income	11.9	76.6[B]	(18.0)[C]	128.6[A]	0.83
AARP Growth + Income	10.9	NA	(19.2)[D]	NA	0.81
Founders Blue Chip	10.1	75.6[B]	(23.1)[D]	128.5[A]	0.94
AMA Classic Growth	9.7	55.6[D]	(24.8)[E]	100.8[C]	0.99
SteinRoe Prime Equities	9.0	NA	(21.9)[D]	NA	NA
Reserve Equity—Cont.	9.0	NA	(30.6)[E]	140.2[A]	0.91
Rushmore S. M. Index Plus	8.9	NA	(21.5)[D]	NA	0.83
Lepercq-Istel	7.0	34.8[E]	(17.1)[C]	74.9[D]	0.69

Continued on next page

Growth & Income Funds
Ranked by 1988 Total Return

Fund	Total Return (%)		Market Cycle Performance (%)		Beta
	1988	5-Year*	Bear*	Bull*	
Continued from previous page					
Wayne Hummer Growth	7.0	72.1[B]	(19.4)[D]	114.2[B]	0.96
Valley Forge	7.0	39.1[E]	(3.6)[C]	31.9[E]	0.14
Flex Income and Growth	6.2	NA	(10.6)[C]	NA	0.42
Calamos Convertible Inc.	6.2	NA	(16.9)[C]	NA	0.64
Noddings Convertible	5.8	NA	(9.1)[C]	NA	0.52
Dividend/Growth—Dividend ...	4.5	44.0[E]	(22.0)[D]	85.0[C]	0.91
Average	**16.2**	**79.8**	**(19.6)**	**108.1**	**0.78**

Superscripts indicate the fund's relative ranking—see key at beginning of this chapter and Chapter 5 for a more complete description.

Balanced Funds
Ranked by 1988 Total Return

Fund	Total Return (%)		Market Cycle Performance (%)		Beta
	1988	5-Year*	Bear*	Bull*	
Mutual Shares	30.7	135.0ᴬ	(15.7)ᶜ	104.7ᶜ	0.61
Mutual Qualified	30.2	135.6ᴬ	(15.6)ᶜ	105.6ᴮ	0.62
Lindner Dividend	24.2	93.2ᴬ	(9.2)ᶜ	65.8ᴰ	0.31
Lehman Opportunity	23.3	102.4ᴬ	(20.0)ᴰ	114.2ᴮ	0.77
Dreyfus Convertible Sec.	23.0	96.3ᴬ	(19.3)ᴰ	103.8ᶜ	0.57
Legg Mason Total Return	21.8	NA	(24.6)ᴱ	NA	0.89
SAFECO Income	19.0	95.3ᴬ	(21.6)ᴰ	118.9ᴮ	0.76
Primary Trend Fund	18.4	NA	(13.2)ᶜ	NA	NA
US Income	16.9	41.5ᴱ	(8.4)ᶜ	36.3ᴱ	0.36
Vanguard Wellington	16.1	99.6ᴬ	(15.2)ᶜ	112.7ᴮ	0.67
Value Line Convertible	16.0	NA	(17.1)ᶜ	NA	0.75
Evergreen Total Return	15.7	90.7ᴬ	(16.3)ᶜ	100.2ᶜ	0.56
Bull & Bear Equity-Inc.	15.4	76.0ᴮ	(18.6)ᴰ	95.5ᶜ	0.70
Financial Industrial Inc.	15.3	98.9ᴬ	(17.9)ᶜ	120.8ᴮ	0.79
Vanguard Wellesley Inc.	13.6	96.0ᴬ	(4.0)ᶜ	78.5ᴰ	0.29
Unified Income	12.7	31.4ᴱ	(18.2)ᶜ	56.6ᴰ	0.54
Value Line Income	12.2	62.0ᶜ	(17.5)ᶜ	94.4ᶜ	0.65
Dodge & Cox Balanced	11.5	98.5ᴬ	(13.4)ᶜ	121.2ᴮ	0.64
Scudder Equity Income	11.3	NA	(15.4)ᶜ	NA	NA
Founders Equity Income	11.1	62.7ᶜ	(13.9)ᶜ	69.3ᴰ	0.55
Stratton Monthly Div.	9.8	83.9ᴮ	(11.3)ᶜ	92.4ᶜ	0.45
Strong Investment	9.2	67.9ᶜ	(6.9)ᶜ	59.7ᴰ	0.31
Axe-Houghton Fund B	9.0	81.9ᴮ	(19.6)ᴰ	120.5ᴮ	0.73
USAA Cornerstone	8.4	NA	(18.5)ᶜ	NA	0.61
SteinRoe Total Return	7.9	67.3ᶜ	(13.2)ᶜ	89.3ᶜ	0.58
BB&K Diversa	6.6	NA	(8.4)ᶜ	NA	NA
Bartlett Strategic Inc.	4.6	NA	(1.3)ᴮ	NA	0.11
Loomis-Sayles Mutual	3.2	109.4ᴬ	(12.9)ᶜ	154.3ᴬ	0.89
ADTEK	1.9	NA	(26.0)ᴱ	NA	0.86
Average	**14.4**	**86.9**	**(14.9)**	**95.9**	**0.60**

*Superscripts indicate the fund's relative ranking—see key at beginning of this chapter and Chapter 5 for a more complete description.

Bond Funds
Ranked by 1988 Total Return

Fund	Total Return (%) 1988	5-Year*	Market Cycle Performance (%) Bear*	Bull*
T. Rowe Price High Yield	17.9	NA	(4.0)ᶜ	NA
Benham Target—2010	15.7	NA	9.3ᴬ	NA
Benham Target—2005	14.5	NA	9.8ᴬ	NA
Northeast Investors Trust	14.1	96.6ᴬ	(5.1)ᶜ	80.7ᶜ
Liberty	13.8	64.6ᶜ	(8.0)ᶜ	60.7ᴰ
Vanguard High Yield Bond	13.5	78.6ᴮ	(2.1)ᶜ	64.1ᴰ
Financial Bond—High Yield	13.4	NA	(2.3)ᶜ	NA
Fidelity High Income	12.6	86.6ᴮ	(4.0)ᶜ	72.8ᴰ
Strong Income	12.5	NA	(1.6)ᴮ	NA
SteinRoe High-Yield Bond	11.6	NA	3.0ᴬ	NA
Nicholas Income	11.5	74.0ᴮ	0.2ᴮ	53.7ᴰ
Benham Target—2000	11.5	NA	7.9ᴬ	NA
Benham Target—2015	11.1	NA	10.3ᴬ	NA
Strong Gov't. Securities	10.5	NA	9.4ᴬ	NA
Financial Bond—Select Income	10.4	66.8ᶜ	0.5ᴮ	57.0ᴰ
GIT Income—Maximum	10.2	58.5ᴰ	(5.9)ᶜ	52.9ᴰ
Strong Short-Term	10.1	NA	3.1ᴬ	NA
Boston Co. Managed Income	10.0	NA	1.8ᴬ	NA
US GNMA	10.0	NA	3.3ᴬ	NA
USAA Income	10.0	73.8ᴮ	2.9ᴬ	50.1ᴰ
Vanguard Investment Grade	9.7	75.0ᴮ	3.8ᴬ	51.9ᴰ
Vanguard U.S. Treasury Bond	9.1	NA	4.0ᴬ	NA
Dreyfus A Bonds Plus	9.0	71.0ᶜ	2.4ᴬ	52.8ᴰ
Scudder Income	8.9	72.0ᶜ	2.7ᴬ	53.8ᴰ
Vanguard GNMA	8.8	70.7ᶜ	3.3ᴬ	50.3ᴰ
Axe-Houghton Income	8.7	87.3ᴮ	1.4ᴬ	70.0ᴰ
Counsellors Fixed Income	8.6	NA	1.2ᴮ	NA
Benham GNMA Income	8.5	NA	3.7ᴬ	NA
Mutual of Omaha America	8.4	58.3ᴰ	3.6ᴬ	37.4ᴱ
20th Century Long-Term Bond	8.3	NA	4.7ᴬ	NA
AARP General Bond	8.1	NA	3.1ᴬ	NA
WPG Government Securities	8.0	NA	3.5ᴬ	NA
Value Line U.S. Government	7.9	70.3ᶜ	3.1ᴬ	52.5ᴰ
Rushmore U.S. Gov't. Long-Term	7.9	NA	3.8ᴬ	NA
Fidelity Flexible Bond	7.9	66.0ᶜ	2.6ᴬ	48.8ᴱ
Benham Target—1995	7.9	NA	4.2ᴬ	NA
SAFECO U.S. Government	7.8	NA	1.2ᴮ	NA
Columbia Fixed Income	7.7	65.4ᶜ	3.1ᴬ	46.1ᴱ
Bartlett Fixed Income	7.7	NA	1.0ᴮ	NA
T. Rowe Price New Inc.	7.6	64.8ᶜ	4.3ᴬ	40.6ᴱ
Vanguard Bond Market	7.4	NA	3.1ᴬ	NA
California U.S. Gov't. Sec.	7.3	NA	2.5ᴬ	NA
SteinRoe Managed Bonds	7.2	73.2ᴮ	3.3ᴬ	51.6ᴰ
GIT Income—A-Rated	7.2	72.6ᴮ	2.7ᴬ	55.9ᴰ
Fidelity Ginnie Mae	7.2	NA	2.5ᴬ	NA
Fidelity Intermediate	7.1	69.8ᶜ	2.7ᴬ	51.4ᴰ

Continued on opposite page

Bond Funds
Ranked by 1988 Total Return

	Total Return (%)		Market Cycle Performance (%)	
Fund	1988	5-Year*	Bear*	Bull*
Continued from opposite page				
Babson Bond Port. L	7.1	69.5ᶜ	3.1ᴬ	50.3ᴰ
AARP GNMA & U.S. Treasury ...	7.1	NA	2.3ᴬ	NA
Vanguard Short Term Bond	6.9	63.2ᶜ	2.8ᴬ	42.9ᴱ
Lexington GNMA Income	6.9	59.4ᴰ	1.7ᴬ	45.6ᴱ
SteinRoe Governments Plus	6.9	NA	3.2ᴬ	NA
Delaware Treasury Reserves	6.9	NA	2.2ᴬ	NA
Neuberger Money Market Plus	6.8	NA	2.2ᴬ	NA
Scudder GNMA	6.8	NA	2.2ᴬ	NA
Rushmore U.S. Gov't. Inter.	6.8	NA	3.3ᴬ	NA
IAI Reserve	6.8	NA	2.1ᴬ	NA
Neuberger Limited Mat.	6.7	NA	2.3ᴬ	NA
Fidelity Mortgage Sec.	6.7	NA	2.6ᴬ	NA
AMA Classic Income	6.6	53.2ᴰ	0.9ᴮ	42.1ᴱ
Boston Co. GNMA	6.5	NA	1.9ᴬ	NA
Legg Mason U.S. Gov't. Inter.	6.4	NA	3.0ᴬ	NA
IAI Bond	6.4	68.9ᶜ	3.0ᴬ	52.3ᴰ
Dreyfus GNMA	6.4	NA	2.1ᴬ	NA
Newton Income	6.4	50.5ᴰ	2.1ᴬ	31.4ᴱ
Permanent T-Bill	6.4	NA	NA	NA
Fidelity Government Sec.	6.3	61.3ᴰ	2.6ᴬ	45.5ᴱ
Value Line Aggressive Inc.	6.3	NA	(8.0)ᶜ	NA
Prudential-Bache Govt. Sec. Int. ..	6.2	NA	3.4ᴬ	NA
Financial Bond—U.S. Gov't.	6.2	NA	(0.3)ᴮ	NA
Scudder Target Gen'l. 1990	6.1	63.3ᶜ	2.2ᴬ	48.8ᴱ
Baker—U.S. Government	5.9	NA	3.5ᴬ	NA
T. Rowe Price GNMA	5.9	NA	1.5ᴬ	NA
UMB Bond	5.9	61.4ᴰ	3.3ᴬ	43.5ᴱ
Dreyfus U.S. Gov't. Int.	5.8	NA	3.4ᴬ	NA
Benham Target—1990	5.8	NA	3.1ᴬ	NA
Vanguard Short Term Gov't.	5.7	NA	NA	NA
Fidelity Short-Term Bond	5.7	NA	2.3ᴬ	NA
20th Century U.S. Gov't.	5.6	52.8ᴰ	3.2ᴬ	35.4ᴱ
T. Rowe Price Short-Term	5.5	NA	3.3ᴬ	NA
Cap. Preservation T-Note	5.2	54.7ᴰ	3.4ᴬ	39.8ᴱ
Avondale Government	5.2	NA	2.3ᴬ	NA
Bull & Bear High Yield	5.0	35.8ᴱ	(9.2)ᶜ	42.8ᴱ
Bull & Bear U.S. Gov't.	4.5	NA	2.1ᴬ	NA
Flex Bond	2.7	NA	(0.3)ᴮ	NA
Treasury First	1.6	NA	5.0ᴬ	NA
Average	**8.1**	**67.0**	**2.1**	**50.8**

*Superscripts indicate the fund's relative ranking—see key at beginning of this
chapter and Chapter 5 for a more complete description.

Tax-Exempt Bond Funds
Ranked by 1988 Total Return

Fund	Total Return (%) 1988	Total Return (%) 5-Year*	Market Cycle Performance (%) Bear*	Market Cycle Performance (%) Bull*
Financial Income	15.1	80.9[B]	(0.1)[B]	52.2[D]
Fidelity Penn. High Yield	14.3	NA	(2.0)[C]	NA
SAFECO Municipal	13.9	82.6[B]	0.4[B]	54.3[D]
Vanguard High-Yield Muni.	13.8	79.0[B]	0.4[B]	50.5[D]
SteinRoe High-Yield Muni.	13.7	NA	(1.0)[B]	NA
Scudder High Yield	13.5	NA	(1.4)[B]	NA
Fidelity Aggressive	13.4	NA	(1.2)[B]	NA
Fidelity Michigan	13.0	NA	(0.6)[B]	NA
Fidelity Ohio	12.9	NA	(0.7)[B]	NA
SAFECO California	12.8	72.0[C]	0.5[B]	50.6[D]
Vanguard—Insured Long-Term	12.8	NA	0.6[B]	NA
Fidelity Minnesota	12.6	NA	(0.9)[B]	NA
Dreyfus New Jersey	12.6	NA	NA	NA
USAA High Yield	12.5	70.6[C]	1.5[A]	41.9[E]
Benham Calif. High-Yield	12.5	NA	(2.7)[C]	NA
Fidelity Texas Tax-Free	12.4	NA	(0.7)[B]	NA
Scudder Massachusetts	12.4	NA	NA	NA
Fidelity Municipal	12.3	73.1[B]	(0.2)[B]	50.1[D]
Scudder Managed Municipal	12.3	69.5[C]	(0.3)[B]	47.1[E]
Vanguard Penn. Insured	12.3	NA	0.9[B]	NA
Vanguard Long-Term Muni.	12.2	73.8[B]	0.9[B]	49.3[E]
AARP Insured General	12.2	NA	0.4[B]	NA
Fidelity High Yield	12.2	72.9[B]	(1.4)[B]	50.6[D]
California Muni Fund	12.2	NA	0.7[B]	NA
Vanguard Calif. Insured	12.1	NA	0.6[B]	NA
US Tax-Free	12.0	NA	1.1[B]	NA
Vanguard New York Insured	12.0	NA	0.6[B]	NA
Fidelity N.Y. High Yield	11.9	NA	(0.4)[B]	NA
Scudder California	11.9	NA	0.2[B]	NA
Fidelity Calif. High Yield	11.8	NA	(0.3)[B]	39.1[E]
Bull & Bear Tax-Free Income	11.6	NA	0.1[B]	52.2[D]
Babson Income Portfolio L	11.6	69.9[C]	0.2[B]	48.0[E]
Fidelity Calif. Insured	11.6	NA	0.6[B]	NA
Dreyfus Tax Exempt	11.5	66.8[C]	(0.4)[B]	45.9[E]
Dreyfus New York Insured	11.3	NA	(1.6)[B]	NA
California Tax-Free Income	11.3	NA	(0.4)[B]	NA
New York Muni	11.3	58.1[D]	(2.0)[C]	39.8[E]
Fidelity N.Y. Insured	11.3	NA	0.5[B]	NA
Benham National—Long-Term	11.2	NA	(2.5)[C]	NA
Fidelity Insured Tax-Free	11.2	NA	0.6[B]	NA
T. Rowe Price TF High Yield	11.2	NA	(0.6)[B]	NA
Value Line High-Yield	11.0	NA	(0.6)[B]	NA
Fidelity N.J. High Yield	10.9	NA	NA	NA
SteinRoe Managed Municipals	10.9	84.6[B]	2.3[A]	53.2[D]
Scudder New York	10.9	NA	0.1[B]	NA
Value Line New York	10.8	NA	0.2[B]	NA
Fidelity Mass. High Yield	10.7	NA	(0.9)[B]	NA

Continued on opposite page

Tax-Exempt Bond Funds
Ranked by 1988 Total Return

Fund	Total Return (%)		Market Cycle Performance (%)	
	1988	5-Year*	Bear*	Bull*
Continued from opposite page				
Dreyfus Massachusetts	10.6	NA	(1.4)^B	NA
T. Rowe Price New York	10.4	NA	0.9^B	NA
Benham Calif. Long Term	10.4	55.3^D	(0.7)^B	41.8^E
20th Century Long-Term	10.3	NA	1.5^A	NA
Kentucky Tax-Free Income	10.3	59.9^D	1.4^A	39.8^E
Lexington Tax Exempt Bond	10.3	NA	0.4^B	NA
Unified Muni.—General	10.3	NA	0.2^B	NA
Unified Muni.—Indiana	10.3	NA	0.5^B	NA
Columbia Municipal	10.2	NA	1.5^A	46.8^E
Dreyfus Insured	10.2	NA	(0.1)^B	NA
Benham Calif. Tax-Free Insured	10.2	NA	(1.0)^B	NA
Dreyfus N.Y. Tax Exempt	10.1	NA	(1.5)^B	NA
Fidelity Connecticut	10.1	NA	NA	NA
Vanguard Intermediate-Term	10.0	67.1^C	1.2^B	44.0^E
Rushmore Long-Term	9.7	54.4^D	(0.2)^B	38.4^E
Dreyfus California	9.7	NA	(0.8)^B	NA
Dreyfus N.Y. Intermediate	9.6	NA	(0.6)^B	NA
T. Rowe Price California	9.5	NA	0.0^B	NA
T. Rowe Price Maryland	8.9	NA	0.8^B	NA
USAA Intermediate	8.7	57.2^D	1.8^A	38.4^E
GIT Tax-Free High Yield	8.5	68.5^C	(0.1)^B	49.9^E
GIT Virginia	8.3	NA	NA	NA
Fidelity Limited Term	8.2	62.5^C	0.3^B	43.2^E
Dreyfus Intermediate	8.0	NA	(0.2)^B	NA
T. Rowe Price Income	7.8	55.1^D	(0.9)^B	41.3^E
Strong Municipal Bond	7.6	NA	2.9^A	NA
Rushmore Intermediate	7.6	46.5^D	0.9^B	29.1^E
Scudder Target 1996	7.5	NA	1.3^B	NA
UST Intermediate	7.0	NA	3.3^A	NA
Benham National—Intermediate	6.6	NA	0.4^B	25.2^E
Counsellors New York	6.4	NA	0.0^B	NA
Vanguard Limited Term	6.4	NA	2.7^A	NA
SteinRoe Intermediate	6.1	NA	0.4^B	NA
USAA Short-Term	6.1	39.6^E	2.4^A	24.0^E
20th Century Intermediate	6.0	NA	0.5^B	NA
General N.Y. Intermediate	6.0	NA	0.5^B	NA
Benham Calif. Intermediate	5.9	44.0^D	0.4^B	32.6^E
Dreyfus Short-Intermediate	5.8	NA	1.3^A	NA
Scudder Target 1993	5.6	52.2^D	0.4^B	38.9^E
Vanguard Short-Term Muni.	5.6	34.9^E	1.2^B	22.0^E
T. Rowe Price Short Int.	4.9	NA	1.1^B	25.4^E
Scudder Target 1990	4.9	43.6^E	0.6^B	31.1^E
Fidelity Short-Term TF	4.9	NA	0.1^B	NA
AARP Insured Short Term	4.6	NA	1.2^B	NA
Average	**10.2**	**62.8**	**0.2**	**41.8**

Superscripts indicate the fund's relative ranking—see key at beginning of this chapter and Chapter 5 for a more complete description.

International Funds
Ranked by 1988 Total Return

Fund	Total Return (%) 1988	5-Year*	Market Cycle Performance (%) Bear*	Bull*	Beta
Ivy International	29.7	NA	(21.6)D	NA	NA
FSP—Pacific Basin	23.2	NA	(27.9)E	252.3A	0.73
Transatlantic Growth	21.0	164.6A	(16.9)C	223.6A	0.59
International Equity Trust	19.5	NA	(18.1)C	NA	0.62
Scudder Japan	19.4	NA	1.2B	NA	NA
Scudder Global	19.2	NA	(22.9)D	NA	NA
Scudder International	18.8	167.1A	(21.8)D	212.3A	0.71
Vanguard Trustees'—Int'l.	18.8	205.8A	(12.8)C	216.4A	0.56
IAI International	18.0	NA	(13.0)C	NA	NA
T. Rowe Price Int'l. Stock	17.9	180.1A	(17.5)C	233.1A	0.64
AMA Global Growth	17.5	NA	(22.1)D	NA	NA
Nomura Pacific Basin	16.4	NA	(9.6)C	NA	0.46
Vanguard World—Int'l.	11.6	NA	(11.0)C	NA	0.57
Pax World	11.6	66.9C	(14.9)C	86.9C	0.60
FSP—European	10.6	NA	(20.3)D	NA	NA
AMA Global Short Term	5.6	NA	2.8A	NA	NA
AMA Global Income	4.8	NA	3.4A	NA	NA
Fidelity Global Bond	3.7	NA	12.9A	NA	NA
T. Rowe Price Int'l. Bond	(1.2)	NA	18.6A	NA	NA
Transatlantic Income	(2.0)	NA	19.2A	NA	NA
Average	**14.2**	**156.9**	**(9.6)**	**204.1**	**60.8**

*Superscripts indicate the fund's relative ranking—see key at beginning of this chapter and Chapter 5 for a more complete description.

Precious Metals Funds
Ranked by 1988 Total Return

Fund	Total Return (%) 1988	5-Year*	Market Cycle Performance (%) Bear*	Bull*
Bull & Bear Gold	(13.5)	16.8E	(23.3)D	125.3B
Vanguard Spec.—Gold & P.M.	(14.2)	NA	(20.1)D	122.9B
Lexington Goldfund	(15.0)	42.1E	(15.5)C	133.6A
USAA Gold	(17.1)	NA	(34.7)E	NA
US New Prospector	(18.8)	NA	(28.2)E	NA
FSP—Gold	(20.0)	NA	(31.3)E	95.2C
US Gold Shares	(35.7)	(40.2)E	(18.3)C	45.7E
Average	**(19.2)**	**41.0**	**(24.5)**	**104.5**

*Superscripts indicate the fund's relative ranking—see key at beginning of this chapter and Chapter 5 for a more complete description.

Mutual Fund Data Summaries

On the following pages, we present in-depth information on no-load mutual funds. The funds are listed alphabetically; their category is indicated at the top of the page under the fund's name. Below are brief definitions and explanations of some of the terms used on the data pages.

For more complete descriptions, see **Chapter 5.**

Years Ending: The fiscal year-end for the per-share data information, which varies. All performance information, however, is calculated on a calendar-year basis.

Annual & Five-Year Total Return: Includes the change in net asset value and all distributions, and assumes reinvestment of distributions when paid. Five-year total returns are also ranked: An "A" indicates the fund was in the top performing group and an "E" indicates the fund was in the lowest group.

Degree of Diversification: Measured relative to the S&P 500. Funds were ranked according to how closely their returns tracked the S&P 500. An "A" indicates the fund was in the group that most closely tracked the market; an "E" indicates the fund was in the group that tracked the market the least.

Beta: A measure of risk relative to the stock market. The market's beta is always 1.0; a beta higher than 1.0 indicates fund returns are more volatile than the market and a beta lower than 1.0 indicates fund returns are less volatile than the market. Beta is not calculated for bond or precious metals funds.

Bull: Fund performance and ranking (A through E) over the most recent bull market, from August 1984 through August 1987.

Bear: Fund performance and ranking (A through E) over the most recent bear market, from September 1987 through December 1987.

Distributions: Months in which distributions are paid were provided when available.

12b-1: Indicates whether the fund has a 12b-1 plan. If the fund has a 12b-1 plan, either the maximum charge is indicated or it is stated that the advisor pays any distribution charges.

Investor Services: IRA, Keogh, Corp, 403(b) and **SEP** indicate the availability of IRA, Keogh, corporate pension and profit-sharing plans, non-profit group retirement plans, and simplified employee pension plans. **Withdraw** indicates if the fund allows for the automatic and systematic withdrawal of monies, and **Deduct** indicates if the fund allows for automatic investments through an investor's checking account. All funds offer automatic reinvestment of distributions.

AARP CAPITAL GROWTH

Growth

Scudder Fund Distributors
160 Federal Street
Boston, MA 02110-1706
(800) 253-2277

	Years Ending 9/30					
	1983	1984	1985	1986 (10 mos.)	1987	1988
Dividends from Net Investment Income ($)	—	—	—	.09	.19	.15
Distributions from Net Realized Capital Gains ($)	—	—	—	.19	.90	1.65
Net Asset Value End of Year ($)	—	—	16.95	21.13	27.55	23.88
Ratio of Expenses to Net Assets (%)	—	—	1.50	1.44	1.24	1.23
Ratio of Net Income to Average Net Assets (%)	—	—	1.95	1.27	.62	.37
Portfolio Turnover Rate (%)	—	—	42	46	54	45
Total Assets End of Year (Millions $)	—	—	20.6	55.7	115.9	91.1
Annual Rate of Return (%) Years Ending 12/31	—	—	—	15.9	0.1	27.3

Five-Year Total Return(%)	NA	Degree of Diversification	C	Beta	1.06	Bull (%)	NA	Bear (%)	(24.7)E

Objective:	Seeks long-term capital appreciation through investment in common stocks and convertible securities. Looks for undervalued stocks with above-average long-term earnings growth potential. Can invest in debt securities and put and call options.
Portfolio:	(9/30/88) Common stocks 94%, short-term securities 8%. Largest stock holdings: media and service 40%, utilities 15%.
Portfolio Mgr:	Andrew H. Massie Jr.—1985
Distributions:	Income: Dec **Capital Gains:** Annually
12b-1:	No
Minimum:	**Initial:** $250 **Subsequent:** None
Min IRA:	**Initial:** $250 **Subsequent:** None
Services:	IRA, Keogh, Withdraw, Deduct
Tel Exchange:	Yes **With MMF:** Yes
Registered:	All states
Ticker:	ACGFX

AARP GENERAL BOND

Bond

Scudder Fund Distributors
160 Federal Street
Boston, MA 02110-1706
(800) 253-2277

	Years Ending 9/30					
	1983	1984	1985 (10 mos.)	1986	1987	1988
Dividends from Net Investment Income ($)	—	—	1.06	1.41	1.22	1.27
Distributions from Net Realized Capital Gains ($)	—	—	—	.05	.23	.11
Net Asset Value End of Year ($)	—	—	15.31	15.87	14.45	14.80
Ratio of Expenses to Net Assets (%)	—	—	1.50	1.30	1.18	1.17
Ratio of Net Income to Average Net Assets (%)	—	—	9.86	8.86	7.81	8.55
Portfolio Turnover Rate (%)	—	—	54	63	193	24
Total Assets End of Year (Millions $)	—	—	45.3	88.4	108.0	123.7
Annual Rate of Return (%) Years Ending 12/31	—	—	—	10.7	1.2	8.1

Five-Year Total Return(%)	NA	Degree of Diversification	NA	Beta	NA	Bull (%)	NA	Bear (%)	3.1^

Objective: Seeks high level of current income consistent with preservation of capital. Invests in short-, intermediate- and long-term government securities and in high quality corporate bonds. Normally has 65% of assets invested in government and corporate bonds.

Portfolio: (9/30/88) Long-term bonds 65%, short-term securities 32%, intermediate-term bonds 6%. Largest holdings: U.S. Treasury and agency 26%, utilities 16%.

Portfolio Mgr: William Hutchinson—1987

Distributions: **Income:** Monthly   **Capital Gains:** Annually

12b-1: No

Minimum: **Initial:** $250   **Subsequent:** None

Min IRA: **Initial:** $250   **Subsequent:** None

Services: IRA, Keogh, Withdraw, Deduct

Tel Exchange: Yes   **With MMF:** Yes

Registered: All states

Ticker: AGBFX

AARP GNMA & U.S. TREASURY
Bond

Scudder Fund Distributors
160 Federal Street
Boston, MA 02110-1706
(800) 253-2277

	Years Ending 9/30					
	1983	**1984**	**1985** (10 mos.)	**1986**	**1987**	**1988**
Dividends from Net Investment Income ($)	—	—	1.17	1.54	1.35	1.37
Distributions from Net Realized Capital Gains ($)	—	—	—	.03	.01	—
Net Asset Value End of Year ($)	—	—	15.52	15.99	14.89	15.11
Ratio of Expenses to Net Assets (%)	—	—	1.03	.90	.88	.81
Ratio of Net Income to Average Net Assets (%)	—	—	10.62	9.49	8.76	9.09
Portfolio Turnover Rate (%)	—	—	67	62	51	85
Total Assets End of Year (Millions $)	—	—	322.1	1,963.0	2,827.6	2,837.8

Annual Rate of Return (%) Years Ending 12/31	—	—	—	11.4	2.0	7.1

Five-Year Total Return(%)	NA	Degree of Diversification	NA	Beta NA	Bull (%)	NA	Bear (%) 2.3ᴬ

Objective: Seeks high level of current income consistent with preservation of capital. Invests primarily in GNMA securities and other debt instruments backed by the U.S. government.

Portfolio: (9/30/88) GNMAs 74%, U.S. Treasury notes 26%, repurchase agreements 1%.

Portfolio Mgr: David H. Glen—1987

Distributions: **Income:** Monthly   **Capital Gains:** Annually

12b-1: No

Minimum: **Initial:** $250   **Subsequent:** None

Min IRA: **Initial:** $250   **Subsequent:** None

Services: IRA, Keogh, Withdraw, Deduct

Tel Exchange: Yes   **With MMF:** Yes

Registered: All states

Ticker: AGNMX

AARP GROWTH & INCOME
Growth & Income

Scudder Fund Distributors
160 Federal Street
Boston, MA 02110-1706
(800) 253-2277

			Years Ending 9/30			
	1983	1984	1985 (10 mos.)	1986	1987	1988
Dividends from Net Investment Income ($)	—	—	.19	.70	.49	.94
Distributions from Net Realized Capital Gains ($)	—	—	—	.09	.88	.77
Net Asset Value End of Year ($)	—	—	16.84	20.88	25.54	20.94
Ratio of Expenses to Net Assets (%)	—	—	1.50	1.21	1.08	1.06
Ratio of Net Income to Average Net Assets (%)	—	—	5.62	4.55	3.81	4.52
Portfolio Turnover Rate (%)	—	—	13	37	43	61
Total Assets End of Year (Millions $)	—	—	26.7	99.3	357.6	228.3

Annual Rate of Return (%) Years Ending 12/31	—	—	—	19.2	0.7	10.9

Five-Year Total Return(%)	NA	Degree of Diversification	A	Beta .81	Bull (%)	NA	Bear (%)	(19.2)C

Objective: Seeks long-term growth of capital, current income and growth of income. Invests primarily in common stocks and convertible securities. Looks for companies with good earnings growth potential that pay dividends.

Portfolio: (9/30/88) Common stocks 78%, convertible preferred stocks 12%, convertible bonds 7%, short-term securities 3%. Largest stock holdings: financial 18%, utilities 14%.

Portfolio Mgr: Robert T. Harvey—1985

Distributions: Income: Apr, July, Oct, Dec **Capital Gains:** Annually

12b-1: No

Minimum: Initial: $250 **Subsequent:** None

Min IRA: Initial: $250 **Subsequent:** None

Services: IRA, Keogh, Withdraw, Deduct

Tel Exchange: Yes **With MMF:** Yes

Registered: All states

Ticker: AGIFX

†ACORN
Growth

Harris Associates, L.P.
Two N. LaSalle St.
Chicago, IL 60602-3790
(312) 621-0630

	Years Ending 12/31					
	1983	**1984**	**1985**	**1986**	**1987**	**1988**
Dividends from Net Investment Income ($)	1.04	.55	.51	.50	.77	.82
Distributions from Net Realized Capital Gains ($)	1.04	1.63	1.86	6.07	5.42	3.18
Net Asset Value End of Year ($)	31.82	30.89	37.82	37.27	32.42	36.36
Ratio of Expenses to Net Assets (%)	.85	.85	.78	.79	.82	.80
Ratio of Net Income to Average Net Assets (%)	1.94	2.31	1.73	1.71	1.85	1.52
Portfolio Turnover Rate (%)	22	33	32	34	52	36
Total Assets End of Year (Millions $)	173.8	210.2	317.5	414.6	417.8	563.4

Annual Rate of Return (%) Years Ending 12/31	25.1	4.5	31.4	16.7	4.3	24.7

Five-Year Total Return(%)	108.5^	Degree of Diversification	D	Beta	.83	Bull (%)	129.4^	Bear (%)	(20.6)^D

Objective:	Seeks capital growth through investment in common stocks and convertibles of smaller companies that are not yet widely recognized as growth companies. May invest in foreign securities.
Portfolio:	(12/31/88) Common stocks 95%, money markets 3%, fixed income 2%. Largest stock holdings: information group 29%, consumer goods and services 17%.
Portfolio Mgr:	Ralph Wanger—1970
Distributions:	**Income:** July, Dec **Capital Gains:** Dec
12b-1:	No
Minimum:	**Initial:** $4,000 **Subsequent:** $1,000
Min IRA:	**Initial:** $200 **Subsequent:** $200
Services:	IRA, Keogh, SEP, Withdraw, Deduct
Tel Exchange:	Yes **With MMF:** Yes
Registered:	All states except AL, AR, ND, NH, NM, VT
Ticker:	ACRNX

† There will be a 2% redemption fee only if shares are redeemed in less than 60 days.

ADTEK
Balanced

Heath, Schneider, Mueller & Toll
4920 W. Vliet St.
Milwaukee, WI 53208
(414) 257-1842

	Years Ending 5/31						12/31
	1983	1984	1985	1986	1987	1988	1988* (7 mos.)
Dividends from Net Investment Income ($)	–	–	–	.29	.41	.38	.36
Distributions from Net Realized Capital Gains ($)	–	–	–	.18	.72	1.56	–
Net Asset Value End of Year ($)	–	–	11.10	12.70	13.45	9.33	9.19
Ratio of Expenses to Net Assets (%)	–	–	1.95	1.87	1.73	1.73	2.14
Ratio of Net Income to Average Net Assets (%)	–	–	3.99	3.41	1.74	2.65	3.60
Portfolio Turnover Rate (%)	–	–	179	232	107	226	150
Total Assets End of Year (Millions $)	–	–	23.9	29.6	39.9	24.7	19.2

Annual Rate of Return (%) Years Ending 12/31	–		–		13.5	16.0	(4.9)	1.9	*

Five-Year Total Return(%)	NA	Degree of Diversification	B	Beta	.86	Bull (%)	NA	Bear (%)	(26.0)ᴱ

* *Fiscal year-end changed from 5/31 to 12/31. All annual return figures are for full years ending 12/31.*

Objective: Seeks long-term capital appreciation and protection of capital through a balance of common stocks of established companies, corporate bonds and money market instruments. The particular balance is determined by economic and market conditions indicated by various technical and fundamental analysis techniques. May enter into repurchase agreements.

Portfolio: (12/31/88) Cash equivalents 58%, common stocks 40%, preferred stocks 1%. Largest stock holdings: drugs 5%, financial 5%.

Portfolio Mgr: Nick Carver, F. Mackey Schneider—1989

Distributions: **Income:** Dec   **Capital Gains:** Dec

12b-1: No

Minimum: **Initial:** $250   **Subsequent:** $50

Min IRA: **Initial:** $250   **Subsequent:** $50

Services: IRA, Keogh, Corp, 403(b), Withdraw, Deduct

Tel Exchange: No

Registered: FL, IL, WI

Ticker: ATKFX

AFUTURE
Growth

Carlisle-Asher Management Co.
122 Willowbrook Lane
West Chester, PA 19382
(800) 523-7594/(215) 344-7910

	Years Ending 12/31					
	1983	**1984**	**1985**	**1986**	**1987**	**1988**
Dividends from Net Investment Income ($)	.82	.09	.08	.11	.12	.26
Distributions from Net Realized Capital Gains ($)	.96	2.01	—	—	2.14	—
Net Asset Value End of Year ($)	15.89	11.08	13.38	12.49	9.27	9.18
Ratio of Expenses to Net Assets (%)	1.60	1.60	1.60	1.40	1.60	1.60
Ratio of Net Income to Average Net Assets (%)	.55	.62	.77	(.01)	.83	2.47
Portfolio Turnover Rate (%)	152	121	193	200	355	283
Total Assets End of Year (Millions $)	34.6	24.9	24.6	16.2	9.9	8.0
Annual Rate of Return (%) Years Ending 12/31	12.2	(19.2)	21.5	(5.9)	(11.0)	1.9

Five-Year Total Return(%) (16.2)[E]	Degree of Diversification C	Beta .90	Bull (%) 39.0[E]	Bear (%) (24.1)[D]

Objective: Capital appreciation through long-term holdings in common stock of large, well-established companies. Current dividend income is not a substantial factor in selecting investments. May take defensive posture in debt securities.

Portfolio: (12/31/88) Common stocks 93%, bonds 6%, other assets 2%. Largest stock holdings: consumer products/services 18%, health care 17%.

Portfolio Mgr: Donald Goebert—1988

Distributions: Income: Jan   **Capital Gains:** Jan

12b-1: No

Minimum: Initial: $500   Subsequent: $30

Min IRA: Initial: $500   Subsequent: $30

Services: IRA, Keogh, Withdraw, Deduct

Tel Exchange: No

Registered: All states except AK, AR, CT, ID, KS, KY, LA, ME, MS, ND, NH, NM, NV, SC, SD, UT, VA, VT, WY

Ticker: AFUTX

AMA CLASSIC GROWTH
Growth

AMA Advisers, Inc.
5 Sentry Pkwy. W., Suite 120
P.O. Box 1111
Blue Bell, PA 19422
(800) 262-3863/(215) 825-0400

	Years Ending 9/30				12/31		
	1983	1984	1985	1986	1986* (3 mos.)	1987	1988
Dividends from Net Investment Income ($)	.26	.26	.38	.16	.05	.16	.20
Distributions from Net Realized Capital Gains ($)	–	–	–	.41	1.79	2.16	–
Net Asset Value End of Year ($)	10.11	9.56	10.23	11.92	10.56	8.22	8.81
Ratio of Expenses to Net Assets (%)	1.26	1.30	1.32	1.34	1.73	1.65	1.63
Ratio of Net Income to Average Net Assets (%)	2.26	3.42	3.05	1.12	1.34	1.25	2.24
Portfolio Turnover Rate (%)	114	129	158	127	146	148	67
Total Assets: End of Year (Millions $)	35.1	29.6	26.9	26.8	37.6	36.3	33.6

Annual Rate of Return (%) Years Ending 12/31	7.5	5.4	23.5	11.0	*	(1.8)	9.7

Five-Year Total Return(%)	55.6ᴰ	Degree of Diversification	A	Beta	.99	Bull (%)	100.8ᶜ	Bear (%)	(24.8)ᴰ

*Fiscal year-end changed from 9/30 to 12/31. All annual return figures are for full
years ending 12/31.*

Objective:	Seeks capital appreciation. Fund favors equity investments in companies that have potential for above-average, long-term growth in sales and earnings on a sustained and predictable basis.
Portfolio:	(12/31/88) Common stocks 85%, commercial paper 24%, other assets 1%. Largest stock holdings: basic materials 23%, energy 16%.
Portfolio Mgr:	John E. Turner—1986
Distributions:	**Income:** Jan, Apr, July, Oct **Capital Gains:** Annually
12b-1:	Yes **Amount:** 0.50%
Minimum:	**Initial:** $1,000 **Subsequent:** None
Min IRA:	**Initial:** $500 **Subsequent:** $50
Services:	IRA, Keogh, SEP, 403(b), Withdraw, Deduct
Tel Exchange:	Yes **With MMF:** Yes
Registered:	All states
Ticker:	AMGFX

AMA CLASSIC INCOME
Bond

AMA Advisers, Inc.
5 Sentry Pkwy. W.
Suite 120, P.O. Box 1111
Blue Bell, PA 19422
(800) 262-3863/(215) 825-0400

	Years Ending 3/31					
	1983	1984	1985	1986	1987	1988
Dividends from Net Investment Income ($)	.89	.79	.87	.80	.63	.64
Distributions from Net Realized Capital Gains ($)	—	—	—	—	—	—
Net Asset Value End of Year ($)	8.91	8.33	8.34	9.44	9.46	8.90
Ratio of Expenses to Net Assets (%)	1.16	1.25	1.50	1.39	1.65	1.62
Ratio of Net Income to Average Net Assets (%)	10.80	9.49	10.50	8.87	6.82	7.17
Portfolio Turnover Rate (%)	256	105	62	147	67	54
Total Assets End of Year (Millions $)	23.7	21.2	19.7	19.2	39.4	38.8

Annual Rate of Return (%) Years Ending 12/31	9.1	8.4	18.3	12.7	(.6)	6.6

Five-Year Total Return(%)	53.2ᴰ	Degree of Diversification	NA	Beta	NA	Bull (%)	42.1ᴱ	Bear (%)	.9ᴮ

Objective: Seeks the highest investment income available consistent with preservation of capital. At least 80% of assets are in short-term money market instruments or marketable debt securities of only the three highest investment ratings. May enter into repurchase agreements comprising no more than 10% of fund's assets.

Portfolio: (9/30/88) Non-convertible bonds, notes and debentures 60%, U.S. Treasury securities 18%, commercial paper 13%, repurchase agreements 5%, CDs 3%, other assets 2%.

Portfolio Mgr: John E. Turner—1986

Distributions: **Income:** Jan, Apr, July, Oct   **Capital Gains:** Annually

12b-1: Yes   **Amount:** 0.50%

Minimum: **Initial:** $1,000   **Subsequent:** None

Min IRA: **Initial:** $500   **Subsequent:** $50

Services: IRA, Keogh, SEP, 403(b), Withdraw, Deduct

Tel Exchange: Yes   **With MMF:** Yes

Registered: All states

Ticker: AINFX

AMA GLOBAL GROWTH
International

AMA Advisers, Inc.
5 Sentry Pkwy. W., Suite 120
P.O. Box 1111
Blue Bell, PA 19422
(800) 523-0864/(215) 825-0400

| | Years Ending 12/31 | | | | | |
	1983	1984	1985	1986	1987 (11 mos.)	1988
Dividends from Net Investment Income ($)	−	−	−	−	.34	.52
Distributions from Net Realized Capital Gains ($)	−	−	−	−	.36	.01
Net Asset Value End of Year ($)	−	−	−	−	17.34	19.84
Ratio of Expenses to Net Assets (%)	−	−	−	−	1.49	1.61
Ratio of Net Income to Average Net Assets (%)	−	−	−	−	1.91	2.60
Portfolio Turnover Rate (%)	−	−	−	−	20	9
Total Assets End of Year (Millions $)	−	−	−	−	110.5	106.8

Annual Rate of Return (%) Years Ending 12/31	−	−	−	−	−	17.5

Five-Year Total Return(%)	NA	Degree of Diversification	NA	Beta	NA	Bull (%)	NA	Bear (%)	(22.1)D

Objective:	Seeks capital appreciation through investment in common stocks traded on exchanges worldwide. 30% of the portfolio may be invested in stocks not listed on American exchanges. May also invest in investment-grade debt securities.
Portfolio:	(12/31/88) Common stocks 86%, commercial paper 10%, repurchase agreements 2%, other assets 2%. Largest stock holdings: financial services 20%, capital goods 10%.
Portfolio Mgr:	John E. Turner—1987
Distributions:	**Income:** Quarterly **Capital Gains:** Annually
12b-1:	Yes **Amount:** 0.50%
Minimum:	**Initial:** $1,000 **Subsequent:** None
Min IRA:	**Initial:** $500 **Subsequent:** $50
Services:	IRA, Keogh, SEP, 403(b), Withdraw, Deduct
Tel Exchange:	Yes **With MMF:** Yes
Registered:	All states
Ticker:	AMASX

AMA GLOBAL INCOME
International

AMA Advisers, Inc.
5 Sentry Pkwy. W.
Suite 120, P.O. Box 1111
Blue Bell, PA 19422
(800) 262-3863/(215) 825-0400

	Years Ending 3/31					
	1983	1984	1985	1986	1987	1988 (11 mos.)
Dividends from Net Investment Income ($)	—	—	—	—	—	.78
Distributions from Net Realized Capital Gains ($)	—	—	—	—	—	—
Net Asset Value End of Year ($)	—	—	—	—	—	20.52
Ratio of Expenses to Net Assets (%)	—	—	—	—	—	1.97
Ratio of Net Income to Average Net Assets (%)	—	—	—	—	—	6.04
Portfolio Turnover Rate (%)	—	—	—	—	—	95
Total Assets End of Year (Millions $)	—	—	—	—	—	16.2
Annual Rate of Return (%) Years Ending 12/31	—	—	—	—	—	4.8

Five-Year Total Return(%)	NA	Degree of Diversification	NA	Beta	NA	Bull (%)	NA	Bear (%)	3.4ᴬ

Objective: Seeks investment income, with capital appreciation a secondary objective. Invests in foreign and domestic investment-grade debt securities. May invest up to 10% of assets in preferred and convertible securities. Will normally be invested in the securities of companies or governments of at least three different countries.

Portfolio: (9/30/88) Non-convertible bonds, notes and debentures 41%, U.S. Treasury securities 25%, temporary investments 24%, Treasury bills 9%, other assets 2%.

Portfolio Mgr: John E. Turner—1987

Distributions: Income: Jan, Apr, July, Oct   **Capital Gains:** Annually

12b-1: Yes   **Amount:** 0.50%

Minimum: Initial: $1,000   Subsequent: None

Min IRA: Initial: $500   Subsequent: None

Services: IRA, Keogh, SEP, 403(b), Withdraw, Deduct

Tel Exchange: Yes   **With MMF:** Yes

Registered: All states

Ticker: AIGIX

AMA GLOBAL SHORT TERM
International

AMA Advisers, Inc.
5 Sentry Pkwy. W.
Suite 120, P.O. Box 1111
Blue Bell, PA 19422
(800) 262-3863/(215) 825-0400

	Years Ending 3/31					
	1983	**1984**	**1985**	**1986**	**1987**	**1988** (11 mos.)
Dividends from Net Investment Income ($)	–	–	–	–	–	.39
Distributions from Net Realized Capital Gains ($)	–	–	–	–	–	–
Net Asset Value End of Year ($)	–	–	–	–	–	10.21
Ratio of Expenses to Net Assets (%)	–	–	–	–	–	1.65
Ratio of Net Income to Average Net Assets (%)	–	–	–	–	–	6.07
Portfolio Turnover Rate (%)	–	–	–	–	–	49
Total Assets End of Year (Millions $)	–	–	–	–	–	29.3
Annual Rate of Return (%) Years Ending 12/31	–	–	–	–	–	5.6

Five-Year Total Return(%)	NA	Degree of Diversification	NA	Beta	NA	Bull (%)	NA	Bear (%)	2.8ᴬ

Objective: Seeks to maximize current income. Invests in foreign and domestic investment-grade debt securities (BBB or better) that mature within two years. Normally, the fund will invest in securities of companies or governments of at least three different countries. May not invest more than 70% of its assets in foreign debt securities.

Portfolio: (9/30/88) U.S. Treasury notes 42%, non-convertible bonds, notes and debentures 32%, temporary investments 15%, other assets 7%, Treasury bills 6%.

Portfolio Mgr: John E. Turner—1987

Distributions: Income: Jan, Apr, July, Oct   **Capital Gains:** Annually

12b-1: Yes   **Amount:** 0.50%

Minimum: Initial: $1,000   **Subsequent:** None

Min IRA: Initial: $500   **Subsequent:** None

Services: IRA, Keogh, SEP, 403(b), Withdraw, Deduct

Tel Exchange: Yes   **With MMF:** Yes

Registered: All states

Ticker: AIGSX

AMA GROWTH PLUS INCOME
Growth & Income

AMA Advisers, Inc.
5 Senry Pkwy. W., Suite 120
P.O. Box 1111
Blue Bell, PA 19422
(800) 262-3863/(215) 825-0400

	Years Ending 12/31					
	1983	1984	1985	1986	1987 (11 mos.)	1988
Dividends from Net Investment Income ($)	—	—	—	—	.42	.60
Distributions from Net Realized Capital Gains ($)	—	—	—	—	—	—
Net Asset Value End of Year ($)	—	—	—	—	16.85	18.34
Ratio of Expenses to Net Assets (%)	—	—	—	—	1.60	1.83
Ratio of Net Income to Average Net Assets (%)	—	—	—	—	2.45	3.24
Portfolio Turnover Rate (%)	—	—	—	—	46	68
Total Assets End of Year (Millions $)	—	—	—	—	13.3	15.3

Annual Rate of Return (%) Years Ending 12/31	—	—	—	—	—	12.5

Five-Year Total Return(%)	NA	Degree of Diversification	NA	Beta	NA	Bull (%)	NA	Bear (%)	(21.2)ᴰ

Objective:	Seeks to achieve growth of capital and, as a secondary objective, investment income. Invests in common stocks, preferred stocks, convertible securities and in-vestment-grade debt securities.
Portfolio:	(12/31/88) Common stock 65%, commercial paper 29%, repurchase agreements 9%, other assets 4%. Largest stock holdings: basic materials 10%, utilities 8%.
Portfolio Mgr:	John E. Turner—1987
Distributions:	**Income:** Jan, Apr, July, Oct **Capital Gains:** Annually
12b-1:	Yes **Amount:** 0.50%
Minimum:	**Initial:** $1,000 **Subsequent:** None
Min IRA:	**Initial:** $500 **Subsequent:** $50
Services:	IRA, Keogh, SEP, 403(b), Withdraw, Deduct
Tel Exchange:	Yes **With MMF:** Yes
Registered:	All states
Ticker:	AGGIX ,

AMERICAN PENSION INVESTORS— GROWTH
Growth

American Pension Investors, Inc.
2316 Atherholt Road
Lynchburg, VA 24501
(800) 544-6060/(800) 533-4115

	Years Ending 5/31					
	1983	1984	1985	1986 (11 mos.)	1987	1988
Dividends from Net Investment Income ($)	–	–	–	.05	.57	.03
Distributions from Net Realized Capital Gains ($)	–	–	–	–	1.60	1.19
Net Asset Value End of Year ($)	–	–	–	13.63	12.16	10.43
Ratio of Expenses to Net Assets (%)	–	–	–	2.59	2.41	2.74
Ratio of Net Income to Average Net Assets (%)	–	–	–	2.00	1.11	.82
Portfolio Turnover Rate (%)	–	–	–	169	190	165
Total Assets End of Year (Millions $)	–	–	–	5.1	19.3	27.0
Annual Rate of Return (%) Years Ending 12/31	–	–	–	13.1	(7.6)	26.0

| Five-Year Total Return(%) | NA | Degree of Diversification | A | Beta | 1.11 | Bull (%) | NA | Bear (%) | (28.9)E |

Objective: Seeks growth of capital, with income as the secondary objective. Assets will be aggressively managed. Invests in temporarily depressed securities of sound, well-managed companies. These securities will appear to be undervalued in relation to the quality of the assets and the long-term earning power of their issuers. Also invests in preferred stocks and convertible securities.

Portfolio: (11/30/88) Common stocks 100%. Largest stock holdings: metals and mining 19%, chemicals 12%.

Portfolio Mgr: David Basten—1985

Distributions: **Income:** Annually   **Capital Gains:** Annually

12b-1: Yes   **Amount:** 1.0%

Minimum: **Initial:** $100   **Subsequent:** $50

Min IRA: **Initial:** $100   **Subsequent:** $50

Services: IRA, Keogh, Corp, SEP, 403(b), Withdraw

Tel Exchange: No   **With MMF:** No

Registered: AL, AZ, CA, CO, CT, DE, DC, FL, GA, HI, IL, IN, KS, LA, MA, MD, ME, MI, MN, MO, MS, NC, NE, NH, NV, NY, OH, OR, PA, RI, SC, TN, TX, VA, VT, WA, WI, WV

Ticker: APITX

ANALYTIC OPTIONED EQUITY
Growth & Income

Analytic Investment Mgmt., Inc.
2222 Martin St., #230
Irvine, CA 92715-1454
(714) 833-0294

	Years Ending 12/31					
	1983	**1984**	**1985**	**1986**	**1987**	**1988**
Dividends from Net Investment Income ($)	.60	.44	.48	.45	.46	.42
Distributions from Net Realized Capital Gains ($)	.24	.02	1.20	2.20	2.48	.66
Net Asset Value End of Year ($)	13.86	14.31	14.84	13.70	11.38	12.06
Ratio of Expenses to Net Assets (%)	1.23	1.30	1.23	1.18	1.17	1.13
Ratio of Net Income to Average Net Assets (%)	3.71	3.65	3.30	2.90	2.68	3.44
Portfolio Turnover Rate (%)	49	45	54	64	84	66
Total Assets End of Year (Millions $)	54.2	76.7	85.5	76.4	74.8	102.3
Annual Rate of Return (%) Years Ending 12/31	19.3	6.7	16.5	10.2	4.2	15.6

Five-Year Total Return(%)	65.2[c]	Degree of Diversification	A	Beta	.54	Bull (%)	67.7[D]	Bear (%)	(11.6)[c]

All per share data is adjusted for a 10-for-1 stock split on 6/30/86.

Objective: Obtain a greater long-term total return and smaller fluctuations in quarterly total return from a diversified, optioned common stock portfolio than would be realized from the same portfolio unoptioned.

Portfolio: (12/31/88) Common stocks 86%, other assets 13%, short-term securities 4%, put and call options 1%. Largest stock holdings: telephone utilities 7%, computer equipment 7%.

Portfolio Mgr: Charles Dobson—1978

Distributions: **Income:** Quarterly   **Capital Gains:** Annually

12b-1: No

Minimum: **Initial:** $5,000   **Subsequent:** $500

Min IRA: **Initial:** None   **Subsequent:** None

Services: IRA, Keogh, Corp, SEP, 403(b), Withdraw

Tel Exchange: No

Registered: All states except AR, MT, ND, NH, NM, OK, RI, SC, VT

Ticker: ANALX

ARMSTRONG ASSOCIATES
Growth

Armstrong Associates, Inc.
1445 Ross Ave.
Lock Box 212, Suite 1490
Dallas, TX 75202
(214) 720-9101

	Years Ending 6/30					
	1983	1984	1985	1986	1987	1988
Dividends from Net Investment Income ($)	.43	.20	.14	.24	.16	.14
Distributions from Net Realized Capital Gains ($)	.38	.38	.76	—	.51	1.91
Net Asset Value End of Year ($)	10.22	7.29	7.65	8.72	9.66	7.17
Ratio of Expenses to Net Assets (%)	1.60	1.60	1.70	1.60	1.70	2.00
Ratio of Net Income to Average Net Assets (%)	2.40	1.90	3.10	1.60	1.00	1.30
Portfolio Turnover Rate (%)	59	96	53	54	51	20
Total Assets End of Year (Millions $)	12.9	9.8	11.0	11.7	12.3	10.4

Annual Rate of Return (%) Years Ending 12/31	11.0	(11.5)	21.0	11.3	0.1	15.5

Five-Year Total Return(%)	37.8[E]	Degree of Diversification	B	Beta	.88	Bull (%)	84.4[C]	Bear (%)	(23.9)[D]

Objective:	Seeks growth of capital through investment in common stock of large companies expected to have growth in earnings over a one- to three-year period. May invest in short-term debt securities as a defensive measure.
Portfolio:	(9/30/88) Common stocks 61%, short-term debt and cash 39%. Largest stock holdings: retail and related 16%, electronics and electrical equipment 12%.
Portfolio Mgr:	C.K. Lawson—1967
Distributions:	**Income:** Dec **Capital Gains:** Dec
12b-1:	No
Minimum:	**Initial:** $250 **Subsequent:** None
Min IRA:	**Initial:** $250 **Subsequent:** None
Services:	IRA, Keogh, Withdraw, Deduct
Tel Exchange:	No
Registered:	AR, TX
Ticker:	ARMSX

†AVONDALE GOVERNMENT SECURITIES

Bond

Herbert R. Smith, Inc.
1105 Holliday
Wichita Falls, TX 76301
(817) 761-3777

	Years Ending 3/31					
	1983	**1984**	**1985**	**1986**	**1987**	**1988** (11 mos.)
Dividends from Net Investment Income ($)	—	—	—	—	—	.69
Distributions from Net Realized Capital Gains ($)	—	—	—	—	—	—
Net Asset Value End of Year ($)	—	—	—	—	—	9.93
Ratio of Expenses to Net Assets (%)	—	—	—	—	—	.60
Ratio of Net Income to Average Net Assets (%)	—	—	—	—	—	7.40
Portfolio Turnover Rate (%)	—	—	—	—	—	214
Total Assets End of Year (Millions $)	—	—	—	—	—	41.5
Annual Rate of Return (%) Years Ending 12/31	—	—	—	—	—	5.2

Five-Year Total Return(%)	NA	Degree of Diversification	NA	Beta	NA	Bull (%)	NA	Bear (%)	2.3ᴬ

Objective: Seeks current income consistent with preservation of capital. Invests in debt obligations issued or guaranteed by the U.S. government and its agencies. May write covered call options and may hedge using interest rate futures and options.

Portfolio: (9/30/88) U.S. Treasury notes 50%, FNMAs 38%, GNMAs 10%, other assets 2%.

Portfolio Mgr: Herbert R. Smith—1987

Distributions: **Income:** Monthly   **Capital Gains:** Annually

12b-1: No

Minimum: **Initial:** $5,000   **Subsequent:** $1,000

Min IRA: **Initial:** $1,000   **Subsequent:** $250

Services: IRA, Keogh, Corp, SEP, 403(b), Withdraw, Deduct

Tel Exchange: Yes   **With MMF:** No

Registered: Call for availability

Ticker: AVGFX

† *On October 1, 1988, the fund added a 1% front-end sales charge.*

AXE-HOUGHTON FUND B

Balanced

Axe-Houghton Management, Inc.
400 Benedict Avenue
Tarrytown, NY 10591
(800) 366-0444/(914) 631-8131

	Years Ending 10/31					
	1983	1984	1985	1986	1987	1988
Dividends from Net Investment Income ($)	.59	.59	.66	.66	.58	.40
Distributions from Net Realized Capital Gains ($)	.13	.13	—	.70	2.86	1.68
Net Asset Value End of Year ($)	9.68	9.49	10.77	13.03	9.55	8.16
Ratio of Expenses to Net Assets (%)	.73	.76	.74	.98	1.18	1.25
Ratio of Net Income to Average Net Assets (%)	6.89	6.60	6.93	5.76	3.81	5.19
Portfolio Turnover Rate (%)	64	88	97	239	324	251
Total Assets End of Year (Millions $)	147.7	141.2	152.6	190.0	172.7	163.7

Annual Rate of Return (%) Years Ending 12/31	11.1	6.3	32.9	23.1	(4.0)	9.0

Five-Year Total Return(%) 81.9ᴮ	Degree of Diversification	B	Beta .73	Bull (%) 120.5ᴮ	Bear (%) (19.6)ᴰ

Objective:	Seeks conservation of capital, reasonable income, and long-term capital growth. May not invest more than 75% of its assets in common stocks. Also invests in bonds and preferred stocks.
Portfolio:	(10/31/88) Bonds and other notes 50%, common stocks 48%, short-term notes 1%, other assets 1%. Largest holdings: food stocks 12%, mortgage-backed securities 11%.
Portfolio Mgr:	Porter Sutro—1987
Distributions:	Income: Jan, Apr, July, Oct **Capital Gains:** Jan
12b-1:	Yes **Amount:** 0.45%
Minimum:	Initial: $1,000 **Subsequent:** None
Min IRA:	Initial: $25 Subsequent: $25
Services:	IRA, Keogh, Corp, 403(b), Withdraw, Deduct
Tel Exchange:	Yes **With MMF:** Yes
Registered:	All states
Ticker:	AXEBX

AXE-HOUGHTON INCOME
Bond

Axe-Houghton Management, Inc.
400 Benedict Avenue
Tarrytown, NY 10591
(800) 366-0444/(914) 631-8131

	Years Ending 11/30					
	1983	1984	1985	1986	1987	1988
Dividends from Net Investment Income ($)	.50	.50	.50	.50	.50	.50
Distributions from Net Realized Capital Gains ($)	—	—	—	—	—	—
Net Asset Value End of Year ($)	4.52	4.59	5.05	5.56	5.12	5.12
Ratio of Expenses to Net Assets (%)	1.01	1.09	1.04	1.37	1.42	1.35
Ratio of Net Income to Average Net Assets (%)	9.97	11.12	10.61	9.05	9.70	9.52
Portfolio Turnover Rate (%)	30	13	90	90	269	258
Total Assets End of Year (Millions $)	33.9	35.3	40.2	48.5	51.9	60.5
Annual Rate of Return (%) Years Ending 12/31	7.5	15.5	26.6	15.8	1.8	8.7

Five-Year Total Return(%)	87.3ᴮ	Degree of Diversification	NA	Beta	NA	Bull (%)	70.0ᴰ	Bear (%)	1.4ᴬ

Objective: Seeks high current income consistent with prudent investment risk. Invests in bonds and debentures, dividend-paying common stocks, convertible preferred stocks and bonds, government notes and short-term money market instruments.

Portfolio: (11/30/88) Bonds and other notes 97%, other assets 3%. Largest holdings: utilities 21%, communications services 14%.

Portfolio Mgr: Robert Manning—1987

Distributions: Income: Jan, Apr, July, Oct   **Capital Gains:** Jan

12b-1: Yes   **Amount:** 0.45%

Minimum: Initial: $1,000   **Subsequent:** None

Min IRA: Initial: $25   **Subsequent:** $25

Services: IRA, Keogh, Corp, 403(b), Withdraw, Deduct

Tel Exchange: Yes   **With MMF:** Yes

Registered: All states

Ticker: AXEAX

AXE-HOUGHTON STOCK
Aggressive Growth

Axe-Houghton Management, Inc.
400 Benedict Avenue
Tarrytown, NY 10591
(800) 366-0444/(914) 631-8131

	Years Ending 12/31					
	1983	1984	1985	1986	1987	1988
Dividends from Net Investment Income ($)	.02	.05	—	.04	.04	.05
Distributions from Net Realized Capital Gains ($)	.20	5.01	—	1.80	2.26	—
Net Asset Value End of Year ($)	14.02	6.85	8.98	8.11	5.53	5.47
Ratio of Expenses to Net Assets (%)	.84	.95	.95	1.28	1.41	1.62
Ratio of Net Income to Average Net Assets (%)	.45	1.42	.77	.07	.27	.76
Portfolio Turnover Rate (%)	119	134	191	218	306	193
Total Assets End of Year (Millions $)	150.8	87	107.3	96.2	65.6	57.9

Annual Rate of Return (%) Years Ending 12/31	23.7	(15.5)	31.1	10.9	(6.2)	(0.2)

Five-Year Total Return(%)	15.1[E]	Degree of Diversification	C	Beta	1.29	Bull (%)	141.6[A]	Bear (%)	(35.8)[E]

Objective: Primary objective is long-term capital growth. Looks to invest in companies with above-average growth prospects. Also invests in convertible preferred and foreign stocks. For defensive purposes the fund can invest in bonds.

Portfolio: (12/31/88) Common stocks 85%, short-term notes 15%, other assets 1%. Largest stock holdings: specialty stores 13%, technology service 12%.

Portfolio Mgr: John Schroeder—1984

Distributions: Income: Jan   **Capital Gains:** Jan

12b-1: Yes   **Amount:** 0.45%

Minimum: Initial: $1,000   **Subsequent:** None

Min IRA: Initial: $25   **Subsequent:** $25

Services: IRA, Keogh, Corp, 403(b), Withdraw, Deduct

Tel Exchange: Yes   **With MMF:** Yes

Registered: All states

Ticker: AXETX

BABSON BOND TRUST PORTFOLIO L
(formerly BABSON BOND TRUST)
Bond

Jones and Babson, Inc.
Three Crown Center
2440 Pershing Rd.
Kansas City, MO 64108
(800) 821-5591/(816) 471-5200

	Years Ending 11/30					
	1983	1984	1985	1986	1987	1988
Dividends from Net Investment Income ($)	.17	.12	.21	.16	.11	.20
Distributions from Net Realized Capital Gains ($)	—	—	—	—	—	—
Net Asset Value End of Year ($)	1.48	1.52	1.58	1.68	1.58	1.52
Ratio of Expenses to Net Assets (%)	.75	.92	.98	.97	.97	.97
Ratio of Net Income to Average Net Assets (%)	11.08	11.31	10.45	9.42	9.29	9.99
Portfolio Turnover Rate (%)	49	42	39	41	54	42
Total Assets End of Year (Millions $)	37.1	42.1	54.7	69.7	65.0	66.4
Annual Rate of Return (%) Years Ending 12/31	9.6	12.9	20.7	13.9	1.9	7.1

Five-Year Total Return(%)	69.5[C]	Degree of Diversification	NA	Beta	NA	Bull (%)	50.3[D]	Bear (%)	3.1[A]

Objective: Seeks current regular income and stability of principal. Long-term capital growth is a secondary aim. Maturity structure is conservative, with all issues rated A or higher. Most agency securities are mortgages.

Portfolio: (11/30/88) Corporate bonds 68%, U.S. government bonds 27%, repurchase agreements 4%, other assets 1%. Largest bond holdings: banks and finance 26%, transportation 12%.

Portfolio Mgr: Edward Martin—1984

Distributions: **Income:** Monthly   **Capital Gains:** Annually

12b-1: No

Minimum: **Initial:** $500   **Subsequent:** $50

Min IRA: **Initial:** $250   **Subsequent:** $25

Services: IRA, Keogh, SEP, Withdraw, Deduct

Tel Exchange: Yes   **With MMF:** Yes

Registered: All states

Ticker: BABIX

BABSON ENTERPRISE
Aggressive Growth

Jones & Babson, Inc.
Three Crown Center
2440 Pershing Rd.
Kansas City, MO 64108
(800) 821-5591/(816) 471-5200

	Years Ending 11/30					
	1983	1984 (11 mos.)	1985	1986	1987	1988
Dividends from Net Investment Income ($)	—	—	.07	.05	.05	.04
Distributions from Net Realized Capital Gains ($)	—	—	.13	.47	1.28	1.67
Net Asset Value End of Year ($)	—	9.30	12.52	13.56	10.12	11.90
Ratio of Expenses to Net Assets (%)	—	1.67	1.58	1.37	1.35	1.37
Ratio of Net Income to Average Net Assets (%)	—	.73	.62	.42	.23	.50
Portfolio Turnover Rate (%)	—	14	38	32	24	41
Total Assets End of Year (Millions $)	—	7.3	34.5	47.9	35.6	52.1
Annual Rate of Return (%) Years Ending 12/31	—	(5.0)	38.6	9.0	(9.5)	32.5

Five-Year Total Return(%)	72.1B	Degree of Diversification	D	Beta	.95	Bull (%)	110.5B	Bear (%)	(28.0)E

Objective:	Seeks long-term capital growth through investment in smaller, faster-growing companies whose capitalization is between $15 million and $300 million.
Portfolio:	(11/30/88) Common stocks 94%, repurchase agreements 4%, short-term corporate notes 2%, other assets 1%. Largest stock holdings: leisure 11%, building and construction 11%.
Portfolio Mgr:	Peter Schliemann—1985
Distributions:	**Income:** Annually **Capital Gains:** Annually
12b-1:	No
Minimum:	**Initial:** $1,000 **Subsequent:** $100
Min IRA:	**Initial:** $250 **Subsequent:** $25
Services:	IRA, Keogh, SEP, Withdraw, Deduct
Tel Exchange:	Yes **With MMF:** Yes
Registered:	All states
Ticker:	BABEX

BABSON GROWTH
Growth

Jones & Babson, Inc.
Three Crown Center
2440 Pershing Rd.
Kansas City, MO 64108
(800) 821-5591/(816) 471-5200

	Years Ending 6/30					
	1983	**1984**	**1985**	**1986**	**1987**	**1988**
Dividends from Net Investment Income ($)	.38	.38	.21	.55	.15	.45
Distributions from Net Realized Capital Gains ($)	.23	1.62	.01	3.21	.60	3.03
Net Asset Value End of Year ($)	14.40	10.85	13.40	13.62	16.25	11.66
Ratio of Expenses to Net Assets (%)	.61	.76	.76	.75	.74	.81
Ratio of Net Income to Average Net Assets (%)	3.13	2.64	3.23	2.65	2.12	2.21
Portfolio Turnover Rate (%)	26	52	35	20	14	26
Total Assets End of Year (Millions $)	249.2	208.2	215.4	253.8	288.8	237.5

Annual Rate of Return (%) Years Ending 12/31	15.9	0.2	29.7	19.0	3.1	16.0

Five-Year Total Return(%)	85.0ᴮ	Degree of Diversification	A	Beta	.99	Bull (%)	138.2ᴬ	Bear (%)	(24.9)ᴱ

Objective: Invests in common stocks that are selected for their long-term possibilities of both capital and income growth. Invests in common stocks of established, well-managed companies in growing industries deemed to have potential for maintaining earnings and dividend growth.

Portfolio: (9/30/88) Common stocks 97%, short-term corporate notes 2%. Largest stock holdings: consumer cyclicals 17%, technology 12%.

Portfolio Mgr: David Kirk—1985

Distributions: **Income:** June, Dec   **Capital Gains:** June, Dec

12b-1: No

Minimum: **Initial:** $500   **Subsequent:** $50

Min IRA: **Initial:** $250   **Subsequent:** $25

Services: IRA, Keogh, SEP, Withdraw, Deduct

Tel Exchange: Yes   **With MMF:** Yes

Registered: All states

Ticker: BABSX

BABSON VALUE
Growth & Income

Jones & Babson, Inc.
Three Crown Center
2440 Pershing Rd.
Kansas City, MO 64108
(800) 821-5591/(816) 471-5200

	Years Ending 11/30					
	1983	1984	1985	1986	1987	1988
Dividends from Net Investment Income ($)	—	—	.09	.87	.63	.03
Distributions from Net Realized Capital Gains ($)	—	—	—	.18	.04	—
Net Asset Value End of Year ($)	—	—	12.59	15.04	13.59	16.85
Ratio of Expenses to Net Assets (%)	—	—	.93	1.20	1.08	1.11
Ratio of Net Income to Average Net Assets (%)	—	—	4.79	3.60	3.31	3.87
Portfolio Turnover Rate (%)	—	—	13	28	52	24
Total Assets End of Year (Millions $)	—	—	2.8	6.9	13.5	10.4

Annual Rate of Return (%) Years Ending 12/31	—	—	26.5	20.7	3.3	19.0

Five-Year Total Return(%)	NA	Degree of Diversification	A	Beta	1.01	Bull (%)	NA	Bear (%)	(25.4)E

Objective: Seeks long-term growth of capital and income through investment in common stocks of companies rated B− or better (by Standard & Poor's or Value Line) in terms of growth and stability of earnings and dividends. Holds contrarian attitude seeking undervalued stocks.

Portfolio: (11/30/88) Common stocks 86%, convertible bonds 7%, repurchase agreements 6%. Largest stock holdings: financial services 14%, office equipment and services 10%.

Portfolio Mgr: Nick Whitridge—1984

Distributions: Income: Annually   **Capital Gains:** Annually

12b-1: No

Minimum: Initial: $1,000   Subsequent: $100

Min IRA: Initial: $250   Subsequent: $25

Services: IRA, Keogh, SEP, Withdraw, Deduct

Tel Exchange: Yes   **With MMF:** Yes

Registered: All states

Ticker: BVALX

BAKER— U.S. GOVERNMENT SERIES
Bond

James Baker & Company
1601 Northwest Expressway
20th Floor
Oklahoma City, OK 73118
(405) 842-1400

	Years Ending 12/31					
	1983	1984	1985	1986 (3 mos.)	1987	1988
Dividends from Net Investment Income ($)	—	—	—	—	.87	1.10
Distributions from Net Realized Capital Gains ($)	—	—	—	—	.01	—
Net Asset Value End of Year ($)	—	—	—	15.65	15.20	14.99
Ratio of Expenses to Net Assets (%)	—	—	—	.98	1.00	1.00
Ratio of Net Income to Average Net Assets (%)	—	—	—	6.28	6.18	7.00
Portfolio Turnover Rate (%)	—	—	—	98	740	581
Total Assets End of Year (Millions $)	—	—	—	3.5	19.1	14.8

Annual Rate of Return (%) Years Ending 12/31	—	—	—	—	4.5	5.9

Five-Year Total Return(%) NA	Degree of Diversification NA	Beta NA	Bull (%) NA	Bear (%) 3.5A

Objective: Seeks both current income and capital appreciation through investment in debt obligations of the U.S. government and its agencies, including Treasury bills, notes and bonds. May emphasize capital appreciation or current income depending on the level of interest rates. May also use put and call options.

Portfolio: (12/31/88) U.S. Treasury bonds and notes 85%, GNMAs 15%, short-term securities 6%.

Portfolio Mgr: Douglas McQueen—1986

Distributions: **Income:** Monthly **Capital Gains:** Annually

12b-1: Yes **Amount:** 0.50%

Minimum: **Initial:** $1,000 **Subsequent:** $100

Min IRA: **Initial:** $1,000 **Subsequent:** $100

Services: IRA, Keogh, Corp, 403(b), Withdraw

Tel Exchange: Yes **With MMF:** No

Registered: Call for availability

Ticker: BAKGX

BARTLETT BASIC VALUE

Growth & Income

Bartlett & Company
36 E. Fourth St.
Cincinnati, OH 45202
(800) 543-0863/(513) 621-0066

	1983	1984 (11 mos.)	1985	1986	1987	1988
Years Ending 3/31						
Dividends from Net Investment Income ($)	—	.46	.57	.49	.45	.36
Distributions from Net Realized Capital Gains ($)	—	—	.18	1.02	1.25	—
Net Asset Value End of Year ($)	—	10.20	10.88	13.13	12.96	12.44
Ratio of Expenses to Net Assets (%)	—	1.99	1.78	1.56	1.28	1.57
Ratio of Net Income to Average Net Assets (%)	—	5.71	6.01	4.05	3.49	2.75
Portfolio Turnover Rate (%)	—	8	36	82	58	97
Total Assets End of Year (Millions $)	—	12.4	22.8	52.7	91.1	80.6
Annual Rate of Return (%) Years Ending 12/31	—	—	25.6	13.7	(3.8)	26.3

Five-Year Total Return(%)	NA	Degree of Diversification	D	Beta	.66	Bull (%)	NA	Bear (%)	(20.9)ᴰ

Objective: Seeks capital appreciation and current income by investing in common stocks and convertible securities that are undervalued and have three years' history. May invest in debt securities and cash as defensive move. May enter into repurchase agreements, invest in foreign securities, lend its securities, and hedge its portfolio with options and futures contracts.

Portfolio: (9/30/88) Common stocks 59%, commercial paper 16%, corporate bonds 9%, mortgage-backed securities 5%, U.S. government obligations 3%, repurchase agreements 3%, preferred stocks 2%, other assets 2%. Largest stock holdings: health care 6%, insurance 5%.

Portfolio Mgr: Donald Schmidt—1983

Distributions: Income: Mar, June, Sep, Dec   **Capital Gains:** Mar

12b-1: Yes   **Amount:** Pd. by Advisor

Minimum: Initial: $5,000   Subsequent: $100

Min IRA: Initial: $250   Subsequent: $50

Services: IRA, Keogh, Corp, 403(b)

Tel Exchange: Yes   **With MMF:** Yes

Registered: AZ, CA, CO, DC, DE, FL, GA, IL, IN, KS, KY, MA, MI, MN, MO, NJ, NY, OH, PA, RI, SC, TX, VA, WV

Ticker: MBBVX

BARTLETT FIXED INCOME

Bond

Bartlett & Company
36 East Fourth Street
Cincinnati, OH 45202
(800) 543-0863/(513) 621-0066

	Years Ending 3/31					
	1983	1984	1985	1986	1987 (11 mos.)	1988
Dividends from Net Investment Income ($)	—	—	—	—	.87	.83
Distributions from Net Realized Capital Gains ($)	—	—	—	—	—	—
Net Asset Value End of Year ($)	—	—	—	—	10.18	9.76
Ratio of Expenses to Net Assets (%)	—	—	—	—	.93	1.00
Ratio of Net Income to Average Net Assets (%)	—	—	—	—	8.57	8.56
Portfolio Turnover Rate (%)	—	—	—	—	192	205
Total Assets End of Year (Millions $)	—	—	—	—	145.2	157.1
Annual Rate of Return (%) Years Ending 12/31	—	—	—	—	2.8	7.7

Five-Year Total Return(%)	NA	Degree of Diversification	NA	Beta	NA	Bull (%)	NA	Bear (%)	1.0ᴮ

Objective: Seeks high level of current income. Capital appreciation is of secondary importance. Invests in a broad range of fixed-income securities including U.S. government, corporate and mortgage-backed bonds. May also invest in high-yielding equity securities.

Portfolio: (9/30/88) U.S. government obligations 72%, corporate obligations 16%, temporary cash investments 13%.

Portfolio Mgr: Dale Rabiner—1986

Distributions: **Income:** Monthly   **Capital Gains:** Annually

12b-1: Yes   **Amount:** Pd. by Advisor

Minimum: **Initial:** $5,000   **Subsequent:** $100

Min IRA: **Initial:** $250   **Subsequent:** $50

Services: IRA, Keogh, Corp, 403(b)

Tel Exchange: Yes   **With MMF:** Yes

Registered: AZ, CA, CO, DC, DE, FL, GA, IL, IN, KS, KY, MA, MI, MN, MO, NJ, NY, OH, PA, RI, SC, TX, VA, WV

Ticker: BFXFX

BARTLETT STRATEGIC INCOME
Balanced

Bartlett & Company
36 East Fourth Street
Cincinnati, OH 45202
(800) 543-0863/(513) 621-0066

			Years Ending 6/30			
	1983	1984	1985 (7 mos.)	1986	1987	1988
Dividends from Net Investment Income ($)	–	–	.06	.09	.08	.08
Distributions from Net Realized Capital Gains ($)	–	–	–	–	–	–
Net Asset Value End of Year ($)	–	–	1.05	1.07	1.04	.98
Ratio of Expenses to Net Assets (%)	–	–	.67	.73	.76	.95
Ratio of Net Income to Average Net Assets (%)	–	–	6.40	8.31	7.66	8.49
Portfolio Turnover Rate (%)	–	–	66	167	169	201
Total Assets End of Year (Millions $)	–	–	8.6	25.2	23.2	18.4
Annual Rate of Return (%) Years Ending 12/31	–	–	15.3	9.3	1.4	4.6

Five-Year Total Return(%)	NA	Degree of Diversification	E	Beta	.11	Bull (%)	NA	Bear (%)	(1.3)B

Objective: Seeks a high level of current income consistent with minimal risk of capital. The fund also offers the potential for moderate capital appreciation. Invests in a broad range of fixed-income and equity securities, which may include U.S. government bonds, corporate bonds, GNMAs and foreign securities.

Portfolio: (12/31/88) U.S. government obligations 41%, preferred stocks 18%, corporate bonds 16%, repurchase agreements 14%, common stocks 8%, other assets 3%. Largest stock holdings: energy 3%, retailing 2%.

Portfolio Mgr: Dale Rabiner—1986

Distributions: **Income:** Monthly   **Capital Gains:** Annually

12b-1: Yes   **Amount:** Pd. by Advisor

Minimum: **Initial:** $5,000   **Subsequent:** $100

Min IRA: **Initial:** $250   **Subsequent:** $50

Services: IRA, Keogh, Corp, 403(b)

Tel Exchange: Yes   **With MMF:** Yes

Registered: CO, DC, DE, FL, GA, IL, IN, KY, MI, NJ, NY, OH, UT, WV

Ticker: MBACX

BB&K DIVERSA
Balanced

Bailard, Biehl & Kaiser, Inc.
2755 Campus Drive, Suite 300
San Mateo, CA 94403
(800) 882-8383/(415) 571-6002

	Years Ending 9/30					
	1983	**1984**	**1985**	**1986**	**1987** (10 mos.)	**1988**
Dividends from Net Investment Income ($)	–	–	–	–	–	.35
Distributions from Net Realized Capital Gains ($)	–	–	–	–	–	.29
Net Asset Value End of Year ($)	–	–	–	–	11.70	10.55
Ratio of Expenses to Net Assets (%)	–	–	–	–	1.02	1.26
Ratio of Net Income to Average Net Assets (%)	–	–	–	–	2.45	5.13
Portfolio Turnover Rate (%)	–	–	–	–	66	89
Total Assets End of Year (Millions $)	–	–	–	–	91.7	105.7

Annual Rate of Return (%) Years Ending 12/31	–	–	–	–	8.2	6.6

Five-Year Total Return(%)	NA	Degree of Diversification	NA	Beta	NA	Bull (%)	NA	Bear (%)	(8.4)ᶜ

Objective: Seeks above-average total return with below-average risk through multiple asset allocation. Invests in five classes of securities: stocks, bonds, foreign securities, real estate and cash. Will hold at least 5% in each category and no more than 50% in any one.

Portfolio: (9/30/88) Domestic fixed income 39%, domestic common stocks 23%, international securities 18%, short-term notes 7%, other assets 7%, domestic real estate portfolio 6%.

Portfolio Mgr: Ronald Kaiser—1986

Distributions: Income: Dec   **Capital Gains:** Dec

12b-1: No

Minimum: Initial: $25,000   Subsequent: $2,000

Min IRA: Initial: $10,000   Subsequent: $2,000

Services: IRA, Keogh, Corp, SEP, Withdraw

Tel Exchange: No

Registered: AZ, CA, CO, GA, HI, MD, ME, NJ, NV, NY, UT, VA, WI—For additional states, call for availability.

Ticker: BBKDX

BEACON HILL MUTUAL
Growth

Beacon Hill Management, Inc.
75 Federal St.
Boston, MA 02110-1904
(617) 482-0795

	Years Ending 6/30					
	1983	1984	1985	1986	1987	1988
Dividends from Net Investment Income ($)	.03	—	—	—	—	—
Distributions from Net Realized Capital Gains ($)	—	—	—	—	.99	—
Net Asset Value End of Year ($)	16.76	15.74	20.31	27.44	29.82	24.70
Ratio of Expenses to Net Assets (%)	3.70	3.40	3.30	3.50	3.70	4.0
Ratio of Net Income to Average Net Assets (%)	.30	(.10)	(.20)	(.90)	(1.60)	(1.60)
Portfolio Turnover Rate (%)	20	0	2	8	0	0
Total Assets End of Year (Millions $)	2.6	2.3	2.9	3.9	3.8	3.1

Annual Rate of Return (%) Years Ending 12/31	16.6	3.8	33.5	6.0	5.4	4.3

Five-Year Total Return(%)	61.4ᴰ	Degree of Diversification	B	Beta	.92	Bull (%)	114.0ᴮ	Bear (%)	(21.8)ᴰ

Objective:	Seeks long-term capital growth through investment in common stocks of well-established companies. As a defensive measure, may hold debt securities.
Portfolio:	(12/31/88) Common stocks 100%. Largest stock holdings: drugs and cosmetics 25%, food products 16%.
Portfolio Mgr:	David L. Stone—1964
Distributions:	**Income:** July **Capital Gains:** July
12b-1:	No
Minimum:	**Initial:** None **Subsequent:** None
Min IRA:	**Initial:** None **Subsequent:** None
Services:	IRA, Keogh, Withdraw, Deduct
Tel Exchange:	No
Registered:	Call for information—many pending
Ticker:	BEHMX

BENHAM GNMA INCOME
Bond

Benham Management Corp.
755 Page Mill Road
Palo Alto, CA 94304-1018
(800) 227-8380/(415) 858-3600

	1983	1984	1985	1986 (6 mos.)	1987	1988
				Years Ending 3/31		
Dividends from Net Investment Income ($)	—	—	—	.58	.93	.95
Distributions from Net Realized Capital Gains ($)	—	—	—	—	—	—
Net Asset Value End of Year ($)	—	—	—	10.42	10.42	9.96
Ratio of Expenses to Net Assets (%)	—	—	—	.29	.74	.73
Ratio of Net Income to Average Net Assets (%)	—	—	—	10.52	8.79	8.94
Portfolio Turnover Rate (%)	—	—	—	264	566	497
Total Assets End of Year (Millions $)	—	—	—	169.7	393.2	259.3
Annual Rate of Return (%) Years Ending 12/31	—	—	—	11.3	2.8	8.5

Five-Year Total Return(%)	NA	Degree of Diversification	NA	Beta	NA	Bull (%)	NA	Bear (%)	3.7ᴬ

Objective: Seeks high level of current income through investment in GNMAs and other U.S. government-backed debt securities. At least 65% of the portfolio must be invested in GNMAs.

Portfolio: (9/30/88) GNMAs 88%, repurchase agreements 12%.

Portfolio Mgr: Randall Merk—1987

Distributions: **Income:** Monthly   **Capital Gains:** Annually

12b-1: No

Minimum: **Initial:** $1,000   **Subsequent:** $100

Min IRA: **Initial:** $100   **Subsequent:** $100

Services: IRA, Keogh

Tel Exchange: Yes   **With MMF:** Yes

Registered: All states

Ticker: BGNMX

BENHAM TARGET MATURITIES TRUST SERIES 1990

Bond

Benham Management Corp.
755 Page Mill Road
Palo Alto, CA 94304
(800) 227-8380/(415) 858-3600

	Years Ending 12/31					
	1983	**1984**	**1985**	**1986**	**1987**	**1988**
Dividends from Net Investment Income ($)	–	–	–	–	–	–
Distributions from Net Realized Capital Gains ($)	–	–	–	–	–	–
Net Asset Value End of Year ($)	–	–	68.16	79.12	81.02	85.70
Ratio of Expenses to Net Assets (%)	–	–	.53	.70	.70	.70
Ratio of Net Income to Average Net Assets (%)	–	–	8.76	7.32	7.07	7.33
Portfolio Turnover Rate (%)	–	–	46	113	88	65
Total Assets End of Year (Millions $)	–	–	4.1	5.9	9.6	19.6

Annual Rate of Return (%) Years Ending 12/31	–	–	–	16.1	2.4	5.8

Five-Year Total Return(%)	NA	Degree of Diversification	NA	Beta	NA	Bull (%)	NA	Bear (%)	3.1[A]

Objective: Seeks highest attainable return through investment in zero coupon U.S. Treasury securities and other full coupon Treasury securities. The trust will terminate on December 31 of its target maturity year of 1990 and will be liquidated during the January following the termination.

Portfolio: (12/31/88) Zero coupon bonds due in 1990, 100%. Largest bond holdings: separate trading of interest and principal of securities (STRIPS) 60%, Treasury receipts (TR) 22%.

Portfolio Mgr: Steven Colton—1987

Distributions: **Income:** Annually   **Capital Gains:** Annually

12b-1: No

Minimum: **Initial:** $1,000   **Subsequent:** $100

Min IRA: **Initial:** $100   **Subsequent:** $100

Services: IRA, Keogh

Tel Exchange: Yes   **With MMF:** Yes

Registered: All states

Ticker: BTMIX

BENHAM TARGET MATURITIES TRUST SERIES 1995
Bond

Benham Management Corp.
755 Page Mill Road
Palo Alto, CA 94304
(800) 227-8380/(415) 858-3600

	Years Ending 12/31					
	1983	1984	1985	1986	1987	1988
Dividends from Net Investment Income ($)	—	—	—	—	—	—
Distributions from Net Realized Capital Gains ($)	—	—	—	—	—	—
Net Asset Value End of Year ($)	—	—	42.99	54.33	52.22	56.33
Ratio of Expenses to Net Assets (%)	—	—	.53	.70	.70	.70
Ratio of Net Income to Average Net Assets (%)	—	—	9.05	7.29	7.70	8.09
Portfolio Turnover Rate (%)	—	—	—	89	86	108
Total Assets End of Year (Millions $)	—	—	2.2	5.1	7.0	15.6

Annual Rate of Return (%) Years Ending 12/31	—	—	—	26.4	(3.9)	7.9

Five-Year Total Return(%)	NA	Degree of Diversification	NA	Beta	NA	Bull (%)	NA	Bear (%)	4.2A

Objective: Seeks highest attainable return through investment in zero coupon U.S. Treasury securities and other full coupon Treasury securities. The trust will terminate on December 31 of its target maturity year of 1995 and will be liquidated the following January.

Portfolio: (12/31/88) Zero coupon bonds due in 1995, 100%. Largest bond holdings: Separate trading of interest and principal of securities (STRIPS) 60%, coupons under book entry safekeeping (CUBES) 20%.

Portfolio Mgr: Steven Colton—1987

Distributions: **Income:** Annually   **Capital Gains:** Annually

12b-1: No

Minimum: **Initial:** $1,000   **Subsequent:** $100

Min IRA: **Initial:** $100   **Subsequent:** $100

Services: IRA, Keogh

Tel Exchange: Yes   **With MMF:** Yes

Registered: All states

Ticker: BTMFX

BENHAM TARGET MATURITIES TRUST SERIES 2000

Bond

Benham Management Corp.
755 Page Mill Road
Palo Alto, CA 94304
(800) 227-8380/(415) 858-3600

	Years Ending 12/31					
	1983	**1984**	**1985**	**1986**	**1987**	**1988**
Dividends from Net Investment Income ($)	–	–	–	–	–	–
Distributions from Net Realized Capital Gains ($)	–	–	–	–	–	–
Net Asset Value End of Year ($)	–	–	26.77	35.44	33.33	37.16
Ratio of Expenses to Net Assets (%)	–	–	.52	.70	.70	.70
Ratio of Net Income to Average Net Assets (%)	–	–	9.30	7.34	8.08	8.33
Portfolio Turnover Rate (%)	–	–	34	39	73	163
Total Assets End of Year (Millions $)	–	–	2.2	5.1	6.3	14.1

Annual Rate of Return (%) Years Ending 12/31	–	–	–	32.4	(6.0)	11.5

Five-Year Total Return(%)	NA	Degree of Diversification	NA	Beta	NA	Bull (%)	NA	Bear (%)	7.9ᴬ

Objective: Seeks highest attainable return through investment in zero coupon U.S. Treasury securities and other full coupon Treasury securities. The trust will terminate on December 31, 2000, and will be liquidated the following January.

Portfolio: (12/31/88) Zero coupon bonds due in 2000, 100%. Largest bond holdings: separate trading of interest and principal of securities (STRIPS) 63%, Treasury receipts (TR) 17%.

Portfolio Mgr: Steven Colton—1987

Distributions: **Income:** Annually   **Capital Gains:** Annually

12b-1: No

Minimum: **Initial:** $1,000   **Subsequent:** $100

Min IRA: **Initial:** $100   **Subsequent:** $100

Services: IRA, Keogh

Tel Exchange: Yes   **With MMF:** Yes

Registered: All states

Ticker: BTMTX

BENHAM TARGET MATURITIES TRUST SERIES 2005

Benham Management Corp.
755 Page Mill Road
Palo Alto, CA 94304
(800) 227-8380/(415) 858-3600

Bond

			Years Ending 12/31			
	1983	**1984**	**1985** (9 mos.)	**1986**	**1987**	**1988**
Dividends from Net Investment Income ($)	–	–	–	–	–	–
Distributions from Net Realized Capital Gains ($)	–	–	–	–	–	–
Net Asset Value End of Year ($)	–	–	16.69	23.74	21.28	24.36
Ratio of Expenses to Net Assets (%)	–	–	.47	.70	.70	.70
Ratio of Net Income to Average Net Assets (%)	–	–	9.27	7.25	8.31	8.44
Portfolio Turnover Rate (%)	–	–	37	50	68	27
Total Assets End of Year (Millions $)	–	–	.8	2.9	3.7	8.9

Annual Rate of Return (%) Years Ending 12/31	–	–	–	42.2	(10.4)	14.5

Five-Year Total Return(%)	NA	Degree of Diversification	NA	Beta	NA	Bull (%)	NA	Bear (%)	9.8ᴬ

Objective: Seeks highest attainable return through investment in zero coupon U.S. Treasury securities and other full coupon Treasury securities. The trust will terminate on December 31, 2005, and will be liquidated the following January.

Portfolio: (12/31/88) Zero coupon bonds due in 2005, 100%. Largest bond holdings: separate trading of registered interest and principal of securities (STRIPS) 78%, Treasury receipts (TR) 11%.

Portfolio Mgr: Steven Colton—1987

Distributions: **Income:** Annually   **Capital Gains:** Annually

12b-1: No

Minimum: **Initial:** $1,000   **Subsequent:** $100

Min IRA: **Initial:** $100   **Subsequent:** $100

Services: IRA, Keogh

Tel Exchange: Yes   **With MMF:** Yes

Registered: All states

Ticker: BTFIX

BENHAM TARGET MATURITIES TRUST SERIES 2010
Bond

Benham Management Corp.
755 Page Mill Road
Palo Alto, CA 94304
(800) 227-8380/(415) 858-3600

	Years Ending 12/31					
	1983	1984	1985	1986	1987	1988
Dividends from Net Investment Income ($)	–	–	–	–	–	–
Distributions from Net Realized Capital Gains ($)	–	–	–	–	–	–
Net Asset Value End of Year ($)	–	–	11.43	17.65	14.96	17.31
Ratio of Expenses to Net Assets (%)	–	–	.49	.70	.70	.70
Ratio of Net Income to Average Net Assets (%)	–	–	9.12	6.71	8.13	8.11
Portfolio Turnover Rate (%)	–	–	18	91	84	259
Total Assets End of Year (Millions $)	–	–	1.2	4.9	9.3	9.6

Annual Rate of Return (%) Years Ending 12/31	–	–	–	54.4	(15.2)	15.7

Five-Year Total Return(%)	NA	Degree of Diversification	NA	Beta	NA	Bull (%)	NA	Bear (%)	9.3ᴬ

Objective: Seeks highest attainable return through investment in zero coupon U.S. Treasury securities and other full coupon Treasury securities. The trust will terminate on December 31, 2010, and will be liquidated the following January.

Portfolio: (12/31/88) Zero coupon bonds due in 2010, 100%. Largest bond holdings: Separate trading of interest and principal of securities (STRIPS) 100%.

Portfolio Mgr: Steven Colton—1987

Distributions: Income: Annually   **Capital Gains:** Annually

12b-1: No

Minimum: Initial: $1,000   Subsequent: $100

Min IRA: Initial: $100   Subsequent: $100

Services: IRA, Keogh

Tel Exchange: Yes   **With MMF:** Yes

Registered: All states

Ticker: BTTNX

BENHAM TARGET MATURITIES TRUST SERIES 2015

Bond

Benham Management Corp.
755 Page Mill Road
Palo Alto, CA 94304
(800) 227-8380/(415) 858-3600

| | \multicolumn{6}{c}{Years Ending 12/31} | | | | | |
	1983	1984	1985	1986 (4 mos.)	1987	1988
Dividends from Net Investment Income ($)	—	—	—	—	—	—
Distributions from Net Realized Capital Gains ($)	—	—	—	—	—	—
Net Asset Value End of Year ($)	—	—	—	14.24	11.37	12.63
Ratio of Expenses to Net Assets (%)	—	—	—	.70	.70	.70
Ratio of Net Income to Average Net Assets (%)	—	—	—	6.06	7.99	7.97
Portfolio Turnover Rate (%)	—	—	—	22	509	188
Total Assets End of Year (Millions $)	—	—	—	.5	2.0	11.8
Annual Rate of Return (%) Years Ending 12/31	—	—	—	—	(19.3)	11.1

Five-Year Total Return(%)	NA	Degree of Diversification	NA	Beta	NA	Bull (%)	NA	Bear (%)	10.3[A]

Objective:	Seeks the highest attainable return. Invests only in zero coupon U.S. Treasury securities and in U.S. Treasury bills, notes, and bonds. The trust will terminate on December 31, 2015, and will be liquidated the following January.
Portfolio:	(12/31/88) Zero coupon bonds due in 2015, 100%. Largest bond holdings: separate trading of interest and principal of securities (STRIPS) 100%.
Portfolio Mgr:	Steven Colton—1987
Distributions:	**Income:** Annually **Capital Gains:** Annually
12b-1:	No
Minimum:	**Initial:** $1,000 **Subsequent:** $100
Min IRA:	**Initial:** $100 **Subsequent:** $100
Services:	IRA, Keogh
Tel Exchange:	Yes **With MMF:** Yes
Registered:	All states
Ticker:	BTFTX

BOSTON CO. CAPITAL APPRECIATION

Growth

The Boston Company Advisors
One Boston Place
Boston, MA 02108
(800) 225-5267/(800) 343-6324

	Years Ending 12/31					
	1983	1984	1985	1986	1987	1988
Dividends from Net Investment Income ($)	.64	.69	.74	.50	1.32	.59
Distributions from Net Realized Capital Gains ($)	.82	2.91	1.56	5.80	5.36	1.88
Net Asset Value End of Year ($)	27.92	25.91	32.11	32.40	26.07	28.65
Ratio of Expenses to Net Assets (%)	.98	1.00	.96	.95	.95	1.31
Ratio of Net Income to Average Net Assets (%)	2.73	3.69	3.60	2.65	2.16	2.14
Portfolio Turnover Rate (%)	47	26	59	37	46	24
Total Assets End of Year (Millions $)	238.1	259.7	369.7	452.9	431.6	542.5

Annual Rate of Return (%) Years Ending 12/31	24.0	6.9	35.0	22.5	0.4	19.6

Five-Year Total Return(%)	112.3[A]	Degree of Diversification	A	Beta	.90	Bull (%)	136.6[A]	Bear (%)	(20.1)[D]

Objective: Seeks long-term growth of capital through investment in companies with strong growth features and that meet other investment criteria based on studies of trends in industries and companies. May engage in repurchase agreements, invest in foreign securities and employ leverage.

Portfolio: (12/31/88) Common stocks 84%, repurchase agreements 14%, U.S. government obligations 1%, corporate bonds 1%. Largest stock holdings: financial services 17%, basic industries 11%.

Portfolio Mgr: Gerald Zukowski—1982

Distributions: **Income:** Jan, Apr, July, Oct   **Capital Gains:** Annually

12b-1: Yes   **Amount:** 0.45%

Minimum: **Initial:** $1,000   **Subsequent:** None

Min IRA: **Initial:** $500   **Subsequent:** None

Services: IRA, Keogh, Corp, Withdraw

Tel Exchange: Yes   **With MMF:** Yes

Registered: All states

Ticker: BCCAX

BOSTON CO. GNMA
Bond

The Boston Company Advisors
One Boston Place
Boston, MA 02108
(800) 225-5267/(800) 343-6324

	Years Ending 12/31					
	1983	1984	1985	1986 (10 mos.)	1987	1988
Dividends from Net Investment Income ($)	—	—	—	.88	.99	.81
Distributions from Net Realized Capital Gains ($)	—	—	—	—	—	—
Net Asset Value End of Year ($)	—	—	—	12.63	11.75	11.66
Ratio of Expenses to Net Assets (%)	—	—	—	.65	1.04	1.63
Ratio of Net Income to Average Net Assets (%)	—	—	—	8.21	8.20	6.91
Portfolio Turnover Rate (%)	—	—	—	85	122	64
Total Assets End of Year (Millions $)	—	—	—	15.4	13.6	13.8
Annual Rate of Return (%) Years Ending 12/31	—	—	—	—	0.7	6.5

Five-Year Total Return(%)	NA	Degree of Diversification	NA	Beta	NA	Bull (%)	NA	Bear (%)	1.9A

Objective: Seeks high current income consistent with preservation of capital. Invests in U.S. government-backed debt obligations—principally GNMA mortgage-backed securities.

Portfolio: (12/31/88) Mortgage-backed securities 57%, U.S. government obligations 21%, repurchase agreements 20%, other assets 1%.

Portfolio Mgr: Thomas Hovey—1986

Distributions: **Income:** Monthly   **Capital Gains:** Annually

12b-1: Yes   **Amount:** 0.45%

Minimum: **Initial:** $1,000   **Subsequent:** None

Min IRA: **Initial:** $500   **Subsequent:** None

Services: IRA, Keogh, Corp, Withdraw

Tel Exchange: Yes   **With MMF:** Yes

Registered: All states

Ticker: BGMFX

BOSTON CO.
MANAGED INCOME
Bond

The Boston Company Advisors
One Boston Place
Boston, MA 02108
(800) 225-5267/(800) 343-6324

	Years Ending 12/31					
	1983	1984	1985*	1986	1987	1988
Dividends from Net Investment Income ($)	–	–	.99	.96	1.20	.96
Distributions from Net Realized Capital Gains ($)	–	–	–	.07	.10	–
Net Asset Value End of Year ($)	–	–	11.80	11.91	11.29	11.43
Ratio of Expenses to Net Assets (%)	–	–	1.48	.88	.94	1.14
Ratio of Net Income to Average Net Assets (%)	–	–	10.77	10.01	10.30	8.81
Portfolio Turnover Rate (%)	–	–	173	71	306	139
Total Assets End of Year (Millions $)	–	–	16.7	49.3	51.8	65.1

Annual Rate of Return (%) Years Ending 12/31	–	–	21.8	14.9	5.7	10.0

Five-Year Total Return(%)	NA	Degree of Diversification	NA	Beta	NA	Bull (%)	NA	Bear (%)	1.8A

Objectives changed Nov. 1984; prior history not meaningful.

Objective: Seeks high current income through investment in debt securities such as corporate bonds, debentures, convertibles, preferred stocks, U.S. government obligations and money market instruments. May engage in repurchase agreements and in foreign securities.

Portfolio: (12/31/88) Corporate bonds 51%, U.S. government and agency obligations 17%, repurchase agreements 14%, preferred stocks 9%, collateralized mortgage securities 6%, other assets 3%, common stocks 1%. Largest bond holdings: banking and finance 19%, industrial 19%.

Portfolio Mgr: Thomas Hovey—1988

Distributions: **Income:** Monthly   **Capital Gains:** Annually

12b-1: Yes   **Amount:** 0.45%

Minimum: **Initial:** $1,000   **Subsequent:** None

Min IRA: **Initial:** $500   **Subsequent:** None

Services: IRA, Keogh, Corp, Withdraw

Tel Exchange: Yes   **With MMF:** Yes

Registered: All states

Ticker: BOSGX

BOSTON CO. SPECIAL GROWTH
Growth

The Boston Company Advisors
One Boston Place
Boston, MA 02108
(800) 225-5267/(800) 343-6324

	Years Ending 12/31					
	1983	1984	1985	1986	1987	1988
Dividends from Net Investment Income ($)	–	.09	.35	.31	.81	.34
Distributions from Net Realized Capital Gains ($)	.61	.11	–	4.96	4.10	–
Net Asset Value End of Year ($)	18.05	15.87	20.95	17.21	12.02	14.27
Ratio of Expenses to Net Assets (%)	1.49	1.50	1.35	1.32	1.49	1.58
Ratio of Net Income to Average Net Assets (%)	4.08	2.38	1.96	1.16	3.25	2.70
Portfolio Turnover Rate (%)	247	261	258	192	322	183
Total Assets End of Year (Millions $)	25.5	27.6	53.6	35.9	30.7	35.2

Annual Rate of Return (%) Years Ending 12/31	38.3	(10.9)	34.7	7.7	(4.4)	22.0

Five-Year Total Return(%)	50.9ᴰ	Degree of Diversification	B	Beta	1.02	Bull (%)	96.8ᶜ	Bear (%)	(25.4)ᴱ

Objective: Seeks above-average growth of capital through investment in securities thought to have significant growth potential—primarily common stocks and convertible securities of smaller companies, and larger, more established companies with above-average growth potential. May engage in repurchase agreements, invest in foreign securities, and employ leverage.

Portfolio: (12/31/88) Common stocks 92%, repurchase agreements 11%, convertible bonds 1%. Largest stock holdings: utilities 19%, consumer services 13%.

Portfolio Mgr: J. David Mills—1982

Distributions: **Income:** Annually   **Capital Gains:** Annually

12b-1: Yes   **Amount:** 0.45%

Minimum: **Initial:** $1,000   **Subsequent:** None

Min IRA: **Initial:** $500   **Subsequent:** None

Services: IRA, Keogh, Corp, Withdraw

Tel Exchange: Yes   **With MMF:** Yes

Registered: All states

Ticker: BOSSX

BRANDYWINE FUND
Growth

Friess Associates, Inc.
3908 Kennett Pike
Greenville, DE 19807
(302) 656-6200

	\multicolumn{6}{c}{Years Ending 9/30}
	1983	1984	1985	1986 (10 mos.)	1987	1988
Dividends from Net Investment Income ($)	–	–	–	–	.03	–
Distributions from Net Realized Capital Gains ($)	–	–	–	–	–	.88
Net Asset Value End of Year ($)	–	–	–	11.01	17.00	12.89
Ratio of Expenses to Net Assets (%)	–	–	–	1.3	1.2	1.2
Ratio of Net Income to Average Net Assets (%)	–	–	–	.71	(.18)	.34
Portfolio Turnover Rate (%)	–	–	–	58	147	107
Total Assets End of Year (Millions $)	–	–	–	58.0	127.8	122.9
Annual Rate of Return (%) Years Ending 12/31	–	–	–	16.4	2.6	17.7

Five-Year Total Return(%)	NA	Degree of Diversification	D	Beta	1.32	Bull (%)	NA	Bear (%)	(29.9)[E]

Objective: Primary objective is to produce long-term capital appreciation through investment in common stocks of lesser-known companies moving from a lower to a higher market share position within their industry groups. No more than 5% of fund's assets may be invested in companies with less than three years' operating history.

Portfolio: (12/31/88) Common stocks 90%, short-term securities 10%. Largest stock holdings: computer systems 15%, retail sales and distributors 12%.

Portfolio Mgr: Foster Friess—1985

Distributions: **Income:** Annually   **Capital Gains:** Annually

12b-1: No

Minimum: **Initial:** $25,000   **Subsequent:** $1,000

Min IRA: **Initial:** NA   **Subsequent:** NA

Services: NA

Tel Exchange: No

Registered: AL, AR, AZ, CA, CO, CT, DE, FL, HI, IN, MA, MD, ME, MI, MO, NC, NJ, NV, NY, OH, PA, SC, TN, TX, UT, VA, WA, WI, WY

Ticker: BRWIX

BRUCE FUND
Aggressive Growth

Bruce and Co.
20 N. Wacker Dr., Suite 1425
Chicago, IL 60606
(312) 236-9160

	Years Ending 6/30					
	1983	1984	1985	1986	1987	1988
Dividends from Net Investment Income ($)	—	3.74	8.25	10.20	1.29	3.65
Distributions from Net Realized Capital Gains ($)	—	29.56	99.23	36.94	—	8.63
Net Asset Value End of Year ($)	—	185.44	120.24	117.47	112.40	93.04
Ratio of Expenses to Net Assets (%)	—	2.92	4.89	2.68	1.64	1.92
Ratio of Net Income to Average Net Assets (%)	—	3.39	4.99	2.30	2.40	2.55
Portfolio Turnover Rate (%)	—	99	85	0	11	5
Total Assets End of Year (Millions $)	—	1.1	1.0	2.9	7.0	4.6

Annual Rate of Return (%) Years Ending 12/31	—	6.2	37.0	29.6	(18.0)	12.9

Five-Year Total Return(%)	74.5[B]	Degree of Diversification	E	Beta	.73	Bull (%)	108.1[B]	Bear (%)	(17.6)[C]

Objective: Seeks long-term capital appreciation; dividend income is a secondary consideration. Can invest in stocks, bonds and convertible securities. May also invest in unseasoned companies where the risks are greater than for established companies.

Portfolio: (9/30/88) Common stocks 51%, U.S. government bonds 40%, municipal bonds 8%, cash 1%. Largest stock holdings: Team Inc. 29%, Lodgistix Inc. 22%.

Portfolio Mgr: Robert Bruce—1983

Distributions: Income: Aug   Capital Gains: Aug

12b-1: No

Minimum: Initial: $1,000   Subsequent: $500

Min IRA: Initial: $1,000   Subsequent: $500

Services: IRA, SEP

Tel Exchange: No

Registered: CA, CO, CT, FL, GA, IL, IN, KY, LA, MA, MD, MI, MN, MO, MS, NC, NJ, NV, NY, OK, OR, PA, SC, TN, TX, VA, WA, WI

Ticker: BRUFX

BULL & BEAR
CAPITAL GROWTH
Aggressive Growth

Bull & Bear Advisers, Inc.
11 Hanover Sq.
New York, NY 10005
(800) 847-4200/(212) 363-1100

	Years Ending 12/31					
	1983	1984	1985	1986	1987	1988
Dividends from Net Investment Income ($)	.23	.30	.13	.20	—	—
Distributions from Net Realized Capital Gains ($)	—	1.96	.35	5.91	1.57	1.01
Net Asset Value End of Year ($)	15.87	12.81	15.81	10.37	8.35	8.50
Ratio of Expenses to Net Assets (%)	1.23	1.33	1.41	2.25	2.20	2.30
Ratio of Net Income to Average Net Assets (%)	1.96	1.16	1.28	(.16)	(.33)	(.45)
Portfolio Turnover Rate (%)	67	94	78	78	112	183
Total Assets End of Year (Millions $)	76.1	63.6	91.8	61.7	64.6	57.4

Annual Rate of Return (%) Years Ending 12/31	15.5	(4.3)	27.8	3.6	(4.3)	13.9

Five-Year Total Return(%)	37.9ᴱ	Degree of Diversification	B	Beta	1.09	Bull (%)	93.7ᶜ	Bear (%)	(28.4)ᴱ

Objective: Seeks long-term capital appreciation through a diversified portfolio consisting primarily of common stocks of emerging growth companies and in special situations. May invest in foreign securities, may employ leverage and may engage in repurchase agreements.

Portfolio: (12/31/88) Common stocks 99%, convertible securities 1%. Largest stock holdings: pharmaceutical and health 18%, business services 13%.

Portfolio Mgr: Brett B. Sneed—1988

Distributions: Income: Dec   **Capital Gains:** Dec

12b-1: Yes   **Amount:** 1.00%

Minimum: Initial: $1,000   **Subsequent:** $100

Min IRA: Initial: $100   **Subsequent:** $100

Services: IRA, Keogh, SEP, 403(b), Withdraw, Deduct

Tel Exchange: Yes   **With MMF:** Yes

Registered: All states

Ticker: BULSX

BULL & BEAR
EQUITY-INCOME
Balanced

Bull & Bear Advisers, Inc.
11 Hanover Sq.
New York, NY 10005
(800) 847-4200/(212) 363-1100

	Years Ending 12/31					
	1983	**1984**	**1985**	**1986**	**1987**	**1988**
Dividends from Net Investment Income ($)	.65	.70	.70	.38	.44	.40
Distributions from Net Realized Capital Gains ($)	—	.25	1.31	2.01	.21	—
Net Asset Value End of Year ($)	11.13	10.93	11.41	11.03	9.90	11.02
Ratio of Expenses to Net Assets (%)	2.03	1.98	2.14	3.00	2.57	2.70
Ratio of Net Income to Average Net Assets (%)	5.86	6.49	6.63	3.52	3.52	3.62
Portfolio Turnover Rate (%)	36	155	103	93	91	18
Total Assets End of Year (Millions $)	5.3	4.5	6.3	11.3	13.3	11.9
Annual Rate of Return (%) Years Ending 12/31	12.4	7.2	25.8	18.7	(4.7)	15.4

Five-Year Total Return(%)	76.0[B]	Degree of Diversification	B	Beta	.70	Bull (%)	95.5[C]	Bear (%)	(18.6)[D]

Objective: Intends to provide current income and long-term growth through investment in large, major corporations' common stock and senior convertibles. May also invest in corporate bonds and money market instruments.

Portfolio: (12/31/88) Common stocks 34%, convertible bonds 32%, convertible preferred stocks 18%, mortgage/asset backed bonds 8%, non-convertible corporate bonds 7%, other assets 1%. Largest stock holdings: consumer products 8%, basic materials 6%.

Portfolio Mgr: Robert Radsch—1982

Distributions: **Income:** Mar, June, Sept, Dec   **Capital Gains:** Dec

12b-1: Yes   **Amount:** 1.00%

Minimum: **Initial:** $1,000   **Subsequent:** $100

Min IRA: **Initial:** $100   **Subsequent:** $100

Services: IRA, Keogh, SEP, 403(b), Withdraw, Deduct

Tel Exchange: Yes   **With MMF:** Yes

Registered: All states

Ticker: BULAX

BULL & BEAR GOLD INVESTORS LTD.
Precious Metals

Bull & Bear Advisers, Inc.
11 Hanover Square
New York, NY 10005
(800) 847-4200/(212) 363-1100

| | Years Ending 6/30 | | | | | |
	1983	1984	1985	1986	1987	1988
Dividends from Net Investment Income ($)	.50	.20	.12	.04	.03	—
Distributions from Net Realized Capital Gains ($)	—	—	—	—	—	1.39
Net Asset Value End of Year ($)	14.11	12.04	10.21	9.98	18.76	14.31
Ratio of Expenses to Net Assets (%)	1.71	1.71	1.74	2.39	2.46	2.33
Ratio of Net Income to Average Net Assets (%)	3.08	1.23	1.08	.18	(.21)	.10
Portfolio Turnover Rate (%)	12	31	30	32	66	62
Total Assets End of Year (Millions $)	23.4	23.0	21.6	20.6	62.2	47.7

Annual Rate of Return (%) Years Ending 12/31	0.6	(25.2)	2.6	35.0	30.3	(13.5)

Five-Year Total Return(%)	16.8[E]	Degree of Diversification	E	Beta	NA	Bull (%)	125.3[B]	Bear (%)	(23.3)[D]

Objective:	Seeks capital appreciation by concentrating its investments in gold bullion and stocks of companies mining, processing or dealing in gold and other foreign securities. May hold any or all of its cash in foreign currencies including gold coins.
Portfolio:	(12/31/88) Common stocks 66%, bullion 23%, convertible bonds 6%, Japan 2%, Canadian 2%. Largest stock holdings: North American mining companies 37%, Pacific Rim mining companies 17%.
Portfolio Mgr:	Robert Radsch—1982
Distributions:	Income: Jan **Capital Gains:** Jan
12b-1:	Yes **Amount:** 1.00%
Minimum:	Initial: $1,000 Subsequent: $100
Min IRA:	Initial: $100 Subsequent: $100
Services:	IRA, Keogh, SEP, 403(b), Withdraw, Deduct
Tel Exchange:	Yes **With MMF:** Yes
Registered:	All states except WI
Ticker:	BULGX

BULL & BEAR HIGH YIELD
Bond

Bull & Bear Advisers, Inc.
11 Hanover Square
New York, NY 10005
(800) 847-4200/(212) 363-1100

	1983	1984 (10 mos.)	1985	1986	1987	1988
			Years Ending 6/30			
Dividends from Net Investment Income ($)	—	1.62	1.94	1.89	1.74	1.43
Distributions from Net Realized Capital Gains ($)	—	—	—	—	.02	—
Net Asset Value End of Year ($)	—	13.25	14.42	14.96	13.04	10.83
Ratio of Expenses to Net Assets (%)	—	.99	1.16	1.37	1.50	1.71
Ratio of Net Income to Average Net Assets (%)	—	13.77	13.86	13.45	12.40	11.96
Portfolio Turnover Rate (%)	—	95	127	77	85	124
Total Assets End of Year (Millions $)	—	8.7	33.5	113.1	206.2	124.1
Annual Rate of Return (%) Years Ending 12/31	—	7.8	20.9	6.0	(6.4)	5.0

Five-Year Total Return(%)	35.8ᴱ	Degree of Diversification	NA	Beta	NA	Bull (%)	42.8ᴱ	Bear (%)	(9.2)ᶜ

Objective: Seeks the highest income over the long term through investment in high-yield fixed-income debt securities of short-, intermediate-, or long-term maturities graded in the lower categories. Value of shares subject to influence by changes in interest rates. May invest up to 15% of assets in foreign securities and may enter into repurchase agreements.

Portfolio: (12/31/88) Corporate bonds 81%, preferred stocks 9%, U.S. government obligations 6%, other assets 4%. Largest holdings: public utilities 9%, retailing 7%.

Portfolio Mgr: Edward G. Webb Jr.—1979

Distributions: **Income:** Monthly   **Capital Gains:** Annually

12b-1: Yes   **Amount:** 0.50%

Minimum: **Initial:** $1,000   **Subsequent:** $100

Min IRA: **Initial:** $100   **Subsequent:** $100

Services: IRA, Keogh, SEP, 403(b), Withdraw, Deduct

Tel Exchange: Yes   **With MMF:** Yes

Registered: All states

Ticker: BULHX

BULL & BEAR
SPECIAL EQUITIES
Aggressive Growth

Bull & Bear Advisers, Inc.
11 Hanover Square
New York, NY 10005
(800) 847-4200/(212) 363-1100

	1983	1984	1985	1986 (9 mos.)	1987	1988
				Years Ending 12/31		
Dividends from Net Investment Income ($)	—	—	—	—	—	—
Distributions from Net Realized Capital Gains ($)	—	—	—	—	—	1.15
Net Asset Value End of Year ($)	—	—	—	16.83	15.75	18.17
Ratio of Expenses to Net Assets (%)	—	—	—	2.97	3.01	6.22
Ratio of Net Income to Average Net Assets (%)	—	—	—	(1.23)	(.82)	(4.75)
Portfolio Turnover Rate (%)	—	—	—	558	751	514
Total Assets End of Year (Millions $)	—	—	—	2.3	2.3	3.0
Annual Rate of Return (%) Years Ending 2/31	—	—	—	—	(6.4)	22.7

Five-Year Total Return(%)	NA	Degree of Diversification	NA	Beta	NA	Bull (%)	NA	Bear (%)	(23.9)ᴰ

Objective: Seeks capital appreciation by investing at least 65% of the fund's portfolio in equity securities. May invest up to 35% of the fund's assets in corporate bonds, debentures or preferred stocks. The fund does not intend to concentrate its investments in any one industry, but has reserved the right to invest up to 25% of the value of its total assets in a particular industry.

Portfolio: (12/31/88) Common stocks 101%. Largest stock holdings: consumer products and services 17%, pharmaceutical and health care 17%.

Portfolio Mgr: David Scofield—1986; Brett B. Sneed—1988

Distributions: Income: Dec   **Capital Gains:** Dec

12b-1: Yes   **Amount:** 1.00%

Minimum: Initial: $1,000   Subsequent: $100

Min IRA: Initial: $100   Subsequent: $100

Services: IRA, Keogh, SEP, 403(b), Withdraw, Deduct

Tel Exchange: Yes   **With MMF:** Yes

Registered: All states except AR

Ticker: BSPEX

BULL & BEAR U.S. GOVERNMENT GUARANTEED SECURITIES
Bond

Bull & Bear Advisers, Inc.
11 Hanover Square
New York, NY 10005
(800) 847-4200/(212) 363-1100

	Years Ending 6/30					
	1983	1984	1985	1986 (4 mos.)	1987	1988
Dividends from Net Investment Income ($)	—	—	—	.47	1.42	1.49
Distributions from Net Realized Capital Gains ($)	—	—	—	—	—	—
Net Asset Value End of Year ($)	—	—	—	14.84	14.68	14.36
Ratio of Expenses to Net Assets (%)	—	—	—	1.21	2.06	1.96
Ratio of Net Income to Average Net Assets (%)	—	—	—	10.40	9.40	9.95
Portfolio Turnover Rate (%)	—	—	—	31	185	174
Total Assets End of Year (Millions $)	—	—	—	8.8	46.8	63.5

Annual Rate of Return (%) Years Ending 12/31	—	—	—	—	5.4	4.5

Five-Year Total Return(%)	NA	Degree of Diversification	NA	Beta	NA	Bull (%)	NA	Bear (%)	2.1ᴬ

Objective: Seeks high level of current income, liquidity, and safety of principal. Invests in U.S. Treasury and government agency securities including bills, notes, bonds, GNMAs, and Federal Housing Administration bonds. Can also write covered call options on securities it owns.

Portfolio: (12/31/88) GNMAs 112%.

Portfolio Mgr: Charles Halsey Jr.—1986

Distributions: **Income:** Monthly   **Capital Gains:** Annually

12b-1: Yes   **Amount:** 0.50%

Minimum: **Initial:** $1,000   **Subsequent:** $100

Min IRA: **Initial:** $100   **Subsequent:** $100

Services: IRA, Keogh, SEP, 403(b), Withdraw, Deduct

Tel Exchange: Yes   **With MMF:** Yes

Registered: All states

Ticker: BBUSX

CALAMOS CONVERTIBLE INCOME
Growth & Income

Calamos Asset Management, Inc.
2001 Spring Road, #750
Oak Brook, IL 60521
(800) 323-9943/(312) 571-7115

	Years Ending 4/30					
	1983	1984	1985	1986 (10 mos.)	1987	1988
Dividends from Net Investment Income ($)	—	—	—	.25	.54	.66
Distributions from Net Realized Capital Gains ($)	—	—	—	—	.53	.11
Net Asset Value End of Year ($)	—	—	—	11.99	11.94	10.56
Ratio of Expenses to Net Assets (%)	—	—	—	2.00	1.30	1.20
Ratio of Net Income to Average Net Assets (%)	—	—	—	4.90	4.60	5.60
Portfolio Turnover Rate (%)	—	—	—	26	45	56
Total Assets End of Year (Millions $)	—	—	—	10.2	23.6	23.2

Annual Rate of Return (%) Years Ending 12/31	—	—	—	16.1	(4.5)	6.2

Five-Year Total Return(%)	NA	Degree of Diversification	D	Beta	.64	Bull (%)	NA	Bear (%)	(16.9)ᶜ

Objective: Seeks high current income. Capital appreciation is a secondary objective. Invests at least 65% of its assets in convertible bonds and preferred stocks. May invest 30% in issues rated BB or lower by Standard & Poor's.

Portfolio: (10/31/88) Convertible bonds 76%, convertible preferred stocks 18%, interest bearing deposits 6%, common stocks 1%. Largest holdings: capital goods—technology 26%, consumer growth staples 14%.

Portfolio Mgr: John Calamos—1985

Distributions: **Income:** Quarterly   **Capital Gains:** Annually

12b-1: No

Minimum: **Initial:** $5,000   **Subsequent:** $500

Min IRA: **Initial:** $2,000   **Subsequent:** $500

Services: IRA, Keogh, Withdraw, Deduct

Tel Exchange: No

Registered: All states except AL, AK, AR, ME, MS, ND, NH, SD, VT, WV, WY

Ticker: NDCIX

CALIFORNIA INVESTMENT TRUST U.S. GOVERNMENT SECURITIES

Bond

CCM Partners
44 Montgomery St., Suite 2200
San Francisco, CA 94104
(800) 826-8166/(415) 398-2727
In California (800) 225-8778

	Years Ending 8/31					
	1983	1984	1985	1986 (9 mos.)	1987	1988
Dividends from Net Investment Income ($)	—	—	—	.50	.91	.87
Distributions from Net Realized Capital Gains ($)	—	—	—	—	—	—
Net Asset Value End of Year ($)	—	—	—	10.26	9.62	9.46
Ratio of Expenses to Net Assets (%)	—	—	—	.04	.34	.59
Ratio of Net Income to Average Net Assets (%)	—	—	—	9.66	8.27	9.24
Portfolio Turnover Rate (%)	—	—	—	279	115	110
Total Assets End of Year (Millions $)	—	—	—	.01	13.1	10.4
Annual Rate of Return (%) Years Ending 12/31	—	—	—	11.9	1.2	7.3

Five-Year Total Return(%)	NA	Degree of Diversification	NA	Beta	NA	Bull (%)	NA	Bear (%)	2.5A

Objective: Seeks safety from credit risk, liquidity, and as high a level of income as is consistent with these objectives by investing in full faith and credit obligations of the U.S. government and its agencies, primarily GNMAs.

Portfolio: (8/31/88) GNMAs 83%, U.S. Treasury notes 13%, repurchase agreements 3%, other 1%.

Portfolio Mgr: Phillip McClanahan—1985

Distributions: **Income:** Monthly   **Capital Gains:** Annually

12b-1: No

Minimum: **Initial:** $10,000   **Subsequent:** $250

Min IRA: **Initial:** None   **Subsequent:** None

Services: IRA, Keogh, Withdraw

Tel Exchange: Yes   **With MMF:** Yes

Registered: CA, HI, NV

Ticker: CAUSX

CALVERT—EQUITY PORTFOLIO
Growth

Calvert Asset Management Co.
1700 Pennsylvania Ave., N.W.
Washington, DC 20006
(800) 368-2748/(301) 951-4820

	Years Ending 9/30					
	1983	1984	1985	1986	1987	1988
Dividends from Net Investment Income ($)	—	.37	.44	.34	.18	.11
Distributions from Net Realized Capital Gains ($)	—	.04	—	—	2.14	3.41
Net Asset Value End of Year ($)	18.89	16.94	16.98	22.16	24.75	17.25
Ratio of Expenses to Net Assets (%)	2.25	2.06	1.98	1.83	1.70	1.87
Ratio of Net Income to Average Net Assets (%)	3.55	2.48	1.56	.84	.42	.57
Portfolio Turnover Rate (%)	12	148	38	56	34	45
Total Assets End of Year (Millions $)	8.6	6.8	5.9	7.6	9.7	7.4
Annual Rate of Return (%) Years Ending 12/31	9.0	(6.7)	23.6	12.1	(8.2)	20.0

Five-Year Total Return(%)	42.5E	Degree of Diversification	B	Beta	1.00	Bull (%)	92.3C	Bear (%)	(28.9)E

Objective: Seeks growth of capital through investment in equity securities considered neither speculative nor conservative. Chosen through analysis of cash flow, book value, dividend growth potential, management quality, and current and future earnings.

Portfolio: (9/30/88) Common stocks 83%, convertible corporate bonds 1%. Largest stock holdings: business equipment and services 14%, banking and financial services 14%.

Portfolio Mgr: Joseph Clorety—1984

Distributions: **Income:** Annually   **Capital Gains:** Annually

12b-1: Yes   **Amount:** 0.75%

Minimum: **Initial:** $2,000   **Subsequent:** $250

Min IRA: **Initial:** $1,000   **Subsequent:** $250

Services: IRA, Keogh, 403(b), Withdraw, Deduct

Tel Exchange: Yes   **With MMF:** Yes

Registered: All states

Ticker: CFEQX

CAPITAL PRESERVATION TREASURY NOTE TRUST
Bond

Benham Management Corp.
755 Page Mill Rd.
Palo Alto, CA 94304-1018
(800) 227-8380/(415) 858-3600

	Years Ending 3/31					
	1983	1984	1985	1986	1987	1988
Dividends from Net Investment Income ($)	.91	1.03	.93	.83	1.69	.95
Distributions from Net Realized Capital Gains ($)	—	—	—	—	—	—
Net Asset Value End of Year ($)	10.35	10.13	10.35	11.97	10.91	10.11
Ratio of Expenses to Net Assets (%)	1.00	1.00	1.00	1.00	.93	.75
Ratio of Net Income to Average Net Assets (%)	9.97	9.44	9.76	8.42	6.26	7.36
Portfolio Turnover Rate (%)	—	—	53	294	396	465
Total Assets End of Year (Millions $)	11.1	9.2	12.5	28.5	43.2	54.2

Annual Rate of Return (%) Years Ending 12/31	7.4	12.0	17.6	13.1	(1.3)	5.2

Five-Year Total Return(%) 54.7ᴅ	Degree of Diversification NA	Beta NA	Bull (%) 39.8ᴱ	Bear (%) 3.4ᴬ

Objective: Seeks high current income consistent with safety of principal; at least 90% of the trust's portfolio is invested in U.S. Treasury notes, and up to 10% in U.S. Treasury bills and repurchase agreements consisting of U.S. Treasury securities.

Portfolio: (9/30/88) U.S. Treasury notes 88%, zero coupon bonds 12%.

Portfolio Mgr: Jeff Tyler—1988

Distributions: Income: Monthly   **Capital Gains:** Dec

12b-1: No

Minimum: Initial: $1,000   **Subsequent:** $100

Min IRA: Initial: $100   **Subsequent:** None

Services: IRA, Keogh

Tel Exchange: Yes   **With MMF:** Yes

Registered: All states

Ticker: CPTNX

CENTURY SHARES TRUST
Growth

Century Shares Trust
One Liberty Square
Boston, MA 02109
(800) 321-1928/(617) 482-3060

	Years Ending 12/31					
	1983	1984	1985	1986	1987	1988
Dividends from Net Investment Income ($)	.64	.60	.54	.51	.50	.54
Distributions from Net Realized Capital Gains ($)	.45	.91	.91	1.11	1.61	1.90
Net Asset Value End of Year ($)	13.62	14.02	18.22	18.30	14.76	14.62
Ratio of Expenses to Net Assets (%)	.94	.95	.84	.77	.81	.87
Ratio of Net Income to Average Net Assets (%)	4.57	4.30	3.14	2.57	2.60	3.45
Portfolio Turnover Rate (%)	4	4	6	6	2	3
Total Assets End of Year (Millions $)	74.4	76.8	123.2	141	109.4	110.4

Annual Rate of Return (%) Years Ending 12/31	21.2	15.6	42.6	9.4	(8.0)	15.7

Five-Year Total Return(%)	91.8[A]	Degree of Diversification	E	Beta	.74	Bull (%)	127.6[A]	Bear (%)	(20.2)[D]

Objective: Seeks long-term growth of capital and current income through investments exclusively in insurance and banking stocks and in bonds and obligations that are legal investments for savings banks in Massachusetts.

Portfolio: (12/31/88) Common stocks 94%, other 6%. Largest stock holdings: insurance 88%, banking 5%.

Portfolio Mgr: Allan W. Fulkerson—1965

Distributions: Income: June, Dec   **Capital Gains:** Dec

12b-1: No

Minimum: Initial: $500   Subsequent: $25

Min IRA: Initial: $500   Subsequent: $25

Services: IRA

Tel Exchange: No

Registered: All states

Ticker: CENSX

COLUMBIA FIXED INCOME SECURITIES
Bond

Columbia Financial Center
1301 S.W. Fifth Ave.
P.O. Box 1350
Portland, OR 97207-1350
(800) 547-1037/(503) 222-3600

	Years Ending 12/31					
	1983	1984	1985	1986	1987	1988
Dividends from Net Investment Income ($)	1.35	1.44	1.40	1.21	1.03	1.04
Distributions from Net Realized Capital Gains ($)	–	–	–	–	.27	–
Net Asset Value End of Year ($)	12.21	12.14	13.05	13.37	12.23	12.11
Ratio of Expenses to Net Assets (%)	1.22	1.05	.88	.79	.82	.77
Ratio of Net Income to Average Net Assets (%)	11.30	12.17	11.03	9.15	8.21	8.44
Portfolio Turnover Rate (%)	46	98	94	97	114	133
Total Assets End of Year (Millions $)	29.4	38.1	83.2	124.4	100.3	102.6

Annual Rate of Return (%) Years Ending 12/31	–	12.3	20.1	12.4	1.4	7.7

Five-Year Total Return(%)	65.4^C	Degree of Diversification	NA	Beta	NA	Bull (%)	46.1^E	Bear (%)	3.1^A

Objective: Seeks high level of current income, consistent with conservation of capital, through investment in a broad range of investment-grade fixed-income securities, amounting to 80% of its assets. Other 20% may be in lower grade debt securities as well as those of the U.S. government.

Portfolio: (12/31/88) U.S. government and agency obligations 68%, corporate bonds 28%, repurchase agreements 3%, cash 1%. Largest bond holdings: financial bonds 17%, industrial bonds 6%.

Portfolio Mgr: Thomas Thomsen—1983

Distributions: **Income:** Monthly   **Capital Gains:** Dec

12b-1: No

Minimum: **Initial:** $1,000   **Subsequent:** $100

Min IRA: **Initial:** $1,000   **Subsequent:** $100

Services: IRA, Keogh, SEP, Withdraw

Tel Exchange: Yes   **With MMF:** Yes

Registered: All states except AL, AR, DE, IN, KS, KY, LA, ME, MS, ND, NE, NH, NM, OK, RI, SC, SD, TN, UT, VT, WI, WV

Ticker: CFISX

COLUMBIA GROWTH
Growth

Columbia Financial Center
1301 S.W. Fifth Ave.
P.O. Box 1350
Portland, OR 97207-1350
(800) 547-1037/(503) 222-3600

	Years Ending 12/31					
	1983	1984	1985	1986	1987	1988
Dividends from Net Investment Income ($)	.12	.19	.33	.40	.61	.52
Distributions from Net Realized Capital Gains ($)	2.42	2.41	—	6.48	5.33	.64
Net Asset Value End of Year ($)	25.45	21.53	28.02	22.88	20.19	21.21
Ratio of Expenses to Net Assets (%)	1.10	1.18	1.06	1.00	1.04	1.04
Ratio of Net Income to Average Net Assets (%)	1.48	1.78	1.81	.78	1.46	2.33
Portfolio Turnover Rate (%)	95	90	93	131	197	179
Total Assets End of Year (Millions $)	145.5	155.1	250.6	200.9	193.5	204.3

Annual Rate of Return (%) Years Ending 12/31	21.5	(5.1)	32.0	6.8	14.7	10.8

Five-Year Total Return(%) 70.1c	Degree of Diversification A	Beta .91	Bull (%) 121.0B	Bear (%) (17.0)c

Objective: Seeks capital growth and preservation through selection of common stocks on the basis of sales trends, earnings and profit margins, new products, industry environment, management and future orientation, all in the framework of the economy and market conditions. May adopt defensive posture in bonds or commercial paper.

Portfolio: (12/31/88) Common stocks 83%, commercial paper 14%, repurchase agreements 3%, cash 1%. Largest stock holdings: technology 15%, health 9%.

Portfolio Mgr: Robert Unger

Distributions: **Income:** Dec   **Capital Gains:** Dec

12b-1: No

Minimum: **Initial:** $1,000   **Subsequent:** $100

Min IRA: **Initial:** $1,000   **Subsequent:** $100

Services: IRA, Keogh, SEP, Withdraw

Tel Exchange: Yes   **With MMF:** Yes

Registered: All states except NH

Ticker: CLMBX

†COLUMBIA SPECIAL
Aggressive Growth

Columbia Financial Center
1301 S.W. Fifth Avenue
P.O. Box 1350
Portland, OR 97207-1350
(800) 547-1037/(503) 222-3600

	Years Ending 12/31					
	1983	1984	1985 (5 mos.)	1986	1987	1988
Dividends from Net Investment Income ($)	—	—	—	—	—	—
Distributions from Net Realized Capital Gains ($)	—	—	—	.74	—	5.60
Net Asset Value End of Year ($)	—	—	23.96	26.97	27.79	33.96
Ratio of Expenses to Net Assets (%)	—	—	1.24	1.54	1.44	1.38
Ratio of Net Income to Average Net Assets (%)	—	—	.94	(.47)	(.63)	.06
Portfolio Turnover Rate (%)	—	—	112	203	333	244
Total Assets End of Year (Millions $)	—	—	3.1	20.4	20.6	30.5

Annual Rate of Return (%) Years Ending 12/31	—	—	—	15.8	3.0	42.5

Five-Year Total Return(%) NA	Degree of Diversification D	Beta 1.25	Bull (%) NA	Bear (%) (30.0)E

Objective: Seeks significant capital appreciation by investing in securities that are riskier than the market. Invests in small companies with capitalizations less than the average of companies in the S&P 500.

Portfolio: (12/31/88) Common stocks 97%, repurchase agreements 4%. Largest stock holdings: consumer nondurables 25%, entertainment and media 18%.

Portfolio Mgr: Alan Folkman—1985

Distributions: Income: Dec   **Capital Gains:** Dec

12b-1: No

Minimum: Initial: $2,000   Subsequent: $100

Min IRA: Initial: $2,000   Subsequent: $100

Services: IRA, Keogh, SEP, Withdraw

Tel Exchange: Yes   **With MMF:** Yes

Registered: All states except AL, AR, CA, DE, IN, KS, KY, LA, ME, MO, MS, ND, NE, NH, NM, OK, RI, SC, SD, TN, UT, VT, WI, WV

Ticker: CLSPX

† *There will be a 2% redemption fee only if shares are redeemed within 60 days after purchase.*

COPLEY FUND
(formerly COPLEY TAX-MANAGED)
Growth

Copley Financial Services Corp.
315 Pleasant Street
P.O. Box 3287
Fall River, MA 02722
(508) 674-8459

	Years Ending 2/28					
	1983	1984	1985	1986	1987	1988
Dividends from Net Investment Income ($)	—	—	—	—	—	—
Distributions from Net Realized Capital Gains ($)	—	—	—	—	—	—
Net Asset Value End of Year ($)	5.68	6.14	7.68	10.04	11.75	10.82
Ratio of Expenses to Net Assets (%)	2.23	1.40	1.50	1.47	1.43	1.90
Ratio of Net Income to Average Net Assets (%)	7.90	8.49	7.90	7.26	5.20	5.58
Portfolio Turnover Rate (%)	56	39	29	19	16	10
Total Assets End of Year (Millions $)	2.7	5.6	8.4	21.6	33.6	25.9
Annual Rate of Return (%) Years Ending 12/31	11.6	23.9	24.6	17.7	(8.3)	19.9

Five-Year Total Return(%)	100.0[A]	Degree of Diversification	E	Beta	.48	Bull (%)	86.7[C]	Bear (%)	(13.2)[C]

Objective: Seeks high income without concern for level of dividend income, as it is tax-free. Set up as a corporation that is entitled to 85% exemption from federal income taxes on dividends received, and the 15% balance can be used as expenses to run the fund. Invests in highly visible companies with strong balance sheets that pay high dividends which have been increasing.

Portfolio: (8/31/88) Common and preferred stocks 98%, short-term securities 1%. Largest stock holdings: electric and gas 22%, electric power 22%.

Portfolio Mgr: Irving Levine—1978

Distributions: Income: NA   **Capital Gains:** NA

12b-1: No

Minimum: Initial: $1,000   Subsequent: $100

Min IRA: Initial: $100   Subsequent: $100

Services: IRA, Keogh, Withdraw

Tel Exchange: None

Registered: All states

Ticker: COPLX

COUNSELLORS CAPITAL APPRECIATION

Growth

Warburg Pincus Counsellors, Inc.
466 Lexington Avenue
New York, NY 10017-3147
(800) 888-6878/(212) 878-0600

	1983	1984	1985	1986	1987 (2 mos.)	1988
Dividends from Net Investment Income ($)	—	—	—	—	—	.14
Distributions from Net Realized Capital Gains ($)	—	—	—	—	—	—
Net Asset Value End of Year ($)	—	—	—	—	7.74	9.47
Ratio of Expenses to Net Assets (%)	—	—	—	—	1.00	1.07
Ratio of Net Income to Average Net Assets (%)	—	—	—	—	1.88	2.00
Portfolio Turnover Rate (%)	—	—	—	—	20	33
Total Assets End of Year (Millions $)	—	—	—	—	17.9	29.3

Annual Rate of Return (%) Years Ending 12/31	—	—	—	—	—	21.4

Five-Year Total Return(%)	NA	Degree of Diversification	NA	Beta	NA	Bull (%)	NA	Bear (%)	(19.2)D

Objective: Seeks long-term capital appreciation. Invests in a broadly diversified portfolio of equity securities of domestic companies. Invests at least 80% of its total assets in common stocks, warrants and convertible securities. May invest up to 20% of its assets in investment-grade debt securities and preferred stocks.

Portfolio: (10/31/88) Common stocks 80%, short-term securities 18%, corporate bonds 1%, other assets 1%. Largest stock holdings: communications and media 13%, financial services 11%.

Portfolio Mgr: John Furth—1987

Distributions: **Income:** Semiannually   **Capital Gains:** Annually

12b-1: No

Minimum: **Initial:** $25,000   **Subsequent:** $5,000

Min IRA: **Initial:** $10,000   **Subsequent:** $2,000

Services: IRA, Keogh, SEP, Withdraw

Tel Exchange: Yes   **With MMF:** Yes

Registered: All states

Ticker: CUCAX

COUNSELLORS FIXED INCOME
Bond

Warburg, Pincus Counsellors, Inc.
466 Lexington Avenue
New York, NY 10017-3147
(800) 888-6878/(212) 878-0600

	Years Ending 10/31					
	1983	1984	1985	1986	1987 (2 mos.)	1988
Dividends from Net Investment Income ($)	—	—	—	—	.19	.88
Distributions from Net Realized Capital Gains ($)	—	—	—	—	—	—
Net Asset Value End of Year ($)	—	—	—	—	9.62	9.93
Ratio of Expenses to Net Assets (%)	—	—	—	—	.70	.74
Ratio of Net Income to Average Net Assets (%)	—	—	—	—	9.10	8.80
Portfolio Turnover Rate (%)	—	—	—	—	30	56
Total Assets End of Year (Millions $)	—	—	—	—	26.3	75.5

Annual Rate of Return (%) Years Ending 12/31	—	—	—	—	—	8.6

Five-Year Total Return(%)	NA	Degree of Diversification	NA	Beta	NA	Bull (%)	NA	Bear (%)	1.2B

Objective: Primary objective is to generate high current income consistent with reasonable risk; capital appreciation is secondary. Invests in corporate bonds, debentures, notes, convertible securities, preferred stocks, government obligations and repurchase agreements. Normally will be 80% invested in fixed-income securities.

Portfolio: (10/31/88) Corporate bonds 60%, U.S. government obligations 23%, zero coupon bonds 8%, agency obligations 7%, short-term securities 2%, preferred stocks 1%.

Portfolio Mgr: Stuart Goode—1987

Distributions: **Income:** Monthly   **Capital Gains:** Annually

12b-1: No

Minimum: **Initial:** $25,000   **Subsequent:** $5,000

Min IRA: **Initial:** $10,000   **Subsequent:** $2,000

Services: IRA, Keogh, SEP, Withdraw

Tel Exchange: Yes   **With MMF:** Yes

Registered: All states

Ticker: CUFIX

CUMBERLAND GROWTH
Growth

Cumberland Advisors
614 Landis Avenue
Vineland, NJ 08360
(800) 257-7013/(609) 692-6690

	Years Ending 12/31					
	1983*	1984	1985	1986*	1987*	1988
Dividends from Net Investment Income ($)	.16	.24	.17	.17	.77	—
Distributions from Net Realized Capital Gains ($)	—	.31	—	—	—	—
Net Asset Value End of Year ($)	9.74	8.61	10.21	10.73	8.87	9.90
Ratio of Expenses to Net Assets (%)	4.1	4.1	3.8	3.4	4.6	5.1
Ratio of Net Income to Average Net Assets (%)	3.5	2.3	2.7	1.3	.1	(1.1)
Portfolio Turnover Rate (%)	219	71	194	187	267	367
Total Assets End of Year (Millions $)	.91	.77	1.6	2.4	2.2	2.1
Annual Rate of Return (%) Years Ending 12/31	16.4	(6.0)	21.5	11.8	(15.0)	11.6

Five-Year Total Return(%)	21.1E	Degree of Diversification	C	Beta	.82	Bull (%)	67.8D	Bear (%)	(25.9)E

Per share data appear as reported in the fund's prospectus and annual report; figures for 1983, 1986 and 1987, however, do not balance.

Objective: Primary objective is capital appreciation; current income is a secondary consideration. Invests primarily in common stocks, but may invest in bonds rated BBB or lower by Standard & Poor's. Can leverage the fund through bank borrowings, and may also sell stock short.

Portfolio: (12/31/88) Common stocks 69%, U.S. government obligations 31%. Largest stock holdings: food and tobacco 8%, financial services 8%.

Portfolio Mgr: Donald Sulam—1985

Distributions: **Income:** Annually   **Capital Gains:** Annually

12b-1: No

Minimum: **Initial:** $1,000   **Subsequent:** $100

Min IRA: **Initial:** $100   **Subsequent:** $100

Services: IRA, Keogh

Tel Exchange: No

Registered: CT, DE, FL, GA, IL, IN, MA, MI, NJ, NY, PA, TX

Ticker: CUGFX

DELAWARE GROUP TREASURY RESERVES INVESTORS SERIES

Bond

Delaware Management Holdings
Ten Penn Center Plaza
Philadelphia, PA 19103
(800) 523-4640/(215) 988-1333

	Years Ending 12/31					
	1983	1984	1985 (1 mo.)	1986	1987	1988
Dividends from Net Investment Income ($)	—	—	.06	.84	.70	.73
Distributions from Net Realized Capital Gains ($)	—	—	—	—	—	—
Net Asset Value End of Year ($)	—	—	10.04	9.98	9.80	9.70
Ratio of Expenses to Net Assets (%)	—	—	—	1.02	1.06	.90
Ratio of Net Income to Average Net Assets (%)	—	—	—	7.85	6.86	7.44
Portfolio Turnover Rate (%)	—	—	—	39	304	146
Total Assets End of Year (Millions $)	—	—	8.1	182.8	138.8	132.8

Annual Rate of Return (%) Years Ending 12/31	—	—	—	7.7	5.3	6.9

Five-Year Total Return(%)	NA	Degree of Diversification	NA	Beta	NA	Bull (%)	NA	Bear (%)	2.2[A]

Objective:	Seeks high stable level of current income while attempting to minimize fluctuations in principal and provide maximum liquidity. Invests in short- and intermediate-term securities guaranteed by the U.S. government. Average maturity of the portfolio is no more than 5 years.
Portfolio:	(12/25/88) U.S. government agency obligations 71%, collateralized mortgage obligations 18%, GNMAs 6%, repurchase agreements 3%, other assets 3%.
Portfolio Mgr:	Dorothea Dutton—1985
Distributions:	**Income:** Monthly **Capital Gains:** Annually
12b-1:	Yes **Amount:** 0.30%
Minimum:	**Initial:** $1,000 **Subsequent:** $25
Min IRA:	**Initial:** $250 **Subsequent:** $25
Services:	IRA, Keogh, Corp, SEP, 403(b), Withdraw, Deduct
Tel Exchange:	Yes **With MMF:** Yes
Registered:	All states
Ticker:	DELXX

DIVIDEND/GROWTH
—DIVIDEND SERIES
Growth & Income

A.I.M. Management
107 N. Adams St.
Rockville, MD 20850
(800) 638-2042/(301) 251-1002

	Years Ending 12/31					
	1983	1984	1985	1986	1987	1988
Dividends from Net Investment Income ($)	1.15	.87	.85	1.50	.55	.60
Distributions from Net Realized Capital Gains ($)	—	—	1.70	1.68	2.13	.05
Net Asset Value End of Year ($)	23.38	25.03	25.80	24.81	22.13	22.44
Ratio of Expenses to Net Assets (%)	2.43	2.00	2.00	2.00	1.99	2.29
Ratio of Net Income to Average Net Assets (%)	3.87	3.86	3.43	2.60	1.90	2.66
Portfolio Turnover Rate (%)	67	56	34	43	34	88
Total Assets End of Year (Millions $)	3.7	4.0	4.3	4.4	3.9	3.1

Annual Rate of Return (%) Years Ending 12/31	15.2	11.4	14.1	8.7	(0.2)	4.5

Five-Year Total Return(%)	44.0ᴱ	Degree of Diversification	A	Beta	.91	Bull (%)	85.0ᶜ	Bear (%)	(22.0)ᴰ

Objective: Seeks income growth with secondary emphasis on growth of capital through investment in income-producing, large, well-established companies that are fundamentally sound. May take short positions, may use leverage and may write covered call options. May invest minor portion in new companies or in special situations.

Portfolio: (12/31/88) Common stocks 59%, U.S Treasury bonds 20%, U.S. Treasury bills 19%, other assets 2%. Largest stock holdings: electric utilities 21%, drugs 13%.

Portfolio Mgr: Gordon Lamb—1980; David Straus—1981

Distributions: **Income:** Feb, May, Aug, Nov **Capital Gains:** Annually

12b-1: No

Minimum: **Initial:** $300   **Subsequent:** $50

Min IRA: **Initial:** $300   **Subsequent:** $50

Services: IRA, Keogh, SEP, Withdraw

Tel Exchange: Yes   **With MMF:** No

Registered: Call for availability

Ticker: DGDSX

DODGE & COX BALANCED
Balanced

Dodge & Cox
One Post St., 35th Flr.
San Francisco, CA 94104
(415) 434-0311

	Years Ending 12/31					
	1983	**1984**	**1985**	**1986**	**1987**	**1988**
Dividends from Net Investment Income ($)	1.72	1.73	1.70	1.62	1.70	1.68
Distributions from Net Realized Capital Gains ($)	.31	.83	.37	3.55	2.67	.46
Net Asset Value End of Year ($)	27.33	25.92	31.93	32.62	30.72	32.09
Ratio of Expenses to Net Assets (%)	.76	.76	.75	.73	.72	.77
Ratio of Net Income to Average Net Assets (%)	6.31	6.76	6.03	4.86	4.69	5.19
Portfolio Turnover Rate (%)	10	7	26	14	15	9
Total Assets End of Year (Millions $)	19.6	19.1	24.5	27.5	34.4	39.0
Annual Rate of Return (%) Years Ending 12/31	17.0	4.7	32.5	19.2	7.7	11.5

Five-Year Total Return(%)	98.5[A]	Degree of Diversification	A	Beta	.64	Bull (%)	121.2[B]	Bear (%)	(13.4)[C]

Objective: To provide shareholders with regular income, conservation of principal and an opportunity for long-term growth of principal and income through investment (no more than 75%) in common stocks of dividend-paying, financially strong companies with sound economic backgrounds. Remaining 25% shall be invested in high-grade bonds and preferred stocks.

Portfolio: (12/31/88) Common stocks 63%, bonds 32%, short-term securities 4%, other assets 1%. Largest stock holdings: finance 10%, public utilities 8%.

Portfolio Mgr: Peter Avenali—1971

Distributions: Income: Mar, June, Sept, Dec   **Capital Gains:** Dec

12b-1: No

Minimum: Initial: $1,000   **Subsequent:** $100

Min IRA: Initial: $1,000   **Subsequent:** $100

Services: IRA, Withdraw

Tel Exchange: No

Registered: CA, CT, DC, GA, HI, MA, MI, NV, NY, OR, UT, WA, WY

Ticker: DODBX

DODGE & COX STOCK
Growth & Income

Dodge & Cox
One Post St., 35th Flr.
San Francisco, CA 94104
(415) 434-0311

	Years Ending 12/31					
	1983	1984	1985	1986	1987	1988
Dividends from Net Investment Income ($)	1.00	1.02	1.01	.94	1.03	1.07
Distributions from Net Realized Capital Gains ($)	.77	1.88	1.23	3.90	1.58	1.11
Net Asset Value End of Year ($)	26.19	24.45	30.95	31.66	32.94	35.26
Ratio of Expenses to Net Assets (%)	.70	.69	.68	.66	.65	.69
Ratio of Net Income to Average Net Assets (%)	4.05	4.26	3.80	2.95	2.68	3.09
Portfolio Turnover Rate (%)	17	14	22	10	12	10
Total Assets End of Year (Millions $)	27.3	27.8	38.5	45.1	67.5	81.6
Annual Rate of Return (%) Years Ending 12/31	26.7	5.1	37.7	18.8	12.5	13.8

Five-Year Total Return(%)	119.9[A]	Degree of Diversification	A	Beta	.95	Bull (%)	165.1[A]	Bear (%)	(20.2)[D]

Objective: Seeks long-term growth of principal and income through investment in dividend-paying, financially strong companies with sound economic backgrounds. Stocks must be from a variety of industries and able to be traded readily. A secondary objective is to achieve some current income.

Portfolio: (12/31/88) Common stocks 96%, short-term securities 3%. Largest stock holdings: finance 15%, public utilities 11%.

Portfolio Mgr: Joseph Fee—1971

Distributions: **Income:** Mar, June, Sept, Dec   **Capital Gains:** Dec

12b-1: No

Minimum: **Initial:** $1,000   **Subsequent:** $100

Min IRA: **Initial:** $1,000   **Subsequent:** $100

Services: IRA, Withdraw

Tel Exchange: No

Registered: CA, CT, DC, GA, HI, MA, MI, NV, NY, OR, UT, WA, WY

Ticker: DODGX

DREYFUS
A BONDS PLUS
Bond

The Dreyfus Corp.
600 Madison Ave.
New York, NY 10022
(800) 645-6561/(718) 895-1206

	Years Ending 3/31					
	1983	1984	1985	1986	1987	1988
Dividends from Net Investment Income ($)	1.57	1.52	1.48	1.42	1.30	1.22
Distributions from Net Realized Capital Gains ($)	–	–	–	–	.25	.22
Net Asset Value End of Year ($)	13.86	12.81	13.10	15.32	15.11	13.78
Ratio of Expenses to Net Assets (%)	.95	.93	.94	.87	.84	.88
Ratio of Net Income to Average Net Assets (%)	11.75	11.29	11.85	10.34	8.72	8.87
Portfolio Turnover Rate (%)	10	5	21	61	79	49
Total Assets End of Year (Millions $)	97.6	105.5	123.3	222.9	319.6	254.3

Annual Rate of Return (%) Years Ending 12/31	7.6	12.4	23.1	13.9	(.4)	9.0

Five-Year Total Return(%)	71.0ᶜ	Degree of Diversification	NA	Beta	NA	Bull (%)	52.8ᴰ	Bear (%)	2.4ᴬ

Objective:	Seeks maximization of current income with preservation of liquidity and capital. Invests 80% of assets in debt obligations rated A or better. The other components must be of high quality as well.
Portfolio:	(9/30/88) Corporate bonds and notes 90%, short-term securities 8%, cash 2%. Largest bond holdings: utilities 15%, banking 10%.
Portfolio Mgr:	Barbara Kenworthy—1985
Distributions:	**Income:** Monthly **Capital Gains:** Annually
12b-1:	No
Minimum:	**Initial:** $2,500 **Subsequent:** $100
Min IRA:	**Initial:** $750 **Subsequent:** None
Services:	IRA, Keogh, Corp, SEP, 403(b), Withdraw, Deduct
Tel Exchange:	Yes **With MMF:** Yes
Registered:	All states
Ticker:	DRBDX

DREYFUS CONVERTIBLE SECURITIES

Balanced

The Dreyfus Corp.
600 Madison Ave.
New York, NY 10022
(800) 645-6561/(718) 895-1206

	Years Ending 4/30					
	1983	1984	1985	1986	1987	1988
Dividends from Net Investment Income ($)	.67	.63	.60	.56	.51	.45
Distributions from Net Realized Capital Gains ($)	.08	.04	.28	.24	.85	.58
Net Asset Value End of Year ($)	7.69	7.77	7.72	9.33	9.49	8.56
Ratio of Expenses to Net Assets (%)	.85	.85	.85	.85	.85	.85
Ratio of Net Income to Average Net Assets (%)	10.47	8.85	8.51	8.64	6.20	6.18
Portfolio Turnover Rate (%)	27	25	32	62	91	45
Total Assets End of Year (Millions $)	83.2	92.2	101.1	143.4	250.1	253.6

Annual Rate of Return (%) Years Ending 12/31	21.0	7.6	23.5	23.7	(3.0)	23.0

Five-Year Total Return(%)	96.3^A	Degree of Diversification	E	Beta	.57	Bull (%)	103.8^C	Bear (%)	(19.3)^D

Objective: Seeks to maximize current income. Invests primarily in bonds, debentures and preferred stocks and secondarily in common stocks with high current dividend and appreciation potential. May lend securities from its portfolio and write (sell) covered call options and invest in foreign securities.

Portfolio: (10/31/88) Equity-related securities 96%, short-term securities 3%, bonds and notes 1%. Largest stock holdings: forest products 12%, consumer/food 6%.

Portfolio Mgr: Barbara Kenworthy—1986

Distributions: **Income:** Quarterly   **Capital Gains:** May

12b-1: No

Minimum: **Initial:** $2,500   **Subsequent:** $100

Min IRA: **Initial:** $750   **Subsequent:** None

Services: IRA, Keogh, Corp, SEP, 403(b), Withdraw, Deduct

Tel Exchange: Yes   **With MMF:** Yes

Registered: All states

Ticker: DRCSX

DREYFUS GNMA
Bond

The Dreyfus Corp.
600 Madison Ave.
New York, NY 10022
(800) 645-6561/(718) 895-1206

	Years Ending 4/30					
	1983	1984	1985	1986 (11 mos.)	1987	1988
Dividends from Net Investment Income ($)	—	—	—	1.32	1.39	1.33
Distributions from Net Realized Capital Gains ($)	—	—	—	—	.03	—
Net Asset Value End of Year ($)	—	—	—	15.81	15.08	14.75
Ratio of Expenses to Net Assets (%)	—	—	—	.96	1.01	1.01
Ratio of Net Income to Average Net Assets (%)	—	—	—	11.23	9.88	9.99
Portfolio Turnover Rate (%)	—	—	—	245	257	288
Total Assets End of Year (Millions $)	—	—	—	1,739.5	2,396.6	1,981.4

Annual Rate of Return (%) Years Ending 12/31	—	—	—	9.5	2.5	6.4

Five-Year Total Return(%)	NA	Degree of Diversification	NA	Beta	NA	Bull (%)	NA	Bear (%)	2.1ᴬ

Objective: Seeks high current income consistent with capital preservation through investing at least 65% of its net assets in GNMAs. May also invest in other U.S. government-backed debt securities.

Portfolio: (10/31/88) GNMAs 83%, short-term securities 13%, U.S. Treasury notes 5%, U.S. Treasury bonds 1%.

Portfolio Mgr: Ina Goodman—1985

Distributions: **Income:** Monthly   **Capital Gains:** Annually

12b-1: Yes   **Amount:** 0.20%

Minimum: **Initial:** $2,500   **Subsequent:** $100

Min IRA: **Initial:** $750   **Subsequent:** None

Services: IRA, Keogh, Corp, SEP, 403(b), Withdraw, Deduct

Tel Exchange: Yes   **With MMF:** Yes

Registered: All states

Ticker: DRGMX

DREYFUS GROWTH OPPORTUNITY

Growth

The Dreyfus Corp.
600 Madison Ave.
New York, NY 10022
(800) 645-6561/(718) 895-1206

	Years Ending 2/28					
	1983	**1984**	**1985**	**1986**	**1987**	**1988**
Dividends from Net Investment Income ($)	.29	.25	.18	.21	.21	.42
Distributions from Net Realized Capital Gains ($)	.81	.34	.88	.34	2.80	2.07
Net Asset Value End of Year ($)	10.59	11.24	9.89	12.21	11.99	9.42
Ratio of Expenses to Net Assets (%)	1.06	.99	1.02	.98	.95	.91
Ratio of Net Income to Average Net Assets (%)	5.49	2.84	3.06	2.85	2.57	4.60
Portfolio Turnover Rate (%)	68	60	44	56	73	129
Total Assets End of Year (Millions $)	251.5	369.7	441.9	478.0	516.3	492.2

Annual Rate of Return (%) Years Ending 12/31	31.5	(12.1)	30.7	15.0	6.4	17.9

Five-Year Total Return(%)	65.6[c]	Degree of Diversification	D	Beta	.84	Bull (%)	108.2[B]	Bear (%)	(22.0)[D]

Objective: Primarily aims to promote growth of capital through investment in established companies. Up to 25% of portfolio may be in foreign companies. Income is secondary but in periods of market weakness the fund will emphasize investment in money markets and other high-yielding securities.

Portfolio: (8/31/88) Common stocks 77%, short-term securities 22%, preferred stocks 6%, bonds 2%. Largest stock holdings: chemicals 25%, petroleum products—domestic 14%.

Portfolio Mgr: Salil K. Banerjee—1987

Distributions: **Income:** Annually **Capital Gains:** Annually

12b-1: No

Minimum: **Initial:** $2,500 **Subsequent:** $100

Min IRA: **Initial:** $750 **Subsequent:** None

Services: IRA, Keogh, Corp, SEP, 403(b), Withdraw, Deduct

Tel Exchange: Yes **With MMF:** Yes

Registered: All states

Ticker: DREQX

DREYFUS NEW LEADERS

Aggressive Growth

The Dreyfus Corp.
600 Madison Ave.
New York, NY 10022
(800) 645-6561/(516) 794-5210

			Years Ending 12/31			
	1983	1984	1985 (11 mos.)	1986	1987	1988
Dividends from Net Investment Income ($)	–	–	–	.01	.17	.22
Distributions from Net Realized Capital Gains ($)	–	–	–	.01	–	–
Net Asset Value End of Year ($)	–	–	18.11	20.36	19.16	23.41
Ratio of Expenses to Net Assets (%)	–	–	1.46	1.30	1.41	1.50
Ratio of Net Income to Average Net Assets (%)	–	–	1.55	.66	.35	.90
Portfolio Turnover Rate (%)	–	–	81	195	177	120
Total Assets End of Year (Millions $)	–	–	5.1	65.1	79.8	112.4

	1983	1984	1985	1986	1987	1988
Annual Rate of Return (%) Years Ending 12/31	–	–	–	12.6	(5.3)	23.3

Five-Year Total Return(%)	NA	Degree of Diversification	C	Beta 1.10	Bull (%)	NA	Bear (%)	(28.5)ᴱ

Objective: The fund's goal is to maximize capital appreciation. Invests in small emerging growth stocks of both foreign and domestic issues. May invest up to 25% of assets in foreign stocks. May also buy and sell put and call options.

Portfolio: (12/31/88) Common stocks 64%, short-term securities 31%, cash 4%, convertible preferred stocks 1%. Largest stock holdings: basic industries 21%, financial 10%.

Portfolio Mgr: Thomas Frank—1986

Distributions: **Income:** Annually   **Capital Gains:** Annually

12b-1: Yes   **Amount:** 0.25%

Minimum: **Initial:** $2,500   **Subsequent:** $100

Min IRA: **Initial:** $750   **Subsequent:** None

Services: IRA, Keogh, Corp, SEP, 403(b), Withdraw, Deduct

Tel Exchange: Yes   **With MMF:** Yes

Registered: All states

Ticker: DNLDX

DREYFUS
THIRD CENTURY
Growth & Income

The Dreyfus Corp.
600 Madison Ave.
New York, NY 10022
(800) 645-6561/(718) 895-1206

| | Years Ending 5/31 | | | | | |
	1983	1984	1985	1986	1987	1988
Dividends from Net Investment Income ($)	.32	.26	.20	.21	.31	.36
Distributions from Net Realized Capital Gains ($)	.45	.55	.53	.51	.96	1.27
Net Asset Value End of Year ($)	7.86	6.42	7.42	8.13	7.73	5.76
Ratio of Expenses to Net Assets (%)	1.01	1.03	1.01	.97	.99	1.02
Ratio of Net Income to Average Net Assets (%)	5.36	3.76	4.40	4.69	3.94	3.96
Portfolio Turnover Rate (%)	63	26	45	63	33	37
Total Assets End of Year (Millions $)	151.5	114.4	174.3	176.7	170.0	152.5

Annual Rate of Return (%) Years Ending 12/31	20.2	1.6	29.5	4.6	2.5	23.2

Five-Year Total Return(%)	73.7[B]	Degree of Diversification	B	Beta .77	Bull (%)	95.8[C]	Bear (%)	(20.1)[D]

Objective: Seeks capital growth through investment in the common stocks of companies that meet traditional investment standards and show evidence of contributing to the enhancement of the quality of life in the United States in four areas: protection and proper use of natural resources, occupational health and safety, consumer protection, and equal employment opportunity.

Portfolio: (11/30/88) Common stocks 47%, short-term securities 39%, cash 10%, convertible preferred stocks 2%, convertible subordinated debentures 1%. Largest stock holdings: health 16%, coal 7%.

Portfolio Mgr: Jeffrey Friedman—1972

Distributions: **Income:** July   **Capital Gains:** July

12b-1: No

Minimum: **Initial:** $2,500   **Subsequent:** $100

Min IRA: **Initial:** $750   **Subsequent:** None

Services: IRA, Keogh, Corp, SEP, 403(b), Withdraw, Deduct

Tel Exchange: Yes   **With MMF:** Yes

Registered: All states

Ticker: DRTHX

DREYFUS U.S. GOVERNMENT INTERMEDIATE SECURITIES, L.P.
Bond

The Dreyfus Corp.
600 Madison Ave.
New York, NY 10022
(800) 645-6561/(718) 895-1206

	Years Ending 12/31					
	1983	1984	1985	1986	1987 (9 mos.)	1988
Dividends from Net Investment Income ($)	—	—	—	—	.99	1.16
Distributions from Net Realized Capital Gains ($)	—	—	—	—	—	—
Net Asset Value End of Year ($)	—	—	—	—	12.66	12.22
Ratio of Expenses to Net Assets (%)	—	—	—	—	—	.47
Ratio of Net Income to Average Net Assets (%)	—	—	—	—	9.93	9.18
Portfolio Turnover Rate (%)	—	—	—	—	5	21
Total Assets End of Year (Millions $)	—	—	—	—	40.7	62.1

Annual Rate of Return (%) Years Ending 12/31	—	—	—	—	—	5.8

Five-Year Total Return(%)	NA	Degree of Diversification	NA	Beta	NA	Bull (%)	NA	Bear (%)	3.4A

Objective: Seeks high level of current income consistent with preservation of capital through investment in debt obligations of the U.S. government and its agencies. The fund is organized as a limited partnership in order to pass to investors state and local tax exemptions afforded to owners of such U.S. government securities.

Portfolio: (12/31/88) U.S. Treasury obligations 95%, cash 4%, short-term securities 1%.

Portfolio Mgr: Barbara Kenworthy—1987

Distributions: Income: Monthly   **Capital Gains:** Annually

12b-1: No

Minimum: Initial: $2,500   Subsequent: $100

Min IRA: Initial: NA   Subsequent: NA

Services: Corp, 403(b), Withdraw

Tel Exchange: Yes   **With MMF:** Yes

Registered: All states

Ticker: DRGIX

ECLIPSE EQUITY
Growth & Income

Towneley Capital Mgmt., Inc.
144 East 30th Street
New York, NY 10016
(800) 872-2710/(404) 631-0414

	Years Ending 12/31					
	1983	1984	1985	1986	1987	1988
Dividends from Net Investment Income ($)	—	—	—	—	.38	.41
Distributions from Net Realized Capital Gains ($)	—	—	—	—	—	—
Net Asset Value End of Year ($)	—	—	—	—	9.35	10.12
Ratio of Expenses to Net Assets (%)	—	—	—	—	1.09	1.12
Ratio of Net Income to Average Net Assets (%)	—	—	—	—	4.91	4.05
Portfolio Turnover Rate (%)	—	—	—	—	14	31
Total Assets End of Year (Millions $)	—	—	—	—	147.1	161.2

Annual Rate of Return (%) Years Ending 12/31	—	—	—	—	—	12.7

Five-Year Total Return(%) NA	Degree of Diversification NA	Beta NA	Bull (%) NA	Bear (%) (6.0)c

Objective: Seeks a high total return from equity investments. Buys stocks based on their intrinsic worth, expected future earnings growth, and current and expected dividend income. Generally invests in smaller companies whose market value is less than the average of the S&P 500.

Portfolio: (12/31/88) Common stocks 68%, U.S. government obligations 24%, repurchase agreements 9%. Largest stock holdings: industrial equipment 8%, insurance 5%.

Portfolio Mgr: Wesley McCain—1987

Distributions: **Income:** Quarterly   **Capital Gains:** Annually

12b-1: No

Minimum: **Initial:** $10,000   **Subsequent:** None

Min IRA: **Initial:** $1,000   **Subsequent:** None

Services: IRA, Corp, SEP

Tel Exchange: Yes   **With MMF:** Yes

Registered: All states

Ticker: EEQFX

EVERGREEN
Aggressive Growth

Saxon Woods Asset Mgmt. Corp.
550 Mamaroneck Ave.
Harrison, NY 10528
(800) 235-0064/(914) 698-5711

	Years Ending 9/30					
	1983	1984	1985	1986	1987	1988
Dividends from Net Investment Income ($)	.19	.17	.16	.14	.13	.25
Distributions from Net Realized Capital Gains ($)	.05	1.20	.41	.66	1.12	1.56
Net Asset Value End of Year ($)	11.51	9.78	11.03	13.55	15.12	12.47
Ratio of Expenses to Net Assets (%)	1.11	1.10	1.08	1.04	1.03	1.03
Ratio of Net Income to Average Net Assets (%)	1.95	1.83	1.73	1.41	1.32	1.70
Portfolio Turnover Rate (%)	78	53	59	48	46	42
Total Assets End of Year (Millions $)	210.4	240.0	334.2	638.6	808.3	751.1

Annual Rate of Return (%) Years Ending 12/31	29.1	0.6	34.6	12.9	(3.5)	23.0

Five-Year Total Return(%) 81.2[B]	Degree of Diversification C	Beta .90	Bull (%) 116.7[B]	Bear (%) (24.7)[E]

Objective: Achieve capital appreciation by investing principally in securities of little-known companies, relatively small companies and companies undergoing changes that are believed favorable.

Portfolio: (9/30/88) Common stocks 84%, short-term securities 15%, other assets 2%. Largest stock holdings: banks 14%, retailing 10%.

Portfolio Mgr: Stephen Lieber—1971

Distributions: **Income:** Annually   **Capital Gains:** Annually

12b-1: No

Minimum: **Initial:** $2,000   **Subsequent:** None

Min IRA: **Initial:** None   **Subsequent:** None

Services: IRA, Keogh, SEP, Withdraw, Deduct

Tel Exchange: Yes   **With MMF:** Yes

Registered: All states

Ticker: EVGRX

EVERGREEN
TOTAL RETURN
Balanced

Saxon Woods Asset Mgmt. Corp.
550 Mamaroneck Ave.
Harrison, NY 10528
(800) 235-0064/(914) 698-5711

	Years Ending 3/31					
	1983	1984	1985	1986	1987	1988
Dividends from Net Investment Income ($)	.79	.86	.96	1.22	1.14	.80
Distributions from Net Realized Capital Gains ($)	.81	.73	1.32	.98	1.11	.88
Net Asset Value End of Year ($)	14.78	15.21	16.63	19.72	20.37	17.11
Ratio of Expenses to Net Assets (%)	1.29	1.09	1.31	1.11	1.02	1.01
Ratio of Net Income to Average Net Assets (%)	6.94	6.21	6.18	6.06	5.68	5.80
Portfolio Turnover Rate (%)	113	67	82	65	44	81
Total Assets End of Year (Millions $)	32.9	47.4	83.7	408.4	1,635.7	1,355.0
Annual Rate of Return (%) Years Ending 12/31	30.3	14.4	31.5	20.3	(8.9)	15.7

Five-Year Total Return(%)	90.7ᴬ	Degree of Diversification	C	Beta	.56	Bull (%)	100.2ᶜ	Bear (%)	(16.3)ᶜ

Objective: The fund invests primarily in common and preferred stocks and fixed-income securities that are established and income-producing, with the objective of obtaining current income and capital appreciation. May write covered call options. Portfolio is usually 75% in equity securities and 25% in debt securities.

Portfolio: (9/30/88) Common stocks 73%, convertible debentures 15%, convertible preferred stocks 10%, other assets 2%, short-term securities 1%. Largest stock holdings: electric utilities 19%, banks 11%.

Portfolio Mgr: Nola M. Falcone—1978

Distributions: **Income:** Apr, July, Oct, Dec   **Capital Gains:** Dec

12b-1: No

Minimum: **Initial:** $2,000   **Subsequent:** None

Min IRA: **Initial:** None   **Subsequent:** None

Services: IRA, Keogh, SEP, Withdraw, Deduct

Tel Exchange: Yes   **With MMF:** Yes

Registered: All states

Ticker: EVTRX

EVERGREEN VALUE TIMING
Growth & Income

Saxon Woods Asset Mgmt.
550 Mamaroneck Ave.
Harrison, NY 10528
(800) 235-0064/(914) 698-5711

	Years Ending 12/31					
	1983	1984	1985	1986	1987	1988
Dividends from Net Investment Income ($)	–	–	–	–	.24	.19
Distributions from Net Realized Capital Gains ($)	–	–	–	–	–	.86
Net Asset Value End of Year ($)	–	–	–	–	9.38	10.62
Ratio of Expenses to Net Assets (%)	–	–	–	–	1.76	1.56
Ratio of Net Income to Average Net Assets (%)	–	–	–	–	1.90	1.70
Portfolio Turnover Rate (%)	–	–	–	–	48	41
Total Assets End of Year (Millions $)	–	–	–	–	21.5	24.4

Annual Rate of Return (%) Years Ending 12/31	–	–	–	–	–	24.6

Five-Year Total Return(%)	NA	Degree of Diversification	NA	Beta	NA	Bull (%)	NA	Bear (%)	(20.2)ᴰ

Objective: Seeks capital appreciation and current income. Invests in the common stocks of companies that the advisor feels are undervalued relative to their assets, breakup value, earnings or potential earnings growth. May also invest in convertible and debt securities.

Portfolio: (12/31/88) Common stocks 82%, short-term securities 11%, preferred stocks 3%, other assets 3%. Largest stock holdings: industrial specialty products 9%, chemicals 9%.

Portfolio Mgr: Stephen Lieber—1986

Distributions: **Income:** Annually **Capital Gains:** Annually

12b-1: No

Minimum: **Initial:** $2,000 **Subsequent:** None

Min IRA: **Initial:** None **Subsequent:** None

Services: IRA, Keogh, SEP, Withdraw, Deduct

Tel Exchange: Yes **With MMF:** Yes

Registered: All states except MO

Ticker: EVVTX

THE FAIRMONT
Aggressive Growth

Morton H. Sachs & Co.
1346 S. Third St.
Louisville, KY 40208
(502) 636-5633

	Years Ending 2/28				12/31		
	1983	1984	1985	1986	1986* (10 mos.)	1987	1988
Dividends from Net Investment Income ($)	1.13	.94	.60	.62	.33	.51	.71
Distributions from Net Realized Capital Gains ($)	3.82	1.93	3.28	7.42	6.20	.23	—
Net Asset Value End of Year ($)	34.59	39.56	45.06	53.64	49.50	44.87	45.56
Ratio of Expenses to Net Assets (%)	1.99	2.15	2.05	1.48	1.26	1.18	1.25
Ratio of Net Income to Average Net Assets (%)	3.77	2.28	1.41	1.22	.71	.91	1.30
Portfolio Turnover Rate (%)	135	103	123	129	124	145	158
Total Assets: End of Year (Millions $)	5.7	14.7	24.5	60.7	79.6	79.0	64.1
Annual Rate of Return (%) Years Ending 12/31	35.9	10.8	32.1	14.0	*	(7.6)	3.1

Five-Year Total Return(%) 59.1ᴰ	Degree of Diversification D	Beta 1.04	Bull (%) 117.4ᴮ	Bear (%) (26.2)ᴱ

*Fiscal year-end changed from 2/28 to 12/31. All annual return figures are for full years ending 12/31.

Objective:	Seeks capital appreciation through investment in common stocks chosen on the basis of economic projections, technical analysis and earnings projections. Market timing is also used. May invest in foreign securities and enter into repurchase agreements. May convert to cash or U.S. government securities for defensive purposes.
Portfolio:	(12/31/88) Common stocks 98%, repurchase agreements 6%, U.S. government securities 2%. Largest stock holdings: transportation 14%, drug and medical 12%.
Portfolio Mgr:	Morton H. Sachs—1981
Distributions:	**Income:** Dec **Capital Gains:** Dec
12b-1:	No
Minimum:	**Initial:** $5,000 **Subsequent:** None
Min IRA:	**Initial:** $1,125 **Subsequent:** None
Services:	IRA, Keogh, Corp, 403(b)
Tel Exchange:	No
Registered:	All states except NH, VT
Ticker:	FAIMX

FIDELITY CONTRAFUND
Growth

Fidelity Investments Co.
82 Devonshire St.
Boston, MA 02109
(800) 544-6666/(617) 523-1919

	Years Ending 12/31					
	1983	**1984**	**1985**	**1986**	**1987**	**1988**
Dividends from Net Investment Income ($)	.45	.29	.25	.25	—	.32
Distributions from Net Realized Capital Gains ($)	.38	1.69	—	2.15	.43	—
Net Asset Value End of Year ($)	12.73	9.77	12.16	11.29	10.72	12.65
Ratio of Expenses to Net Assets (%)	.96	.99	.95	.88	.92	.98
Ratio of Net Income to Average Net Assets (%)	3.61	2.82	3.84	1.68	1.26	3.01
Portfolio Turnover Rate (%)	452	234	135	190	196	250
Total Assets End of Year (Millions $)	86.2	80.8	86.7	84.0	86.7	105.7
Annual Rate of Return (%) Years Ending 12/31	23.2	(8.3)	27.0	12.8	(2.1)	21.0

Five-Year Total Return(%)	55.7[D]	Degree of Diversification	B	Beta	1.08	Bull (%)	132.8[A]	Bear (%)	(30.3)[E]

Objective: Seeks capital growth through investment in securities believed to be undervalued due to an overly pessimistic appraisal by the public. Income received from investments is incidental to the objective.

Portfolio: (12/31/88) Common stocks 85%, short-term obligations 8%, U.S. government obligations 5%, preferred stocks 1%, units 1%. Largest stock holdings: utilities 26%, finance 10%.

Portfolio Mgr: Stuart Williams—1987

Distributions: **Income:** Annually   **Capital Gains:** Annually

12b-1: Yes   **Amount:** Pd. by Advisor

Minimum: **Initial:** $1,000   **Subsequent:** $250

Min IRA: **Initial:** $500   **Subsequent:** $250

Services: IRA, Keogh, Corp, SEP, 403(b), Withdraw, Deduct

Tel Exchange: Yes   **With MMF:** Yes

Registered: All states

Ticker: FCNTX

FIDELITY CONVERTIBLE SECURITIES

Growth & Income

Fidelity Investments Co.
82 Devonshire St.
Boston, MA 02109
(800) 544-6666/(617) 523-1919

	Years Ending 11/30					
	1983	1984	1985	1986	1987 (11 mos.)	1988
Dividends from Net Investment Income ($)	—	—	—	—	.24	.60
Distributions from Net Realized Capital Gains ($)	—	—	—	—	—	—
Net Asset Value End of Year ($)	—	—	—	—	9.05	10.01
Ratio of Expenses to Net Assets (%)	—	—	—	—	1.60	1.60
Ratio of Net Income to Average Net Assets (%)	—	—	—	—	5.45	6.20
Portfolio Turnover Rate (%)	—	—	—	—	233	191
Total Assets End of Year (Millions $)	—	—	—	—	39.5	44.6

Annual Rate of Return (%) Years Ending 12/31	—	—	—	—	—	15.9

Five-Year Total Return(%)	NA	Degree of Diversification	NA	Beta	NA	Bull (%)	NA	Bear (%)	(17.4)c

Objective: Seeks a high level of total return from current income and capital appreciation primarily through investment in convertible securities. Invests at least 65% of assets in convertibles including bonds, debentures, notes and preferred stocks.

Portfolio: (11/30/88) Convertible bonds 36%, convertible preferred stocks 30%, short-term obligations 12%, U.S. government obligations 11%, common stocks 10%. Largest holdings: finance 9%, utilities 8%.

Portfolio Mgr: Andrew Midler—1988

Distributions: **Income:** Quarterly   **Capital Gains:** Annually

12b-1: Yes   **Amount:** Pd. by Advisor

Minimum: **Initial:** $2,500   **Subsequent:** $250

Min IRA: **Initial:** $500   **Subsequent:** $250

Services: IRA, Keogh, Corp, SEP, 403(b), Withdraw, Deduct

Tel Exchange: Yes   **With MMF:** Yes

Registered: All states

Ticker: FCVSX

FIDELITY FLEXIBLE BOND
Bond

Fidelity Investments Co.
82 Devonshire St.
Boston, MA 02109
(800) 544-6666/(617) 523-1919

	Years Ending 4/30					
	1983	1984	1985	1986	1987	1988
Dividends from Net Investment Income ($)	.80	.76	.79	.74	.67	.61
Distributions from Net Realized Capital Gains ($)	—	—	—	—	—	—
Net Asset Value End of Year ($)	7.29	6.34	6.60	7.46	7.00	6.77
Ratio of Expenses to Net Assets (%)	.81	.77	.79	.67	.69	.76
Ratio of Net Income to Average Net Assets (%)	11.74	11.40	12.22	10.53	9.17	8.95
Portfolio Turnover Rate (%)	378	164	164	243	127	118
Total Assets End of Year (Millions $)	169.2	134.6	166.5	250.5	383.5	315.7

Annual Rate of Return (%) Years Ending 12/31	6.6	11.8	21.1	13.5	.1	7.9

Five-Year Total Return(%)	66.0^C	Degree of Diversification	NA	Beta	NA	Bull (%)	48.8^E	Bear (%)	2.6^A

Objective: Seeks current income and security of shareholders' capital. At least 80% of assets are in investment-grade (BBB or higher) debt securities.

Portfolio: (10/31/88) U.S. government obligations 40%, corporate bonds 27%, Canadian obligations 14%, short-term obligations 12%, supranational obligations 5%, foreign obligations 2%.

Portfolio Mgr: Michael Gray—1987

Distributions: **Income:** Monthly   **Capital Gains:** Annually

12b-1: Yes   **Amount:** Pd. by Advisor

Minimum: **Initial:** $2,500   **Subsequent:** $250

Min IRA: **Initial:** $500   **Subsequent:** $250

Services: IRA, Keogh, Corp, SEP, 403(b), Withdraw, Deduct

Tel Exchange: Yes   **With MMF:** Yes

Registered: All states

Ticker: FBNDX

FIDELITY FREEDOM
Aggressive Growth

Fidelity Investments Co.
82 Devonshire St.
Boston, MA 02109
(800) 544-6666/(617) 523-1919

	Years Ending 11/30					
	1983 (8 mos.)	1984	1985	1986	1987	1988
Dividends from Net Investment Income ($)	—	.04	.24	.35	.14	.23
Distributions from Net Realized Capital Gains ($)	—	.42	.15	.98	3.50	3.18
Net Asset Value End of Year ($)	12.68	12.15	14.88	16.93	12.94	12.55
Ratio of Expenses to Net Assets (%)	1.26	1.13	1.14	1.07	.97	1.09
Ratio of Net Income to Average Net Assets (%)	1.47	3.08	2.86	1.11	1.25	1.79
Portfolio Turnover Rate (%)	116	97	100	161	171	156
Total Assets End of Year (Millions $)	141.3	388.3	600.5	916.0	993.0	1,244.1

Annual Rate of Return (%) Years Ending 12/31	—	3.4	28.5	13.7	8.9	15.5

Five-Year Total Return(%)	90.0[B]	Degree of Diversification	B	Beta 1.09	Bull (%) 143.9[A]	Bear (%) (25.5)[E]

Objective: Seeks long- and short-term capital gains by investing in common stocks of well-known and established companies as well as small companies. Best suited to retirement plans where the tax status of distributions is immaterial.

Portfolio: (11/30/88) Common stocks 91%, short-term obligations 8%, preferred stocks 1%. Largest stock holdings: conglomerates 14%, energy 13%.

Portfolio Mgr: Stuart Williams—1988

Distributions: Income: Dec   **Capital Gains:** Dec

12b-1: Yes   **Amount:** Pd. by Advisor

Minimum: Initial: $500   **Subsequent:** $250

Min IRA: Initial: $500   **Subsequent:** $250

Services: IRA, Keogh, Corp, SEP, 403(b), Withdraw, Deduct

Tel Exchange: Yes   **With MMF:** Yes

Registered: All states

Ticker: FDFFX

FIDELITY FUND
Growth & Income

Fidelity Investments Co.
82 Devonshire St.
Boston, MA 02109
(800) 544-6666/(617) 523-1919

	Years Ending 12/31					
	1983	1984	1985	1986	1987	1988
Dividends from Net Investment Income ($)	.84	.71	.72	.66	.48	.56
Distributions from Net Realized Capital Gains ($)	1.97	4.40	.05	4.08	2.72	—
Net Asset Value End of Year ($)	19.89	14.82	18.08	16.05	13.58	15.42
Ratio of Expenses to Net Assets (%)	.71	.66	.66	.60	.67	.67
Ratio of Net Income to Average Net Assets (%)	4.34	5.06	4.25	3.48	2.75	3.69
Portfolio Turnover Rate (%)	210	200	215	214	211	175
Total Assets End of Year (Millions $)	668.9	617.6	761.5	780.7	869.8	891.6
Annual Rate of Return (%) Years Ending 12/31	22.4	1.4	28.0	15.4	3.1	17.9

Five-Year Total Return(%)	82.1[B]	Degree of Diversification	A	Beta	.97	Bull (%)	124.5[B]	Bear (%)	(23.2)[D]

Objective: Seeks long-term capital growth. In order to provide a reasonable current return, invests in securities selected for their current income characteristics. Companies are well-established, dividend-paying and from a variety of industries that show potential for stability and reliability of earnings.

Portfolio: (12/31/88) Common stocks 76%, U.S. government obligations 9%, short-term obligations 7%, corporate bonds 5%, convertible preferred stocks 3%. Largest stock holdings: utilities 13%, basic industries 11%.

Portfolio Mgr: Barry Greenfield—1981

Distributions: Income: Mar, June, Sept, Dec   **Capital Gains:** Dec

12b-1: Yes   **Amount:** Pd. by Advisor

Minimum: Initial: $1,000   Subsequent: $250

Min IRA: Initial: $500   Subsequent: $250

Services: IRA, Keogh, Corp, SEP, 403(b), Withdraw, Deduct

Tel Exchange: Yes   **With MMF:** Yes

Registered: All states

Ticker: FFIDX

FIDELITY GINNIE MAE
Bond

Fidelity Investments Co.
82 Devonshire St.
Boston, MA 02109
(800) 544-6666/(617) 523-1919

			Years Ending 7/31			
	1983	1984	1985	1986 (9 mos.)	1987	1988
Dividends from Net Investment Income ($)	—	—	—	.72	.87	.86
Distributions from Net Realized Capital Gains ($)	—	—	—	—	.01	—
Net Asset Value End of Year ($)	—	—	—	10.58	10.23	10.02
Ratio of Expenses to Net Assets (%)	—	—	—	.75	.79	.87
Ratio of Net Income to Average Net Assets (%)	—	—	—	9.13	8.28	8.57
Portfolio Turnover Rate (%)	—	—	—	106	177	361
Total Assets End of Year (Millions $)	—	—	—	652.9	868.9	721.6
Annual Rate of Return (%) Years Ending 12/31	—	—	—	13.0	1.2	7.2

Five-Year Total Return(%)	NA	Degree of Diversification	NA	Beta	NA	Bull (%)	NA	Bear (%)	2.5ᴬ

Objective: Seeks high level of current income through investment primarily in GNMAs and other debt securities guaranteed by the U.S. government. May hedge the portfolio with futures contracts and put options.

Portfolio: (7/31/88) GNMAs 72%, short-term securities 20%, U.S. Treasury notes 8%.

Portfolio Mgr: Jim Wolfson—1986

Distributions: **Income:** Monthly   **Capital Gains:** Annually

12b-1: Yes   **Amount:** Pd. by Advisor

Minimum: **Initial:** $1,000   **Subsequent:** $250

Min IRA: **Initial:** $500   **Subsequent:** $250

Services: IRA, Keogh, Corp, SEP, 403(b), Withdraw, Deduct

Tel Exchange: Yes   **With MMF:** Yes

Registered: All states

Ticker: FGMNX

FIDELITY GLOBAL BOND
International

Fidelity Investments Co.
82 Devonshire St.
Boston, MA 02109
(800) 544-6666/(617) 523-1919

	Years Ending 10/31					
	1983	1984	1985	1986	1987 (10 mos.)	1988
Dividends from Net Investment Income ($)	–	–	–	–	.56	.13
Distributions from Net Realized Capital Gains ($)	–	–	–	–	–	–
Net Asset Value End of Year ($)	–	–	–	–	10.45	11.47
Ratio of Expenses to Net Assets (%)	–	–	–	–	.95	1.14
Ratio of Net Income to Average Net Assets (%)	–	–	–	–	7.14	7.61
Portfolio Turnover Rate (%)	–	–	–	–	297	227
Total Assets End of Year (Millions $)	–	–	–	–	43.8	59.2

Annual Rate of Return (%) Years Ending 12/31	–	–	–	–	–	3.7

Five-Year Total Return(%)	NA	Degree of Diversification	NA	Beta	NA	Bull (%)	NA	Bear (%)	12.9ᴬ

Objective: Seeks high total return through investment in debt securities issued worldwide. Will invest at least 65% of assets in debt securities rated not less than BB by Standard & Poor's. Considers factors such as currency relationships, interest rates and inflation. May invest in interest rate futures contracts.

Portfolio: (10/31/88) Bonds 91%, repurchase agreements 9%. Largest holdings: U.S. Treasury securities 34%, Australian bonds 13%.

Portfolio Mgr: Judy Pagliuca—1986

Distributions: **Income:** Annually **Capital Gains:** Annually

12b-1: Yes **Amount:** Pd. by Advisor

Minimum: **Initial:** $2,500 **Subsequent:** $250

Min IRA: **Initial:** $500 **Subsequent:** $250

Services: IRA, Keogh, Corp, SEP, 403(b), Withdraw, Deduct

Tel Exchange: Yes **With MMF:** Yes

Registered: All states

Ticker: FGBDX

FIDELITY GOVERNMENT SECURITIES
Bond

Fidelity Investments Co.
82 Devonshire St.
Boston, MA 02109
(800) 544-6666/(617) 523-1919

	Years Ending 12/31					
	1983	1984	1985	1986	1987	1988
Dividends from Net Investment Income ($)	.94	1.01	.98	.90	.85	.84
Distributions from Net Realized Capital Gains ($)	.28	—	—	—	—	—
Net Asset Value End of Year ($)	9.28	9.24	9.80	10.28	9.52	9.27
Ratio of Expenses to Net Assets (%)	.88	.85	.81	.84	.87	.79
Ratio of Net Income to Average Net Assets (%)	9.92	11.14	10.46	8.72	8.68	8.87
Portfolio Turnover Rate (%)	NA	NA	137	138	253	283
Total Assets End of Year (Millions $)	85.6	89.2	269.6	751.7	682.7	568.0

Annual Rate of Return (%) Years Ending 12/31	6.0	11.3	17.6	14.7	1.0	6.3

Five-Year Total Return(%)	61.3ᴰ	Degree of Diversification	NA	Beta	NA	Bull (%)	45.5ᴱ	Bear (%)	2.6ᴬ

Objective: Seeks income from investment in U.S. government obligations. Income is exempt from state and local income taxes in all states.

Portfolio: (12/31/88) U.S. government and agency obligations 100%.

Portfolio Mgr: Jim Wolfson—1986

Distributions: **Income:** Monthly **Capital Gains:** Dec

12b-1: Yes **Amount:** Pd. by Advisor

Minimum: **Initial:** $1,000 **Subsequent:** $250

Min IRA: **Initial:** NA* **Subsequent:** NA

Services: Withdraw, Deduct

Tel Exchange: Yes **With MMF:** Yes

Registered: All states

Ticker: FGOVX

Fund is structured as a limited partnership.

FIDELITY HIGH INCOME
Bond

Fidelity Investments Co.
82 Devonshire St.
Boston, MA 02109
(800) 544-6666/(617) 523-1919

	Years Ending 11/30				4/30	
	1983	1984	1985	1986	1987* (5 mos.)	1988
Dividends from Net Investment Income ($)	1.10	1.16	1.15	1.10	.45	1.03
Distributions from Net Realized Capital Gains ($)	–	–	–	.13	.26	.20
Net Asset Value End of Year ($)	9.01	8.68	9.24	9.94	9.62	8.72
Ratio of Expenses to Net Assets (%)	.87	.85	.83	.80	.78	.88
Ratio of Net Income to Average Net Assets (%)	12.45	13.51	12.54	11.30	10.99	11.38
Portfolio Turnover Rate (%)	129	71	157	104	116	68
Total Assets End of Year (Millions $)	261.1	395.9	782.9	1,645.7	1,720.2	1,529.9

Annual Rate of Return (%) Years Ending 12/31	18.5	10.5	25.5	18.0	1.2	12.6

Five-Year Total Return(%)	86.6[B]	Degree of Diversification	NA	Beta	NA	Bull (%)	72.8[D]	Bear (%)	(4.0)[C]

Fiscal year-end changed from 11/30 to 4/30.

Objective: Seeks high current income through investments in high-yielding, fixed-income corporate securities that are rated Baa (BBB) or lower and securities unrated by rating services. Securities are further screened for future potential financial strength of the issuing company.

Portfolio: (10/31/88) Corporate bonds 80%, short-term obligations 18%, U.S. government obligations 1%, non-convertible preferred stocks 1%. Largest bond holdings: media and leisure 17%, retail and wholesale 12%.

Portfolio Mgr: William Pike—1981

Distributions: **Income:** Monthly   **Capital Gains:** Annually

12b-1: Yes   **Amount:** Pd. by Advisor

Minimum: **Initial:** $2,500   **Subsequent:** $250

Min IRA: **Initial:** $500   **Subsequent:** $250

Services: IRA, Keogh, Corp, SEP, 403(b), Withdraw, Deduct

Tel Exchange: Yes   **With MMF:** Yes

Registered: All states

Ticker: FAGIX

FIDELITY INTERMEDIATE BOND

Bond

Fidelity Investments Co.
82 Devonshire St.
Boston, MA 02109
(800) 544-6666/(617) 523-1919

	Years Ending 12/31					
	1983	1984	1985	1986	1987	1988
Dividends from Net Investment Income ($)	1.03	1.10	.74	.66	1.61	.87
Distributions from Net Realized Capital Gains ($)	—	—	—	.22	.10	—
Net Asset Value End of Year ($)	9.72	9.83	11.01	11.55	10.04	9.87
Ratio of Expenses to Net Assets (%)	.69	.73	.79	.75	.86	.87
Ratio of Net Income to Average Net Assets (%)	10.43	11.62	10.73	9.27	9.17	8.76
Portfolio Turnover Rate (%)	238	80	68	101	67	59
Total Assets End of Year (Millions $)	114.2	151.7	244.1	367.9	370.4	504.3

Annual Rate of Return (%) Years Ending 12/31	9.4	13.5	20.9	13.1	2.1	7.1

Five-Year Total Return(%)	69.8^C	Degree of Diversification	NA	Beta	NA	Bull (%)	51.4^D	Bear (%)	2.7^A

Objective: Seeks current income through investment in corporate bonds rated A or better, government securities and money market instruments. Average maturity is less than 10 years.

Portfolio: (12/31/88) U.S. government and agency obligations 46%, short-term obligations 24%, corporate bonds 19%, Canadian obligations 7%, supranational obligations 3%, foreign obligations 1%.

Portfolio Mgr: Michael Gray—1987

Distributions: **Income:** Monthly   **Capital Gains:** Annually

12b-1: Yes   **Amount:** Pd. by Advisor

Minimum: **Initial:** $1,000   **Subsequent:** $250

Min IRA: **Initial:** $500   **Subsequent:** $250

Services: IRA, Keogh, Corp, SEP, 403(b), Withdraw, Deduct

Tel Exchange: Yes   **With MMF:** Yes

Registered: All states

Ticker: FTHRX

FIDELITY MORTGAGE SECURITIES
Bond

Fidelity Investments Co.
82 Devonshire St.
Boston, MA 02109
(800) 544-6666/(617) 523-1919

	Years Ending 7/31					
	1983	1984	1985 (7 mos.)	1986	1987	1988
Dividends from Net Investment Income ($)	—	—	.70	1.06	.91	.86
Distributions from Net Realized Capital Gains ($)	—	—	—	—	.03	—
Net Asset Value End of Year ($)	—	—	10.10	10.49	10.10	9.91
Ratio of Expenses to Net Assets (%)	—	—	.75	.75	.80	.90
Ratio of Net Income to Average Net Assets (%)	—	—	11.53	10.11	8.79	8.96
Portfolio Turnover Rate (%)	—	—	72	59	160	245
Total Assets End of Year (Millions $)	—	—	140.6	642.3	603.4	484.5
Annual Rate of Return (%) Years Ending 12/31	—	—	19.6	11.5	2.6	6.7

Five-Year Total Return(%)	NA	Degree of Diversification	NA	Beta	NA	Bull (%)	NA	Bear (%)	2.6ᴬ

Objective: Seeks high level of current income through investment in mortgage-related securities such as GNMAs, FNMAs, FHLMCs and CMOs, which comprise 65% of the portfolio. The remaining 35% can be long- or short-term debt.

Portfolio: (7/31/88) Mortgage-related securities 75%, short-term obligations 14%, U.S. Treasury notes 7%, U.S. Treasury bonds 4%.

Portfolio Mgr: Jim Wolfson—1986

Distributions: **Income:** Monthly **Capital Gains:** Annually

12b-1: Yes **Amount:** Pd. by Advisor

Minimum: **Initial:** $1,000 **Subsequent:** $250

Min IRA: **Initial:** $500 **Subsequent:** $250

Services: IRA, Keogh, Corp, SEP, 403(b), Withdraw, Deduct

Tel Exchange: Yes **With MMF:** Yes

Registered: All states

Ticker: FMSFX

FIDELITY SHORT-TERM BOND
Bond

Fidelity Investments Co.
82 Devonshire St.
Boston, MA 02109
(800) 544-6666/(617) 523-1919

| | Years Ending 4/30 | | | | | |
	1983	1984	1985	1986	1987 (7 mos.)	1988
Dividends from Net Investment Income ($)	–	–	–	–	.48	.84
Distributions from Net Realized Capital Gains ($)	–	–	–	–	–	–
Net Asset Value End of Year ($)	–	–	–	–	9.67	9.47
Ratio of Expenses to Net Assets (%)	–	–	–	–	.90	.88
Ratio of Net Income to Average Net Assets (%)	–	–	–	–	8.40	8.77
Portfolio Turnover Rate (%)	–	–	–	–	149	251
Total Assets End of Year (Millions $)	–	–	–	–	137.1	382.1

Annual Rate of Return (%) Years Ending 12/31	–	–	–	–	3.9	5.7

Five-Year Total Return(%)	NA	Degree of Diversification	NA	Beta	NA	Bull (%)	NA	Bear (%)	2.3A

Objective: Seeks high level of current income consistent with preservation of capital. Average maturity of portfolio cannot exceed three years. Invests in investment-grade fixed-income securities rated BBB or higher by Standard & Poor's, including government notes, commercial paper and bankers' acceptances.

Portfolio: (10/31/88) Corporate bonds 44%, U.S. government obligations 29%, Canadian obligations 12%, foreign obligations 10%, supranational obligations 3%, short-term obligations 1%.

Portfolio Mgr: Alan Bembenek—1987

Distributions: **Income:** Monthly   **Capital Gains:** Annually

12b-1: Yes   **Amount:** Pd. by Advisor

Minimum: **Initial:** $1,000   **Subsequent:** $250

Min IRA: **Initial:** $500   **Subsequent:** $250

Services: IRA, Keogh, Corp, SEP, 403(b), Withdraw, Deduct

Tel Exchange: Yes   **With MMF:** Yes

Registered: All states

Ticker: FSHBX

FIDELITY TREND
Growth

Fidelity Investments Co.
82 Devonshire St.
Boston, MA 02109
(800) 544-6666/(617) 523-1919

	Years Ending 12/31					
	1983	**1984**	**1985**	**1986**	**1987**	**1988**
Dividends from Net Investment Income ($)	.78	.83	.79	.61	.44	.52
Distributions from Net Realized Capital Gains ($)	—	—	1.25	10.64	6.20	1.06
Net Asset Value End of Year ($)	38.56	36.86	45.02	39.83	31.40	37.43
Ratio of Expenses to Net Assets (%)	.66	.56	.52	.52	.49	.47
Ratio of Net Income to Average Net Assets (%)	2.60	2.90	2.40	2.00	1.49	2.01
Portfolio Turnover Rate (%)	71	57	62	71	128	49
Total Assets End of Year (Millions $)	637.6	602.4	712.7	669.1	599.0	701.6

Annual Rate of Return (%) Years Ending 12/31	25.2	(2.2)	28.2	13.5	(4.2)	24.3

Five-Year Total Return(%)	69.4[C]	Degree of Diversification	B	Beta 1.13	Bull (%) 119.4[B]	Bear (%) (28.4)[E]

Objective: Seeks growth of capital through investment in securities of both well-established companies and smaller firms. Decisions based on studies of momentum in trends of earnings and security prices of individual companies, industries and the market. May loan its portfolio securities, use leverage and engage in repurchase agreements. Income return is incidental to the objective of capital growth.

Portfolio: (12/31/88) Common stocks 91%, short-term obligations 8%, convertible preferred stocks 1%, corporate bonds 1%. Largest stock holdings: utilities 20%, basic industries 13%.

Portfolio Mgr: Alan Leifer—1987

Distributions: **Income:** Annually   **Capital Gains:** Annually

12b-1: Yes   **Amount:** Pd. by Advisor

Minimum: **Initial:** $1,000   **Subsequent:** $250

Min IRA: **Initial:** $500   **Subsequent:** $250

Services: IRA, Keogh, Corp, SEP, 403(b), Withdraw, Deduct

Tel Exchange: Yes   **With MMF:** Yes

Registered: All states

Ticker: FTRNX

FIDELITY VALUE
Growth

Fidelity Investments Co.
82 Devonshire St.
Boston, MA 02109
(800) 544-6666/(617) 523-1919

	Years Ending 10/31					
	1983	1984	1985	1986	1987	1988
Dividends from Net Investment Income ($)	—	.27	.49	.42	.15	—
Distributions from Net Realized Capital Gains ($)	—	3.63	—	—	2.36	—
Net Asset Value End of Year ($)	23.04	18.53	20.29	26.49	21.01	27.18
Ratio of Expenses to Net Assets (%)	.88	1.26	1.13	1.07	1.07	1.11
Ratio of Net Income to Average Net Assets (%)	2.87	4.84	3.43	2.20	1.02	4.74
Portfolio Turnover Rate (%)	353	389	246	281	442	480
Total Assets End of Year (Millions $)	96.9	114.0	100.8	142.8	92.0	134.5

Annual Rate of Return (%) Years Ending 12/31	31.9	(8.7)	22.1	15.1	(8.6)	29.0

Five-Year Total Return(%) 51.4ᴰ	Degree of Diversification C	Beta .92	Bull (%) 95.4ᶜ	Bear (%) (26.2)ᴱ

Objective: Seeks capital growth through investment in securities of companies that possess valuable fixed assets, or securities that fund management believes to be undervalued in the marketplace because of changes in the company, the economy, or the industry. May loan its portfolio securities and engage in repurchase agreements.

Portfolio: (10/31/88) Common stocks 95%, short-term obligations 6%. Largest stock holdings: media and leisure 28%, nondurables 25%.

Portfolio Mgr: Ernest Wiggins—1986

Distributions: Income: Dec   **Capital Gains:** Dec

12b-1: Yes   **Amount:** Pd. by Advisor

Minimum: Initial: $1,000   **Subsequent:** $250

Min IRA: Initial: $500   **Subsequent:** $250

Services: IRA, Keogh, Corp, SEP, 403(b), Withdraw, Deduct

Tel Exchange: Yes   **With MMF:** Yes

Registered: All states

Ticker: FDVLX

FIDUCIARY CAPITAL GROWTH

Aggressive Growth

Fiduciary Management, Inc.
222 E. Mason St.
Milwaukee, WI 53202
(414) 271-6666

	Years Ending 9/30					
	1983	1984	1985	1986	1987	1988
Dividends from Net Investment Income ($)	.25	.16	.31	.19	.10	.14
Distributions from Net Realized Capital Gains ($)	—	.30	.20	.03	3.68	3.45
Net Asset Value End of Year ($)	19.40	17.94	19.10	22.51	21.96	15.19
Ratio of Expenses to Net Assets (%)	1.80	1.50	1.30	1.2	1.1	1.3
Ratio of Net Income to Average Net Assets (%)	1.90	2.00	1.20	.40	.60	.30
Portfolio Turnover Rate (%)	30	26	38	57	83	43
Total Assets End of Year (Millions $)	20.8	28.5	41.5	51.9	55.2	41.6

Annual Rate of Return (%) Years Ending 12/31	29.0	(4.2)	29.8	(.4)	(9.0)	18.8

Five-Year Total Return(%)	33.9ᴱ	Degree of Diversification	D	Beta	1.00	Bull (%)	70.4ᴰ	Bear (%)	(27.0)ᴱ

Objective: Seeks long-term capital appreciation principally through investing in common stocks underpriced relative to growth prospects, and in unseasoned companies and companies in special situations such as mergers. May invest in foreign securities.

Portfolio: (9/30/88) Common stocks 91%, short-term securities 8%, convertible debentures 1%. Largest stock holdings: electronics 12%, energy and energy services 9%.

Portfolio Mgr: Ted Kellner—1981

Distributions: Income: Oct, Dec   **Capital Gains:** Oct, Dec

12b-1: No

Minimum: Initial: $1,000   Subsequent: $100

Min IRA: Initial: $1,000   Subsequent: $100

Services: IRA, Keogh, Corp, Withdraw

Tel Exchange: No

Registered: All states except AK, AR, ID, ME, MS, MT, NC, ND, NE, NH, SD, VT, WV, WY

Ticker: FCGFX

FINANCIAL BOND SHARES—HIGH YIELD PORTFOLIO
Bond

Financial Programs, Inc.
P.O. Box 2040
Denver, CO 80201
(800) 525-8085/(303) 779-1233

	Years Ending 12/31					
	1983	1984 (10 mos.)	1985	1986	1987	1988
Dividends from Net Investment Income ($)	—	.81	1.03	1.01	.94	.93
Distributions from Net Realized Capital Gains ($)	—	—	—	.17	—	—
Net Asset Value End of Year ($)	—	7.51	8.37	8.38	7.75	7.82
Ratio of Expenses to Net Assets (%)	—	.43	.93	.76	.86	.82
Ratio of Net Income to Average Net Assets (%)	—	10.72	12.97	11.35	11.22	11.72
Portfolio Turnover Rate (%)	—	35	96	134	89	42
Total Assets End of Year (Millions $)	—	3.8	18.3	46.6	37.9	60.5

Annual Rate of Return (%) Years Ending 12/31	—	—	26.6	14.5	3.6	13.4

Five-Year Total Return(%)	NA	Degree of Diversification	NA	Beta	NA	Bull (%)	NA	Bear (%)	(2.3)c

Objective: Seeks high current income through investment in bonds and other debt securities and preferred stock rated low and medium (BBB/Baa or lower). More than 25% of its assets may be concentrated in the public utility industry.

Portfolio: (12/31/88) Corporate bonds 96%, corporate short-term notes 3%, preferred stocks 1%. Largest bond holdings: manufacturing 13%, retail 13%.

Portfolio Mgr: William Veronda—1984

Distributions: Income: Monthly **Capital Gains:** Annually

12b-1: No

Minimum: Initial: $250 Subsequent: $50

Min IRA: Initial: $250 Subsequent: $50

Services: IRA, Keogh, Corp, SEP, 403(b), Withdraw, Deduct

Tel Exchange: Yes **With MMF:** Yes

Registered: All states

Ticker: FHYPX

FINANCIAL BOND SHARES—SELECT INCOME PORTFOLIO
Bond

Financial Programs, Inc.
P.O. Box 2040
Denver, CO 80201
(800) 525-8085/(303) 779-1233

	Years Ending 12/31					
	1983	1984	1985	1986	1987	1988
Dividends from Net Investment Income ($)	.78	.73	.72	.68	.64	.61
Distributions from Net Realized Capital Gains ($)	.05	—	—	.32	—	—
Net Asset Value End of Year ($)	6.65	6.22	6.84	7.10	6.36	6.39
Ratio of Expenses to Net Assets (%)	0	.23	.97	.85	.99	1.00
Ratio of Net Income to Average Net Assets (%)	11.03	11.74	11.10	9.19	9.36	9.47
Portfolio Turnover Rate (%)	33	188	146	153	131	143
Total Assets End of Year (Millions $)	8.5	8.1	15.1	24.7	19.8	29.9
Annual Rate of Return (%) Years Ending 12/31	5.1	5.2	22.7	18.8	(1.5)	10.4

Five-Year Total Return(%)	66.8ᶜ	Degree of Diversification	NA	Beta	NA	Bull (%)	57.0ᴰ	Bear (%)	0.5ᴮ

Objective: Seeks a high level of current income through investment in bonds and other debt securities of established companies and of government and municipal issues. 50% of assets invested in investment grade securities (Baa/BBB or higher). Remaining 50% invested in lower grade or unrated securities.

Portfolio: (12/31/88) Corporate bonds 51%, U.S. government obligations 42%, U.S. government agency obligations 3%, municipal bonds 3%. Largest bond holdings: savings and loan 6%, retail 5%.

Portfolio Mgr: William Veronda—1984

Distributions: **Income:** Monthly   **Capital Gains:** Annually

12b-1: No

Minimum: **Initial:** $250   **Subsequent:** $50

Min IRA: **Initial:** $250   **Subsequent:** $50

Services: IRA, Keogh, Corp, SEP, 403(b), Withdraw, Deduct

Tel Exchange: Yes   **With MMF:** Yes

Registered: All states

Ticker: FBDSX

FINANCIAL BOND SHARES— U.S. GOVERNMENT

Bond

Financial Programs, Inc.
P.O. Box 2040
Denver, CO 80201
(800) 525-8085/(303) 779-1233

	Years Ending 12/31					
	1983	1984	1985	1986	1987	1988
Dividends from Net Investment Income ($)	—	—	—	.61	.53	.54
Distributions from Net Realized Capital Gains ($)	—	—	—	.03	—	—
Net Asset Value End of Year ($)	—	—	—	7.90	6.98	6.87
Ratio of Expenses to Net Assets (%)	—	—	—	.74	1.29	1.19
Ratio of Net Income to Average Net Assets (%)	—	—	—	7.53	7.06	7.75
Portfolio Turnover Rate (%)	—	—	—	61	284	221
Total Assets End of Year (Millions $)	—	—	—	7.2	7.9	9.4
Annual Rate of Return (%) Years Ending 12/31	—	—	—	—	(5.1)	6.2

Five-Year Total Return(%)	NA	Degree of Diversification	NA	Beta	NA	Bull (%)	NA	Bear (%)	(0.3)[B]

Objective:	Seeks high level of current income by investing in U.S. government and government agency debt obligations. These include bills, notes, bonds, and GNMA mortgage-backed securities. May also buy and sell interest rate futures contracts to hedge the portfolio.
Portfolio:	(12/31/88) U.S. government agency obligations 50%, U.S. government obligations 32%, repurchase agreements 18%.
Portfolio Mgr:	William Veronda—1986
Distributions:	**Income:** Monthly **Capital Gains:** Annually
12b-1:	No
Minimum:	**Initial:** $250 **Subsequent:** $50
Min IRA:	**Initial:** $250 **Subsequent:** $50
Services:	IRA, Keogh, Corp, SEP, 403(b), Withdraw, Deduct
Tel Exchange:	Yes **With MMF:** Yes
Registered:	All states
Ticker:	FBDGX

FINANCIAL DYNAMICS

Aggressive Growth

Financial Programs, Inc.
P.O. Box 2040
Denver, CO 80201
(800) 525-8085/(303) 779-1233

	Years Ending 4/30					
	1983	1984	1985	1986	1987	1988
Dividends from Net Investment Income ($)	.18	.15	.09	.06	.02	.02
Distributions from Net Realized Capital Gains ($)	.99	1.38	–	1.24	1.75	.47
Net Asset Value End of Year ($)	10.02	6.87	7.28	8.59	8.42	6.65
Ratio of Expenses to Net Assets (%)	.66	.66	.78	.90	.92	1.02
Ratio of Net Income to Average Net Assets (%)	2.07	1.44	1.30	.63	.27	.28
Portfolio Turnover Rate (%)	114	56	152	246	234	199
Total Assets End of Year (Millions $)	94.5	66.6	73.8	87.7	91.0	83.6

Annual Rate of Return (%) Years Ending 12/31	13.1	(13.8)	29.1	6.4	3.7	9.1

Five-Year Total Return(%) 34.1ᴱ	Degree of Diversification C	Beta 1.28	Bull (%) 116.5ᴮ	Bear (%) (30.3)ᴱ

Objective:	Seeks capital growth through aggressive investment policies. Invests primarily in common stocks appearing to be in an early stage of growth; gives no consideration to immediate income return. Stocks are chosen by fundamental analysis techniques. May use leverage.
Portfolio:	(10/31/88) Common stocks 98%, corporate short-term notes 2%. Largest stock holdings: utilities 14%, recreation services 8%.
Portfolio Mgr:	Daniel Leonard—1985
Distributions:	**Income:** April **Capital Gains:** April
12b-1:	No
Minimum:	**Initial:** $250 **Subsequent:** $50
Min IRA:	**Initial:** $250 **Subsequent:** $50
Services:	IRA, Keogh, Corp, SEP, 403(b), Withdraw, Deduct
Tel Exchange:	Yes **With MMF:** Yes
Registered:	All states
Ticker:	FIDYX

FINANCIAL INDUSTRIAL
Growth

Financial Programs, Inc.
P.O. Box 2040
Denver, CO 80201
(800) 525-8085/(303) 779-1233

	Years Ending 8/31					
	1983	1984	1985	1986	1987	1988
Dividends from Net Investment Income ($)	.20	.16	.14	.12	.08	.07
Distributions from Net Realized Capital Gains ($)	.89	.04	.46	1.02	.64	—
Net Asset Value End of Year ($)	4.49	4.09	4.09	4.14	4.64	3.48
Ratio of Expenses to Net Assets (%)	.63	.64	.72	.74	.77	.81
Ratio of Net Income to Average Net Assets (%)	3.47	3.87	3.27	2.16	1.56	1.84
Portfolio Turnover Rate (%)	88	80	133	227	250	116
Total Assets End of Year (Millions $)	363.8	336.2	342.3	397.1	480.5	327.7

Annual Rate of Return (%) Years Ending 12/31	15.3	(1.2)	28.2	8.4	0.0	5.9

Five-Year Total Return(%)	45.3[D]	Degree of Diversification	A	Beta	1.04	Bull (%)	112.3[B]	Bear (%)	(25.9)[E]

Objective:	Seeks long-term capital growth and a reasonable degree of current income through investment in well-established, dividend-paying companies from major fields of business and industrial activity.
Portfolio:	(8/31/88) Common stocks 89%, corporate short-term notes 10%, fixed-income securities 1%. Largest stock holdings: oil & gas related 11%, pharmaceuticals 10%.
Portfolio Mgr:	R. Dalton—1987
Distributions:	**Income:** Feb, May, Aug, Nov **Capital Gains:** Aug
12b-1:	No
Minimum:	**Initial:** $250 **Subsequent:** $50
Min IRA:	**Initial:** $250 **Subsequent:** $50
Services:	IRA, Keogh, Corp, SEP, 403(b), Withdraw, Deduct
Tel Exchange:	Yes **With MMF:** Yes
Registered:	All states
Ticker:	FLRFX

FINANCIAL INDUSTRIAL INCOME

Balanced

Financial Programs, Inc.
P.O. Box 2040
Denver, CO 80201
(800) 525-8085/(303) 779-1233

	Years Ending 6/30					
	1983	**1984**	**1985**	**1986**	**1987**	**1988**
Dividends from Net Investment Income ($)	.48	.54	.48	.48	.36	.36
Distributions from Net Realized Capital Gains ($)	.56	.96	.66	1.89	1.06	.35
Net Asset Value End of Year ($)	8.97	7.30	8.42	9.10	8.85	7.98
Ratio of Expenses to Net Assets (%)	.63	.64	.68	.71	.74	.78
Ratio of Net Income to Average Net Assets (%)	5.48	5.92	5.72	4.85	3.96	4.29
Portfolio Turnover Rate (%)	57	54	54	160	195	148
Total Assets End of Year (Millions $)	222.7	182.7	249.3	341.7	451.1	381.1

Annual Rate of Return (%) Years Ending 12/31	23.5	9.7	30.8	14.6	4.8	15.3

Five-Year Total Return(%)	98.9ᴬ	Degree of Diversification	A	Beta	.79	Bull (%)	120.8ᴮ	Bear (%)	(17.9)ᶜ

Objective: Seeks current income through investment in common and preferred stocks and convertible bonds of well-established, dividend-paying companies as well as debt securities with high payments.

Portfolio: (9/20/88) Common stocks 70%, fixed-income securities 23%, short-term corporate notes 5%, preferred stocks 3%. Largest stock holdings: drug, manufacturing.

Portfolio Mgr: John Kaweske—1985

Distributions: Income: Mar, June, Sept, Dec   **Capital Gains:** Dec

12b-1: No

Minimum: Initial: $250   Subsequent: $50

Min IRA: Initial: $250   Subsequent: $50

Services: IRA, Keogh, Corp, SEP, 403(b), Withdraw, Deduct

Tel Exchange: Yes   **With MMF:** Yes

Registered: All states

Ticker: FIIIX

FINANCIAL STRATEGIC PORTFOLIO— ENERGY

Aggressive Growth

Financial Programs, Inc.
P.O. Box 2040
Denver, CO 80201
(800) 525-8085/(303) 779-1233

	Years Ending 10/31					
	1983	1984 (9 mos.)	1985	1986	1987	1988
Dividends from Net Investment Income ($)	—	.13	.16	.14	.11	.17
Distributions from Net Realized Capital Gains ($)	—	—	—	.17	.53	.11
Net Asset Value End of Year ($)	—	7.49	8.29	8.33	8.22	9.29
Ratio of Expenses to Net Assets (%)	—	1.17	1.50	1.50	1.30	1.90
Ratio of Net Income to Average Net Assets (%)	—	2.58	2.34	2.85	1.32	.99
Portfolio Turnover Rate (%)	—	28	235	629	452	177
Total Assets End of Year (Millions $)	—	.3	.5	1.7	12.0	5.8

Annual Rate of Return (%) Years Ending 12/31	—	—	13.6	7.2	4.9	15.0

Five-Year Total Return(%)	NA	Degree of Diversification	E	Beta	.88	Bull (%)	102.5B	Bear (%)	(28.2)E

Objective:	Seeks capital appreciation through investment in energy-related stocks. These include companies that explore, develop, produce or distribute known sources of energy such as oil, gas, coal, uranium, geothermal or solar.
Portfolio:	(10/31/88) Common stocks 100%. Largest stock holdings: oil and gas—exploration/production 53%, oil and gas—production/pipeline 25%.
Portfolio Mgr:	Steven Markusen—1986
Distributions:	**Income:** Annually **Capital Gains:** Annually
12b-1:	No
Minimum:	**Initial:** $250 **Subsequent:** $50
Min IRA:	**Initial:** $250 **Subsequent:** $50
Services:	IRA, Keogh, Corp, SEP, 403(b), Withdraw, Deduct
Tel Exchange:	Yes **With MMF:** Yes
Registered:	All states
Ticker:	FSTEX

FINANCIAL STRATEGIC PORTFOLIO— EUROPEAN

International

Financial Programs, Inc.
P.O. Box 2040
Denver, CO 80201
(800) 525-8085/(303) 779-1233

	Years Ending 10/31					
	1983	1984	1985	1986 (5 mos.)	1987	1988
Dividends from Net Investment Income ($)	—	—	—	.01	.05	.08
Distributions from Net Realized Capital Gains ($)	—	—	—	—	.01	—
Net Asset Value End of Year ($)	—	—	—	8.31	7.98	9.04
Ratio of Expenses to Net Assets (%)	—	—	—	.63	1.50	1.88
Ratio of Net Income to Average Net Assets (%)	—	—	—	.11	1.44	1.08
Portfolio Turnover Rate (%)	—	—	—	4	131	75
Total Assets End of Year (Millions $)	—	—	—	.8	9.5	6.8

Annual Rate of Return (%) Years Ending 12/31	—	—	—	—	(4.6)	10.6

Five-Year Total Return(%)	NA	Degree of Diversification	NA	Beta	NA	Bull (%)	NA	Bear (%)	(20.3)ᴰ

Objective: Seeks capital appreciation through investment in foreign securities located on principal exchanges in Europe, including England, France, West Germany and Italy. May enter into forward foreign currency contracts to hedge against exchange rate fluctuations.

Portfolio: (10/31/88) Common stocks 80%, corporate short-term notes 20%. Largest stock holdings: chemicals and plastic products 7%, pharmaceuticals 7%.

Portfolio Mgr: Jerry Mill—1986

Distributions: **Income:** Annually **Capital Gains:** Annually

12b-1: No

Minimum: **Initial:** $250 **Subsequent:** $50

Min IRA: **Initial:** $250 **Subsequent:** $50

Services: IRA, Keogh, Corp, SEP, 403(b), Withdraw, Deduct

Tel Exchange: Yes **With MMF:** Yes

Registered: All states

Ticker: FEURX

FINANCIAL STRATEGIC PORTFOLIO— FINANCIAL SERVICES

Growth

Financial Programs, Inc.
P.O. Box 2040
Denver, CO 80201
(800) 525-8085/(303) 779-1233

| | \multicolumn{6}{c}{Years Ending 10/31} |
	1983	1984	1985	1986 (5 mos.)	1987	1988
Dividends from Net Investment Income ($)	—	—	—	.03	.06	.13
Distributions from Net Realized Capital Gains ($)	—	—	—	—	.12	—
Net Asset Value End of Year ($)	—	—	—	7.74	6.37	7.55
Ratio of Expenses to Net Assets (%)	—	—	—	.63	1.50	1.95
Ratio of Net Income to Average Net Assets (%)	—	—	—	.48	1.18	1.71
Portfolio Turnover Rate (%)	—	—	—	76	284	175
Total Assets End of Year (Millions $)	—	—	—	.5	1.2	2.3

Annual Rate of Return (%) Years Ending 12/31	—	—	—	—	(11.0)	17.1

Five-Year Total Return(%)	NA	Degree of Diversification	NA	Beta	NA	Bull (%)	NA	Bear (%)	(18.4)[c]

Objective:	Seeks capital appreciation through investment in companies in the financial services industry. These include banks, savings and loans, securities brokers, and insurance companies.
Portfolio:	(10/31/88) Common stocks 91%, corporate short-term notes 5%, preferred stocks 2%, fixed-income securities 2%. Largest stock holdings: banking 45%, insurance 23%.
Portfolio Mgr:	William Keithler—1987
Distributions:	**Income:** Annually **Capital Gains:** Annually
12b-1:	No
Minimum:	**Initial:** $250 **Subsequent:** $50
Min IRA:	**Initial:** $250 **Subsequent:** $50
Services:	IRA, Keogh, Corp, SEP, 403(b), Withdraw, Deduct
Tel Exchange:	Yes **With MMF:** Yes
Registered:	All states
Ticker:	FSFSX

FINANCIAL STRATEGIC PORTFOLIO— GOLD

Precious Metals

Financial Programs, Inc.
P.O. Box 2040
Denver, CO 80201
(800) 525-8085/(303) 779-1233

	Years Ending 10/31					
	1983	1984 (9 mos.)	1985	1986	1987	1988
Dividends from Net Investment Income ($)	—	.06	.11	.08	.06	.02
Distributions from Net Realized Capital Gains ($)	—	—	—	.05	.04	—
Net Asset Value End of Year ($)	—	4.91	3.99	5.08	5.60	5.03
Ratio of Expenses to Net Assets (%)	—	1.17	1.50	1.50	1.15	1.58
Ratio of Net Income to Average Net Assets (%)	—	1.63	2.72	2.35	.98	.62
Portfolio Turnover Rate (%)	—	110	46	232	124	47
Total Assets End of Year (Millions $)	—	1.2	2.4	5.2	37.8	32.5

Annual Rate of Return (%) Years Ending 12/31	—	—	(4.4)	38.7	16.0	(20.0)

Five-Year Total Return(%)	NA	Degree of Diversification	E	Beta	NA	Bull (%)	95.2C	Bear (%)	(31.3)E

Objective:	Seeks capital appreciation through investment in companies involved in the gold industry. These include companies engaged in mining, exploration, processing, dealing or investing in gold.
Portfolio:	(10/31/88) Common stocks 85%, corporate short-term notes 15%. Largest stock holdings: mining 85%.
Portfolio Mgr:	Steven Markusen—1986
Distributions:	**Income:** Annually **Capital Gains:** Annually
12b-1:	No
Minimum:	**Initial:** $250 **Subsequent:** $50
Min IRA:	**Initial:** $250 **Subsequent:** $50
Services:	IRA, Keogh, Corp, SEP, 403(b), Withdraw, Deduct
Tel Exchange:	Yes **With MMF:** Yes
Registered:	All states
Ticker:	FGLDX

FINANCIAL STRATEGIC PORTFOLIO— HEALTH SCIENCES

Aggressive Growth

Financial Programs, Inc.
P.O. Box 2040
Denver, CO 80201
(800) 525-8085/(303) 779-1233

	Years Ending 10/31					
	1983	1984 (9 mos.)	1985	1986	1987	1988
Dividends from Net Investment Income ($)	—	.03	.01	—	—	—
Distributions from Net Realized Capital Gains ($)	—	—	—	1.37	.90	.03
Net Asset Value End of Year ($)	—	8.13	9.75	12.78	11.69	14.29
Ratio of Expenses to Net Assets (%)	—	1.17	1.50	1.50	1.42	1.65
Ratio of Net Income to Average Net Assets (%)	—	.65	.19	(.28)	(.17)	(.48)
Portfolio Turnover Rate (%)	—	101	203	479	364	280
Total Assets End of Year (Millions $)	—	.3	1.4	4.1	10.4	10.0

Annual Rate of Return (%) Years Ending 12/31	—	—	31.5	29.5	7.1	16.0

Five-Year Total Return(%) NA	Degree of Diversification D	Beta 1.21	Bull (%) 166.4^A	Bear (%) (24.9)^E

Objective: Primary objective is capital appreciation through investment in companies engaged in the development, production or distribution of products or services related to the health sciences industry, including pharmaceutical companies, R&D companies and hospital chains.

Portfolio: (10/31/88) Common stocks 98%, corporate short-term notes 2%. Largest stock holdings: pharmaceuticals 33%, biotechnology 29%.

Portfolio Mgr: John Kaweske—1985

Distributions: **Income:** Annually   **Capital Gains:** Annually

12b-1: No

Minimum: **Initial:** $250   **Subsequent:** $50

Min IRA: **Initial:** $250   **Subsequent:** $50

Services: IRA, Keogh, Corp, SEP, 403(b), Withdraw, Deduct

Tel Exchange: Yes   **With MMF:** Yes

Registered: All states

Ticker: FHLSX

FINANCIAL STRATEGIC PORTFOLIO— LEISURE

Aggressive Growth

Financial Programs, Inc.
P.O. Box 2040
Denver, CO 80201
(800) 525-8085/(303) 779-1233

	Years Ending 10/31					
	1983	1984 (9 mos.)	1985	1986	1987	1988
Dividends from Net Investment Income ($)	–	.06	.04	–	–	–
Distributions from Net Realized Capital Gains ($)	–	–	–	2.76	1.43	–
Net Asset Value End of Year ($)	–	8.47	10.03	11.38	9.00	11.99
Ratio of Expenses to Net Assets (%)	–	1.17	1.50	1.50	1.50	1.89
Ratio of Net Income to Average Net Assets (%)	–	1.40	.57	(.11)	(.37)	.16
Portfolio Turnover Rate (%)	–	23	160	458	376	136
Total Assets End of Year (Millions $)	–	.3	1.2	2.8	2.7	5.6

Annual Rate of Return (%) Years Ending 12/31	–	–	32.3	18.8	0.7	28.5

Five-Year Total Return(%) NA	Degree of Diversification C	Beta 1.10	Bull (%) 127.7A	Bear (%) (25.0)E

Objective: Seeks capital appreciation through investment in companies engaged in the design, production or distribution of products or services related to the leisure-time activities of individuals, including companies in the motion picture, casino, and recreation industries.

Portfolio: (10/31/88) Common stocks 92%, corporate short-term notes 8%. Largest stock holdings: retail 32%, recreation products 20%.

Portfolio Mgr: Steven Markusen—1986

Distributions: Income: Annually　　　　**Capital Gains:** Annually

12b-1: No

Minimum: Initial: $250　　Subsequent: $50

Min IRA: Initial: $250　　Subsequent: $50

Services: IRA, Keogh, Corp, SEP, 403(b), Withdraw, Deduct

Tel Exchange: Yes　　**With MMF:** Yes

Registered: All states

Ticker: FLISX

FINANCIAL STRATEGIC PORTFOLIO— PACIFIC BASIN
International

Financial Programs, Inc.
P.O. Box 2040
Denver, CO 80201
(800) 525-8085/(303) 779-1233

	Years Ending 10/31					
	1983	1984 (9 mos.)	1985	1986	1987	1988
Dividends from Net Investment Income ($)	—	.09	.04	.04	.07	—
Distributions from Net Realized Capital Gains ($)	—	—	—	1.73	3.12	—
Net Asset Value End of Year ($)	—	7.05	8.39	11.52	9.68	12.24
Ratio of Expenses to Net Assets (%)	—	1.17	1.50	1.47	1.26	1.62
Ratio of Net Income to Average Net Assets (%)	—	2.13	.99	.39	.39	(.12)
Portfolio Turnover Rate (%)	—	99	161	199	155	69
Total Assets End of Year (Millions $)	—	.8	2.9	8.5	36.0	28.4
Annual Rate of Return (%) Years Ending 12/31	—	—	27.3	71.8	9.8	23.2

Five-Year Total Return(%)	NA	Degree of Diversification	E	Beta	.73	Bull (%)	252.3A	Bear (%)	(27.9)E

Objective: Seeks capital appreciation through investment in companies domiciled in Far Eastern or Western Pacific countries, including Japan, Australia, Hong Kong, Singapore and the Philippines. May use currency futures to hedge the portfolio.

Portfolio: (10/31/88) Common stocks 92%, corporate short-term notes 7%, fixed-income securities 1%. Largest stock holdings: diversified companies 15%, real estate related 14%.

Portfolio Mgr: William Keithler—1986

Distributions: **Income:** Annually   **Capital Gains:** Annually

12b-1: No

Minimum: **Initial:** $250   **Subsequent:** $50

Min IRA: **Initial:** $250   **Subsequent:** $50

Services: IRA, Keogh, Corp, SEP, 403(b), Withdraw, Deduct

Tel Exchange: Yes   **With MMF:** Yes

Registered: All states

Ticker: FPBSX

FINANCIAL STRATEGIC PORTFOLIO— TECHNOLOGY

Aggressive Growth

Financial Programs, Inc.
P.O. Box 2040
Denver, CO 80201
(800) 525-8085/(303) 779-1233

	Years Ending 10/31					
	1983	**1984** (9 mos.)	**1985**	**1986**	**1987**	**1988**
Dividends from Net Investment Income ($)	–	.02	–	–	–	–
Distributions from Net Realized Capital Gains ($)	–	–	–	1.07	.01	–
Net Asset Value End of Year ($)	–	7.11	7.59	9.29	8.49	10.11
Ratio of Expenses to Net Assets (%)	–	1.17	1.50	1.50	1.47	1.72
Ratio of Net Income to Average Net Assets (%)	–	.55	.03	(.71)	(.68)	(.90)
Portfolio Turnover Rate (%)	–	91	175	368	556	356
Total Assets End of Year (Millions $)	–	1.0	2.5	4.7	9.3	9.7

Annual Rate of Return (%) Years Ending 12/31	–	–	27.3	22.0	(5.3)	14.2

Five-Year Total Return(%)	NA	Degree of Diversification	E	Beta 1.28	Bull (%) 114.9[B]	Bear (%) (30.4)[E]

Objective: Primary objective is capital appreciation through investment in companies in the technology industries. These companies derive at least 25% of their sales from technology-related areas such as computers, communications, video, electronics and robotics.

Portfolio: (10/31/88) Common stocks 100%. Largest stock holdings: computer software 13%, recreation services 13%.

Portfolio Mgr: Daniel Leonard—1985

Distributions: **Income:** Annually   **Capital Gains:** Annually

12b-1: No

Minimum: **Initial:** $250   **Subsequent:** $50

Min IRA: **Initial:** $250   **Subsequent:** $50

Services: IRA, Keogh, Corp, SEP, 403(b), Withdraw, Deduct

Tel Exchange: Yes   **With MMF:** Yes

Registered: All states

Ticker: FTCHX

FINANCIAL STRATEGIC PORTFOLIO— UTILITIES

Growth & Income

Financial Programs, Inc.
P.O. Box 2040
Denver, CO 80201
(800) 525-8085/(303) 779-1233

			Years Ending 10/31			
	1983	1984	1985	1986 (5 mos.)	1987	1988
Dividends from Net Investment Income ($)	—	—	—	.06	.40	.40
Distributions from Net Realized Capital Gains ($)	—	—	—	.01	.01	—
Net Asset Value End of Year ($)	—	—	—	8.74	8.05	8.59
Ratio of Expenses to Net Assets (%)	—	—	—	.63	1.39	1.39
Ratio of Net Income to Average Net Assets (%)	—	—	—	1.69	5.07	4.93
Portfolio Turnover Rate (%)	—	—	—	69	84	164
Total Assets End of Year (Millions $)	—	—	—	7.5	16.1	18.4

Annual Rate of Return (%) Years Ending 12/31	—	—	—	—	(4.9)	14.2

Five-Year Total Return(%)	NA	Degree of Diversification	NA	Beta	NA	Bull (%)	NA	Bear (%)	(11.0)c

Objective:	Seeks capital appreciation through investment in public utility companies. These include companies that manufacture, produce, generate, transmit or sell gas or electric energy. Also invests in telephone and other communication utilities.
Portfolio:	(10/31/88) Common stocks 92%, corporate short-term notes 8%. Largest stock holdings: power 65%, telephone 14%.
Portfolio Mgr:	Jerry Mill—1988
Distributions:	**Income:** Jan, Apr, July, Oct **Capital Gains:** Annually
12b-1:	No
Minimum:	**Initial:** $250 **Subsequent:** $50
Min IRA:	**Initial:** $250 **Subsequent:** $50
Services:	IRA, Keogh, Corp, SEP, 403(b), Withdraw, Deduct
Tel Exchange:	Yes **With MMF:** Yes
Registered:	All states
Ticker:	FSTUX

FLEX BOND
Bond

R. Meeder & Associates, Inc.
6000 Memorial Drive
P.O. Box 7177
Dublin, OH 43017
(800) 325-3539/(614) 766-7000

	Years Ending 12/31					
	1983	1984	1985 (8 mos.)	1986	1987	1988
Dividends from Net Investment Income ($)	–	–	1.21	1.83	1.66	1.49
Distributions from Net Realized Capital Gains ($)	–	–	–	.17	.31	–
Net Asset Value End of Year ($)	–	–	20.84	21.31	19.22	18.25
Ratio of Expenses to Net Assets (%)	–	–	1.05	.78	.75	.83
Ratio of Net Income to Average Net Assets (%)	–	–	8.20	8.74	8.31	7.85
Portfolio Turnover Rate (%)	–	–	239	150	258	188
Total Assets End of Year (Millions $)	–	–	4.2	13.6	13.4	6.3
Annual Rate of Return (%) Years Ending 12/31	–	–	–	12.5	(0.7)	2.7

Five-Year Total Return(%)	NA	Degree of Diversification	NA	Beta	NA	Bull (%)	NA	Bear (%)	(0.3)B

Objective: Seeks to maximize current income through investment in fixed-income securities. Investments will be limited to debt obligations of the U.S. government and its agencies and high-grade corporate bonds rated A or better by Standard & Poor's. For defensive purposes the fund can invest in money market securities.

Portfolio: (12/31/88) U.S. Treasury obligations 75%, short-term securities 23%, other assets 2%.

Portfolio Mgr: Philip Voelker—1988

Distributions: **Income:** Monthly   **Capital Gains:** Annually

12b-1: Yes   **Amount:** 0.20%

Minimum: **Initial:** $2,500   **Subsequent:** $100

Min IRA: **Initial:** $500   **Subsequent:** $100

Services: IRA, Keogh, Corp, SEP, Withdraw

Tel Exchange: Yes   **With MMF:** Yes

Registered: AL, AZ, CA, CO, CT, DC, FL, GA, HI, IL, IN, MA, MD, MI, MN, MO, NC, NJ, NY, OH, PA, SC, TN, TX, VA, WA, WI

Ticker: FLXBX

FLEX GROWTH
Growth

R. Meeder & Associates, Inc.
6000 Memorial Drive
P.O. Box 7177
Dublin, OH 43017
(800) 325-3539/(614) 766-7000

	Years Ending 12/31					
	1983	1984	1985 (9 mos.)	1986	1987	1988
Dividends from Net Investment Income ($)	–	–	–	.28	.05	.78
Distributions from Net Realized Capital Gains ($)	–	–	–	1.15	–	.19
Net Asset Value End of Year ($)	–	–	10.69	10.52	11.27	9.67
Ratio of Expenses to Net Assets (%)	–	–	1.62	1.49	1.48	1.50
Ratio of Net Income to Average Net Assets (%)	–	–	4.34	2.32	1.79	2.06
Portfolio Turnover Rate (%)	–	–	218	152	326	313
Total Assets End of Year (Millions $)	–	–	6.9	10.2	12.8	4.5
Annual Rate of Return (%) Years Ending 12/31	–	–	–	10.6	7.6	(5.8)

Five-Year Total Return(%)	NA	Degree of Diversification	E	Beta	.70	Bull (%)	NA	Bear (%)	(13.4)c

Objective: Seeks capital appreciation through investment in common stocks of smaller companies that have above normal prospects for growth and earnings. Primarily buys the securities of companies listed on the New York Stock Exchange. For defensive purposes the fund can invest in debt obligations or money market securities.

Portfolio: (12/31/88) Short term securities 71%, common stocks 58%. Largest stock holdings: tobacco 3%, restaurants 3%.

Portfolio Mgr: Richard Peterson—1985; Philip Voelker—1989

Distributions: **Income:** Annually   **Capital Gains:** Annually

12b-1: Yes   **Amount:** 0.20%

Minimum: **Initial:** $2,500   **Subsequent:** $100

Min IRA: **Initial:** $500   **Subsequent:** $100

Services: IRA, Keogh, Corp, SEP, Withdraw

Tel Exchange: Yes   **With MMF:** Yes

Registered: AL, AZ, CA, CO, CT, DC, FL, GA, HI, IL, IN, MA, MD, MI, MN, MO, NC, NJ, NY, OH, PA, SC, TN, TX, VA, WA, WI

Ticker: FLCGX

FLEX INCOME AND GROWTH
Growth & Income

R. Meeder & Associates, Inc.
6000 Memorial Drive
P.O. Box 7177
Dublin, OH 43017
(800) 325-3539/(614) 766-7000

	Years Ending 12/31					
	1983	**1984**	**1985** (1mo.)	**1986**	**1987**	**1988**
Dividends from Net Investment Income ($)	—	—	—	1.04	1.51	1.17
Distributions from Net Realized Capital Gains ($)	—	—	—	.74	—	—
Net Asset Value End of Year ($)	—	—	20.44	22.00	18.85	18.83
Ratio of Expenses to Net Assets (%)	—	—	1.74	1.01	1.00	1.00
Ratio of Net Income to Average Net Assets (%)	—	—	8.52	5.95	6.06	6.31
Portfolio Turnover Rate (%)	—	—	0	219	259	140
Total Assets End of Year (Millions $)	—	—	2.2	7.9	3.6	2.1

Annual Rate of Return (%) Years Ending 12/31	—	—	—	16.7	(7.6)	6.2

Five-Year Total Return(%)	NA	Degree of Diversification	E	Beta	.42	Bull (%)	NA	Bear (%)	(10.6)c

Objective: Seeks current dividend income and long-term growth of capital through investment in high-yielding common and preferred stocks. May also invest in bonds and money market instruments for defensive purposes.

Portfolio: (12/31/88) Common stocks 69%, short-term securities 28%, other assets 3%. Largest stock holdings: Central electric utilities 14%, Eastern electric utilities 12%.

Portfolio Mgr: Richard Peterson—1985

Distributions: **Income:** Monthly　　　　**Capital Gains:** Annually

12b-1: Yes　　　　**Amount:** 0.20%

Minimum: **Initial:** $2,500　　**Subsequent:** $100

Min IRA: **Initial:** $500　　**Subsequent:** $100

Services: IRA, Keogh, Corp, SEP, Withdraw

Tel Exchange: Yes　　　　**With MMF:** Yes

Registered: AL, AZ, CA, CO, CT, DC, FL, GA, HI, IL, IN, MA, MD, MI, MN, MO, NC, NJ, NY, OH, PA, SC, TN, TX, VA, WA, WI

Ticker: FLIGX

†FLEX RETIREMENT GROWTH
Growth

R. Meeder & Associates, Inc.
6000 Memorial Drive
P.O. Box 7177
Dublin, OH 43017
(800) 325-3539/(614) 766-7000

	Years Ending 12/31					
	1983	1984	1985	1986	1987	1988
Dividends from Net Investment Income ($)	.05	.41	.52	.42	.07	.84
Distributions from Net Realized Capital Gains ($)	—	1.06	—	1.27	—	.28
Net Asset Value End of Year ($)	12.14	10.48	11.45	10.91	11.94	9.72
Ratio of Expenses to Net Assets (%)	1.51	1.48	1.50	1.44	1.34	1.37
Ratio of Net Income to Average Net Assets (%)	4.58	5.85	3.50	2.53	2.38	2.84
Portfolio Turnover Rate (%)	201	143	244	141	274	345
Total Assets End of Year (Millions $)	39.6	52.7	48.4	59.0	89.4	36.0

Annual Rate of Return (%) Years Ending 12/31	18.6	(1.2)	14.1	10.2	10.1	(9.7)

Five-Year Total Return(%)	23.6E	Degree of Diversification	D	Beta	.65	Bull (%)	59.3D	Bear (%)	(14.0)C

Objective: Seeks capital appreciation through investment in common stocks of companies with market values above $100 million and records of financial strength and strong earnings. Intended for retirement accounts, so will not avoid ordinary income or short-term capital gains. May convert entire portfolio to cash during down markets.

Portfolio: (12/31/88) Repurchase agreements 82%, common stocks 51%, commercial paper 5%, U.S. Treasury bills 4%. Largest stock holdings: machine tool 3%, restaurants 3%.

Portfolio Mgr: Philip Voelker—1982

Distributions: **Income:** Annually   **Capital Gains:** Annually

12b-1: Yes   **Amount:** 0.20%

Minimum: **Initial:** $2,500   **Subsequent:** $100

Min IRA: **Initial:** $500   **Subsequent:** $100

Services: IRA, Keogh, Corp, SEP, Withdraw

Tel Exchange: Yes   **With MMF:** Yes

Registered: AL, AZ, CA, CO, CT, DC, FL, GA, HI, IL, IN, MA, MD, MI, MN, MO, NC, NJ, NY, OH, PA, SC, TN, TX, VA, WA, WI

Ticker: FLFDX

† *The fund merged into Flex Growth on March 11, 1989.*

†44 WALL STREET
Aggressive Growth

MDB Asset Management Corp.
26 Broadway
New York, NY 10004
(800) 543-2620/(212) 248-8080

	Years Ending 6/30					
	1983	1984	1985	1986	1987	1988
Dividends from Net Investment Income ($)	—	—	—	—	—	—
Distributions from Net Realized Capital Gains ($)	1.09	4.02	.58	—	—	—
Net Asset Value End of Year ($)	22.11	7.56	3.93	4.21	3.81	2.12
Ratio of Expenses to Net Assets (%)	2.77	4.06	5.09	7.31	8.50	13.40
Ratio of Net Income to Average Net Assets (%)	(1.54)	(3.18)	(4.07)	(5.79)	(6.96)	(10.13)
Portfolio Turnover Rate (%)	113	95	163	104	57	118
Total Assets End of Year (Millions $)	248.5	82.0	55.4	34.3	19.2	6.7
Annual Rate of Return (%) Years Ending 12/31	9.7	(58.6)	(20.1)	(16.3)	(34.6)	19.3

Five-Year Total Return(%) (78.4)E	Degree of Diversification E	Beta 1.48	Bull (%) (37.1)E	Bear (%) (42.1)E

Objective: Seeks to achieve growth of capital through investment in a limited number of securities selected for relatively long-term performance. The fund intends to be fully invested in common stocks. For defensive purposes, the fund may invest in U.S. government securities. May invest up to 10% of its net assets in non-liquid assets.

Portfolio: (6/30/88) Common stocks 48%, short-term securities 39%, bonds 13%. Largest stock holdings: services 9%, airlines 8%.

Portfolio Mgr: Mark D. Beckerman—1988

Distributions: **Income:** Annually　　**Capital Gains:** Annually

12b-1: No

Minimum: **Initial:** $1,000　　**Subsequent:** $100

Min IRA: **Initial:** $1,000　　**Subsequent:** $100

Services: IRA, SEP, 403(b), Withdraw, Deduct

Tel Exchange: Yes　　**With MMF:** Yes

Registered: AZ, CO, CT, DC, DE, FL, GA, HI, IL, MA, MD, MI, MN, MO,NE, NJ, NM, NY, OK, OR, PA, VA, WA

Ticker: FWALX

† *The fund charges a 0.25% redemption fee.*

†FOUNDERS BLUE CHIP
Growth & Income

Founders Mutual Depositor Corp.
3033 E. First Ave., #810
Denver, CO 80206
(800) 525-2440/(303) 394-4404

	Years Ending 9/30					12/31	
	1983	1984	1985	1986	1987	1987* (3 mos.)	1988
Dividends from Net Investment Income ($)	.40	.31	.38	.32	.26	.05	.19
Distributions from Net Realized Capital Gains ($)	.71	—	1.17	1.85	3.22	1.71	.25
Net Asset Value End of Year ($)	10.68	10.48	10.01	10.68	9.98	6.14	6.31
Ratio of Expenses to Net Assets (%)	.42	.74	.70	.74	.87	.98	1.00
Ratio of Net Income to Average Net Assets (%)	3.96	3.90	3.69	2.64	2.11	2.41	2.81
Portfolio Turnover Rate (%)	—	16	18	42	56	31	58
Total Assets: End of Year (Millions $)	143.6	134.9	138.8	175.0	239.7	174.6	173.2

Annual Rate of Return (%) Years Ending 12/31	25.0	1.6	31.3	16.8	2.4	*	10.1

Five-Year Total Return(%) 75.6[B]	Degree of Diversification	A	Beta	.94	Bull (%) 128.5[A]	Bear (%) (23.1)[D]

Fiscal year-end changed from 9/30 to 12/31. All annual return figures are for full years ending 12/31.

Objective:	Seeks long-term growth of income and capital through investment in common stocks of companies that have at least $500 million in revenues, have proven earnings records and are in sound financial condition. May invest in foreign securities.
Portfolio:	(12/31/88) Common stocks 89%, corporate short-term notes 9%, cash 2%. Largest stock holdings: publishing and broadcasting 11%, consumer products 8%.
Portfolio Mgr:	Jay Tracey—1988
Distributions:	**Income:** Mar, June, Sept, Dec **Capital Gains:** Dec
12b-1:	Yes **Amount:** 0.25%
Minimum:	**Initial:** $1,000 **Subsequent:** $100
Min IRA:	**Initial:** $500 **Subsequent:** $100
Services:	IRA, Keogh, Corp, SEP, 403(b), Withdraw, Deduct
Tel Exchange:	Yes **With MMF:** Yes
Registered:	All states except NH
Ticker:	FRMUX

† *Fund was a unit investment trust prior to December 1, 1983.*

FOUNDERS
EQUITY INCOME
Balanced

Founders Mutual Depositor Corp.
3033 E. First Ave., #810
Denver, CO 80206
(800) 525-2440/(303) 394-4404

	Years Ending 9/30					12/31	
	1983	1984	1985	1986	1987	1987* (3 mos.)	1988
Dividends from Net Investment Income ($)	.29	.50	.46	.37	.42	.08	.38
Distributions from Net Realized Capital Gains ($)	—	.25	.32	.15	.44	.87	—
Net Asset Value End of Year ($)	7.48	7.19	7.26	7.89	8.72	6.55	6.89
Ratio of Expenses to Net Assets (%)	1.50	1.50	1.50	1.59	1.66	1.84	1.64
Ratio of Net Income to Average Net Assets (%)	6.14	6.67	5.88	4.44	4.03	4.16	5.39
Portfolio Turnover Rate (%)	159	145	126	178	133	141	182
Total Assets: End of Year (Millions $)	7.3	7.3	10.0	12.1	16.9	13.2	12.6

Annual Rate of Return (%) Years Ending 12/31	15.4	11.5	12.7	14.5	1.9	*	11.1

Five-Year Total Return(%)	62.7c	Degree of Diversification	D	Beta	.55	Bull (%)	69.3D	Bear (%)	(13.9)c

Fiscal year-end changed from 9/30 to 12/31. All annual return figures are for full years ending 12/31.

Objective:	Intends to provide as high income as is consistent with investment quality of companies that are well established and pay dividends. Debt investments will yield interest income. May invest in foreign securities.
Portfolio:	(12/31/88) Corporate short-term notes 47%, common stocks 44%, U.S. Treasury obligations 17%. Largest stock holdings: oil and gas 11%, telecommunications 9%.
Portfolio Mgr:	Michael Haines—1988
Distributions:	**Income:** Mar, June, Sept, Dec **Capital Gains:** Dec
12b-1:	Yes **Amount:** 0.25%
Minimum:	**Initial:** $1,000 **Subsequent:** $100
Min IRA:	**Initial:** $500 **Subsequent:** $100
Services:	IRA, Keogh, Corp, SEP, 403(b), Withdraw, Deduct
Tel Exchange:	Yes **With MMF:** Yes
Registered:	All states except NH
Ticker:	FRINX

FOUNDERS FRONTIER
Aggressive Growth

Founders Mutual Depositor Corp.
3033 East First Ave., #810
Denver, CO 80206
(800) 525-2440/(303) 394-4404

	Years Ending 12/31					
	1983	**1984**	**1985**	**1986**	**1987** (11 mos.)	**1988**
Dividends from Net Investment Income ($)	–	–	–	–	–	–
Distributions from Net Realized Capital Gains ($)	–	–	–	–	.58	.78
Net Asset Value End of Year ($)	–	–	–	–	11.03	13.45
Ratio of Expenses to Net Assets (%)	–	–	–	–	2.25	1.89
Ratio of Net Income to Average Net Assets (%)	–	–	–	–	(.74)	(.43)
Portfolio Turnover Rate (%)	–	–	–	–	588	312
Total Assets End of Year (Millions $)	–	–	–	–	3.3	8.8

Annual Rate of Return (%) Years Ending 12/31	–	–	–	–	–	29.2

Five-Year Total Return(%)	NA	Degree of Diversification	NA	Beta	NA	Bull (%)	NA	Bear (%)	(17.8)c

Objective: Seeks capital appreciation through investment in common stocks of small- and medium-sized companies, both foreign and domestic. Can invest up to 100% of the fund's assets in either foreign or domestic stocks, but it cannot have more than 25% invested in one foreign country. May also invest in put and call options.

Portfolio: (12/31/88) Common stocks 95%, cash 4%, warrants 1%. Largest stock holdings: retail 19%, telecommunications 11%.

Portfolio Mgr: Stuart Roberts—1987

Distributions: Income: Dec   **Capital Gains:** Dec

12b-1: Yes   **Amount:** 0.25%

Minimum: Initial: $1,000   Subsequent: $100

Min IRA: Initial: $500   Subsequent: $100

Services: IRA, Keogh, Corp, SEP, 403(b), Withdraw, Deduct

Tel Exchange: Yes   **With MMF:** Yes

Registered: All states except NH

Ticker: FOUNX

FOUNDERS GROWTH
Growth

Founders Mutual Depositor Corp.
3033 E. First Ave., #810
Denver, CO 80206
(800) 525-2440/(303) 394-4404

	Years Ending 10/31					12/31	
	1983	1984	1985	1986	1987	1987* (2 mos.)	1988
Dividends from Net Investment Income ($)	.29	.16	.18	.17	.11	.13	.15
Distributions from Net Realized Capital Gains ($)	.34	2.51	—	—	1.34	1.61	—
Net Asset Value End of Year ($)	10.08	6.59	7.47	9.87	8.91	7.41	7.61
Ratio of Expenses to Net Assets (%)	1.24	1.22	1.17	1.27	1.25	1.54	1.38
Ratio of Net Income to Average Net Assets (%)	1.64	2.52	2.49	1.19	.99	2.43	1.74
Portfolio Turnover Rate (%)	150	203	186	142	147	20	179
Total Assets: End of Year (Millions $)	46.6	41.3	42.7	61.6	58.3	69.0	53.0

Annual Rate of Return (%) Years Ending 12/31	18.9	(11.1)	28.8	19.3	10.2	*	4.8

Five-Year Total Return(%)	57.9ᴰ	Degree of Diversification	B	Beta	.99	Bull (%)	131.7ᴬ	Bear (%)	(21.4)ᴰ

Fiscal year-end changed from 10/31 to 12/31. All annual return figures are for full years ending 12/31.

Objective:	Seeks capital appreciation by investing in common stocks of established companies. Current dividends are considered but are not a major factor in stock selection. Engages in short-term trading so that portfolio turnover usually exceeds 100% and brokerage commission expenses are correspondingly high.
Portfolio:	(12/31/88) Common stocks 89%, corporate short-term notes 5%, cash 4%, preferred stocks 2%. Largest stock holdings: retail 11%, building materials 9%.
Portfolio Mgr:	Stuart Roberts—1985
Distributions:	**Income:** Dec **Capital Gains:** Dec
12b-1:	Yes **Amount:** 0.25%
Minimum:	**Initial:** $1,000 **Subsequent:** $100
Min IRA:	**Initial:** $500 **Subsequent:** $100
Services:	IRA, Keogh, Corp, SEP, 403(b), Withdraw, Deduct
Tel Exchange:	Yes **With MMF:** Yes
Registered:	All states except NH
Ticker:	FRGRX

FOUNDERS SPECIAL
Aggressive Growth

Founders Mutual Depositor Corp.
3033 E. First Ave., #810
Denver, CO 80206
(800) 525-2440/(303) 394-4404

	Years Ending 12/31					
	1983*	1984*	1985*	1986*	1987	1988
Dividends from Net Investment Income ($)	.05	.11	.05	.06	.03	.03
Distributions from Net Realized Capital Gains ($)	.61	—	—	.69	.72	.31
Net Asset Value End of Year ($)	5.46	4.68	5.34	5.60	5.14	5.47
Ratio of Expenses to Net Assets (%)	1.20	1.11	1.02	1.06	1.14	1.12
Ratio of Net Income to Average Net Assets (%)	.90	2.20	.85	.73	.45	.59
Portfolio Turnover Rate (%)	141	191	192	138	210	160
Total Assets End of Year (Millions $)	94.5	81.3	95.4	70.2	66.8	63.0
Annual Rate of Return (%) Years Ending 12/31	23.4	(12.2)	15.2	18.9	5.3	13.2

Five-Year Total Return(%)	43.3ᴱ	Degree of Diversification	C	Beta	1.08	Bull (%)	102.4ᶜ	Bear (%)	(24.2)ᴰ

*Prices reflect an adjustment for a 5-for-1 stock split on 8/31/87.

Objective:	Seeks above-average capital growth by investing in common stocks of smaller companies that are rapidly growing. Dividends play a minor role in the fund's strategy.
Portfolio:	(12/31/88) Common stocks 94%, corporate short-term notes 6%. Largest stock holdings: telecommunications 21%, retail 12%.
Portfolio Mgr:	Stuart Roberts—1985
Distributions:	**Income:** Dec **Capital Gains:** Dec
12b-1:	No
Minimum:	**Initial:** $1,000 **Subsequent:** $100
Min IRA:	**Initial:** $500 **Subsequent:** $100
Services:	IRA, Keogh, Corp, SEP, 403(b), Withdraw, Deduct
Tel Exchange:	Yes **With MMF:** Yes
Registered:	All states except NH
Ticker:	FRSPX

GATEWAY GROWTH PLUS
Growth

Gateway Investment Advisors
P.O. Box 458167
Cincinnati, OH 45245
(800) 354-6339/(513) 248-2700

	Years Ending 12/31					
	1983	1984	1985	1986 (8 mos.)	1987	1988
Dividends from Net Investment Income ($)	–	–	–	–	.11	.09
Distributions from Net Realized Capital Gains ($)	–	–	–	–	.01	–
Net Asset Value End of Year ($)	–	–	–	10.00	9.96	9.67
Ratio of Expenses to Net Assets (%)	–	–	–	1.47	1.49	1.49
Ratio of Net Income to Average Net Assets (%)	–	–	–	1.33	.27	.78
Portfolio Turnover Rate (%)	–	–	–	96	157	132
Total Assets End of Year (Millions $)	–	–	–	3.2	4.4	3.6

Annual Rate of Return (%) Years Ending 12/31	–	–	–	–	0.7	(2.0)

Five-Year Total Return(%)	NA	Degree of Diversification	NA	Beta	NA	Bull (%)	NA	Bear (%)	(22.8)ᴰ

Objective: Seeks long-term growth of capital with secondary objective of conserving capital. Normally will invest in New York or American Stock Exchange-listed issues that have market capitalizations above $50 million and revenues exceeding $100 million. Can also invest in index options.

Portfolio: (12/31/88) Common stocks 92%, repurchase agreements 22%. Largest stock holdings: capital goods 15%, consumer cyclicals 14%.

Portfolio Mgr: Peter Williams—1988

Distributions: Income: Dec   **Capital Gains:** Dec

12b-1: No

Minimum: Initial: $500   Subsequent: $100

Min IRA: Initial: $500   Subsequent: $100

Services: IRA, SEP, Withdraw

Tel Exchange: Yes   **With MMF:** No

Registered: AL, AZ, CA, CO, CT, DC, DE, FL, GA, HI, IA, IL, IN, KS, KY, MA, MD, ME, MI, MN, MO, NC, NJ, NV, NY, OH, OR, PA, SC, TN, TX, UT, VA, WI, WV, WY

Ticker: GATGX

GATEWAY OPTION INDEX
Growth & Income

Gateway Investment Advisors
P.O. Box 458167
Cincinnati, OH 45245
(800) 354-6339/(513) 248-2700

	Years Ending 12/31					
	1983	**1984**	**1985***	**1986**	**1987**	**1988**
Dividends from Net Investment Income ($)	.55	.57	.46	.34	.33	.21
Distributions from Net Realized Capital Gains ($)	1.31	.65	1.22	1.46	1.92	—
Net Asset Value End of Year ($)	14.91	14.23	14.69	14.63	11.60	13.67
Ratio of Expenses to Net Assets (%)	1.41	1.45	1.50	1.49	1.48	2.08
Ratio of Net Income to Average Net Assets (%)	3.50	3.84	2.81	2.23	1.83	1.75
Portfolio Turnover Rate (%)	170	103	96	85	175	10
Total Assets End of Year (Millions $)	26.9	21.6	28.4	45.3	27.4	27.3

Annual Rate of Return (%) Years Ending 12/31	14.9	4.0	16.0	12.6	(5.7)	19.8

Five-Year Total Return(%)	53.3ᴰ	Degree of Diversification	D	Beta	.53	Bull (%)	61.1ᴰ	Bear (%)	(16.5)ᶜ

*Changed objective March 1985.

Objective:	Seeks a high current return at a reduced level of risk, primarily by investing in the common stocks listed in the S&P 100 index and selling call options on that index. May engage in repurchase agreements as well.
Portfolio:	(12/31/88) Common stocks 102%, short call options 3%. Largest stock holdings: consumer growth 16%, energy 15%.
Portfolio Mgr:	Peter Thayer—1977
Distributions:	**Income:** Mar, June, Sept, Dec **Capital Gains:** Dec
12b-1:	No
Minimum:	**Initial:** $500 **Subsequent:** $100
Min IRA:	**Initial:** $500 **Subsequent:** $100
Services:	IRA, SEP, Withdraw
Tel Exchange:	Yes **With MMF:** No
Registered:	AL, AZ, CA, CO, CT, DC, DE, FL, GA, HI, IA, IL, IN, KS, KY, MA, MD, ME, MI, MN, MO, NC, NJ, NM, NV, NY, OH, OK, OR, PA, SC, TN, TX, UT, VA, WI, WV, WY
Ticker:	GATEX

GENERAL SECURITIES
Growth & Income

Craig-Hallum, Inc.
701 Fourth Ave. South
Minneapolis, MN 55415
(612) 332-1212

	Years Ending 11/30					
	1983	1984	1985	1986	1987	1988
Dividends from Net Investment Income ($)	.58	.51	.30	.38	.70	.22
Distributions from Net Realized Capital Gains ($)	1.50	.87	1.25	2.13	.31	.82
Net Asset Value End of Year ($)	12.09	10.17	11.84	11.71	10.05	10.91
Ratio of Expenses to Net Assets (%)	1.50	1.50	1.50	1.45	1.49	1.46
Ratio of Net Income to Average Net Assets (%)	4.64	3.91	2.61	4.89	3.27	2.23
Portfolio Turnover Rate (%)	13	70	76	68	77	78
Total Assets End of Year (Millions $)	11.6	10.9	13.6	14.2	14.4	15.6
Annual Rate of Return (%) Years Ending 12/31	8.9	(0.9)	38.6	9.0	2.0	14.0

Five-Year Total Return(%)	74.2[B]	Degree of Diversification	E	Beta	.47	Bull (%)	87.9[C]	Bear (%)	(9.0)[C]

Objective: Seeks long-term capital appreciation and security of principal by investing primarily in common stocks of large, seasoned companies. May write covered call options. May adopt defensive posture in debt securities.

Portfolio: (11/30/88) Common stocks 78%, U.S. Treasury notes 24%, cash 2%. Largest stock holdings: chemicals 19%, retail and wholesale 10%.

Portfolio Mgr: Jack Robinson—1951

Distributions: Income: Feb, May, Aug, Nov   **Capital Gains:** Dec

12b-1: No

Minimum: Initial: $100   Subsequent: $10

Min IRA: Initial: $100   Subsequent: $10

Services: IRA, Keogh, SEP, Withdraw

Tel Exchange: No

Registered: All states except AL, AR, FL, HI, KY, LA, MA, MO, MS, MT, ND, SC, TN, TX, WI

Ticker: GSECX

GINTEL CAPITAL APPRECIATION

Aggressive Growth

Gintel Equity Management, Inc.
Greenwich Office Park OP-6
Greenwich, CT 06830
(800) 243-5808/(203) 622-6400

	1983	1984	1985	1986 (12 mos.)	1987	1988
Dividends from Net Investment Income ($)	–	–	–	–	.23	–
Distributions from Net Realized Capital Gains ($)	–	–	–	.91	.01	–
Net Asset Value End of Year ($)	–	–	–	11.07	10.00	13.56
Ratio of Expenses to Net Assets (%)	–	–	–	1.9	1.8	2.2
Ratio of Net Income to Average Net Assets (%)	–	–	–	1.4	1.0	1.0
Portfolio Turnover Rate (%)	–	–	–	119	125	135
Total Assets End of Year (Millions $)	–	–	–	21.8	21.6	27.6
Annual Rate of Return (%) Years Ending 12/31	–	–	–	19.1	(7.1)	35.6

Five-Year Total Return(%)	NA	Degree of Diversification	D	Beta	.86	Bull (%)	NA	Bear (%)	(21.4)D

Objective: Seeks capital appreciation through investment in common stocks of major companies listed on the NYSE or Amex and up to 25% of total assets in the OTC. May concentrate investments in 12 issues or four industry groups; and may invest in foreign securities, employ leverage, lend its securities and make short sales of securities it holds.

Portfolio: (12/31/88) Common stocks 104%. Largest stock holdings: copper producer 33%, diversified chemical producer 12%.

Portfolio Mgr: Robert Gintel, Ernest Mysogland—1986

Distributions: Income: Annually   **Capital Gains:** Annually

12b-1: Yes   **Amount:** 0.50%

Minimum: Initial: $5,000   **Subsequent:** None

Min IRA: Initial: $2,000   **Subsequent:** None

Services: IRA, Keogh, Corp, SEP, 403(b), Withdraw

Tel Exchange: Yes   **With MMF:** Yes

Registered: Call for availability

Ticker: GINCX

GINTEL ERISA
Growth & Income

Gintel Equity Management, Inc.
Greenwich Office Park OP-6
Greenwich, CT 06830
(800) 243-5808/(203) 622-6400

	Years Ending 12/31					
	1983	1984	1985	1986	1987	1988
Dividends from Net Investment Income ($)	1.43	.85	1.10	1.08	1.99	—
Distributions from Net Realized Capital Gains ($)	1.19	2.75	1.88	1.47	13.41	—
Net Asset Value End of Year ($)	37.57	34.70	39.48	45.29	29.79	36.34
Ratio of Expenses to Net Assets (%)	1.40	1.40	1.30	1.30	1.20	1.30
Ratio of Net Income to Average Net Assets (%)	3.10	3.70	3.00	1.80	2.90	2.50
Portfolio Turnover Rate (%)	59	109	100	69	109	100
Total Assets End of Year (Millions $)	54.3	71.9	85.4	88.6	75.0	81.3

Annual Rate of Return (%) Years Ending 12/31	27.5	2.6	23.9	21.8	(1.1)	22.0

Five-Year Total Return(%)	86.7[B]	Degree of Diversification	D	Beta	.82	Bull (%)	97.7[C]	Bear (%)	(18.4)[C]

Objective:	An investment vehicle exclusively for tax-exempt investors or retirement plans. The fund seeks long-term capital growth, investment income, and short-term capital gains by investing in common stocks of major corporations listed on the NYSE or Amex, or traded in the OTC, and having at least three years of continuous operation.
Portfolio:	(12/31/88) Common stocks 98%, cash equivalents 2%, other assets 1%. Largest stock holdings: copper producer 17%, supermarkets 14%.
Portfolio Mgr:	Robert Gintel, Ernest Mysogland—1982
Distributions:	**Income:** Dec **Capital Gains:** Dec
12b-1:	Yes **Amount:** 0.20% fund, 0.20% Advisor
Minimum:	**Initial:** $10,000 **Subsequent:** None
Min IRA:	**Initial:** $2,000 **Subsequent:** None
Services:	IRA, Keogh, Corp, SEP, 403(b), Withdraw
Tel Exchange:	No
Registered:	Call for availability
Ticker:	GINTX

GIT EQUITY— SPECIAL GROWTH

Aggressive Growth

Bankers Finance Investment
Management Corp.
1655 N. Fort Myer Drive
Arlington, VA 22209
(800) 336-3063/(703) 528-6500

	Years Ending 3/31					
	1983	1984 (10 mos.)	1985	1986	1987	1988
Dividends from Net Investment Income ($)	—	.20	.09	.12	.14	.13
Distributions from Net Realized Capital Gains ($)	—	—	—	.25	.13	2.62
Net Asset Value End of Year ($)	—	9.21	11.47	16.44	18.02	15.12
Ratio of Expenses to Net Assets (%)	—	.36	1.09	1.35	1.50	1.50
Ratio of Net Income to Average Net Assets (%)	—	3.85	1.29	1.38	0.92	0.73
Portfolio Turnover Rate (%)	—	18	30	35	8	29
Total Assets End of Year (Millions $)	—	.64	2.5	10.7	19.6	15.5

Annual Rate of Return (%) Years Ending 12/31	—	(1.2)	47.2	15.1	(1.4)	24.7

Five-Year Total Return(%) 105.8ᴬ	Degree of Diversification D	Beta .88	Bull (%) 119.6ᴮ	Bear (%) (20.0)ᴰ

Objective: Seeks maximum capital appreciation through investment in small growth companies. Current income is not a consideration. Designed for investors who can assume an above-average level of risk from investment in common stock.

Portfolio: (9/30/88) Common stocks 76%, repurchase agreements 20%, convertible bonds 4%. Largest stock holdings: building 9%, food distribution 6%.

Portfolio Mgr: Richard Carney—1983

Distributions: **Income:** Semiannually   **Capital Gains:** Annually

12b-1: No

Minimum: **Initial:** $1,000   **Subsequent:** None

Min IRA: **Initial:** $500   **Subsequent:** None

Services: IRA, Keogh, Withdraw, Deduct

Tel Exchange: Yes   **With MMF:** Yes

Registered: All states except AK, MT, ND, NH, OK, SD, UT

Ticker: GTSGX

GIT INCOME—
A-RATED
Bond

Bankers Finance Investment
Management Corp.
1655 N. Fort Myer Dr.
Arlington, VA 22209
(800) 336-3063/(703) 528-6500

		Years Ending 3/31				
	1983	1984 (11 mos.)	1985	1986	1987	1988
Dividends from Net Investment Income ($)	—	.84	1.11	1.04	.91	.86
Distributions from Net Realized Capital Gains ($)	—	—	—	—	—	.47
Net Asset Value End of Year ($)	—	9.21	9.55	11.49	11.39	10.18
Ratio of Expenses to Net Assets (%)	—	—	.89	1.12	1.41	1.47
Ratio of Net Income to Average Net Assets (%)	—	12.90	11.78	9.82	7.99	8.18
Portfolio Turnover Rate (%)	—	—	63	26	31	36
Total Assets End of Year (Millions $)	—	2.9	4.4	7.8	9.3	6.3

Annual Rate of Return (%) Years Ending 12/31	—	14.7	24.9	13.6	(1.1)	7.2

Five-Year Total Return(%)	72.6[B]	Degree of Diversification	NA	Beta	NA	Bull (%)	55.9[D]	Bear (%)	2.7[A]

Objective: Seeks to obtain high level of current income through investment in bonds rated A or above by Standard & Poor's. Cannot invest more than 25% of fund assets in the securities of issuers in a single industry.

Portfolio: (9/30/88) U.S. government and agency obligations 46%, repurchase agreements 36%, corporate bonds 18%. Largest bond holdings: electric utilities 11%, bank and finance 3%.

Portfolio Mgr: Richard Gunn—1985

Distributions: **Income:** Monthly　　**Capital Gains:** Annually

12b-1: No

Minimum: **Initial:** $1,000　　**Subsequent:** None

Min IRA: **Initial:** $500　　**Subsequent:** None

Services: IRA, Keogh, Withdraw, Deduct

Tel Exchange: Yes　　**With MMF:** Yes

Registered: All states except ND, NE, SC, UT

Ticker: GTTAX

GIT INCOME—MAXIMUM

Bond

Bankers Finance Investment
Mgmt. Corp.
1655 N. Fort Myer Dr.
Arlington, VA 22209
(800) 336-3063/(703) 528-6500

	Years Ending 3/31					
	1983	1984	1985	1986	1987	1988
Dividends from Net Investment Income ($)	—	.91	1.23	1.16	1.06	.93
Distributions from Net Realized Capital Gains ($)	—	—	—	—	—	—
Net Asset Value End of Year ($)	—	9.09	8.99	9.97	9.66	8.43
Ratio of Expenses to Net Assets (%)	—	—	.93	1.10	1.39	1.45
Ratio of Net Income to Average Net Assets (%)	—	13.47	13.75	12.23	10.87	10.48
Portfolio Turnover Rate (%)	—	16	66	47	127	78
Total Assets End of Year (Millions $)	—	3.3	7.3	12.9	16.7	11.1

Annual Rate of Return (%) Years Ending 12/31	—	9.6	22.0	10.6	(2.8)	10.2

Five-Year Total Return(%)	58.5ᴰ	Degree of Diversification	NA	Beta	NA	Bull (%)	52.9ᴰ	Bear (%)	(5.9)ᶜ

Objective: Seeks high current income through investment in long-term lower-medium-grade (BB) and low-grade (Caa/CCC) debt securities of the U.S. government, corporations and foreign governments. May enter into repurchase agreements and may temporarily hold short-term debt securities and cash for defensive purposes.

Portfolio: (9/30/88) Corporate bonds 75%, U.S. government and agency obligations 14%, repurchase agreements 12%. Largest bond holdings: manufacturing 14%, communications 9%.

Portfolio Mgr: Richard Gunn—1985

Distributions: **Income:** Monthly   **Capital Gains:** Annually

12b-1: No

Minimum: **Initial:** $1,000   **Subsequent:** None

Min IRA: **Initial:** $500   **Subsequent:** None

Services: IRA, Keogh, Withdraw, Deduct

Tel Exchange: Yes   **With MMF:** Yes

Registered: All states except ND, NE, SC, UT

Ticker: GITMX

GRADISON ESTABLISHED GROWTH
Growth

Gradison & Co.
The 580 Building
6th & Walnut Streets
Cincinnati, OH 45202-3198
(800) 543-1818/(513) 579-5700

		Years Ending 4/30				
	1983	1984 (8 mos.)	1985	1986	1987	1988
Dividends from Net Investment Income ($)	—	.10	.26	.30	.34	.50
Distributions from Net Realized Capital Gains ($)	—	—	—	—	1.18	1.44
Net Asset Value End of Year ($)	—	10.17	11.66	15.04	17.69	16.27
Ratio of Expenses to Net Assets (%)	—	2.00	2.00	1.72	1.61	1.57
Ratio of Net Income to Average Net Assets (%)	—	3.71	2.68	2.63	2.50	2.67
Portfolio Turnover Rate (%)	—	20	71	80	76	26
Total Assets End of Year (Millions $)	—	6.7	12.6	30.7	53.8	69.2
Annual Rate of Return (%) Years Ending 12/31	—	4.5	28.8	22.0	12.4	15.1

Five-Year Total Return(%)	112.6^A	Degree of Diversification	C	Beta	.82	Bull (%)	134.9^A	Bear (%)	(13.1)^C

Objective:	Seeks long-term growth of capital by investing in common stocks of established companies in the S&P 500 stock index. Employs computer model to screen companies on basis of earnings, P/E ratios, rate of return, etc.
Portfolio:	(10/31/88) Common stocks 75%, repurchase agreements 25%. Largest stock holdings: metal refining 12%, forest/paper products 11%.
Portfolio Mgr:	William Leugers—1983
Distributions:	Inc: Feb, May, Aug, Nov **Cap Gains:** Semiannually
12b-1:	Yes **Amount:** 0.25%
Minimum:	Initial: $1,000 Subsequent: $50
Min IRA:	Initial: $1,000 Subsequent: $50
Services:	IRA, Withdraw
Tel Exchange:	Yes **With MMF:** Yes
Registered:	AZ, CA, CO, CT, FL, GA, IL, IN, KY, LA, MA, MD, MI, MN, MO, NC, NJ, NY, OH, PA, SC, TN, TX, UT, VA, WA
Ticker:	GETGX

GRADISON OPPORTUNITY GROWTH
Aggressive Growth

Gradison & Co.
The 580 Building
6th & Walnut Streets
Cincinnati, OH 45202-3198
(800) 543-1818/(513) 579-5700

	1983	1984 (8 mos.)	1985	1986	1987	1988
Years Ending 4/30						
Dividends from Net Investment Income ($)	—	.01	Nil	.03	.04	.12
Distributions from Net Realized Capital Gains ($)	—	—	—	—	.80	.13
Net Asset Value End of Year ($)	—	8.04	9.30	13.16	13.23	12.97
Ratio of Expenses to Net Assets (%)	—	2.00	2.00	2.00	1.73	1.83
Ratio of Net Income to Average Net Assets (%)	—	.25	.29	.26	.90	1.22
Portfolio Turnover Rate (%)	—	108	99	83	65	74
Total Assets End of Year (Millions $)	—	3.9	4.8	14.4	20.3	17.7
Annual Rate of Return (%) Years Ending 12/31	—	(3.2)	28.1	13.0	(5.4)	23.6

Five-Year Total Return(%)	63.8[c]	Degree of Diversification	D	Beta	.86	Bull (%)	93.4[c]	Bear (%)	(22.0)[D]

Objective: Seeks long-term capital growth through investment in common stocks of smaller companies (under $350 million) that show dynamic growth potential.

Portfolio: (10/31/88) Common stocks 78%, repurchase agreements 21%, other assets 1%. Largest stock holdings: business/industrial products and services 12%, banks, savings and loans 11%.

Portfolio Mgr: William Leugers—1983

Distributions: **Income:** May, Nov   **Capital Gains:** Semiannually

12b-1: Yes   **Amount:** 0.25%

Minimum: **Initial:** $1,000   **Subsequent:** $50

Min IRA: **Initial:** $1,000   **Subsequent:** $50

Services: IRA, Withdraw

Tel Exchange: Yes   **With MMF:** Yes

Registered: CA, CO, CT, FL, GA, IL, IN, KY, LA, MA, MD, MI, MN, MO, NC, NJ, NY, OH, PA, SC, TX, UT, VA, WA

Ticker: GOGFX

GROWTH INDUSTRY SHARES
Growth

William Blair and Co.
135 S. LaSalle St.
Chicago, IL 60603
(312) 346-4830

	Years Ending 12/31					
	1983	**1984**	**1985**	**1986**	**1987**	**1988**
Dividends from Net Investment Income ($)	.19	.19	.23	.22	.14	.16
Distributions from Net Realized Capital Gains ($)	.34	.70	.57	3.52	1.37	.80
Net Asset Value End of Year ($)	11.69	10.29	11.82	9.10	8.21	7.81
Ratio of Expenses to Net Assets (%)	.87	.92	.95	.90	.87	.92
Ratio of Net Income to Average Net Assets (%)	1.76	2.06	1.96	1.69	1.46	1.46
Portfolio Turnover Rate (%)	10	13	43	26	22	18
Total Assets End of Year (Millions $)	63.5	58.4	72.2	68.6	66.3	59.8
Annual Rate of Return (%) Years Ending 12/31	13.5	(4.1)	23.3	9.2	6.6	7.1

Five-Year Total Return(%)	47.5D	Degree of Diversification	B	Beta	.92	Bull (%)	85.4C	Bear (%)	(18.5)D

Objective: Seeks long-term capital growth by investing in well-managed companies in growth industries. Secondary objective is growth of income. Companies chosen on eight criteria: leader in field, unique or specialty company, quality products, outstanding marketing, value-based pricing, competitive internationally, above-average return on equity, sound financial practices.

Portfolio: (12/31/88) Common stocks 91%, temporary investments 9%, convertible securities 1%. Largest stock holdings: consumer services and products 22%, industrial technology 19%.

Portfolio Mgr: Neal Seltzer—1985

Distributions: **Income:** May, Aug, Nov, Dec   **Capital Gains:** Dec

12b-1: No

Minimum: **Initial:** $1,000   **Subsequent:** $250

Min IRA: **Initial:** $1,000   **Subsequent:** $250

Services: IRA, Keogh, SEP, Withdraw, Deduct

Tel Exchange: No

Registered: All states except NH

Ticker: GRINX

GUARDIAN MUTUAL
Growth & Income

Neuberger and Berman Mgmt.
342 Madison Ave.
New York, NY 10173
(800) 877-9700/(212) 850-8300

	Years Ending 10/31					
	1983	**1984**	**1985**	**1986**	**1987**	**1988**
Dividends from Net Investment Income ($)	1.45	1.43	1.76	1.51	1.24	1.07
Distributions from Net Realized Capital Gains ($)	2.38	1.12	6.44	4.50	3.94	3.95
Net Asset Value End of Year ($)	36.92	37.59	36.54	39.52	33.25	36.94
Ratio of Expenses to Net Assets (%)	.67	.77	.76	.73	.74	.84
Ratio of Net Income to Average Net Assets (%)	3.92	3.81	4.58	3.59	2.72	2.80
Portfolio Turnover Rate (%)	50	32	57	70	91	73
Total Assets End of Year (Millions $)	276.1	344.9	388.5	531.8	461.1	539.0

Annual Rate of Return (%) Years Ending 12/31	25.3	7.5	25.3	11.9	(1.0)	28.0

Five-Year Total Return(%)	91.0[A]	Degree of Diversification	B	Beta	.96	Bull (%)	121.0[B]	Bear (%)	(26.2)[E]

Objective: Seeks capital appreciation through investment in common stocks of dividend-paying, seasoned companies. Current income is a secondary objective. May invest in foreign securities, lend its securities, engage in repurchase agreements, and write covered call options.

Portfolio: (10/31/88) Common stocks 94%, short-term corporate notes 4%, U.S. government obligations 4%. Largest stock holdings: drugs 11%, telephone utilities 10%.

Portfolio Mgr: Kent Simons—1981

Distributions: Income: Apr, July, Oct, Dec **Capital Gains:** Oct

12b-1: No

Minimum: Initial: $1,000 **Subsequent:** $100

Min IRA: Initial: $250 **Subsequent:** $50

Services: IRA, Keogh, Withdraw, Deduct

Tel Exchange: Yes **With MMF:** Yes

Registered: All states except NH

Ticker: GUARX

HARBOR GROWTH
Growth

Harbor Capital Advisors, Inc.
One SeaGate
Toledo, OH 43666
(800) 422-1050/(419) 247-2477

	Years Ending 10/31					
	1983	1984	1985	1986	1987 (11 mos.)	1988
Dividends from Net Investment Income ($)	—	—	—	—	—	.10
Distributions from Net Realized Capital Gains ($)	—	—	—	—	.26	.79
Net Asset Value End of Year ($)	—	—	—	—	10.25	11.04
Ratio of Expenses to Net Assets (%)	—	—	—	—	1.33	1.06
Ratio of Net Income to Average Net Assets (%)	—	—	—	—	.72	1.14
Portfolio Turnover Rate (%)	—	—	—	—	56	53
Total Assets End of Year (Millions $)	—	—	—	—	98.7	116.0
Annual Rate of Return (%) Years Ending 12/31	—	—	—	—	2.9	14.3

Five-Year Total Return(%)	NA	Degree of Diversification	NA	Beta	NA	Bull (%)	NA	Bear (%)	(25.2)E

Objective: Primary objective is to achieve long-term growth of capital through investment in common stocks. Uses computer-generated forecasts of earnings and return-on-investment to select above-average growth companies.

Portfolio: (10/31/88) Common stocks 99%, short-term securities 2%. Largest stock holdings: drugs and hospital supplies 7%, chemicals 7%.

Portfolio Mgr: Bartley Madden—1986

Distributions: **Income:** Annually   **Capital Gains:** Annually

12b-1: No

Minimum: **Initial:** $2,000   **Subsequent:** $500

Min IRA: **Initial:** $2,000   **Subsequent:** $500

Services: IRA, Corp, SEP, Withdraw, Deduct

Tel Exchange: Yes   **With MMF:** Yes

Registered: All states

Ticker: HAGWX

HARBOR
U.S. EQUITIES
Growth & Income

Harbor Capital Advisors, Inc.
One SeaGate
Toledo, OH 43666
(800) 422-1050/(419) 247-2477

	Years Ending 10/31					
	1983	1984	1985	1986	1987	1988 (10 mos.)
Dividends from Net Investment Income ($)	—	—	—	—	—	—
Distributions from Net Realized Capital Gains ($)	—	—	—	—	—	—
Net Asset Value End of Year ($)	—	—	—	—	—	11.67
Ratio of Expenses to Net Assets (%)	—	—	—	—	—	.99
Ratio of Net Income to Average Net Assets (%)	—	—	—	—	—	1.48
Portfolio Turnover Rate (%)	—	—	—	—	—	48
Total Assets End of Year (Millions $)	—	—	—	—	—	46.4
Annual Rate of Return (%) Years Ending 12/31	—	—	—	—	—	15.4

Five-Year Total Return(%)	NA	Degree of Diversification	NA	Beta	NA	Bull (%)	NA	Bear (%)	NA

Objective: Seeks capital growth and income through investment in a portfolio consisting primarily of equity securities of large, established companies. Invests primarily in common stocks, convertible securities and other equity securities of companies that have market capitalizations of at least $700 million. May also invest a portion of its assets in cash for defensive purposes.

Portfolio: (10/31/88) Common stocks 100%. Largest stock holdings: pharmaceuticals 7%, retailing 5%.

Portfolio Mgr: Bartley Madden—1987

Distributions: **Income:** Annually   **Capital Gains:** Annually

12b-1: No

Minimum: **Initial:** $2,000   **Subsequent:** $500

Min IRA: **Initial:** $2,000   **Subsequent:** $500

Services: IRA, Corp, SEP, Withdraw, Deduct

Tel Exchange: Yes   **With MMF:** Yes

Registered: All states

Ticker: HAEQX

IAI APOLLO
Growth

Investment Advisers, Inc.
1100 Dain Tower, P.O. Box 357
Minneapolis, MN 55440
(612) 371-2884

	Years Ending 3/31					
	1983	1984 (10 mos.)	1985	1986	1987	1988
Dividends from Net Investment Income ($)	–	–	.22	.20	.18	.17
Distributions from Net Realized Capital Gains ($)	–	–	.14	.20	.34	1.67
Net Asset Value End of Year ($)	–	10.21	10.07	11.46	12.51	10.75
Ratio of Expenses to Net Assets (%)	–	1.00	1.00	1.00	1.00	1.00
Ratio of Net Income to Average Net Assets (%)	–	2.90	2.60	2.10	1.30	1.00
Portfolio Turnover Rate (%)	–	20	36	85	86	63
Total Assets End of Year (Millions $)	–	12.9	18.2	24.7	22.3	20.5

Annual Rate of Return (%) Years Ending 12/31	–	–	12.7	2.0	13.9	24.3

Five-Year Total Return(%)	NA	Degree of Diversification	C	Beta	.93	Bull (%)	NA	Bear (%)	(20.3)ᴰ

Objective: Seeks long-term capital appreciation through investment in common stocks of companies that are unpopular, undervalued or in severe financial difficulties. A minor portion may be invested in Ba (BB) or lower-rated debt securities. May enter into repurchase agreements and invest in venture capital limited partnerships, restricted securities and foreign securities.

Portfolio: (9/30/88) Common stocks 84%, short-term securities 12%, restricted securities 6%. Largest stock holdings: telecommunications 12%, office equipment 11%.

Portfolio Mgr: Richard Tschudy—1983

Distributions: **Income:** June, Dec   **Capital Gains:** June, Dec

12b-1: No

Minimum: **Initial:** $5,000   **Subsequent:** $1,000

Min IRA: **Initial:** $100   **Subsequent:** $100

Services: IRA, Keogh, Corp, 403(b), Withdraw

Tel Exchange: No

Registered: AZ, CA, CO, DC, HI, IA, IL, MD, MI, MN, MO, MT, ND, NE, NY, PA, SD, TN, TX, WA, WI, WY

Ticker: NSAFX

IAI BOND
Bond

Investment Advisers, Inc.
1100 Dain Tower, P.O. Box 357
Minneapolis, MN 55440
(612) 371-2884

	Years Ending 3/31					
	1983	1984	1985	1986	1987	1988
Dividends from Net Investment Income ($)	1.00	.91	1.00	.95	.89	.95
Distributions from Net Realized Capital Gains ($)	—	—	—	—	.28	.10
Net Asset Value End of Year ($)	9.57	8.99	9.41	10.72	10.29	9.63
Ratio of Expenses to Net Assets (%)	.90	.80	.70	.70	.70	.80
Ratio of Net Income to Average Net Assets (%)	11.30	10.40	11.20	9.60	8.50	7.70
Portfolio Turnover Rate (%)	83	40	22	76	35	20
Total Assets End of Year (Millions $)	11.2	16.8	22.8	31.5	46.1	41.1
Annual Rate of Return (%) Years Ending 12/31	8.0	15.5	20.1	12.1	2.1	6.4

Five-Year Total Return(%)	68.9ᶜ	Degree of Diversification	NA	Beta	NA	Bull (%)	52.3ᴰ	Bear (%)	3.0ᴬ

Objective: Seeks high level of current income and preservation of capital through investment in a diversified portfolio of investment grade bonds and other debt securities of similar quality. May enter into repurchase agreements and invest in foreign securities.

Portfolio: (9/30/88) Long-term government and corporate bonds 94%, short-term securities 4%. Largest bond holdings: U.S. government and its agencies 75%, industrial 11%.

Portfolio Mgr: Larry Hill—1984

Distributions: **Income:** Mar, June, Sept, Dec   **Capital Gains:** June

12b-1: No

Minimum: **Initial:** $5,000   **Subsequent:** $1,000

Min IRA: **Initial:** $100   **Subsequent:** $100

Services: IRA, Keogh, Corp, 403(b), Withdraw

Tel Exchange: No

Registered: AZ, CA, CO, DC, HI, IA, IL, MD, MI, MN, MO, MT, ND, NE, NY, PA, SD, TN, TX, WA, WI, WY

Ticker: NSBFX

IAI INTERNATIONAL
International

Investment Advisers, Inc.
1100 Dain Tower
P.O. Box 357
Minneapolis, MN 55440
(612) 371-2884

	Years Ending 3/31					
	1983	1984	1985	1986	1987	1988 (11 mos.)
Dividends from Net Investment Income ($)	–	–	–	–	–	–
Distributions from Net Realized Capital Gains ($)	–	–	–	–	–	–
Net Asset Value End of Year ($)	–	–	–	–	–	9.82
Ratio of Expenses to Net Assets (%)	–	–	–	–	–	2.13
Ratio of Net Income to Average Net Assets (%)	–	–	–	–	–	(.16)
Portfolio Turnover Rate (%)	–	–	–	–	–	53
Total Assets End of Year (Millions $)	–	–	–	–	–	11.9

Annual Rate of Return (%) Years Ending 12/31	–	–	–	–	–	18.0

Five-Year Total Return(%)	NA	Degree of Diversification	NA	Beta	NA	Bull (%)	NA	Bear (%)	(13.0)c

Objective: Seeks capital appreciation through investment in foreign equity securities; income is a secondary objective. Under normal conditions the fund will invest 95% of its assets in foreign equities. Can also invest in put and call options, foreign currency futures and other financial futures.

Portfolio: (9/30/88) Common stocks 89%, short-term debt securities 8%. Largest country holdings: Japan 25%, United Kingdom 23%.

Portfolio Mgr: David Tilles—1987

Distributions: **Income:** Semiannually   **Capital Gains:** Annually

12b-1: No

Minimum: **Initial:** $5,000   **Subsequent:** $1,000

Min IRA: **Initial:** $100   **Subsequent:** $100

Services: IRA, Keogh, Corp, SEP, 403(b), Withdraw

Tel Exchange: No

Registered: AZ, CA, CO, DC, HI, IA, IL, MD, MI, MN, MO, MT, ND, NE, NY, PA, SD, TN, TX, WA, WI, WY

Ticker: NSTIX

IAI REGIONAL
Growth

Investment Advisers, Inc.
1100 Dain Tower, P.O. Box 357
Minneapolis, MN 55440
(612) 371-2884

	Years Ending 3/31					
	1983	1984	1985	1986	1987	1988
Dividends from Net Investment Income ($)	.45	.40	.48	.43	.42	.40
Distributions from Net Realized Capital Gains ($)	.03	1.19	1.11	.40	6.45	3.21
Net Asset Value End of Year ($)	18.30	16.61	17.29	23.44	21.19	17.11
Ratio of Expenses to Net Assets (%)	1.00	.90	.80	.80	.80	.80
Ratio of Net Income to Average Net Assets (%)	3.10	2.60	3.00	2.10	1.80	1.60
Portfolio Turnover Rate (%)	116	77	80	112	133	85
Total Assets End of Year (Millions $)	38.4	44.9	56.5	77.8	101.9	85.7
Annual Rate of Return (%) Years Ending 12/31	13.1	(2.1)	38.4	22.8	5.0	18.6

Five-Year Total Return(%)	107.0ᴬ	Degree of Diversification	B	Beta	.86	Bull (%)	139.2ᴬ	Bear (%)	(18.1)ᶜ

Objective: Seeks capital appreciation through investment of at least 80% of its equity investments in companies headquartered in MN, WI, IA, NE, MT, ND or SD. For defensive purposes, may convert entire portfolio to debt securities. May enter into repurchase agreements and invest in restricted securities, venture capital, limited partnerships and foreign securities.

Portfolio: (9/30/88) Common stocks 81%, short-term securities 20%, restricted securities 5%. Largest stock holdings: paper 9%, utilities 7%.

Portfolio Mgr: Julian Carlin—1980

Distributions: **Income:** June, Dec   **Capital Gains:** June, Dec

12b-1: No

Minimum: **Initial:** $5,000   **Subsequent:** $1,000

Min IRA: **Initial:** $100   **Subsequent:** $100

Services: IRA, Keogh, Corp, 403(b), Withdraw

Tel Exchange: No

Registered: AZ, CA, CO, DC, HI, IA, IL, MA, MD, MI, MN, MO, MT, ND, NE, NY, PA, SD, TN, TX, WA, WI, WY

Ticker: NSRFX

IAI RESERVE
Bond

Investment Advisers, Inc.
1100 Dain Tower, P.O. Box 357
Minneapolis, MN 55440
(612) 371-2884

	Years Ending 3/31					
	1983	1984	1985	1986 (2 mos.)	1987	1988
Dividends from Net Investment Income ($)	—	—	—	—	.47	.71
Distributions from Net Realized Capital Gains ($)	—	—	—	—	—	—
Net Asset Value End of Year ($)	—	—	—	10.10	10.19	10.08
Ratio of Expenses to Net Assets (%)	—	—	—	.90	.80	.80
Ratio of Net Income to Average Net Assets (%)	—	—	—	4.90	5.60	5.90
Portfolio Turnover Rate (%)	—	—	—	—	30	—
Total Assets End of Year (Millions $)	—	—	—	25.5	35.0	67.5

Annual Rate of Return (%) Years Ending 12/31	—	—	—	—	5.9	6.8

Five-Year Total Return(%) NA	Degree of Diversification NA	Beta NA	Bull (%) NA	Bear (%) 2.1[A]

Objective:	Seeks a high level of capital stability and liquidity, with a secondary objective of high current income. Invests in investment-grade government and commercial paper. Will not purchase securities with a maturity date more than 25 months from the date of acquisition.
Portfolio:	(9/30/88) Short-term securities 78%, long-term government and corporate bonds 21%.
Portfolio Mgr:	Larry Hill—1986
Distributions:	**Income:** Mar, June, Sept, Dec **Capital Gains:** June
12b-1:	No
Minimum:	**Initial:** $5,000 **Subsequent:** $1,000
Min IRA:	**Initial:** $100 **Subsequent:** $100
Services:	IRA, Keogh, Corp, 403(b), Withdraw
Tel Exchange:	No
Registered:	AZ, CA, CO, DC, HI, IA, IL, MD, MI, MN, MO, MT, ND, NE, NY, PA, SD, TN, TX, WA, WI, WY
Ticker:	NSRSX

IAI STOCK
Growth

Investment Advisers, Inc.
1100 Dain Tower, P.O. Box 357
Minneapolis, MN 55440
(612) 371-2884

	Years Ending 3/31					
	1983	1984	1985	1986	1987	1988
Dividends from Net Investment Income ($)	.48	.35	.41	.48	.37	.37
Distributions from Net Realized Capital Gains ($)	.64	.62	1.39	.46	1.80	1.34
Net Asset Value End of Year ($)	13.86	13.53	13.25	16.09	17.32	14.80
Ratio of Expenses to Net Assets (%)	.80	.70	.70	.70	.80	.80
Ratio of Net Income to Average Net Assets (%)	3.80	3.00	3.90	2.90	2.10	1.70
Portfolio Turnover Rate (%)	81	69	62	50	68	36
Total Assets End of Year (Millions $)	35.3	48.7	60.2	69.1	83.7	83.3

Annual Rate of Return (%) Years Ending 12/31	19.4	3.7	23.2	12.9	15.4	8.4

Five-Year Total Return(%)	80.6[B]	Degree of Diversification	B	Beta	.87	Bull (%)	121.0[B]	Bear (%)	(18.3)[C]

Objective:	Seeks capital appreciation, and income secondarily, through investment primarily in common stocks of widely-known companies. May enter into repurchase agreements and invest in restricted securities, REITs and venture capital limited partnerships.
Portfolio:	(9/30/88) Common stocks 83%, restricted securities 8%, short-term securities 8%, corporate bonds 2%. Largest stock holdings: telecommunications 10%, office equipment 10%.
Portfolio Mgr:	Richard Tschudy—1970
Distributions:	**Income:** June, Dec **Capital Gains:** June, Dec
12b-1:	No
Minimum:	**Initial:** $5,000 **Subsequent:** $1,000
Min IRA:	**Initial:** $100 **Subsequent:** $100
Services:	IRA, Keogh, Corp, 403(b), Withdraw
Tel Exchange:	No
Registered:	AZ, CA, CO, DC, HI, IA, IL, MD, MI, MN, MO, MT, ND, NE, NY, PA, SD, TN, TX, WA, WI, WY
Ticker:	NSSFX

INTERNATIONAL EQUITY TRUST
International

Furman Selz
230 Park Ave.
New York, NY 10169
(800) 845-8406/(212) 309-8400

	Years Ending 9/30					
	1983	1984	1985	1986 (9 mos.)	1987	1988
Dividends from Net Investment Income ($)	–	–	–	–	.02	–
Distributions from Net Realized Capital Gains ($)	–	–	–	–	.67	1.33
Net Asset Value End of Year ($)	–	–	–	14.07	18.02	14.40
Ratio of Expenses to Net Assets (%)	–	–	–	2.47	1.64	1.30
Ratio of Net Income to Average Net Assets (%)	–	–	–	.12	.42	.38
Portfolio Turnover Rate (%)	–	–	–	78	85	86
Total Assets End of Year (Millions $)	–	–	–	9.2	32.6	29.9
Annual Rate of Return (%) Years Ending 12/31	–	–	–	49.6	3.3	19.5

Five-Year Total Return(%)	NA	Degree of Diversification	E	Beta	.62	Bull (%)	NA	Bear (%)	(18.1)c

Objective: Seeks long-term capital appreciation through investment in securities markets outside the United States. The fund will normally have 65% of its assets invested in foreign equity securities. May also invest in foreign debt obligations and use currency futures to hedge the portfolio.

Portfolio: (9/30/88) Common stocks 90%, commercial paper 7%, preferred stocks 2%. Largest country holdings: Japan 37%, United Kingdom 11%.

Portfolio Mgr: Edward Kong—1985

Distributions: **Income:** Semiannually **Capital Gains:** Annually

12b-1: Yes **Amount:** 0.50%

Minimum: **Initial:** $2,500 **Subsequent:** $100

Min IRA: **Initial:** $250 **Subsequent:** $100

Services: IRA, Keogh, Corp, 403(b), Withdraw

Tel Exchange: No

Registered: All states except AR, NH

Ticker: FTIEX

IVY GROWTH
Growth & Income

Ivy Management Inc.
South Shore Park
40 Industrial Park Rd.
Hingham, MA 02043
(800) 235-3322/(617) 749-1416

	Years Ending 12/31					
	1983	1984	1985	1986	1987	1988
Dividends from Net Investment Income ($)	.74	.78	.96	.46	.91	.38
Distributions from Net Realized Capital Gains ($)	.38	1.78	.76	4.48	.30	—
Net Asset Value End of Year ($)	15.49	13.88	15.90	13.44	12.09	13.21
Ratio of Expenses to Net Assets (%)	1.22	1.29	1.27	1.29	1.27	1.35
Ratio of Net Income to Average Net Assets (%)	5.90	5.40	4.70	4.50	2.40	2.80
Portfolio Turnover Rate (%)	59	97	132	95	74	84
Total Assets End of Year (Millions $)	114.4	63.5*	136.7	158.1	173.1	172.2

Annual Rate of Return (%) Years Ending 12/31	30.1	7.9	29.4	16.8	(1.8)	12.4

Five-Year Total Return(%)	79.9[B]	Degree of Diversification	B	Beta	.74	Bull (%)	117.4[B]	Bear (%)	(21.7)[D]

Change in size reflects halving of total assets in the forming of the other fund in this series, Ivy Institutional Investors Fund.

Objective: Seeks long-term growth of capital primarily through investment in equity securities of large, well-established companies. May write covered call options and may convert portfolio to debt investments as a defensive posture.

Portfolio: (12/31/88) Domestic common stocks 72%, short-term securities 13%, foreign common stocks 13%, cash 2%, convertible preferred stocks 1%. Largest stock holdings: banking and credit 11%, drugs and hospital supply 6%.

Portfolio Mgr: Michael Peers—1986

Distributions: **Income:** Dec   **Capital Gains:** Dec

12b-1: No

Minimum: **Initial:** $1,000   **Subsequent:** None

Min IRA: **Initial:** None   **Subsequent:** None

Services: IRA, Keogh, Corp, SEP, Withdraw

Tel Exchange: Yes   **With MMF:** Yes

Registered: All states

Ticker: IVYFX

IVY INTERNATIONAL
International

Ivy Management Inc.
South Shore Park
40 Industrial Park Rd.
Hingham, MA 02043
(800) 235-3322/(617) 749-1416

	Years Ending 12/31					
	1983	1984	1985	1986	1987	1988
Dividends from Net Investment Income ($)	–	–	–	.07	.05	.11
Distributions from Net Realized Capital Gains ($)	–	–	–	–	1.87	–
Net Asset Value End of Year ($)	–	–	–	12.40	12.90	16.62
Ratio of Expenses to Net Assets (%)	–	–	–	2.00	1.90	1.90
Ratio of Net Income to Average Net Assets (%)	–	–	–	.30	.40	.80
Portfolio Turnover Rate (%)	–	–	–	20	47	45
Total Assets End of Year (Millions $)	–	–	–	9.6	21.1	23.6

Annual Rate of Return (%) Years Ending 12/31	–	–	–	–	19.6	29.7

Five-Year Total Return(%)	NA	Degree of Diversification	NA	Beta	NA	Bull (%)	NA	Bear (%)	(21.6)D

Objective: Seeks long-term capital appreciation through investment in foreign equity securities, primarily those traded in European and Pacific Basin markets. For defensive purposes the fund may invest in U.S. equity securities. Current income is a secondary objective.

Portfolio: (12/31/88) Common stocks 95%, convertible preferred stocks 2%, short-term securities 1%, corporate bonds 1%, cash 1%. Largest country holdings: United Kingdom 19%, Japan 16%.

Portfolio Mgr: Hakan Castegren—1986

Distributions: **Income:** Dec   **Capital Gains:** Dec

12b-1: No

Minimum: **Initial:** $1,000   **Subsequent:** None

Min IRA: **Initial:** None   **Subsequent:** None

Services: IRA, Keogh, Corp, SEP, Withdraw

Tel Exchange: Yes   **With MMF:** Yes

Registered: All states

Ticker: IVINX

JANUS FUND
Growth

Janus Capital Corp.
100 Fillmore Street, Suite 300
Denver, CO 80206-4923
(800) 525-3713/(303) 333-3863

	Years Ending 10/31					
	1983	**1984**	**1985**	**1986**	**1987**	**1988**
Dividends from Net Investment Income ($)	.25	.14	.48	.47	.38	.32
Distributions from Net Realized Capital Gains ($)	.14	1.03	—	.80	2.49	1.61
Net Asset Value End of Year ($)	13.11	12.19	13.42	14.77	12.39	12.11
Ratio of Expenses to Net Assets (%)	1.11	1.06	1.03	1.00	1.01	.98
Ratio of Net Income to Average Net Assets (%)	2.07	4.26	4.01	2.82	1.55	4.99
Portfolio Turnover Rate (%)	94	162	163	254	214	175
Total Assets End of Year (Millions $)	264.7	319.1	410.7	474.4	387.5	391.6
Annual Rate of Return (%) Years Ending 12/31	26.1	(0.1)	24.5	11.2	3.9	16.6

Five-Year Total Return(%)	67.7[c]	Degree of Diversification	C	Beta	.66	Bull (%)	85.1[c]	Bear (%)	(17.1)[c]

Objective: Seeks long-term capital growth by investing in securities selected solely for their capital appreciation. Emphasizes companies, their divisions, or new products in early growth stage. Companies may be quite new or small. May convert portfolio to debt securities as a defensive posture.

Portfolio: (10/31/88) Common stocks 85%, corporate bonds 8%, U.S. Treasury bonds 3%, other assets 2%, preferred stocks 1%. Largest stock holdings: communications 15%, financial services 11%.

Portfolio Mgr: James Craig III—1986

Distributions: **Income:** Dec   **Capital Gains:** Dec

12b-1: Yes   **Amount:** Pd. by Advisor

Minimum: **Initial:** $1,000   **Subsequent:** $50

Min IRA: **Initial:** $500   **Subsequent:** $50

Services: IRA, Keogh, Withdraw, Deduct

Tel Exchange: Yes   **With MMF:** Yes

Registered: All states

Ticker: JANSX

JANUS VALUE
Growth

Janus Capital Corp.
100 Fillmore Street, Suite 300
Denver, CO 80206-4923
(800) 525-3713/(303) 333-3863

	Years Ending 5/31					
	1983	1984	1985 (7 mos.)	1986	1987	1988
Dividends from Net Investment Income ($)	–	–	–	.23	.25	.41
Distributions from Net Realized Capital Gains ($)	–	–	–	.31	1.37	1.18
Net Asset Value End of Year ($)	–	–	11.57	14.27	13.69	9.66
Ratio of Expenses to Net Assets (%)	–	–	1.99	2.00	1.79	1.70
Ratio of Net Income to Average Net Assets (%)	–	–	5.68	3.55	2.98	3.35
Portfolio Turnover Rate (%)	–	–	68	152	202	317
Total Assets End of Year (Millions $)	–	–	2.5	10.1	18.9	13.5
Annual Rate of Return (%) Years Ending 12/31	–	–	–	11.5	(11.7)	19.1

Five-Year Total Return(%)	NA	Degree of Diversification	D	Beta	.91	Bull (%)	NA	Bear (%)	(26.1)E

Objective: Seeks capital appreciation through investment in common stocks chosen primarily from a "contrarian" viewpoint, including companies with a strong financial position and low price-earnings ratio. May invest 25% of assets in ADRs of foreign issues.

Portfolio: (11/30/88) Common stocks 82%, preferred stocks 8%, short-term corporate notes 8%, other assets 2%. Largest stock holdings: communications 27%, financial services 7%.

Portfolio Mgr: Thomas Marsico—1988

Distributions: **Income:** Dec   **Capital Gains:** Dec

12b-1: Yes   **Amount:** Pd. by Advisor

Minimum: **Initial:** $1,000   **Subsequent:** $50

Min IRA: **Initial:** $500   **Subsequent:** $50

Services: IRA, Keogh, Withdraw, Deduct

Tel Exchange: Yes   **With MMF:** Yes

Registered: All states except NH

Ticker: JAVLX

JANUS VENTURE
Aggressive Growth

Janus Capital Corp.
100 Fillmore Street, Suite 300
Denver, CO 80206-4923
(800) 525-3713/(303) 333-3863

	1983	1984	1985 (3 mos.)	1986	1987	1988
Years Ending 7/31						
Dividends from Net Investment Income ($)	—	—	—	.18	.19	.15
Distributions from Net Realized Capital Gains ($)	—	—	—	1.20	2.33	4.17
Net Asset Value End of Year ($)	—	—	24.17	30.78	34.63	28.11
Ratio of Expenses to Net Assets (%)	—	—	2.00	1.90	1.44	1.41
Ratio of Net Income to Average Net Assets (%)	—	—	2.03	1.47	.40	5.11
Portfolio Turnover Rate (%)	—	—	293	248	250	299
Total Assets End of Year (Millions $)	—	—	4.1	30.9	46.3	34.4

Annual Rate of Return (%) Years Ending 12/31	—	—	—	20.2	5.1	19.6

Five-Year Total Return(%)	NA	Degree of Diversification	D	Beta .67	Bull (%)	NA	Bear (%)	(17.3)c

Objective:	Seeks capital appreciation through investment primarily in common stocks of small companies with less than $250 million in annual revenues. May also invest in larger companies with strong growth potential, and in foreign companies through ADRs.
Portfolio:	(7/31/88) Common stocks 54%, short-term corporate notes 39%, cash and other assets 5%, corporate bonds 2%. Largest stock holdings: medical 14%, insurance 7%.
Portfolio Mgr:	James Craig III—1984

Distributions: **Income:** Dec   **Capital Gains:** Dec

12b-1: Yes   **Amount:** Pd. by Advisor

Minimum: **Initial:** $1,000   **Subsequent:** $50

Min IRA: **Initial:** $500   **Subsequent:** $50

Services: IRA, Keogh, Withdraw, Deduct

Tel Exchange: Yes   **With MMF:** Yes

Registered: All states except NH

Ticker: JAVTX

†KAUFMANN FUND
Aggressive Growth

Edgemont Asset Mgmt. Corp.
17 Battery Place, Suite 2624
New York, NY 10004
(212) 344-3337

	Years Ending 12/31					
	1983	1984	1985	1986	1987	1988
Dividends from Net Investment Income ($)	–	–	–	–	.01	–
Distributions from Net Realized Capital Gains ($)	–	–	–	–	–	–
Net Asset Value End of Year ($)	–	–	–	1.13	.70	1.11
Ratio of Expenses to Net Assets (%)	–	–	–	1.48	2.00	2.00
Ratio of Net Income to Average Net Assets (%)	–	–	–	1.67	.92	(.23)
Portfolio Turnover Rate (%)	–	–	–	125	228	343
Total Assets End of Year (Millions $)	–	–	–	3.3	1.9	5.7

Annual Rate of Return (%) Years Ending 12/31	–	–	–	–	(37.2)	58.6

Five-Year Total Return(%)	NA	Degree of Diversification	NA	Beta	NA	Bull (%)	NA	Bear (%)	(37.7)ᴱ

Objective: The fund's objective is capital appreciation. Invests in common stocks, convertible preferred stocks and convertible bonds. May invest 25% of its assets in warrants and 10% in options, and can also go short. The fund is a non-diversified investment company, meaning it is less limited in the amount of assets it can invest in any one issue. Looks at growth prospects and the economic outlook for companies.

Portfolio: (12/31/88) Common stocks 73%, other assets 21%, bonds 6%. Largest stock holdings: drugs 14%, communication equipment and services 13%.

Portfolio Mgr: Lawrence Auriana, Hans Utsch—1986

Distributions: **Income:** Annually   **Capital Gains:** Annually

12b-1: Yes   **Amount:** 1.00%

Minimum: **Initial:** $1,000   **Subsequent:** $100

Min IRA: **Initial:** $100   **Subsequent:** None

Services: IRA, Keogh, Corp, Withdraw, Deduct

Tel Exchange: Yes   **With MMF:** Yes

Registered: CA, CO, CT, DE, FL, GA, HI, IL, MA, MD, MI, NJ, NM, NV, NY, PA, UT, VA, WA, WY

Ticker: KAUFX

† *The fund charges a 0.2% redemption fee.*

LEGG MASON SPECIAL INVESTMENT TRUST

Aggressive Growth

Legg Mason Wood Walker, Inc.
111 South Calvert Street
Baltimore, MD 21202
(800) 822-5544/(301) 539-3400

	Years Ending 3/31					
	1983	1984	1985	1986 (3 mos.)	1987	1988
Dividends from Net Investment Income ($)	—	—	—	—	.02	.08
Distributions from Net Realized Capital Gains ($)	—	—	—	—	.22	.89
Net Asset Value End of Year ($)	—	—	—	11.53	12.80	10.14
Ratio of Expenses to Net Assets (%)	—	—	—	2.5	2.5	2.5
Ratio of Net Income to Average Net Assets (%)	—	—	—	1.20	—	1.00
Portfolio Turnover Rate (%)	—	—	—	41	77	159
Total Assets End of Year (Millions $)	—	—	—	34.3	55.8	43.6
Annual Rate of Return (%) Years Ending 12/31	—	—	—	7.5	(10.6)	19.7

Five-Year Total Return(%)	NA	Degree of Diversification	C	Beta	1.05	Bull (%)	NA	Bear (%)	(29.8)E

Objective:	Seeks capital appreciation through investment in equity securities of out-of-favor companies that are not followed closely by analysts. Current income is not a consideration. Also invests in companies involved in reorganization or restructuring.
Portfolio:	(9/30/88) Common stocks 72%, short-term securities 16%, bonds 9%, preferred stocks 2%. Largest stock holdings: insurance 13%, technology 8%.
Portfolio Mgr:	William Miller III—1985
Distributions:	**Income:** Annually **Capital Gains:** Annually
12b-1:	Yes **Amount:** 1.00%
Minimum:	**Initial:** $1,000 **Subsequent:** $500
Min IRA:	**Initial:** $1,000 **Subsequent:** $500
Services:	IRA, Keogh, Corp, SEP, 403(b), Withdraw, Deduct
Tel Exchange:	Yes **With MMF:** Yes
Registered:	All states except AK, CA, MO
Ticker:	LMASX

LEGG MASON TOTAL RETURN TRUST
Growth & Income

Legg Mason Wood Walker, Inc.
111 South Calvert Street
Baltimore, MD 21202
(800) 822-5544/(301) 539-3400

	Years Ending 3/31					
	1983	1984	1985	1986 (4 mos.)	1987	1988
Dividends from Net Investment Income ($)	–	–	–	–	.19	.21
Distributions from Net Realized Capital Gains ($)	–	–	–	–	.04	1.39
Net Asset Value End of Year ($)	–	–	–	10.78	11.63	8.86
Ratio of Expenses to Net Assets (%)	–	–	–	2.2	2.4	2.3
Ratio of Net Income to Average Net Assets (%)	–	–	–	3.80	1.70	1.90
Portfolio Turnover Rate (%)	–	–	–	40	83	50
Total Assets End of Year (Millions $)	–	–	–	44.3	47.0	35.4
Annual Rate of Return (%) Years Ending 12/31	–	–	–	1.4	(7.5)	21.8

Five-Year Total Return(%)	NA	Degree of Diversification	B	Beta	.89	Bull (%)	NA	Bear (%)	(24.6)E

Objective:	Seeks capital appreciation and current income in order to achieve an attractive total return consistent with reasonable risk. Invests primarily in dividend-paying common stocks, convertible securities and bonds. Will invest no more than 25% of assets in bonds rated BBB or less.
Portfolio:	(9/30/88) Common stocks 91%, short-term securities 5%, preferred stocks 2%, corporate bonds 1%. Largest stock holdings: banking 22%, multi-industry 12%.
Portfolio Mgr:	Ernest Kiehne—1985
Distributions:	**Income:** Jan, May, July, Oct **Capital Gains:** Dec
12b-1:	Yes **Amount:** 1.00%
Minimum:	**Initial:** $1,000 **Subsequent:** $500
Min IRA:	**Initial:** $1,000 **Subsequent:** $500
Services:	IRA, Keogh, Corp, SEP, 403(b), Withdraw, Deduct
Tel Exchange:	Yes **With MMF:** Yes
Registered:	All states except AK
Ticker:	LMTRX

LEGG MASON U.S. GOVERNMENT INTERMEDIATE-TERM

Bond

Legg Mason Wood Walker, Inc.
111 South Calvert Street
Baltimore, MD 21203-1476
(800) 822-5544/(301) 539-3400

	Years Ending 12/31					
	1983	1984	1985	1986	1987 (5 mos.)	1988
Dividends from Net Investment Income ($)	—	—	—	—	.30	.74
Distributions from Net Realized Capital Gains ($)	—	—	—	—	—	.01
Net Asset Value End of Year ($)	—	—	—	—	9.92	9.79
Ratio of Expenses to Net Assets (%)	—	—	—	—	1.00	1.00
Ratio of Net Income to Average Net Assets (%)	—	—	—	—	7.40	7.40
Portfolio Turnover Rate (%)	—	—	—	—	66	133
Total Assets End of Year (Millions $)	—	—	—	—	16.6	27.1

Annual Rate of Return (%) Years Ending 12/31	—	—	—	—	—	6.4

Five-Year Total Return(%)	NA	Degree of Diversification	NA	Beta	NA	Bull (%)	NA	Bear (%)	3.0ᴬ

Objective: Seeks to provide high income consistent with prudent investment risk and liquidity needs. Invests at least 75% of its assets in U.S. government or agency securities, including repurchase agreements. Expects to maintain average maturity of three to 10 years. Invests up to 25% of its assets in cash, commercial paper and investment-grade debt securities of domestic issuers.

Portfolio: (12/31/88) U.S. government and agency obligations 71%, corporate bonds and notes 24%, short-term securities 3%. Largest bond holdings: banking and finance 13%, utilities 6%.

Portfolio Mgr: Rita Hildebrandt—1987

Distributions:	**Income:** Monthly	**Capital Gains:** Annually
12b-1:	Yes	**Amount:** 0.50%
Minimum:	**Initial:** $1,000	**Subsequent:** $500
Min IRA:	**Initial:** $1,000	**Subsequent:** $500
Services:	IRA, Keogh, Corp, SEP, 403(b), Withdraw, Deduct	
Tel Exchange:	Yes	**With MMF:** Yes
Registered:	All states except AK	
Ticker:	LGINX	

LEGG MASON VALUE TRUST
Growth

Legg Mason Wood Walker, Inc.
111 South Calvert Street
Baltimore, MD 21202
(800) 822-5544/(301) 539-3400

	Years Ending 3/31					
	1983 (13 mos.)	1984	1985	1986	1987	1988
Dividends from Net Investment Income ($)	.20	.27	.34	.36	.40	.41
Distributions from Net Realized Capital Gains ($)	—	.05	.34	.86	2.78	2.78
Net Asset Value End of Year ($)	16.16	18.82	23.09	30.68	30.14	24.28
Ratio of Expenses to Net Assets (%)	2.50	2.50	2.41	2.07	2.00	1.97
Ratio of Net Income to Average Net Assets (%)	3.30	2.50	2.30	2.00	1.50	1.50
Portfolio Turnover Rate (%)	6	18	38	33	43	45
Total Assets End of Year (Millions $)	15.1	61.1	163.4	599.1	819.3	665.8

Annual Rate of Return (%) Years Ending 12/31	42.8	12.0	31.7	9.4	(7.2)	25.8

Five-Year Total Return(%)	88.4[B]	Degree of Diversification	B	Beta	.95	Bull (%)	116.2[B]	Bear (%)	(26.4)[E]

Objective:	Seeks long-term capital growth through investment in undervalued companies that are temporarily depressed due to any of a variety of factors, but are deemed to have potential for superior performance.
Portfolio:	(9/30/88) Common stocks 92%, short-term securities 7%. Largest stock holdings: banking 18%, insurance 11%.
Portfolio Mgr:	Ernest Kiehne—1982
Distributions:	Income: Jan, May, July, Oct **Capital Gains:** Dec
12b-1:	Yes **Amount:** 0.95%
Minimum:	Initial: $1,000 **Subsequent:** $500
Min IRA:	Initial: $1,000 **Subsequent:** $500
Services:	IRA, Keogh, Corp, SEP, 403(b), Withdraw, Deduct
Tel Exchange:	Yes **With MMF:** Yes
Registered:	All states except AK
Ticker:	LMVTX

LEHMAN OPPORTUNITY
Aggressive Growth

Lehman Management Co.
55 Water St.
New York, NY 10041
(800) 221-5350/(212) 668-8578

	Years Ending 8/31					
	1983	1984	1985	1986	1987	1988
Dividends from Net Investment Income ($)	.48	.43	.41	.48	.59	.76
Distributions from Net Realized Capital Gains ($)	—	1.39	1.37	1.40	2.79	2.95
Net Asset Value End of Year ($)	19.78	20.30	23.73	27.87	29.53	23.39
Ratio of Expenses to Net Assets (%)	1.30	1.23	1.23	1.16	1.16	1.20
Ratio of Net Income to Average Net Assets (%)	2.88	2.44	2.71	2.44	1.92	2.29
Portfolio Turnover Rate (%)	46	32	24	28	25	29
Total Assets End of Year (Millions $)	38.7	48.5	71.2	110.1	113.6	92.6

Annual Rate of Return (%) Years Ending 12/31	38.9	11.1	32.8	6.4	4.5	23.3

Five-Year Total Return(%)	102.4[A]	Degree of Diversification	B	Beta	.77	Bull (%) 114.2[B]	Bear (%) (20.0)[D]

Objective: Seeks above-average long-term capital appreciation by investing principally in common stocks and convertible securities of both seasoned, established companies and small, new companies. May invest up to 5% of its assets in foreign securities, and may use leverage.

Portfolio: (8/31/88) Common stocks 89%, corporate short-term notes 9%, preferred stocks 1%. Largest stock holdings: insurance 23%, finance 16%.

Portfolio Mgr: Irving Brilliant—1979

Distributions: **Income:** Annually   **Capital Gains:** Annually

12b-1: No

Minimum: **Initial:** $1,000   **Subsequent:** $100

Min IRA: **Initial:** $250   **Subsequent:** $50

Services: IRA, Keogh, Withdraw

Tel Exchange: No

Registered: All states

Ticker: LOPPX

LEPERCQ-ISTEL
Growth & Income

Lepercq, de Neuflize & Co.
345 Park Ave.
New York, NY 10154
(212) 702-0175

	Years Ending 12/31					
	1983	1984	1985	1986	1987	1988
Dividends from Net Investment Income ($)	.95	.60	.74	.64	.57	.54
Distributions from Net Realized Capital Gains ($)	–	.73	1.47	1.08	.85	.23
Net Asset Value End of Year ($)	15.69	13.58	13.89	13.29	12.23	12.33
Ratio of Expenses to Net Assets (%)	1.02	1.04	1.12	1.67	1.44	1.50
Ratio of Net Income to Average Net Assets (%)	4.02	3.77	3.81	3.01	2.69	4.13
Portfolio Turnover Rate (%)	27	26	28	45	67	72
Total Assets End of Year (Millions $)	111.1	91.9	28.7	23.6	22.3	20.1

Annual Rate of Return (%) Years Ending 12/31	17.1	(5.1)	20.0	8.2	2.3	7.0

Five-Year Total Return(%)	34.8ᴇ	Degree of Diversification	C	Beta	.69	Bull (%)	74.9ᴰ	Bear (%)	(17.1)ᶜ

Objective: Seeks long-term growth of capital and reasonable current income from investment in securities of companies that through fundamental analysis show potential for growth and value. Fund chooses a few companies from each industry group that show promise in the prevailing industrial and economic environment. Looks for promising geographical regions. May invest in international securities. May write covered call options.

Portfolio: (12/31/88) Common stocks 49%, U.S. government obligations 41%, short-term securities 14%. Largest stock holdings: natural gas and oil 18%, financial services 12%.

Portfolio Mgr: Bruno Desforges—1986

Distributions: Income: July, Dec   **Capital Gains:** Dec

12b-1: Yes   **Amount:** 1.00%

Minimum: Initial: $500   **Subsequent:** 1 full share

Min IRA: Initial: $500   **Subsequent:** 1 full share

Services: IRA, Withdraw

Tel Exchange: No

Registered: All states

Ticker: ISTLX

LEVERAGE FUND OF BOSTON
Aggressive Growth

Eaton Vance Management, Inc.
24 Federal St.
Boston, MA 02110
(800) 225-6265/(617) 482-8260

	Years Ending 12/31					
	1983	**1984**	**1985**	**1986**	**1987**	**1988**
Dividends from Net Investment Income ($)	—	—	—	—	—	—
Distributions from Net Realized Capital Gains ($)	3.04	.50	—	1.53	1.50	—
Net Asset Value End of Year ($)	8.29	6.70	8.84	7.26	5.41	5.92
Ratio of Expenses to Net Assets (%)	3.47	4.30	2.73	2.76	2.50	2.09
Ratio of Net Income to Average Net Assets (%)	(.75)	(2.28)	(.06)	(1.11)	(1.77)	(.41)
Portfolio Turnover Rate (%)	75	48	78	53	115	70
Total Assets End of Year (Millions $)	41.5	28.9	33.2	23.4	18.8	18.3
Annual Rate of Return (%) Years Ending 12/31	16.1	(13.1)	32.1	(0.7)	(4.0)	9.4

Five-Year Total Return(%) 19.7ᴱ	Degree of Diversification D	Beta 1.33	Bull (%) 126.8ᴬ	Bear (%) (34.9)ᴱ

Objective: Seeks growth of capital primarily through investment in equity securities of large and small companies that show growth promise because of new products, other changes or special situations. May employ leverage by borrowing money to purchase securities but must have assets representing three times borrowings. May invest in foreign securities and engage in repurchase agreements.

Portfolio: (12/31/88) Common stocks 100%. Largest stock holdings: medical products and services 13%, metals and mining 9%.

Portfolio Mgr: Michael Chapman—1987

Distributions: **Income:** Semiannually   **Capital Gains:** Annually

12b-1: No

Minimum: **Initial:** $1,000   **Subsequent:** $50

Min IRA: **Initial:** $50   **Subsequent:** $50

Services: IRA, Keogh, Corp, 403(b), Withdraw, Deduct

Tel Exchange: Yes   **With MMF:** Yes

Registered: All states

Ticker: LEVGX

LEXINGTON
GNMA INCOME
Bond

Lexington Management Corp.
P.O. Box 1515
Park 80 W. Plaza 2
Saddle Brook, NJ 07662
(800) 526-0056

	Years Ending 12/31					
	1983	1984	1985	1986	1987	1988
Dividends from Net Investment Income ($)	.80	.82	.93	.75	.73	.64
Distributions from Net Realized Capital Gains ($)	–	–	–	–	.03	–
Net Asset Value End of Year ($)	7.72	7.74	8.06	8.22	7.58	7.45
Ratio of Expenses to Net Assets (%)	1.47	1.22	1.01	.86	.98	1.07
Ratio of Net Income to Average Net Assets (%)	10.77	11.89	11.06	9.30	8.49	8.31
Portfolio Turnover Rate (%)	207	133	168	300	89	233
Total Assets End of Year (Millions $)	22.4	25.4	87.4	141.4	107.6	97.1

Annual Rate of Return (%) Years Ending 12/31	7.6	11.9	18.3	11.7	0.8	6.9

Five-Year Total Return(%)	59.4ᴰ	Degree of Diversification	NA	Beta	NA	Bull (%)	45.6ᴱ	Bear (%)	1.7ᴬ

Objective: Seeks high level of current income, retaining liquidity and safety of principal. At least 80% of assets invested in GNMA certificates with balance in other U.S. government securities. May buy repurchase agreements.

Portfolio: (12/31/88) GNMA 95%, U.S. government obligations 6%, repurchase agreements 1%.

Portfolio Mgr: Denis Jamison—1981

Distributions: **Income:** Monthly **Capital Gains:** Dec

12b-1: No

Minimum: **Initial:** $1,000 **Subsequent:** $50

Min IRA: **Initial:** $250 **Subsequent:** $50

Services: IRA, Keogh, Corp, SEP, 403(b), Withdraw, Deduct

Tel Exchange: Yes **With MMF:** Yes

Registered: All states

Ticker: LEXNX

LEXINGTON GOLDFUND
Precious Metals

Lexington Management Corp.
P.O. Box 1515
Park 80 W. Plaza 2
Saddle Brook, NJ 07662
(800) 526-0056

	Years Ending 12/31					
	1983	1984	1985	1986	1987	1988
Dividends from Net Investment Income ($)	.06	.04	.04	.02	.05	.05
Distributions from Net Realized Capital Gains ($)	.05	.10	—	—	.32	—
Net Asset Value End of Year ($)	4.14	3.05	3.40	4.49	6.20	5.21
Ratio of Expenses to Net Assets (%)	1.51	1.52	1.52	1.52	1.29	1.61
Ratio of Net Income to Average Net Assets (%)	2.24	1.14	.71	1.11	.57	.78
Portfolio Turnover Rate (%)	16	17	30	15	14	20
Total Assets: End of Year (Millions $)	7.0	7.5	12.4	24.6	104.9	92.9

Annual Rate of Return (%) Years Ending 12/31	(6.4)	(23.7)	13.0	32.7	46.3	(15.0)

Five-Year Total Return(%)	42.1ᴱ	Degree of Diversification	E	Beta	NA	Bull (%)	133.6ᴬ	Bear (%)	(15.5)ᶜ

Objective: Seeks capital appreciation and a hedge against inflation through investment in gold bullion and debt and equity securities of domestic and foreign firms engaged in mining or processing gold. May buy repurchase agreements and CDs.

Portfolio: (12/31/88) Common stocks 64%, gold bullion 23%, short-term securities 8%, demand notes 4%, other assets 1%. Largest stock holdings: North American gold mining 34%, Australian gold mining 14%.

Portfolio Mgr: Caesar Bryan—1987

Distributions: **Income:** Semiannually   **Capital Gains:** Dec

12b-1: No

Minimum: **Initial:** $1,000   **Subsequent:** $50

Min IRA: **Initial:** $250   **Subsequent:** $50

Services: IRA, Keogh, Corp, SEP, 403(b), Withdraw, Deduct

Tel Exchange: Yes   **With MMF:** Yes

Registered: All states except NH, WI

Ticker: LEXMX

LEXINGTON GROWTH
Growth

Lexington Management Corp.
P.O. Box 1515
Park 80 W. Plaza 2
Saddle Brook, NJ 07662
(800) 526-0056

	Years Ending 12/31					
	1983	1984	1985	1986	1987	1988
Dividends from Net Investment Income ($)	.11	.30	.12	.20	.38	.12
Distributions from Net Realized Capital Gains ($)	.06	.73	—	—	3.67	—
Net Asset Value End of Year ($)	10.24	7.98	9.96	11.80	8.01	8.72
Ratio of Expenses to Net Assets (%)	1.21	1.50	1.43	1.32	1.34	1.33
Ratio of Net Income to Average Net Assets (%)	2.00	1.78	2.00	1.24	1.26	1.27
Portfolio Turnover Rate (%)	57	141	151	54	83	48
Total Assets End of Year (Millions $)	35.0	22.7	28.0	29.9	25.6	26.4

Annual Rate of Return (%) Years Ending 12/31	9.9	(12.0)	26.7	20.6	0.0	10.5

Five-Year Total Return(%)	48.5ᴰ	Degree of Diversification	A	Beta	1.00	Bull (%)	135.1ᴬ	Bear (%)	(25.9)ᴱ

Objective: Seeks capital growth. May invest in securities of newer, less seasoned companies, companies whose earnings are cyclically depressed but have good potential for recovery, or established companies experiencing important changes, such as product innovation. May also buy repurchase agreements.

Portfolio: (12/31/88) Common stocks 88%, short-term securities 9%, bonds 3%. Largest stock holdings: drugs and health care 14%, consumer products 8%.

Portfolio Mgr: Carolyn Croney—1985

Distributions: Income: Dec   **Capital Gains:** Dec

12b-1: No

Minimum: Initial: $1,000   **Subsequent:** $50

Min IRA: Initial: $250   **Subsequent:** $50

Services: IRA, Keogh, Corp, SEP, 403(b), Withdraw, Deduct

Tel Exchange: Yes   **With MMF:** Yes

Registered: All states except NH

Ticker: LEXGX

LEXINGTON RESEARCH
Growth & Income

Lexington Management Corp.
P.O. Box 1515
Park 80 W. Plaza 2
Saddle Brook, NJ 07662
(800) 526-0056

	Years Ending 12/31					
	1983	1984	1985	1986	1987	1988
Dividends from Net Investment Income ($)	.72	.80	.60	.66	.51	.45
Distributions from Net Realized Capital Gains ($)	1.11	2.73	.11	2.33	5.52	—
Net Asset Value End of Year ($)	20.02	15.37	18.62	19.16	13.58	14.39
Ratio of Expenses to Net Assets (%)	.95	1.00	1.00	.95	.96	1.10
Ratio of Net Income to Average Net Assets (%)	3.99	4.20	3.52	2.52	2.37	3.20
Portfolio Turnover Rate (%)	64	59	86	82	95	81
Total Assets End of Year (Millions $)	111.7	100.0	114.3	124.7	112.8	111.1

Annual Rate of Return (%) Years Ending 12/31	28.7	(4.3)	26.3	20.2	0.0	9.5

Five-Year Total Return(%)	59.0[D]	Degree of Diversification	A	Beta	.88	Bull (%)	120.7[B]	Bear (%)	(22.9)[D]

Objective: Seeks capital growth over the long-term through investments in stocks of large, ably-managed and well-financed companies. Income is a secondary objective. May buy repurchase agreements.

Portfolio: (12/31/88) Common stocks 87%, short-term securities 11%, bonds 4%. Largest stock holdings: drugs and health care 11%, electronics and electrical equipment 10%.

Portfolio Mgr: James Fargis—1985

Distributions: Income: Feb, May, Aug, Dec **Capital Gains:** Dec

12b-1: No

Minimum: Initial: $1,000 Subsequent: $50

Min IRA: Initial: $250 Subsequent: $50

Services: IRA, Keogh, Corp, SEP, 403(b), Withdraw, Deduct

Tel Exchange: Yes **With MMF:** Yes

Registered: All states except NH

Ticker: LEXRX

†LIBERTY
Bond

Neuberger and Berman Mgmt.
342 Madison Avenue
New York, NY 10173
(800) 877-9700/(212) 850-8300

	Years Ending 3/31					
	1983	1984	1985	1986	1987	1988
Dividends from Net Investment Income ($)	.36	.30	.40	.32	.38	.47
Distributions from Net Realized Capital Gains ($)	—	—	—	—	—	—
Net Asset Value End of Year ($)	3.89	3.97	3.93	4.61	4.86	4.28
Ratio of Expenses to Net Assets (%)	1.50	1.50	2.00	2.00	1.98	1.97
Ratio of Net Income to Average Net Assets (%)	9.43	8.95	9.69	7.38	9.18	9.45
Portfolio Turnover Rate (%)	171	225	110	256	186	156
Total Assets End of Year (Millions $)	8.6	8.1	8.0	9.9	12.3	12.1
Annual Rate of Return (%) Years Ending 12/31	16.7	6.1	20.9	18.2	(4.6)	13.8

Five-Year Total Return(%)	64.6ᶜ	Degree of Diversification	NA	Beta	NA	Bull (%)	60.7ᴰ	Bear (%)	(8.0)ᶜ

Objective: Seeks a high level of current income by investing in a diversified portfolio of higher-yielding, lower-rated (BBB or lower) fixed-income securities. May invest in foreign securities.

Portfolio: (9/30/88) Corporate bonds 78%, corporate short-term notes 16%, preferred stocks 8%. Largest bond holdings: consumer goods and products 22%, manufacturing 15%.

Portfolio Mgr: Irwin Lainoff—1976

Distributions: Income: Apr, July, Oct, Dec   **Capital Gains:** Dec

12b-1: No

Minimum: Initial: $1,000   Subsequent: $100

Min IRA: Initial: $250   Subsequent: $50

Services: IRA, Keogh, Withdraw, Deduct

Tel Exchange: Yes   **With MMF:** Yes

Registered: All states except AZ, IA, IL, LA, ME, MS, NC, NH, TN

Ticker: CNALX

†*The fund merged into T. Rowe Price High Yield Fund as of March 31, 1989.*

†LINDNER
Growth

Lindner Management Corp.
200 South Bemiston Ave.
P.O. Box 11208
St. Louis, MO 63105
(314) 727-5305

	Years Ending 6/30					
	1983	1984	1985	1986	1987	1988
Dividends from Net Investment Income ($)	.66	.86	1.63	.11	1.49	.98
Distributions from Net Realized Capital Gains ($)	.32	.45	1.58	.87	4.09	1.61
Net Asset Value End of Year ($)	18.63	18.30	19.00	21.16	19.15	17.74
Ratio of Expenses to Net Assets (%)	.78	.89	.65	.58	.89	1.07
Ratio of Net Income to Average Net Assets (%)	6.13	6.22	7.44	5.83	4.56	3.76
Portfolio Turnover Rate (%)	15	40	46	33	39	21
Total Assets End of Year (Millions $)	270.8	339.8	397.9	390.9	405.8	404.4

Annual Rate of Return (%) Years Ending 12/31	24.7	12.8	19.5	14.1	8.8	20.4

Five-Year Total Return(%)	101.4^	Degree of Diversification	D	Beta	.57	Bull (%)	91.5c	Bear (%)	(14.9)c

Objective: Seeks to achieve long-term capital appreciation; income is secondary. Invests in common stocks or securities convertible into common stocks. May also invest in non-convertible preferred stocks and debt securities.

Portfolio: (9/30/88) Common stocks 85%, corporate bonds 12%, U.S. Treasury bills 2%, preferred shares 1%, other assets 1%. Largest stock holdings: financial services 14%, electric and gas utilities 11%.

Portfolio Mgr: Robert Lange—1977

Distributions: **Income:** August   **Capital Gains:** August

12b-1: No

Minimum: **Initial:** $2,000   **Subsequent:** $100

Min IRA: **Initial:** $250   **Subsequent:** $100

Services: IRA, Withdraw

Tel Exchange: No

Registered: AL, AZ, CA, CO, CT, DC, FL, GA, HI, IL, IN, MA, MD, MI, MN, MO, NC, NJ, NM, NV, NY, OH, OR, PA, TN, TX, VA, WA, WI

Ticker: LDNRX

† *There will be a 2% redemption fee only if shares are redeemed within 60 days after purchase.*

LINDNER DIVIDEND FUND
Balanced

Lindner Management Corp.
200 South Bemiston
P.O. Box 11208
St. Louis, MO 63105
(314) 727-5305

	9/30	Years Ending 2/28				
	1983	1984* (5 mos.)	1985	1986	1987	1988
Dividends from Net Investment Income ($)	1.47	.31	1.38	1.79	2.17	1.87
Distributions from Net Realized Capital Gains ($)	—	5.24	.86	.01	3.26	1.16
Net Asset Value End of Year ($)	26.02	21.53	22.88	24.90	24.49	21.19
Ratio of Expenses to Net Assets (%)	.94	.42	1.14	.95	1.00	1.04
Ratio of Net Income to Average Net Assets (%)	6.23	2.83	8.40	8.08	7.43	7.43
Portfolio Turnover Rate (%)	14	1	11	26	56	17
Total Assets End of Year (Millions $)	1.3	1.2	51.6	67.1	67.0	52.3

Annual Rate of Return (%) Years Ending 12/31	43.8	14.9	16.8	20.8	(4.1)	24.2

Five-Year Total Return(%)	93.2ᴬ	Degree of Diversification	E	Beta	.31	Bull (%)	65.8ᴰ	Bear (%)	(9.2)ᶜ

Fiscal year-end changed from 9/30 to 2/28.

Objective: Seeks current income; capital appreciation is a secondary objective. Invests in high-yielding common stocks, preferred stocks, convertible securities and bonds. Under normal circumstances, the fund will invest at least 65% of its assets in common and preferred stocks.

Portfolio: (8/31/88) Preferred stocks 37%, common stocks 29%, non-convertible bonds 14%, convertible bonds 13%, U.S. Treasury bills 5%, other assets 1%. Largest holdings: electric and gas utilities 39%, oil 10%.

Portfolio Mgr: Eric Ryback—1984

Distributions: **Income:** Apr, June, Sept, Dec   **Capital Gains:** Apr

12b-1: No

Minimum: **Initial:** $2,000   **Subsequent:** $100

Min IRA: **Initial:** $250   **Subsequent:** $100

Services: IRA, Withdraw

Tel Exchange: No

Registered: CA, CO, GA, HI, IL, MA, MI, MO, NC, NJ, NV, NY, PA, TX, VA

Ticker: LDDVX

LMH
Growth & Income

Heine Management Group, Inc.
253 Post Rd. West
P.O. Box 830
Westport, CT 06881
(800) 225-8558/(203) 222-1624

	Years Ending 6/30					
	1983	**1984**	**1985**	**1986**	**1987**	**1988**
Dividends from Net Investment Income ($)	—	—	.11	.52	1.10	2.37
Distributions from Net Realized Capital Gains ($)	—	—	.11	.80	4.42	3.12
Net Asset Value End of Year ($)	—	20.55	25.30	29.20	25.49	18.83
Ratio of Expenses to Net Assets (%)	—	2.60	1.42	1.25	1.29	1.44
Ratio of Net Income to Average Net Assets (%)	—	2.82	3.24	3.83	4.11	4.09
Portfolio Turnover Rate (%)	—	13	25	50	19	72
Total Assets End of Year (Millions $)	—	30.5	77.1	83.9	76.7	40.0
Annual Rate of Return (%) Years Ending 12/31	—	9.4	22.8	14.1	(6.4)	18.0

Five-Year Total Return(%) 69.1[c]	Degree of Diversification C	Beta .48	Bull (%) 71.2[D]	Bear (%) (14.5)[c]

Objective: Seeks capital appreciation through investment in common stocks of well-established, dividend-paying companies that are currently undervalued, considering the strength of their financial position. May also invest in preferred stocks and convertible securities, and up to 10% of total assets may be invested in U.S.-traded foreign securities.

Portfolio: (9/30/88) Common stocks 65%, commercial paper 23%, U.S. government obligations 12%. Largest stock holdings: conglomerates 8%, automotive 7%.

Portfolio Mgr: Leonard M. Heine Jr.—1983

Distributions: **Income:** Annually   **Capital Gains:** Annually

12b-1: No

Minimum: **Initial:** $2,500   **Subsequent:** $1,000

Min IRA: **Initial:** $500   **Subsequent:** $500

Services: IRA, Keogh

Tel Exchange: No

Registered: All states except AL, TX

Ticker: LMHFX

†LOOMIS-SAYLES CAPITAL DEVELOPMENT

Aggressive Growth

Loomis, Sayles & Company, Inc.
P.O. Box 449, Back Bay Annex
Boston, MA 02117
(800) 345-4048/(617) 578-1333

	Years Ending 12/31					
	1983	**1984**	**1985**	**1986**	**1987**	**1988**
Dividends from Net Investment Income ($)	.47	.11	.18	.16	.14	.62
Distributions from Net Realized Capital Gains ($)	2.50	6.15	—	7.46	10.09	.02
Net Asset Value End of Year ($)	25.21	17.28	25.02	23.12	16.56	15.87
Ratio of Expenses to Net Assets (%)	.76	.70	.79	.74	.82	.92
Ratio of Net Income to Average Net Assets (%)	.44	1.18	.66	.45	.70	3.89
Portfolio Turnover Rate (%)	174	129	209	208	187	301
Total Assets End of Year (Millions $)	143.7	130.9	170.5	210.0	231.8	194.2

Annual Rate of Return (%) Years Ending 12/31	15.4	(7.3)	46.2	27.5	15.9	(0.3)

Five-Year Total Return(%)	99.8ᴬ	Degree of Diversification	D	Beta	1.28	Bull (%)	188.2ᴬ	Bear (%)	(18.8)ᴰ

Objective: Seeks long-term capital appreciation. Invests in common stocks and securities convertible into common stock. Will maintain flexibility as to the sizes and types of companies in which it will invest. Invests in well-established companies with records of above-average growth and smaller companies with good management and attractive prospects. May hold a portion of its assets in cash or fixed-income investments.

Portfolio: (12/31/88) Short-term securities 53%, common stocks 46%, cash 1%. Largest stock holdings: airline/air freight 11%, metals and mining 6%.

Portfolio Mgr: G. Kenneth Heebner—1976

Distributions: Income: Dec   **Capital Gains:** Dec

12b-1: No

Minimum: Initial: $1,000   Subsequent: $50

Min IRA: Initial: $250   Subsequent: $25

Services: IRA, Keogh, Withdraw, Deduct

Tel Exchange: Yes   **With MMF:** Yes

Registered: All states

Ticker: LOMCX

† *As of January 25, 1989, the fund is closed to new investors.*

LOOMIS-SAYLES MUTUAL
Balanced

Loomis Sayles & Co., Inc.
P.O. Box 449, Back Bay Annex
Boston, MA 02117
(800) 345-4048/(617) 578-1333

	Years Ending 12/31					
	1983	**1984**	**1985**	**1986**	**1987**	**1988**
Dividends from Net Investment Income ($)	1.09	.95	1.08	.94	1.06	1.10
Distributions from Net Realized Capital Gains ($)	—	1.86	—	2.75	4.52	—
Net Asset Value End of Year ($)	18.81	17.01	21.53	22.86	20.40	19.94
Ratio of Expenses to Net Assets (%)	.87	.85	.86	.84	.94	1.01
Ratio of Net Income to Average Net Assets (%)	5.14	6.67	5.10	3.81	3.69	5.25
Portfolio Turnover Rate (%)	194	135	186	127	197	218
Total Assets End of Year (Millions $)	95.5	90.6	121.1	203.4	303.0	292.7

Annual Rate of Return (%) Years Ending 12/31	10.0	6.4	34.4	24.8	13.6	3.2

Five-Year Total Return(%) 109.4^A	Degree of Diversification D	Beta .89	Bull (%) 154.3^A	Bear (%) (12.9)^C

Objective: Seeks high total return from income and capital growth by investing in a diversified portfolio of stocks and bonds of seasoned, well-established, dividend-paying companies.

Portfolio: (12/31/88) Common stocks 49%, short-term securities 39%, bonds and notes 13%. Largest stock holdings: airlines 7%, fertilizer producers 6%.

Portfolio Mgr: G. Kenneth Heebner—1976

Distributions: Income: Quarterly   **Capital Gains:** Dec

12b-1: No

Minimum: Initial: $1,000   Subsequent: $50

Min IRA: Initial: $250   Subsequent: $25

Services: IRA, Keogh, Withdraw, Deduct

Tel Exchange: Yes   **With MMF:** Yes

Registered: All states

Ticker: LOMMX

MANHATTAN
Growth

Neuberger and Berman Mgmt.
342 Madison Ave.
New York, NY 10173
(800) 877-9700/(212) 850-8300

	Years Ending 12/31					
	1983	1984	1985	1986	1987	1988
Dividends from Net Investment Income ($)	.17	.18	.11	.08	.26	.16
Distributions from Net Realized Capital Gains ($)	—	—	—	1.24	.95	.04
Net Asset Value End of Year ($)	6.32	6.56	8.86	8.95	7.81	9.04
Ratio of Expenses to Net Assets (%)	1.30	1.50	1.40	1.10	1.0	1.20
Ratio of Net Income to Average Net Assets (%)	1.70	1.90	1.80	1.30	1.60	1.60
Portfolio Turnover Rate (%)	173	186	155	96	111	70
Total Assets End of Year (Millions $)	75.5	79.4	158.9	293.6	329.2	341.8

Annual Rate of Return (%) Years Ending 12/31	26.8	7.1	37.1	17.0	0.4	18.3

Five-Year Total Return(%)	104.0[A]	Degree of Diversification	A	Beta	1.10	Bull (%)	153.8[A]	Bear (%)	(27.5)[E]

Objective:	Seeks capital growth; any income received is incidental to growth objective. May invest in preferred stocks and debt securities without limitation as a defensive tactic. Common stock investment is in well-established, leading companies with maximum growth potential.
Portfolio:	(12/31/88) Common stocks 96%, cash 3%, short-term corporate notes 2%. Largest stock holdings: oil and gas 10%, health care 9%.
Portfolio Mgr:	Irwin Lainoff—1979
Distributions:	**Income:** Dec **Capital Gains:** Dec
12b-1:	No
Minimum:	**Initial:** $1,000 **Subsequent:** $100
Min IRA:	**Initial:** $250 **Subsequent:** $50
Services:	IRA, Keogh, Withdraw, Deduct
Tel Exchange:	Yes **With MMF:** Yes
Registered:	All states
Ticker:	CNAMX

MATHERS
Growth

Mathers & Company, Inc.
100 Corporate North, Suite 201
Bannockburn, IL 60015
(800) 962-3863/(312) 295-7400

	Years Ending 12/31					
	1983	1984	1985	1986	1987	1988
Dividends from Net Investment Income ($)	.63	.86	.55	.81	.88	.33
Distributions from Net Realized Capital Gains ($)	1.49	2.68	1.82	7.38	5.97	.50
Net Asset Value End of Year ($)	24.07	19.97	22.65	16.96	14.46	15.60
Ratio of Expenses to Net Assets (%)	.60	.69	.74	.77	.82	.98
Ratio of Net Income to Average Net Assets (%)	3.54	2.90	3.69	1.76	2.37	2.18
Portfolio Turnover Rate (%)	85	71	278	174	202	148
Total Assets End of Year (Millions $)	217.2	182.1	187.3	134.8	151.5	201.0
Annual Rate of Return (%) Years Ending 12/31	16.1	(1.5)	27.5	12.9	26.2	13.7

Five-Year Total Return(%)	103.8[A]	Degree of Diversification	E	Beta	.71	Bull (%)	117.3[B]	Bear (%)	(3.7)[C]

Objective: Long-term capital appreciation principally through investment in common stocks of growth companies and a small percentage of companies in special situations (mergers, etc.) or that are unseasoned. Current income is a secondary consideration.

Portfolio: (12/31/88) Common stocks 99%, short-term notes 3%. Largest stock holdings: pollution control 15%, transportation 9%.

Portfolio Mgr: Henry G. Van der Eb Jr.—1975

Distributions: **Income:** Dec   **Capital Gains:** Dec

12b-1: No

Minimum: **Initial:** $1,000   **Subsequent:** $200

Min IRA: **Initial:** None   **Subsequent:** None

Services: IRA, Keogh

Tel Exchange: No

Registered: All states except ME, MT, ND, NH, SD, VT

Ticker: MATRX

MEDICAL TECHNOLOGY
Aggressive Growth

AMA Advisers, Inc.
5 Sentry Pkwy. West
Suite 120, P.O. Box 1111
Blue Bell, PA 19422
(800) 262-3863/(215) 825-0400

	Years Ending 6/30					
	1983	1984	1985	1986	1987	1988
Dividends from Net Investment Income ($)	.02	.02	—	.02	—	—
Distributions from Net Realized Capital Gains ($)	.02	.04	.07	.06	.19	4.22
Net Asset Value End of Year ($)	13.00	8.46	10.41	15.87	16.62	10.43
Ratio of Expenses to Net Assets (%)	1.40	1.56	1.49	1.44	1.90	2.26
Ratio of Net Income to Average Net Assets (%)	—	(.13)	.17	(.16)	(.84)	(.53)
Portfolio Turnover Rate (%)	8	23	21	15	6	2
Total Assets End of Year (Millions $)	72.7	49.8	66.7	97.6	59.0	40.6

Annual Rate of Return (%) Years Ending 12/31	(0.7)	(12.5)	39.0	15.3	(1.9)	4.6

Five-Year Total Return(%)	44.0E	Degree of Diversification	C	Beta	1.10	Bull (%)	126.1B	Bear (%)	(25.2)E

Objective: Seeks capital appreciation through concentration of investments in companies engaged in the design, manufacture or sale of products or services that are derived from technology for use in medicine or health care. May move up to 75% of assets into defensive positions. May invest in foreign securities.

Portfolio: (9/30/88) Common stocks 87%, commercial paper 12%, other assets 2%. Largest stock holdings: therapeutic technology 37%, supplies and equipment 24%.

Portfolio Mgr: Jennifer L. Byrne—1985

Distributions: **Income:** July   **Capital Gains:** July

12b-1: Yes   **Amount:** 0.50%

Minimum: **Initial:** $1,000   **Subsequent:** None

Min IRA: **Initial:** $500   **Subsequent:** $50

Services: IRA, Keogh, Corp, SEP, 403(b), Withdraw, Deduct

Tel Exchange: Yes   **With MMF:** Yes

Registered: All states

Ticker: ATCFX

M.S.B. FUND
Growth

Savings Banks Trust Company
330 Madison Avenue
New York, NY 10017
(212) 551-1800

	Years Ending 12/31					
	1983	1984	1985	1986	1987	1988
Dividends from Net Investment Income ($)	.71	.71	.61	.48	.33	.37
Distributions from Net Realized Capital Gains ($)	1.11	1.70	1.43	3.70	3.88	2.11
Net Asset Value End of Year ($)	21.12	19.00	21.97	20.60	17.23	16.40
Ratio of Expenses to Net Assets (%)	.38	.50	.79	.94	.98	1.19
Ratio of Net Income to Average Net Assets (%)	3.43	3.70	2.94	2.08	1.32	2.06
Portfolio Turnover Rate (%)	12	19	21	8	37	19
Total Assets End of Year (Millions $)	57.6	43.7	51.3	50.0	48.8	49.1
Annual Rate of Return (%) Years Ending 12/31	18.1	2.2	27.0	12.7	4.7	9.8

Five-Year Total Return(%) 68.2[C]	Degree of Diversification	B	Beta 1.08	Bull (%) 121.8[B]	Bear (%) (24.9)[E]

Objective: Seeks to achieve capital appreciation. Income is a secondary objective. Invests all of its assets in equity securities, primarily common stocks and, to a lesser extent, corporate debt securities convertible into common stock. For defensive purposes, the fund may invest in non-equity securities such as investment-grade corporate bonds, commercial paper and government securities.

Portfolio: (12/31/88) Common stocks 96%, commercial paper 4%. Largest stock holdings: electrical equipment 9%, conglomerates 8%.

Portfolio Mgr: Catherine Jacobson—1984

Distributions: Income: Quarterly   **Capital Gains:** Annually

12b-1: No

Minimum: Initial: $50   **Subsequent:** $25

Min IRA: Initial: NA

Services: Withdraw

Tel Exchange: No

Registered: CT, NJ, NY

Ticker: MSBFX

MUTUAL OF OMAHA AMERICA
Bond

Mutual of Omaha Fund
  Management Co.
10235 Regency Circle
Omaha, NE 68114
(800) 228-9596/(402) 397-8555

	Years Ending 12/31					
	1983	1984	1985	1986	1987	1988
Dividends from Net Investment Income ($)	.94	1.03	.91	.92	.83	.81
Distributions from Net Realized Capital Gains ($)	–	–	–	–	.03	.04
Net Asset Value End of Year ($)	9.74	9.77	10.44	10.65	9.85	9.80
Ratio of Expenses to Net Assets (%)	1.21	1.11	1.05	.98	.98	1.03
Ratio of Net Income to Average Net Assets (%)	9.84	10.52	8.95	8.49	8.10	8.30
Portfolio Turnover Rate (%)	NA	NA	168	76	35	33
Total Assets End of Year (Millions $)	20.4	19.1	28.3	49.1	53.1	52.4

Annual Rate of Return (%) Years Ending 12/31	6.6	11.7	16.9	11.1	0.7	8.4

Five-Year Total Return(%) 58.3D	Degree of Diversification NA	Beta NA	Bull (%) 37.4E	Bear (%) 3.6A

Objective:	Seeks current income through investing at least 80% of its total assets in the securities of the U.S. government or its instrumentalities.
Portfolio:	(12/31/88) U.S. government and agency securities 46%, U.S. government sponsored securities 41%, short-term securities 34%.
Portfolio Mgr:	Shirley Lang—1986
Distributions:	**Income:** Mar, June, Sept, Dec **Capital Gains:** Dec
12b-1:	No
Minimum:	**Initial:** $250 **Subsequent:** $50
Min IRA:	**Initial:** $250 **Subsequent:** $50
Services:	IRA, Keogh, Corp, 403(b), Withdraw, Deduct
Tel Exchange:	Yes **With MMF:** Yes
Registered:	All states
Ticker:	MOMAX

MUTUAL QUALIFIED FUND
(formerly MUTUAL QUALIFIED INCOME)
Balanced

Heine Securities Corporation
51 John F. Kennedy Parkway
Short Hills, NJ 07078
(800) 448-3863/(201) 912-2100

	Years Ending 12/31					
	1983	1984	1985	1986	1987	1988
Dividends from Net Investment Income ($)	.39	.35	.61	.85	.88	.83
Distributions from Net Realized Capital Gains ($)	1.33	1.13	1.17	1.56	1.44	1.62
Net Asset Value End of Year ($)	15.91	16.75	19.15	20.06	19.37	22.71
Ratio of Expenses to Net Assets (%)	1.11	.81	.70	.68	.71	.62
Ratio of Net Income to Average Net Assets (%)	2.83	3.58	4.27	4.55	3.43	3.96
Portfolio Turnover Rate (%)	79	107	96	124	74	85
Total Assets End of Year (Millions $)	56.3	178.1	432.5	561.4	686.3	1,093.8

Annual Rate of Return (%) Years Ending 12/31	34.9	14.7	25.5	16.9	7.6	30.2

Five-Year Total Return(%)	135.6^A	Degree of Diversification	D	Beta	.62	Bull (%)	105.6^B	Bear (%)	(15.6)^C

Objective: Primary objective is capital appreciation from either short- or long-term investment in companies involved in prospective mergers, consolidations, liquidations and re-organizations. Current income is a secondary objective.

Portfolio: (12/31/88) Common stocks 47%, temporary investments 29%, corporate bonds 10%, foreign investments 5%, preferred stocks 4%, bonds and notes in reorganization 3%, companies in liquidation 1%. Largest stock holdings: food and beverages 7%, natural resources 6%.

Portfolio Mgr: Michael Price—1980

Distributions: **Income:** Semiannually   **Capital Gains:** Semiannually

12b-1: No

Minimum: **Initial:** $1,000   **Subsequent:** $50

Min IRA: **Initial:** $1,000   **Subsequent:** $50

Services: IRA, Keogh, SEP, 403(b), Withdraw, Deduct

Tel Exchange: No

Registered: All states

Ticker: MQIFX

MUTUAL SHARES
Balanced

Heine Securities Corporation
51 John F. Kennedy Parkway
Short Hills, NJ 07078
(800) 448-3863/(201) 912-2100

	Years Ending 12/31					
	1983	1984	1985	1986	1987	1988
Dividends from Net Investment Income ($)	1.37	1.42	1.88	2.34	2.52	2.63
Distributions from Net Realized Capital Gains ($)	4.63	4.83	4.12	4.52	4.09	5.05
Net Asset Value End of Year ($)	49.49	50.30	57.57	60.43	57.83	67.77
Ratio of Expenses to Net Assets (%)	.83	.73	.67	.70	.69	.67
Ratio of Net Income to Average Net Assets (%)	3.20	3.42	4.08	4.07	3.32	4.16
Portfolio Turnover Rate (%)	70	102	91	122	78	90
Total Assets End of Year (Millions $)	241.1	496.0	1,076.2	1,402.6	1,684.6	2,551.7

Annual Rate of Return (%) Years Ending 12/31	37.0	14.4	26.6	16.9	6.2	30.7

Five-Year Total Return(%) 135.0[A]	Degree of Diversification	D	Beta	.61	Bull (%) 104.7[B]	Bear (%) (15.7)[C]

Objective: Primary objective is capital appreciation from either short- or long-term investment in the debt or equity securities of companies involved in prospective mergers, consolidations, liquidations and reorganizations. Income is secondary objective.

Portfolio: (12/31/88) Common stocks 49%, temporary investments 29%, corporate bonds 8%, foreign investments 5%, preferred stocks 4%, bonds and notes in reorganization 3%, companies in liquidation 1%. Largest stock holdings: food and beverages 8%, natural resources 6%.

Portfolio Mgr: Michael Price—1975

Distributions: **Income:** Semiannually   **Capital Gains:** Semiannually

12b-1: No

Minimum: **Initial:** $5,000   **Subsequent:** $100

Min IRA: **Initial:** $2,000   **Subsequent:** $100

Services: IRA, Keogh, SEP, 403(b), Withdraw, Deduct

Tel Exchange: No

Registered: All states

Ticker: MUTHX

NAESS & THOMAS SPECIAL

Aggressive Growth

Vanguard Group
Vanguard Financial Center
Valley Forge, PA 19482
(800) 662-7447/(215) 648-6000

	Years Ending 9/30					
	1983	**1984**	**1985**	**1986**	**1987**	**1988**
Dividends from Net Investment Income ($)	.91	—	.45	—	—	—
Distributions from Net Realized Capital Gains ($)	2.76	7.53	2.31	—	5.67	3.64
Net Asset Value End of Year ($)	59.31	39.45	35.04	39.71	47.20	35.87
Ratio of Expenses to Net Assets (%)	1.41	1.05	1.00	.92	.92	.95
Ratio of Net Income to Average Net Assets (%)	(.54)	1.11	(.28)	(.06)	(.25)	.24
Portfolio Turnover Rate (%)	83	100	103	88	92	68
Total Assets End of Year (Millions $)	41.2	37.1	31.6	30.8	35.1	27.0

Annual Rate of Return (%) Years Ending 12/31	17.9	(25.1)	21.7	0.0	(7.2)	24.6

Five-Year Total Return(%)	5.5ᴱ	Degree of Diversification	D	Beta 1.16	Bull (%) 60.5ᴰ	Bear (%) (31.6)ᴱ

Objective: Fund is intended for that portion of an investor's funds that can be appropriately invested in special risks of various kinds; the basic aim is growth of principal. Invests in securities of small companies from different sectors of the economy. May invest up to 25% of assets in foreign securities.

Portfolio: (9/30/88) Common stocks 83%, repurchase agreements 22%. Largest stock holdings: technology 16%, health care 14%.

Portfolio Mgr: Ronald Mischner—1984

Distributions: Income: Dec   **Capital Gains:** Dec

12b-1: No

Minimum: Initial: $3,000   Subsequent: $100

Min IRA: Initial: $500   Subsequent: $100

Services: IRA, Keogh, Corp, SEP, 403(b), Withdraw, Deduct

Tel Exchange: No

Registered: All states

Ticker: NAESX

NATIONAL INDUSTRIES FUND
Growth

Stonebridge Capital Mgmt., Inc.
5990 Greenwood Plaza Blvd.
Englewood, CO 80111
(303) 220-8500

	Years Ending 11/30					
	1983	1984	1985	1986	1987	1988
Dividends from Net Investment Income ($)	.61	.39	.34	.25	.13	.10
Distributions from Net Realized Capital Gains ($)	.43	1.17	.18	.50	1.32	1.15
Net Asset Value End of Year ($)	13.96	11.59	12.31	13.08	11.04	11.70
Ratio of Expenses to Net Assets (%)	1.67	1.70	1.70	1.68	1.65	1.70
Ratio of Net Income to Average Net Assets (%)	2.78	2.83	2.01	.89	.64	1.04
Portfolio Turnover Rate (%)	50	57	70	74	68	32
Total Assets End of Year (Millions $)	31.2	27.8	27.9	28.0	24.3	26.8

Annual Rate of Return (%) Years Ending 12/31	11.3	(2.3)	10.5	9.8	2.6	12.6

Five-Year Total Return(%)	37.0[E]	Degree of Diversification	B	Beta	.92	Bull (%)	70.9[D]	Bear (%) (22.0)[D]

Objective: Seeks long-term capital appreciation and growth in income. Current income is a secondary consideration. Invests in companies that appear to have good prospects for increased earnings and dividends.

Portfolio: (11/30/88) Common stocks 88%, cash 5%, U.S. government obligations 4%, short-term securities 3%. Largest stock holdings: pharmaceuticals 15%, food and beverages 10%.

Portfolio Mgr: Richard Barrett—1984

Distributions: Income: Dec   **Capital Gains:** Dec

12b-1: No

Minimum: Initial: $250   Subsequent: $25

Min IRA: Initial: NA   Subsequent: NA

Services: Withdraw

Tel Exchange: No

Registered: All states

Ticker: NAIDX

NEUBERGER & BERMAN LIMITED MATURITY BOND

Bond

Neuberger & Berman Mgmt.
342 Madison Avenue
New York, NY 10173
(800) 877-9700/(212) 850-8300

	Years Ending 2/28					
	1983	1984	1985	1986	1987 (9 mos.)	1988
Dividends from Net Investment Income ($)	—	—	—	—	.48	.69
Distributions from Net Realized Capital Gains ($)	—	—	—	—	—	—
Net Asset Value End of Year ($)	—	—	—	—	10.17	10.00
Ratio of Expenses to Net Assets (%)	—	—	—	—	.50	.50
Ratio of Net Income to Average Net Assets (%)	—	—	—	—	7.21	7.47
Portfolio Turnover Rate (%)	—	—	—	—	41	158
Total Assets End of Year (Millions $)	—	—	—	—	69.6	107.3
Annual Rate of Return (%) Years Ending 12/31	—	—	—	—	3.6	6.7

Five-Year Total Return(%)	NA	Degree of Diversification	NA	Beta	NA	Bull (%)	NA	Bear (%)	2.3ᴬ

Objective: Seeks the highest current income consistent with low risk to principal and liquidity. As a secondary objective the fund seeks capital appreciation. Invests in a diversified portfolio of limited maturity debt securities. These are short- to intermediate-term debt securities with actual remaining maturities of five and a half years or less.

Portfolio: (8/31/88) U.S. Treasury obligations 42%, corporate commercial paper 26%, time deposits 14%, mortgage-backed securities 12%, corporate debt securities 4%, banks and financial institutions 2%.

Portfolio Mgr: Theresa Havell—1986

Distributions: **Income:** Monthly   **Capital Gains:** Annually

12b-1: Yes   **Amount:** 0.15%

Minimum: **Initial:** $10,000   **Subsequent:** $200

Min IRA: **Initial:** $10,000   **Subsequent:** $200

Services: IRA Rollover Account, Keogh, Withdraw, Deduct

Tel Exchange: Yes   **With MMF:** Yes

Registered: All states except NH

Ticker: NLMBX

NEUBERGER & BERMAN MONEY MARKET PLUS
Bond

Neuberger & Berman Mgmt.
342 Madison Ave.
New York, NY 10173
(800) 877-9700/(212) 850-8300

| | Years Ending 2/28 | | | | | |
	1983	1984	1985	1986	1987 (4 mos.)	1988
Dividends from Net Investment Income ($)	–	–	–	–	.18	.66
Distributions from Net Realized Capital Gains ($)	–	–	–	–	–	–
Net Asset Value End of Year ($)	–	–	–	–	9.98	9.93
Ratio of Expenses to Net Assets (%)	–	–	–	–	.50	.50
Ratio of Net Income to Average Net Assets (%)	–	–	–	–	6.53	7.22
Portfolio Turnover Rate (%)	–	–	–	–	39	121
Total Assets End of Year (Millions $)	–	–	–	–	66.8	125.3

Annual Rate of Return (%) Years Ending 12/31	–	–	–	–	5.5	6.8

Five-Year Total Return(%)	NA	Degree of Diversification	NA	Beta	NA	Bull (%)	NA	Bear (%)	2.2^A

Objective: Seeks a higher total return than a conventional money market fund, while providing liquidity and a minimal risk to principal. The fund's average maturity can be expected to vary from 30 days to one year. Invests in short-term U.S. government securities and commerical paper.

Portfolio: (8/31/88) Corporate commerical paper 24%, certificates of deposit 20%, bankers' acceptances 18%, U.S. Treasury obligations 15%, U.S. government agency securities 8%, mortgage-backed securities 8%, corporate debt securities 3%, banks and financial institutions 3%.

Portfolio Mgr: Theresa Havell—1986

Distributions: **Income:** Monthly **Capital Gains:** Annually

12b-1: No

Minimum: **Initial:** $5,000 **Subsequent:** $200

Min IRA: **Initial:** $250 **Subsequent:** $200

Services: IRA, Keogh, Withdraw, Deduct

Tel Exchange: Yes **With MMF:** Yes

Registered: All states

Ticker: NBMMX

NEUBERGER & BERMAN PARTNERS FUND
(formerly PARTNERS)

Growth & Income

Neuberger and Berman Mgmt.
342 Madison Ave.
New York, NY 10173
(800) 877-9700/(212) 850-8300

	Years Ending 6/30					
	1983	**1984**	**1985**	**1986**	**1987**	**1988**
Dividends from Net Investment Income ($)	1.11	.84	.72	.65	.44	.70
Distributions from Net Realized Capital Gains ($)	—	1.96	.27	1.27	2.25	2.79
Net Asset Value End of Year ($)	17.21	14.13	17.42	20.63	20.83	16.84
Ratio of Expenses to Net Assets (%)	.97	.91	.93	.89	.86	.95
Ratio of Net Income to Average Net Assets (%)	6.29	5.44	4.80	3.23	2.93	3.28
Portfolio Turnover Rate (%)	232	227	146	181	169	210
Total Assets End of Year (Millions $)	139.3	146.3	221.9	433.3	757.8	718.7

Annual Rate of Return (%) Years Ending 12/31	19.1	8.2	29.8	17.3	4.2	15.5

Five-Year Total Return(%)	98.1[A]	Degree of Diversification	A	Beta	.77	Bull (%)	122.3[B]	Bear (%)	(19.5)[D]

Objective: Seeks capital growth by investing primarily in securities of large, established, dividend-paying companies that are believed to offer appreciation potential. Seeks short-term gains. May invest in investment-grade debt securities, re-purchase agreements and foreign securities. May also write covered call options.

Portfolio: (9/30/88) Common stocks 66%, U.S. government obligations 28%, corporate short-term notes 4%, corporate debt 1%. Largest stock holdings: oil and gas 17%, consumer goods and services 8%.

Portfolio Mgr: Robert C. Vitale—1988; Dietrich Weismann—1984

Distributions: Income: Aug   **Capital Gains:** Aug

12b-1: No

Minimum: Initial: $1,000   Subsequent: $100

Min IRA: Initial: $250   Subsequent: $50

Services: IRA, Keogh, Withdraw, Deduct

Tel Exchange: Yes   **With MMF:** Yes

Registered: All states except NH

Ticker: PARTX

NEUBERGER & BERMAN SELECTED SECTORS PLUS ENERGY
(formerly ENERGY)

Growth & Income

Neuberger & Berman Mgmt.
342 Madison Ave.
New York, NY 10173
(800) 877-9700/(212) 850-8300

	Years Ending 9/30					
	1983	1984	1985	1986	1987	1988
Dividends from Net Investment Income ($)	1.01	.86	.92	.88	.49	.47
Distributions from Net Realized Capital Gains ($)	.79	.66	.93	1.66	3.31	.51
Net Asset Value End of Year ($)	18.04	17.47	17.46	17.96	20.10	16.60
Ratio of Expenses to Net Assets (%)	.83	.88	.89	.88	.86	1.01
Ratio of Net Income to Average Net Assets (%)	5.32	4.70	4.60	4.08	2.21	2.64
Portfolio Turnover Rate (%)	32	22	18	28	88	66
Total Assets End of Year (Millions $)	334.6	337.9	333.9	376.5	481.2	375.2

Annual Rate of Return (%) Years Ending 12/31	22.1	4.8	22.6	10.1	0.6	16.5

Five-Year Total Return(%)	65.8c	Degree of Diversification	C	Beta	.83	Bull (%)	97.2c	Bear (%)	(23.8)D

Objective:	Seeks long-term capital growth. Will select 90% or more of its investments from 13 economic sectors, including the energy sector, each consisting of several industries. Invests at least 25% of its assets in the energy sector.
Portfolio:	(9/30/88)* Common stocks 91%, short-term corporate notes 9%. Largest stock holdings: oil 25%, general growth 17%.
Portfolio Mgr:	Bernard Stein—1955; Lawrence Marx III—1988
Distributions:	**Income:** Sept **Capital Gains:** Sept
12b-1:	No
Minimum:	**Initial:** $1,000 **Subsequent:** $100
Min IRA:	**Initial:** $250 **Subsequent:** $50
Services:	IRA, Keogh, Withdraw, Deduct
Tel Exchange:	Yes **With MMF:** Yes
Registered:	All states except NH
Ticker:	ENEGX

The portfolio composition will change due to the new objective stated here.

NEUWIRTH
Aggressive Growth

Wood, Struthers & Winthrop
Mgmt. Corp.
140 Broadway
New York, NY 10005
(800) 225-8011/(816) 283-1700

	Years Ending 12/31					
	1983	1984	1985	1986	1987	1988
Dividends from Net Investment Income ($)	.16	—	.08	.04	—	.01
Distributions from Net Realized Capital Gains ($)	—	.37	—	3.21	.54	2.28
Net Asset Value End of Year ($)	12.56	10.98	15.21	13.35	11.52	12.64
Ratio of Expenses to Net Assets (%)	1.58	1.64	1.55	1.78	1.69	1.93
Ratio of Net Income to Average Net Assets (%)	(.26)	.66	.38	(.45)	(.49)	.13
Portfolio Turnover Rate (%)	81	83	86	74	117	108
Total Assets End of Year (Millions $)	23.0	18.2	23.9	23.3	21.1	21.8
Annual Rate of Return (%) Years Ending 12/31	15	(8.0)	39.1	8.7	(10.7)	29.6

Five-Year Total Return(%)	60.9[D]	Degree of Diversification	D	Beta	1.09	Bull (%)	110.8[B]	Bear (%)	(29.4)[E]

Objective: Seeks capital growth through investment in securities of established companies in growth industries. May invest in lesser-known emerging growth companies, and up to 20% of total assets may be invested in foreign securities. May write put and call options.

Portfolio: (12/30/88) Common stocks 82%, short-term obligations 14%, U.S. government obligations 5%. Largest stock holdings: technology 21%, consumer cyclicals 19%.

Portfolio Mgr: Leighton McIlvaine Jr.—1980

Distributions: Income: Dec   **Capital Gains:** Dec

12b-1: No

Minimum: Initial: $1,000   Subsequent: $100

Min IRA: Initial: $250   Subsequent: $100

Services: IRA, Keogh, Withdraw, Deduct

Tel Exchange: No

Registered: All states except AR, AZ, CA

Ticker: NEUFX

NEW BEGINNING GROWTH

Aggressive Growth

Sit Investment Associates, Inc.
1714 First Bank Place West
Minneapolis, MN 55402
(800) 332-5580/(612) 332-3223

	Years Ending 6/30					
	1983	1984	1985	1986	1987	1988
Dividends from Net Investment Income ($)	.08	.17	.23	—	.05	.03
Distributions from Net Realized Capital Gains ($)	1.01	.39	.76	—	3.82	2.95
Net Asset Value End of Year ($)	23.01	18.88	22.97	32.76	33.52	27.91
Ratio of Expenses to Net Assets (%)	1.50	1.50	1.50	1.32	1.20	1.21
Ratio of Net Income to Average Net Assets (%)	.85	1.18	2.65	.19	.09	.57
Portfolio Turnover Rate (%)	67	80	130	99	81	78
Total Assets End of Year (Millions $)	9.4	13.3	19.6	40.8	56.1	48.1
Annual Rate of Return (%) Years Ending 12/31	27.0	(3.1)	43.6	10.4	5.5	9.8

Five-Year Total Return(%)	78.1[B]	Degree of Diversification	C	Beta	1.10	Bull (%)	132.9[A]	Bear (%)	(24.6)[D]

Objective: Seeks to maximize long-term capital appreciation. Invests primarily in the common stock of small emerging-growth companies. For defensive purposes, can invest 100% of assets in corporate or government fixed-income securities.

Portfolio: (9/30/88) Common stocks 89%, short-term securities 8%, convertible bonds 2%, other assets 1%. Largest stock holdings: financial 19%, capital goods/construction 18%.

Portfolio Mgr: Douglas Jones—1981

Distributions: **Income:** Annually   **Capital Gains:** Annually

12b-1: No

Minimum: **Initial:** $2,000   **Subsequent:** $100

Min IRA: **Initial:** None   **Subsequent:** None

Services: IRA, Keogh, Corp, SEP, Withdraw, Deduct

Tel Exchange: Yes   **With MMF:** No

Registered: CA, CO, CT, DC, DE, FL, GA, IA, IL, IN, KS, MA, MD, MI, MN, MO, MS, NJ, NY, OH, PA, TX, VA, WA, WI, WY

Ticker: NBNGX

NEWTON GROWTH
Growth

M&I Investment Mgmt. Corp.
330 E. Kilbourn Ave.
Two Plaza East, #1150
Milwaukee, WI 53202
(800) 247-7039/(414) 347-1141

	Years Ending 12/31					
	1983	**1984**	**1985**	**1986**	**1987**	**1988**
Dividends from Net Investment Income ($)	.19	.52	—	1.06	.27	.40
Distributions from Net Realized Capital Gains ($)	1.89	—	—	11.73	1.30	—
Net Asset Value End of Year ($)	27.06	24.35	31.29	20.74	18.42	20.37
Ratio of Expenses to Net Assets (%)	1.16	1.17	1.18	1.23	1.20	1.27
Ratio of Net Income to Average Net Assets (%)	.70	2.19	2.22	1.51	.96	2.00
Portfolio Turnover Rate (%)	55	44	143	136	96	51
Total Assets End of Year (Millions $)	31.5	30.0	33.9	33.9	31.9	32.0
Annual Rate of Return (%) Years Ending 12/31	23.5	(8.2)	28.7	9.1	(3.6)	12.8

Five-Year Total Return(%)	40.0ᴱ	Degree of Diversification	C	Beta	1.07	Bull (%)	105.7ᴮ	Bear (%)	(31.2)ᴱ

Objective: Long-term growth of capital through investment primarily in common stocks of large, established, dividend-paying companies. Current income is of lesser importance.

Portfolio: (12/31/88) Common stocks 82%, short-term securities 20%. Largest stock holdings: capital goods 24%, consumer goods and services 22%.

Portfolio Mgr: James Heubner—1988

Distributions: Income: Dec   **Capital Gains:** Dec

12b-1: Yes   **Amount:** 0.25%

Minimum: Initial: $1,000   Subsequent: $50

Min IRA: Initial: $500   Subsequent: $50

Services: IRA, Keogh, Corp, SEP, 403(b), Withdraw, Deduct

Tel Exchange: Yes   **With MMF:** Yes

Registered: All states except DC, DE, KY, NE, OK, SC, SD, VT

Ticker: NEWTX

NEWTON INCOME
Bond

M&I Investment Mgmt. Corp.
330 E. Kilbourn Ave.
Two Plaza East, #1150
Milwaukee, WI 53202
(800) 247-7039/(414) 347-1141

	Years Ending 7/31					
	1983	**1984**	**1985**	**1986**	**1987**	**1988**
Dividends from Net Investment Income ($)	.87	.82	.77	.60	.66	.64
Distributions from Net Realized Capital Gains ($)	—	—	—	—	—	—
Net Asset Value End of Year ($)	7.89	7.92	8.22	8.54	8.19	8.00
Ratio of Expenses to Net Assets (%)	1.49	1.66	1.60	1.51	1.46	1.44
Ratio of Net Income to Average Net Assets (%)	10.73	10.42	9.78	8.88	7.48	7.29
Portfolio Turnover Rate (%)	41	0	480	56	15	48
Total Assets End of Year (Millions $)	6.3	7.1	11.7	11.5	13.9	16.1
Annual Rate of Return (%) Years Ending 12/31	11.6	12.2	12.8	9.0	2.5	6.4

Five-Year Total Return(%)	50.5ᴰ	Degree of Diversification	NA	Beta	NA	Bull (%)	31.4ᴱ	Bear (%)	2.1ᴬ

Objective:	Seeks above-average income through investment in investment-grade bonds (rated Baa, BBB or better) of varying maturity as fits current economic conditions. May invest in income-producing common stocks.
Portfolio:	(7/31/88) U.S. government securities 36%, corporate bonds 33%, short-term securities 14%, federal agency securities 12%, other assets 4%.
Portfolio Mgr:	David Schulz—1985
Distributions:	Income: Mar, June, Sept, Dec **Capital Gains:** Dec
12b-1:	Yes **Amount:** 0.25%
Minimum:	Initial: $1,000 **Subsequent:** $50
Min IRA:	Initial: $500 **Subsequent:** $50
Services:	IRA, Keogh, Corp, SEP, 403(b), Withdraw, Deduct
Tel Exchange:	Yes **With MMF:** Yes
Registered:	All states except DE, ID, KY, ME, MS, MT, NE, OK, SC, SD, VT
Ticker:	NWTNX

NICHOLAS
Growth

Nicholas Company, Inc.
700 N. Water St., #1010
Milwaukee, WI 53202
(800) 227-5987/(414) 272-6133

	Years Ending 3/31					
	1983	1984	1985	1986	1987	1988
Dividends from Net Investment Income ($)	.62	.64	.64	.57	.88	1.84
Distributions from Net Realized Capital Gains ($)	1.01	1.07	1.58	.61	.19	4.03
Net Asset Value End of Year ($)	25.08	24.47	29.24	35.26	39.94	32.15
Ratio of Expenses to Net Assets (%)	.95	.87	.82	.86	.86	.86
Ratio of Net Income to Average Net Assets (%)	4.05	2.69	3.24	4.11	3.13	3.04
Portfolio Turnover Rate (%)	31	22	14	14	27	32
Total Assets End of Year (Millions $)	126.1	153.4	309.0	955.5	1,298.9	1,117.7

Annual Rate of Return (%) Years Ending 12/31	23.9	9.9	29.7	11.7	(1.3)	18.0

Five-Year Total Return(%)	85.5ᴮ	Degree of Diversification	B	Beta	.67	Bull (%)	101.5ᶜ	Bear (%)	(19.1)ᴰ

Objective: Seeks capital appreciation through investment primarily in common stocks with favorable long-term prospects. Investment in unseasoned companies is limited to 5%.

Portfolio: (9/30/88) Common stocks 88%, short-term securities 9%, convertible bonds 2%, convertible preferred stocks 1%. Largest stock holdings: insurance 16%, banks, savings and loans 15%.

Portfolio Mgr: Albert Nicholas—1969

Distributions: **Income:** Annually   **Capital Gains:** Annually

12b-1: No

Minimum: **Initial:** $500   **Subsequent:** $100

Min IRA: **Initial:** $500   **Subsequent:** $100

Services: IRA, Keogh, Corp, SEP, Withdraw, Deduct

Tel Exchange: Yes   **With MMF:** Yes

Registered: All states

Ticker: NICSX

NICHOLAS II
Growth

Nicholas Company, Inc.
700 N. Water St., #1010
Milwaukee, WI 53202
(800) 227-5987/(414) 272-6133

	1983	1984	1985	1986	1987	1988
Dividends from Net Investment Income ($)	—	—	.09	.16	.42	.34
Distributions from Net Realized Capital Gains ($)	—	—	.19	.06	.51	1.30
Net Asset Value End of Year ($)	—	11.66	14.39	16.90	21.01	18.58
Ratio of Expenses to Net Assets (%)	—	1.85	1.11	.79	.74	.77
Ratio of Net Income to Average Net Assets (%)	—	1.98	3.29	2.70	1.37	1.97
Portfolio Turnover Rate (%)	—	29	10	15	26	18
Total Assets End of Year (Millions $)	—	11.4	140.1	299.2	432.3	380.3
Annual Rate of Return (%) Years Ending 12/31	—	16.9	33.8	10.3	7.2	17.3

Years Ending 9/30

Five-Year Total Return(%) 116.9ᴬ	Degree of Diversification C	Beta .81	Bull (%) 124.2ᴮ	Bear (%) (19.1)ᴰ

Objective:	Primary objective is long-term growth; current income is a secondary consideration. Invests primarily in common stocks that are believed to have favorable long-term growth prospects. May invest 5% of the fund's assets in unseasoned companies that have an operating history of less than three years.
Portfolio:	(9/30/88) Common stocks 95%, short-term securities 4%, Largest stock holdings: banks, savings and loans 13%, consumer products 13%.
Portfolio Mgr:	Albert Nicholas—1983
Distributions:	**Income:** Annually **Capital Gains:** Annually
12b-1:	No
Minimum:	**Initial:** $1,000 **Subsequent:** $100
Min IRA:	**Initial:** $1,000 **Subsequent:** $100
Services:	IRA, Keogh, Corp, SEP, Withdraw, Deduct
Tel Exchange:	Yes **With MMF:** Yes
Registered:	All states
Ticker:	NCTWX

NICHOLAS INCOME
Bond

Nicholas Company, Inc.
700 N. Water St., #1010
Milwaukee, WI 53202
(800) 227-5987/(414) 272-6133

	Years Ending 12/31					
	1983	1984	1985	1986	1987	1988
Dividends from Net Investment Income ($)	.44	.44	.42	.38	.47	.37
Distributions from Net Realized Capital Gains ($)	—	—	—	—	—	—
Net Asset Value End of Year ($)	3.67	3.65	3.96	4.01	3.64	3.68
Ratio of Expenses to Net Assets (%)	1.00	1.00	1.00	.96	.86	.83
Ratio of Net Income to Average Net Assets (%)	12.09	12.82	12.57	10.22	9.79	10.03
Portfolio Turnover Rate (%)	19	14	12	20	48	12
Total Assets End of Year (Millions $)	14.6	16.9	34.8	65.0	69.7	78.1

Annual Rate of Return (%) Years Ending 12/31	12.4	12.6	21.2	11.4	2.6	11.5

Five-Year Total Return(%)	74.0D	Degree of Diversification	NA	Beta	NA	Bull (%)	53.7D	Bear (%)	0.2B

Objective: Seeks high level of current income and consistent conservation of capital. Must invest at least 25% of total assets in geographically diversified and state-regulated electric utilities and systems. Balance is invested in investment-grade debt securities. May include repurchase agreements and other cash investments.

Portfolio: (12/31/88) Non-convertible bonds 88%, convertible bonds 5%, common stocks 3%, cash 2%, short-term securities 1%, preferred stocks 1%.

Portfolio Mgr: Albert Nicholas—1977

Distributions: Income: April, July, Oct, Dec   **Capital Gains:** Dec

12b-1: No

Minimum: Initial: $500   Subsequent: $50

Min IRA: Initial: $500   Subsequent: $50

Services: IRA, Keogh, Corp, SEP, Withdraw, Deduct

Tel Exchange: No

Registered: All states

Ticker: NCINX

NICHOLAS LIMITED EDITION
Growth

Nicholas Company, Inc.
700 N. Water St., #1010
Milwaukee, WI 53202
(800) 227-5987/(414) 272-6133

	Years Ending 12/31					
	1983	1984	1985	1986	1987 (7 mos.)	1988
Dividends from Net Investment Income ($)	—	—	—	—	.09	.10
Distributions from Net Realized Capital Gains ($)	—	—	—	—	—	.25
Net Asset Value End of Year ($)	—	—	—	—	9.15	11.29
Ratio of Expenses to Net Assets (%)	—	—	—	—	1.48	1.32
Ratio of Net Income to Average Net Assets (%)	—	—	—	—	2.21	1.03
Portfolio Turnover Rate (%)	—	—	—	—	0	31
Total Assets End of Year (Millions $)	—	—	—	—	19.3	33.0

Annual Rate of Return (%) Years Ending 12/31	—	—	—	—	—	27.3

Five-Year Total Return(%)	NA	Degree of Diversification	NA	Beta	NA	Bull (%)	NA	Bear (%)	(13.8)c

Objective: Seeks long-term capital appreciation through investment in common stocks. Income is a secondary consideration. Invests in small- to medium-sized companies that the advisor feels will have superior growth in sales and earnings. May also invest in debt securities and preferred stock.

Portfolio: (12/31/88) Common stocks 88%, short-term securities 12%. Largest stock holdings: industrial products and services 14%, insurance 13%.

Portfolio Mgr: Albert Nicholas—1987

Distributions: **Income:** Annually   **Capital Gains:** Annually

12b-1: No

Minimum: **Initial:** $2,000   **Subsequent:** $100

Min IRA: **Initial:** $2,000   **Subsequent:** $100

Services: IRA, Keogh, Corp, SEP, Withdraw, Deduct

Tel Exchange: No

Registered: All states

Ticker: NCLEX

NODDINGS CONVERTIBLE STRATEGIES
Growth & Income

Noddings Investment Group, Inc.
Two Mid America Plaza
Suite 920
Oakbrook Terrace, IL 60181
(800) 544-7785/(312) 954-1322

	Years Ending 4/30					10/31	
	1983	1984	1985	1986 (10 mos.)	1987	1987* (6 mos.)	1988
Dividends from Net Investment Income ($)	—	—	—	.15	.42	.20	.65
Distributions from Net Realized Capital Gains ($)	—	—	—	—	.60	.21	1.78
Net Asset Value End of Year ($)	—	—	—	11.77	11.53	10.60	8.53
Ratio of Expenses to Net Assets (%)	—	—	—	2.00	1.70	1.70	2.00
Ratio of Net Income to Average Net Assets (%)	—	—	—	5.40	4.60	5.10	6.40
Portfolio Turnover Rate (%)	—	—	—	37	62	40	54
Total Assets: End of Year (Millions $)	—	—	—	5.4	12.7	8.7	7.3

Annual Rate of Return (%) Years Ending 12/31	—	—	—	15.6	(2.7)	*	5.8

Five-Year Total Return(%)	NA	Degree of Diversification	E	Beta	.52	Bull (%)	NA	Bear (%)	(9.1)c

Fiscal year-end changed from 4/30 to 10/31. All annual return figures are for full years ending 12/31.

Objective:	Seeks long-term capital appreciation through investment in a diversified portfolio of convertible securities. At least 65% of the fund's assets will usually be invested in convertibles, some of which are rated BB or lower by S&P. May also sell stocks short against their convertible positions.
Portfolio:	(10/31/88) Convertible bonds 94%, other assets 11%, warrants 1%, index put options 1%, preferred stocks 1%, short position −8%. Largest holdings: electronics 9%, retail/special lines 7%.
Portfolio Mgr:	Carol Sachs, Thomas C. Noddings—1985
Distributions:	**Income:** Quarterly **Capital Gains:** Annually
12b-1:	No
Minimum:	**Initial:** $2,000 **Subsequent:** $100
Min IRA:	**Initial:** $2,000 **Subsequent:** $100
Services:	IRA, SEP, Withdraw, Deduct
Tel Exchange:	No
Registered:	Call for availability
Ticker:	NDCGX

NOMURA PACIFIC BASIN
International

Nomura Capital Mgmt., Inc.
180 Maiden Lane
New York, NY 10038
(800) 833-0018/(212) 208-9366

| | Years Ending 3/31 | | | | | |
	1983	1984	1985	1986 (9 mos.)	1987	1988
Dividends from Net Investment Income ($)	–	–	–	–	–	.08
Distributions from Net Realized Capital Gains ($)	–	–	–	–	.36	10.46
Net Asset Value End of Year ($)	–	–	–	15.68	24.20	20.59
Ratio of Expenses to Net Assets (%)	–	–	–	1.50	1.45	1.22
Ratio of Net Income to Average Net Assets (%)	–	–	–	.88	.14	.28
Portfolio Turnover Rate (%)	–	–	–	3	46	61
Total Assets End of Year (Millions $)	–	–	–	32.4	81.8	94.8
Annual Rate of Return (%) Years Ending 12/31	–	–	–	74.5	33.8	16.4

Five-Year Total Return(%)	NA	Degree of Diversification	E	Beta	.46	Bull (%)	NA	Bear (%)	(9.6)c

Objective: Seeks long-term capital appreciation by investing 70% of the fund's assets in equity securities of corporations located in the Pacific Basin, including Japan, Australia and the Philippines. Companies will range from large and well-established to small and unseasoned.

Portfolio: (9/30/88) Common stocks 95%, short-term securities 5%. Largest country holdings: Japan 79%, Australia 7%.

Portfolio Mgr: Takeo Nakamura—1985

Distributions: **Income:** Semiannually   **Capital Gains:** Annually

12b-1: Yes   **Amount:** Pd. by Advisor

Minimum: **Initial:** $10,000   **Subsequent:** $5,000

Min IRA: **Initial:** $10,000   **Subsequent:** $5,000

Services: IRA

Tel Exchange: No

Registered: AK, AL, AZ, CA, CO, CT, DE, FL, GA, HI, ID, IL, IN, KS, MA, MD, MI, MN, MO, MS, NE, NJ, NV, NY, OH, OR, PA, TN, TX, UT, VA, WA, WI, WV, WY

Ticker: NPBFX

NORTHEAST INVESTORS GROWTH

Growth

Northeast Management &
Research Co., Inc.
50 Congress Street
Boston, MA 02109
(800) 225-6704/(617) 523-3588

	Years Ending 12/31					
	1983	**1984**	**1985**	**1986**	**1987**	**1988**
Dividends from Net Investment Income ($)	.21	.12	.05	.13	.12	.27
Distributions from Net Realized Capital Gains ($)	.15	.30	.09	.52	.62	.47
Net Asset Value End of Year ($)	11.36	11.36	15.24	18.23	16.84	18.28
Ratio of Expenses to Net Assets (%)	2.01	2.02	2.00	1.87	1.60	1.74
Ratio of Net Income to Average Net Assets (%)	.89	1.25	.92	.53	.60	1.25
Portfolio Turnover Rate (%)	63	34	37	13	36	16
Total Assets End of Year (Millions $)	4.0	4.1	6.4	20.5	20.8	19.2

Annual Rate of Return (%) Years Ending 12/31	9.6	3.9	36.7	24.3	(4.3)	12.8

Five-Year Total Return(%) 90.6[A]	Degree of Diversification B	Beta .96	Bull (%) 149.7[A]	Bear (%) (27.2)[E]

Objective: Seeks long-term growth of both capital and future income. Invests in stocks, bonds and short-term money market instruments. Ordinarily no more than 25% of the fund's assets will be invested in fixed-income securities.

Portfolio: (12/31/88) Common stocks 94%, repurchase agreements 4%. Largest stock holdings: food and beverages 21%, drug companies and health 20%.

Portfolio Mgr: William Oates Jr.—1980

Distributions: **Income:** Annually   **Capital Gains:** Annually

12b-1: No

Minimum: **Initial:** $1,000   **Subsequent:** None

Min IRA: **Initial:** $500   **Subsequent:** None

Services: IRA, Keogh, 403(b)

Tel Exchange: Yes   **With MMF:** No

Registered: All states except AL, IA

Ticker: NTHFX

NORTHEAST INVESTORS TRUST
Bond

Trustees, Northeast
Investors Trust
50 Congress St.
Boston, MA 02109
(800) 225-6704/(617) 523-3588

	Years Ending 9/30					
	1983	1984	1985	1986	1987	1988
Dividends from Net Investment Income ($)	1.44	1.46	1.46	1.46	1.46	1.94
Distributions from Net Realized Capital Gains ($)	–	–	–	–	–	–
Net Asset Value End of Year ($)	11.83	10.98	12.19	13.60	12.89	12.16
Ratio of Expenses to Net Assets (%)	.67	.67	.72	.72	.76	.75
Ratio of Net Income to Average Net Assets (%)	12.42	12.92	12.70	11.53	11.59	13.16
Portfolio Turnover Rate (%)	30	14	22	43	52	17
Total Assets End of Year (Millions $)	169.4	168.2	218.1	313.3	347.9	404.5

Annual Rate of Return (%) Years Ending 12/31	11.2	13.9	25.6	20.4	0.1	14.1

Five-Year Total Return(%)	96.6^	Degree of Diversification	NA	Beta NA	Bull (%)	80.7^C	Bear (%)	(5.1)^C

Objective:	Seeks production of income, with capital growth as a secondary objective. Between 25% and 50% of the trust's assets will be invested in the electric utility industry. Common stock investments will be in established, dividend-paying companies. May use leverage.
Portfolio:	(9/30/88) Corporate bonds 103%. Largest bond holdings: retail 17%, banks and finance 16%.
Portfolio Mgr:	Ernest Monrad—1969
Distributions:	**Income:** Feb, May, Aug, Nov **Capital Gains:** Sept
12b-1:	No
Minimum:	**Initial:** $1,000 **Subsequent:** None
Min IRA:	**Initial:** $500 **Subsequent:** None
Services:	IRA, Keogh, 403(b)
Tel Exchange:	Yes **With MMF:** No
Registered:	All states except AL, IA
Ticker:	NTHEX

100 FUND
Aggressive Growth

Berger Associates, Inc.
899 Logan St., Suite 211
Denver, CO 80203
(800) 333-1001/(303) 837-1020

	Years Ending 9/30					
	1983	**1984**	**1985**	**1986**	**1987**	**1988**
Dividends from Net Investment Income ($)	.13	—	.34	—	—	—
Distributions from Net Realized Capital Gains ($)	—	—	—	—	1.16	4.75
Net Asset Value End of Year ($)	20.49	14.47	15.02	20.15	24.64	18.43
Ratio of Expenses to Net Assets (%)	1.70	1.90	2.00	1.71	1.61	1.72
Ratio of Net Income to Average Net Assets (%)	(.51)	1.95	(.59)	(.47)	(.27)	(.57)
Portfolio Turnover Rate (%)	155	272	130	122	106	166
Total Assets End of Year (Millions $)	14.4	9.6	8.9	10.6	11.7	10.6
Annual Rate of Return (%) Years Ending 12/31	17.0	(20.1)	25.7	20.0	15.7	1.7

Five-Year Total Return(%)	41.8[E]	Degree of Diversification	E	Beta	.86	Bull (%)	88.1[C]	Bear (%)	(10.7)[C]

Objective: Seeks long-term capital appreciation through investment in common stocks of established companies on the basis of fundamental analysis, industry trends and earnings trends in relation to the current market environment.

Portfolio: (9/30/88) Common stocks 93%, other assets 5%, warrants 1%. Largest stock holdings: chemicals 13%, medical instruments 9%.

Portfolio Mgr: William Berger—1966

Distributions: Income: Dec   **Capital Gains:** Annually

12b-1: Yes   **Amount:** 0.30%

Minimum: Initial: $250   Subsequent: $50

Min IRA: Initial: $250   Subsequent: $50

Services: IRA, Keogh, Withdraw

Tel Exchange: Yes   **With MMF:** No

Registered: CA, CO, FL, GA, HI, LA, MA, MD, MI, MN, MS, NJ, NY, TX, WA

Ticker: BEONX

101 FUND
Growth

Berger Associates, Inc.
899 Logan St., Suite 211
Denver, CO 80203
(800) 333-1001/(303) 837-1020

	Years Ending 9/30					
	1983	1984	1985	1986	1987	1988
Dividends from Net Investment Income ($)	.48	.45	.43	.57	.60	.59
Distributions from Net Realized Capital Gains ($)	—	1.00	—	.29	3.00	1.36
Net Asset Value End of Year ($)	14.90	13.28	14.29	17.86	17.22	12.91
Ratio of Expenses to Net Assets (%)	2.00	2.00	2.00	1.96	1.79	2.00
Ratio of Net Income to Average Net Assets (%)	3.75	4.24	2.42	3.65	4.04	3.48
Portfolio Turnover Rate (%)	168	267	166	187	241	159
Total Assets End of Year (Millions $)	1.3	1.4	1.6	2.7	2.8	2.2

Annual Rate of Return (%) Years Ending 12/31	35.2	(0.3)	29.1	15.0	(2.6)	5.3

Five-Year Total Return(%)	51.9[D]	Degree of Diversification	C	Beta	.77	Bull (%)	84.8[C]	Bear (%)	(19.2)[D]

Objective: Seeks capital appreciation and a moderate level of current income through investment in dividend-paying common stocks of large, established companies and senior debt securities.

Portfolio: (9/30/88) Common stocks 70%, convertible debentures 28%, warrants 2%, other assets 1%. Largest stock holdings: drugs 10%, beverages 6%.

Portfolio Mgr: William Berger—1966

Distributions: Income: Quarterly   **Capital Gains:** Annually

12b-1: Yes   **Amount:** 0.30%

Minimum: Initial: $250   **Subsequent:** $50

Min IRA: Initial: $250   **Subsequent:** $50

Services: IRA, Keogh, Withdraw

Tel Exchange: Yes   **With MMF:** No

Registered: CA, CO, FL, HI, LA, MA, MD, MI, MN, MS, NJ, NY, TX, WA

Ticker: BEOOX

PAX WORLD

International

Pax World Management Corp.
224 State St.
Portsmouth, NH 03801
(603) 431-8022

	Years Ending 12/31					
	1983	**1984**	**1985**	**1986**	**1987**	**1988**
Dividends from Net Investment Income ($)	.49	.51	.52	.50	.75	.61
Distributions from Net Realized Capital Gains ($)	.28	.77	.37	.71	1.24	.37
Net Asset Value End of Year ($)	11.97	11.47	13.34	13.19	11.58	11.92
Ratio of Expenses to Net Assets (%)	1.40	1.50	1.40	1.20	1.10	1.10
Ratio of Net Income to Average Net Assets (%)	4.30	6.50	4.30	3.20	4.10	5.00
Portfolio Turnover Rate (%)	29	34	48	57	124	58
Total Assets End of Year (Millions $)	12.2	16.9	32.7	53.8	65.8	73.6
Annual Rate of Return (%) Years Ending 12/31	24.1	7.5	25.5	8.4	2.2	11.6

Five-Year Total Return(%)	66.9c	Degree of Diversification	B	Beta	.60	Bull (%)	86.9c	Bear (%)	(14.9)c

Objective: Primarily seeks income, and secondarily seeks long-term capital growth. Endeavors to contribute to world peace through investment in companies producing life-supportive goods and services. Will not invest in companies engaging in or contributing to military activities or those in the liquor, gambling or tobacco industries.

Portfolio: (12/31/88) Common stocks 60%, government bonds 39%, cash 2%. Largest stock holdings: drugs 17%, natural gas 15%.

Portfolio Mgr: Anthony Brown—1971

Distributions: Income: July, Dec   **Capital Gains:** Dec

12b-1: Yes   **Amount:** 0.25%

Minimum: Initial: $250   Subsequent: $50

Min IRA: Initial: $250   Subsequent: $50

Services: IRA, Keogh, SEP, 403(b), Withdraw

Tel Exchange: No

Registered: All states except ND, NE, NV, SD, UT, WY

Ticker: PAXWX

†PENNSYLVANIA MUTUAL FUND
Growth

Quest Advisory Corp.
1414 Avenue of the Americas
New York, NY 10019
(800) 221-4268/(212) 355-7311

	Years Ending 12/31					
	1983	1984	1985	1986	1987	1988
Dividends from Net Investment Income ($)	.03	.07	.09	.13	.33	.12
Distributions from Net Realized Capital Gains ($)	.60	.55	.16	1.11	1.30	.28
Net Asset Value End of Year ($)	6.55	6.09	7.43	6.98	5.47	6.41
Ratio of Expenses to Net Assets (%)	1.29	1.18	1.03	.98	.99	1.01
Ratio of Net Income to Average Net Assets (%)	1.73	2.44	2.17	1.85	2.02	2.35
Portfolio Turnover Rate (%)	35	15	15	19	23	24
Total Assets End of Year (Millions $)	108.6	226.7	354.3	333.0	276.4	444.5
Annual Rate of Return (%) Years Ending 12/31	40.5	3.1	26.8	11.2	1.4	24.6

Five-Year Total Return(%)	83.6ᴮ	Degree of Diversification	D	Beta	.66	Bull (%)	90.0ᶜ	Bear (%)	(17.3)ᶜ

Objective: Seeks long-term capital growth through investment in small- and medium-sized companies. Invests in common stocks and convertible stocks and bonds, and for defensive purposes may also invest in short-term securities.

Portfolio: (12/31/88) Common stocks 69%, repurchase agreements 21%, U.S. Treasury obligations 7%, other assets 1%, preferred stocks 1%, corporate bonds 1%. Largest stock holdings: business and industrial products 19%, business and industrial services 11%.

Portfolio Mgr: Thomas Ebright—1978; Charles Royce—1973

Distributions: Income: Dec **Capital Gains:** Dec

12b-1: No

Minimum: Initial: $10,000 Subsequent: $50

Min IRA: Initial: $2,000 Subsequent: $50

Services: IRA, 403(b), Withdraw, Deduct

Tel Exchange: No

Registered: AL, AK, AZ, CA, CO, CT, DC, DE, FL, GA, HI, KY, MA, MD, MI, MT, NC, NE, NJ, NM, NV, NY, OK, OR, PA, RI, SC, TN, TX, UT, VA, VT, WA, WV, WY

Ticker: PENNX

† *The fund charges a 1% redemption fee on shares sold within one year of purchase.*

†PERMANENT PORTFOLIO
Growth

World Money Managers
7 Fourth Street, Suite 14
Petaluma, CA 94952
(800) 531-5142/(512) 453-7558

	12/31	Years Ending 1/31				
	1983	1984* (1 mo.)	1985	1986	1987	1988
Dividends from Net Investment Income ($)	—	Nil	—	—	—	—
Distributions from Net Realized Capital Gains ($)	—	Nil	—	—	—	.12
Net Asset Value End of Year ($)	11.88	11.75	10.82	11.88	13.66	14.71
Ratio of Expenses to Net Assets (%)	.92	.92	.90	.90	1.17	1.15
Ratio of Net Income to Average Net Assets (%)	3.31	2.81	3.53	3.00	2.51	2.53
Portfolio Turnover Rate (%)	2	0	11	17	31	22
Total Assets End of Year (Millions $)	69.9	68.9	71.1	73.0	72.5	90.2

Annual Rate of Return (%) Years Ending 12/31	5.5	(12.9)	12.2	13.6	13.1	1.3

Five-Year Total Return(%)	27.2ᴱ	Degree of Diversification	E	Beta	.22	Bull (%)	48.1ᴱ	Bear (%)	(3.5)ᶜ

*Fiscal year-end changed from 12/31 to 1/31.

Objective: Invests a fixed "target percentage" of its net assets in gold, silver, Swiss francs, real estate and natural resource company stocks, and other stocks with the aim of preserving and increasing "purchasing power." Strives for long-term asset appreciation.

Portfolio: (7/31/88) U.S. government securities 35%, common stocks 30%, silver and gold 25%, Swiss franc assets 9%. Largest stock holdings: real estate 9%, natural resources 6%.

Portfolio Mgr: Terry Coxon—1982

Distributions: **Income:** Dec   **Capital Gains:** Dec

12b-1: Yes   **Amount:** 0.25%

Minimum: **Initial:** $1,000   **Subsequent:** $100

Min IRA: **Initial:** $1,000   **Subsequent:** $100

Services: IRA, Withdraw

Tel Exchange: Yes   **With MMF:** Yes

Registered: All states

Ticker: PRPFX

† *The fund has a one-time $35 start-up fee.*

PERMANENT TREASURY BILL PORTFOLIO

Bond

World Money Managers
7 Fourth Street, Suite 14
Petaluma CA 94952
(800) 531-5142/(512) 453-7558

	Years Ending 1/31					
	1983	1984	1985	1986	1987	1988 (8 mos.)
Dividends from Net Investment Income ($)	–	–	–	–	–	–
Distributions from Net Realized Capital Gains ($)	–	–	–	–	–	–
Net Asset Value End of Year ($)	–	–	–	–	–	51.54
Ratio of Expenses to Net Assets (%)	–	–	–	–	–	.50
Ratio of Net Income to Average Net Assets (%)	–	–	–	–	–	5.32
Portfolio Turnover Rate (%)	–	–	–	–	–	0
Total Assets End of Year (Millions $)	–	–	–	–	–	6.5
Annual Rate of Return (%) Years Ending 12/31	–	–	–	–	–	6.4

Five-Year Total Return(%)	NA	Degree of Diversification	NA	Beta	NA	Bull (%)	NA	Bear (%)	NA

Objective:	Invests in short-term U.S. Treasury bills. Seeks to earn high current income consistent with safety of principal. May also invest in U.S. Treasury bonds and notes having a remaining maturity of 13 months or less.
Portfolio:	(7/31/88) U.S. government securities 108%.
Portfolio Mgr:	Terry Coxon—1987
Distributions:	Income: Dec **Capital Gains:** Dec
12b-1:	Yes **Amount:** 0.25%
Minimum:	**Initial:** $1,000 **Subsequent:** $100
Min IRA:	**Initial:** $1,000 **Subsequent:** $100
Services:	IRA, Withdraw
Tel Exchange:	Yes **With MMF:** Yes
Registered:	All states
Ticker:	PRTBX

PINE STREET
Growth & Income

Wood, Struthers & Winthrop
Management Corp.
140 Broadway
New York, NY 10005
(800) 225-8011/(816) 283-1700

	Years Ending 6/30					
	1983	1984	1985	1986	1987	1988
Dividends from Net Investment Income ($)	.56	.47	.56	.55	.37	.42
Distributions from Net Realized Capital Gains ($)	1.33	1.45	1.26	1.96	1.10	.93
Net Asset Value End of Year ($)	14.17	10.97	13.10	14.38	14.58	11.64
Ratio of Expenses to Net Assets (%)	1.15	1.15	1.09	1.17	1.14	1.17
Ratio of Net Income to Average Net Assets (%)	4.36	3.47	4.43	3.93	3.23	3.35
Portfolio Turnover Rate (%)	103	104	65	90	48	38
Total Assets End of Year (Millions $)	45.0	39.3	52.1	65.9	70.8	55.4

Annual Rate of Return (%) Years Ending 12/31	19.1	5.1	30.7	14.3	(5.8)	16.2

Five-Year Total Return(%)	72.0ᶜ	Degree of Diversification	A	Beta	.92	Bull (%)	112.5ᴮ	Bear (%)	(24.8)ᴱ

Objective: Seeks to combine continuity of income with opportunity for growth through investment in common stocks of well-established companies. May invest in debt or equity securities of foreign countries.

Portfolio: (9/30/88) Common stocks 67%, U.S. government obligations 20%, commercial paper 7%, convertible bonds 5%, convertible preferred stocks 1%. Largest stock holdings: business equipment 9%, oil and gas 8%.

Portfolio Mgr: James Engle—1986

Distributions: Income: Apr, July, Oct, Dec   **Capital Gains:** Dec

12b-1: No

Minimum: **Initial:** $1,000   **Subsequent:** $100

Min IRA: **Initial:** $250   **Subsequent:** $100

Services: IRA, Keogh, Withdraw, Deduct

Tel Exchange: No

Registered: All states

Ticker: PINSX

T. ROWE PRICE CAPITAL APPRECIATION

Aggressive Growth

T. Rowe Price Associates
100 East Pratt Street
Baltimore, MD 21202
(800) 638-5660/(301) 547-2308

	Years Ending 12/31					
	1983	1984	1985	1986 (6 mos.)	1987	1988
Dividends from Net Investment Income ($)	−	−	−	−	.48	.28
Distributions from Net Realized Capital Gains ($)	−	−	−	−	1.85	.37
Net Asset Value End of Year ($)	−	−	−	10.85	9.15	10.42
Ratio of Expenses to Net Assets (%)	−	−	−	1.20	1.20	1.50
Ratio of Net Income to Average Net Assets (%)	−	−	−	2.16	3.03	2.76
Portfolio Turnover Rate (%)	−	−	−	375	291	166
Total Assets End of Year (Millions $)	−	−	−	69.0	63.9	101.3

Annual Rate of Return (%) Years Ending 12/31	−	−	−	−	5.9	21.2

Five-Year Total Return(%)	NA	Degree of Diversification	NA	Beta	NA	Bull (%)	NA	Bear (%)	(10.8)c

Objective: Seeks capital appreciation through investment primarily in common stocks. Portfolio consists of two categories: long-term "core" holdings of undervalued growth stocks, and short-term holdings where the stock price is expected to rise over the short term. Can invest up to 35% of the fund's assets in corporate debt.

Portfolio: (12/31/88) Common stocks 70%, short-term securities 23%, preferred stocks 6%, other assets 1%. Largest stock holdings: consumer services 17%, consumer nondurables 14%.

Portfolio Mgr: Richard H. Fontaine−1986; Richard Howard−1989

Distributions: Income: Annually   Capital Gains: Annually

12b-1: No

Minimum: Initial: $1,000   Subsequent: $100

Min IRA: Initial: $500   Subsequent: $50

Services: IRA, Keogh, Corp, SEP, 403(b), Withdraw, Deduct

Tel Exchange: Yes   With MMF: Yes

Registered: All states

Ticker: PRWCX

T. ROWE PRICE EQUITY INCOME

Growth & Income

T. Rowe Price Associates
100 East Pratt Street
Baltimore, MD 21202
(800) 638-5660/(301) 547-2308

	Years Ending 12/31					
	1983	1984	1985 (2 mos.)	1986	1987	1988
Dividends from Net Investment Income ($)	—	—	—	.65	.82	.62
Distributions from Net Realized Capital Gains ($)	—	—	—	.26	1.35	.38
Net Asset Value End of Year ($)	—	—	11.00	12.96	11.29	13.38
Ratio of Expenses to Net Assets (%)	—	—	1.00	1.00	1.10	1.30
Ratio of Net Income to Average Net Assets (%)	—	—	7.62	5.16	4.58	4.83
Portfolio Turnover Rate (%)	—	—	37	73	80	36
Total Assets End of Year (Millions $)	—	—	16.6	94.0	185.0	500.7

Annual Rate of Return (%) Years Ending 12/31	—	—	—	26.6	3.5	27.6

Five-Year Total Return(%)	NA	Degree of Diversification	B	Beta	.67	Bull (%)	NA	Bear (%)	(15.8)[c]

Objective: Seeks high level of income through investment in dividend-paying common stocks of established companies that also have capital appreciation potential. May invest in investment grade (BBB or higher) debt securities without limit. Will invest at least 65% of fund's assets in income-producing common stocks.

Portfolio: (12/31/88) Common stocks 67%, short-term securities 23%, convertible bonds 4%, corporate bonds 2%, convertible preferred stocks 1%, preferred stocks 1%, U.S. government and agency obligations 1%. Largest stock holdings: consumer nondurables 10%, process industries 9%.

Portfolio Mgr: Tom Broadus—1985

Distributions: Income: Quarterly   **Capital Gains:** Annually

12b-1: No

Minimum: Initial: $1,000   **Subsequent:** $100

Min IRA: Initial: $500   **Subsequent:** $50

Services: IRA, Keogh, Corp, SEP, 403(b), Withdraw, Deduct

Tel Exchange: Yes   **With MMF:** Yes

Registered: All states

Ticker: PRFDX

T. ROWE PRICE GNMA

Bond

T. Rowe Price Associates, Inc.
100 E. Pratt St.
Baltimore, MD 21202
(800) 638-5660/(301) 547-2308

	Years Ending 2/28					
	1983	**1984**	**1985**	**1986** (3 mos.)	**1987**	**1988**
Dividends from Net Investment Income ($)	–	–	–	.26	.90	.92
Distributions from Net Realized Capital Gains ($)	–	–	–	–	–	.02
Net Asset Value End of Year ($)	–	–	–	10.12	10.27	9.55
Ratio of Expenses to Net Assets (%)	–	–	–	1.00	1.00	.99
Ratio of Net Income to Average Net Assets (%)	–	–	–	10.06	8.82	9.56
Portfolio Turnover Rate (%)	–	–	–	51	226	193
Total Assets End of Year (Millions $)	–	–	–	123.6	377.5	369.0

Annual Rate of Return (%) Years Ending 12/31	–	–	–	11.0	.8	5.9

Five-Year Total Return(%)	NA	Degree of Diversification	NA	Beta	NA	Bull (%)	NA	Bear (%)	1.5A

Objective:	Seeks high level of current income consistent with preservation of capital. Invests in securities backed by the U.S. government, principally GNMAs.
Portfolio:	(8/31/88) U.S. government guaranteed obligations 90%, U.S. Treasury bonds 8%, U.S. Treasury notes 5%, repurchase agreements 2%.
Portfolio Mgr:	Peter Van Dyke—1988
Distributions:	**Income:** Monthly **Capital Gains:** Annually
12b-1:	No
Minimum:	**Initial:** $2,000 **Subsequent:** $100
Min IRA:	**Initial:** $1,000 **Subsequent:** $50
Services:	IRA, Keogh, Corp, SEP, 403(b), Withdraw, Deduct
Tel Exchange:	Yes **With MMF:** Yes
Registered:	All states
Ticker:	PRGMX

T. ROWE PRICE GROWTH & INCOME

Growth & Income

T. Rowe Price Associates
100 E. Pratt St.
Baltimore, MD 21202
(800) 638-5660/(301) 547-2308

	Years Ending 12/31					
	1983	**1984**	**1985**	**1986**	**1987**	**1988**
Dividends from Net Investment Income ($)	.60	.79	.61	.71	.88	.49
Distributions from Net Realized Capital Gains ($)	—	.06	—	1.57	1.04	.47
Net Asset Value End of Year ($)	13.05	12.44	14.18	12.98	10.63	12.32
Ratio of Expenses to Net Assets (%)	.90	.94	.94	.96	1.03	1.04
Ratio of Net Income to Average Net Assets (%)	5.91	6.63	4.53	5.26	4.80	3.94
Portfolio Turnover Rate (%)	48	52	121	100	114	50
Total Assets End of Year (Millions $)	234.5	309.1	356.8	388.6	365.6	444.6

Annual Rate of Return (%) Years Ending 12/31	32.6	1.9	19.7	7.9	(4.3)	25.1

Five-Year Total Return(%)	57.7D	Degree of Diversification	B	Beta	.87	Bull (%)	86.3C	Bear (%)	(23.2)D

Objective: Seeks long-term growth of capital, a reasonable level of current income, and an increase in future income through investment primarily in income-producing equity securities that have prospects for both capital growth and dividend income.

Portfolio: (12/31/88) Common stocks 85%, convertible bonds 7%, short-term securities 4%, convertible preferred stocks 3%, preferred stocks 1%. Largest stock holdings: financial 19%, consumer cyclicals 13%.

Portfolio Mgr: Stephen Bosel—1987

Distributions: **Income:** Apr, July, Oct, Dec   **Capital Gains:** Dec

12b-1: No

Minimum: **Initial:** $1,000   **Subsequent:** $100

Min IRA: **Initial:** $500   **Subsequent:** $50

Services: IRA, Keogh, Corp, SEP, 403(b), Withdraw, Deduct

Tel Exchange: Yes   **With MMF:** Yes

Registered: All states

Ticker: PRGIX

T. ROWE PRICE GROWTH STOCK
Growth

T. Rowe Price Associates, Inc.
100 E. Pratt St.
Baltimore, MD 21202
(800) 638-5660/(301) 547-2308

	Years Ending 12/31					
	1983	1984	1985	1986	1987	1988
Dividends from Net Investment Income ($)	.50	.36	.34	.38	.63	.32
Distributions from Net Realized Capital Gains ($)	–	.45	.64	4.18	2.66	.26
Net Asset Value End of Year ($)	15.21	14.20	17.95	16.96	14.27	14.55
Ratio of Expenses to Net Assets (%)	.50	.52	.52	.57	.67	.77
Ratio of Net Income to Average Net Assets (%)	2.15	2.53	2.32	1.79	1.71	2.08
Portfolio Turnover Rate (%)	63	60	69	60	51	41
Total Assets End of Year (Millions $)	1,013.0	965.5	1,158.4	1,273.2	1,267.9	1,294.5

Annual Rate of Return (%) Years Ending 12/31	12.3	(0.7)	35.1	21.7	3.3	6.1

Five-Year Total Return(%) 78.8[B]	Degree of Diversification B	Beta .92	Bull (%) 142.5[A]	Bear (%) (22.1)[D]

Objective: Seeks long-term capital appreciation primarily through investment in common stocks of well-established growth companies. May invest up to 25% of assets in foreign securities and write covered call options.

Portfolio: (12/31/88) Common, preferred and convertible stocks 96%, short-term securities 4%, convertible bonds 1%. Largest stock holdings: foreign 21%, technology 18%.

Portfolio Mgr: M. David Testa—1984

Distributions: Income: Dec   **Capital Gains:** Dec

12b-1: No

Minimum: Initial: $1,000   Subsequent: $100

Min IRA: Initial: $500   Subsequent: $50

Services: IRA, Keogh, Corp, SEP, 403(b), Withdraw, Deduct

Tel Exchange: Yes   **With MMF:** Yes

Registered: All states

Ticker: PRGFX

T. ROWE PRICE HIGH YIELD
Bond

T. Rowe Price Associates, Inc.
100 E. Pratt St.
Baltimore, MD 21202
(800) 638-5660/(301) 547-2308

	1983	**1984**	**1985** (2 mos.)	**1986**	**1987**	**1988**
				Years Ending 2/28		
Dividends from Net Investment Income ($)	—	—	.22	1.37	1.28	1.25
Distributions from Net Realized Capital Gains ($)	—	—	—	—	.13	.14
Net Asset Value End of Year ($)	—	—	9.99	10.99	11.26	10.21
Ratio of Expenses to Net Assets (%)	—	—	1.00	1.00	.99	.99
Ratio of Net Income to Average Net Assets (%)	—	—	16.69	13.01	11.57	12.10
Portfolio Turnover Rate (%)	—	—	6	164	166	138
Total Assets End of Year (Millions $)	—	—	22.5	456.7	939.5	840.2

Annual Rate of Return (%) Years Ending 12/31	—	—	22.5	15.1	2.9	17.9

Five-Year Total Return(%)	NA	Degree of Diversification	NA	Beta	NA	Bull (%)	NA	Bear (%)	(4.0)c

Objective: Seeks high level of current income by investing in long-term, high-yielding, lower and medium quality fixed-income securities. May lend its securities, write options, and purchase foreign debt securities.

Portfolio: (8/31/88) Corporate bonds and notes 82%, U.S. Treasury obligations 6%, foreign bonds 5%, common stocks and warrants 2%, preferred stocks 2%, other assets 2%, convertible bonds 1%.

Portfolio Mgr: Richard Swingle—1984

Distributions: **Income:** Monthly **Capital Gains:** Annually

12b-1: No

Minimum: **Initial:** $2,000 **Subsequent:** $100

Min IRA: **Initial:** $1,000 **Subsequent:** $50

Services: IRA, Keogh, Corp, SEP, 403(b), Withdraw, Deduct

Tel Exchange: Yes **With MMF:** Yes

Registered: All states

Ticker: PRHYX

T. ROWE PRICE INTERNATIONAL BOND

International

T. Rowe Price Associates, Inc.
100 East Pratt Street
Baltimore, MD 21202
(800) 638-5660/(301) 547-2308

	Years Ending 12/31					
	1983	1984	1985	1986 (4 mos.)	1987	1988
Dividends from Net Investment Income ($)	—	—	—	.28	1.01	.91
Distributions from Net Realized Capital Gains ($)	—	—	—	—	.05	.26
Net Asset Value End of Year ($)	—	—	—	10.01	11.60	10.25
Ratio of Expenses to Net Assets (%)	—	—	—	1.25	1.25	1.20
Ratio of Net Income to Average Net Assets (%)	—	—	—	9.48	9.47	8.73
Portfolio Turnover Rate (%)	—	—	—	218	284	368
Total Assets End of Year (Millions $)	—	—	—	70.0	400.0	407.1

Annual Rate of Return (%) Years Ending 12/31		—	—	—	—	28.1	(1.2)

Five-Year Total Return(%)	NA	Degree of Diversification	NA	Beta	NA	Bull (%)	NA	Bear (%)	18.6[A]

Objective: To achieve a high level of current income through investment in foreign bonds. Also seeks capital appreciation and protection of its principal through actively managing its maturity structure and currency exposure.

Portfolio: (12/31/88) Netherlands 24%, France 21%, United States 16%, Japan 16%, United Kingdom 12%, Australia 5%, West Germany 3%.

Portfolio Mgr: Edward A. Taber III—1986

Distributions: **Income:** Monthly   **Capital Gains:** Annually

12b-1: No

Minimum: **Initial:** $1,000   **Subsequent:** $100

Min IRA: **Initial:** $500   **Subsequent:** $50

Services: IRA, Keogh, Corp, SEP, 403(b), Withdraw, Deduct

Tel Exchange: Yes   **With MMF:** Yes

Registered: All states

Ticker: RPIBX

T. ROWE PRICE INTERNATIONAL STOCK

International

T. Rowe Price Associates
100 E. Pratt St.
Baltimore, MD 21202
(800) 638-5660/(301) 547-2308

	Years Ending 12/31					
	1983	**1984**	**1985**	**1986**	**1987**	**1988**
Dividends from Net Investment Income ($)	.11	.08	.15	.11	.23	.16
Distributions from Net Realized Capital Gains ($)	—	.08	.23	1.38	4.98	.93
Net Asset Value End of Year ($)	7.16	6.59	9.04	12.89	8.54	8.97
Ratio of Expenses to Net Assets (%)	1.14	1.11	1.11	1.10	1.14	1.16
Ratio of Net Income to Average Net Assets (%)	1.24	2.29	1.54	.89	.93	1.78
Portfolio Turnover Rate (%)	69	38	62	56	77	42
Total Assets End of Year (Millions $)	130.0	180.6	376.9	790.0	642.5	629.8

Annual Rate of Return (%) Years Ending 12/31	28.4	(5.6)	45.2	60.5	8.0	17.9

Five-Year Total Return(%) 180.1ᴬ	Degree of Diversification	E	Beta .64	Bull (%) 233.1ᴬ	Bear (%) (17.5)ᶜ

Objective: Seeks long-term capital growth and income by investing in a diversified portfolio of marketable securities of established non-U.S. issuers.

Portfolio: (12/31/88) United Kingdom 21%, Japan 19%, West Germany 9%, Netherlands 8%, other countries 37%.

Portfolio Mgr: Martin G. Wade—1980

Distributions: **Income:** Dec   **Capital Gains:** Dec

12b-1: No

Minimum: **Initial:** $1,000   **Subsequent:** $100

Min IRA: **Initial:** $500   **Subsequent:** $50

Services: IRA, Keogh, Corp, SEP, 403(b), Withdraw, Deduct

Tel Exchange: Yes   **With MMF:** Yes

Registered: All states

Ticker: PRITX

T. ROWE PRICE NEW AMERICA GROWTH

Growth

T. Rowe Price Associates
100 East Pratt Street
Baltimore, MD 21202
(800) 638-5660/(301) 547-2308

	Years Ending 12/31					
	1983	1984	1985 (3 mos.)	1986	1987	1988
Dividends from Net Investment Income ($)	–	–	–	.10	.06	–
Distributions from Net Realized Capital Gains ($)	–	–	–	.30	1.39	–
Net Asset Value End of Year ($)	–	–	11.85	13.14	10.45	12.38
Ratio of Expenses to Net Assets (%)	–	–	1.00	1.00	1.23	1.50
Ratio of Net Income to Average Net Assets (%)	–	–	3.40	.38	(.08)	(.36)
Portfolio Turnover Rate (%)	–	–	49	81	72	45
Total Assets End of Year (Millions $)	–	–	30.5	83.4	62.4	66.4

Annual Rate of Return (%) Years Ending 12/31	–	–	–	14.3	(9.9)	18.5

Five-Year Total Return(%)	NA	Degree of Diversification	C	Beta 1.15	Bull (%)	NA	Bear (%)	(26.4)E

Objective: Seeks long-term growth of capital through investment primarily in common stocks of companies that operate in the service sector of the economy. Will invest at least 75% of net assets in service sector stocks. May also write covered call options and buy puts.

Portfolio: (12/31/88) Common stocks 93%, short-term securities 6%, other assets 1%. Largest stock holdings: consumer services 41%, business services 33%.

Portfolio Mgr: John Laporte—1985

Distributions: Income: Dec   **Capital Gains:** Dec

12b-1: No

Minimum: Initial: $1,000   Subsequent: $100

Min IRA: Initial: $500   Subsequent: $50

Services: IRA, Keogh, Corp, SEP, 403(b), Withdraw, Deduct

Tel Exchange: Yes   **With MMF:** Yes

Registered: All states

Ticker: PRWAX

T. ROWE PRICE NEW ERA

Growth

T. Rowe Price Associates
100 E. Pratt St.
Baltimore, MD 21202
(800) 638-5660/(301) 547-2308

	Years Ending 12/31					
	1983	1984	1985	1986	1987	1988
Dividends from Net Investment Income ($)	.81	.61	.68	.50	.98	.53
Distributions from Net Realized Capital Gains ($)	.07	1.29	1.41	3.25	1.77	.61
Net Asset Value End of Year ($)	18.44	17.13	18.67	17.76	18.08	18.79
Ratio of Expenses to Net Assets (%)	.68	.68	.69	.73	.82	.89
Ratio of Net Income to Average Net Assets (%)	3.45	3.96	2.76	1.98	3.11	2.41
Portfolio Turnover Rate (%)	37	39	37	32	30	16
Total Assets End of Year (Millions $)	485.1	472.1	529.4	496.2	756.7	726.6
Annual Rate of Return (%) Years Ending 12/31	26.4	3.5	22.9	16.2	17.5	10.3

Five-Year Total Return(%)	91.6ᴬ	Degree of Diversification	C	Beta	.93	Bull (%)	131.3ᴬ	Bear (%)	(19.1)ᴰ

Objective: Seeks long-term growth of capital through investment primarily in common stocks of companies that own or develop natural resources, and selected growth companies with capable management, sound financial and accounting policies, effective R&D, and efficient service. May invest in foreign securities, loan its portfolio securities (up to 30% of assets), and write covered call options.

Portfolio: (12/31/88) Common stocks 91%, short-term securities 9%, convertible preferred stocks 1%. Largest stock holdings: integrated petroleum 17%, precious metals 10%.

Portfolio Mgr: George Roche—1979

Distributions: Income: Dec   **Capital Gains:** Dec

12b-1: No

Minimum: Initial: $1,000   Subsequent: $100

Min IRA: Initial: $500   Subsequent: $50

Services: IRA, Keogh, Corp, SEP, 403(b), Withdraw, Deduct

Tel Exchange: Yes   **With MMF:** Yes

Registered: All states

Ticker: PRNEX

T. ROWE PRICE NEW HORIZONS
Aggressive Growth

T. Rowe Price Associates
100 E. Pratt St.
Baltimore, MD 21202
(800) 638-5660/(301) 547-2308

	Years Ending 12/31					
	1983	1984	1985	1986	1987	1988
Dividends from Net Investment Income ($)	.20	.16	.14	.09	.06	.07
Distributions from Net Realized Capital Gains ($)	.76	3.72	.52	2.64	1.93	.03
Net Asset Value End of Year ($)	17.90	12.78	15.13	12.38	9.51	10.74
Ratio of Expenses to Net Assets (%)	.61	.71	.70	.73	.78	.84
Ratio of Net Income to Average Net Assets (%)	.83	1.15	.63	.10	.23	.67
Portfolio Turnover Rate (%)	45	32	31	35	50	43
Total Assets End of Year (Millions $)	1,355.1	1,273.2	1,474.9	1,033.9	855.8	914.9

Annual Rate of Return (%) Years Ending 12/31	19.7	(11.8)	24.0	(0.2)	(7.6)	14.0

Five-Year Total Return(%)	15.1E	Degree of Diversification	C	Beta	1.14	Bull (%)	65.5D	Bear (%)	(28.4)E

Objective: Seeks long-term growth of capital through investment primarily in common stocks of small growth companies that have the potential to become major companies in the future.

Portfolio: (12/31/88) Common stocks 89%, short-term securities 11%, convertible bonds 1%. Largest stock holdings: business services and transportation 23%, consumer services 22%.

Portfolio Mgr: John Laporte—1987

Distributions: Income: Dec   **Capital Gains:** Dec

12b-1: No

Minimum: Initial: $1,000   Subsequent: $100

Min IRA: Initial: $500   Subsequent: $50

Services: IRA, Keogh, Corp, SEP, 403(b), Withdraw, Deduct

Tel Exchange: Yes   **With MMF:** Yes

Registered: All states

Ticker: PRNHX

T. ROWE PRICE NEW INCOME
Bond

T. Rowe Price Associates, Inc.
100 E. Pratt St.
Baltimore, MD 21202
(800) 638-5660/(301) 547-2308

	Years Ending 2/28					
	1983* (2 mos.)	1984	1985	1986	1987	1988
Dividends from Net Investment Income ($)	.17	.95	.94	.88	.75	.76
Distributions from Net Realized Capital Gains ($)	—	—	—	—	—	—
Net Asset Value End of Year ($)	8.56	8.24	8.18	8.95	9.17	8.76
Ratio of Expenses to Net Assets (%)	.57	.62	.64	.66	.65	.80
Ratio of Net Income to Average Net Assets (%)	12.10	11.13	11.53	10.39	8.22	8.77
Portfolio Turnover Rate (%)	67	84	155	185	125	158
Total Assets End of Year (Millions $)	640.3	695.5	707.8	936.0	938.9	834.8
Annual Rate of Return (%) Years Ending 12/31	9.7	11.9	17.6	14.0	2.1	7.6

Five-Year Total Return(%)	64.8ᶜ	Degree of Diversification	NA	Beta	NA	Bull (%)	40.6ᴱ	Bear (%)	4.3ᴬ

Fiscal year-end changed from 12/31 to 2/28.

Objective: Seeks high current income with reasonable stability through investment in high grade fixed-income securities.

Portfolio: (8/31/88) U.S. government securities 58%, corporate bonds and notes 22%, foreign bonds 10%, Canadian bonds 4%, commercial paper 3%, other assets 3%. Largest bond holdings: finance and credit 10%, banking 4%.

Portfolio Mgr: Charles Smith—1986

Distributions: **Income:** Monthly   **Capital Gains:** Annually

12b-1: No

Minimum: **Initial:** $2,000   **Subsequent:** $100

Min IRA: **Initial:** $1,000   **Subsequent:** $50

Services: IRA, Keogh, Corp, SEP, 403(b), Withdraw, Deduct

Tel Exchange: Yes   **With MMF:** Yes

Registered: All states

Ticker: PRCIX

T. ROWE PRICE SCIENCE & TECHNOLOGY
Aggressive Growth

T. Rowe Price Associates
100 E. Pratt St.
Baltimore, MD 21202
(800) 638-5660/(301) 547-2308

	Years Ending 12/31					
	1983	1984	1985	1986	1987 (3 mos.)	1988
Dividends from Net Investment Income ($)	—	—	—	—	.04	.07
Distributions from Net Realized Capital Gains ($)	—	—	—	—	—	.44
Net Asset Value End of Year ($)	—	—	—	—	8.02	8.57
Ratio of Expenses to Net Assets (%)	—	—	—	—	1.20	1.20
Ratio of Net Income to Average Net Assets (%)	—	—	—	—	2.09	.68
Portfolio Turnover Rate (%)	—	—	—	—	22	92
Total Assets End of Year (Millions $)	—	—	—	—	9.6	12.4

Annual Rate of Return (%) Years Ending 12/31	—	—	—	—	—	13.3

Five-Year Total Return(%)	NA	Degree of Diversification	NA	Beta	NA	Bull (%)	NA	Bear (%)	NA

Objective: Seeks long-term growth of capital through investment in the common stocks of companies that are expected to benefit from the development, advancement and use of science and technology. Looks for high-growth companies in the health care, information processing, waste management, synthetic materials, and communications industries.

Portfolio: (12/31/88) Common stocks 93%, short-term securities 6%, other assets 1%. Largest stock holdings: computer software and services 21%, computer systems 14%.

Portfolio Mgr: John Laporte—1988

Distributions: Income: Dec   **Capital Gains:** Dec

12b-1: No

Minimum: Initial: $1,000   Subsequent: $100

Min IRA: Initial: $500   Subsequent: $50

Services: IRA, Keogh, Corp, SEP, 403(b), Withdraw, Deduct

Tel Exchange: Yes   With MMF: Yes

Registered: All states

Ticker: PRSCX

T. ROWE PRICE SHORT-TERM BOND

Bond

T. Rowe Price Associates, Inc.
100 E. Pratt St.
Baltimore, MD 21202
(800) 638-5660/(301) 547-2308

	1983	1984	1985	1986	1987	1988
			Years Ending 2/28			
Dividends from Net Investment Income ($)	—	—	.53	.47	.40	.39
Distributions from Net Realized Capital Gains ($)	—	—	—	—	—	—
Net Asset Value End of Year ($)	—	—	4.97	5.17	5.21	5.08
Ratio of Expenses to Net Assets (%)	—	—	.90	1.31	.94	.91
Ratio of Net Income to Average Net Assets (%)	—	—	10.73	9.12	7.58	7.85
Portfolio Turnover Rate (%)	—	—	73	21	7	203
Total Assets End of Year (Millions $)	—	—	42.0	96.1	218.2	284.4
Annual Rate of Return (%) Years Ending 12/31	—	—	12.8	9.0	5.2	5.5

Five-Year Total Return(%)	NA	Degree of Diversification	NA	Beta	NA	Bull (%)	NA	Bear (%)	3.3A

Objective:	Seeks high level of income with minimum fluctuation of principal value and liquidity. Portfolio will consist of short- and intermediate-term securities.
Portfolio:	(8/31/88) CDs 29%, U.S. government securities 29%, corporate bonds and notes 23%, commercial paper 13%, foreign bonds 4%, other assets 2%. Largest bond holdings: banking 13%, finance and credit 4%.
Portfolio Mgr:	Edward A. Taber III—1984
Distributions:	**Income:** Monthly **Capital Gains:** Annually
12b-1:	No
Minimum:	**Initial:** $2,000 **Subsequent:** $100
Min IRA:	**Initial:** $1,000 **Subsequent:** $50
Services:	IRA, Keogh, Corp, SEP, 403(b), Withdraw, Deduct
Tel Exchange:	Yes **With MMF:** Yes
Registered:	All states
Ticker:	PRWBX

PRIMARY TREND FUND

Growth & Income

Arnold Investment Counsel, Inc.
First Financial Centre
700 North Water Street
Milwaukee, WI 53202
(800) 443-6544/(414) 271-7870

	Years Ending 6/30					
	1983	1984	1985	1986	1987 (9 mos.)	1988
Dividends from Net Investment Income ($)	–	–	–	–	–	.35
Distributions from Net Realized Capital Gains ($)	–	–	–	–	–	.07
Net Asset Value End of Year ($)	–	–	–	–	11.62	11.82
Ratio of Expenses to Net Assets (%)	–	–	–	–	1.3	1.2
Ratio of Net Income to Average Net Assets (%)	–	–	–	–	3.90	6.40
Portfolio Turnover Rate (%)	–	–	–	–	20	17
Total Assets End of Year (Millions $)	–	–	–	–	31.3	44.7

Annual Rate of Return (%) Years Ending 12/31	–	–	–	–	3.7	18.4

Five-Year Total Return(%) NA	Degree of Diversification NA	Beta NA	Bull (%) NA	Bear (%) (13.2)c

Objective: Seeks to maximize total return without exposing capital to undue risk. Invests in common stock and convertible and fixed-income securities. Attempts to align the portfolio with primary market trends that can last from several quarters up to several years.

Portfolio: (12/31/88) Common stocks 97%, short-term securities 2%, other assets 1%. Largest stock holdings: USX Corporation 6%, NIPSCO Industries, Inc. 6%.

Portfolio Mgr: James Arnold, Sr.—1986

Distributions: **Income:** Semiannually   **Capital Gains:** Semiannually

12b-1: No

Minimum: **Initial:** $5,000   **Subsequent:** $100

Min IRA: **Initial:** $2,000   **Subsequent:** $100

Services: IRA, Keogh, Corp, SEP, 403(b), Withdraw, Deduct

Tel Exchange: No

Registered: All states

Ticker: PTFDX

†PRUDENTIAL-BACHE GOVERNMENT SECURITIES INTERMEDIATE TERM
Bond

The Prudential Insurance Co.
of America
One Seaport Plaza
New York, NY 10292
(800) 225-1852

	Years Ending 11/30					
	1983	1984	1985	1986	1987	1988
Dividends from Net Investment Income ($)	—	—	—	.99	.78	.95
Distributions from Net Realized Capital Gains ($)	—	—	—	.16	.16	—
Net Asset Value End of Year ($)	—	—	—	10.97	10.24	9.92
Ratio of Expenses to Net Assets (%)	—	—	—	.75	.72	.83
Ratio of Net Income to Average Net Assets (%)	—	—	—	8.51	8.30	9.39
Portfolio Turnover Rate (%)	—	—	—	139	59	28
Total Assets End of Year (Millions $)	—	—	—	866.5	633.9	474.1
Annual Rate of Return (%) Years Ending 12/31	—	—	—	13.7	2.6	6.2

Five-Year Total Return(%)	NA	Degree of Diversification	NA	Beta	NA	Bull (%)	NA	Bear (%)	3.4^

Objective: Seeks to achieve a high level of income consistent with providing reasonable safety. Invests in U.S. government securities or government guaranteed securities that mature no later than 10 years from date of purchase.

Portfolio: (11/30/88) U.S. Treasury notes 68%, Federal Home Loan Bank 14%, FNMA 7%, Federal Home Loan Mortgage Corporation 5%, repurchase agreements 3%, other assets 2%, corporate obligations 1%.

Portfolio Mgr: Elena Walsh—1986

Distributions: **Income:** Monthly   **Capital Gains:** Annually

12b-1: Yes   **Amount:** 0.25%

Minimum: **Initial:** $1,000   **Subsequent:** $100

Min IRA: **Initial:** None   **Subsequent:** None

Services: IRA, Keogh, Corp, SEP, 403(b), Withdraw, Deduct

Tel Exchange: Yes   **With MMF:** Yes

Registered: All states

Ticker: PBGVX

† *Prior to 7/85, this fund had a front-end sales charge of 1%.*

PRUDENT SPECULATOR LEVERAGED FUND

Aggressive Growth

Prudent Speculator Group
P.O. Box 75231
Los Angeles, CA 90075-0231
(800) 444-4778

			Years Ending 10/31			
	1983	1984	1985	1986	1987 (4 mos.)	1988
Dividends from Net Investment Income ($)	–	–	–	–	–	–
Distributions from Net Realized Capital Gains ($)	–	–	–	–	–	–
Net Asset Value End of Year ($)	–	–	–	–	6.93	7.54
Ratio of Expenses to Net Assets (%)	–	–	–	–	2.68	2.81
Ratio of Net Income to Average Net Assets (%)	–	–	–	–	.31	(.08)
Portfolio Turnover Rate (%)	–	–	–	–	–	16
Total Assets End of Year (Millions $)	–	–	–	–	7.7	9.8

Annual Rate of Return (%) Years Ending 12/31	–	–	–	–	–	12.7

Five-Year Total Return(%)	NA	Degree of Diversification	NA	Beta	NA	Bull (%)	NA	Bear (%)	NA

Objective: Seeks long-term capital growth; current income is not an investment objective. Under normal conditions, at least 80% of the fund's assets will be invested in a diversified portfolio of common stocks. Looks for stocks that have lower than average price-earnings ratios, price-to-book-value ratios and price-to-sales ratios.

Portfolio: (10/31/88) Common stocks 97%, short-term obligations 3%. Largest stock holdings: savings and loans 16%, insurance 10%.

Portfolio Mgr: Al Frank—1987

Distributions: Income: Dec   **Capital Gains:** Dec

12b-1: Yes   **Amount:** 0.25%

Minimum: Initial: $5,000   **Subsequent:** $500

Min IRA: Initial: $2,000   **Subsequent:** $200

Services: IRA, Keogh, Withdraw, Deduct

Tel Exchange: Yes   **With MMF:** Yes

Registered: All states except NE, NH

Ticker: PSLFX

RAINBOW
Growth

Furman, Anderson & Co.
19 Rector St.
New York, NY 10006
(212) 509-8532

	Years Ending 5/31						10/31
	1983	1984	1985	1986	1987	1988	1988* (5 mos.)
Dividends from Net Investment Income ($)	–	–	–	–	–	–	–
Distributions from Net Realized Capital Gains ($)	–	–	–	–	–	.76	–
Net Asset Value End of Year ($)	4.01	3.71	4.26	5.45	6.18	4.86	5.44
Ratio of Expenses to Net Assets (%)	4.65	4.32	3.02	3.46	3.27	3.53	1.39
Ratio of Net Income to Average Net Assets (%)	(.22)	.54	2.84	.00	(.85)	(.20)	(.28)
Portfolio Turnover Rate (%)	291	247	164	190	113	133	90
Total Assets End of Year (Millions $)	1.8	1.5	1.7	2.0	2.2	1.9	2.1

Annual Rate of Return (%) Years Ending 12/31	22.2	(4.9)	20.7	15.8	(4.0)	18.1	*

Five-Year Total Return(%) 50.6ᴰ	Degree of Diversification D	Beta .91	Bull (%) 88.4ᶜ	Bear (%) (24.7)ᴱ

*Fiscal year-end changed from 5/31 to 10/31. All annual return figures are for full
years ending 12/31.*

Objective:	Seeks capital appreciation through investment in common stocks of established companies. Employs speculative market techniques such as listed put and call options. May write covered and uncovered put and call options, and buy and write options on stock indexes. May sell securities short, and invest up to 20% of its assets in warrants and up to 25% in foreign securities.
Portfolio:	(10/31/88) Common stocks 89%, other assets 11%. Largest stock holdings: chemicals 18%, consumer retail 11%.
Portfolio Mgr:	Robert Furman—1974
Distributions:	**Income:** Annually **Capital Gains:** Annually
12b-1:	No
Minimum:	**Initial:** $300 **Subsequent:** $50
Min IRA:	**Initial:** $300 **Subsequent:** $50
Services:	IRA, Keogh
Tel Exchange:	No
Registered:	NJ, NY
Ticker:	RBOWX

REICH & TANG EQUITY

Aggressive Growth

Reich & Tang, Inc.
100 Park Avenue
New York, NY 10017
(212) 370-1252

	Years Ending 12/31					
	1983	1984	1985 (11 mos.)	1986	1987	1988
Dividends from Net Investment Income ($)	—	—	.30	.28	.40	.44
Distributions from Net Realized Capital Gains ($)	—	—	—	.63	1.78	1.53
Net Asset Value End of Year ($)	—	—	13.44	14.50	13.11	14.11
Ratio of Expenses to Net Assets (%)	—	—	.99	1.21	1.11	1.11
Ratio of Net Income to Average Net Assets (%)	—	—	3.70	2.51	2.07	2.87
Portfolio Turnover Rate (%)	—	—	20	35	43	27
Total Assets End of Year (Millions $)	—	—	54.2	110.5	101.6	102.4

Annual Rate of Return (%) Years Ending 12/31	—	—	—	14.7	5.1	22.9

Five-Year Total Return(%)	NA	Degree of Diversification	A	Beta	.88	Bull (%)	NA	Bear (%)	(19.6)ᴰ

Objective: Seeks long-term capital appreciation; current income is a secondary consideration. Invests in common stocks of undervalued companies showing good growth potential. May convert entirely to debt securities and money market instruments for defensive purposes. May enter into repurchase agreements, buy warrants, invest in foreign securities and restricted securities.

Portfolio: (12/31/88) Common stocks 76%, short-term securities 23%, preferred stocks 2%. Largest stock holdings: consumer products 11%, communications 10%.

Portfolio Mgr: Robert Hoerle—1985

Distributions: **Income:** Semiannually   **Capital Gains:** Annually

12b-1: Yes   **Amount:** 0.05%

Minimum: **Initial:** $5,000   **Subsequent:** None

Min IRA: **Initial:** $250   **Subsequent:** None

Services: IRA, Corp, Withdraw

Tel Exchange: Yes   **With MMF:** Yes

Registered: All states except AK, AZ, IA, ID, KS, LA, MS, ND, SD, RI, WV

Ticker: RCHTX

†RESERVE EQUITY TRUST— CONTRARIAN PORTFOLIO

Growth & Income

Reserve Management Co., Inc.
810 Seventh Avenue
New York, NY 10019
(800) 421-0261/(212) 977-9675

	Years Ending 5/31					
	1983	1984 (4 mos.)	1985	1986	1987	1988
Dividends from Net Investment Income ($)	—	—	.30	.49	.27	.31
Distributions from Net Realized Capital Gains ($)	—	—	—	.01	.46	1.34
Net Asset Value End of Year ($)	—	9.28	12.63	16.89	18.05	13.65
Ratio of Expenses to Net Assets (%)	—	1.00	1.00	1.00	1.50	1.44
Ratio of Net Income to Average Net Assets (%)	—	5.05	4.22	3.04	2.16	2.77
Portfolio Turnover Rate (%)	—	5	6	26	25	2
Total Assets End of Year (Millions $)	—	.2	5.3	20.9	27.3	8.2

Annual Rate of Return (%) Years Ending 12/31	—	—	40.5	10.8	(6.8)	9.0

Five-Year Total Return(%)	NA	Degree of Diversification	B	Beta	.91	Bull (%)	140.2ᴬ	Bear (%)	(30.6)ᴱ

Objective: Seeks dividend income and capital appreciation through investment in securities believed to be undervalued and those overlooked due to pessimistic appraisals by the public.

Portfolio: (11/30/88) Repurchase agreements 97%, common stocks 3%. Largest stock holdings: communications 1%, medical services and supplies 1%.

Portfolio Mgr: Bruce Bent—1988

Distributions: **Income:** Quarterly   **Capital Gains:** Annually

12b-1: Yes   **Amount:** 0.25%

Minimum: **Initial:** $10,000   **Subsequent:** $1,000

Min IRA: **Initial:** $1,000   **Subsequent:** $250

Services: IRA

Tel Exchange: Yes   **With MMF:** Yes

Registered: All states except AR, KS, KY, ME, MT, NE, NH, NM, OK, OR, SD, UT

Ticker: RETCX

† *A front-end sales charge of 4% has been approved, however, management has not put the charge into effect.*

RIGHTIME
Growth

Rightime Econometrics, Inc.
Forst Pavilion
218 Glenside Ave.
Wyncote, PA 19095-1595
(800) 242-1421/(215) 887-8111

	Years Ending 10/31					
	1983	1984	1985 (2 mos.)	1986	1987	1988
Dividends from Net Investment Income ($)	–	–	–	.05	–	.67
Distributions from Net Realized Capital Gains ($)	–	–	–	.20	1.94	3.97
Net Asset Value End of Year ($)	–	–	25.87	32.05	34.35	31.86
Ratio of Expenses to Net Assets (%)	–	–	3.19	2.77	2.55	2.58
Ratio of Net Income to Average Net Assets (%)	–	–	(.60)	(1.63)	1.20	.53
Portfolio Turnover Rate (%)	–	–	–	231	166	187
Total Assets End of Year (Millions $)	–	–	14.7	145.2	211.3	235.0
Annual Rate of Return (%) Years Ending 12/31	–	–	–	10.7	19.5	(1.3)

Five-Year Total Return(%)	NA	Degree of Diversification	E	Beta	.50	Bull (%)	NA	Bear (%)	2.5ᴬ

Objective: Seeks high total return through investment in other investment companies. Looks at past performance and investment structure. Investment companies may be open- or closed-end, load or no-load.

Portfolio: (10/31/88) Equity funds 97%, short-term securities 3%. Largest fund holdings: Vanguard Index Trust 9%, Putnam Voyager Fund 7%

Portfolio Mgr: David Rights—1985

Distributions: **Income:** Annually   **Capital Gains:** Annually

12b-1: Yes   **Amount:** 1.20%

Minimum: **Initial:** $2,000   **Subsequent:** $100

Min IRA: **Initial:** None   **Subsequent:** None

Services: IRA, Keogh, 403(b), Withdraw

Tel Exchange: Yes   **With MMF:** No

Registered: All states except CA, NH, TX, WI

Ticker: RTFDX

RUSHMORE OVER-THE-COUNTER INDEX PLUS

Growth

Money Management Associates
4922 Fairmont Avenue
Bethesda, MD 20814
(800) 343-3355/(301) 657-1500

	Years Ending 8/31					
	1983	1984	1985	1986 (8 mos.)	1987	1988
Dividends from Net Investment Income ($)	—	—	—	.04	.11	.13
Distributions from Net Realized Capital Gains ($)	—	—	—	.03	.03	—
Net Asset Value End of Year ($)	—	—	—	11.42	15.32	11.77
Ratio of Expenses to Net Assets (%)	—	—	—	1.00	.76	.95
Ratio of Net Income to Average Net Assets (%)	—	—	—	.64	1.18	.93
Portfolio Turnover Rate (%)	—	—	—	5	42	252
Total Assets End of Year (Millions $)	—	—	—	.8	6.1	4.0

Annual Rate of Return (%) Years Ending 12/31	—	—	—	7.9	6.3	9.2

Five-Year Total Return(%)	NA	Degree of Diversification	C	Beta 1.20	Bull (%)	NA	Bear (%)	(26.3)ᴱ

Objective: Seeks to provide investment results that closely correlate to the performance of the common stocks represented by the NASDAQ-100 index. May also invest in options transactions as part of its effort to correlate its performance with the index.

Portfolio: (8/31/88) Common stocks 71%, repurchase agreements 28%, options 1%. Largest stock holdings: Apple Computer, Inc. 6%, MCI Communications Corp. 5%.

Portfolio Mgr: Daniel Ryczek—1985

Distributions: **Income:** Monthly   **Capital Gains:** Annually

12b-1: No

Minimum: **Initial:** $2,500   **Subsequent:** None

Min IRA: **Initial:** $500   **Subsequent:** None

Services: IRA, Keogh, SEP

Tel Exchange: Yes   **With MMF:** Yes

Registered: All states

Ticker: RSOIX

RUSHMORE STOCK MARKET INDEX PLUS

Growth & Income

Money Management Associates
4922 Fairmont Avenue
Bethesda, MD 20814
(800) 343-3355/(301) 657-1500

	Years Ending 8/31					
	1983	1984	1985	1986 (8 mos.)	1987	1988
Dividends from Net Investment Income ($)	—	—	—	.18	.29	.44
Distributions from Net Realized Capital Gains ($)	—	—	—	—	—	.81
Net Asset Value End of Year ($)	—	—	—	11.78	15.75	11.59
Ratio of Expenses to Net Assets (%)	—	—	—	1.00	.75	.90
Ratio of Net Income to Average Net Assets (%)	—	—	—	3.13	3.08	3.41
Portfolio Turnover Rate (%)	—	—	—	7	188	621
Total Assets End of Year (Millions $)	—	—	—	1.2	29.0	10.4
Annual Rate of Return (%) Years Ending 12/31	—	—	—	17.6	8.9	8.9

Five-Year Total Return(%)	NA	Degree of Diversification	A	Beta	.83	Bull (%)	NA	Bear (%)	(21.5)ᴅ

Objective: The fund's objective is to provide investment results that closely correlate to the performance of the common stocks comprising the Standard & Poor's 100 index. Index options are also used in an attempt to enhance the performance of the fund.

Portfolio: (8/31/88) Common stocks 83%, repurchase agreements 16%, options 1%.

Portfolio Mgr: Daniel Ryczek—1985

Distributions: Income: Monthly   **Capital Gains:** Annually

12b-1: No

Minimum: Initial: $2,500   Subsequent: None

Min IRA: Initial: $500   Subsequent: None

Services: IRA, Keogh, SEP

Tel Exchange: Yes   **With MMF:** Yes

Registered: All states

Ticker: RSSIX

RUSHMORE U.S. GOVERNMENT INTERMEDIATE-TERM SECURITIES

Bond

Money Management Associates
4922 Fairmont Avenue
Bethesda, MD 20814
(800) 343-3355/(301) 657-1500

	Years Ending 8/31					
	1983	1984	1985	1986 (8 mos.)	1987	1988
Dividends from Net Investment Income ($)	—	—	—	.46	.63	.80
Distributions from Net Realized Capital Gains ($)	—	—	—	—	—	—
Net Asset Value End of Year ($)	—	—	—	10.47	9.70	9.53
Ratio of Expenses to Net Assets (%)	—	—	—	1.00	.78	.81
Ratio of Net Income to Average Net Assets (%)	—	—	—	6.50	6.18	8.14
Portfolio Turnover Rate (%)	—	—	—	—	87	1,754
Total Assets End of Year (Millions $)	—	—	—	.4	.9	1.1
Annual Rate of Return (%) Years Ending 12/31	—	—	—	10.5	0.8	6.8

Five-Year Total Return(%)	NA	Degree of Diversification	NA	Beta	NA	Bull (%)	NA	Bear (%)	3.3A

Objective:	Seeks to provide investors with maximum current income consistent with safety of principal. Invest in government securities with maturities of 10 years or less.
Portfolio:	(8/31/88) U.S. government obligations 96%, repurchase agreements 4%.
Portfolio Mgr:	Daniel Ryczek—1986
Distributions:	**Income:** Monthly **Capital Gains:** Annually
12b-1:	No
Minimum:	**Initial:** $2,500 **Subsequent:** None
Min IRA:	**Initial:** $500 **Subsequent:** None
Services:	IRA, Keogh, SEP
Tel Exchange:	Yes **With MMF:** Yes
Registered:	All states
Ticker:	RSUIX

RUSHMORE
U.S. GOVERNMENT
LONG-TERM
SECURITIES
Bond

Money Management Associates
4922 Fairmont Avenue
Bethesda, MD 20814
(800) 343-3355/(301) 657-1500

			Years Ending 8/31		
	1983	1984	1985	1986 (8 mos.)	1987	1988
Dividends from Net Investment Income ($)	—	—	—	.61	.77	.75
Distributions from Net Realized Capital Gains ($)	—	—	—	—	—	—
Net Asset Value End of Year ($)	—	—	—	9.97	9.19	8.96
Ratio of Expenses to Net Assets (%)	—	—	—	1.00	.78	.83
Ratio of Net Income to Average Net Assets (%)	—	—	—	8.83	7.90	8.05
Portfolio Turnover Rate (%)	—	—	—	44	226	829
Total Assets End of Year (Millions $)	—	—	—	7.7	10.8	7.2
Annual Rate of Return (%) Years Ending 12/31	—	—	—	8.9	0.4	7.9

Five-Year Total Return(%)	NA	Degree of Diversification	NA	Beta	NA	Bull (%)	NA	Bear (%)	3.8ᴬ

Objective: Seeks to provide investors with maximum current income that is consistent with safety of principal. Invests in government securities with maturities of 10 years or more.

Portfolio: (8/31/88) U.S. government obligations 99%, repurchase agreements 1%.

Portfolio Mgr: Daniel Ryczek—1985

Distributions: **Income:** Monthly   **Capital Gains:** Annually

12b-1: No

Minimum: **Initial:** $2,500   **Subsequent:** None

Min IRA: **Initial:** $500   **Subsequent:** None

Services: IRA, Keogh, SEP

Tel Exchange: Yes   **With MMF:** Yes

Registered: All states

Ticker: RSGVX

SAFECO EQUITY
Growth & Income

SAFECO Asset Management Co.
SAFECO Plaza
Seattle, WA 98185
(800) 426-6730/(206) 545-5530

	Years Ending 9/30					
	1983	1984	1985	1986	1987	1988
Dividends from Net Investment Income ($)	.52	.45	.41	.34	.22	.23
Distributions from Net Realized Capital Gains ($)	.83	.58	.72	1.22	2.03	1.85
Net Asset Value End of Year ($)	10.62	9.79	10.25	11.44	12.23	8.51
Ratio of Expenses to Net Assets (%)	.65	.64	.68	.88	.97	1.00
Ratio of Net Income to Average Net Assets (%)	4.78	4.66	3.97	2.55	1.92	2.16
Portfolio Turnover Rate (%)	16	20	56	86	85	88
Total Assets End of Year (Millions $)	34.5	31.4	34.9	46.7	64.7	45.6

Annual Rate of Return (%) Years Ending 12/31	21.1	2.8	32.6	12.6	(4.8)	25.3

Five-Year Total Return(%)	83.2[B]	Degree of Diversification	B	Beta	1.05	Bull (%)	130.2[A]	Bear (%)	(29.2)[E]

Objective:	Seeks reasonable balance of long-term growth of capital and reasonable current income for shareholders. Fund invests primarily in common stocks or convertibles of well-established, dividend-paying companies.
Portfolio:	(9/30/88) Common stocks 98%, short-term securities 2%, corporate bonds 1%. Largest stock holdings: electrical equipment and electronics 11%, health care 10%.
Portfolio Mgr:	Thomas Maguire, Doug Johnson—1984
Distributions:	**Income:** Mar, June, Sept, Dec **Capital Gains:** Sept, Dec
12b-1:	No
Minimum:	**Initial:** $1,000 **Subsequent:** $100
Min IRA:	**Initial:** $250 **Subsequent:** $100
Services:	IRA, SEP, Withdraw, Deduct
Tel Exchange:	Yes **With MMF:** Yes
Registered:	All states except ME, NH, VT
Ticker:	SAFQX

SAFECO GROWTH
Growth

SAFECO Asset Management Co.
SAFECO Plaza
Seattle, WA 98185
(800) 426-6730/(206) 545-5530

	Years Ending 9/30					
	1983	**1984**	**1985**	**1986**	**1987**	**1988**
Dividends from Net Investment Income ($)	.44	.46	.56	.42	.23	.48
Distributions from Net Realized Capital Gains ($)	.67	1.20	1.16	2.98	1.59	2.06
Net Asset Value End of Year ($)	20.38	16.87	16.86	15.40	18.13	14.95
Ratio of Expenses to Net Assets (%)	.61	.61	.63	.85	.92	.98
Ratio of Net Income to Average Net Assets (%)	2.35	2.89	2.94	1.90	1.46	2.37
Portfolio Turnover Rate (%)	19	23	29	46	24	19
Total Assets End of Year (Millions $)	64.5	63.5	66.3	68.4	82.7	74.3
Annual Rate of Return (%) Years Ending 12/31	31.8	(7.0)	19.6	1.8	7.0	22.1

Five-Year Total Return(%)	48.0ᴰ	Degree of Diversification	B	Beta	.91	Bull (%)	80.4ᴰ	Bear (%)	(19.8)ᴰ

Objective: Seeks capital growth and increased shareholder income through investment in large, well-established, dividend-paying companies. Short-term investments are only made when deemed beneficial. The aim is to keep portfolio turnover rates low.

Portfolio: (9/30/88) Common stocks 71%, short-term securities 29%, corporate bonds 2%. Largest stock holdings: office equipment 10%, insurance 5%.

Portfolio Mgr: Gary Aster—1984

Distributions: **Income:** Mar, June, Sept, Dec   **Capital Gains:** Sept

12b-1: No

Minimum: **Initial:** $1,000   **Subsequent:** $100

Min IRA: **Initial:** $250   **Subsequent:** $100

Services: IRA, SEP, Withdraw, Deduct

Tel Exchange: Yes   **With MMF:** Yes

Registered: All states except ME, NH, VT

Ticker: SAFGX

SAFECO INCOME
Balanced

SAFECO Asset Management Co.
SAFECO Plaza
Seattle, WA 98185
(800) 426-6730/(206) 545-5530

	1983	1984	1985	1986	1987	1988
			Years Ending 9/30			
Dividends from Net Investment Income ($)	.83	.85	.80	.79	.78	.98
Distributions from Net Realized Capital Gains ($)	.44	.87	1.17	.56	.73	.84
Net Asset Value End of Year ($)	13.44	12.63	12.96	15.52	17.16	14.32
Ratio of Expenses to Net Assets (%)	.63	.63	.73	.95	.94	.97
Ratio of Net Income to Average Net Assets (%)	6.85	7.02	6.41	5.08	4.53	5.58
Portfolio Turnover Rate (%)	32	34	29	29	33	34
Total Assets End of Year (Millions $)	21.5	19.8	31.5	102.3	313.2	231.7
Annual Rate of Return (%) Years Ending 12/31	28.3	10.7	31.4	19.9	(5.9)	19.0

Five-Year Total Return(%)	95.3[A]	Degree of Diversification	A	Beta	.76	Bull (%)	118.9[B]	Bear (%)	(21.6)[D]

Objective: Seeks high current income and capital growth through investments in common stocks and convertible securities of medium- to large-sized companies that pay dividends.

Portfolio: (9/30/88) Common stocks 68%, corporate bonds 24%, preferred stocks 7%, short-term securities 1%. Largest stock holdings: banking and finance 10%, utilities/telephone 8%.

Portfolio Mgr: Arley Hudson—1978

Distributions: **Income:** Mar, June, Sept, Dec **Capital Gains:** Sept

12b-1: No

Minimum: **Initial:** $1,000 **Subsequent:** $100

Min IRA: **Initial:** $250 **Subsequent:** $100

Services: IRA, SEP, Withdraw, Deduct

Tel Exchange: Yes **With MMF:** Yes

Registered: All states except ME, NH, VT

Ticker: SAFIX

SAFECO
U.S. GOVERNMENT
SECURITIES
Bond

SAFECO Asset Management Co.
SAFECO Plaza
Seattle, WA 98185
(800) 426-6730/(206) 545-5530

	Years Ending 9/30					
	1983	1984	1985	1986 (5 mos.)	1987	1988
Dividends from Net Investment Income ($)	–	–	–	.33	.82	.87
Distributions from Net Realized Capital Gains ($)	–	–	–	–	–	–
Net Asset Value End of Year ($)	–	–	–	10.00	9.13	9.06
Ratio of Expenses to Net Assets (%)	–	–	–	1.25	1.05	1.06
Ratio of Net Income to Average Net Assets (%)	–	–	–	8.01	8.59	9.51
Portfolio Turnover Rate (%)	–	–	–	33	101	110
Total Assets End of Year (Millions $)	–	–	–	8.1	20.3	27.7

Annual Rate of Return (%) Years Ending 12/31	–	–	–	–	0.9	7.8

Five-Year Total Return(%)	NA	Degree of Diversification	NA	Beta	NA	Bull (%)	NA	Bear (%)	1.2B

Objective: Seeks high level of current income consistent with the preservation of capital through investment in the U.S. government's and its agencies' debt obligations. During normal market conditions the fund will invest at least 65% of its assets in U.S. government securities, principally GNMAs. May invest in other no-load government bond funds.

Portfolio: (9/30/88) U.S. government and agency obligations 98%, short-term securities 2%.

Portfolio Mgr: Paul Stevenson—1988

Distributions: **Income:** Monthly   **Capital Gains:** Sept, Dec

12b-1: No

Minimum: **Initial:** $1,000   **Subsequent:** $100

Min IRA: **Initial:** $250   **Subsequent:** $100

Services: IRA, SEP, Withdraw, Deduct

Tel Exchange: Yes   **With MMF:** Yes

Registered: All states except ME, NH, VT

Ticker: SFUSX

†SALEM GROWTH
Growth

Salem Funds
99 High Street
Boston, MA 02110
(800) 343-3424/(704) 331-0710

	1983	1984	1985 (7 mos.)	1986	1987	1988
			Years Ending 3/31			
Dividends from Net Investment Income ($)	—	—	—	.20	.13	.26
Distributions from Net Realized Capital Gains ($)	—	—	—	—	.09	.53
Net Asset Value End of Year ($)	—	—	10.04	12.35	14.66	12.83
Ratio of Expenses to Net Assets (%)	—	—	2.00	2.00	1.97	1.74
Ratio of Net Income to Average Net Assets (%)	—	—	6.47	2.34	1.41	1.92
Portfolio Turnover Rate (%)	—	—	0	20	20	16
Total Assets End of Year (Millions $)	—	—	.1	5.6	23.2	21.9

Annual Rate of Return (%) Years Ending 12/31	—	—	—	16.6	1.6	20.2

Five-Year Total Return(%)	NA	Degree of Diversification	A	Beta	.83	Bull (%)	NA	Bear (%)	(21.6)ᴰ

Objective: Primary objective is long-term capital growth; income is a secondary objective. Invests in companies with at least $100 million in equity. Will also invest in convertible securities rated at least BBB by Standard & Poor's.

Portfolio: (9/30/88) Common stocks 96%, short-term securities 2%, other assets 2%. Largest stock holdings: consumer staples 17%, industrial intermediates 14%.

Portfolio Mgr: Edward Outen—1985

Distributions: **Income:** Feb, May, Aug, Nov   **Capital Gains:** May

12b-1: Yes   **Amount:** 0.75%

Minimum: **Initial:** $1,000   **Subsequent:** None

Min IRA: **Initial:** $1,000   **Subsequent:** None

Services: IRA, Keogh, Withdraw, Deduct

Tel Exchange: Yes   **With MMF:** Yes

Registered: AL, DC, FL, GA, IL, KY, MD, MI, MS, NC, NY, OH, PA, SC, TN, VA

Ticker: SALGX

† *A contingent deferred sales charge of 2% payable to the fund's principal underwriter may be imposed on shares of the Growth Portfolio redeemed within four years of purchase. However, for the foreseeable future no contingent deferred sales charge will be imposed.*

SBSF
GROWTH FUND
(formerly SBSF FUND)
Growth

Spears, Benzak, Salomon & Farrell
45 Rockefeller Plaza
New York, NY 10111
(800) 422-7273/(212) 903-1200

	Years Ending 11/30					
	1983	1984	1985	1986	1987	1988
Dividends from Net Investment Income ($)	—	.18	.40	.32	.37	.48
Distributions from Net Realized Capital Gains ($)	—	—	—	.55	1.05	.40
Net Asset Value End of Year ($)	—	10.81	13.53	14.16	11.80	13.31
Ratio of Expenses to Net Assets (%)	—	1.37	1.40	1.17	1.10	1.16
Ratio of Net Income to Average Net Assets (%)	—	4.11	1.96	1.80	1.67	3.12
Portfolio Turnover Rate (%)	—	87	80	65	66	47
Total Assets End of Year (Millions $)	—	23.5	60.7	90.1	83.3	81.0

Annual Rate of Return (%) Years Ending 12/31	—	11.8	28.3	8.1	(3.1)	17.2

Five-Year Total Return(%) 76.1[B]	Degree of Diversification B	Beta .70	Bull (%) 92.0[C]	Bear (%) (20.6)[D]

Objective: Seeks high total return over the long term, consistent with reasonable risk. Using common stocks, bonds and convertible securities, the fund looks for above-average capital appreciation during up markets and capital preservation during down markets.

Portfolio: (11/30/88) Common stocks 70%, short-term securities 15%, U.S. government securities 5%, corporate bonds 5%, cash 3%, convertible preferred stocks 3%. Largest stock holdings: insurance 16%, oil and gas 11%.

Portfolio Mgr: Louis R. Benzak—1983

Distributions: **Income:** June, Dec   **Capital Gains:** Dec

12b-1: Yes   **Amount:** 0.25%

Minimum: **Initial:** None   **Subsequent:** None

Min IRA: **Initial:** $500   **Subsequent:** None

Services: IRA, Keogh, Withdraw

Tel Exchange: Yes   **With MMF:** Yes

Registered: All states except MO, SD

Ticker: SBFFX

†SCHRODER U.S. EQUITY
Growth

Schroder Capital Mgmt.
International, Inc.
787 Seventh Avenue
New York, NY 10019
(212) 422-6550

	Years Ending 10/31					
	1983	1984	1985	1986	1987	1988
Dividends from Net Investment Income ($)	.80	.25	.30	.24	.25	.18
Distributions from Net Realized Capital Gains ($)	.63	4.74	.36	.73	2.53	2.94
Net Asset Value End of Year ($)	15.42	10.49	10.86	12.55	10.15	7.49
Ratio of Expenses to Net Assets (%)	.89	1.12	1.16	1.16	1.30	1.60
Ratio of Net Income to Average Net Assets (%)	2.30	2.56	2.66	2.25	1.60	1.89
Portfolio Turnover Rate (%)	82	44	59	41	43	18
Total Assets End of Year (Millions $)	99.0	54.8	51.3	46.6	29.7	25.6

Annual Rate of Return (%) Years Ending 12/31	8.4	(1.6)	23.7	11.9	0.5	12.2

Five-Year Total Return(%) 53.6ᴰ	Degree of Diversification	A	Beta 1.02	Bull (%) 111.5ᴮ	Bear (%) (26.5)ᴱ

Objective: Seeks growth of capital, with income as a secondary objective. Invests substantially all its assets in common stock and securities convertible into common stock. The fund may invest up to 10% of the value of its assets in securities that are subject to legal or contractual restrictions on resale. May also invest to a limited degree in non-convertible preferred and debt securities.

Portfolio: (10/31/88) Common stocks 91%, other assets 8%, collateralized mortgage obligations 1%. Largest stock holdings: technology 13%, capital goods/construction 13%.

Portfolio Mgr: Mark J. Smith—1986

Distributions: Income: Quarterly   **Capital Gains:** Annually

12b-1: No

Minimum: Initial: $500   **Subsequent:** $100

Min IRA: Initial: NA   **Subsequent:** NA

Services: None

Tel Exchange: No

Registered: DC, HI, NJ, NV, NY, WY

Ticker: SUSEX

† *Prior to 2/12/88, Schroder U.S. Equity was called Cheapside Dollar Fund Limited. Cheapside Dollar Fund was only available to foreign investors.*

SCUDDER
CAPITAL GROWTH
Growth

Scudder, Stevens & Clark
175 Federal St.
Boston, MA 02110
(800) 225-2470/(617) 439-4640

	Years Ending 9/30					
	1983	1984	1985	1986	1987	1988
Dividends from Net Investment Income ($)	–	.26	.29	.23	.23	.20
Distributions from Net Realized Capital Gains ($)	–	.72	.51	1.88	2.46	2.38
Net Asset Value End of Year ($)	15.22	13.70	15.35	17.17	20.41	16.10
Ratio of Expenses to Net Assets (%)	.82	.90	.86	.84	.88	.95
Ratio of Net Income to Average Net Assets (%)	2.12	2.17	1.74	1.50	.86	.63
Portfolio Turnover Rate (%)	48	36	58	56	58	49
Total Assets End of Year (Millions $)	237.5	236.3	302.4	413.9	583.0	490.7

Annual Rate of Return (%) Years Ending 12/31	22.1	0.5	36.2	16.5	(0.8)	29.7

Five-Year Total Return(%) 105.2ᴬ	Degree of Diversification	B	Beta 1.07	Bull (%) 133.0ᴬ	Bear (%) (25.4)ᴱ

Objective: Seeks to maximize long-term growth of capital by investing in common stocks with growth potential, in companies with special situations and in foreign companies. The fund may also invest in debt securities for defensive purposes.

Portfolio: (9/30/88) Common stocks 91%, short-term securities 10%. Largest stock holdings: media and services 38%, utilities 17%.

Portfolio Mgr: Andrew H. Massie Jr.—1982

Distributions: **Income:** Annually   **Capital Gains:** Annually

12b-1: No

Minimum: **Initial:** $1,000   **Subsequent:** $100

Min IRA: **Initial:** $500   **Subsequent:** $50

Services: IRA, Keogh, Corp, SEP, 403(b), Withdraw, Deduct

Tel Exchange: Yes   **With MMF:** Yes

Registered: All states

Ticker: SCDUX

SCUDDER DEVELOPMENT
Aggressive Growth

Scudder, Stevens & Clark
175 Federal St.
Boston, MA 02110-2267
(800) 225-2470/(617) 439-4640

	Years Ending 6/30					
	1983	1984	1985	1986	1987	1988
Dividends from Net Investment Income ($)	.45	.34	.28	.17	—	—
Distributions from Net Realized Capital Gains ($)	—	.44	.35	.92	1.33	1.90
Net Asset Value End of Year ($)	23.51	18.57	20.41	25.12	25.39	22.00
Ratio of Expenses to Net Assets (%)	1.26	1.31	1.29	1.25	1.27	1.30
Ratio of Net Income to Average Net Assets (%)	2.16	1.62	.90	(.03)	(.33)	(.44)
Portfolio Turnover Rate (%)	22	20	26	29	24	39
Total Assets End of Year (Millions $)	253.0	206.4	254.0	358.7	386.5	355.6
Annual Rate of Return (%) Years Ending 12/31	18.2	(10.3)	19.8	7.6	(1.6)	11.1

Five-Year Total Return(%)	26.4E	Degree of Diversification	C	Beta	1.15	Bull (%)	80.1D	Bear (%)	(26.5)E

Objective:	Seeks long-term capital growth by investing in marketable equity securities of small or little-known companies with promise of expanding in size and profitability, and/or of gaining increased market recognition for their securities. May invest in restricted securities and foreign securities. May convert to debt instruments as a defensive measure.
Portfolio:	(9/30/88) Common stocks 95%, short-term securities 4%. Largest stock holdings: technology 29%, health 19%.
Portfolio Mgr:	Roy C. McKay—1988
Distributions:	**Income:** Aug, Dec **Capital Gains:** Aug, Dec
12b-1:	No
Minimum:	**Initial:** $1,000 **Subsequent:** $100
Min IRA:	**Initial:** $500 **Subsequent:** $50
Services:	IRA, Keogh, Corp, SEP, 403(b), Withdraw, Deduct
Tel Exchange:	Yes **With MMF:** Yes
Registered:	All states
Ticker:	SCDVX

SCUDDER EQUITY INCOME

Balanced

Scudder, Stevens & Clark
175 Federal Sreet
Boston, MA 02110-2267
(800) 225-2470/(617) 426-8300

	Years Ending 9/30					
	1983	1984	1985	1986	1987 (5 mos.)	1988
Dividends from Net Investment Income ($)	−	−	−	−	.18	.36
Distributions from Net Realized Capital Gains ($)	−	−	−	−	−	−
Net Asset Value End of Year ($)	−	−	−	−	11.97	11.01
Ratio of Expenses to Net Assets (%)	−	−	−	−	1.00	1.00
Ratio of Net Income to Average Net Assets (%)	−	−	−	−	6.17	6.03
Portfolio Turnover Rate (%)	−	−	−	−	−	44
Total Assets End of Year (Millions $)	−	−	−	−	12.3	14.6
Annual Rate of Return (%) Years Ending 12/31	−	−	−	−	−	11.3

Five-Year Total Return(%)	NA	Degree of Diversification	NA	Beta	NA	Bull (%)	NA	Bear (%)	(15.4)c

Objective: Seeks high level of current income, primarily by investing in high-yielding common stocks and convertible securities. A secondary objective is growth of capital and income. Looks for stocks with price-earnings ratios lower than the S&P 500, and with below-average stock market risk. May also invest in debt securities.

Portfolio: (9/30/88) Common stocks 54%, short-term securities 20%, convertible bonds 12%, long-term bonds 5%, convertible preferred stocks 5%, intermediate-term notes 3%, other assets 1%. Largest stock holdings: utilities 17%, financial 13%.

Portfolio Mgr: Charles S. Boit−1987

Distributions: Income: Apr, July, Oct, Dec   **Capital Gains:** Dec

12b-1: No

Minimum: Initial: $1,000   Subsequent: $100

Min IRA: Initial: $500   Subsequent: $50

Services: IRA, Keogh, Corp, SEP, 403(b), Withdraw, Deduct

Tel Exchange: Yes   **With MMF:** Yes

Registered: All states

Ticker: SEINX

SCUDDER GLOBAL
International

Scudder, Stevens & Clark
175 Federal Street
Boston, MA 02110-2267
(800) 225-2470/(617) 439-4640

	1983	1984	1985	1986	1987 (11 mos.)	1988
Dividends from Net Investment Income ($)	–	–	–	–	–	.06
Distributions from Net Realized Capital Gains ($)	–	–	–	–	–	.25
Net Asset Value End of Year ($)	–	–	–	–	15.42	14.47
Ratio of Expenses to Net Assets (%)	–	–	–	–	1.84	1.71
Ratio of Net Income to Average Net Assets (%)	–	–	–	–	.63	1.23
Portfolio Turnover Rate (%)	–	–	–	–	32	54
Total Assets End of Year (Millions $)	–	–	–	–	101.9	80.7

(table header spanning: Years Ending 6/30)

Annual Rate of Return (%) Years Ending 12/31	–	–	–	–	2.9	19.2

Five-Year Total Return(%)	NA	Degree of Diversification	NA	Beta	NA	Bull (%)	NA	Bear (%)	(22.9)ᴰ

Objective: Seeks long-term growth of capital through worldwide investment in equity securities. Will be invested in at least three different countries, one of which will be the U.S. Income is an incidental consideration. Can buy and sell index and foreign currency futures as a hedge.

Portfolio: (9/30/88) Common stocks 86%, bonds 7%, commercial paper 2%, preferred stocks 2%, convertible bonds 1%, other assets 1%. Largest country holdings: United States 40%, United Kingdom 14%.

Portfolio Mgr: William Holzer—1986

Distributions: **Income:** Aug, Dec   **Capital Gains:** Aug, Dec

12b-1: No

Minimum: **Initial:** $1,000   **Subsequent:** $100

Min IRA: **Initial:** $500   **Subsequent:** $50

Services: IRA, Keogh, Corp, SEP, 403(b), Withdraw, Deduct

Tel Exchange: Yes   **With MMF:** Yes

Registered: All states

Ticker: SCOBX

SCUDDER GNMA
Bond

Scudder, Stevens & Clark
175 Federal St.
Boston, MA 02110
(800) 225-2470/(617) 439-4640

	Years Ending 3/31					
	1983	1984	1985	1986 (8 mos.)	1987	1988
Dividends from Net Investment Income ($)	—	—	—	1.12	1.34	1.30
Distributions from Net Realized Capital Gains ($)	—	—	—	—	.08	—
Net Asset Value End of Year ($)	—	—	—	15.41	15.44	14.61
Ratio of Expenses to Net Assets (%)	—	—	—	1.02	1.05	1.04
Ratio of Net Income to Average Net Assets (%)	—	—	—	10.11	8.63	8.93
Portfolio Turnover Rate (%)	—	—	—	124	59	92
Total Assets End of Year (Millions $)	—	—	—	153.8	293.8	251.5
Annual Rate of Return (%) Years Ending 12/31	—	—	—	11.3	1.5	6.8

Five-Year Total Return(%)	NA	Degree of Diversification	NA	Beta	NA	Bull (%)	NA	Bear (%)	2.2A

Objective: Seeks high current income and safety of principal by investing at least 65% of its net assets in GNMA securities. Invests in other U.S. government-backed securities. May also buy and sell options and futures contracts.

Portfolio: (9/30/88) GNMAs 82%, U.S. Treasury notes 19%, repurchase agreements 2%.

Portfolio Mgr: David H. Glen—1987

Distributions: Income: Monthly   **Capital Gains:** May, Dec

12b-1: No

Minimum: Initial: $1,000   **Subsequent:** $100

Min IRA: Initial: $500   **Subsequent:** $50

Services: IRA, Keogh, Corp, SEP, 403(b), Withdraw, Deduct

Tel Exchange: Yes   **With MMF:** Yes

Registered: All states

Ticker: SGMSX

SCUDDER GROWTH & INCOME
Growth & Income

Scudder, Stevens & Clark
175 Federal St.
Boston, MA 02110-2267
(800) 225-2470/(617) 439-4640

	Years Ending 12/31					
	1983	1984*	1985	1986	1987	1988
Dividends from Net Investment Income ($)	.43	.40	.58	.68	.68	.59
Distributions from Net Realized Capital Gains ($)	.49	1.78	—	2.28	2.64	—
Net Asset Value End of Year ($)	14.79	11.90	15.35	15.02	12.31	13.18
Ratio of Expenses to Net Assets (%)	.92	.89	.84	.83	.89	.92
Ratio of Net Income to Average Net Assets (%)	3.11	3.56	4.35	4.19	4.24	4.63
Portfolio Turnover Rate (%)	84	79	73	45	60	48
Total Assets End of Year (Millions $)	260.1	223.6	302.1	384.5	391.8	401.6
Annual Rate of Return (%) Years Ending 12/31	13.3	(3.7)	34.5	17.8	3.4	11.9

Five-Year Total Return(%)	76.6[B]	Degree of Diversification	A	Beta	.83	Bull (%)	128.6[A]	Bear (%)	(18.0)[C]

Changed name and objectives.

Objective: Seeks long-term capital growth and current income by purchasing seasoned and readily marketable dividend-paying securities of leading companies. May invest in foreign securities and sell covered call options and futures contracts. May also lend portfolio securities and enter into repurchase agreements.

Portfolio: (12/31/88) Common stocks 77%, convertible preferred stocks 11%, convertible bonds 7%, short-term securities 6%. Largest stock holdings: financial 14%, utilities 13%.

Portfolio Mgr: Benjamin W. Thorndike—1987

Distributions: Income: Apr, July, Oct, Dec   **Capital Gains:** Dec

12b-1: No

Minimum: Initial: $1,000   Subsequent: $100

Min IRA: Initial: $500   Subsequent: $50

Services: IRA, Keogh, Corp, SEP, 403(b), Withdraw, Deduct

Tel Exchange: Yes   **With MMF:** Yes

Registered: All states

Ticker: SCDGX

SCUDDER INCOME
Bond

Scudder, Stevens & Clark
175 Federal St.
Boston, MA 02110-2267
(800) 225-2470/(617) 439-4640

	Years Ending 12/31					
	1983	1984	1985	1986	1987	1988
Dividends from Net Investment Income ($)	1.25	1.25	1.29	1.22	1.10	1.07
Distributions from Net Realized Capital Gains ($)	—	—	—	—	—	—
Net Asset Value End of Year ($)	11.64	11.70	12.82	13.41	12.40	12.41
Ratio of Expenses to Net Assets (%)	.97	1.02	.91	.88	.94	.94
Ratio of Net Income to Average Net Assets (%)	10.61	11.04	10.57	9.12	8.37	8.53
Portfolio Turnover Rate (%)	40	40	30	24	34	20
Total Assets End of Year (Millions $)	110.5	122.9	171.7	248.5	241.8	244.8
Annual Rate of Return (%) Years Ending 12/31	10.8	12.3	21.7	14.6	0.8	8.9

Five-Year Total Return(%)	72.0[C]	Degree of Diversification	NA	Beta	NA	Bull (%)	53.8[D]	Bear (%)	2.7[A]

Objective: Seeks current income through investment in fixed-income securities, dividend-paying common stocks and government obligations. May invest in foreign securities and CDs of both foreign and domestic banks. May sell covered call options and enter into repurchase agreements.

Portfolio: (12/31/88) Long term bonds 46%, intermediate-term bonds 27%, short-term securities 21%, preferred stocks 2%, other assets 2%, convertible bonds 1%. Largest bond holdings: utilities 17%, financial 10%.

Portfolio Mgr: William Hutchinson—1986

Distributions: **Income:** Apr, July, Oct, Dec   **Capital Gains:** Annually

12b-1: No

Minimum: **Initial:** $1,000   **Subsequent:** $100

Min IRA: **Initial:** $500   **Subsequent:** $50

Services: IRA, Keogh, Corp, SEP, 403(b), Withdraw, Deduct

Tel Exchange: Yes   **With MMF:** Yes

Registered: All states

Ticker: SCSBX

SCUDDER INTERNATIONAL

International

Scudder, Stevens & Clark
175 Federal St.
Boston, MA 02110
(800) 225-2470/(617) 439-4640

	7/31	Years Ending 3/31				
	1983	1984* (8 mos.)	1985	1986	1987	1988
Dividends from Net Investment Income ($)	.54	.31	.10	.41	.49	.82
Distributions from Net Realized Capital Gains ($)	–	–	.58	.13	5.93	9.39
Net Asset Value End of Year ($)	21.21	24.29	23.03	36.93	44.05	33.43
Ratio of Expenses to Net Assets (%)	1.13	1.05	1.04	.99	1.09	1.21
Ratio of Net Income to Average Net Assets (%)	2.23	1.02	2.34	2.60	1.19	1.16
Portfolio Turnover Rate (%)	39	17	20	36	67	55
Total Assets End of Year (Millions $)	110.8	188.9	222.9	597	791.3	558.8
Annual Rate of Return (%) Years Ending 12/31	29.2	(0.7)	48.9	50.5	1.0	18.8

Five-Year Total Return(%) 167.1^	Degree of Diversification E	Beta .71	Bull (%) 212.3^	Bear (%) (21.8)^D

Fiscal year-end changed from 7/31 to 3/31.

Objective: Seeks long-term capital growth through investment in marketable equity securities of established non-U.S. companies and economies with prospects for growth. Also invests in fixed-income securities of foreign governments and companies with a view toward total investment return.

Portfolio: (9/30/88) Common stocks 88%, convertible bonds 4%, short-term securities 4%, bonds 2%, other assets 1%, preferred stocks 1%, convertible preferred stocks 1%. Largest country holdings: Japan 18%, United Kingdom 14%.

Portfolio Mgr: Nicholas Bratt—1976

Distributions: **Income:** May, Dec   **Capital Gains:** May, Dec

12b-1: No

Minimum: **Initial:** $1,000   **Subsequent:** $100

Min IRA: **Initial:** $500   **Subsequent:** $50

Services: IRA, Keogh, Corp, SEP, 403(b), Withdraw, Deduct

Tel Exchange: Yes   **With MMF:** Yes

Registered: All states

Ticker: SCINX

SCUDDER JAPAN
International

Scudder, Stevens & Clark
175 Federal Street
Boston, MA 02110-2267
(800) 535-2726/(617) 439-4640

	Years Ending 12/31					
	1983*	1984*	1985*	1986*	1987*	1988
Dividends from Net Investment Income ($)	—	—	—	—	—	.02
Distributions from Net Realized Capital Gains ($)	—	—	—	—	—	3.88
Net Asset Value End of Year ($)	—	—	—	—	—	16.24
Ratio of Expenses to Net Assets (%)	—	—	—	—	—	1.01
Ratio of Net Income to Average Net Assets (%)	—	—	—	—	—	.28
Portfolio Turnover Rate (%)	—	—	—	—	—	39
Total Assets End of Year (Millions $)	—	—	—	—	—	403.9

Annual Rate of Return (%) Years Ending 12/31	*	*	*	*	*	19.4

Five-Year Total Return(%)	NA	Degree of Diversification	NA	Beta	NA	Bull (%)	NA	Bear (%)	1.2B

Prior to 1988, the fund was a closed-end investment company traded on the NYSE.

Objective: Seeks capital appreciation by investing in the common stocks of Japanese companies. The fund will invest at least 80% of its assets in Japan, but may keep up to 20% in short-term cash investments if conditions warrant. May also invest in Japanese debt securities and enter into foreign currency futures contracts.

Portfolio: (12/31/88) Common stock 93%, short-term securities 8%. Largest stock holdings: industrial goods 24%, retail 22%.

Portfolio Mgr: Laura Luckyn-Malone—1986

Distributions: **Income:** Annually **Capital Gains:** Annually

12b-1: No

Minimum: **Initial:** $1,000 **Subsequent:** $100

Min IRA: **Initial:** $500 **Subsequent:** $50

Services: IRA, Keogh, Corp, SEP, 403(b), Withdraw, Deduct

Tel Exchange: Yes **With MMF:** Yes

Registered: All states

Ticker: SJPNX

SCUDDER TARGET GENERAL 1990
Bond

Scudder, Stevens & Clark
175 Federal St.
Boston, MA 02110-2267
(800) 225-2470/(617) 439-4640

	10/31		Years Ending 12/31				
	1983	**1984**	**1984*** (2 mos.)	**1985**	**1986**	**1987**	**1988**
Dividends from Net Investment Income ($)	.59	.82	.14	.83	.66	.56	.58
Distributions from Net Realized Capital Gains ($)	—	—	—	—	.39	.12	.06
Net Asset Value End of Year ($)	9.33	9.38	9.53	10.38	10.53	10.16	10.13
Ratio of Expenses to Net Assets (%)	1.00	1.06	1.00	1.00	1.25	1.41	1.50
Ratio of Net Income to Average Net Assets (%)	8.63	9.07	8.75	8.33	6.16	5.34	5.63
Portfolio Turnover Rate (%)	4	13	0	49	35	41	33
Total Assets: End of Year (Millions $)	6.0	8.8	9.3	12.5	16.2	15.4	13.3

Annual Rate of Return (%) Years Ending 12/31	(0.4)	12.9	*	18.3	12.0	2.9	6.1

Five-Year Total Return(%) 63.3ᶜ	Degree of Diversification NA	Beta NA	Bull (%) 48.8ᴱ	Bear (%) 2.2ᴬ

*Fiscal year-end changed from 10/31 to 12/31. All annual return figures are for full years ending 12/31.

Objective:	Seeks current income plus preservation of capital. Invests in high-grade corporate bonds and notes plus U.S. Treasury securities. The portfolio is designed to be liquidated in 1990.
Portfolio:	(12/31/88) Corporate bonds 75%, U.S. Treasury obligations 22%, U.S. government-backed obligations 4%. Largest bond holdings: utilities 32%, financial 21%.
Portfolio Mgr:	Samuel Thorne Jr.—1988
Distributions:	**Income:** Monthly **Capital Gains:** Annually
12b-1:	No
Minimum:	**Initial:** $1,000 **Subsequent:** $100
Min IRA:	**Initial:** $500 **Subsequent:** $50
Services:	IRA, Keogh, Corp, SEP, 403(b), Withdraw, Deduct
Tel Exchange:	Yes **With MMF:** Yes
Registered:	All states
Ticker:	SGNIX

SELECTED AMERICAN SHARES
Growth & Income

Prescott Asset Mgmt., Inc.
230 W. Monroe St., 28th Flr.
Chicago, IL 60606
(800) 553-5533/(312) 641-7862

	Years Ending 12/31					
	1983	1984	1985	1986	1987	1988
Dividends from Net Investment Income ($)	.56	.48	.40	.48	.42	.26
Distributions from Net Realized Capital Gains ($)	–	.05	.17	2.29	.92	–
Net Asset Value End of Year ($)	9.68	10.54	13.35	12.65	11.43	13.67
Ratio of Expenses to Net Assets (%)	.94	.99	.87	.85	1.11	1.11
Ratio of Net Income to Average Net Assets (%)	5.80	4.58	4.42	3.07	2.38	2.07
Portfolio Turnover Rate (%)	66	49	33	40	45	35
Total Assets End of Year (Millions $)	81.3	84.3	122.6	160.5	263.2	284.7

Annual Rate of Return (%) Years Ending 12/31	22.6	13.9	33.2	17.0	0.2	22.0

Five-Year Total Return(%) 117.0[A]	Degree of Diversification	B	Beta	.81	Bull (%) 126.3[B]	Bear (%) (21.4)[D]

Objective:	To provide growth of capital and income. The fund invests in varying proportions of common stocks and fixed-income securities of companies with large capitalizations and long records of earnings growth and dividends. May lend portfolio securities and write covered call options.
Portfolio:	(12/31/88) Common stocks 98%, short-term securities 1%. Largest stock holdings: insurance 17%, tobacco 13%.
Portfolio Mgr:	Donald Yacktman—1983
Distributions:	**Income:** Mar, June, Sept, Dec **Capital Gains:** Annually
12b-1:	Yes **Amount:** 1.00%
Minimum:	**Initial:** $1,000 **Subsequent:** $100
Min IRA:	**Initial:** $1,000 **Subsequent:** $100
Services:	IRA, Keogh, Corp, SEP, Withdraw, Deduct
Tel Exchange:	Yes **With MMF:** Yes
Registered:	All states
Ticker:	PAMAX

SELECTED SPECIAL SHARES
Growth

Prescott Asset Mgmt., Inc.
230 W. Monroe St., 28th Flr.
Chicago, IL 60606
(800) 553-5533/(312) 641-7862

	Years Ending 12/31					
	1983	1984	1985	1986	1987	1988
Dividends from Net Investment Income ($)	.38	.56	.49	.64	.64	.20
Distributions from Net Realized Capital Gains ($)	—	4.28	.65	3.45	1.40	1.75
Net Asset Value End of Year ($)	23.28	17.70	20.55	17.83	15.91	17.04
Ratio of Expenses to Net Assets (%)	1.21	1.38	1.23	1.08	1.10	1.24
Ratio of Net Income to Average Net Assets (%)	2.72	2.67	3.23	2.47	.85	1.09
Portfolio Turnover Rate (%)	101	68	73	133	89	71
Total Assets End of Year (Millions $)	36.6	32.7	35.9	32.8	36.1	34.9

Annual Rate of Return (%) Years Ending 12/31	28.0	(4.2)	23.5	7.2	0.6	19.6

Five-Year Total Return(%)	52.6[D]	Degree of Diversification	B	Beta 1.02	Bull (%) 102.4[C]	Bear (%) (26.7)[E]

Objective: Seeks growth of capital through investment in common stocks and convertible securities of growing companies that are undervalued. Looks for strong management and growth record. Current income is incidental to this objective.

Portfolio: (12/31/88) Common stocks 99%, short-term securities 2%. Largest stock holdings: retailing 13%, distribution 13%.

Portfolio Mgr: Ronald Ball—1986

Distributions: Income: Dec   **Capital Gains:** Dec

12b-1: Yes   **Amount:** 1.00%

Minimum: Initial: $1,000   Subsequent: $100

Min IRA: Initial: $1,000   Subsequent: $100

Services: IRA, Keogh, Corp, SEP, Withdraw, Deduct

Tel Exchange: Yes   **With MMF:** Yes

Registered: All states

Ticker: PAMSX

†SEQUOIA
Growth

Ruane, Cunniff & Co., Inc.
1370 Avenue of the Americas
New York, NY 10019
(212) 245-4500

	Years Ending 12/31					
	1983	1984	1985	1986	1987	1988
Dividends from Net Investment Income ($)	1.64	1.43	1.51	1.61	2.21	1.39
Distributions from Net Realized Capital Gains ($)	1.30	2.58	3.77	8.54	1.59	2.23
Net Asset Value End of Year ($)	37.11	39.26	44.01	39.29	38.43	38.81
Ratio of Expenses to Net Assets (%)	1.0	1.0	1.0	1.0	1.0	1.0
Ratio of Net Income to Average Net Assets (%)	5.0	4.3	3.8	3.9	3.3	3.6
Portfolio Turnover Rate (%)	17	39	44	40	43	39
Total Assets End of Year (Millions $)	350.7	443.2	599.6	696.7	720.5	714.2

Annual Rate of Return (%) Years Ending 12/31	27.0	18.7	27.7	12.6	7.2	11.0

Five-Year Total Return(%) 103.1ᴬ	Degree of Diversification D	Beta .50	Bull (%) 97.4ᶜ	Bear (%) (11.7)ᶜ

Objective: Seeks to provide growth of capital. Invests primarily in common stocks and securities convertible into common stock. May invest in foreign securities, restricted securities, and special situations including reorganizations and liquidations.

Portfolio: (12/31/88) Common stocks 54%, U.S. government obligations 39%, preferred stocks 8%. Largest stock holdings: paper manufacturing 15%, broadcasting 13%.

Portfolio Mgr: William Ruane—1970

Distributions: Income: Aug, Dec　　　　　**Capital Gains:** Dec

12b-1: No

Minimum: Initial: NA　　　Subsequent: $50

Min IRA: Initial: NA　　　Subsequent: None

Services: IRA, Withdraw

Tel Exchange: No

Registered: CA, CT, FL, IA, IL, IN, MA, MD, MI, MN, NC, NE, NJ, NV, NY, PA, TX, WI

Ticker: SEQUX

† *Closed to new investors.*

SHADOW STOCK FUND

Aggressive Growth

Jones & Babson, Inc.
Three Crown Center
2440 Pershing Road
Kansas City, MO 64108
(800) 821-5591/(816) 471-5200

	Years Ending 6/30					
	1983	1984	1985	1986	1987	1988 (10 mos.)
Dividends from Net Investment Income ($)	—	—	—	—	—	.08
Distributions from Net Realized Capital Gains ($)	—	—	—	—	—	—
Net Asset Value End of Year ($)	—	—	—	—	—	8.69
Ratio of Expenses to Net Assets (%)	—	—	—	—	—	1.51
Ratio of Net Income to Average Net Assets (%)	—	—	—	—	—	1.57
Portfolio Turnover Rate (%)	—	—	—	—	—	7
Total Assets End of Year (Millions $)	—	—	—	—	—	16.3
Annual Rate of Return (%) Years Ending 12/31	—	—	—	—	—	22.5

Five-Year Total Return(%)	NA	Degree of Diversification	NA	Beta	NA	Bull (%)	NA	Bear (%)	NA

Objective: Seeks long-term growth of capital by investing in the stocks of small, neglected companies. These companies will have market capitalizations of between $20 million and $110 million and will have annual net profits of at least $1 million for the three most recent fiscal years. The fund will include more than 400 stocks.

Portfolio: (9/30/88) Common stocks 94%, repurchase agreements 9%. Largest stock holdings: consumer cyclical 22%, technology 18%.

Portfolio Mgr: Peter Schliemann, Nick Whitridge—1987

Distributions: **Income:** June   **Capital Gains:** June

12b-1: No

Minimum: **Initial:** $2,500   **Subsequent:** $100

Min IRA: **Initial:** $250   **Subsequent:** $25

Services: IRA, Keogh, SEP, Withdraw, Deduct

Tel Exchange: Yes   **With MMF:** Yes

Registered: All states

Ticker: SHSTX

SHERMAN, DEAN
Aggressive Growth

Sherman, Dean
Management and Research Corp.
6061 N.W. Expressway, Suite 465
San Antonio, TX 78201
(512) 735-7700

	Years Ending 5/31					
	1983	1984	1985	1986	1987	1988
Dividends from Net Investment Income ($)	.12	.03	.01	.04	–	–
Distributions from Net Realized Capital Gains ($)	–	–	–	–	–	–
Net Asset Value End of Year ($)	9.12	6.86	6.11	5.21	8.14	6.14
Ratio of Expenses to Net Assets (%)	1.91	2.01	2.04	2.36	3.38	2.75
Ratio of Net Income to Average Net Assets (%)	.70	.23	.00	(1.90)	(3.34)	(1.98)
Portfolio Turnover Rate (%)	4	12	21	13	0	0
Total Assets End of Year (Millions $)	5.1	4.3	3.8	2.3	2.9	2.2

Annual Rate of Return (%) Years Ending 12/31	(3.8)	(32.0)	13.1	(4.6)	.2	25.7

Five-Year Total Return(%)	(7.5)E	Degree of Diversification	E	Beta	.56	Bull (%)	47.3E	Bear (%)	(37.9)E

Objective: Seeks long-term capital appreciation through investment in common stocks of companies that show unusually favorable prospects, including small, unseasoned and special situation companies. May concentrate 50% of assets in two companies—25% each.

Portfolio: (11/30/88) Common stocks 97%, bonds 2%, cash and other assets 1%. Largest stock holdings: mining 51%, shipping 20%.

Portfolio Mgr: J. Walter Sherman—1967

Distributions: Income: June   **Capital Gains:** June

12b-1: Yes   **Amount:** 0.25%

Minimum: Initial: $1,000   Subsequent: $100

Min IRA: Initial: NA   Subsequent: NA

Services: None

Tel Exchange: No

Registered: CA, CO, CT, DC, FL, GA, HI, IL, IN, MA, MD, MI, MN, MO, NJ, NY, OR, PA, TX, VA, WA, WI, WY

Ticker: SHDNX

SOUND SHORE
Growth

Sound Shore Management, Inc.
P.O. Box 1810
8 Sound Shore Drive
Greenwich, CT 06836
(203) 629-1980

| | Years Ending 3/31 | | | | | 12/31 | |
	1983	1984	1985	1986	1987	1987* (9 mos.)	1988
Dividends from Net Investment Income ($)	—	—	—	.14	.08	.18	.18
Distributions from Net Realized Capital Gains ($)	—	—	—	—	.39	1.21	1.18
Net Asset Value End of Year ($)	—	—	—	13.67	15.97	11.58	12.67
Ratio of Expenses to Net Assets (%)	—	—	—	1.48	1.45	1.36	1.40
Ratio of Net Income to Average Net Assets (%)	—	—	—	2.55	1.14	1.06	1.57
Portfolio Turnover Rate (%)	—	—	—	82	91	85	134
Total Assets End of Year (Millions $)	—	—	—	13.9	31.5	23.8	28.5

Annual Rate of Return (%) Years Ending 12/31	—	—	—	20.5	(3.7)	*	21.1

Five-Year Total Return(%) NA	Degree of Diversification C	Beta .81	Bull (%) NA	Bear (%) (21.6)ᴰ

Fiscal year-end changed from 3/31 to 12/31. All annual return figures are for full years ending 12/31.

Objective: Seeks capital growth with current income as a secondary objective. Invests in a diversified group of growth stocks selected on the basis of price, earnings expectations, balance sheet characteristics, and perceived management skills. May not invest more than 25% of net assets in any particular industry.

Portfolio: (12/31/88) Common stocks 87%, short-term securities 15%. Largest stock holdings: savings and loan 13%, consumer products 10%.

Portfolio Mgr: Harry Burn III—1985

Distributions: **Income:** Semiannually   **Capital Gains:** Annually

12b-1: Yes   **Amount:** 1.00%

Minimum: **Initial:** $20,000   **Subsequent:** None

Min IRA: **Initial:** $250   **Subsequent:** None

Services: IRA, Withdraw

Tel Exchange: Yes   **With MMF:** Yes

Registered: All states

Ticker: SSHFX

STEINROE CAPITAL OPPORTUNITIES

Aggressive Growth

Stein Roe & Farnham
P.O. Box 1143
Chicago, IL 60690
(800) 338-2550/(312) 368-7800

	Years Ending 12/31					9/30
	1983	1984	1985	1986	1987	1988* (9 mos.)
Dividends from Net Investment Income ($)	.19	.12	.29	.20	.09	—
Distributions from Net Realized Capital Gains ($)	.65	2.55	—	.85	6.73	—
Net Asset Value End of Year ($)	26.43	19.37	23.81	26.75	21.23	21.55
Ratio of Expenses to Net Assets (%)	.89	.92	.95	.95	.95	1.01
Ratio of Net Income to Average Net Assets (%)	.45	1.21	.94	.19	.18	.34
Portfolio Turnover Rate (%)	72	85	90	116	133	164
Total Assets End of Year (Millions $)	292.5	176.1	176.1	191.4	171.9	194.1

Annual Rate of Return (%) Years Ending 12/31	11.9	(16.8)	24.6	16.8	8.7	(3.9)

Five-Year Total Return(%) 26.5ᴱ	Degree of Diversification D	Beta 1.16	Bull (%) 119.7ᴮ	Bear (%) (27.0)ᴱ

Fiscal year-end changed from 12/31 to 9/30.

Objective:	To provide long-term capital appreciation by investing in selected common stocks of both seasoned and smaller companies that have potential for success with new products or services, technological developments, or management shifts. May invest in foreign securities.
Portfolio:	(9/30/88) Common stocks 82%, short-term obligations 19%. Largest stock holdings: distribution 18%, health care 13%.
Portfolio Mgr:	Ronald Lewison, Gloria Santella—1989
Distributions:	**Income:** Dec **Capital Gains:** Dec
12b-1:	No
Minimum:	**Initial:** $1,000 **Subsequent:** $100
Min IRA:	**Initial:** $500 **Subsequent:** $50
Services:	IRA, Keogh, SEP, Withdraw
Tel Exchange:	Yes **With MMF:** Yes
Registered:	All states
Ticker:	SRFCX

STEINROE DISCOVERY

Aggressive Growth

Stein Roe & Farnham
P.O. Box 1143
Chicago, IL 60690
(800) 338-2550/(312) 368-7800

	Years Ending 6/30					12/31	9/30
	1983	1984 (11 mos.)	1985	1986	1987	1987* (6 mos.)	1988* (9 mos.)
Dividends from Net Investment Income ($)	—	—	.03	.04	.04	.02	—
Distributions from Net Realized Capital Gains ($)	—	—	—	—	.03	2.56	—
Net Asset Value End of Year ($)	—	7.49	10.22	13.76	13.24	8.13	8.95
Ratio of Expenses to Net Assets (%)	—	1.49	1.42	1.29	1.36	1.51	1.50
Ratio of Net Income to Average Net Assets (%)	—	.32	.71	.31	.21	(.93)	.95
Portfolio Turnover Rate (%)	—	64	101	157	207	84	231
Total Assets End of Year (Millions $)	—	33.2	97.2	133.4	65.7	37.1	39.2

Annual Rate of Return (%) Years Ending 12/31	—	(12.2)	45.3	(5.3)	(3.2)	*	11.8

Five-Year Total Return(%)	30.7ᴱ	Degree of Diversification	D	Beta	1.27	Bull (%)	100.9ᶜ	Bear (%)	(28.1)ᴱ

Fiscal year-end changed. All annual return figures are for full years ending 12/31.

Objective: Seeks long-term capital appreciation by investing in the common stock of smaller companies with less than $250 million in market capitalization and in larger companies with new products, technological developments or other favorable business developments. May include new issues. May write covered call options and enter into repurchase agreements.

Portfolio: (9/30/88) Common stocks 94%, short-term obligations 4%, other assets 2%. Largest stock holdings: health care 18%, distribution 17%.

Portfolio Mgr: Ronald Lewison, Gloria Santella—1988

Distributions: **Income:** Dec   **Capital Gains:** Dec

12b-1: No

Minimum: **Initial:** $1,000   **Subsequent:** $100

Min IRA: **Initial:** $500   **Subsequent:** $50

Services: IRA, Keogh, SEP, Withdraw

Tel Exchange: Yes   **With MMF:** Yes

Registered: All states except CA

Ticker: SRDFX

STEINROE GOVERNMENTS PLUS
Bond

Stein Roe & Farnham
P.O. Box 1143
Chicago, IL 60690
(800) 338-2550/(312) 368-7800

	Years Ending 6/30					
	1983	1984	1985	1986 (4 mos.)	1987	1988
Dividends from Net Investment Income ($)	–	–	–	.24	.72	.74
Distributions from Net Realized Capital Gains ($)	–	–	–	–	–	.05
Net Asset Value End of Year ($)	–	–	–	10.10	9.79	9.59
Ratio of Expenses to Net Assets (%)	–	–	–	1.00	1.00	1.00
Ratio of Net Income to Average Net Assets (%)	–	–	–	7.61	7.13	7.68
Portfolio Turnover Rate (%)	–	–	–	91	205	237
Total Assets End of Year (Millions $)	–	–	–	12.0	22.6	26.9

Annual Rate of Return (%) Years Ending 12/31	–	–	–	–	0.1	6.9

Five-Year Total Return(%)	NA	Degree of Diversification	NA	Beta	NA	Bull (%)	NA	Bear (%)	3.2^A

Objective: Seeks to provide a high level of current income. Invests primarily in securities issued or guaranteed by the U.S. government or its agencies. Fund may invest a significantly large portion of its assets in mortgage-backed debt securities. Under normal market conditions, invests at least 80% of its assets in government securities. May also invest up to 20% of its assets in other types of debt securities.

Portfolio: (12/31/88) Long-term obligations 89%, short-term obligations 13%. Largest holdings: GNMAs 58%, FNMAs 14%.

Portfolio Mgr: Michael Kennedy—1988

Distributions: Income: Monthly   **Capital Gains:** Annually

12b-1: No

Minimum: Initial: $1,000   Subsequent: $100

Min IRA: Initial: $500   Subsequent: $50

Services: IRA, Keogh, SEP, Withdraw

Tel Exchange: Yes   With MMF: Yes

Registered: All states

Ticker: SRGPX

STEINROE HIGH-YIELD BONDS

Bond

Stein Roe & Farnham
P.O. Box 1143
Chicago, IL 60690
(800) 338-2550/(312) 368-7800

	Years Ending 6/30					
	1983	**1984**	**1985**	**1986** (4 mos.)	**1987**	**1988**
Dividends from Net Investment Income ($)	—	—	—	.30	.98	.95
Distributions from Net Realized Capital Gains ($)	—	—	—	—	—	—
Net Asset Value End of Year ($)	—	—	—	9.94	9.71	9.60
Ratio of Expenses to Net Assets (%)	—	—	—	1.00	.96	.91
Ratio of Net Income to Average Net Assets (%)	—	—	—	10.07	9.90	10.08
Portfolio Turnover Rate (%)	—	—	—	84	153	158
Total Assets End of Year (Millions $)	—	—	—	32.0	91.9	96.6

Annual Rate of Return (%) Years Ending 12/31	—	—	—	—	4.0	11.6

Five-Year Total Return(%)	NA	Degree of Diversification	NA	Beta	NA	Bull (%)	NA	Bear (%) 3.0ᴬ

Objective: Seeks high level of current income; capital appreciation and capital preservation are of secondary importance. Invests at least 60% of the fund's assets in medium- or higher-quality debt securities. May invest up to 35% of its assets in preferred and common stocks.

Portfolio: (12/31/88) Long-term obligations 90%, short-term obligations 6%, other assets 4%. Largest holdings: electric utilities 22%, financial 11%.

Portfolio Mgr: Jerry Paul—1987

Distributions: **Income:** Monthly   **Capital Gains:** Annually

12b-1: No

Minimum: **Initial:** $1,000   **Subsequent:** $100

Min IRA: **Initial:** $500   **Subsequent:** $50

Services: IRA, Keogh, SEP, Withdraw

Tel Exchange: Yes   **With MMF:** Yes

Registered: All states

Ticker: SRHBX

STEINROE MANAGED BONDS
Bond

Stein Roe & Farnham
P.O. Box 1143
Chicago, IL 60690
(800) 338-2550/(312) 368-7800

	Years Ending 6/30					
	1983	1984	1985	1986	1987	1988
Dividends from Net Investment Income ($)	.97	.94	.89	.84	.74	.68
Distributions from Net Realized Capital Gains ($)	–	.21	–	–	.74	.14
Net Asset Value End of Year ($)	9.00	7.75	8.89	9.92	8.77	8.51
Ratio of Expenses to Net Assets (%)	.81	.78	.70	.69	.68	.73
Ratio of Net Income to Average Net Assets (%)	10.68	11.15	10.65	9.03	7.94	7.97
Portfolio Turnover Rate (%)	185	152	286	334	230	273
Total Assets End of Year (Millions $)	84.1	86.5	134.6	183.4	188.7	162.3

Annual Rate of Return (%) Years Ending 12/31	6.9	11.8	22.9	16.3	1.1	7.2

Five-Year Total Return(%) 73.2[B]	Degree of Diversification NA	Beta NA	Bull (%) 51.6[D]	Bear (%) 3.3[A]

Objective: Seeks to provide a high level of current income, consistent with the preservation of capital. Under normal conditions, will invest at least 65% of its assets in convertible and non-convertible bonds. All bonds in the portfolio will be investment-grade corporates or Treasury securities.

Portfolio: (12/31/88) Long-term obligations 92%, short-term obligations 7%, other assets 1%. Largest holdings: U.S. government and agency obligations 62%, financial 9%.

Portfolio Mgr: Michael Kennedy—1988

Distributions: **Income:** Monthly   **Capital Gains:** Annually

12b-1: No

Minimum: **Initial:** $1,000   **Subsequent:** $100

Min IRA: **Initial:** $500   **Subsequent:** $50

Services: IRA, Keogh, SEP, Withdraw

Tel Exchange: Yes   **With MMF:** Yes

Registered: All states

Ticker: SRBFX

STEINROE PRIME EQUITIES
Growth & Income

Stein Roe & Farnham
P.O. Box 1143
Chicago, IL 60690
(800) 338-2550/(312) 368-7800

	Years Ending 9/30					
	1983	1984	1985	1986	1987 (6 mos.)	1988
Dividends from Net Investment Income ($)	–	–	–	–	.03	.14
Distributions from Net Realized Capital Gains ($)	–	–	–	–	–	–
Net Asset Value End of Year ($)	–	–	–	–	10.49	8.88
Ratio of Expenses to Net Assets (%)	–	–	–	–	1.91	1.47
Ratio of Net Income to Average Net Assets (%)	–	–	–	–	1.43	2.03
Portfolio Turnover Rate (%)	–	–	–	–	32	105
Total Assets End of Year (Millions $)	–	–	–	–	22.9	23.0

Annual Rate of Return (%) Years Ending 12/31	–	–	–	–	–	9.0

Five-Year Total Return(%)	NA	Degree of Diversification	NA	Beta	NA	Bull (%)	NA	Bear (%)	(21.9)ᴰ

Objective: Primary objective is growth of capital. Normally invests at least 65% of net assets in well-established companies with market capitalizations above $1 billion. May invest up to 10% of its assets in foreign securities. May also purchase fixed-income securities, and options and futures contracts.

Portfolio: (9/30/88) Common stocks 87%, commercial paper 11%, convertible subordinated debentures 2%, convertible preferred stocks 2%. Largest stock holdings: food, beverage and tobacco 8%, energy 8%.

Portfolio Mgr: Ralph Segall, Carlene Murphy—1983

Distributions: **Income:** Quarterly   **Capital Gains:** Dec

12b-1: No

Minimum: **Initial:** $1,000   **Subsequent:** $100

Min IRA: **Initial:** $500   **Subsequent:** $50

Services: IRA, Keogh, SEP, Withdraw

Tel Exchange: Yes   **With MMF:** Yes

Registered: All states

Ticker: SRPEX

STEINROE SPECIAL

Aggressive Growth

Stein Roe & Farnham
P.O. Box 1143
Chicago, IL 60690
(800) 338-2550/(312) 368-7800

	Years Ending 12/31					9/30
	1983	1984	1985	1986	1987	1988* (9 mos.)
Dividends from Net Investment Income ($)	.23	.23	.19	.34	.57	.01
Distributions from Net Realized Capital Gains ($)	.57	2.29	.54	3.80	3.90	–
Net Asset Value End of Year ($)	17.73	14.88	18.41	16.95	12.83	15.12
Ratio of Expenses to Net Assets (%)	.93	.96	.92	.92	.96	.99
Ratio of Net Income to Average Net Assets (%)	1.88	1.99	2.07	1.75	1.32	1.31
Portfolio Turnover Rate (%)	81	89	96	116	103	42
Total Assets End of Year (Millions $)	145.2	152.0	278.0	253.7	187.9	224.5

Annual Rate of Return (%) Years Ending 12/31	32.9	0.0	29.4	14.8	3.5	20.2

Five-Year Total Return(%) 84.8[B]	Degree of Diversification B	Beta .97	Bull (%) 122.8[B]	Bear (%) (21.6)[D]

Fiscal year-end changed from 12/31 to 9/30.

Objective:	Seeks capital appreciation through investment in the common stocks of companies expected to benefit from special factors or trends or having unusual capital appreciation potential, including new issues.
Portfolio:	(9/30/88) Common stocks 84%, short-term obligations 11%, convertible subordinated debentures 3%, bonds and notes 1%, convertible preferred stocks 1%. Largest stock holdings: media 20%, industrial products 11%.
Portfolio Mgr:	Richard Weiss, Carlene Murphy—1983
Distributions:	**Income:** Dec **Capital Gains:** Dec
12b-1:	No
Minimum:	**Initial:** $1,000 **Subsequent:** $100
Min IRA:	**Initial:** $500 **Subsequent:** $50
Services:	IRA, Keogh, SEP, Withdraw
Tel Exchange:	Yes **With MMF:** Yes
Registered:	All states
Ticker:	SRSPX

STEINROE STOCK

Aggressive Growth

Stein Roe & Farnham
P.O. Box 1143
Chicago, IL 60690
(800) 338-2550/(312) 368-7800

	Years Ending 12/31					9/30
	1983	**1984**	**1985**	**1986**	**1987**	**1988*** (9 mos.)
Dividends from Net Investment Income ($)	.28	.38	.30	.25	.29	.15
Distributions from Net Realized Capital Gains ($)	1.43	4.70	—	3.22	2.71	—
Net Asset Value End of Year ($)	21.36	14.04	17.43	16.97	14.67	14.60
Ratio of Expenses to Net Assets (%)	.63	.67	.67	.67	.65	.76
Ratio of Net Income to Average Net Assets (%)	1.13	2.55	1.89	1.34	1.25	1.62
Portfolio Turnover Rate (%)	173	195	114	137	143	84
Total Assets End of Year (Millions $)	269.3	216.5	224.4	226.6	232.7	195.7

Annual Rate of Return (%) Years Ending 12/31	14.0	(9.8)	26.5	17.3	5.1	0.7

Five-Year Total Return(%) 41.7ᴱ	Degree of Diversification A	Beta 1.10	Bull (%) 127.3ᴬ	Bear (%) (26.1)ᴱ

**Fiscal year-end changed from 12/31 to 9/30.*

Objective: Seeks long-term capital appreciation through investment primarily in common stocks and convertible securities of established companies. May write covered call options on up to 25% of assets.

Portfolio: (9/30/88) Common stocks 92%, short-term obligations 8%. Largest stock holdings: computer-related equipment 8%, food, beverages and tobacco 7%.

Portfolio Mgr: Michael Carey—1988

Distributions: Income: Feb, May, Aug, Nov   **Capital Gains:** Dec

12b-1: No

Minimum: Initial: $1,000   Subsequent: $100

Min IRA: Initial: $500   Subsequent: $50

Services: IRA, Keogh, SEP, Withdraw

Tel Exchange: Yes   **With MMF:** Yes

Registered: All states

Ticker: SRFSX

STEINROE
TOTAL RETURN
Balanced

Stein Roe & Farnham
P.O. Box 1143
Chicago, IL 60690
(800) 338-2550/(312) 368-7800

	Years Ending 12/31					9/30
	1983	1984	1985	1986	1987	1988* (9 mos.)
Dividends from Net Investment Income ($)	1.26	1.41	1.42	1.35	1.63	.90
Distributions from Net Realized Capital Gains ($)	—	1.55	.19	2.70	1.45	.11
Net Asset Value End of Year ($)	23.40	21.37	25.04	25.07	22.25	22.66
Ratio of Expenses to Net Assets (%)	.73	.73	.77	.79	.80	.87
Ratio of Net Income to Average Net Assets (%)	5.55	6.94	6.30	5.21	5.12	5.68
Portfolio Turnover Rate (%)	79	50	100	108	86	85
Total Assets End of Year (Millions $)	93.0	95.7	128.7	149.8	140.2	134.2

Annual Rate of Return (%) Years Ending 12/31	13.5	5.2	25.6	16.9	0.4	7.9

Five-Year Total Return(%)	67.3c	Degree of Diversification	A	Beta	.58	Bull (%)	89.3c	Bear (%)	(13.2)c

Fiscal year-end changed from 12/31 to 9/30.

Objective: To maintain and increase the purchasing power of invested capital while providing income by investing in high-quality bonds, preferred stocks and common stocks of established companies. Stocks will comprise no more than 75% of assets. May write (sell) covered call options.

Portfolio: (9/30/88) Bonds and notes 32%, common stocks 29%, convertible subordinated debentures 20%, short-term obligations 11%, convertible preferred stocks 7%, other assets 1%. Largest stock holdings: petroleum 4%, food, beverages and tobacco 4%.

Portfolio Mgr: Robert Christensen—1981

Distributions: **Income:** Feb, May, Aug, Nov   **Capital Gains:** Annually

12b-1: No

Minimum: **Initial:** $1,000   **Subsequent:** $100

Min IRA: **Initial:** $500   **Subsequent:** $50

Services: IRA, Keogh, SEP, Withdraw

Tel Exchange: Yes   **With MMF:** Yes

Registered: All states

Ticker: SRFBX

STEINROE UNIVERSE
Growth

Stein Roe & Farnham
P.O. Box 1143
Chicago, IL 60690
(800) 338-2550/(312) 368-7800

	Years Ending 6/30					12/31	9/30
	1983	1984	1985	1986	1987	1987* (6 mos.)	1988* (9 mos.)
Dividends from Net Investment Income ($)	.36	.17	.28	.27	.21	.27	—
Distributions from Net Realized Capital Gains ($)	—	.64	—	—	3.62	5.48	—
Net Asset Value End of Year ($)	22.45	14.98	18.05	24.34	21.64	12.60	13.30
Ratio of Expenses to Net Assets (%)	1.10	1.09	1.19	1.20	1.19	1.37	1.55
Ratio of Net Income to Average Net Assets (%)	1.21	1.23	1.27	.87	1.13	.63	.02
Portfolio Turnover Rate (%)	75	130	179	147	242	87	156
Total Assets End of Year (Millions $)	336.4	182.5	116.8	114.7	94.4	45.5	20.4

Annual Rate of Return (%) Years Ending 12/31	20.6	(18.8)	28.3	13.2	(1.6)	*	2.1

Five-Year Total Return(%)	18.5ᴱ	Degree of Diversification	C	Beta	1.08	Bull (%)	100.3ᶜ	Bear (%)	(26.7)ᴱ

Fiscal year-end changed. All annual return figures are for full years ending 12/31.

Objective: Seeks capital appreciation primarily through investment in common stocks of growth companies including small and unseasoned companies or securities convertible into common stocks. Selection made by computerized database, which includes financial forecasts and estimates of indicated market value. May write covered call options, invest in foreign securities and enter into repurchase agreements.

Portfolio: (9/30/88) Common stocks 96%, short-term obligations 6%. Largest stock holdings: distribution 14%, tires, rubber and related products 7%.

Portfolio Mgr: Stephen McNally—1988

Distributions: Income: Dec   **Capital Gains:** Dec

12b-1: No

Minimum: Initial: $1,000   **Subsequent:** $100

Min IRA: Initial: $500   **Subsequent:** $50

Services: IRA, Keogh, SEP, Withdraw

Tel Exchange: Yes   **With MMF:** Yes

Registered: All states except CA

Ticker: SRUFX

STRATTON GROWTH
Growth & Income

Stratton Management Co.
Plymouth Mtg. Exec. Campus
610 W. Germantown Pike
Suite 361
Plymouth Meeting, PA 19462
(800) 634-5726/(215) 941-0255

	Years Ending 5/31					
	1983	1984	1985	1986	1987	1988
Dividends from Net Investment Income ($)	.29	.13	.14	.20	.28	.70
Distributions from Net Realized Capital Gains ($)	—	—	.70	.61	2.07	1.53
Net Asset Value End of Year ($)	17.92	15.67	18.85	24.25	22.24	19.48
Ratio of Expenses to Net Assets (%)	1.80	1.61	1.61	1.49	1.50	1.48
Ratio of Net Income to Average Net Assets (%)	1.17	.88	1.22	1.40	1.74	2.80
Portfolio Turnover Rate (%)	70	36	35	29	23	34
Total Assets End of Year (Millions $)	11.8	11.4	14.3	19.3	19.3	16.9
Annual Rate of Return (%) Years Ending 12/31	26.3	(4.6)	27.2	10.7	(4.3)	22.6

Five-Year Total Return(%)	57.6[D]	Degree of Diversification	C	Beta	.88	Bull (%)	89.9[C]	Bear (%)	(22.7)[D]

Objective:	Seeks growth of capital with current income as a secondary consideration. The fund will normally invest in common stocks and convertible securities of medium to large, well-established, dividend-paying companies.
Portfolio:	(11/30/88) Common stocks 91%, convertible debentures 5%, cash 4%. Largest stock holdings: banking 15%, consumer goods/services 15%.
Portfolio Mgr:	James W. Stratton—1972; John A. Afflack—1979
Distributions:	**Income:** July, Dec **Capital Gains:** July, Dec
12b-1:	No
Minimum:	**Initial:** $1,000 **Subsequent:** $100
Min IRA:	**Initial:** None **Subsequent:** None
Services:	IRA, Keogh, 403(b), Withdraw
Tel Exchange:	Yes **With MMF:** No
Registered:	CA, CO, CT, DC, DE, FL, GA, HI, IL, IN, MA, MD, MI, MN, NE, NJ, NY, OH, OR, PA, RI, TX, VA, WA, WY
Ticker:	STRGX

STRATTON MONTHLY DIVIDEND SHARES
Balanced

Stratton Management Co.
Plymouth Meeting Exec. Campus
610 W. Germantown, Suite 361
Plymouth Meeting, PA 19462
(800) 634-5726/(215) 941-0255

	Years Ending 1/31					
	1983	1984	1985	1986	1987	1988
Dividends from Net Investment Income ($)	1.83	1.93	2.05	2.17	2.28	2.06
Distributions from Net Realized Capital Gains ($)	—	—	—	—	.10	.27
Net Asset Value End of Year ($)	20.59	20.32	22.47	27.82	31.09	25.11
Ratio of Expenses to Net Assets (%)	1.98	1.74	1.72	1.49	1.24	1.21
Ratio of Net Income to Average Net Assets (%)	10.33	9.03	9.77	8.36	6.90	7.52
Portfolio Turnover Rate (%)	33	30	28	14	15	24
Total Assets End of Year (Millions $)	8.5	9.0	10.4	21.3	53.6	36.3

Annual Rate of Return (%) Years Ending 12/31	11.8	21.0	29.7	20.4	(11.3)	9.8

Five-Year Total Return(%)	83.9[B]	Degree of Diversification	E	Beta	.45	Bull (%)	92.4[C]	Bear (%)	(11.3)[C]

Objective: Seeks high dividend and interest income from common stocks and convertible securities. Of these investments, 25% must be in public utility companies—electric energy, gas, water or telephone service. May convert to cash equivalents for defensive purposes.

Portfolio: (7/31/88) Common stocks 56%, convertible debentures 27%, convertible preferred stocks 14%, cash 3%. Largest stock holdings: electric utilities 33%, electric and gas utilities 12%.

Portfolio Mgr: James W. Stratton—1980; Gerard E. Hefferman—1980

Distributions: **Income:** Monthly   **Capital Gains:** Annually

12b-1: No

Minimum: **Initial:** $2,000   **Subsequent:** $100

Min IRA: **Initial:** None   **Subsequent:** None

Services: IRA, Keogh, 403(b), Withdraw

Tel Exchange: Yes   **With MMF:** No

Registered: AL, AZ, CA, CO, CT, DC, DE, FL, GA, HI, IL, IN, KS, KY, MA, MD, MI, MN, MO, NJ, NY, OH, OR, PA, RI, TN, TX, VA, WA, WI, WY

Ticker: STMDX

STRONG GOVERNMENT SECURITIES

Bond

Strong/Corneliuson Capital Mgmt.
100 Heritage Reserve
Menomonee Falls, WI 53051
(800) 368-3863/(414) 359-1400

	Years Ending 12/31					
	1983	1984	1985	1986 (2 mos.)	1987	1988
Dividends from Net Investment Income ($)	−	−	−	.13	.65	.68
Distributions from Net Realized Capital Gains ($)	−	−	−	−	−	.09
Net Asset Value End of Year ($)	−	−	−	10.09	9.75	9.98
Ratio of Expenses to Net Assets (%)	−	−	−	.60	1.00	.40
Ratio of Net Income to Average Net Assets (%)	−	−	−	7.20	6.60	6.90
Portfolio Turnover Rate (%)	−	−	−	0	715	1,728
Total Assets End of Year (Millions $)	−	−	−	.9	11.4	25.4

Annual Rate of Return (%) Years Ending 12/31	−	−	−	−	3.4	10.5

Five-Year Total Return(%)	NA	Degree of Diversification	NA	Beta	NA	Bull (%)	NA	Bear (%)	9.4A

Objective:	Seeks high level of current income from investments in the debt obligations of the U.S. government and its agencies. Can use futures contracts and options to hedge the portfolio. May invest in short-term cash instruments and repurchase agreements.
Portfolio:	(12/31/88) U.S. government issues 81%, commercial paper 20%.
Portfolio Mgr:	Richard Strong, William Corneliuson—1986
Distributions:	**Income:** Monthly **Capital Gains:** Annually
12b-1:	No
Minimum:	**Initial:** $1,000 **Subsequent:** $200
Min IRA:	**Initial:** $250 **Subsequent:** None
Services:	IRA, Keogh, Corp, SEP, 403(b), Withdraw, Deduct
Tel Exchange:	Yes **With MMF:** Yes
Registered:	All states
Ticker:	STVSX

STRONG INCOME
Balanced

Strong/Corneliuson Capital Mgmt.
100 Heritage Reserve
Menomonee Falls, WI 53051
(800) 368-3863/(414) 359-1400

	Years Ending 12/31					
	1983	1984	1985 (1 mo.)	1986	1987	1988
Dividends from Net Investment Income ($)	—	—	—	.71	1.53	1.17
Distributions from Net Realized Capital Gains ($)	—	—	—	—	.04	—
Net Asset Value End of Year ($)	—	—	10.30	12.65	11.64	11.88
Ratio of Expenses to Net Assets (%)	—	—	1.10	1.00	1.10	1.20
Ratio of Net Income to Average Net Assets (%)	—	—	23.50	11.30	10.60	9.80
Portfolio Turnover Rate (%)	—	—	7	205	245	400
Total Assets End of Year (Millions $)	—	—	2.5	118.7	137.8	202.6

Annual Rate of Return (%) Years Ending 12/31		—	—	—	29.9	4.3	12.5

Five-Year Total Return(%)	NA	Degree of Diversification	NA	Beta	NA	Bull (%)	NA	Bear (%)	(1.6)B

Objective: Seeks high level of current income from investments in a diversified portfolio of fixed-income securities and divident-paying common stocks. The fixed-income securities may be unrated or as low as CC. May also enter into repurchase agreements and invest in foreign securities, convertibles and preferred stocks.

Portfolio: (12/31/88) Short-term securities 44%, corporate bonds 40%, common stocks 5%. U.S. government issues 5%.

Portfolio Mgr: Richard Strong, William Corneliuson—1986

Distributions: **Income:** Monthly   **Capital Gains:** Annually

12b-1: No

Minimum: **Initial:** $1,000   **Subsequent:** $200

Min IRA: **Initial:** $250   **Subsequent:** None

Services: IRA, Keogh, Corp, SEP, 403(b), Withdraw, Deduct

Tel Exchange: Yes   **With MMF:** Yes

Registered: All states

Ticker: SRNCX

†STRONG INVESTMENT
Balanced

Strong/Corneliuson Capital Mgmt.
815 E. Mason St.
Milwaukee, WI 53202
(800) 368-3863/(414) 765-0620

	Years Ending 12/31					
	1983	1984	1985	1986	1987	1988
Dividends from Net Investment Income ($)	.43	.31	.75	.95	1.78	1.38
Distributions from Net Realized Capital Gains ($)	.90	1.10	.04	.42	2.95	.23
Net Asset Value End of Year ($)	17.48	17.62	20.12	22.18	17.60	17.57
Ratio of Expenses to Net Assets (%)	1.7	1.2	1.1	1.1	1.1	1.2
Ratio of Net Income to Average Net Assets (%)	5.4	8.4	5.4	4.7	4.2	7.5
Portfolio Turnover Rate (%)	162	77	144	80	337	426
Total Assets End of Year (Millions $)	23.1	146.0	220.6	339.4	273.0	256.1
Annual Rate of Return (%) Years Ending 12/31	45.1	9.8	19.4	17.7	(0.3)	9.2

Five-Year Total Return(%)	67.9c	Degree of Diversification	E	Beta	.31	Bull (%)	59.7D	Bear (%)	(6.9)c

Objective: Seeks a combination of income and capital appreciation that will produce the highest total return consistent with the conservation of capital. Invests in common stocks, bonds and convertible securities. Investments in common stocks and convertibles may not exceed 65% of the value of the fund's assets.

Portfolio: (12/31/88) Short-term securities 77%, common stocks 22%. Largest stock holdings: food, beverage and tobacco 12%, health care 5%.

Portfolio Mgr: William Corneliuson, Richard Strong—1981

Distributions: **Income:** Quarterly   **Capital Gains:** Annually

12b-1: No

Minimum: **Initial:** $250   **Subsequent:** $200

Min IRA: **Initial:** $250   **Subsequent:** None

Services: IRA, Keogh, Corp, SEP, 403(b), Withdraw, Deduct

Tel Exchange: Yes   **With MMF:** Yes

Registered: All states

Ticker: STIFX

† *The fund has a 1% front-end sales charge.*

STRONG SHORT-TERM BOND

Bond

Strong/Corneliuson Capital Mgmt.
100 Heritage Reserve
Menomonee Falls, WI 53051
(800) 368-3863/(414) 359-1400

	Years Ending 12/31					
	1983	1984	1985	1986	1987 (4 mos.)	1988
Dividends from Net Investment Income ($)	—	—	—	—	.27	.86
Distributions from Net Realized Capital Gains ($)	—	—	—	—	.01	.07
Net Asset Value End of Year ($)	—	—	—	—	10.03	10.09
Ratio of Expenses to Net Assets (%)	—	—	—	—	.10	1.00
Ratio of Net Income to Average Net Assets (%)	—	—	—	—	8.80	8.50
Portfolio Turnover Rate (%)	—	—	—	—	136	461
Total Assets End of Year (Millions $)	—	—	—	—	17.1	102.1

Annual Rate of Return (%) Years Ending 12/31	—	—	—	—	—	10.1

Five-Year Total Return(%)	NA	Degree of Diversification	NA	Beta	NA	Bull (%)	NA	Bear (%)	3.1A

Objective: Seeks to provide investors with the highest level of income consistent with minimum fluctuation in principal value and current liquidity. Invests in debt securities with maturities of up to 10 years. Under normal circumstances, 65% of the fund's assets will be invested in corporate bonds and securities issued or guaranteed by the U.S. government.

Portfolio: (12/31/88) Commercial paper 67%, corporate bonds 32%, corporate obligations 1%.

Portfolio Mgr: Richard Strong, William Corneliuson—1987

Distributions: **Income:** Monthly   **Capital Gains:** Annually

12b-1: No

Minimum: **Initial:** $1,000   **Subsequent:** $200

Min IRA: **Initial:** $250   **Subsequent:** None

Services: IRA, Keogh, Corp, SEP, 403(b), Withdraw, Deduct

Tel Exchange: Yes   **With MMF:** Yes

Registered: All states

Ticker: SSTBX

†STRONG TOTAL RETURN
Growth & Income

Strong/Corneliuson Capital Mgmt.
815 E. Mason St.
Milwaukee, WI 53202
(800) 368-3863/(414) 765-0620

	Years Ending 12/31					
	1983	**1984**	**1985**	**1986**	**1987**	**1988**
Dividends from Net Investment Income ($)	.52	.37	.58	.70	1.65	1.96
Distributions from Net Realized Capital Gains ($)	1.13	1.29	.20	1.04	3.17	.25
Net Asset Value End of Year ($)	16.48	16.35	19.56	21.61	18.37	18.96
Ratio of Expenses to Net Assets (%)	1.8	1.3	1.1	1.1	1.1	1.2
Ratio of Net Income to Average Net Assets (%)	5.7	8.1	5.0	4.3	5.2	10.1
Portfolio Turnover Rate (%)	222	184	305	154	224	281
Total Assets End of Year (Millions $)	18.4	106.7	233.9	518.7	802.2	1,005.2

Annual Rate of Return (%) Years Ending 12/31	41.3	10.4	25.5	20.0	6.0	15.6

Five-Year Total Return(%) 103.8ᴬ	Degree of Diversification	C	Beta	.67	Bull (%) 101.1ᶜ	Bear (%) (14.8)ᶜ

Objective: Seeks a combination of income and capital appreciation that will produce the highest total return, while assuming reasonable risks. Invests in common stocks, bonds, convertible securities and short-term money market instruments. Common stock investments may be either growth or income oriented.

Portfolio: (12/31/88) Common stocks 35%, corporate bonds 31%, short-term securities 27%, preferred stocks 4%. Largest stock holdings: food, beverage and tobacco 13%, health care 6%.

Portfolio Mgr: William Corneliuson, Richard Strong—1981

Distributions: **Income:** Quarterly   **Capital Gains:** Annually

12b-1: No

Minimum: **Initial:** $250   **Subsequent:** $200

Min IRA: **Initial:** $250   **Subsequent:** None

Services: IRA, Keogh, Corp, SEP, 403(b), Withdraw, Deduct

Tel Exchange: Yes   **With MMF:** Yes

Registered: All states

Ticker: STRFX

† *The fund has a 1% front-end sales charge.*

TRANSATLANTIC GROWTH
International

Kleinwort Benson International
200 Park Ave., 24th Floor
New York, NY 10166
(800) 237-4218/(212) 687-2515

	Years Ending 12/31					
	1983	1984	1985	1986	1987	1988
Dividends from Net Investment Income ($)	.17	.03	.06	—	—	—
Distributions from Net Realized Capital Gains ($)	.06	1.00	.16	4.18	11.82	1.27
Net Asset Value End of Year ($)	14.86	11.87	17.95	22.92	13.21	14.66
Ratio of Expenses to Net Assets (%)	1.28	1.53	1.94	1.49	1.72	2.31
Ratio of Net Income to Average Net Assets (%)	1.29	.55	.69	.29	.38	(.33)
Portfolio Turnover Rate (%)	96	60	73	76	59	55
Total Assets End of Year (Millions $)	35.4	28.0	41.3	92.6	53.8	59.8

Annual Rate of Return (%) Years Ending 12/31	32.9	(14.4)	54.2	51.7	9.2	21.0

Five-Year Total Return(%)	164.6^	Degree of Diversification	E	Beta	.59	Bull (%)	223.6^	Bear (%)	(16.9)^C

Objective: Seeks long-term capital growth through investment in equity securities of companies domiciled in countries other than the United States. For defensive purposes, can invest all or a portion of assets in U.S. government securities or other domestic issues.

Portfolio: (12/31/88) Common stocks and convertible securities 99%, bank deposits 1%. Largest country holdings: Japan 42%, United Kingdom 16%.

Portfolio Mgr: Henry de Vismes—1969

Distributions: **Income:** Semiannually   **Capital Gains:** Annually

12b-1: Yes   **Amount:** 0.20%

Minimum: **Initial:** $1,000   **Subsequent:** $500

Min IRA: **Initial:** $500   **Subsequent:** $500

Services: IRA

Tel Exchange: Yes   **With MMF:** No

Registered: Call for availability

Ticker: TRANX

TRANSATLANTIC INCOME
International

Kleinwort Benson International
200 Park Ave., 24th Floor
New York, NY 10166
(800) 237-4218/(212) 687-2515

	Years Ending 12/31					
	1983	1984	1985	1986	1987 (11 mos.)	1988
Dividends from Net Investment Income ($)	—	—	—	—	.43	.54
Distributions from Net Realized Capital Gains ($)	—	—	—	—	.29	.23
Net Asset Value End of Year ($)	—	—	—	—	11.69	10.66
Ratio of Expenses to Net Assets (%)	—	—	—	—	2.20	2.50
Ratio of Net Income to Average Net Assets (%)	—	—	—	—	4.88	5.72
Portfolio Turnover Rate (%)	—	—	—	—	412	130
Total Assets End of Year (Millions $)	—	—	—	—	8.6	10.4

Annual Rate of Return (%) Years Ending 12/31	—	—	—	—	—	(2.0)

Five-Year Total Return(%)	NA	Degree of Diversification	NA	Beta	NA	Bull (%)	NA	Bear (%)	19.2A

Objective: Seeks high current income through investment in foreign and domestic fixed-income securities. Normally invests in three different currencies, but does not have more than 40% of assets in any one currency.

Portfolio: (12/31/88) Bank deposits 61%, fixed-income securities 31%, other assets 9%. Largest holdings: French francs 14%, Dutch guilders 10%.

Portfolio Mgr: Richard Watt—1987

Distributions: **Income:** Semiannually   **Capital Gains:** Annually

12b-1: Yes   **Amount:** 0.20%

Minimum: **Initial:** $1,000   **Subsequent:** $500

Min IRA: **Initial:** $500   **Subsequent:** $500

Services: IRA

Tel Exchange: Yes   **With MMF:** No

Registered: Call for availability

Ticker: TAINX

TREASURY FIRST
Bond

Vintage Advisors, Inc.
29 W. Susquehanna Ave.
Suite 112
Towson, MD 21204
(800) 234-4111/(301) 494-8488

	Years Ending 10/31					
	1983	**1984**	**1985**	**1986**	**1987** (11 mos.)	**1988**
Dividends from Net Investment Income ($)	—	—	—	—	.72	.83
Distributions from Net Realized Capital Gains ($)	—	—	—	—	.05	.02
Net Asset Value End of Year ($)	—	—	—	—	10.07	9.40
Ratio of Expenses to Net Assets (%)	—	—	—	—	.54	1.05
Ratio of Net Income to Average Net Assets (%)	—	—	—	—	8.54	8.41
Portfolio Turnover Rate (%)	—	—	—	—	307	276
Total Assets End of Year (Millions $)	—	—	—	—	24.4	25.0
Annual Rate of Return (%) Years Ending 12/31	—	—	—	—	8.9	1.6

Five-Year Total Return(%)	NA	Degree of Diversification	NA	Beta	NA	Bull (%)	NA	Bear (%)	5.0ᴬ

Objective: Seeks to achieve a high level of current income, consistent with the preservation of capital and the maintenance of liquidity. Invests in debt obligations issued or guaranteed by the U.S. government, its agencies or instrumentalities. Intends to invest in puts, calls, interest rate futures contracts and options.

Portfolio: (10/31/88) GNMAs 91%, U.S. Treasury notes 6%, options 3%.

Portfolio Mgr: John Vogt—1986

Distributions: **Income:** Monthly   **Capital Gains:** Annually

12b-1: Yes   **Amount:** 0.25%

Minimum: **Initial:** $10,000   **Subsequent:** None

Min IRA: **Initial:** $1,000   **Subsequent:** None

Services: IRA, Keogh, SEP

Tel Exchange: No

Registered: AR, CA, CO, CT, DC, DE, FL, GA, IA, IL, IN, MD, MN, MO, MS, NC, NJ, NY, TN, VA, WI

Ticker: TRFRX

TUDOR
Aggressive Growth

Tudor Management Co.
One New York Plaza
New York, NY 10004
(800) 223-3332/(212) 908-9582

	3/31	Years Ending 12/31					
	1983	1983* (9 mos.)	1984	1985	1986	1987	1988
Dividends from Net Investment Income ($)	.22	.28	.11	.37	.07	—	.03
Distributions from Net Realized Capital Gains ($)	—	.54	1.56	—	5.48	1.69	.75
Net Asset Value End of Year ($)	19.94	20.92	17.67	22.75	20.08	18.82	20.90
Ratio of Expenses to Net Assets (%)	1.35	1.01	1.01	.95	1.01	1.03	1.14
Ratio of Net Income to Average Net Assets (%)	2.41	.09	2.42	.63	(.16)	(.19)	.22
Portfolio Turnover Rate (%)	99	55	83	123	128	113	89
Total Assets: End of Year (Millions $)	53.3	91.5	94.0	155.9	163.8	142.5	157.3

Annual Rate of Return (%) Years Ending 12/31	28.4	*	(7.2)	31.2	12.3	1.1	15.3

Five-Year Total Return(%) 59.5[D]	Degree of Diversification C	Beta 1.18	Bull (%) 126.8[A]	Bear (%) (27.7)[E]

*Fiscal year-end changed from 3/31 to 12/31. All annual return figures are for full years ending 12/31.

Objective:	Seeks capital appreciation through investment in common stocks. The fund invests approximately 50% of its assets in "special situations" and may write covered call options. May enter into repurchase agreements.
Portfolio:	(12/31/88) Common stocks 90%, repurchase agreements 9%, warrants 2%, other investments 2%, bonds 1%, preferred stocks 1%. Largest stock holdings: basic industries 9%, business services 9%.
Portfolio Mgr:	Melville Straus—1973
Distributions:	**Income:** Mar, Aug **Capital Gains:** Annually
12b-1:	No
Minimum:	**Initial:** $1,000 **Subsequent:** $50
Min IRA:	**Initial:** $250 **Subsequent:** $50
Services:	IRA, Keogh, Withdraw
Tel Exchange:	Yes **With MMF:** Yes
Registered:	All states
Ticker:	TUDRX

†20TH CENTURY GIFTRUST

Aggressive Growth

Investors Research Corp.
4500 Main Street
P.O. Box 419200
Kansas City, MO 64141-6200
(800) 345-2021/(816) 531-5575

	1983	1984 (11 mos.)	1985	1986	1987	1988
Years Ending 10/31						
Dividends from Net Investment Income ($)	—	—	.02	—	—	—
Distributions from Net Realized Capital Gains ($)	—	—	—	.18	1.25	.86
Net Asset Value End of Year ($)	—	4.23	5.75	8.19	6.67	6.84
Ratio of Expenses to Net Assets (%)	—	1.01	1.01	1.01	1.00	1.00
Ratio of Net Income to Average Net Assets (%)	—	.90	(.30)	(.40)	(.50)	(.10)
Portfolio Turnover Rate (%)	—	135	134	123	130	157
Total Assets End of Year (Millions $)	—	1.9	3.5	7.1	9.6	13.2
Annual Rate of Return (%) Years Ending 12/31	—	(14.3)	55.4	28.0	8.7	11.1

Five-Year Total Return(%) 105.9ᴬ	Degree of Diversification D	Beta 1.36	Bull (%) 205.9ᴬ	Bear (%) (23.2)ᴰ

Objective: Seeks capital growth by investing primarily in common stocks that are considered by management to have better-than-average prospects for appreciation. Giftrust shares are held in trust by an independent trustee until the maturity date that the investor specifies.

Portfolio: (10/31/88) Common stocks 98%, temporary cash investments 3%. Largest stock holdings: retail 16%, industrial equipment and machinery 14%.

Portfolio Mgr: James E. Stowers Jr. and associates—1983.

Distributions: **Income:** Dec   **Capital Gains:** Dec

12b-1: No

Minimum: **Initial:** $100   **Subsequent:** None

Min IRA: **Initial:** NA   **Subsequent:** NA

Services: Deduct

Tel Exchange: No   **With MMF:** No

Registered: All states

Ticker: TWGTX

† *Accounts are opened on behalf of others, not one's self.*

20TH CENTURY GROWTH

Aggressive Growth

Investors Research Corp.
4500 Main Street
P.O. Box 419200
Kansas City, MO 64141-6200
(800) 345-2021/(816) 531-5575

	Years Ending 10/31					
	1983	**1984**	**1985**	**1986**	**1987**	**1988**
Dividends from Net Investment Income ($)	.05	.05	.15	.18	.09	.05
Distributions from Net Realized Capital Gains ($)	–	1.82	–	–	5.08	3.46
Net Asset Value End of Year ($)	15.77	12.29	14.16	19.47	15.62	12.54
Ratio of Expenses to Net Assets (%)	1.02	1.01	1.01	1.01	1.00	1.00
Ratio of Net Income to Average Net Assets (%)	.50	1.40	1.30	.60	.20	2.40
Portfolio Turnover Rate (%)	98	132	116	105	114	143
Total Assets End of Year (Millions $)	659.1	678.2	759.9	964.5	1,187.6	1,228.4
Annual Rate of Return (%) Years Ending 12/31	24.5	(10.2)	33.9	19.4	13.0	2.7

Five-Year Total Return(%)	66.6[C]	Degree of Diversification	B	Beta	1.26	Bull (%)	168.3[A]	Bear (%)	(26.8)[E]

Objective: Capital growth through investment in common stocks of larger companies that management considers to possess better than average growth prospects based on fundamental and technical analysis and three-year history.

Portfolio: (10/31/88) Common stocks 95%, temporary cash investments 3%, other assets 2%. Largest stock holdings: broadcasting and publishing 10%, leisure 9%.

Portfolio Mgr: James E. Stowers Jr. and associates—1958

Distributions: Income: Dec   **Capital Gains:** Dec

12b-1: No

Minimum: Initial: None   Subsequent: None

Min IRA: Initial: None   Subsequent: None

Services: IRA, Keogh, Corp, 403(b), Withdraw, Deduct

Tel Exchange: Yes   **With MMF:** Yes

Registered: All states

Ticker: TWCGX

20TH CENTURY HERITAGE
Growth

Investors Research Corp.
4500 Main Street
P.O. Box 419200
Kansas City, MO 64141-6200
(800) 345-2021/(816) 531-5575

	Years Ending 10/31					
	1983	1984	1985	1986	1987	1988
Dividends from Net Investment Income ($)	—	—	—	—	—	.01
Distributions from Net Realized Capital Gains ($)	—	—	—	—	—	—
Net Asset Value End of Year ($)	—	—	—	—	—	6.21
Ratio of Expenses to Net Assets (%)	—	—	—	—	—	1.00
Ratio of Net Income to Average Net Assets (%)	—	—	—	—	—	1.40
Portfolio Turnover Rate (%)	—	—	—	—	—	130
Total Assets End of Year (Millions $)	—	—	—	—	—	55.4
Annual Rate of Return (%) Years Ending 12/31	—	—	—	—	—	16.4

Five-Year Total Return(%)	NA	Degree of Diversification	NA	Beta	NA	Bull (%)	NA	Bear (%)	NA

Objective: Seeks capital growth by investing primarily in common stocks that are considered by management to have better-than-average prospects for appreciation. Common stocks chosen must have a record of paying cash dividends, but growth is the primary consideration, and the dividends may not be significant. Invests in smaller companies with smaller share trading volume.

Portfolio: (10/31/88) Common stocks 98%, temporary cash investments 2%. Largest stock holdings: steel 14%, chemicals 10%.

Portfolio Mgr: James E. Stowers Jr. and associates—1987

Distributions: **Income:** Dec   **Capital Gains:** Dec

12b-1: No

Minimum: **Initial:** None   **Subsequent:** None

Min IRA: **Initial:** None   **Subsequent:** None

Services: IRA, Keogh, Corp, 403(b), Withdraw, Deduct

Tel Exchange: Yes   **With MMF:** Yes

Registered: All states

Ticker: TWHIX

20TH CENTURY LONG-TERM BOND
Bond

Investors Research Corp.
4500 Main Street
P.O. Box 419200
Kansas City, MO 64141-6200
(800) 345-2021/(816) 531-5575

	Years Ending 10/31					
	1983	1984	1985	1986	1987 (8 mos.)	1988
Dividends from Net Investment Income ($)	–	–	–	–	4.76	8.36
Distributions from Net Realized Capital Gains ($)	–	–	–	–	–	–
Net Asset Value End of Year ($)	–	–	–	–	89.55	91.85
Ratio of Expenses to Net Assets (%)	–	–	–	–	1.00	1.00
Ratio of Net Income to Average Net Assets (%)	–	–	–	–	8.10	9.15
Portfolio Turnover Rate (%)	–	–	–	–	146	280
Total Assets End of Year (Millions $)	–	–	–	–	9.4	25.8

Annual Rate of Return (%) Years Ending 12/31	–	–	–	–	–	8.3

Five-Year Total Return(%)	NA	Degree of Diversification	NA	Beta	NA	Bull (%)	NA	Bear (%)	4.7A

Objective: Seeks high level of income from investment in longer-term bonds, which generally have greater price volatility than short- or intermediate-term bonds. During normal conditions the average weighted maturity of the portfolio will be 15 to 25 years. Invests in medium- to high-grade corporate bonds and U.S. government bonds.

Portfolio: (10/31/88) Corporate bonds 54%, U.S. government securities 27%, sovereign governments 8%, mortgage-backed securities 8%, U.S. government agency securities 4%, repurchase agreements 3%. Largest bond holdings: energy 11%, food and beverage 7%.

Portfolio Mgr: Charles M. Duboc—1987

Distributions: **Income:** Monthly   **Capital Gains:** Dec

12b-1: No

Minimum: **Initial:** None   **Subsequent:** None

Min IRA: **Initial:** None   **Subsequent:** None

Services: IRA, Keogh, Corp, 403(b), Withdraw, Deduct

Tel Exchange: Yes   **With MMF:** Yes

Registered: All states

Ticker: TWLBX

20TH CENTURY SELECT

Aggressive Growth

Investors Research Corp.
4500 Main Street
P.O. Box 419200
Kansas City, MO 64141-6200
(800) 345-2021/(816) 531-5575

	Years Ending 10/31					
	1983	1984	1985	1986	1987	1988
Dividends from Net Investment Income ($)	.14	.14	.47	.52	.38	.48
Distributions from Net Realized Capital Gains ($)	—	.69	—	—	3.46	6.37
Net Asset Value End of Year ($)	25.46	22.35	26.48	35.40	32.69	27.85
Ratio of Expenses to Net Assets (%)	1.02	1.01	1.01	1.01	1.00	1.00
Ratio of Net Income to Average Net Assets (%)	1.40	2.40	2.50	1.60	1.10	2.20
Portfolio Turnover Rate (%)	57	112	119	85	123	140
Total Assets End of Year (Millions $)	648.9	840.5	1,143.1	1,978.4	2,416.9	2,366.6
Annual Rate of Return (%) Years Ending 12/31	30.0	(7.6)	33.8	20.7	5.7	5.6

Five-Year Total Return(%)	66.6[c]	Degree of Diversification	A	Beta	1.09	Bull (%)	147.3[a]	Bear (%)	(23.9)[d]

Objective: Seeks capital growth by investing primarily in common stocks. Invests in securities of companies with above-average growth prospects that also pay dividends or interest. However, the income characteristics are only a secondary consideration.

Portfolio: (10/31/88) Common stocks 99%, temporary cash investments 2%. Largest stock holdings: transportation 5%, retail 5%.

Portfolio Mgr: James E. Stowers Jr. and associates—1958

Distributions: **Income:** Dec   **Capital Gains:** Dec

12b-1: No

Minimum: **Initial:** None   **Subsequent:** None

Min IRA: **Initial:** None   **Subsequent:** None

Services: IRA, Keogh, Corp, 403(b), Withdraw, Deduct

Tel Exchange: Yes   **With MMF:** Yes

Registered: All states

Ticker: TWCIX

20TH CENTURY ULTRA

Aggressive Growth

Investors Research Corp.
4500 Main Street
P.O. Box 419200
Kansas City, MO 64141-6200
(800) 345-2021/(816) 531-5575

	Years Ending 10/31					
	1983	1984	1985	1986	1987	1988
Dividends from Net Investment Income ($)	—	—	—	.01	.01	—
Distributions from Net Realized Capital Gains ($)	—	.26	—	—	—	3.26
Net Asset Value End of Year ($)	7.98	6.57	7.13	9.06	8.76	6.86
Ratio of Expenses to Net Assets (%)	1.02	1.01	1.01	1.01	1.00	1.00
Ratio of Net Income to Average Net Assets (%)	(.40)	(.30)	.10	—	(.50)	(.30)
Portfolio Turnover Rate (%)	58	93	100	99	137	140
Total Assets End of Year (Millions $)	506.0	445.6	385.4	314.8	236.0	258.5
Annual Rate of Return (%) Years Ending 12/31	26.3	(19.3)	26.2	10.3	6.7	13.3

Five-Year Total Return(%)	35.7E	Degree of Diversification	D	Beta	1.39	Bull (%)	115.7B	Bear (%)	(27.6)E

Objective: Seeks capital growth by investing primarily in common stocks that are considered by management to have better-than-average prospects for appreciation. Seeks maximum growth over time with little or no income. Invests in shares of smaller companies.

Portfolio: (10/31/88) Common stocks 90%, temporary cash investments 7%, other assets 4%. Largest stock holdings: retail (specialty) 20%, broadcasting and publishing 7%.

Portfolio Mgr: James E. Stowers Jr. and associates—1981

Distributions: **Income:** Dec   **Capital Gains:** Dec

12b-1: No

Minimum: **Initial:** None   **Subsequent:** None

Min IRA: **Initial:** None   **Subsequent:** None

Services: IRA, Keogh, Corp, SEP, 403(b), Withdraw, Deduct

Tel Exchange: Yes   **With MMF:** Yes

Registered: All states

Ticker: TWCUX

20TH CENTURY U.S. GOVERNMENTS

Bond

Investors Research Corp.
4500 Main Street
P.O. Box 419200
Kansas City, MO 64141-6200
(800) 345-2021/(816) 531-5575

	Years Ending 10/31					
	1983 (10 mos.)	1984	1985	1986	1987	1988
Dividends from Net Investment Income ($)	8.02	10.25	9.97	8.71	7.92	8.15
Distributions from Net Realized Capital Gains ($)	—	—	—	.56	1.22	—
Net Asset Value End of Year ($)	97.58	96.79	99.51	101.58	95.48	94.15
Ratio of Expenses to Net Assets (%)	1.02	1.01	1.01	1.01	1.00	1.00
Ratio of Net Income to Average Net Assets (%)	10.08	10.72	10.10	8.54	8.10	8.60
Portfolio Turnover Rate (%)	403	352	573	464	468	578
Total Assets End of Year (Millions $)	34.7	58.8	98.8	254.7	335.6	440.3

Annual Rate of Return (%) Years Ending 12/31	7.0	12.3	12.9	9.9	3.8	5.6

Five-Year Total Return(%)	52.8ᴅ	Degree of Diversification	NA	Beta	NA	Bull (%)	35.4ᴇ	Bear (%)	3.2ᴬ

Objective: Seeks income through investment in U.S. government securities, with its portfolio maturity averaging four years or less.

Portfolio: (10/31/88) U.S. government securities 82%, U.S. government agency securities 11%, repurchase agreements 6%, other assets 1%.

Portfolio Mgr: Charles M. Duboc—1982

Distributions: **Income:** Monthly   **Capital Gains:** Dec

12b-1: No

Minimum: **Initial:** None   **Subsequent:** None

Min IRA: **Initial:** None   **Subsequent:** None

Services: IRA, Keogh, Corp, 403(b), Withdraw, Deduct

Tel Exchange: Yes   **With MMF:** Yes

Registered: All states

Ticker: TWUSX

20TH CENTURY VISTA

Aggressive Growth

Investors Research Corp.
4500 Main Street
P.O. Box 419200
Kansas City, MO 64141-6200
(800) 345-2021/(816) 531-5575

	1983	1984 (11 mos.)	1985	1986	1987	1988
Dividends from Net Investment Income ($)	—	—	.01	—	—	—
Distributions from Net Realized Capital Gains ($)	—	—	—	—	.65	.46
Net Asset Value End of Year ($)	—	4.43	4.68	6.88	5.73	5.91
Ratio of Expenses to Net Assets (%)	—	1.01	1.01	1.01	1.00	1.00
Ratio of Net Income to Average Net Assets (%)	—	.40	(.20)	(.30)	(.70)	.20
Portfolio Turnover Rate (%)	—	97	174	121	123	145
Total Assets End of Year (Millions $)	—	105.1	99.4	159.8	187.3	206.3

Annual Rate of Return (%) Years Ending 12/31	—	(16.3)	22.5	26.3	6.0	2.4

Five-Year Total Return(%)	40.7ᴱ	Degree of Diversification	E	Beta	1.44	Bull (%)	129.7ᴬ	Bear (%)	(25.4)ᴱ

Objective: Seeks capital growth by investing primarily in common stocks that are considered by management to have better-than-average prospects for appreciation. Seeks maximum growth over time with little or no income. Invests in smaller companies. Fund is more volatile than most of 20th Century's stock funds, and it is one of the most aggressive.

Portfolio: (10/31/88) Common stocks 98%, temporary cash investments 2%. Largest stock holdings: computer software and services 18%, medical services and supplies 9%.

Portfolio Mgr: James E. Stowers Jr. and associates—1983

Distributions: Income: Dec   **Capital Gains:** Dec

12b-1: No

Minimum: Initial: None   Subsequent: None

Min IRA: Initial: None   Subsequent: None

Services: IRA, Keogh, Corp, 403(b), Withdraw, Deduct

Tel Exchange: Yes   **With MMF:** Yes

Registered: All states

Ticker: TWCVX

UMB BOND
Bond

Jones & Babson, Inc.
Three Crown Center
2440 Pershing Road
Kansas City, MO 64108
(800) 821-5591/(816) 471-5200

	Years Ending 6/30					
	1983 (7 mos.)	1984	1985	1986	1987	1988
Dividends from Net Investment Income ($)	.36	1.06	.46	1.29	.40	.85
Distributions from Net Realized Capital Gains ($)	—	—	—	.08	—	.01
Net Asset Value End of Year ($)	9.98	9.07	10.79	10.86	10.98	10.85
Ratio of Expenses to Net Assets (%)	.85	.87	.88	.88	.87	.87
Ratio of Net Income to Average Net Assets (%)	8.94	9.85	9.21	8.11	7.36	7.47
Portfolio Turnover Rate (%)	—	—	51	23	12	7
Total Assets End of Year (Millions $)	4.6	6.0	9.8	19.0	31.1	29.6

Annual Rate of Return (%) Years Ending 12/31	4.8	13.5	16.2	12.3	2.9	5.9

Five-Year Total Return(%)	61.4ᴰ	Degree of Diversification	NA	Beta	NA	Bull (%)	43.5ᴱ	Bear (%)	3.3ᴬ

Objective: To provide maximum current income while preserving capital. Invests in the guaranteed obligations of the U.S. government and its agencies, including Treasury securities and GNMAs. Will also invest in corporate debt rated A or better by Standard & Poor's.

Portfolio: (9/30/88) Corporate bonds 44%, government sponsored enterprises 31%, U.S. government securities 13%, U.S. government agency 4%, short-term corporate notes 3%, repurchase agreements 2%, other assets 2%.

Portfolio Mgr: George Root—1982

Distributions: **Income:** Semiannually   **Capital Gains:** Annually

12b-1: No

Minimum: **Initial:** $1,000   **Subsequent:** $100

Min IRA: **Initial:** $250   **Subsequent:** $25

Services: IRA, Keogh, Corp, SEP, 403(b), Withdraw

Tel Exchange: Yes   **With MMF:** Yes

Registered: AR, CA, DC, FL, IA, IL, IN, KS, MA, MN, MO, MT, NE, OH, OK, PA, SD

Ticker: UMBBX

UMB STOCK
Growth & Income

Jones & Babson, Inc.
Three Crown Center
2440 Pershing Road
Kansas City, MO 64108
(800) 821-5591/(816) 471-5200

	Years Ending 6/30					
	1983 (7 mos.)	1984	1985	1986	1987	1988
Dividends from Net Investment Income ($)	.19	.60	.25	.71	.20	.43
Distributions from Net Realized Capital Gains ($)	.42	.54	—	1.11	.40	1.12
Net Asset Value End of Year ($)	11.50	10.09	12.29	13.52	15.26	13.07
Ratio of Expenses to Net Assets (%)	.85	.87	.88	.87	.87	.86
Ratio of Net Income to Average Net Assets (%)	3.95	4.38	4.36	3.75	3.08	3.41
Portfolio Turnover Rate (%)	76	80	65	38	50	33
Total Assets End of Year (Millions $)	6.8	11.2	18.3	31.7	42.3	43.4
Annual Rate of Return (%) Years Ending 12/31	23.7	5.9	23.1	12.3	5.1	13.9

Five-Year Total Return(%)	75.2[B]	Degree of Diversification	A	Beta	.86	Bull (%)	102.8[C]	Bear (%)	(19.4)[D]

Objective: Seeks long-term growth of both capital and dividend income. Normally will invest 80% of its assets in common stocks that have demonstrated a consistent and above-average ability to increase earnings and dividends.

Portfolio: (9/30/88) Common stocks 76%, short-term corporate notes 17%, convertible corporate bonds 6%, convertible preferred stocks 1%, repurchase agreements 1%. Largest stock holdings: consumer staples 15%, basic materials 15%.

Portfolio Mgr: David Anderson—1982

Distributions: Income: Semiannually   **Capital Gains:** Annually

12b-1: No

Minimum: Initial: $1,000   **Subsequent:** $100

Min IRA: Initial: $250   **Subsequent:** $25

Services: IRA, Keogh, Corp, SEP, 403(b), Withdraw

Tel Exchange: Yes   **With MMF:** Yes

Registered: AR, CA, DC, FL, IA, IL, IN, KS, MA, MN, MO, MT, NE, OH, OK, PA, SD

Ticker: UMBSX

UNIFIED GROWTH
Growth

Unified Management Corp.
429 N. Pennsylvania St.
Indianapolis, IN 46204-1897
(800) 862-7283/(317) 634-3300

	Years Ending 4/30					
	1983	**1984**	**1985**	**1986**	**1987**	**1988**
Dividends from Net Investment Income ($)	.33	.55	.40	.35	.33	.27
Distributions from Net Realized Capital Gains ($)	1.08	—	—	—	2.45	1.83
Net Asset Value End of Year ($)	16.71	15.31	18.56	24.21	23.69	17.92
Ratio of Expenses to Net Assets (%)	1.28	1.16	1.10	1.00	1.01	1.06
Ratio of Net Income to Average Net Assets (%)	3.09	3.57	2.68	1.99	1.39	1.20
Portfolio Turnover Rate (%)	99	16	37	27	61	70
Total Assets End of Year (Millions $)	8.5	10.9	15.0	25.5	28.1	18.9
Annual Rate of Return (%) Years Ending 12/31	11.3	7.5	26.0	13.5	(11.6)	18.2

Five-Year Total Return(%)	60.7[D]	Degree of Diversification	C	Beta	.98	Bull (%)	99.1[C]	Bear (%)	(26.7)[E]

Objective: Seeks long-term appreciation by investing primarily in common stocks and convertible securities of medium-sized and smaller companies with attractive profit margins and high returns on equity. Current income is a secondary consideration. May take defensive posture with debt instruments.

Portfolio: (10/31/88) Common stocks 93%, short-term notes 5%, commercial paper 2%. Largest stock holdings: chemical/specialty 13%, medical supplies 11%.

Portfolio Mgr: Nicholas Kaiser—1970

Distributions: Income: April, Dec   **Capital Gains:** April, Dec

12b-1: No

Minimum: Initial: $200   Subsequent: $25

Min IRA: Initial: $25   Subsequent: $25

Services: IRA, Keogh, Corp, 403(b), Withdraw, Deduct

Tel Exchange: Yes   **With MMF:** Yes

Registered: CA, DC, FL, HI, IN, NJ, OH, PA, WY

Ticker: UNGFX

UNIFIED INCOME
Balanced

Unified Management Corp.
429 N. Pennsylvania St.
Indianapolis, IN 46204-1897
(800) 862-7283/(317) 634-3300

	Years Ending 10/31					
	1983	1984	1985	1986	1987	1988
Dividends from Net Investment Income ($)	.90	1.16	1.10	.89	.90	.77
Distributions from Net Realized Capital Gains ($)	.44	–	–	–	–	–
Net Asset Value End of Year ($)	12.16	11.17	11.75	12.75	10.47	11.05
Ratio of Expenses to Net Assets (%)	1.33	1.30	1.22	1.12	1.10	1.35
Ratio of Net Income to Average Net Assets (%)	8.70	9.84	9.25	7.39	6.74	6.54
Portfolio Turnover Rate (%)	19	25	18	49	75	118
Total Assets End of Year (Millions $)	7.5	7.1	8.7	13.6	11.2	9.4

Annual Rate of Return (%) Years Ending 12/31	17.9	(0.5)	20.5	9.8	(11.6)	12.7

Five-Year Total Return(%)	31.4[E]	Degree of Diversification	C	Beta	.54	Bull (%)	56.6[D]	Bear (%)	(18.2)[C]

Objective: Seeks current income and preservation of capital by investing in fixed and convertible corporate debt, common and preferred stock, and short-term instruments.

Portfolio: (10/31/88) Corporate bonds 55%, common stocks 37%, convertible preferred stocks 6%, convertible corporate bonds 3%. Largest stock holdings: electric utility 5%, drug manufacturing 5%.

Portfolio Mgr: Nicholas Kaiser—1977

Distributions: Income: Apr, Oct   **Capital Gains:** Oct

12b-1: No

Minimum: Initial: $500   Subsequent: $25

Min IRA: Initial: $25   Subsequent: $25

Services: IRA, Keogh, Corp, 403(b), Withdraw, Deduct

Tel Exchange: Yes   **With MMF:** Yes

Registered: CA, DC, FL, HI, IN, NJ, OH, WY
Call for additional states

Ticker: UNIIX

UNIFIED MUTUAL SHARES
Growth & Income

Unified Management Corp.
429 N. Pennsylvania St.
Indianapolis, IN 46204-1897
(800) 862-7283/(317) 634-3300

	Years Ending 7/31					
	1983	1984	1985	1986	1987	1988
Dividends from Net Investment Income ($)	.50	.59	.55	.59	.59	.57
Distributions from Net Realized Capital Gains ($)	—	—	—	.17	2.25	.97
Net Asset Value End of Year ($)	12.00	10.88	14.39	16.80	17.20	13.99
Ratio of Expenses to Net Assets (%)	1.23	1.21	1.11	1.02	1.03	1.10
Ratio of Net Income to Average Net Assets (%)	4.74	4.91	4.27	4.04	3.12	3.63
Portfolio Turnover Rate (%)	51	12	5	41	49	85
Total Assets End of Year (Millions $)	9.8	8.8	12.6	18.9	23.5	17.2
Annual Rate of Return (%) Years Ending 12/31	21.7	8.5	30.8	11.6	(2.3)	14.2

Five-Year Total Return(%)	76.8[B]	Degree of Diversification	A	Beta	.75	Bull (%)	106.9[B]	Bear (%)	(19.3)[D]

Objective: The fund seeks capital growth and current income principally through the purchase of high-quality, income-producing common stocks and convertible securities whose markets, profit margins and rates of return indicate future growth potentials. May write covered options.

Portfolio: (7/31/88) Common stocks 85%, short-term securities 9%, bonds 5%, convertible preferred stocks 2%. Largest stock holdings: drug manufacturing, ethical & consumer 12%, electric utility 8%.

Portfolio Mgr: Nicholas Kaiser—1963

Distributions: **Income:** Jan, July **Capital Gains:** July

12b-1: No

Minimum: **Initial:** $200 **Subsequent:** $25

Min IRA: **Initial:** $25 **Subsequent:** $25

Services: IRA, Keogh, Corp, 403(b), Withdraw, Deduct

Tel Exchange: Yes **With MMF:** Yes

Registered: CA, DC, FL, HI, IN, ND, NJ, WY

Ticker: UNFMX

USAA AGGRESSIVE GROWTH
(formerly USAA SUNBELT ERA)
Aggressive Growth

USAA Investment Mgmt. Co.
9800 Fredericksburg Rd.
San Antonio, TX 78288
(800) 531-8000/(512) 498-8000

	Years Ending 9/30					
	1983	1984	1985	1986	1987	1988
Dividends from Net Investment Income ($)	.04	.06	.08	.11	.07	.12
Distributions from Net Realized Capital Gains ($)	–	.25	–	–	.35	1.86
Net Asset Value End of Year ($)	18.27	14.20	14.78	17.29	21.79	17.23
Ratio of Expenses to Net Assets (%)	1.06	1.06	1.11	1.05	.97	1.00
Ratio of Net Income to Average Net Assets (%)	.75	.75	.66	.37	.54	.82
Portfolio Turnover Rate (%)	49	52	74	57	35	68
Total Assets End of Year (Millions $)	79.9	98.2	108.9	119.0	149.8	139.2
Annual Rate of Return (%) Years Ending 12/31	23.9	(18.1)	23.0	5.5	(0.8)	14.3

Five-Year Total Return(%)	20.4[E]	Degree of Diversification	C	Beta	1.12	Bull (%)	85.4[C]	Bear (%)	(26.1)[E]

Objective:	Seeks appreciation of capital through investment primarily in common stocks of smaller, emerging companies located in or doing business in the sunbelt region of the United States.
Portfolio:	(9/30/88) Common stocks 92%, short-term notes 13%, preferred stocks 1%. Largest stock holdings: computer services 13%, electronics 12%.
Portfolio Mgr:	Stuart Wester—1988
Distributions:	Income: Nov **Capital Gains:** Annually
12b-1:	No
Minimum:	Initial: $1,000 Subsequent: $50
Min IRA:	Initial: $1,000 Subsequent: $50
Services:	IRA, SEP, 403(b), Withdraw, Deduct
Tel Exchange:	Yes **With MMF:** Yes
Registered:	All states
Ticker:	USAUX

USAA CORNERSTONE
Balanced

USAA Investment Mgmt. Co.
9800 Fredericksburg Rd.
San Antonio, TX 78288
(800) 531-8000/(512) 498-8000

	Years Ending 9/30					
	1983	1984 (1 mo.)	1985	1986	1987	1988
Dividends from Net Investment Income ($)	—	—	.04	.32	.30	.36
Distributions from Net Realized Capital Gains ($)	—	—	.02	.06	.21	.02
Net Asset Value End of Year ($)	—	9.98	10.58	14.49	19.76	16.71
Ratio of Expenses to Net Assets (%)	—	1.90	1.50	1.50	1.07	1.21
Ratio of Net Income to Average Net Assets (%)	—	6.98	5.03	3.68	3.41	3.54
Portfolio Turnover Rate (%)	—	9	15	70	15	28
Total Assets End of Year (Millions $)	—	3.3	13.6	29.0	822.6	544.0

Annual Rate of Return (%) Years Ending 12/31	—	—	14.7	40.7	9.0	8.4

Five-Year Total Return(%)	NA	Degree of Diversification	E	Beta	.61	Bull (%)	NA	Bear (%)	(18.5)c

Objective: Seeks to preserve purchasing power of capital and achieve reasonably stable value of fund shares and positive, inflation-adjusted rate of return despite shifting inflation and volatility in markets. Will invest 20% in each of five asset categories: gold stocks, foreign stocks, real estate stocks, basic value stocks and U.S. government securities.

Portfolio: (9/30/88) Common stocks 80%, U.S. government and agency issues 20%. Largest stock holdings: basic value stocks 21%, real estate stocks 21%.

Portfolio Mgr: David Peebles—1988

Distributions: **Income:** Annually   **Capital Gains:** Annually

12b-1: No

Minimum: **Initial:** $1,000   **Subsequent:** $50

Min IRA: **Initial:** $1,000   **Subsequent:** $50

Services: IRA, SEP, 403(b), Withdraw, Deduct

Tel Exchange: Yes   **With MMF:** Yes

Registered: All states

Ticker: USCRX

USAA GOLD
Precious Metals

USAA Investment Mgmt. Co.
9800 Fredericksburg Rd.
San Antonio, TX 78288
(800) 531-8000/(512) 498-8000

	Years Ending 9/30					
	1983	1984 (1 mo.)	1985	1986	1987	1988
Dividends from Net Investment Income ($)	–	–	.02	.12	.10	.05
Distributions from Net Realized Capital Gains ($)	–	–	–	–	–	.51
Net Asset Value End of Year ($)	–	9.20	6.83	8.27	17.07	8.22
Ratio of Expenses to Net Assets (%)	–	1.93	1.50	1.50	1.14	1.42
Ratio of Net Income to Average Net Assets (%)	–	4.84	3.71	1.50	.73	.50
Portfolio Turnover Rate (%)	–	–	–	62	54	27
Total Assets End of Year (Millions $)	–	3.3	15.1	29.5	309.9	174.5

Annual Rate of Return (%) Years Ending 12/31	–	–	(20.7)	55.6	15.8	17.1

Five-Year Total Return(%)	NA	Degree of Diversification	E	Beta	.08	Bull (%)	NA	Bear (%)	(34.7)[E]

Objective: Seeks long-term capital appreciation and protection of capital against inflation through investment in common stock of companies engaged in gold exploration, mining or processing. Up to 20% of assets may be in other precious metals, diamonds or minerals.

Portfolio: (9/30/88) Common stocks 92%, U.S. government and agency issues 14%. Largest stock holdings: North American gold mines 49%, Australian gold mines 42%.

Portfolio Mgr: David Ullom—1988

Distributions: Income: Annually   **Capital Gains:** Annually

12b-1: No

Minimum: Initial: $1,000   Subsequent: $50

Min IRA: Initial: $1,000   Subsequent: $50

Services: IRA, SEP, 403(b), Withdraw, Deduct

Tel Exchange: Yes   **With MMF:** Yes

Registered: All states

Ticker: USAGX

USAA GROWTH
Growth

USAA Investment Mgmt. Co.
9800 Fredericksburg Rd.
San Antonio, TX 78288
(800) 531-8000/(512) 498-8000

	Years Ending 9/30					
	1983	1984	1985	1986	1987	1988
Dividends from Net Investment Income ($)	.32	.14	.23	.28	.19	.37
Distributions from Net Realized Capital Gains ($)	—	.47	—	.31	1.59	3.88
Net Asset Value End of Year ($)	15.91	13.08	13.76	15.94	19.63	11.68
Ratio of Expenses to Net Assets (%)	1.03	1.00	1.06	1.09	1.09	1.22
Ratio of Net Income to Average Net Assets (%)	1.19	2.25	1.86	1.37	2.14	2.40
Portfolio Turnover Rate (%)	94	69	128	110	124	109
Total Assets End of Year (Millions $)	107.2	128.6	145.2	173.8	272.3	208.1
Annual Rate of Return (%) Years Ending 12/31	15.8	(7.5)	19.9	10.1	5.5	6.6

Five-Year Total Return(%)	37.4[E]	Degree of Diversification	A	Beta	.98	Bull (%)	97.2[C]	Bear (%)	(21.9)[D]

Objective: Long-term growth of capital. Invests in common stocks of companies that are established and have substantial capitalizations along with exceptional prospects for growth in earnings. May invest up to 10% of its assets in foreign securities listed on U.S. exchanges.

Portfolio: (9/30/88) Common stocks 93%, short-term notes 3%, bonds 3%. Largest stock holdings: electronics 9%, telephone utilities 8%.

Portfolio Mgr: William Fries—1989

Distributions: Income: Nov   **Capital Gains:** Annually

12b-1: No

Minimum: Initial: $1,000   Subsequent: $50

Min IRA: Initial: $1,000   Subsequent: $50

Services: IRA, SEP, 403(b), Withdraw, Deduct

Tel Exchange: Yes   **With MMF:** Yes

Registered: All states

Ticker: USAAX

USAA INCOME
Bond

USAA Investment Mgmt. Co.
9800 Fredericksburg Rd.
San Antonio, TX 78288
(800) 531-8000/(512) 498-8000

	Years Ending 9/30					
	1983	1984	1985	1986	1987	1988
Dividends from Net Investment Income ($)	1.05	1.06	1.21	1.12	1.24	1.06
Distributions from Net Realized Capital Gains ($)	–	.12	–	.02	.06	.26
Net Asset Value End of Year ($)	10.93	10.68	11.46	12.08	10.89	11.20
Ratio of Expenses to Net Assets (%)	1.09	.75	.68	.65	.61	.61
Ratio of Net Income to Average Net Assets (%)	10.58	10.97	10.96	9.70	9.13	9.57
Portfolio Turnover Rate (%)	166	116	79	38	36	11
Total Assets End of Year (Millions $)	39.0	92.1	138.8	213.6	249.9	284.6

Annual Rate of Return (%) Years Ending 12/31	10.7	13.9	19.0	12.6	3.5	10.0

Five-Year Total Return(%)	73.8[B]	Degree of Diversification	NA	Beta	NA	Bull (%)	50.1[D]	Bear (%)	2.9[A]

Objective: Seeks high yields from marketable income-producing securities with a mix of maturities and qualities. May invest in restricted securities.

Portfolio: (9/30/88) U.S. government and agency issues 48%, corporate bonds 34%, common stocks 14%, short-term notes 1%.

Portfolio Mgr: John Saunders—1985

Distributions: **Income:** Monthly   **Capital Gains:** Annually

12b-1: No

Minimum: **Initial:** $1,000   **Subsequent:** $50

Min IRA: **Initial:** $1,000   **Subsequent:** $50

Services: IRA, SEP, 403(b), Withdraw, Deduct

Tel Exchange: Yes   **With MMF:** Yes

Registered: All states

Ticker: USAIX

USAA
INCOME STOCK
Growth & Income

USAA Investment Mgmt. Co.
9800 Fredericksburg Rd.
San Antonio, TX 78288
(800) 531-8000/(512) 498-8000

	Years Ending 9/30					
	1983	1984	1985	1986	1987 (5 mos.)	1988
Dividends from Net Investment Income ($)	—	—	—	—	.03	.42
Distributions from Net Realized Capital Gains ($)	—	—	—	—	—	.02
Net Asset Value End of Year ($)	—	—	—	—	10.74	10.26
Ratio of Expenses to Net Assets (%)	—	—	—	—	1.00	1.00
Ratio of Net Income to Average Net Assets (%)	—	—	—	—	5.22	4.72
Portfolio Turnover Rate (%)	—	—	—	—	7	28
Total Assets End of Year (Millions $)	—	—	—	—	21.7	31.2

Annual Rate of Return (%) Years Ending 12/31	—	—	—	—	—	19.4

Five-Year Total Return(%)	NA	Degree of Diversification	NA	Beta	NA	Bull (%)	NA	Bear (%)	(15.5)c

Objective: Seeks current income with the prospect of increasing dividend income and the potential for capital appreciation. Invests in the common stocks of well-established, large companies that pay higher-than-average dividends. May also invest in convertibles.

Portfolio: (9/30/88) Common stocks 96%, short-term notes 7%. Largest stock holdings: telephone utilities 17%, electric utilities 15%.

Portfolio Mgr: Harry Miller—1989

Distributions: **Income:** Quarterly   **Capital Gains:** Annually

12b-1: No

Minimum: **Initial:** $1,000   **Subsequent:** $50

Min IRA: **Initial:** $1,000   **Subsequent:** $50

Services: IRA, SEP, 403(b), Withdraw, Deduct

Tel Exchange: Yes   **With MMF:** Yes

Registered: All states

Ticker: USISX

†U.S. BOSTON GROWTH & INCOME

Growth & Income

U.S. Boston Investment Mgmt.
Six New England Executive Park
Burlington, MA 01803
(617) 272-6420

	Years Ending 3/31					
	1983	**1984**	**1985**	**1986** (11 mos.)	**1987**	**1988**
Dividends from Net Investment Income ($)	–	–	–	–	.12	.35
Distributions from Net Realized Capital Gains ($)	–	–	–	–	–	2.66
Net Asset Value End of Year ($)	–	–	–	12.82	15.64	11.30
Ratio of Expenses to Net Assets (%)	–	–	–	1.65	1.92	1.83
Ratio of Net Income to Average Net Assets (%)	–	–	–	1.99	1.25	1.44
Portfolio Turnover Rate (%)	–	–	–	34	99	124
Total Assets End of Year (Millions $)	–	–	–	15.3	35.0	25.9
Annual Rate of Return (%) Years Ending 12/31	–	–	–	19.3	1.5	17.0

Five-Year Total Return(%)	NA	Degree of Diversification	A	Beta	.97	Bull (%)	NA	Bear (%)	(23.7)D

Objective: Seeks long-term growth of capital and income. Invests primarily in common stocks of large companies having substantial equity capital and currently paying dividends. May also invest in convertible debentures, bonds, convertible preferred stocks and investment-grade fixed-income securities.

Portfolio: (9/30/88) Common stocks 99%, short-term securities 1%. Largest stock holdings: consumer basics 14%, technology 13%.

Portfolio Mgr: Kim Dow—1985

Distributions: **Income:** Annually   **Capital Gains:** Annually

12b-1: Yes   **Amount:** 0.60%

Minimum: **Initial:** $5,000   **Subsequent:** None

Min IRA: **Initial:** None   **Subsequent:** None

Services: IRA, 403(b), Withdraw, Deduct

Tel Exchange: Yes   **With MMF:** No

Registered: CA, CO, CT, FL, IN, MA, ME, MI, MN, MT, NH, NJ, NY, PA, RI, TN, VT, WA

Ticker: USBOX

† *The fund has a 1% redemption fee.*

US GNMA
Bond

United Services Advisors, Inc.
P.O. Box 29467
San Antonio, TX 78229-0467
(800) 873-8637/(512) 696-1234

	Years Ending 6/30					
	1983	1984	1985	1986 (3 mos.)	1987	1988
Dividends from Net Investment Income ($)	—	—	—	.11	.78	.87
Distributions from Net Realized Capital Gains ($)	—	—	—	—	—	.06
Net Asset Value End of Year ($)	—	—	—	9.90	9.47	9.31
Ratio of Expenses to Net Assets (%)	—	—	—	—	(.08)	—
Ratio of Net Income to Average Net Assets (%)	—	—	—	6.50	8.24	8.78
Portfolio Turnover Rate (%)	—	—	—	—	107	90
Total Assets End of Year (Millions $)	—	—	—	.8	6.7	6.8

Annual Rate of Return (%) Years Ending 12/31	—	—	—	—	(1.3)	10.0

Five-Year Total Return(%)	NA	Degree of Diversification	NA	Beta	NA	Bull (%)	NA	Bear (%)	3.3ᴬ

Objective: Seeks to provide a high level of current income, consistent with safety of principal and maintenance of liquidity. At least 65% of the fund's assets will be invested in GNMAs. Also uses put and call options to hedge the portfolio.

Portfolio: (9/30/88) Long-term U.S. government-guaranteed obligations 97%, other assets 2%, short-term U.S. government obligations 1%.

Portfolio Mgr: J. David Edwards—1987

Distributions: **Income:** Monthly   **Capital Gains:** Dec

12b-1: No

Minimum: **Initial:** $100   **Subsequent:** $50

Min IRA: **Initial:** None   **Subsequent:** None

Services: IRA, Keogh, Corp, SEP, 403(b), Withdraw, Deduct

Tel Exchange: Yes   **With MMF:** No

Registered: All states

Ticker: UNGMX

US GOLD SHARES
Precious Metals

United Services Advisors, Inc.
P.O. Box 29467
San Antonio, TX 78229-0467
(800) 873-8637/(512) 696-1234

	Years Ending 6/30					
	1983	1984	1985	1986	1987	1988
Dividends from Net Investment Income ($)	.34	.41	.29	.26	.35	.40
Distributions from Net Realized Capital Gains ($)	—	—	.06	—	—	—
Net Asset Value End of Year ($)	8.97	7.92	5.33	3.32	6.32	3.74
Ratio of Expenses to Net Assets (%)	1.11	1.06	1.15	1.27	1.32	1.31
Ratio of Net Income to Average Net Assets (%)	6.34	5.69	4.47	6.90	6.45	5.10
Portfolio Turnover Rate (%)	4	11	10	14	24	18
Total Assets End of Year (Millions $)	314.9	443.1	389.6	214.8	407.7	237.9
Annual Rate of Return (%) Years Ending 12/31	1.2	(29.7)	(26.9)	37.5	31.6	(35.7)

Five-Year Total Return(%) (40.2)ᴱ	Degree of Diversification	E	Beta	NA	Bull (%)	45.7ᴱ	Bear (%)	(18.3)ᶜ

Objective: Seeks long-term capital growth as well as protection against inflation and monetary instability. Fund concentrates its investments in common stocks of companies involved in exploration for, mining of, processing of, or dealing in gold, with emphasis on stocks of foreign companies.

Portfolio: (9/30/88) Common stocks 76%, repurchase agreements 24%. Largest holdings: long-life gold mines 26%, gold-uranium mines 17%.

Portfolio Mgr: J. David Edwards—1987

Distributions: **Income:** June, Dec   **Capital Gains:** Dec

12b-1: No

Minimum: **Initial:** $100   **Subsequent:** $50

Min IRA: **Initial:** None   **Subsequent:** None

Services: IRA, Keogh, Corp, SEP, 403(b), Withdraw, Deduct

Tel Exchange: Yes   **With MMF:** Yes

Registered: All states

Ticker: USERX

US GOOD AND BAD TIMES

Growth

United Services Advisors
P.O. Box 29467
San Antonio, TX 78229-0467
(800) 873-8637/(512) 696-1234

	Years Ending 6/30					
	1983	**1984**	**1985**	**1986**	**1987**	**1988**
Dividends from Net Investment Income ($)	.15	.11	.49	.17	.38	.74
Distributions from Net Realized Capital Gains ($)	—	—	—	—	—	—
Net Asset Value End of Year ($)	12.93	11.96	14.55	18.38	20.24	16.44
Ratio of Expenses to Net Assets (%)	2.20	1.45	1.50	1.40	1.35	1.43
Ratio of Net Income to Average Net Assets (%)	2.08	2.54	2.38	1.98	1.68	1.68
Portfolio Turnover Rate (%)	156	92	99	91	58	180
Total Assets End of Year (Millions $)	15.3	12.8	36.1	32.7	36.4	16.8

Annual Rate of Return (%) Years Ending 12/31	11.1	2.7	23.9	11.3	0.6	(3.1)

Five-Year Total Return(%)	38.0ᴱ	Degree of Diversification	B	Beta	.93	Bull (%)	100.3ᶜ	Bear (%)	(23.6)ᴰ

Objective: Invests in common stock of industrial corporations with little or no debt that are believed to be able to have capital appreciation in good economic times and preservation of capital in bad economic times. May invest up to 50% of assets in debt instruments as a defensive tactic.

Portfolio: (9/30/88) Common stocks 49%, U.S. government obligations 40%, repurchase agreements 11%. Largest stock holdings: printing and paper products 9%, communications 7%.

Portfolio Mgr: J. David Edwards—1987

Distributions: **Income:** June, Dec   **Capital Gains:** Dec

12b-1: No

Minimum: **Initial:** $100   **Subsequent:** $50

Min IRA: **Initial:** None   **Subsequent:** None

Services: IRA, Keogh, Corp, SEP, 403(b), Withdraw, Deduct

Tel Exchange: Yes   **With MMF:** Yes

Registered: All states

Ticker: GBTFX

US GROWTH
Aggressive Growth

United Services Advisors
P.O. Box 29467
San Antonio, TX 78229-0467
(800) 873-8637/(512) 696-1234

	Years Ending 6/30					
	1983	1984	1985	1986	1987	1988
Dividends from Net Investment Income ($)	—	—	.07	.06	.07	.11
Distributions from Net Realized Capital Gains ($)	—	—	—	—	—	1.55
Net Asset Value End of Year ($)	—	7.62	7.60	9.87	10.13	7.13
Ratio of Expenses to Net Assets (%)	—	1.45	1.67	1.52	1.71	2.03
Ratio of Net Income to Average Net Assets (%)	—	1.74	.97	.52	.62	.47
Portfolio Turnover Rate (%)	—	161	163	60	64	94
Total Assets End of Year (Millions $)	—	6.3	12.7	11.9	9.2	6.3
Annual Rate of Return (%) Years Ending 12/31	—	(25.6)	21.0	11.5	(11.2)	10.5

Five-Year Total Return(%)	(1.6)ᴱ	Degree of Diversification	C	Beta	1.02	Bull (%)	57.6ᴰ	Bear (%)	(27.2)ᴱ

Objective: Seeks capital appreciation through investment in common stocks of established, well-known and newer, less-seasoned companies. Fundamental analysis is employed to identify underpriced stocks, cyclical companies and companies that seem to be changing for the better. May invest up to 25% of assets in foreign securities traded on U.S. exchanges.

Portfolio: (9/30/88) Common stocks 60%, U.S. government obligations 43%, warrants 1%. Largest stock holdings: computer systems and services 12%, health care 8%.

Portfolio Mgr: J. David Edwards—1987

Distributions: Income: June, Dec   **Capital Gains:** Dec

12b-1: No

Minimum: Initial: $100   Subsequent: $50

Min IRA: Initial: None   Subsequent: None

Services: IRA, Keogh, Corp, SEP, 403(b), Withdraw, Deduct

Tel Exchange: Yes   **With MMF:** Yes

Registered: All states

Ticker: GRTHX

US INCOME
Balanced

United Services Advisors, Inc.
P.O. Box 29467
San Antonio, TX 78229-0467
(800) 873-8637/(512) 696-1234

	1983	1984 (8 mos.)	1985	1986	1987	1988
		Years Ending 6/30				
Dividends from Net Investment Income ($)	—	.11	.61	.38	.50	.76
Distributions from Net Realized Capital Gains ($)	—	—	—	.07	.56	.35
Net Asset Value End of Year ($)	—	9.19	10.42	11.20	10.50	9.64
Ratio of Expenses to Net Assets (%)	—	1.80	1.66	1.63	1.60	1.73
Ratio of Net Income to Average Net Assets (%)	—	6.34	5.58	3.27	6.14	6.19
Portfolio Turnover Rate (%)	—	279	271	179	174	127
Total Assets End of Year (Millions $)	—	1.2	2.5	2.9	3.6	4.5
Annual Rate of Return (%) Years Ending 12/31	—	3.9	15.3	5.5	(4.3)	16.9

Five-Year Total Return(%)	41.5[E]	Degree of Diversification	E	Beta	.36	Bull (%)	36.3[E]	Bear (%)	(8.4)[C]

Objective: Seeks preservation of capital and current income. Secondarily, seeks capital appreciation through investment in common stocks of companies with a long record of paying cash dividends, and U.S. Treasury debt securities and convertibles. May write covered call options.

Portfolio: (9/30/88) Common stocks 89%, U.S. government obligations 22%. Largest stock holdings: electric, water and gas utilities 46%, telephone services 29%.

Portfolio Mgr: J. David Edwards—1987

Distributions: **Income:** Mar, June, Sep, Dec   **Capital Gains:** Dec

12b-1: No

Minimum: **Initial:** $100   **Subsequent:** $50

Min IRA: **Initial:** None   **Subsequent:** None

Services: IRA, Keogh, Corp, SEP, 403(b), Withdraw, Deduct

Tel Exchange: Yes   **With MMF:** Yes

Registered: All states

Ticker: USINX

†US LOCAP
Aggressive Growth

United Services Advisors
P.O. Box 29467
San Antonio, TX 78229-0467
(800) 873-8637/(512) 696-1234

	Years Ending 6/30					
	1983	1984	1985 (5 mos.)	1986	1987	1988
Dividends from Net Investment Income ($)	–	–	–	.02	.02	–
Distributions from Net Realized Capital Gains ($)	–	–	–	–	–	–
Net Asset Value End of Year ($)	–	–	7.64	8.43	8.39	6.76
Ratio of Expenses to Net Assets (%)	–	–	1.67	1.84	2.27	2.43
Ratio of Net Income to Average Net Assets (%)	–	–	1.22	.31	(.82)	(.76)
Portfolio Turnover Rate (%)	–	–	6	70	52	39
Total Assets End of Year (Millions $)	–	–	2.1	3.2	4.3	2.6

Annual Rate of Return (%) Years Ending 12/31	–	–	–	(6.6)	(13.2)	3.4

Five-Year Total Return(%)	NA	Degree of Diversification	E	Beta	.85	Bull (%)	NA	Bear (%)	(33.6)ᴱ

Objective: To provide above-average capital appreciation. Current income is not a consideration. Invests in companies with a market capitalization in the bottom 10% of the combined group of common stocks listed on the New York and American stock exchanges.

Portfolio: (9/30/88) Common stocks 84%, U.S. government obligations 14%, other assets 2%. Largest stock holdings: electronics, electrical and supplies 14%, energy and related equipment 11%.

Portfolio Mgr: J. David Edwards—1987

Distributions: Income: Dec   **Capital Gains:** Dec

12b-1: No

Minimum: Initial: $100   Subsequent: $50

Min IRA: Initial: None   Subsequent: None

Services: IRA, Keogh, Corp, SEP, 403(b), Withdraw, Deduct

Tel Exchange: Yes   **With MMF:** Yes

Registered: All states

Ticker: LOCFX

† *There will be a 2% redemption fee only if shares are redeemed within six months after purchase.*

†US NEW PROSPECTOR

Precious Metals

United Services Advisors
P.O. Box 29467
San Antonio, TX 78229-0467
(800) 873-8637/(512) 696-1234

	Years Ending 6/30					
	1983	1984	1985	1986 (7 mos.)	1987	1988
Dividends from Net Investment Income ($)	–	–	–	–	–	–
Distributions from Net Realized Capital Gains ($)	–	–	–	–	.02	.23
Net Asset Value End of Year ($)	–	–	–	.96	2.05	1.40
Ratio of Expenses to Net Assets (%)	–	–	–	1.51	1.47	1.47
Ratio of Net Income to Average Net Assets (%)	–	–	–	.01	(.05)	.04
Portfolio Turnover Rate (%)	–	–	–	31	44	39
Total Assets End of Year (Millions $)	–	–	–	27.3	127.0	104.1

Annual Rate of Return (%) Years Ending 12/31	–	–	–	38.5	31.1	(18.8)

Five-Year Total Return(%)	NA	Degree of Diversification	E	Beta	NA	Bull (%)	NA	Bear (%)	(28.2)E

Objective: Seeks long-term growth of capital as well as protection against inflation and monetary instability. Current income is not a consideration. Invests in companies involved in the natural resource industry, including gold, silver, timber and oil.

Portfolio: (9/30/88) Common stocks 84%, repurchase agreements 14%, warrants 1%, convertible bonds 1%. Largest stock holdings: major gold-producing companies 43%, other gold-producing companies 27%.

Portfolio Mgr: J. David Edwards—1987

Distributions: **Income:** Dec   **Capital Gains:** Dec

12b-1: No

Minimum: **Initial:** $100   **Subsequent:** $50

Min IRA: **Initial:** None   **Subsequent:** None

Services: IRA, Keogh, Corp, SEP, 403(b), Withdraw, Deduct

Tel Exchange: Yes   **With MMF:** Yes

Registered: All states

Ticker: UNWPX

† *There will be a 2% redemption fee only if shares are redeemed within six months after purchase.*

US REAL ESTATE FUND
Growth

United Services Advisors
P.O. Box 29467
San Antonio, TX 78229-0467
(800) 873-8637/(512) 696-1234

	Years Ending 6/30					
	1983	**1984**	**1985**	**1986**	**1987**	**1988**
Dividends from Net Investment Income ($)	–	–	–	–	–	.38
Distributions from Net Realized Capital Gains ($)	–	–	–	–	–	–
Net Asset Value End of Year ($)	–	–	–	–	–	9.29
Ratio of Expenses to Net Assets (%)	–	–	–	–	–	–
Ratio of Net Income to Average Net Assets (%)	–	–	–	–	–	6.76
Portfolio Turnover Rate (%)	–	–	–	–	–	51
Total Assets End of Year (Millions $)						3.2

Annual Rate of Return (%) Years Ending 12/31	–	–	–	–	–	20.8

Five-Year Total Return(%)	NA	Degree of Diversification	NA	Beta	NA	Bull (%)	NA	Bear (%)	(19.5)D

Objective: Seeks long-term capital appreciation. Invests at least 65% of its assets in companies that have 50% of their assets in, or derive 50% of their revenues from, the ownership, construction, management or sale of residential, commercial or industrial real estate. May write covered call options.

Portfolio: (9/30/88) Common stocks 83%, U.S. government obligations 14%, other assets 3%. Largest stock holdings: real estate investment trusts 60%.

Portfolio Mgr: J. David Edwards—1987

Distributions: Income: June, Dec   **Capital Gains:** Dec

12b-1: No

Minimum: Initial: $100   Subsequent: $50

Min IRA: Initial: None   Subsequent: None

Services: IRA, Keogh, Corp, SEP, 403(b), Withdraw, Deduct

Tel Exchange: Yes   **With MMF:** Yes

Registered: All states

Ticker: UNREX

†VALLEY FORGE
Growth & Income

Valley Forge Mgmt. Corp.
P.O. Box 262
Valley Forge, PA 19481
(215) 688-6839

	Years Ending 12/31					
	1983	**1984**	**1985**	**1986**	**1987**	**1988**
Dividends from Net Investment Income ($)	.42	.54	.47	.69	1.31	.62
Distributions from Net Realized Capital Gains ($)	.78	.96	.06	.41	.19	.06
Net Asset Value End of Year ($)	11.53	10.71	11.16	10.67	9.63	9.57
Ratio of Expenses to Net Assets (%)	1.60	1.70	1.40	1.40	1.30	1.40
Ratio of Net Income to Average Net Assets (%)	6.0	7.1	5.6	5.9	6.9	5.5
Portfolio Turnover Rate (%)	39	70	87	40	56	97
Total Assets End of Year (Millions $)	3.2	7.8	10.1	9.2	9.4	9.0
Annual Rate of Return (%) Years Ending 12/31	17.9	6.7	10.5	5.5	4.6	7.0

Five-Year Total Return(%)	39.1ᴱ	Degree of Diversification	E	Beta	.14	Bull (%)	31.9ᴱ	Bear (%)	(3.6)ᶜ

Objective: Seeks capital appreciation and, secondarily, current income through investment in common stocks of established companies chosen on the basis of fundamental analysis and technical market considerations. May convert to short-term debt securities during adverse stock market conditions.

Portfolio: (12/31/88) Short-term money market securities 79%, common stocks 14%, bonds 4%, preferred stocks 3%. Largest stock holdings: American Telephone & Telegraph Corp. 5%, energy and related 2%.

Portfolio Mgr: Bernard Klawans—1971

Distributions: **Income:** Dec   **Capital Gains:** Dec

12b-1: No

Minimum: **Initial:** $2,500   **Subsequent:** $100

Min IRA: **Initial:** $1,000   **Subsequent:** $100

Services: IRA

Tel Exchange: No

Registered: All states

Ticker: VAFGX

† *There will be a 1% redemption fee only if shares are redeemed within six months after purchase.*

VALUE LINE AGGRESSIVE INCOME
Bond

Value Line, Inc.
711 Third Avenue
New York, NY 10017
(800) 223-0818/(212) 687-3965

| | Years Ending 1/31 | | | | | |
	1983	1984	1985	1986	1987 (11 mos.)	1988
Dividends from Net Investment Income ($)	–	–	–	–	1.16	1.15
Distributions from Net Realized Capital Gains ($)	–	–	–	–	–	–
Net Asset Value End of Year ($)	–	–	–	–	9.90	8.28
Ratio of Expenses to Net Assets (%)	–	–	–	–	1.33	1.22
Ratio of Net Income to Average Net Assets (%)	–	–	–	–	12.02	12.29
Portfolio Turnover Rate (%)	–	–	–	–	110	134
Total Assets End of Year (Millions $)	–	–	–	–	57.5	54.2

Annual Rate of Return (%) Years Ending 12/31	–	–	–	–	(2.0)	6.3

Five-Year Total Return(%)	NA	Degree of Diversification	NA	Beta	NA	Bull (%)	NA	Bear (%)	(8.0)c

Objective: Seeks to maximize current income; capital appreciation is of secondary importance. Invests primarily in high-yielding fixed-income corporate securities issued by companies rated B++ or lower for relative strength in the Value Line Investment Survey.

Portfolio: (7/31/88) Corporate bonds 79%, U.S. Treasury obligations 20%, repurchase agreements 2%. Largest corporate holdings: multiform 8%, petroleum—integrated 7%.

Portfolio Mgr: Terence Dwyer—1988

Distributions: **Income:** Monthly   **Capital Gains:** Annually

12b-1: No

Minimum: **Initial:** $1,000   **Subsequent:** $250

Min IRA: **Initial:** $1,000   **Subsequent:** $250

Services: IRA, Keogh, Corp, SEP, 403(b), Withdraw, Deduct

Tel Exchange: Yes   **With MMF:** Yes

Registered: All states

Ticker: VAGIX

VALUE LINE CONVERTIBLE
Balanced

Value Line Inc.
711 Third Ave.
New York, NY 10017
(800) 223-0818/(212) 687-3965

	Years Ending 4/30					
	1983	1984	1985	1986 (10 mos.)	1987	1988
Dividends from Net Investment Income ($)	—	—	—	.24	.54	.68
Distributions from Net Realized Capital Gains ($)	—	—	—	—	.71	.48
Net Asset Value End of Year ($)	—	—	—	12.45	12.36	10.28
Ratio of Expenses to Net Assets (%)	—	—	—	1.31	1.04	1.06
Ratio of Net Income to Average Net Assets (%)	—	—	—	5.37	5.12	4.78
Portfolio Turnover Rate (%)	—	—	—	164	234	257
Total Assets End of Year (Millions $)	—	—	—	49.8	89.2	64.7
Annual Rate of Return (%) Years Ending 12/31	—	—	—	16.1	(6.1)	16.0

Five-Year Total Return(%)	NA	Degree of Diversification	D	Beta	.75	Bull (%)	NA	Bear (%)	(17.1)c

Objective: Seeks high current income and capital appreciation through investment primarily in convertible securities. May also invest in non-convertible debt and equity securities.

Portfolio: (10/31/88) Convertible subordinated debentures 51%, convertible preferred stocks 27%, repurchase agreements 13%, other assets 8%, common stocks 1%. Largest holdings: paper & forest products 7%, copper 7%.

Portfolio Mgr: Alan Lyons—1985

Distributions: **Income:** Quarterly   **Capital Gains:** Annually

12b-1: No

Minimum: **Initial:** $1,000   **Subsequent:** $250

Min IRA: **Initial:** $1,000   **Subsequent:** $250

Services: IRA, Keogh, Corp, SEP, 403(b), Withdraw, Deduct

Tel Exchange: Yes   **With MMF:** Yes

Registered: All states

Ticker: VALCX

VALUE LINE FUND
Growth

Value Line, Inc.
711 Third Ave.
New York, NY 10017
(800) 223-0818/(212) 687-3965

	Years Ending 12/31					
	1983	**1984**	**1985**	**1986**	**1987**	**1988**
Dividends from Net Investment Income ($)	.55	.20	.20	.23	.27	.32
Distributions from Net Realized Capital Gains ($)	.75	—	—	1.75	2.64	.24
Net Asset Value End of Year ($)	12.87	10.77	14.27	14.68	12.51	13.15
Ratio of Expenses to Net Assets (%)	.77	.83	.81	.73	.69	.71
Ratio of Net Income to Average Net Assets (%)	2.04	1.67	1.62	1.44	1.53	2.67
Portfolio Turnover Rate (%)	97	110	129	145	118	108
Total Assets End of Year (Millions $)	203.2	166.5	206.0	212.6	204.7	180.9
Annual Rate of Return (%) Years Ending 12/31	(1.3)	(14.7)	34.6	16.7	4.7	9.7

Five-Year Total Return(%)	53.8ᴰ	Degree of Diversification	B	Beta 1.04	Bull (%) 126.7ᴬ	Bear (%) (20.2)ᴰ

Objective:	Primary objective is long-term growth of capital through investment in common stocks chosen on the basis of the Value Line Ranking System for Timeliness. May write covered call options, invest in restricted securities, and enter into repurchase agreements. May take defensive posture in debt investments.
Portfolio:	(12/31/88) Common stocks 78%, repurchase agreements 15%, U.S. government agency obligations 6%, U.S. Treasury obligations 2%. Largest stock holdings: medical supplies 5%, drugs 4%.
Portfolio Mgr:	Frank Korth—1988
Distributions:	**Income:** Quarterly **Capital Gains:** Annually
12b-1:	No
Minimum:	**Initial:** $1,000 **Subsequent:** $100
Min IRA:	**Initial:** $1,000 **Subsequent:** $100
Services:	IRA, Keogh, Corp, SEP, 403(b), Withdraw, Deduct
Tel Exchange:	Yes **With MMF:** Yes
Registered:	All states
Ticker:	VLIFX

VALUE LINE INCOME

Balanced

Value Line, Inc.
711 Third Ave.
New York, NY 10017
(800) 223-0818/(212) 687-3965

	Years Ending 12/31					
	1983	1984	1985	1986	1987	1988
Dividends from Net Investment Income ($)	.56	.48	.48	.48	.43	.40
Distributions from Net Realized Capital Gains ($)	.14	.26	—	.91	.69	—
Net Asset Value End of Year ($)	6.77	6.16	7.09	6.81	5.57	5.84
Ratio of Expenses to Net Assets (%)	.78	.89	.83	.77	.76	.80
Ratio of Net Income to Average Net Assets (%)	5.52	7.17	7.62	6.43	5.95	6.76
Portfolio Turnover Rate (%)	72	114	148	167	96	83
Total Assets End of Year (Millions $)	125.9	117.9	134.4	162.8	140.2	133.1
Annual Rate of Return (%) Years Ending 12/31	6.7	2.9	23.7	16.3	(2.4)	12.2

Five-Year Total Return(%)	62.0c	Degree of Diversification	A	Beta	.65	Bull (%)	94.4c	Bear (%)	(17.5)c

Objective: Seeks current income but considers capital appreciation to be an important secondary objective. Substantially all its investments are in common stocks or convertibles chosen on the basis of the Value Line Ranking System for Timeliness. May shift portfolio to debt investments as defensive posture. May invest in repurchase agreements and restricted securities, and may write covered call options.

Portfolio: (12/31/88) Common stocks 40%, corporate bonds 23%, repurchase agreements 18%, U.S. government agency obligations 17%, U.S. Treasury obligations 3%. Largest stock holdings: telecommunications 6%, insurance—diversified 6%.

Portfolio Mgr: Lydia Miller—1988

Distributions: **Income:** Quarterly   **Capital Gains:** Annually

12b-1: No

Minimum: **Initial:** $1,000   **Subsequent:** $100

Min IRA: **Initial:** $1,000   **Subsequent:** $100

Services: IRA, Keogh, Corp, SEP, 403(b), Withdraw, Deduct

Tel Exchange: Yes   **With MMF:** Yes

Registered: All states

Ticker: VALIX

VALUE LINE LEVERAGED GROWTH

Growth

Value Line, Inc.
711 Third Ave.
New York, NY 10017
(800) 223-0818/(212) 687-3965

	Years Ending 12/31					
	1983	1984	1985	1986	1987	1988
Dividends from Net Investment Income ($)	.65	.31	.13	.34	.46	.44
Distributions from Net Realized Capital Gains ($)	.02	.99	—	2.60	4.93	—
Net Asset Value End of Year ($)	19.66	16.56	20.90	22.80	18.15	18.87
Ratio of Expenses to Net Assets (%)	.80	.86	.80	.96	.95	.97
Ratio of Net Income to Average Net Assets (%)	2.24	.90	1.51	.98	1.05	1.99
Portfolio Turnover Rate (%)	105	89	121	115	148	143
Total Assets End of Year (Millions $)	216.1	181.5	228.6	290.0	282.9	235.3
Annual Rate of Return (%) Years Ending 12/31	7.9	(8.8)	27.1	23.3	3.0	6.4

Five-Year Total Return(%)	56.8[D]	Degree of Diversification	A	Beta 1.11	Bull (%) 136.2[A]	Bear (%) (23.4)[D]

Objective:	Seeks capital growth through investment in common stocks chosen on the basis of Value Line Ranking System for Timeliness. No consideration is given to current income in the choice of investments. May employ leverage from banks and may write covered call options. May enter into repurchase agreements.
Portfolio:	(12/31/88) Common stocks 76%, U.S. Treasury obligations 25%. Largest stock holdings: tobacco 9%, medical supplies 5%.
Portfolio Mgr:	David Campbell—1988
Distributions:	**Income:** Annually **Capital Gains:** Annually
12b-1:	No
Minimum:	**Initial:** $1,000 **Subsequent:** $100
Min IRA:	**Initial:** $1,000 **Subsequent:** $100
Services:	IRA, Keogh, Corp, SEP, 403(b), Withdraw, Deduct
Tel Exchange:	Yes **With MMF:** Yes
Registered:	All states
Ticker:	VALLX

VALUE LINE SPECIAL SITUATIONS
Aggressive Growth

Value Line, Inc.
711 Third Ave.
New York, NY 10017
(800) 223-0818/(212) 687-3965

	Years Ending 12/31					
	1983	1984	1985	1986	1987	1988
Dividends from Net Investment Income ($)	.45	.02	.05	.04	.12	.09
Distributions from Net Realized Capital Gains ($)	—	.08	—	—	2.56	—
Net Asset Value End of Year ($)	16.11	11.91	14.37	15.07	10.99	11.25
Ratio of Expenses to Net Assets (%)	1.00	1.06	1.07	1.02	1.01	1.16
Ratio of Net Income to Average Net Assets (%)	.66	.60	.22	.29	.26	.68
Portfolio Turnover Rate (%)	63	75	88	73	41	59
Total Assets End of Year (Millions $)	337.9	240.1	242.7	193.6	123.8	112.3

Annual Rate of Return (%) Years Ending 12/31	19.4	(25.5)	21.1	5.1	(9.8)	3.3

Five-Year Total Return(%) (11.7)E	Degree of Diversification	C	Beta 1.22	Bull (%) 65.3D	Bear (%) (29.1)E

Objective: Seeks long-term capital growth. Experiences wider than average price fluctuations and a period of years without substantial current investment income; 80% of its assets are invested in securities of companies in special situations (unusual developments in the operations of the company such as a new product or a merger). Uses Value Line Ranking System for Timeliness for determining possible undervaluation.

Portfolio: (12/31/88) Common stocks 67%, U.S. Treasury obligations 22%, repurchase agreements 12%, units 1%. Largest stock holdings: medical supplies 8%, computer and peripherals 6%.

Portfolio Mgr: Peter Shraga—1987

Distributions: **Income:** Annually   **Capital Gains:** Annually

12b-1: No

Minimum: **Initial:** $1,000   **Subsequent:** $100

Min IRA: **Initial:** $1,000   **Subsequent:** $100

Services: IRA, Keogh, Corp, SEP, 403(b), Withdraw, Deduct

Tel Exchange: Yes   **With MMF:** Yes

Registered: All states

Ticker: VALSX

VALUE LINE U.S. GOVERNMENT SECURITIES
Bond

Value Line, Inc.
711 Third Ave.
New York, NY 10017
(800) 223-0818/(212) 687-3965

	Years Ending 8/31					
	1983	**1984**	**1985**	**1986**	**1987**	**1988**
Dividends from Net Investment Income ($)	1.36	1.28	1.30	1.32	1.23	1.08
Distributions from Net Realized Capital Gains ($)	—	.28	—	.15	.23	—
Net Asset Value End of Year ($)	11.77	11.18	12.61	12.95	11.91	11.85
Ratio of Expenses to Net Assets (%)	.82	.92	.86	.76	.72	.67
Ratio of Net Income to Average Net Assets (%)	10.93	11.63	11.01	10.10	9.49	10.09
Portfolio Turnover Rate (%)	7	31	64	73	48	54
Total Assets End of Year (Millions $)	48.6	51.4	68.3	112.4	217.7	246.5
Annual Rate of Return (%) Years Ending 12/31	6.0	13.7	21.2	10.7	3.4	7.9

Five-Year Total Return(%)	70.3[C]	Degree of Diversification	NA	Beta	NA	Bull (%)	52.5[D]	Bear (%)	3.1[A]

Objective: Seeks to obtain maximum income without undue risk to principal. Invests at least 80% of its assets in issues of the U.S. government and its agencies and instrumentalities. Capital preservation and possible capital appreciation are secondary objectives. May lend its portfolio's securities and engage in repurchase agreements.

Portfolio: (8/31/88) U.S. government agency obligations 86%, U.S. Treasury obligations 12%, cash 1%, repurchase agreements 1%.

Portfolio Mgr: Milton Schlein—1986

Distributions: **Income:** Quarterly   **Capital Gains:** Annually

12b-1: No

Minimum: **Initial:** $1,000   **Subsequent:** $250

Min IRA: **Initial:** $1,000   **Subsequent:** $250

Services: IRA, Keogh, Corp, SEP, 403(b), Withdraw, Deduct

Tel Exchange: Yes   **With MMF:** Yes

Registered: All states

Ticker: VALBX

VANGUARD
BOND MARKET
Bond

Vanguard Group
Vanguard Financial Center
Valley Forge, PA 19482
(800) 662-7447/(215) 648-6000

			Years Ending 12/31			
	1983	1984	1985	1986 (1 mo.)	1987	1988
Dividends from Net Investment Income ($)	—	—	—	.03	.83	.81
Distributions from Net Realized Capital Gains ($)	—	—	—	—	—	—
Net Asset Value End of Year ($)	—	—	—	9.94	9.20	9.05
Ratio of Expenses to Net Assets (%)	—	—	—	0	.14	.30
Ratio of Net Income to Average Net Assets (%)	—	—	—	6.82	9.01	8.84
Portfolio Turnover Rate (%)	—	—	—	0	77	21
Total Assets End of Year (Millions $)	—	—	—	2.7	43.3	58.1

Annual Rate of Return (%) Years Ending 12/31	—	—	—	—	1.2	7.4

Five-Year Total Return(%)	NA	Degree of Diversification	NA	Beta	NA	Bull (%)	NA	Bear (%)	3.1ᴬ

Objective: This is an index fund. Its objective is to duplicate the total return of the Salomon Brothers broad investment-grade bond index. Bonds in the index have maturities greater than one year, have a minimum rating of BBB, and have general availability in the marketplace. Included are Treasury bonds, GNMAs and corporate bonds.

Portfolio: (12/31/88) U.S. government and agency obligations 75%, corporate bonds 14%, repurchase agreements 8%, foreign bonds 2%, other assets 1%. Largest bond holdings: finance 6%, utilities 5%.

Portfolio Mgr: Ian MacKinnon—1986

Distributions: **Income:** Monthly   **Capital Gains:** Annually

12b-1: No

Minimum: **Initial:** $3,000   **Subsequent:** $100

Min IRA: **Initial:** $500   **Subsequent:** $100

Services: IRA, Keogh, Corp, SEP, 403(b), Withdraw, Deduct

Tel Exchange: Yes   **With MMF:** Yes

Registered: All states

Ticker: VBMFX

VANGUARD CONVERTIBLE SECURITIES

Growth & Income

Vanguard Group
Vanguard Financial Center
Valley Forge, PA 19482
(800) 662-7447/(215) 648-6000

	Years Ending 11/30					
	1983	1984	1985	1986 (5 mos.)	1987	1988
Dividends from Net Investment Income ($)	—	—	—	.17	.51	.56
Distributions from Net Realized Capital Gains ($)	—	—	—	—	—	.12
Net Asset Value End of Year ($)	—	—	—	9.80	7.94	8.71
Ratio of Expenses to Net Assets (%)	—	—	—	.80	.85	.88
Ratio of Net Income to Average Net Assets (%)	—	—	—	6.02	6.13	6.52
Portfolio Turnover Rate (%)	—	—	—	13	13	24
Total Assets End of Year (Millions $)	—	—	—	72.8	72.8	69.2
Annual Rate of Return (%) Years Ending 12/31	—	—	—	—	(10.7)	15.7

Five-Year Total Return(%)	NA	Degree of Diversification	NA	Beta	NA	Bull (%)	NA	Bear (%)	(19.2)ᴰ

Objective: Seeks high level of current income together with long-term capital appreciation. At least 80% of the fund's assets will be invested in convertible bonds, debentures, corporate notes, and preferred stocks. Can invest up to 20% of assets in non-convertible corporate or government debt securities.

Portfolio: (11/30/88) Convertible bonds 92%, repurchase agreements 4%, convertible preferred stocks 3%, other assets 2%, common stocks 1%. Largest bond holdings: technology 17%, retailing 11%.

Portfolio Mgr: Rohit Desai—1986

Distributions: **Income:** Jan, Apr, July, Oct   **Capital Gains:** Annually

12b-1: No

Minimum: **Initial:** $3,000   **Subsequent:** $100

Min IRA: **Initial:** $500   **Subsequent:** $100

Services: IRA, Keogh, Corp, SEP, 403(b), Withdraw, Deduct

Tel Exchange: Yes   **With MMF:** Yes

Registered: All states

Ticker: VCVCX

†VANGUARD EXPLORER

Aggressive Growth

Vanguard Group
Vanguard Financial Center
Valley Forge, PA 19482
(800) 662-7447/(215) 648-6000

	Years Ending 10/31					
	1983	1984	1985	1986	1987	1988
Dividends from Net Investment Income ($)	.24	.64	.38	.33	.02	.11
Distributions from Net Realized Capital Gains ($)	.58	1.66	.20	1.29	3.27	1.96
Net Asset Value End of Year ($)	38.35	31.10	32.56	31.59	25.06	29.64
Ratio of Expenses to Net Assets (%)	.88	1.00	.80	.76	.62	.65
Ratio of Net Income to Average Net Assets (%)	2.02	1.27	1.02	.05	.28	.99
Portfolio Turnover Rate (%)	16	8	19	15	9	28
Total Assets End of Year (Millions $)	237.2	260.9	334.7	271.6	210.4	265.8

Annual Rate of Return (%) Years Ending 12/31	20.3	(19.5)	22.2	(8.5)	(7.0)	25.8

Five-Year Total Return(%)	5.4ᴱ	Degree of Diversification	E	Beta	.89	Bull (%)	38.4ᴱ	Bear (%)	(25.4)ᴱ

Objective: Seeks to provide long-term capital appreciation by investing in the common stocks of relatively small, unseasoned or new companies. Stocks are selected principally for their long-term capital growth potential and current income. Short-term market fluctuations are not considerations in the selection of investments.

Portfolio: (10/31/88) Common stocks 90%, repurchase agreements 9%, other assets 1%. Largest stock holdings: industrial systems and equipment 14%, defense products and services 12%.

Portfolio Mgr: Frank Wisneski—1979

Distributions: Income: Dec   **Capital Gains:** Dec

12b-1: No

Minimum: Initial: $3,000   Subsequent: $100

Min IRA: Initial: $500   Subsequent: $100

Services: IRA, Keogh, Corp, SEP, 403(b), Withdraw, Deduct

Tel Exchange: No

Registered: All states

Ticker: VEXPX

† Closed to new investors.

VANGUARD EXPLORER II
Aggressive Growth

Vanguard Group
Vanguard Financial Center
Valley Forge, PA 19482
(800) 662-7447/(215) 648-6000

	Years Ending 10/31					
	1983	1984	1985 (4 mos.)	1986	1987	1988
Dividends from Net Investment Income ($)	–	–	–	.08	.04	.05
Distributions from Net Realized Capital Gains ($)	–	–	–	–	.47	1.44
Net Asset Value End of Year ($)	–	–	19.25	20.08	16.91	20.00
Ratio of Expenses to Net Assets (%)	–	–	1.06	1.17	.62	.73
Ratio of Net Income to Average Net Assets (%)	–	–	1.68	.24	.26	.33
Portfolio Turnover Rate (%)	–	–	3	27	4	38
Total Assets End of Year (Millions $)	–	–	13.8	36.5	45.1	70.0

Annual Rate of Return (%) Years Ending 12/31	–	–	–	(7.3)	(4.5)	22.0

Five-Year Total Return(%)	NA	Degree of Diversification	D	Beta	1.11	Bull (%)	NA	Bear (%)	(27.5)E

Objective: Seeks long-term growth of capital by investing in common stocks of small, unseasoned companies with less than $100 million in annual revenues and more than three years of operating history.

Portfolio: (10/31/88) Common stocks 87%, temporary cash investments 11%, convertible bonds 3%. Largest stock holdings: medical and biotechnology 16%, electronic instrumentation 12%.

Portfolio Mgr: John Granahan—1985

Distributions: Income: Annually   **Capital Gains:** Annually

12b-1: No

Minimum: Initial: $3,000   Subsequent: $100

Min IRA: Initial: $500   Subsequent: $100

Services: IRA, Keogh, Corp, SEP, 403(b), Withdraw, Deduct

Tel Exchange: No

Registered: All states

Ticker: VEIIX

VANGUARD GNMA
Bond

Vanguard Group
Vanguard Financial Center
Valley Forge, PA 19482
(800) 662-7447/(215) 648-6000

	Years Ending 1/31					
	1983	1984	1985	1986	1987	1988
Dividends from Net Investment Income ($)	1.11	1.07	1.08	1.04	.97	.89
Distributions from Net Realized Capital Gains ($)	—	—	—	—	.01	—
Net Asset Value End of Year ($)	9.21	9.20	9.25	9.92	10.10	9.69
Ratio of Expenses to Net Assets (%)	.57	.58	.58	.50	.38	.35
Ratio of Net Income to Average Net Assets (%)	11.89	11.31	11.90	10.16	9.41	9.35
Portfolio Turnover Rate (%)	41	21	23	32	28	22
Total Assets End of Year (Millions $)	84.7	172.4	298.9	1,262.1	2,380.3	1,908.6
Annual Rate of Return (%) Years Ending 12/31	9.7	14.0	20.6	11.5	2.3	8.8

Five-Year Total Return(%)	70.7C	Degree of Diversification	NA	Beta	NA	Bull (%)	50.3D	Bear (%)	3.3A

Objective: Seeks current income through investing at least 80% of assets in GNMA mortgage-backed securities whose interest and principal payment is guaranteed by the U.S. government. Balance invested in other U.S. government guaranteed securities.

Portfolio: (7/31/88) GNMA obligations 96%, repurchase agreements 5%.

Portfolio Mgr: Paul G. Sullivan—1980

Distributions: Income: Monthly   **Capital Gains:** Annually

12b-1: No

Minimum: Initial: $3,000   Subsequent: $100

Min IRA: Initial: $500   Subsequent: $100

Services: IRA, Keogh, Corp, SEP, 403(b), Withdraw, Deduct

Tel Exchange: Yes   **With MMF:** Yes

Registered: All states

Ticker: VFIIX

VANGUARD HIGH YIELD BOND

Bond

Vanguard Group
Vanguard Financial Center
Valley Forge, PA 19482
(800) 662-7447/(215) 648-6000

	Years Ending 1/31					
	1983	1984	1985	1986	1987	1988
Dividends from Net Investment Income ($)	1.28	1.20	1.18	1.14	1.08	1.01
Distributions from Net Realized Capital Gains ($)	–	–	–	–	.12	–
Net Asset Value End of Year ($)	8.96	8.97	8.52	8.84	9.33	8.53
Ratio of Expenses to Net Assets (%)	.71	.68	.65	.60	.45	.41
Ratio of Net Income to Average Net Assets (%)	13.58	12.75	13.61	12.51	11.43	11.47
Portfolio Turnover Rate (%)	52	82	71	61	67	82
Total Assets End of Year (Millions $)	51.2	116.8	252.5	634.6	1,370.0	993.7

Annual Rate of Return (%) Years Ending 12/31	15.7	7.5	21.9	16.9	2.7	13.5

Five-Year Total Return(%)	78.6[B]	Degree of Diversification	NA	Beta	NA	Bull (%)	64.1[D]	Bear (%)	(2.1)[C]

Objective: Seeks current income primarily from investment in high-yielding, medium- and lower-quality bonds. Normally only 20% can be in debt securities rated below B, convertibles, preferred stocks or short-term investments. May invest in foreign securities and restricted securities. Fund performs own credit analysis.

Portfolio: (7/31/88) Corporate bonds 84%, government obligations 9%, repurchase agreements 4%, preferred stocks 2%, other assets 1%. Largest corporate holdings: industrial 61%, communications and entertainment 9%.

Portfolio Mgr: Earl McEvoy—1984

Distributions: Income: Monthly   **Capital Gains:** Annually

12b-1: No

Minimum: Initial: $3,000   Subsequent: $100

Min IRA: Initial: $500   Subsequent: $100

Services: IRA, Keogh, Corp, SEP, 403(b), Withdraw, Deduct

Tel Exchange: Yes   **With MMF:** Yes

Registered: All states

Ticker: VWEHX

†VANGUARD HIGH YIELD STOCK
Growth & Income

Vanguard Group
Vanguard Financial Center
Valley Forge, PA 19482
(800) 662-7447/(215) 648-6000

	Years Ending 10/31					
	1983	1984	1985	1986	1987	1988
Dividends from Net Investment Income ($)	1.05	1.32	1.41	1.37	1.36	1.49
Distributions from Net Realized Capital Gains ($)	.89	1.81	.92	1.95	3.29	2.82
Net Asset Value End of Year ($)	17.68	17.06	19.17	20.58	16.33	14.52
Ratio of Expenses to Net Assets (%)	.76	.67	.56	.52	.50	.54
Ratio of Net Income to Average Net Assets (%)	7.84	9.07	7.34	6.95	6.65	8.72
Portfolio Turnover Rate (%)	59	65	60	70	70	17
Total Assets End of Year (Millions $)	52.3	87.6	159.5	180.8	158.9	163.4

Annual Rate of Return (%) Years Ending 12/31	32.8	25.5	30.1	21.6	(4.7)	26.2

Five-Year Total Return(%) 138.7ᴬ	Degree of Diversification D	Beta .54	Bull (%) 132.5ᴬ	Bear (%) (18.7)ᴰ

Objective: Seeks to provide a high level of dividend income while also seeking growth of capital. Invests in high-yielding, domestic common stocks or equity related securities with capital appreciation potential. Invests in companies whose earnings growth potential is such that increases in dividend rates may be expected in the future. May also invest in preferred stocks, bonds and cash equivalents.

Portfolio: (10/31/88) Common stocks 61%, preferred stocks 23%, repurchase agreements 9%, government and agency obligations 6%, other assets 1%. Largest stock holdings: electric utilities 18%, banks 17%.

Portfolio Mgr: John Neff—1975

Distributions: **Income:** Quarterly   **Capital Gains:** Annually

12b-1: No

Minimum: **Initial:** $3,000   **Subsequent:** $100

Min IRA: **Initial:** $500   **Subsequent:** $100

Services: IRA, Keogh, Corp, SEP, 403(b), Withdraw, Deduct

Tel Exchange: Yes   **With MMF:** Yes

Registered: All states

Ticker: VQDIX

† *Closed to new investors.*

†VANGUARD INDEX TRUST— EXTENDED MARKET PORTFOLIO

Growth

Vanguard Group
Vanguard Financial Center
Valley Forge, PA 19482
(800) 662-7447/(215) 648-6000

	Years Ending 12/31					
	1983	1984	1985	1986	1987 (1 mo.)	1988
Dividends from Net Investment Income ($)	–	–	–	–	–	.20
Distributions from Net Realized Capital Gains ($)	–	–	–	–	–	.16
Net Asset Value End of Year ($)	–	–	–	–	9.99	11.60
Ratio of Expenses to Net Assets (%)	–	–	–	–	–	.24
Ratio of Net Income to Average Net Assets (%)	–	–	–	–	–	2.90
Portfolio Turnover Rate (%)	–	–	–	–	0	26
Total Assets End of Year (Millions $)	–	–	–	–	5.2	34.6

Annual Rate of Return (%) Years Ending 12/31	–	–	–	–	–	19.7

Five-Year Total Return(%)	NA	Degree of Diversification	NA	Beta	NA	Bull (%)	NA	Bear (%)	NA

Objective: Seeks to provide investment results that correspond to the aggregate price and yield performance of the Wilshire 4500 index. This index is heavily weighted toward stocks with mid-sized and small market capitalizations that are not included in the S&P 500 index.

Portfolio: (12/31/88) Common stocks 97%, repurchase agreements 4%.

Portfolio Mgr: George U. Sauter—1987

Distributions: Income: Dec   **Capital Gains:** Dec

12b-1: No

Minimum: Initial: $3,000   Subsequent: $100

Min IRA: Initial: $500   Subsequent: $100

Services: IRA, Keogh, Corp, SEP, 403(b), Withdraw, Deduct

Tel Exchange: No

Registered: All states

Ticker: VEXMX

† *The fund charges a portfolio transaction fee of 1% at the time of purchase.*

VANGUARD INDEX TRUST—500 PORTFOLIO
(formerly VANGUARD INDEX 500)

Vanguard Group
Vanguard Financial Center
Valley Forge, PA 19482
(800) 662-7447/(215) 648-6000

Growth & Income

	Years Ending 12/31					
	1983	**1984**	**1985**	**1986**	**1987**	**1988**
Dividends from Net Investment Income ($)	.87	.88	.91	.89	.69	1.10
Distributions from Net Realized Capital Gains ($)	.71	.48	1.61	2.02	.17	.32
Net Asset Value End of Year ($)	19.70	19.52	22.99	24.27	24.65	27.18
Ratio of Expenses to Net Assets (%)	.28	.27	.28	.28	.26	.22
Ratio of Net Income to Average Net Assets (%)	4.22	4.53	4.09	3.40	3.15	4.08
Portfolio Turnover Rate (%)	35	14	36	29	15	10
Total Assets End of Year (Millions $)	233.7	289.7	394.2	485.0	826.5	1,055.0
Annual Rate of Return (%) Years Ending 12/31	21.3	6.2	31.1	18.3	4.7	16.2

Five-Year Total Return(%)	100.5[A]	Degree of Diversification	A	Beta	1.00	Bull (%)	143.5[A]	Bear (%)	(24.5)[D]

Objective: Seeks to duplicate stock market price and yield performance by owning all stocks in the Standard & Poor's 500 stock index. Established fund shareholders may exchange their shares of S&P 500 stocks for fund shares.

Portfolio: (12/31/88) Common stocks 95%, temporary cash investments 5%.

Portfolio Mgr: George U. Sauter—1987

Distributions: **Income:** Mar, June, Sept, Dec   **Capital Gains:** Dec

12b-1: No

Minimum: **Initial:** $3,000   **Subsequent:** $100

Min IRA: **Initial:** $500   **Subsequent:** $100

Services: IRA, Keogh, Corp, SEP, 403(b), Withdraw, Deduct

Tel Exchange: No

Registered: All states

Ticker: VFINX

VANGUARD INVESTMENT GRADE BOND

Bond

Vanguard Group
Vanguard Financial Center
Valley Forge, PA 19482
(800) 662-7447/(215) 648-6000

	Years Ending 1/31					
	1983	1984	1985	1986	1987	1988
Dividends from Net Investment Income ($)	.96	.95	.96	.92	.85	.77
Distributions from Net Realized Capital Gains ($)	—	—	—	—	.12	—
Net Asset Value End of Year ($)	8.00	7.84	7.84	8.42	8.77	8.11
Ratio of Expenses to Net Assets (%)	.75	.67	.62	.55	.41	.37
Ratio of Net Income to Average Net Assets (%)	12.16	11.80	12.50	10.78	9.41	9.40
Portfolio Turnover Rate (%)	122	62	55	56	47	63
Total Assets End of Year (Millions $)	62.5	68.6	106.5	318.3	753.2	664.6

Annual Rate of Return (%) Years Ending 12/31	6.7	14.2	21.9	14.3	.3	9.7

Five-Year Total Return(%) 75.0ᴮ	Degree of Diversification NA	Beta NA	Bull (%) 51.9ᴰ	Bear (%) 3.8ᴬ

Objective: Seeks current income through investment primarily in long-term corporate bonds with coupons of Baa grade or higher. Fund performs own credit analysis. May invest in foreign securities and restricted securities and engage in repurchase agreements of similar quality.

Portfolio: (7/31/88) Corporate bonds 80%, government obligations 16%, repurchase agreements 3%, other assets 2%. Largest corporate holdings: industrial 34%, banks and finance 15%.

Portfolio Mgr: Paul Sullivan—1976

Distributions: **Income:** Monthly   **Capital Gains:** Annually

12b-1: No

Minimum: **Initial:** $3,000   **Subsequent:** $100

Min IRA: **Initial:** $500   **Subsequent:** $100

Services: IRA, Keogh, Corp, SEP, 403(b), Withdraw, Deduct

Tel Exchange: Yes   **With MMF:** Yes

Registered: All states

Ticker: VWESX

VANGUARD PRIMECAP
Growth

Vanguard Group
Vanguard Financial Center
Valley Forge, PA 19482
(800) 662-7447/(215) 648-6000

	Years Ending 12/31					
	1983	1984 (2 mos.)	1985	1986	1987	1988
Dividends from Net Investment Income ($)	—	—	.03	.56	.40	.38
Distributions from Net Realized Capital Gains ($)	—	—	—	.73	.94	1.00
Net Asset Value End of Year ($)	—	26.22	35.56	42.57	40.23	44.74
Ratio of Expenses to Net Assets (%)	—	—	.98	.82	.83	.83
Ratio of Net Income to Average Net Assets (%)	—	2.12	1.44	1.00	.91	.83
Portfolio Turnover Rate (%)	—	51	14	15	21	26
Total Assets End of Year (Millions $)	—	1.8	54.1	132.6	164.9	185.7

Annual Rate of Return (%) Years Ending 12/31	—	—	35.8	23.5	(2.3)	14.7

Five-Year Total Return(%)	NA	Degree of Diversification	C	Beta 1.04	Bull (%)	NA	Bear (%)	(24.3)ᴰ

Objective: Seeks long-term growth of capital, income is not an objective. Under normal conditions the fund will invest 80% of its assets in equity securities, including common stocks and convertibles. Looks for companies with superior earnings growth and consistency. May also invest in out-of-favor cyclical stocks.

Portfolio: (12/31/88) Common stocks 96%, repurchase agreements 2%, other assets 1%. Largest stock holdings: electronic components and instruments 16%, computer and related 14%.

Portfolio Mgr: Howard Schow—1984

Distributions: Income: Dec   **Capital Gains:** Dec

12b-1: No

Minimum: Initial: $10,000   Subsequent: $1,000

Min IRA: Initial: $500   Subsequent: $100

Services: IRA, Keogh, Corp, SEP, 403(b), Withdraw, Deduct

Tel Exchange: Yes   **With MMF:** Yes

Registered: All states

Ticker: VPMCX

VANGUARD QUANTITATIVE PORTFOLIOS

Growth & Income

Vanguard Group
Vanguard Financial Center
Valley Forge, PA 19482
(800) 662-7447/(215) 648-6000

	Years Ending 12/31					
	1983	**1984**	**1985**	**1986**	**1987**	**1988**
Dividends from Net Investment Income ($)	–	–	–	–	.25	.35
Distributions from Net Realized Capital Gains ($)	–	–	–	–	.06	–
Net Asset Value End of Year ($)	–	–	–	9.69	9.80	11.08
Ratio of Expenses to Net Assets (%)	–	–	–	0	.64	.64
Ratio of Net Income to Average Net Assets (%)	–	–	–	5.15	2.79	3.38
Portfolio Turnover Rate (%)	–	–	–	0	73	50
Total Assets End of Year (Millions $)	–	–	–	7.4	149.1	143.5

Annual Rate of Return (%) Years Ending 12/31	–	–	–	–	3.3	16.6

Five-Year Total Return(%)	NA	Degree of Diversification	NA	Beta	NA	Bull (%)	NA	Bear (%)	(24.4)D

Objective: Seeks to provide a total return greater than the total return of the S&P 500 stock index. Over 65% of the fund's assets are invested in companies that are also included in the S&P 500. The advisor uses quantitative analysis to weight the portfolio toward the most attractive stocks in the universe of stocks monitored.

Portfolio: (12/31/88) Common stocks 96%, temporary cash investments 4%. Largest stock holdings: IBM Corp. 4%, Exxon Corp. 3%.

Portfolio Mgr: John Nagorniak—1986

Distributions: Income: July, Dec   **Capital Gains:** Dec

12b-1: No

Minimum: Initial: $3,000   Subsequent: $100

Min IRA: Initial: $500   Subsequent: $100

Services: IRA, Keogh, Corp, SEP, 403(b), Withdraw, Deduct

Tel Exchange: No   **With MMF:** No

Registered: All states

Ticker: VQNPX

VANGUARD SHORT TERM BOND

Bond

Vanguard Group
Vanguard Financial Center
Valley Forge, PA 19482
(800) 662-7447/(215) 648-6000

	Years Ending 1/31					
	1983 (3 mos.)	1984	1985	1986	1987	1988
Dividends from Net Investment Income ($)	.27	1.02	1.07	1.00	.88	.76
Distributions from Net Realized Capital Gains ($)	—	—	—	—	.18	—
Net Asset Value End of Year ($)	10.05	9.94	10.17	10.55	10.67	10.43
Ratio of Expenses to Net Assets (%)	.51	.56	.62	.49	.38	.33
Ratio of Net Income to Average Net Assets (%)	10.33	10.23	11.26	9.50	7.79	7.36
Portfolio Turnover Rate (%)	65	121	270	460	278	258
Total Assets End of Year (Millions $)	64.1	135.8	119.1	198.5	400.7	428.8
Annual Rate of Return (%) Years Ending 12/31	9.1	14.2	14.9	11.3	4.4	6.9

Five-Year Total Return(%)	63.2[c]	Degree of Diversification	NA	Beta	NA	Bull (%)	42.9[E]	Bear (%)	2.8[A]

Objective: The fund invests primarily in short-term investment-grade bonds with maturities ranging from less than one year to four years. Has objective of obtaining the highest possible income consistent with minimum fluctuation in principal. May engage in repurchase agreements and invest up to 20% of assets in foreign securities.

Portfolio: (7/31/88) Corporate bonds 67%, foreign securities 13%, temporary cash investments 11%, government and agency obligations 7%, other assets 2%. Largest corporate holdings: finance—banks 16%, finance—diversified 16%.

Portfolio Mgr: Ian MacKinnon—1982

Distributions: **Income:** Monthly   **Capital Gains:** Annually

12b-1: No

Minimum: **Initial:** $3,000   **Subsequent:** $100

Min IRA: **Initial:** $500   **Subsequent:** $100

Services: IRA, Keogh, Corp, SEP, 403(b), Withdraw, Deduct

Tel Exchange: Yes   **With MMF:** Yes

Registered: All states

Ticker: VFSTX

VANGUARD SHORT TERM GOVERNMENT BOND

Bond

Vanguard Group
Vanguard Financial Center
Valley Forge, PA 19482
(800) 662-7447/(215) 648-6000

	Years Ending 1/31					
	1983	1984	1985	1986	1987	1988 (1 mo.)
Dividends from Net Investment Income ($)	—	—	—	—	—	.05
Distributions from Net Realized Capital Gains ($)	—	—	—	—	—	—
Net Asset Value End of Year ($)	—	—	—	—	—	10.05
Ratio of Expenses to Net Assets (%)	—	—	—	—	—	—
Ratio of Net Income to Average Net Assets (%)	—	—	—	—	—	—
Portfolio Turnover Rate (%)	—	—	—	—	—	—
Total Assets End of Year (Millions $)	—	—	—	—	—	6.1

Annual Rate of Return (%) Years Ending 12/31	—	—	—	—	—	5.7

Five-Year Total Return(%)	NA	Degree of Diversification	NA	Beta	NA	Bull (%)	NA	Bear (%)	NA

Objective: Seeks to provide the highest level of current income consistent with safety of principal, minimum fluctuation in principal value, and current liquidity. Invests in short-term U.S. government obligations and U.S. government agency securities with an average maturity ranging from no less than one year to not more than four years.

Portfolio: (7/31/88) Government and agency obligations 94%, temporary cash investments 5%, other assets 2%.

Portfolio Mgr: Ian MacKinnon—1987

Distributions: **Income:** Monthly   **Capital Gains:** Annually

12b-1: No

Minimum: **Initial:** $3,000   **Subsequent:** $100

Min IRA: **Initial:** $500   **Subsequent:** $100

Services: IRA, Keogh, Corp, SEP, 403(b), Withdraw, Deduct

Tel Exchange: Yes   **With MMF:** Yes

Registered: All states

Ticker: VSGBX

†VANGUARD SPECIALIZED PORTFOLIOS— ENERGY

Growth & Income

Vanguard Group
Vanguard Financial Center
Valley Forge, PA 19482
(800) 662-7447/(215) 648-6000

	Years Ending 1/31					
	1983	1984	1985 (7 mos.)	1986	1987	1988
Dividends from Net Investment Income ($)	—	—	—	.14	.44	.76
Distributions from Net Realized Capital Gains ($)	—	—	—	.08	.05	1.41
Net Asset Value End of Year ($)	—	—	9.81	9.93	12.42	10.22
Ratio of Expenses to Net Assets (%)	—	—	.55	.92	.65	.38
Ratio of Net Income to Average Net Assets (%)	—	—	3.75	4.40	3.43	3.70
Portfolio Turnover Rate (%)	—	—	34	156	34	84
Total Assets End of Year (Millions $)	—	—	1.0	2.1	28.6	35.6
Annual Rate of Return (%) Years Ending 12/31	—	—	14.4	12.7	6.1	21.4

Five-Year Total Return(%)	NA	Degree of Diversification	E	Beta	.85	Bull (%)	117.6ᴮ	Bear (%)	(26.4)ᴱ

Objective:	Capital appreciation is the primary objective. Invests in companies engaged in the production, transmission, marketing, control or measurement of energy or energy fuels. Energy sources include oil, gas, coal, solar power, nuclear and geothermal. Does not invest in electric utilities.
Portfolio:	(7/31/88) Common stocks 91%, convertible bonds and stocks 5%, cash 4%. Largest stock holdings: domestic oil producers 25%, natural gas transmission 14%.
Portfolio Mgr:	Ernst von Metzsch—1984
Distributions:	**Income:** Annually **Capital Gains:** Annually
12b-1:	No
Minimum:	**Initial:** $3,000 **Subsequent:** $100
Min IRA:	**Initial:** $500 **Subsequent:** $50
Services:	IRA, Keogh, SEP, Withdraw, Deduct
Tel Exchange:	Yes **With MMF:** Yes
Registered:	All states
Ticker:	VGENX

† *The fund has a 1% redemption fee that is reinvested in the fund.*

†VANGUARD SPECIALIZED PORTFOLIOS— GOLD AND PRECIOUS METALS

Precious Metals

Vanguard Group
Vanguard Financial Center
Valley Forge, PA 19482
(800) 662-7447/(215) 648-6000

	Years Ending 1/31					
	1983	1984	1985 (7 mos.)	1986	1987	1988
Dividends from Net Investment Income ($)	—	—	—	.06	.21	.48
Distributions from Net Realized Capital Gains ($)	—	—	—	—	—	1.14
Net Asset Value End of Year ($)	—	—	6.60	7.60	10.50	9.35
Ratio of Expenses to Net Assets (%)	—	—	.87	.73	.59	.47
Ratio of Net Income to Average Net Assets (%)	—	—	3.25	3.86	3.36	2.71
Portfolio Turnover Rate (%)	—	—	11	40	32	44
Total Assets End of Year (Millions ($)	—	—	6.9	30.5	69.9	128.0

Annual Rate of Return (%) Years Ending 12/31	—	—	(5.0)	49.9	38.7	(14.2)

Five-Year Total Return(%)	NA	Degree of Diversification	E	Beta	NA	Bull (%)	122.9B	Bear (%)	(20.1)D

Objective: Capital appreciation is the primary objective. Invests in companies engaged in the exploration, mining, fabrication, processing, or dealing in gold, silver, platinum, diamonds or other precious metals and minerals. May also invest in gold bullion and coins.

Portfolio: (7/31/88) Common stocks 76%, precious metals 15%, cash 8%. Largest holdings: North American gold stocks 27%, Australian gold stocks 24%.

Portfolio Mgr: David Hutchins—1986

Distributions: Income: Annually   **Capital Gains:** Annually

12b-1: No

Minimum: Initial: $3,000   **Subsequent:** $100

Min IRA: Initial: $500   **Subsequent:** $50

Services: IRA, Keogh, SEP, Withdraw, Deduct

Tel Exchange: Yes   **With MMF:** Yes

Registered: All states

Ticker: VGPMX

† *The fund has a 1% redemption fee that is reinvested in the fund.*

†VANGUARD SPECIALIZED PORTFOLIOS— HEALTH CARE

Growth

Vanguard Group
Vanguard Financial Center
Valley Forge, PA 19482
(800) 662-7447/(215) 648-6000

	Years Ending 1/31					
	1983	**1984**	**1985** (7 mos.)	**1986**	**1987**	**1988**
Dividends from Net Investment Income ($)	—	—	—	.07	.13	.57
Distributions from Net Realized Capital Gains ($)	—	—	—	.11	.80	1.39
Net Asset Value End of Year ($)	—	—	11.85	15.61	19.53	17.53
Ratio of Expenses to Net Assets (%)	—	—	.59	.83	.61	.51
Ratio of Net Income to Average Net Assets (%)	—	—	2.41	1.52	1.47	1.65
Portfolio Turnover Rate (%)	—	—	23	59	27	41
Total Assets End of Year (Millions $)	—	—	2.7	22.5	49.1	54.2
Annual Rate of Return (%) Years Ending 12/31	—	—	45.8	21.4	(0.5)	28.4

Five-Year Total Return(%)	NA	Degree of Diversification	C	Beta	.98	Bull (%)	169.7ᴬ	Bear (%)	(26.5)ᴱ

Objective:	Capital appreciation is the primary objective. Invests in companies engaged in the development, production or distribution of products related to the treatment or prevention of diseases and other medical infirmities. Companies include pharmaceutical companies, medical supply firms, and hospital and healthcare facility operators.
Portfolio:	(7/31/88) Common stocks 94%, cash 4%, preferred stocks and convertibles 2%. Largest stock holdings: pharmaceuticals 66%, medical technology and services 27%.
Portfolio Mgr:	Edward Owens—1984
Distributions:	**Income:** Annually **Capital Gains:** Annually
12b-1:	No
Minimum:	**Initial:** $3,000 **Subsequent:** $100
Min IRA:	**Initial:** $500 **Subsequent:** $50
Services:	IRA, Keogh, SEP, Withdraw, Deduct
Tel Exchange:	Yes **With MMF:** Yes
Registered:	All states
Ticker:	VGHCX

† *The fund has a 1% redemption fee that is reinvested in the fund.*

†VANGUARD SPECIALIZED PORTFOLIOS— SERVICE ECONOMY

Growth

Vanguard Group
Vanguard Financial Center
Valley Forge, PA 19482
(800) 662-7447/(215) 648-6000

			Years Ending 1/31			
	1983	1984	1985 (7 mos.)	1986	1987	1988
Dividends from Net Investment Income ($)	–	–	–	.09	.16	.85
Distributions from Net Realized Capital Gains ($)	–	–	–	.12	.70	2.05
Net Asset Value End of Year ($)	–	–	12.69	16.88	19.45	13.63
Ratio of Expenses to Net Assets (%)	–	–	.58	.57	.48	.44
Ratio of Net Income to Average Net Assets (%)	–	–	2.92	2.24	1.61	2.08
Portfolio Turnover Rate (%)	–	–	125	54	96	49
Total Assets End of Year (Millions $)	–	–	3.5	33.7	49.0	24.3
Annual Rate of Return (%) Years Ending 12/31	–	–	43.7	12.8	(13.0)	19.1

Five-Year Total Return(%)	NA	Degree of Diversification	B	Beta 1.11	Bull (%) 130.6ᴬ	Bear (%) (31.8)ᴱ

Objective: Capital appreciation is the primary objective. Invests in companies that provide financial, information and media, business and consumer services. Companies include banks, insurance companies, publishers, motion picture companies, computer service and waste management. May also invest in drug and catalog retailers.

Portfolio: (7/31/88) Common stocks 95%, cash 3%, other 2%. Largest stock holdings: financial 29%, business 23%.

Portfolio Mgr: William Hicks—1984

Distributions: **Income:** Annually   **Capital Gains:** Annually

12b-1: No

Minimum: **Initial:** $3,000   **Subsequent:** $100

Min IRA: **Initial:** $500   **Subsequent:** $50

Services: IRA, Keogh, SEP, Withdraw, Deduct

Tel Exchange: Yes   **With MMF:** Yes

Registered: All states

Ticker: VGSEX

† *The fund has a 1% redemption fee that is reinvested in the fund.*

†VANGUARD SPECIALIZED PORTFOLIOS— TECHNOLOGY

Growth

Vanguard Group
Vanguard Financial Center
Valley Forge, PA 19482
(800) 662-7447/(215) 648-6000

	Years Ending 1/31					
	1983	1984	1985 (7 mos.)	1986	1987	1988
Dividends from Net Investment Income ($)	—	—	—	.05	.08	.18
Distributions from Net Realized Capital Gains ($)	—	—	—	.05	.30	.53
Net Asset Value End of Year ($)	—	—	11.57	11.73	13.77	10.23
Ratio of Expenses to Net Assets (%)	—	—	.53	.72	.65	.39
Ratio of Net Income to Average Net Assets (%)	—	—	1.85	1.35	.82	1.02
Portfolio Turnover Rate (%)	—	—	65	85	108	129
Total Assets End of Year (Millions $)	—	—	5.1	12.6	25.5	18.2
Annual Rate of Return (%) Years Ending 12/31	—	—	13.9	5.7	(11.9)	9.5

Five-Year Total Return(%)	NA	Degree of Diversification	D	Beta	1.26	Bull (%)	64.2D	Bear (%)	(32.6)E

Objective: Capital appreciation is the primary objective. Invests in companies that develop, produce or distribute products and services related to advances in technology. Companies include computer hardware, peripheral, services and supplies; telecommunications; semiconductors; aerospace and defense; medical technology; consumer electronics.

Portfolio: (7/31/88) Common stocks 91%, cash 9%. Largest holdings: computer equipment 32%, semiconductors 18%.

Portfolio Mgr: Perry Traquina—1984

Distributions: **Income:** Annually   **Capital Gains:** Annually

12b-1: No

Minimum: **Initial:** $3,000   **Subsequent:** $100

Min IRA: **Initial:** $500   **Subsequent:** $50

Services: IRA, Keogh, SEP, Withdraw, Deduct

Tel Exchange: Yes   **With MMF:** Yes

Registered: All states

Ticker: VGTCX

† *The fund has a 1% redemption fee that is reinvested in the fund.*

VANGUARD STAR
Growth

Vanguard Group
Vanguard Financial Center
Valley Forge, PA 19482
(800) 662-7447/(215) 648-6000

	Years Ending 12/31					
	1983	1984	1985 (9 mos.)	1986	1987	1988
Dividends from Net Investment Income ($)	–	–	.05	.86	.85	.69
Distributions from Net Realized Capital Gains ($)	–	–	–	.71	.75	.03
Net Asset Value End of Year ($)	–	–	11.45	11.34	9.98	11.12
Ratio of Expenses to Net Assets (%)	–	–	0	0	0	0
Ratio of Net Income to Average Net Assets (%)	–	–	7.04	5.44	6.08	5.87
Portfolio Turnover Rate (%)	–	–	–	–	–	21
Total Assets End of Year (Millions $)	–	–	112.3	454.7	567.7	681.5

Annual Rate of Return (%) Years Ending 12/31	–	–	–	13.8	1.6	19.0

Five-Year Total Return(%)	NA	Degree of Diversification	B	Beta	.55	Bull (%)	NA	Bear (%)	(13.4)c

Objective: Designed as a retirement portfolio. The fund invests in other Vanguard mutual funds, which in turn invest in common stocks and bonds. Seeks maximum total investment return. Will invest at least 60% in equity funds and not more than 40% in bond funds. May also invest in repurchase agreements.

Portfolio: (12/31/88) Largest holdings: Windsor II 33%, Windsor Fund 21%, Money Market Reserves—Prime Portfolio 13%, GNMA Portfolio 12%.

Portfolio Mgr: Dan Gross—1985

Distributions: **Income:** July, Dec   **Capital Gains:** Dec

12b-1: No

Minimum: **Initial:** $3,000   **Subsequent:** $100

Min IRA: **Initial:** $500   **Subsequent:** $100

Services: IRA, Keogh, Corp, SEP, 403(b), Withdraw, Deduct

Tel Exchange: Yes   **With MMF:** Yes

Registered: All states

Ticker: VGSTX

VANGUARD TRUSTEES' COMMINGLED— INTERNATIONAL PORTFOLIO
International

Vanguard Group
Vanguard Financial Center
Valley Forge, PA 19482
(800) 662-7447/(215) 648-6000

	Years Ending 12/31					
	1983 (7 mos.)	1984	1985	1986	1987	1988
Dividends from Net Investment Income ($)	.44	1.09	.93	1.03	.75	.99
Distributions from Net Realized Capital Gains ($)	.02	.11	2.54	6.55	18.32	4.58
Net Asset Value End of Year ($)	25.98	24.59	30.91	38.68	28.66	28.27
Ratio of Expenses to Net Assets (%)	.90	.63	.56	.52	.50	.51
Ratio of Net Income to Average Net Assets (%)	3.35	3.89	3.11	2.65	2.44	2.55
Portfolio Turnover Rate (%)	-0-	8	29	24	48	90
Total Assets End of Year (Millions $)	65.3	317.1	581.6	718.7	657.3	467.0

Annual Rate of Return (%) Years Ending 12/31	—	(0.7)	40.2	49.9	23.4	18.8

Five-Year Total Return(%) 205.8ᴬ	Degree of Diversification E	Beta .56	Bull (%) 216.4ᴬ	Bear (%) (12.8)ᶜ

Objective: Invests primarily in non-U.S. securities concentrating on areas apparently undervalued to achieve long-term total return. The contrarian approach is employed as well as computer modeling. May lend its portfolio securities.

Portfolio: (12/31/88) Common stocks 93%, temporary cash investments 7%, other assets 1%. Largest country holdings: Japan 29%, Canada 13%.

Portfolio Mgr: John Wagstaff-Callahan—1984

Distributions: Income: Mar, June, Sept, Dec　　**Capital Gains:** Dec

12b-1: No

Minimum: Initial: $10,000　Subsequent: $1,000

Min IRA: Initial: $500　Subsequent: $100

Services: IRA, Keogh, Corp, SEP, 403(b), Withdraw, Deduct

Tel Exchange: Yes　　**With MMF:** Yes

Registered: All states

Ticker: VTRIX

VANGUARD TRUSTEES' COMMINGLED— U.S. PORTFOLIO

Growth & Income

Vanguard Group
Vanguard Financial Center
Valley Forge, PA 19482
(800) 662-7447/(215) 648-6000

	Years Ending 12/31					
	1983	1984	1985	1986	1987	1988
Dividends from Net Investment Income ($)	1.52	1.57	1.45	1.16	.72	.97
Distributions from Net Realized Capital Gains ($)	2.15	2.51	4.10	6.15	5.88	1.00
Net Asset Value End of Year ($)	35.72	30.56	31.15	28.69	22.77	26.35
Ratio of Expenses to Net Assets (%)	.50	.53	.48	.52	.52	.58
Ratio of Net Income to Average Net Assets (%)	4.19	4.74	4.42	3.46	2.77	3.86
Portfolio Turnover Rate (%)	30	33	25	19	44	27
Total Assets End of Year (Millions $)	269.9	271.6	201.6	162.5	122.1	115.4
Annual Rate of Return (%) Years Ending 12/31	29.1	(2.9)	20.4	15.6	1.6	24.6

Five-Year Total Return(%)	71.2[C]	Degree of Diversification	B	Beta	1.03	Bull (%)	122.3[B]	Bear (%)	(27.3)[E]

Objective: Seeks long-term total return. Looks for securities of industries or companies unpopular in the marketplace, stocks not widely held by other institutions with low price-to-book value, and undervalued companies with under-utilized borrowing power.

Portfolio: (12/31/88) Common stocks 94%, temporary cash investments 4%, other assets 2%. Largest stock holdings: General Motors Corp. 4%, McDonnell Douglas Corp. 3%.

Portfolio Mgr: John Wagstaff-Callahan—1980

Distributions: **Income:** Mar, June, Sept, Dec   **Capital Gains:** Dec

12b-1: No

Minimum: **Initial:** $10,000   **Subsequent:** $1,000

Min IRA: **Initial:** $500   **Subsequent:** $100

Services: IRA, Keogh, Corp, SEP, 403(b), Withdraw, Deduct

Tel Exchange: Yes   **With MMF:** Yes

Registered: All states

Ticker: VTRSX

VANGUARD U.S. TREASURY BOND

Bond

Vanguard Group
Vanguard Financial Center
Valley Forge, PA 19482
(800) 662-7447/(215) 648-6000

	Years Ending 1/31					
	1983	1984	1985	1986	1987 (8 mos.)	1988
Dividends from Net Investment Income ($)	—	—	—	—	.53	.78
Distributions from Net Realized Capital Gains ($)	—	—	—	—	.03	—
Net Asset Value End of Year ($)	—	—	—	—	10.28	9.49
Ratio of Expenses to Net Assets (%)	—	—	—	—	—	.32
Ratio of Net Income to Average Net Assets (%)	—	—	—	—	6.93	8.10
Portfolio Turnover Rate (%)	—	—	—	—	182	182
Total Assets End of Year (Millions $)	—	—	—	—	34.7	82.7

Annual Rate of Return (%) Years Ending 12/31	—	—	—	—	(2.9)	9.1

Five-Year Total Return(%) NA	Degree of Diversification NA	Beta NA	Bull (%) NA	Bear (%) 4.0ᴬ

Objective:	Seeks high level of current income consistent with safety of principal and liquidity. Invests at least 85% of its assets in long-term U.S. Treasury bonds and other "full faith and credit" obligations of the U.S. government. Can invest in zero coupon Treasury bonds and interest rate futures.
Portfolio:	(7/31/88) U.S. Treasury securities 91%, repurchase agreements 6%, other assets 3%.
Portfolio Mgr:	Ian MacKinnon—1986
Distributions:	**Income:** Monthly **Capital Gains:** Annually
12b-1:	No
Minimum:	**Initial:** $3,000 **Subsequent:** $100
Min IRA:	**Initial:** $500 **Subsequent:** $100
Services:	IRA, Keogh, Corp, SEP, 403(b), Withdraw, Deduct
Tel Exchange:	Yes **With MMF:** Yes
Registered:	All states
Ticker:	VUSTX

VANGUARD WELLESLEY INCOME
(formerly VANGUARD WELLESLEY)
Balanced

Vanguard Group
Vanguard Financial Center
Valley Forge, PA 19482
(800) 662-7447/(215) 648-6000

	Years Ending 12/31					
	1983	1984	1985	1986	1987	1988
Dividends from Net Investment Income ($)	1.31	1.37	1.38	1.33	1.04	1.23
Distributions from Net Realized Capital Gains ($)	–	–	.10	.47	.38	–
Net Asset Value End of Year ($)	12.66	13.28	15.31	16.27	14.57	15.26
Ratio of Expenses to Net Assets (%)	.70	.71	.60	.58	.49	.51
Ratio of Net Income to Average Net Assets (%)	10.23	10.68	9.36	7.74	7.83	8.14
Portfolio Turnover Rate (%)	38	36	21	31	40	20
Total Assets End of Year (Millions $)	105.4	114.6	224.1	510.2	495.0	567.1

Annual Rate of Return (%) Years Ending 12/31	18.6	16.6	27.4	18.4	(1.9)	13.6

Five-Year Total Return(%)	96.0[A]	Degree of Diversification	E	Beta	.29	Bull (%)	78.5[D]	Bear (%)	(4.0)[C]

Objective: Seeks to provide as much current income as management believes is consistent with reasonable risk. Invests approximately 70% of assets in investment grade fixed-income securities, with the balance invested in high yielding common stocks. May lend its portfolio securities and engage in repurchase agreements.

Portfolio: (12/31/88) Corporate bonds 40%, common stocks 37%, U.S. government agency obligations 21%, repurchase agreements 1%, other assets 1%. Largest stock holdings: GTE Corp. 2%, General Motors Corp. 2%.

Portfolio Mgr: Earl McEvoy—1982; John Ryan—1987

Distributions: **Income:** Mar, June, Sept, Dec   **Capital Gains:** Dec

12b-1: No

Minimum: **Initial:** $3,000   **Subsequent:** $100

Min IRA: **Initial:** $500   **Subsequent:** $100

Services: IRA, Keogh, Corp, SEP, 403(b), Withdraw, Deduct

Tel Exchange: Yes   **With MMF:** Yes

Registered: All states

Ticker: VWINX

VANGUARD WELLINGTON
Balanced

Vanguard Group
Vanguard Financial Center
Valley Forge, PA 19482
(800) 662-7447/(215) 648-6000

	Years Ending 11/30					
	1983	**1984**	**1985**	**1986**	**1987**	**1988**
Dividends from Net Investment Income ($)	.91	.92	.92	.94	.54	.98
Distributions from Net Realized Capital Gains ($)	.44	.48	.30	.34	—	.14
Net Asset Value End of Year ($)	12.49	12.08	13.99	16.06	14.92	16.82
Ratio of Expenses to Net Assets (%)	.64	.59	.64	.53	.43	.47
Ratio of Net Income to Average Net Assets (%)	7.09	7.52	6.84	5.88	5.56	5.88
Portfolio Turnover Rate (%)	30	27	27	25	27	28
Total Assets End of Year (Millions $)	617.3	604.2	783.8	1,102.1	1,273.6	1,527.5

Annual Rate of Return (%) Years Ending 12/31	24.6	10.7	28.4	18.2	2.3	16.1

Five-Year Total Return(%)	99.6[A]	Degree of Diversification	C	Beta	.67	Bull (%) 112.7[B]	Bear (%) (15.2)[C]

Objective: Seeks to provide conservation of principal, reasonable income return, and profits without undue risk through balanced investments in common stocks, bonds and preferred stocks of well-established, dividend-paying companies. Common stocks generally make up 60% to 70% of total portfolio.

Portfolio: (11/30/88) Common stocks 65%, bonds 21%, U.S. government and agency obligations 12%, repurchase agreements 1%, other assets 1%. Largest stock holdings: basic industries 19%, consumer products and services 11%.

Portfolio Mgr: Vincent Bajakian—1972

Distributions: **Income:** Feb, May, Aug, Nov   **Capital Gains:** Nov

12b-1: No

Minimum: **Initial:** $3,000   **Subsequent:** $100

Min IRA: **Initial:** $500   **Subsequent:** $100

Services: IRA, Keogh, Corp, SEP, 403(b), Withdraw, Deduct

Tel Exchange: Yes   **With MMF:** Yes

Registered: All states

Ticker: VWELX

†VANGUARD WINDSOR

Growth & Income

Vanguard Group
Vanguard Financial Center
Valley Forge, PA 19482
(800) 662-7447/(215) 648-6000

	Years Ending 10/31					
	1983	1984	1985	1986	1987	1988
Dividends from Net Investment Income ($)	.70	.76	.79	.85	.30	.87
Distributions from Net Realized Capital Gains ($)	1.03	.48	.74	2.59	–	2.21
Net Asset Value End of Year ($)	11.50	12.12	13.39	13.85	14.22	14.13
Ratio of Expenses to Net Assets (%)	.67	.63	.53	.52	.43	.46
Ratio of Net Income to Average Net Assets (%)	6.31	6.72	6.19	5.28	4.86	5.08
Portfolio Turnover Rate (%)	48	23	23	51	46	24
Total Assets End of Year (Millions $)	1,665.9	2,337.6	3,814.3	4,862.3	4,849.2	5,921.4

Annual Rate of Return (%) Years Ending 12/31	30.1	19.5	28.0	20.2	1.4	28.7

Five-Year Total Return(%)	139.9ᴬ	Degree of Diversification	C	Beta	.82	Bull (%)	143.6ᴬ	Bear (%)	(22.3)ᴰ

Objective: Seeks long-term growth of capital and income. Current income is a secondary objective. Invests primarily in equity securities; bonds and preferred stocks may be held. Equity investments are selected principally on the basis of fundamental investment value. Key to the valuation process is the relationship of a company's underlying earning power and dividend payout to the market price of its stock.

Portfolio: (10/31/88) Common stocks 91%, temporary cash investments 5%, government and agency obligations 4%, other assets 1%. Largest stock holdings: automotive 22%, banks 16%.

Portfolio Mgr: John Neff—1964

Distributions: Income: May, Dec **Capital Gains:** Dec

12b-1: No

Minimum: Initial: $10,000 Subsequent: $100

Min IRA: Initial: $2,000 Subsequent: $100

Services: IRA, Keogh, Corp, SEP, 403(b), Withdraw, Deduct

Tel Exchange: Yes **With MMF:** Yes

Registered: All states

Ticker: VWNDX

† *On January 3, 1989, the fund opened to new investors.*

VANGUARD WINDSOR II
Growth & Income

Vanguard Group
Vanguard Financial Center
Valley Forge, PA 19482
(800) 662-7447/(215) 648-6000

	Years Ending 10/31					
	1983	1984	1985 (4 mos.)	1986	1987	1988
Dividends from Net Investment Income ($)	—	—	.11	.43	.20	.61
Distributions from Net Realized Capital Gains ($)	—	—	—	.52	—	.80
Net Asset Value End of Year ($)	—	—	9.91	12.48	12.41	13.23
Ratio of Expenses to Net Assets (%)	—	—	.80	.65	.49	.58
Ratio of Net Income to Average Net Assets (%)	—	—	4.56	4.33	4.11	4.94
Portfolio Turnover Rate (%)	—	—	1	50	46	27
Total Assets End of Year (Millions $)	—	—	133.0	814.0	1,322.8	1,485.7

Annual Rate of Return (%) Years Ending 12/31	—	—	—	21.4	(2.1)	24.7

Five-Year Total Return(%)	NA	Degree of Diversification	B	Beta	.90	Bull (%)	NA	Bear (%)	(23.4)ᴰ

Objective: Seeks long-term growth of capital and income through investment in common stocks characterized by above average income yields and below average price-earnings ratios. May hold cash or fixed-income securities for defensive purposes and engage in repurchase agreements or lend its securities.

Portfolio: (10/31/88) Common stocks 93%, repurchase agreements 7%. Largest stock holdings: banks 13%, electric utilities 13%.

Portfolio Mgr: James Barrow—1985; William Starke—1987

Distributions: **Income:** May, Dec   **Capital Gains:** Dec

12b-1: No

Minimum: **Initial:** $3,000   **Subsequent:** $100

Min IRA: **Initial:** $500   **Subsequent:** $100

Services: IRA, Keogh, Corp, SEP, 403(b), Withdraw, Deduct

Tel Exchange: Yes   **With MMF:** Yes

Registered: All states

Ticker: VWNFX

VANGUARD
W.L. MORGAN
GROWTH

Growth

Vanguard Group
Vanguard Financial Center
Valley Forge, PA 19482
(800) 662-7447/(215) 648-6000

	Years Ending 12/31					
	1983	**1984**	**1985**	**1986**	**1987**	**1988**
Dividends from Net Investment Income ($)	.25	.31	.25	.43	.20	.24
Distributions from Net Realized Capital Gains ($)	1.04	1.39	.60	2.88	2.45	.98
Net Asset Value End of Year ($)	13.84	11.45	13.82	11.50	9.39	10.27
Ratio of Expenses to Net Assets (%)	.85	.68	.60	.54	.46	.55
Ratio of Net Income to Average Net Assets (%)	2.33	2.51	1.96	1.49	1.52	2.20
Portfolio Turnover Rate (%)	31	38	41	31	43	32
Total Assets End of Year (Millions $)	401.7	467.8	665.0	594.3	538.0	622.0
Annual Rate of Return (%) Years Ending 12/31	28.0	(5.1)	29.5	7.8	4.7	22.3

Five-Year Total Return(%)	69.8[C]	Degree of Diversification	C	Beta	1.03	Bull (%)	117.0[B]	Bear (%)	(25.2)[E]

Objective: Primarily long-term capital growth. Fund follows a "three-tier" strategy of investing in established growth, emerging growth and cyclical growth companies chosen on the basis of greater than average earnings growth potential and quality of management.

Portfolio: (12/31/88) Common stocks 95%, temporary cash investments 4%. Largest stock holdings: established growth companies 55%, cyclical growth and other companies 22%.

Portfolio Mgr: Frank Wisneski—1979

Distributions: Income: Dec   **Capital Gains:** Dec

12b-1: No

Minimum: Initial: $3,000   Subsequent: $100

Min IRA: Initial: $500   Subsequent: $100

Services: IRA, Keogh, Corp, SEP, 403(b), Withdraw, Deduct

Tel Exchange: Yes   **With MMF:** Yes

Registered: All states

Ticker: VMRGX

VANGUARD WORLD–INTERNATIONAL GROWTH

International

Vanguard Group
Vanguard Financial Center
Valley Forge, PA 19482
(800) 662-7447/(215) 648-6000

	Years Ending 8/31					
	1983	1984	1985	1986 (11 mos.)	1987	1988
Dividends from Net Investment Income ($)	—	—	—	—	.07	.13
Distributions from Net Realized Capital Gains ($)	—	—	—	—	.80	2.43
Net Asset Value End of Year ($)	—	—	—	11.67	14.21	10.45
Ratio of Expenses to Net Assets (%)	—	—	—	.78	.66	.67
Ratio of Net Income to Average Net Assets (%)	—	—	—	1.10	1.00	1.39
Portfolio Turnover Rate (%)	—	—	—	39	77	71
Total Assets End of Year (Millions $)	—	—	—	451.3	606.7	453.9
Annual Rate of Return (%) Years Ending 12/31	—	—	—	56.6	12.4	11.6

Five-Year Total Return(%)	NA	Degree of Diversification	E	Beta	.57	Bull (%)	NA	Bear (%)	(11.0)c

Objective: Seeks long-term capital appreciation through investment in common stocks of seasoned foreign companies from a wide diversity of countries. May enter into foreign currency futures contracts and may lend its securities.

Portfolio: (8/31/88) Common stocks 97%, repurchase agreements 2%, other assets 1%. Largest country holdings: Japan 40%, Switzerland 13%.

Portfolio Mgr: Richard Foulkes—1981

Distributions: Income: Dec   **Capital Gains:** Dec

12b-1: No

Minimum: Initial: $3,000   Subsequent: $100

Min IRA: Initial: $500   Subsequent: $100

Services: IRA, Keogh, Corp, SEP, 403(b), Withdraw, Deduct

Tel Exchange: Yes   **With MMF:** Yes

Registered: All states

Ticker: VWIGX

VANGUARD WORLD—U.S. GROWTH

Growth

Vanguard Group
Vanguard Financial Center
Valley Forge, PA 19482
(800) 662-7447/(215) 648-6000

	Years Ending 8/31					
	1983	1984	1985	1986	1987	1988
Dividends from Net Investment Income ($)	–	–	–	–	.28	.31
Distributions from Net Realized Capital Gains ($)	–	–	–	–	1.94	3.26
Net Asset Value End of Year ($)	–	–	–	13.21	12.74	7.17
Ratio of Expenses to Net Assets (%)	–	–	–	.80	.65	.88
Ratio of Net Income to Average Net Assets (%)	–	–	–	2.27	2.41	1.23
Portfolio Turnover Rate (%)	–	–	–	77	142	38
Total Assets End of Year (Millions $)	–	–	–	188.0	184.1	130.2
Annual Rate of Return (%) Years Ending 12/31	–	–	–	7.6	(6.1)	8.8

Five-Year Total Return(%)	NA	Degree of Diversification	A	Beta	.92	Bull (%)	NA	Bear (%)	(23.9)^D

Objective:	Seeks long-term capital appreciation through investment in common stock of primarily seasoned companies. May also invest in special situations and newer companies and, for defensive purposes, debt securities.
Portfolio:	(8/31/88) Common stocks 94%, other assets 4%, repurchase agreements 2%. Largest stock holdings: finance and insurance 17%, consumer 15%.
Portfolio Mgr:	J. Parker Hall—1987
Distributions:	Income: Dec **Capital Gains:** Dec
12b-1:	No
Minimum:	Initial: $3,000 Subsequent: $100
Min IRA:	Initial: $500 Subsequent: $100
Services:	IRA, Keogh, Corp, SEP, (403)b, Withdraw, Deduct
Tel Exchange:	Yes **With MMF:** Yes
Registered:	All states
Ticker:	VWUSX

WAYNE HUMMER GROWTH
Growth

Wayne Hummer Mgmt. Co.
175 W. Jackson Blvd.
Chicago, IL 60604-2884
(800) 621-4477/(312) 431-1700

	1983	1984 (3 mos.)	1985	1986	1987	1988
Dividends from Net Investment Income ($)	—	—	.33	.30	.24	.29
Distributions from Net Realized Capital Gains ($)	—	—	—	.01	.35	1.11
Net Asset Value End of Year ($)	—	9.83	10.67	13.85	16.14	13.79
Ratio of Expenses to Net Assets (%)	—	1.50	1.50	1.50	1.50	1.50
Ratio of Net Income to Average Net Assets (%)	—	5.09	4.12	2.44	1.64	1.73
Portfolio Turnover Rate (%)	—	0	26	27	28	10
Total Assets End of Year (Millions $)	—	1.7	4.3	10.1	18.8	20.5

Annual Rate of Return (%) Years Ending 12/31	—	4.0	24.4	13.8	9.3	7.0

Five-Year Total Return(%) 72.1[B]	Degree of Diversification A	Beta .96	Bull (%) 114.2[B]	Bear (%) (19.4)[D]

Objective: Seeks long-term capital growth and, secondarily, current income through investment in the common stock, preferred stock, bonds or convertibles of established dividend-paying companies. May temporarily invest in investment-grade debt securities as a defensive move.

Portfolio: (9/30/88) Common stocks 92%, commercial paper 7%, other assets 1%. Largest stock holdings: chemical 12%, auto and machinery 11%.

Portfolio Mgr: Allan Bird—1983; Thomas Rowland—1987

Distributions: **Income:** April, July, Oct, Dec **Capital Gains:** April, Dec

12b-1: No

Minimum: **Initial:** $1,000 **Subsequent:** $500

Min IRA: **Initial:** $500 **Subsequent:** $200

Services: IRA, Keogh, SEP

Tel Exchange: Yes **With MMF:** Yes

Registered: All states except DE, ID, NH

Ticker: WHGRX

WEALTH MONITORS
Growth

Wealth Monitors, Inc.
1001 East 101st Terrace, Suite 220
Kansas City, MO 64131
(816) 941-7990

	Years Ending 3/31					
	1983	**1984**	**1985**	**1986**	**1987** (8 mos.)	**1988**
Dividends from Net Investment Income ($)	–	–	–	–	–	.01
Distributions from Net Realized Capital Gains ($)	–	–	–	–	–	.46
Net Asset Value End of Year ($)	–	–	–	–	9.92	6.57
Ratio of Expenses to Net Assets (%)	–	–	–	–	1.77	3.54
Ratio of Net Income to Average Net Assets (%)	–	–	–	–	.10	.90
Portfolio Turnover Rate (%)	–	–	–	–	119	152
Total Assets End of Year (Millions $)	–	–	–	–	6.1	3.7

Annual Rate of Return (%) Years Ending 12/31	–	–	–	–	(23.0)	7.0

Five-Year Total Return(%)	NA	Degree of Diversification	NA	Beta	NA	Bull (%)	NA	Bear (%)	(37.2)E

Objective: Seeks to obtain capital appreciation over the long term. Income from dividends or interest on portfolio securities is a secondary consideration. Invests in equity securities of domestic and foreign issuers. Equity securities consist of listed or unlisted common stocks, convertible securities or warrants. The fund may also write put and call options and purchase put options.

Portfolio: (9/30/88) Common stocks 86%, convertible preferred stocks 7%, temporary cash investments 6%, other assets 2%. Largest stock holdings: financial services 16%, radio/TV broadcasting 11%.

Portfolio Mgr: Michael W. Lamb—1986

Distributions: **Income:** May, Dec   **Capital Gains:** May, Dec

12b-1: Yes   **Amount:** 0.50%

Minimum: **Initial:** $1,000   **Subsequent:** $100

Min IRA: **Initial:** NA   **Subsequent:** NA

Services: None

Tel Exchange: No

Registered: CA, CO, CT, DE, FL, GA, IA, IL, IN, KS, MA, MD, MI, MN, MO, NE, NJ, NY, OH, OK, PA

Ticker: WLTHX

WPG
Growth

Weiss, Peck & Greer
One New York Plaza, 30th Flr.
New York, NY 10004
(800) 223-3332/(212) 908-9582

	Years Ending 12/31					
	1983	**1984**	**1985**	**1986**	**1987**	**1988**
Dividends from Net Investment Income ($)	.47	.57	.65	.15	.15	.17
Distributions from Net Realized Capital Gains ($)	.01	.54	—	6.55	3.36	.48
Net Asset Value End of Year ($)	20.84	19.32	24.42	20.64	18.73	19.95
Ratio of Expenses to Net Assets (%)	1.32	1.17	1.21	1.23	1.19	1.53
Ratio of Net Income to Average Net Assets (%)	1.57	3.79	2.28	1.88	.65	.82
Portfolio Turnover Rate (%)	63	104	108	71	84	42
Total Assets End of Year (Millions $)	33.0	32.7	42.1	36.1	34.8	34.1

Annual Rate of Return (%) Years Ending 12/31	18.5	(1.6)	30.5	11.2	6.8	9.3

Five-Year Total Return(%)	66.7[C]	Degree of Diversification	A	Beta	1.06	Bull (%)	123.8[B]	Bear (%)	(22.9)[D]

Objective: Seeks both current income and capital growth. Portfolio generally consists of 75% equity securities and 25% debt securities of well-known, seasoned, established, dividend-paying companies. May write covered call options, buy options, lend its portfolio securities, and enter into repurchase agreements.

Portfolio: (12/31/88) Common stocks 94%, repurchase agreements 7%, other investments 3%, preferred stocks 1%. Largest stock holdings: basic industries 12%, capital goods 9%.

Portfolio Mgr: Gerald Levine—1985

Distributions: Income: Mar, June, Sept, Dec   **Capital Gains:** Dec

12b-1: No

Minimum: Initial: $1,000   Subsequent: $50

Min IRA: Initial: $250   Subsequent: $50

Services: IRA, Keogh, Withdraw

Tel Exchange: Yes   **With MMF:** Yes

Registered: All states

Ticker: WPGFX

WPG GOVERNMENT SECURITIES
Bond

Weiss, Peck & Greer
One New York Plaza, 30th Flr.
New York, NY 10004
(800) 223-3332/(212) 908-9582

	Years Ending 12/31					
	1983	1984	1985	1986 (10 mos.)	1987	1988
Dividends from Net Investment Income ($)	–	–	–	.30	.72	.78
Distributions from Net Realized Capital Gains ($)	–	–	–	.17	.07	–
Net Asset Value End of Year ($)	–	–	–	10.33	9.77	9.74
Ratio of Expenses to Net Assets (%)	–	–	–	1.16	.87	.82
Ratio of Net Income to Average Net Assets (%)	–	–	–	6.09	7.41	7.97
Portfolio Turnover Rate (%)	–	–	–	203	108	130
Total Assets End of Year (Millions $)	–	–	–	48.7	76.0	79.3

Annual Rate of Return (%) Years Ending 12/31	–	–	–	–	2.5	8.0

Five-Year Total Return(%)	NA	Degree of Diversification	NA	Beta	NA	Bull (%)	NA	Bear (%)	3.5ᴬ

Objective: Seeks high level of current income consistent with preservation of capital. Invests primarily in U.S. government securities having remaining maturities of one year or more. May also write (sell) and buy covered put and call options.

Portfolio: (12/31/88) Mortgage-backed securities 44%, U.S. Treasury notes 29%, U.S. Treasury bonds 16%, U.S. government agencies 6%, repurchase agreements 3%, other assets 2%.

Portfolio Mgr: David Hoyle—1986

Distributions: **Income:** Monthly   **Capital Gains:** Annually

12b-1: Yes   **Amount:** 0.05%

Minimum: **Initial:** $1,000   **Subsequent:** $50

Min IRA: **Initial:** $250   **Subsequent:** $50

Services: IRA, Keogh, Withdraw

Tel Exchange: Yes   **With MMF:** Yes

Registered: All states

Ticker: WPGVX

Tax-Exempt Bond Funds

On the following pages, we present 91 tax-exempt bond funds, listed alphabetically. All return figures are based on a calendar year-end, and reinvestment of distributions when paid. We did not calculate beta figures or degrees of diversification for tax-exempt bond funds, since they are measures relative to the stock market and are thus less meaningful for these funds.

AARP INSURED TAX FREE GENERAL BOND

Scudder Fund Distributors
160 Federal Street
Boston, MA 02110-1706
(800) 253-2277

	1983	1984	1985 (10 mos.)	1986	1987	1988
Dividends, Income ($)	—	—	.64	1.01	1.07	1.08
Distributions, Cap. Gains ($)	—	—	—	.06	.20	—
Net Asset Value ($)	—	—	15.12	16.69	15.00	16.02
Expense Ratio (%)	—	—	1.29	1.13	1.00	.92
Ratio of Net Income to Average Net Assets (%)	—	—	6.11	6.40	6.58	6.95
Portfolio Turnover Rate (%)	—	—	91	36	135	164
Total Assets (Millions $)	—	—	62.3	129.3	238.0	312.5
Annual Rate of Return (%) Years Ending 12/31	—	—	—	16.9	(1.4)	12.2

Years Ending 9/30

Distr: Income: Monthly
    Capital Gains: Annually
Minimum: Initial: $250
    Subsequent: None
Portfolio Mgr: David L. Murphy—1988

Telephone Exchange: Yes
    With MMF: Yes
Registered In: All states
12b-1: No
Ticker: AITGX

AARP INSURED TAX FREE SHORT TERM

Scudder Fund Distributors
160 Federal Street
Boston, MA 02110-1706
(800) 253-2277

	1983	1984	1985 (10 mos.)	1986	1987	1988
Dividends, Income ($)	—	—	.47	.73	.75	.83
Distributions, Cap. Gains ($)	—	—	—	—	.05	—
Net Asset Value ($)	—	—	15.11	15.58	15.13	15.29
Expense Ratio (%)	—	—	1.50	1.48	1.31	1.27
Ratio of Net Income to Average Net Assets (%)	—	—	4.51	4.72	4.80	5.47
Portfolio Turnover Rate (%)	—	—	—	23	22	63
Total Assets (Millions $)	—	—	30.1	48.1	70.5	79.2
Annual Rate of Return (%) Years Ending 12/31	—	—	—	8.3	3.3	4.6

Years Ending 9/30

Distr: Income: Monthly
    Capital Gains: Annually
Minimum: Initial: $250
    Subsequent: None
Portfolio Mgr: Donald Carleton—1988

Telephone Exchange: Yes
    With MMF: Yes
Registered In: All states
12b-1: No
Ticker: AITSX

BABSON TAX-FREE INCOME— PORTFOLIO L

Jones & Babson, Inc.
Three Crown Center
2440 Pershing Rd.
Kansas City, MO 64108
(800) 821-5591/(816) 471-5200

	Years Ending 6/30					
	1983	1984	1985	1986	1987	1988
Dividends, Income ($)	.74	.73	.72	.71	.63	.64
Distributions, Cap. Gains ($)	—	—	—	—	.60	.19
Net Asset Value ($)	8.30	7.66	8.76	9.45	8.64	8.41
Expense Ratio (%)	.75	.92	1.00	1.00	.99	1.00
Ratio of Net Income to Average Net Assets (%)	9.15	8.94	8.82	7.75	6.80	7.54
Portfolio Turnover Rate (%)	27	27	32	46	123	168
Total Assets (Millions $)	10.6	11.9	16.0	20.9	22.0	21.3
Annual Rate of Return (%) Years Ending 12/31	9.0	9.1	20.4	18.2	(1.9)	11.6

Distr: Income: Monthly
Capital Gains: Dec
Minimum: Initial: $1,000
Subsequent: $100
Portfolio Mgr: Edward Martin—1984

Telephone Exchange: Yes
With MMF: Yes
Registered In: All states
12b-1: No
Ticker: BALTX

BENHAM CALIFORNIA TAX-FREE HIGH-YIELD

Benham Management Corp.
755 Page Mill Road
Palo Alto, CA 94304
(800) 227-8380/(415) 858-3600

	Years Ending 8/31					
	1983	1984	1985	1986	1987 (8 mos.)	1988
Dividends, Income ($)	—	—	—	—	.45	.65
Distributions, Cap. Gains ($)	—	—	—	—	—	—
Net Asset Value ($)	—	—	—	—	8.69	8.45
Expense Ratio (%)	—	—	—	—	0	0
Ratio of Net Income to Average Net Assets (%)	—	—	—	—	7.50	7.85
Portfolio Turnover Rate (%)	—	—	—	—	57	143
Total Assets (Millions $)	—	—	—	—	8.4	13.2
Annual Rate of Return (%) Years Ending 12/31	—	—	—	—	—	12.5

Distr: Income: Monthly
Capital Gains: Annually
Minimum: Initial: $1,000
Subsequent: $100
Portfolio Mgr: Steven Permut—1986

Telephone Exchange: Yes
With MMF: Yes
Registered In: AK, AZ, CA, HI, NV, OR, WA
12b-1: No
Ticker: BCHYX

BENHAM CALIFORNIA TAX-FREE INSURED

Benham Management Corp.
755 Page Mill Road
Palo Alto, CA 94304
(800) 227-8380/(415) 858-3600

	Years Ending 8/31					
	1983	1984	1985	1986	1987 (8 mos.)	1988
Dividends, Income ($)	—	—	—	—	.44	.62
Distributions, Cap. Gains ($)	—	—	—	—	—	—
Net Asset Value ($)	—	—	—	—	9.07	8.80
Expense Ratio (%)	—	—	—	—	0	0
Ratio of Net Income to Average Net Assets (%)	—	—	—	—	7.11	7.39
Portfolio Turnover Rate (%)	—	—	—	—	21	145
Total Assets (Millions $)	—	—	—	—	12.8	29.5
Annual Rate of Return (%) Years Ending 12/31	—	—	—	—	—	10.2

Distr: Income: Monthly
Capital Gains: Annually
Minimum: Initial: $1,000
Subsequent: $100
Portfolio Mgr: Katharine Gordon—1986

Telephone Exchange: Yes
With MMF: Yes
Registered In: AK, AZ, CA, HI, NV, OR, WA
12b-1: No
Ticker: BCINX

BENHAM CALIFORNIA TAX-FREE INTERMEDIATE

Benham Management Corp.
755 Page Mill Road
Palo Alto, CA 94304
(800) 227-8380/(415) 858-3600

	Years Ending 8/31					
	1983	1984	1985	1986	1987	1988
Dividends, Income ($)	—	.58	.69	.69	.62	.63
Distributions, Cap. Gains ($)	—	—	—	—	—	—
Net Asset Value ($)	—	9.56	9.86	10.56	10.30	10.06
Expense Ratio (%)	—	.97	.96	.74	.67	.64
Ratio of Net Income to Average Net Assets (%)	—	7.47	7.11	6.71	5.92	6.19
Portfolio Turnover Rate (%)	—	93	48	23	52	47
Total Assets (Millions $)	—	30.4	56.3	124.9	166.9	157.3
Annual Rate of Return (%) Years Ending 12/31	—	5.3	13.8	12.7	.8	5.9

Distr: Income: Monthly
Capital Gains: Annually
Minimum: Initial: $1,000
Subsequent: $100
Portfolio Mgr: Katharine Gordon—1983

Telephone Exchange: Yes
With MMF: Yes
Registered In: AK, AZ, CA, HI, NV, OR, WA
12b-1: No
Ticker: BCITX

BENHAM CALIFORNIA TAX-FREE LONG TERM

Benham Management Corp.
755 Page Mill Road
Palo Alto, CA 94304
(800) 227-8380/(415) 858-3600

	Years Ending 8/31					
	1983	1984	1985	1986	1987	1988
Dividends, Income ($)	—	.71	.84	.83	.85	.74
Distributions, Cap. Gains ($)	—	—	—	—	—	—
Net Asset Value ($)	—	9.54	10.15	11.42	10.54	10.36
Expense Ratio (%)	—	.97	.95	.74	.65	.63
Ratio of Net Income to Average Net Assets (%)	—	9.08	8.58	7.70	6.87	7.19
Portfolio Turnover Rate (%)	—	107	91	48	82	35
Total Assets (Millions $)	—	27.5	83.9	196.6	179.5	143.2
Annual Rate of Return (%) Years Ending 12/31	—	5.7	17.6	18.7	(4.6)	10.4

Distr: Income: Monthly
 Capital Gains: Annually
Minimum: Initial: $1,000
 Subsequent: $100
Portfolio Mgr: Katharine Gordon—1983

Telephone Exchange: Yes
 With MMF: Yes
Registered In: AK, AZ, CA, HI, NV, OR, WA
12b-1: No
Ticker: BCLTX

BENHAM NATIONAL TAX-FREE TRUST INTERMEDIATE-TERM

Benham Management Corp.
755 Page Mill Road
Palo Alto, CA 94304
(800) 227-8380/(415) 858-3600

	Years Ending 5/31					
	1983	1984	1985 (10 mos.)	1986	1987	1988
Dividends, Income ($)	—	—	.64	.72	.64	.63
Distributions, Cap. Gains ($)	—	—	—	—	—	—
Net Asset Value ($)	—	—	9.55	9.91	9.87	9.98
Expense Ratio (%)	—	—	—	.27	.50	.50
Ratio of Net Income to Average Net Assets (%)	—	—	8.26	7.41	6.27	6.34
Portfolio Turnover Rate (%)	—	—	77	44	26	54
Total Assets (Millions $)	—	—	3.1	12.2	19.5	20.1
Annual Rate of Return (%) Years Ending 12/31	—	—	12.5	14.2	2.2	6.6

Distr: Income: Monthly
 Capital Gains: Annually
Minimum: Initial: $1,000
 Subsequent: $100
Portfolio Mgr: Katharine Gordon—1983

Telephone Exchange: Yes
 With MMF: Yes
Registered In: All states
12b-1: No
Ticker: BNTIX

BENHAM NATIONAL TAX-FREE TRUST LONG-TERM

Benham Management Corp.
755 Page Mill Road
Palo Alto, CA 94304
(800) 227-8380/(415) 858-3600

	1983	1984	1985 (10 mos.)	1986	1987	1988
Dividends, Income ($)	—	—	.82	.94	.84	.77
Distributions, Cap. Gains ($)	—	—	—	—	—	—
Net Asset Value ($)	—	—	10.56	11.37	10.79	10.51
Expense Ratio (%)	—	—	—	.26	.50	.50
Ratio of Net Income to Average Net Assets (%)	—	—	9.70	8.61	7.11	7.27
Portfolio Turnover Rate (%)	—	—	33	57	102	76
Total Assets (Millions $)	—	—	7.1	22.8	24.0	25.2
Annual Rate of Return (%) Years Ending 12/31	—	—	19.2	18.7	(6.7)	11.2

Distr: Income: Monthly
    Capital Gains: Annually
Minimum: Initial: $1,000
    Subsequent: $100
Portfolio Mgr: Katharine Gordon—1983

Telephone Exchange: Yes
    With MMF: Yes
Registered In: All states
12b-1: No
Ticker: BTFLX

BULL & BEAR TAX-FREE INCOME

Bull & Bear Advisers, Inc.
11 Hanover Square
New York, NY 10005
(800) 847-4200/(212) 363-1100

	1983	1984 (10 mos.)	1985	1986	1987	1988
Dividends, Income ($)	—	1.10	1.39	1.31	1.26	1.19
Distributions, Cap. Gains ($)	—	—	—	.58	—	—
Net Asset Value ($)	—	15.04	16.88	18.17	16.74	17.44
Expense Ratio (%)	—	.82	1.02	1.18	1.18	1.27
Ratio of Net Income to Average Net Assets (%)	—	8.05	8.70	7.29	7.18	7.11
Portfolio Turnover Rate (%)	—	67	46	60	62	70
Total Assets (Millions $)	—	4.2	11.0	21.8	16.1	19.3
Annual Rate of Return (%) Years·Ending 12/31	—	—	22.4	19.6	(0.9)	11.6

Distr: Income: Monthly
    Capital Gains: Dec
Minimum: Initial: $1,000
    Subsequent: $100
Portfolio Mgr: Charles Adams III—1987

Telephone Exchange: Yes
    With MMF: Yes
Registered In: All states
12b-1: Yes **Amount:** 0.50%
Ticker: BLTFX

CALIFORNIA MUNI

Fundamental Portfolio Advisors
111 Broadway, Suite 1107
New York, NY 10006
(800) 225-6864/(212) 608-6864

	1983	1984 (3 mos.)	1985	1986	1987	1988
Years Ending 12/31						
Dividends, Income ($)	—	.28	.81	.76	.67	.60
Distributions, Cap. Gains ($)	—	—	—	1.66	.17	.05
Net Asset Value ($)	—	9.46	10.58	9.23	8.52	8.87
Expense Ratio (%)	—	NA	3.02	2.33	1.61	1.55
Ratio of Net Income to Average Net Assets (%)	—	11.5	7.78	7.16	7.66	6.88
Portfolio Turnover Rate (%)	—	NA	228	34	32	58
Total Assets (Millions $)	—	NA	10.7	6.3	7.8	10.3
Annual Rate of Return (%) Years Ending 12/31	—	—	21.2	10.5	1.4	12.2

Distr: Income: Monthly
    Capital Gains: Annually
Minimum: Initial: $1,000
    Subsequent: $100
Portfolio Mgr: Lance Brofman—1984

Telephone Exchange: Yes
    With MMF: Yes
Registered In: CA
12b-1: Yes **Amount:** 0.50%
Ticker: CAMFX

CALIFORNIA TAX-FREE INCOME

CCM Partners
44 Montgomery St., Suite 2200
San Francisco, CA 94104
(800) 826-8166/(415) 398-2727
In California (800) 225-8778

	1983	1984	1985	1986 (9 mos.)	1987	1988
Years Ending 8/31						
Dividends, Income ($)	—	—	—	.50	.85	.81
Distributions, Cap. Gains ($)	—	—	—	—	—	—
Net Asset Value ($)	—	—	—	11.72	11.25	11.06
Expense Ratio (%)	—	—	—	.03	.39	.61
Ratio of Net Income to Average Net Assets (%)	—	—	—	8.01	7.22	7.43
Portfolio Turnover Rate (%)	—	—	—	50	87	102
Total Assets (Millions $)	—	—	—	20.8	37.4	39.4
Annual Rate of Return (%) Years Ending 12/31	—	—	—	22.7	(1.2)	11.3

Distr: Income: Monthly
    Capital Gains: Annually
Minimum: Initial: $10,000
    Subsequent: $250
Portfolio Mgr: Phillip McClanahan—1985

Telephone Exchange: Yes
    With MMF: Yes
Registered In: CA, HI, NV
12b-1: No
Ticker: CFNTX

†COLUMBIA MUNICIPAL BOND

Columbia Financial Center
1301 S.W. Fifth Avenue
P.O. Box 1350
Portland, OR 97207-1350
(800) 547-1037/(503) 222-3600

	1983	1984 (7 mos.)	1985	1986	1987	1988
Dividends, Income ($)	—	.89	.88	.84	.77	.77
Distributions, Cap. Gains ($)	—	—	—	—	—	.03
Net Asset Value ($)	—	9.83	10.82	11.75	11.11	11.42
Expense Ratio (%)	—	.96	.76	.65	.66	.63
Ratio of Net Income to Average Net Assets (%)	—	8.86	8.51	7.17	6.84	6.71
Portfolio Turnover Rate (%)	—	111	17	3	21	10
Total Assets (Millions $)	—	14.9	57.5	118.3	118.5	140.9
Annual Rate of Return (%) Years Ending 12/31	—	—	19.8	16.8	1.2	10.2

Years Ending 12/31

Distr: Income: Monthly
    Capital Gains: Dec
Minimum: Initial: $1,000
    Subsequent: $100
Portfolio Mgr: Thomas Thomsen—1984

Telephone Exchange: Yes
    With MMF: Yes
Registered In: CO, DC, HI, ID, NJ, NV, OR, PA, WA
12b-1: No
Ticker: CMBFX

† *There will be a 2% redemption fee for shares redeemed within six months after purchase.*

COUNSELLORS NEW YORK MUNICIPAL BOND

Warburg, Pincus Counsellors, Inc.
466 Lexington Avenue
New York, NY 10017-3147
(800) 888-6878/(212) 878-0600

Years Ending 10/31

	1983	1984	1985	1986	1987 (7 mos.)	1988
Dividends, Income ($)	—	—	—	—	.30	.55
Distributions, Cap. Gains ($)	—	—	—	—	—	—
Net Asset Value ($)	—	—	—	—	9.39	9.71
Expense Ratio (%)	—	—	—	—	.50	.54
Ratio of Net Income to Average Net Assets (%)	—	—	—	—	5.50	5.70
Portfolio Turnover Rate (%)	—	—	—	—	28	145
Total Assets (Millions $)	—	—	—	—	10.4	27.6
Annual Rate of Return (%) Years Ending 12/31	—	—	—	—	—	6.4

Distr: Income: Monthly
    Capital Gains: Annually
Minimum: Initial: $25,000
    Subsequent: $5,000
Portfolio Mgr: Stuart Goode—1987

Telephone Exchange: Yes
    With MMF: Yes
Registered In: CA, CT, NJ, NY
12b-1: No
Ticker: CNMBX

DREYFUS CALIFORNIA TAX EXEMPT BOND

The Dreyfus Corp.
600 Madison Ave.
New York, NY 10022
(800) 645-6561/(718) 895-1206

	\multicolumn{6}{c}{Years Ending 5/31}
	1983	1984 (10 mos.)	1985	1986	1987	1988
Dividends, Income ($)	—	1.02	1.15	1.12	1.08	1.07
Distributions, Cap. Gains ($)	—	—	—	—	—	—
Net Asset Value ($)	—	12.54	13.87	14.70	14.45	14.15
Expense Ratio (%)	—	.55	.75	.72	.70	.71
Ratio of Net Income to Average Net Assets (%)	—	9.47	9.50	8.57	7.78	8.08
Portfolio Turnover Rate (%)	—	36	27	19	32	60
Total Assets (Millions $)	—	216.1	529.3	973.2	1,175.2	1,174.9
Annual Rate of Return (%) Years Ending 12/31	—	—	18.0	17.7	(1.7)	9.7

Distr: Income: Monthly
Capital Gains: Annually
Minimum: Initial: $2,500
Subsequent: $100
Portfolio Mgr: Larry Troutman—1987

Telephone Exchange: Yes
With MMF: Yes
Registered In: All states
12b-1: No
Ticker: DRCAX

DREYFUS INSURED TAX EXEMPT BOND

The Dreyfus Corp.
600 Madison Ave.
New York, NY 10022
(800) 645-6561/(718) 895-1206

	\multicolumn{6}{c}{Years Ending 4/30}
	1983	1984	1985	1986 (10 mos.)	1987	1988
Dividends, Income ($)	—	—	—	1.14	1.24	1.20
Distributions, Cap. Gains ($)	—	—	—	—	—	—
Net Asset Value ($)	—	—	—	18.03	17.38	16.86
Expense Ratio (%)	—	—	—	.73	.84	.90
Ratio of Net Income to Average Net Assets (%)	—	—	—	8.33	7.62	8.01
Portfolio Turnover Rate (%)	—	—	—	51	75	96
Total Assets (Millions $)	—	—	—	144.3	197.6	177.1
Annual Rate of Return (%) Years Ending 12/31	—	—	—	17.1	(1.9)	10.2

Distr: Income: Monthly
Capital Gains: Annually
Minimum: Initial: $2,500
Subsequent: $100
Portfolio Mgr: Larry Troutman—1987

Telephone Exchange: Yes
With MMF: Yes
Registered In: All states
12b-1: Yes **Amount:** 0.20%
Ticker: DTBDX

DREYFUS INTERMEDIATE TAX EXEMPT BOND

Dreyfus Corp.
600 Madison Ave.
New York, NY 10022
(800) 645-6561/(718) 895-1206

	\multicolumn{6}{c}{Years Ending 5/31}
	1983	1984 (9 mos.)	1985	1986	1987	1988
Dividends, Income ($)	—	.82	1.02	1.03	.99	.97
Distributions, Cap. Gains ($)	—	—	—	—	—	—
Net Asset Value ($)	—	11.84	12.93	13.47	13.46	13.36
Expense Ratio (%)	—	.69	.81	.75	.71	.73
Ratio of Net Income to Average Net Assets (%)	—	9.00	9.04	8.51	7.78	7.94
Portfolio Turnover Rate (%)	—	29	21	34	50	49
Total Assets (Millions $)	—	228.5	548.7	920.2	1,089.9	1,014.8
Annual Rate of Return (%) Years Ending 12/31	—	—	16.1	15.4	1.1	8.0

Distr: Income: Monthly
    Capital Gains: Annually
Minimum: Initial: $2,500
    Subsequent: $100
Portfolio Mgr: Monica Wiebolt—1984

Telephone Exchange: Yes
    With MMF: Yes
Registered In: All states
12b-1: No
Ticker: DITEX

DREYFUS MASSACHUSETTS TAX EXEMPT BOND

The Dreyfus Corp.
600 Madison Ave.
New York, NY 10022
(800) 645-6561/(718) 895-1206

	\multicolumn{6}{c}{Years Ending 5/31}
	1983	1984	1985	1986	1987	1988
Dividends, Income ($)	—	—	—	1.17	1.12	1.10
Distributions, Cap. Gains ($)	—	—	—	—	—	—
Net Asset Value ($)	—	—	—	15.89	15.48	15.22
Expense Ratio (%)	—	—	—	.26	.64	.79
Ratio of Net Income to Average Net Assets (%)	—	—	—	7.92	7.39	7.97
Portfolio Turnover Rate (%)	—	—	—	103	39	71
Total Assets (Millions $)	—	—	—	54.7	81.7	84.2
Annual Rate of Return (%) Years Ending 12/31	—	—	—	17.9	(3.4)	10.6

Distr: Income: Monthly
    Capital Gains: Annually
Minimum: Initial: $2,500
    Subsequent: $100
Portfolio Mgr: Larry Troutman—1987
Ticker: DMEBX

Telephone Exchange: Yes
    With MMF: Yes
Registered In: AL, AZ, CA, CT, DC, DE, FL, HI, IN, KY, MA, MD, ME, MN, NC, NH, NJ, NY, OR, PA, RI, SC, TN, TX, VA, VT, WY
12b-1: No

DREYFUS NEW JERSEY TAX EXEMPT BOND

The Dreyfus Corp.
600 Madison Ave.
New York, NY 10022
(800) 645-6561/(718) 895-1206

	Years Ending 12/31					
	1983	1984	1985	1986	1987 (2 mos.)	1988
Dividends, Income ($)	—	—	—	—	.14	.88
Distributions, Cap. Gains ($)	—	—	—	—	—	—
Net Asset Value ($)	—	—	—	—	11.62	12.16
Expense Ratio (%)	—	—	—	—	—	.39
Ratio of Net Income to Average Net Assets (%)	—	—	—	—	8.02	7.75
Portfolio Turnover Rate (%)	—	—	—	—	—	61
Total Assets (Millions $)	—	—	—	—	37.8	174.7
Annual Rate of Return (%) Years Ending 12/31	—	—	—	—	—	12.6

Distr: Income: Monthly
Capital Gains: Annually
Minimum: Initial: $2,500
Subsequent: $100
Portfolio Mgr: Samuel Weinstock—1988

Telephone Exchange: Yes
With MMF: Yes
Registered In: CT, DC, FL, HI, MA, NH, NJ, NY, PA, RI, VT, WY
12b-1: Yes **Amount:** 0.25%
Ticker: DRNJX

DREYFUS NEW YORK INSURED TAX EXEMPT BOND

The Dreyfus Corp.
600 Madison Ave.
New York, NY 10022
(800) 645-6561/(718) 895-1206

	Years Ending 12/31					
	1983	1984	1985	1986	1987 (10 mos.)	1988
Dividends, Income ($)	—	—	—	—	.64	.73
Distributions, Cap. Gains ($)	—	—	—	—	—	—
Net Asset Value ($)	—	—	—	—	10.17	10.56
Expense Ratio (%)	—	—	—	—	—	.23
Ratio of Net Income to Average Net Assets (%)	—	—	—	—	7.12	7.00
Portfolio Turnover Rate (%)	—	—	—	—	49	32
Total Assets (Millions $)	—	—	—	—	25.8	44.6
Annual Rate of Return (%) Years Ending 12/31	—	—	—	—	—	11.3

Distr: Income: Monthly
Capital Gains: Annually
Minimum: Initial: $2,500
Subsequent: $100
Portfolio Mgr: Larry Troutman—1987

Telephone Exchange: Yes
With MMF: Yes
Registered In: CT, DC, HI, MA, NH, NJ, NV, NY, PA, RI, VT, WY
12b-1: Yes **Amount:** 0.25%
Ticker: DNYBX

DREYFUS NEW YORK TAX EXEMPT BOND

The Dreyfus Corp.
600 Madison Ave.
New York, NY 10022
(800) 645-6561/(718) 895-1206

	Years Ending 5/31					
	1983	1984 (10 mos.)	1985	1986	1987	1988
Dividends, Income ($)	—	.97	1.16	1.15	1.10	1.08
Distributions, Cap. Gains ($)	—	—	—	—	—	—
Net Asset Value ($)	—	12.41	14.10	15.05	14.73	14.41
Expense Ratio (%)	—	.77	.76	.71	.71	.72
Ratio of Net Income to Average Net Assets (%)	—	9.38	9.50	8.54	7.75	8.13
Portfolio Turnover Rate (%)	—	44	29	15	38	57
Total Assets (Millions $)	—	252.1	652.9	1,246	1,538	1,463.0
Annual Rate of Return (%) Years Ending 12/31	—	—	20.6	17.1	(2.7)	10.1

Distr: Income: Monthly
Capital Gains: Annually
Minimum: Initial: $2,500
Subsequent: $100
Portfolio Mgr: Monica Wiebolt—1984

Telephone Exchange: Yes
With MMF: Yes
Registered In: All states
12b-1: No
Ticker: DRNYX

DREYFUS NEW YORK TAX EXEMPT INTERMEDIATE BOND

The Dreyfus Corp.
600 Madison Avenue
New York, NY 10022
(800) 645-6561/(516) 794-5210

	Years Ending 5/31					
	1983	1984	1985	1986	1987	1988 (11 mos.)
Dividends, Income ($)	—	—	—	—	—	1.02
Distributions, Cap. Gains ($)	—	—	—	—	—	—
Net Asset Value ($)	—	—	—	—	—	16.19
Expense Ratio (%)	—	—	—	—	—	—
Ratio of Net Income to Average Net Assets (%)	—	—	—	—	—	6.58
Portfolio Turnover Rate (%)	—	—	—	—	—	1
Total Assets (Millions $)	—	—	—	—	—	25.1
Annual Rate of Return (%) Years Ending 12/31	—	—	—	—	—	9.6

Distr: Income: Monthly
Capital Gains: Annually
Minimum: Initial: $2,500
Subsequent: $100
Portfolio Mgr: Monica Wieboldt—1987

Telephone Exchange: Yes
With MMF: Yes
Registered In: CT, DC, FL, HI, MA, NH, NJ, NV, NY, PA, RI, VT, WY
12b-1: Yes **Amount:** 0.25%
Ticker: DRNIX

DREYFUS SHORT-INTERMEDIATE TAX EXEMPT BOND

The Dreyfus Corp.
600 Madison Avenue
New York, NY 10022
(800) 645-6561/(718) 895-1206

	Years Ending 3/31					
	1983	1984	1985	1986	1987	1988 (11 mos.)
Dividends, Income ($)	–	–	–	–	–	.66
Distributions, Cap. Gains ($)	–	–	–	–	–	–
Net Asset Value ($)	–	–	–	–	–	12.63
Expense Ratio (%)	–	–	–	–	–	–
Ratio of Net Income to Average Net Assets (%)	–	–	–	–	–	5.81
Portfolio Turnover Rate (%)	–	–	–	–	–	63
Total Assets (Millions $)	–	–	–	–	–	47.0
Annual Rate of Return (%) Years Ending 12/31	–	–	–	–	–	5.8

Distr: Income: Monthly
    Capital Gains: Annually
Minimum: Initial: $2,500
    Subsequent: $100
Portfolio Mgr: Samuel Weinstock—1987

Telephone Exchange: Yes
    With MMF: Yes
Registered In: All states
12b-1: Yes **Amount:** 0.10%
Ticker: DSIBX

DREYFUS TAX EXEMPT

The Dreyfus Corporation
600 Madison Ave.
New York, NY 10022
(800) 645-6561/(718) 895-1206

	Years Ending 8/31					
	1983	1984	1985	1986	1987	1988
Dividends, Income ($)	1.00	1.01	1.02	.99	.94	.91
Distributions, Cap. Gains ($)	–	–	–	–	–	–
Net Asset Value ($)	10.97	10.84	11.60	12.87	12.22	12.03
Expense Ratio (%)	.73	.71	.69	.69	.68	.71
Ratio of Net Income to Average Net Assets (%)	9.05	9.22	9.11	8.16	7.34	7.68
Portfolio Turnover Rate (%)	37	22	28	53	67	51
Total Assets (Millions $)	1,780.1	2,020.9	2,724.7	3,648.9	3,527.7	3,244.8
Annual Rate of Return (%) Years Ending 12/31	11.6	8.6	19.4	17.4	(1.7)	11.5

Distr: Income: Monthly
    Capital Gains: Annually
Minimum: Initial: $2,500
    Subsequent: $100
Portfolio Mgr: Richard Moynihan—1976

Telephone Exchange: Yes
    With MMF: Yes
Registered In: All states
12b-1: No
Ticker: DRTAX

†FIDELITY AGGRESSIVE TAX-FREE

Fidelity Investments Co.
82 Devonshire St.
Boston, MA 02109
(800) 544-6666/(617) 523-1919

	Years Ending 12/31					
	1983	**1984**	**1985** (3 mos.)	**1986**	**1987**	**1988**
Dividends, Income ($)	—	—	.31	.93	.90	.89
Distributions, Cap. Gains ($)	—	—	—	—	—	—
Net Asset Value ($)	—	—	10.66	11.56	10.82	11.33
Expense Ratio (%)	—	—	.60	.65	.74	.73
Ratio of Net Income to Average Net Assets (%)	—	—	10.17	8.17	8.06	7.98
Portfolio Turnover Rate (%)	—	—	4	17	68	46
Total Assets (Millions $)	—	—	101.4	394.1	352.8	455.8
Annual Rate of Return (%) Years Ending 12/31	—	—	—	17.6	1.4	13.4

Distr: Income: Monthly
Capital Gains: Annually
Minimum: Initial: $2,500
Subsequent: $250
Portfolio Mgr: Ann Punzak—1985

Telephone Exchange: Yes
With MMF: Yes
Registered In: All states
12b-1: Yes **Amount:** Pd. by Advisor
Ticker: FATFX

† *There will be a 1% redemption fee for shares redeemed in less than six months.*

FIDELITY CALIFORNIA TAX-FREE HIGH YIELD

Fidelity Investments Co.
82 Devonshire Street
Boston, MA 02109
(800) 544-6666/(617) 523-1919

	Years Ending 4/30					
	1983	**1984**	**1985** (10 mos.)	**1986**	**1987**	**1988**
Dividends, Income ($)	—	—	.77	.88	.78	.76
Distributions, Cap. Gains ($)	—	—	—	—	.05	.05
Net Asset Value ($)	—	—	10.43	11.51	10.95	10.62
Expense Ratio (%)	—	—	1.00	.72	.68	.73
Ratio of Net Income to Average Net Assets (%)	—	—	9.53	7.75	6.68	7.15
Portfolio Turnover Rate (%)	—	—	14	16	46	52
Total Assets (Millions $)	—	—	30.2	323.5	460.8	399.2
Annual Rate of Return (%) Years Ending 12/31	—	—	16.6	17.7	(3.6)	11.8

Distr: Income: Monthly
Capital Gains: Annually
Minimum: Initial: $2,500
Subsequent: $250
Portfolio Mgr: Jack Haley—1984

Telephone Exchange: Yes
With MMF: Yes
Registered In: CA
12b-1: Yes **Amount:** Pd. by Advisor
Ticker: FCTFX

FIDELITY CALIFORNIA TAX-FREE INSURED

Fidelity Investments Co.
82 Devonshire Street
Boston, MA 02109
(800) 544-6666/(617) 523-1919

		Years Ending 4/30				
	1983	1984	1985	1986	1987 (7 mos.)	1988
Dividends, Income ($)	—	—	—	—	.37	.61
Distributions, Cap. Gains ($)	—	—	—	—	—	—
Net Asset Value ($)	—	—	—	—	9.28	9.20
Expense Ratio (%)	—	—	—	—	.45	.65
Ratio of Net Income to Average Net Assets (%)	—	—	—	—	6.27	6.70
Portfolio Turnover Rate (%)	—	—	—	—	28	76
Total Assets (Millions $)	—	—	—	—	35.2	42.9
Annual Rate of Return (%) Years Ending 12/31	—	—	—	—	(4.5)	11.6

Distr: Income: Monthly
    Capital Gains: Annually
Minimum: Initial: $2,500
    Subsequent: $250
Portfolio Mgr: Jack Haley—1986

Telephone Exchange: Yes
    With MMF: Yes
Registered In: CA
12b-1: Yes **Amount:** Pd. by Advisor
Ticker: FCXIX

FIDELITY CONNECTICUT TAX-FREE

Fidelity Investments Co.
82 Devonshire Street
Boston, MA 02109
(800) 544-6666/(617) 523-1919

		Years Ending 11/30				
	1983	1984	1985	1986	1987 (1 mo.)	1988
Dividends, Income ($)	—	—	—	—	.05	.69
Distributions, Cap. Gains ($)	—	—	—	—	—	—
Net Asset Value ($)	—	—	—	—	10.03	10.30
Expense Ratio (%)	—	—	—	—	.65	.11
Ratio of Net Income to Average Net Assets (%)	—	—	—	—	6.15	7.10
Portfolio Turnover Rate (%)	—	—	—	—	—	11
Total Assets (Millions $)	—	—	—	—	3.9	73.9
Annual Rate of Return (%) Years Ending 12/31	—	—	—	—	—	10.1

Distr: Income: Monthly
    Capital Gains: Annually
Minimum: Initial: $2,500
    Subsequent: $250
Portfolio Mgr: Peter Allegrini—1987

Telephone Exchange: Yes
    With MMF: Yes
Registered In: CT, NJ, NY
12b-1: Yes **Amount:** Pd. by Advisor
Ticker: FICNX

FIDELITY HIGH YIELD MUNICIPALS

Fidelity Investments Co.
82 Devonshire St.
Boston, MA 02109
(800) 544-6666/(617) 523-1919

	Years Ending 11/30					
	1983	1984	1985	1986	1987	1988
Dividends, Income ($)	1.07	1.07	1.04	1.00	.94	.90
Distributions, Cap. Gains ($)	—	—	—	.04	.52	—
Net Asset Value ($)	11.17	11.0	12.29	13.77	11.75	12.21
Expense Ratio (%)	.65	.59	.56	.57	.71	.60
Ratio of Net Income to Average Net Assets (%)	9.44	9.75	8.83	7.63	7.38	7.48
Portfolio Turnover Rate (%)	81	73	57	49	80	47
Total Assets (Millions $)	750.2	1,040.2	1,600.8	2,449.3	1,609.7	1,573.7
Annual Rate of Return (%) Years Ending 12/31	15.9	9.9	21.4	18.9	(2.9)	12.2

Distr: Income: Monthly
    Capital Gains: Annually
Minimum: Initial: $2,500
    Subsequent: $250
Portfolio Mgr: Guy Wickwire—1981

Telephone Exchange: Yes
    With MMF: Yes
Registered In: All states
12b-1: Yes **Amount:** Pd. by Advisor
Ticker: FHIGX

FIDELITY INSURED TAX-FREE

Fidelity Investments Co.
82 Devonshire Street
Boston, MA 02109
(800) 544-6666/(617) 523-1919

	Years Ending 12/31					
	1983	1984	1985 (2 mos.)	1986	1987	1988
Dividends, Income ($)	—	—	.07	.73	.72	.71
Distributions, Cap. Gains ($)	—	—	—	—	.01	—
Net Asset Value ($)	—	—	10.23	11.33	10.36	10.78
Expense Ratio (%)	—	—	.60	.60	.62	.70
Ratio of Net Income to Average Net Assets (%)	—	—	7.89	6.52	6.73	6.64
Portfolio Turnover Rate (%)	—	—	—	23	57	35
Total Assets (Millions $)	—	—	9.5	146.2	145.0	153.7
Annual Rate of Return (%) Years Ending 12/31	—	—	—	18.1	(2.2)	11.2

Distr: Income: Monthly
    Capital Gains: Annually
Minimum: Initial: $2,500
    Subsequent: $250
Portfolio Mgr: Gary Swayze—1985

Telephone Exchange: Yes
    With MMF: Yes
Registered In: All states
12b-1: Yes **Amount:** Pd. by Advisor
Ticker: FMUIX

FIDELITY LIMITED TERM MUNICIPALS

Fidelity Investments Co.
82 Devonshire St.
Boston, MA 02109
(800) 544-6666/(617) 523-1919

			Years Ending 12/31			
	1983	1984	1985	1986	1987	1988
Dividends, Income ($)	.62	.64	.63	.62	.58	.60
Distributions, Cap. Gains ($)	—	—	—	—	—	—
Net Asset Value ($)	8.03	8.15	8.88	9.58	9.10	9.23
Expense Ratio (%)	.83	.79	.71	.68	.74	.67
Ratio of Net Income to Average Net Assets (%)	7.71	7.93	7.41	6.55	6.29	6.51
Portfolio Turnover Rate (%)	146	152	73	30	59	30
Total Assets (Millions $)	182.0	214.2	315.8	580.2	459.0	440.5
Annual Rate of Return (%) Years Ending 12/31	9.9	9.9	17.3	15.2	1.1	8.2

Distr: Income: Monthly
    Capital Gains: Annually
Minimum: Initial: $2,500
    Subsequent: $250
Portfolio Mgr: Jack Haley—1984

Telephone Exchange: Yes
    With MMF: Yes
Registered In: All states
12b-1: Yes **Amount:** Pd. by Advisor
Ticker: FLTMX

FIDELITY MASSACHUSETTS TAX-FREE HIGH YIELD
(formerly FIDELITY MASSFREE HIGH YIELD)

Fidelity Investments Co.
82 Devonshire St.
Boston, MA 02109
(800) 544-6666/(617) 523-1919

			Years Ending 7/31			
	1983	1984 (8 mos.)	1985	1986	1987	1988
Dividends, Income ($)	—	.72	.92	.87	.79	.81
Distributions, Cap. Gains ($)	—	—	—	—	—	.03
Net Asset Value ($)	—	9.64	10.54	11.18	11.12	10.82
Expense Ratio (%)	—	.89	.76	.64	.64	.61
Ratio of Net Income to Average Net Assets (%)	—	10.02	9.01	7.82	6.85	7.56
Portfolio Turnover Rate (%)	—	102	12	13	36	25
Total Assets (Millions $)	—	56.2	203.1	500.2	641.9	580.1
Annual Rate of Return (%) Years Ending 12/31	—	—	19.6	16.9	(1.3)	10.7

Distr: Income: Monthly
    Capital Gains: Annually
Minimum: Initial: $2,500
    Subsequent: $250
Portfolio Mgr: Guy Wickwire—1983

Telephone Exchange: Yes
    With MMF: Yes
Registered In: MA
12b-1: Yes **Amount:** Pd. by Advisor
Ticker: FDMMX

FIDELITY MICHIGAN TAX-FREE

Fidelity Investments Co.
82 Devonshire St.
Boston, MA 02109
(800) 544-6666/(617) 523-1919

	Years Ending 12/31					
	1983	1984	1985 (2 mos.)	1986	1987	1988
Dividends, Income ($)	—	—	.09	.79	.77	.75
Distributions, Cap. Gains ($)	—	—	—	—	.04	—
Net Asset Value ($)	—	—	10.27	11.38	10.25	10.79
Expense Ratio (%)	—	—	.60	.60	.72	.75
Ratio of Net Income to Average Net Assets (%)	—	—	8.43	7.03	7.25	7.12
Portfolio Turnover Rate (%)	—	—	9	24	44	24
Total Assets (Millions $)	—	—	6.6	127.6	128.3	170.7
Annual Rate of Return (%) Years Ending 12/31	—	—	—	18.7	(3.2)	13.0

Distr: Income: Monthly
    Capital Gains: Annually
Minimum: Initial: $2,500
    Subsequent: $250
Portfolio Mgr: Peter Allegrini—1985

Telephone Exchange: Yes
    With MMF: Yes
Registered In: MI
12b-1: Yes **Amount:** Pd. by Advisor
Ticker: FMHTX

FIDELITY MINNESOTA TAX-FREE

Fidelity Investments Co.
82 Devonshire St.
Boston, MA 02109
(800) 544-6666/(617) 523-1919

	Years Ending 12/31					
	1983	1984	1985 (1 mo.)	1986	1987	1988
Dividends, Income ($)	—	—	.07	.77	.72	.71
Distributions, Cap. Gains ($)	—	—	—	—	.03	—
Net Asset Value ($)	—	—	10.09	10.99	9.82	10.31
Expense Ratio (%)	—	—	.60	.60	.79	.82
Ratio of Net Income to Average Net Assets (%)	—	—	8.06	7.05	7.04	7.06
Portfolio Turnover Rate (%)	—	—	—	23	63	31
Total Assets (Millions $)	—	—	5.1	93.7	79.1	99.6
Annual Rate of Return (%) Years Ending 12/31	—	—	—	17.0	(4.1)	12.6

Distr: Income: Monthly
    Capital Gains: Annually
Minimum: Initial: $2,500
    Subsequent: $250
Portfolio Mgr: Peter Allegrini—1985

Telephone Exchange: Yes
    With MMF: Yes
Registered In: MN
12b-1: Yes **Amount:** Pd. by Advisor
Ticker: FIMIX

FIDELITY MUNICIPAL BOND

Fidelity Investments Co.
82 Devonshire St.
Boston, MA 02109
(800) 544-6666/(617) 523-1919

	Years Ending 12/31					
	1983	1984	1985	1986	1987	1988
Dividends, Income ($)	.60	.59	.58	.55	.55	.56
Distributions, Cap. Gains ($)	—	—	—	—	—	—
Net Asset Value ($)	6.72	6.70	7.42	8.28	7.60	7.95
Expense Ratio (%)	.59	.53	.46	.51	.57	.51
Ratio of Net Income to Average Net Assets (%)	8.74	8.98	8.06	6.90	7.03	7.11
Portfolio Turnover Rate (%)	52	93	145	72	72	46
Total Assets (Millions $)	703.5	741.2	905.8	1,141.3	903.2	983.6
Annual Rate of Return (%) Years Ending 12/31	9.3	9.0	20.1	19.5	(1.5)	12.3

Distr: Income: Monthly
Capital Gains: Annually
Minimum: Initial: $2,500
Subsequent: $250
Portfolio Mgr: Gary Swayze—1985

Telephone Exchange: Yes
With MMF: Yes
Registered In: All states
12b-1: Yes **Amount:** Pd. by Advisor
Ticker: FMBDX

FIDELITY NEW JERSEY TAX-FREE HIGH YIELD

Fidelity Investments Co.
82 Devonshire Street
Boston, MA 02109
(800) 544-6666/(617) 523-1919

	Years Ending 11/30					
	1983	1984	1985	1986	1987	1988 (11 mos.)
Dividends, Income ($)	—	—	—	—	—	.67
Distributions, Cap. Gains ($)	—	—	—	—	—	—
Net Asset Value ($)	—	—	—	—	—	10.19
Expense Ratio (%)	—	—	—	—	—	0
Ratio of Net Income to Average Net Assets (%)	—	—	—	—	—	7.52
Portfolio Turnover Rate (%)	—	—	—	—	—	140
Total Assets (Millions $)	—	—	—	—	—	89.7
Annual Rate of Return (%) Years Ending 12/31	—	—	—	—	—	10.9

Distr: Income: Monthly
Capital Gains: Annually
Minimum: Initial: $2,500
Subsequent: $250
Portfolio Mgr: Robert MacIntosh—1988

Telephone Exchange: Yes
With MMF: Yes
Registered In: NJ, NY, PA
12b-1: Yes **Amount:** Pd. by Advisor
Ticker: FNJHX

FIDELITY NEW YORK TAX-FREE HIGH YIELD

Fidelity Investments Co.
82 Devonshire St.
Boston, MA 02109
(800) 544-6666/(617) 523-1919

	1983	1984	1985 (10 mos.)	1986	1987	1988
Dividends, Income ($)	—	—	.74	.89	.82	.79
Distributions, Cap. Gains ($)	—	—	—	—	.17	.10
Net Asset Value ($)	—	—	10.69	11.98	11.48	11.16
Expense Ratio (%)	—	—	1.00	.67	.60	.67
Ratio of Net Income to Average Net Assets (%)	—	—	9.05	7.61	6.76	7.10
Portfolio Turnover Rate (%)	—	—	8	62	51	64
Total Assets (Millions $)	—	—	28.0	202.7	352.3	311.7
Annual Rate of Return (%) Years Ending 12/31	—	—	20.8	16.8	(2.4)	11.9

Distr: Income: Monthly
Capital Gains: Annually
Minimum: Initial: $2,500
Subsequent: $250
Portfolio Mgr: Gary Swayze—1984

Telephone Exchange: Yes
With MMF: Yes
Registered In: NY
12b-1: Yes **Amount:** Pd. by Advisor
Ticker: FTFMX

FIDELITY NEW YORK TAX-FREE INSURED

Fidelity Investments Co.
82 Devonshire St.
Boston, MA 02109
(800) 544-6666/(617) 523-1919

	1983	1984	1985	1986 (7 mos.)	1987	1988
Dividends, Income ($)	—	—	—	.41	.70	.69
Distributions, Cap. Gains ($)	—	—	—	—	.01	—
Net Asset Value ($)	—	—	—	10.96	10.47	10.29
Expense Ratio (%)	—	—	—	.60	.60	.67
Ratio of Net Income to Average Net Assets (%)	—	—	—	6.81	6.31	6.72
Portfolio Turnover Rate (%)	—	—	—	8	30	29
Total Assets (Millions $)	—	—	—	63.9	172.1	155.0
Annual Rate of Return (%) Years Ending 12/31	—	—	—	17.3	(3.2)	11.3

Distr: Income: Monthly
Capital Gains: Annually
Minimum: Initial: $2,500
Subsequent: $250
Portfolio Mgr: Gary Swayze—1985

Telephone Exchange: Yes
With MMF: Yes
Registered In: NY
12b-1: Yes **Amount:** Pd. by Advisor
Ticker: FNTIX

FIDELITY OHIO TAX-FREE

Fidelity Investments Co.
82 Devonshire St.
Boston, MA 02109
(800) 544-6666/(617) 523-1919

	Years Ending 12/31					
	1983	1984	1985 (2 mos.)	1986	1987	1988
Dividends, Income ($)	–	–	.09	.77	.74	.72
Distributions, Cap. Gains ($)	–	–	–	–	–	–
Net Asset Value ($)	–	–	10.12	10.97	9.97	10.50
Expense Ratio (%)	–	–	.60	.60	.79	.73
Ratio of Net Income to Average Net Assets (%)	–	–	8.74	7.01	7.09	7.08
Portfolio Turnover Rate (%)	–	–	54	32	36	23
Total Assets (Millions $)	–	–	4.4	107.1	116.7	153.0
Annual Rate of Return (%) Years Ending 12/31	–	–	–	16.4	(2.4)	12.9

Distr: Income: Monthly
    Capital Gains: Annually
Minimum: Initial: $2,500
    Subsequent: $250
Portfolio Mgr: Peter Allegrini—1985

Telephone Exchange: Yes
    With MMF: Yes
Registered In: OH
12b-1: Yes **Amount:** Pd. by Advisor
Ticker: FOHFX

FIDELITY PENNSYLVANIA TAX-FREE HIGH YIELD

Fidelity Investments Co.
82 Devonshire St.
Boston, MA 02109
(800) 544-6666/(617) 523-1919

	Years Ending 12/31					
	1983	1984	1985	1986 (5 mos.)	1987	1988
Dividends, Income ($)	–	–	–	.27	.70	.66
Distributions, Cap. Gains ($)	–	–	–	–	–	–
Net Asset Value ($)	–	–	–	10.35	9.07	9.66
Expense Ratio (%)	–	–	–	.30	.63	.84
Ratio of Net Income to Average Net Assets (%)	–	–	–	6.66	7.28	7.05
Portfolio Turnover Rate (%)	–	–	–	38	54	31
Total Assets (Millions $)	–	–	–	24.3	41.7	62.5
Annual Rate of Return (%) Years Ending 12/31	–	–	–	–	(5.8)	14.3

Distr: Income: Monthly
    Capital Gains: Annually
Minimum: Initial: $2,500
    Subsequent: $250
Portfolio Mgr: Peter Allegrini—1986

Telephone Exchange: Yes
    With MMF: Yes
Registered In: PA
12b-1: Yes **Amount:** Pd. by Advisor
Ticker: FPXTX

FIDELITY SHORT-TERM TAX-FREE

Fidelity Investments Co.
82 Devonshire St.
Boston, MA 02109
(800) 544-6666/(617) 523-1919

	Years Ending 12/31					
	1983	1984	1985	1986 (1 mo.)	1987	1988
Dividends, Income ($)	—	—	—	.01	.43	.52
Distributions, Cap. Gains ($)	—	—	—	—	—	—
Net Asset Value ($)	—	—	—	9.92	9.51	9.45
Expense Ratio (%)	—	—	—	.60	.60	.35
Ratio of Net Income to Average Net Assets (%)	—	—	—	4.00	4.58	5.48
Portfolio Turnover Rate (%)	—	—	—	—	180	96
Total Assets (Millions $)	—	—	—	2.5	59.2	76.7
Annual Rate of Return (%) Years Ending 12/31	—	—	—	—	0.2	4.9

Distr: Income: Monthly
Capital Gains: Annually
Minimum: Initial: $2,500
Subsequent: $250
Portfolio Mgr: Robert MacIntosh—1987

Telephone Exchange: Yes
With MMF: Yes
Registered In: All states
12b-1: Yes **Amount:** Pd. by Advisor
Ticker: FSTFX

FIDELITY TEXAS TAX-FREE

Fidelity Investments Co.
82 Devonshire Street
Boston, MA 02109
(800) 544-6666/(617) 523-1919

	Years Ending 12/31					
	1983	1984	1985	1986 (11 mos.)	1987	1988
Dividends, Income ($)	—	—	—	.70	.74	.70
Distributions, Cap. Gains ($)	—	—	—	—	—	—
Net Asset Value ($)	—	—	—	10.38	9.58	10.02
Expense Ratio (%)	—	—	—	.65	1.04	1.15
Ratio of Net Income to Average Net Assets (%)	—	—	—	7.42	7.31	7.21
Portfolio Turnover Rate (%)	—	—	—	13	64	32
Total Assets (Millions $)	—	—	—	29.8	26.5	31.8
Annual Rate of Return (%) Years Ending 12/31	—	—	—	—	(0.7)	12.4

Distr: Income: Monthly
Capital Gains: Annually
Minimum: Initial: $2,500
Subsequent: $250
Portfolio Mgr: Peter Allegrini—1986

Telephone Exchange: Yes
With MMF: Yes
Registered In: TX
12b-1: Yes **Amount:** Pd. by Advisor
Ticker: FETAX

FINANCIAL TAX-FREE INCOME SHARES

Financial Programs, Inc.
P.O. Box 2040
Denver, CO 80201
(800) 525-8085/(303) 779-1233

	Years Ending 6/30					
	1983	1984	1985	1986	1987	1988
Dividends, Income ($)	1.31	1.24	1.27	1.21	1.09	1.00
Distributions, Cap. Gains ($)	.15	.08	.70	.80	1.06	—
Net Asset Value ($)	14.47	13.07	14.32	15.20	13.86	13.82
Expense Ratio (%)	.56	.59	.65	.68	.70	.77
Ratio of Net Income to Average Net Assets (%)	9.09	8.87	9.05	7.86	7.04	7.33
Portfolio Turnover Rate (%)	52	88	156	92	98	41
Total Assets (Millions $)	61.7	60.3	85.5	108.5	117.9	109.1
Annual Rate of Return (%) Years Ending 12/31	8.0	9.1	22.9	22.1	(4.0)	15.1

Distr: Income: Monthly
    Capital Gains: Annually
Minimum: Initial: $250
    Subsequent: $50
Portfolio Mgr: Wm. Veronda—1984

Telephone Exchange: Yes
    With MMF: Yes
Registered In: All states
12b-1: No
Ticker: FTIFX

GENERAL NEW YORK TAX EXEMPT INTERMEDIATE BOND
(formerly PARK AVENUE NEW YORK TAX EXEMPT— INTERMEDIATE)

The Dreyfus Corp.
600 Madison Ave.
New York, NY 10022
(800) 645-6561/(718) 895-1206

	Years Ending 10/31					
	1983	1984	1985 (11 mos.)	1986	1987	1988
Dividends, Income ($)	—	—	1.22	1.19	1.06	1.02
Distributions, Cap. Gains ($)	—	—	—	—	—	—
Net Asset Value ($)	—	—	17.39	18.97	17.87	18.48
Expense Ratio (%)	—	—	.21	.46	.89	1.10
Ratio of Net Income to Average Net Assets (%)	—	—	7.68	6.90	6.55	6.59
Portfolio Turnover Rate (%)	—	—	32	38	67	32
Total Assets (Millions $)	—	—	13.9	57.0	53.4	46.9
Annual Rate of Return (%) Years Ending 12/31	—	—	14.9	14.2	1.4	6.0

Distr: Income: Monthly
    Capital Gains: Annually
Minimum: Initial: $2,500
    Subsequent: $100
Portfolio Mgr: Barbara Kolk—1988

Telephone Exchange: Yes
    With MMF: Yes
Registered In: CT, DC, FL, HI, NJ, NV, NY, WY
12b-1: Yes **Amount:** 0.20%
Ticker: PABFX

GIT TAX-FREE HIGH YIELD

Bankers Finance Investment Mgmt.
1655 N. Fort Myer Dr.
Arlington, VA 22209
(800) 336-3063/(703) 528-6500

	1983 (10 mos.)	1984	1985	1986	1987	1988
Dividends, Income ($)	.81	.89	.89	.86	.74	.76
Distributions, Cap. Gains ($)	—	—	—	.81	.08	—
Net Asset Value ($)	10.32	9.87	10.49	11.20	10.38	10.76
Expense Ratio (%)	0.95	1.14	1.29	1.16	.99	1.16
Ratio of Net Income to Average Net Assets (%)	9.03	8.84	8.54	7.60	7.18	7.15
Portfolio Turnover Rate (%)	222	252	173	117	66	77
Total Assets (Millions $)	25.4	27.1	34.3	43.2	44.7	39.8
Annual Rate of Return (%) Years Ending 12/31	—	9.8	19.2	19.4	(0.6)	8.5

Distr: Income: Monthly
    Capital Gains: Annually
Minimum: Initial: $1,000
    Subsequent: None
Portfolio Mgr: Richard Gunn—1985

Telephone Exchange: Yes
    With MMF: Yes
Registered In: All states except IN, LA, ME, MT, NH, NM, OK
12b-1: Yes **Amount:** 1.00%
Ticker: GTFHX

GIT TAX-FREE VIRGINIA PORTFOLIO

Bankers Finance Investment Mgmt.
1655 N. Ft. Myer Dr.
Arlington, VA 22209-3108
(800) 336-3063/(703) 528-6500

	1983	1984	1985	1986	1987	1988
Dividends, Income ($)	—	—	—	—	—	.71
Distributions, Cap. Gains ($)	—	—	—	—	—	—
Net Asset Value ($)	—	—	—	—	—	11.05
Expense Ratio (%)	—	—	—	—	—	.72
Ratio of Net Income to Average Net Assets (%)	—	—	—	—	—	6.41
Portfolio Turnover Rate (%)	—	—	—	—	—	58
Total Assets (Millions $)	—	—	—	—	—	18.6
Annual Rate of Return (%) Years Ending 12/31	—	—	—	—	—	8.3

Distr: Income: Monthly
    Capital Gains: Annually
Minimum: Initial: $1,000
    Subsequent: None
Portfolio Mgr: Richard Gunn—1987

Telephone Exchange: Yes
    With MMF: Yes
Registered In: All states
12b-1: No
Ticker: GTVAX

KENTUCKY TAX-FREE INCOME

Dupree & Co.
167 W. Main St.
Lexington, KY 40507
(800) 432-9518/(606) 254-7741

	Years Ending 6/30					
	1983	1984	1985	1986	1987	1988
Dividends, Income ($)	.58	.58	.57	.55	.50	.48
Distributions, Cap. Gains ($)	—	—	—	—	—	—
Net Asset Value ($)	6.26	6.01	6.38	6.62	6.59	6.52
Expense Ratio (%)	.79	.81	.76	.78	.79	.81
Ratio of Net Income to Average Net Assets (%)	9.56	9.40	9.31	8.39	7.32	7.40
Portfolio Turnover Rate (%)	59	57	30	28	54	87
Total Assets (Millions $)	6.9	10.0	19.4	36.3	61.8	60.5
Annual Rate of Return (%) Years Ending 12/31	12.2	8.1	15.8	16.9	(1.0)	10.3

Distr: Income: Mar, June, Sep, Dec
Capital Gains: Semiannually
Minimum: Initial: $2,500
Subsequent: $100
Portfolio Mgr: Fred Dupree Jr.—1979

Telephone Exchange: Yes
With MMF: No
Registered In: KY
12b-1: No
Ticker: KYTFX

LEXINGTON TAX EXEMPT BOND TRUST

Lexington Management Corp.
P.O. Box 1515
Park 80 W. Plaza 2
Saddle Brook, NJ 07662
(800) 526-0056

	Years Ending 12/31					
	1983	1984	1985	1986 (6 mos.)	1987	1988
Dividends, Income ($)	—	—	—	.32	.80	.63
Distributions, Cap. Gains ($)	—	—	—	—	—	—
Net Asset Value ($)	—	—	—	10.55	9.67	10.03
Expense Ratio (%)	—	—	—	0	0	1.33
Ratio of Net Income to Average Net Assets (%)	—	—	—	7.30	7.95	6.33
Portfolio Turnover Rate (%)	—	—	—	0	67	67
Total Assets (Millions $)	—	—	—	8.4	3.3	13.1
Annual Rate of Return (%) Years Ending 12/31	—	—	—	—	0.0	10.3

Distr: Income: Monthly
Capital Gains: Dec
Minimum: Initial: $1,000
Subsequent: $50
Portfolio Mgr: Denis Jamison—1986

Telephone Exchange: Yes
With MMF: Yes
Registered In: All states
12b-1: No
Ticker: LEBDX

NEW YORK MUNI

Fundamental Portfolio Advisors
111 Broadway, Suite 1107
New York, NY 10006
(800) 225-6864/(212) 608-6864

	Years Ending 12/31					
	1983	**1984**	**1985**	**1986**	**1987**	**1988**
Dividends, Income ($)	.09	.08	.09	.09	.08	.07
Distributions, Cap. Gains ($)	—	—	—	.06	.03	—
Net Asset Value ($)	1.07	1.07	1.19	1.25	1.05	1.09
Expense Ratio (%)	1.53	1.62	1.60	1.48	2.04	1.74
Ratio of Net Income to Average Net Assets (%)	8.05	7.82	7.88	6.91	6.97	6.94
Portfolio Turnover Rate (%)	109	157	424	334	549	463
Total Assets (Millions $)	79.4	129.2	174.4	261.2	220.3	229.9
Annual Rate of Return (%) Years Ending 12/31	NA	8.1	20.3	17.7	(7.3)	11.3

Distr: Income: Monthly
     Capital Gains: Dec
Minimum: Initial: $1,000
     Subsequent: $100
Portfolio Mgr: Lance Brofman—1981

Telephone Exchange: Yes
     With MMF: Yes
Registered In: CT, FL, NJ, NY, PA
12b-1: Yes **Amount:** 0.50%
Ticker: NYMFX

T. ROWE PRICE CALIFORNIA TAX-FREE BOND

T. Rowe Price Associates, Inc.
100 E. Pratt Street
Baltimore, MD 21202
(800) 638-5660/(301) 547-2308

	Years Ending 2/28					
	1983	**1984**	**1985**	**1986**	**1987** (5 mos.)	**1988**
Dividends, Income ($)	—	—	—	—	.29	.57
Distributions, Cap. Gains ($)	—	—	—	—	—	—
Net Asset Value ($)	—	—	—	—	10.48	9.44
Expense Ratio (%)	—	—	—	—	.85	1.00
Ratio of Net Income to Average Net Assets (%)	—	—	—	—	6.10	6.19
Portfolio Turnover Rate (%)	—	—	—	—	88	152
Total Assets (Millions $)	—	—	—	—	43.6	36.4
Annual Rate of Return (%) Years Ending 12/31	—	—	—	—	(6.8)	9.5

Distr: Income: Monthly
     Capital Gains: Annually
Minimum: Initial: $2,000
     Subsequent: $100
Portfolio Mgr: Peter Gordon—1986

Telephone Exchange: Yes
     With MMF: Yes
Registered In: AZ, CA, DC, HI, MD, NJ, NV, OR, WY
12b-1: No
Ticker: PRXCX

T. ROWE PRICE MARYLAND TAX-FREE BOND

T. Rowe Price Associates, Inc.
100 E. Pratt St.
Baltimore, MD 21202
(800) 638-5660/(301) 547-2308

	Years Ending 2/28					
	1983	1984	1985	1986	1987	1988 (11 mos.)
Dividends, Income ($)	–	–	–	–	–	.51
Distributions, Cap. Gains ($)	–	–	–	–	–	–
Net Asset Value ($)	–	–	–	–	–	9.40
Expense Ratio (%)	–	–	–	–	–	.85
Ratio of Net Income to Average Net Assets (%)	–	–	–	–	–	6.15
Portfolio Turnover Rate (%)	–	–	–	–	–	178
Total Assets (Millions $)	–	–	–	–	–	63.2
Annual Rate of Return (%) Years Ending 12/31	–	–	–	–	–	8.9

Distr: Income: Monthly
Capital Gains: Annually
Minimum: Initial: $2,000
Subsequent: $100
Portfolio Mgr: Patrice Berchtenbreiter —1987

Telephone Exchange: Yes
With MMF: Yes
Registered In: DC, DE, FL, HI, MD, NJ, PA, VA, VT, WV, WY
12b-1: No
Ticker: MDXBX

T. ROWE PRICE NEW YORK TAX-FREE BOND

T. Rowe Price Associates, Inc.
100 E. Pratt St.
Baltimore, MD 21202
(800) 638-5660/(301) 547-2308

	Years Ending 2/28					
	1983	1984	1985	1986	1987 (6 mos.)	1988
Dividends, Income ($)	–	–	–	–	.33	.60
Distributions, Cap. Gains ($)	–	–	–	–	–	–
Net Asset Value ($)	–	–	–	–	10.34	9.67
Expense Ratio (%)	–	–	–	–	.85	1.00
Ratio of Net Income to Average Net Assets (%)	–	–	–	–	6.16	6.44
Portfolio Turnover Rate (%)	–	–	–	–	126	147
Total Assets (Millions $)	–	–	–	–	24.3	28.3
Annual Rate of Return (%) Years Ending 12/31	–	–	–	–	(2.5)	10.4

Distr: Income: Monthly
Capital Gains: Annually
Minimum: Initial: $2,000
Subsequent: $100
Portfolio Mgr: Peter Gordon—1986
Ticker: PRNYX

Telephone Exchange: Yes
With MMF: Yes
Registered In: CT, DC, DE, FL, HI, MA, MD, NJ, NY, PA, RI, VA,VT, WV, WY
12b-1: No

T. ROWE PRICE TAX-FREE HIGH YIELD

T. Rowe Price Associates, Inc.
100 E. Pratt St.
Baltimore, MD 21202
(800) 638-5660/(301) 547-2308

	Years Ending 2/28					
	1983	1984	1985	1986	1987	1988
Dividends, Income ($)	—	—	—	.87	.87	.83
Distributions, Cap. Gains ($)	—	—	—	—	—	.25
Net Asset Value ($)	—	—	—	11.43	12.21	11.19
Expense Ratio (%)	—	—	—	1.00	.98	.96
Ratio of Net Income to Average Net Assets (%)	—	—	—	8.47	7.45	7.49
Portfolio Turnover Rate (%)	—	—	—	157	111	128
Total Assets (Millions $)	—	—	—	168.2	324.2	280.6
Annual Rate of Return (%) Years Ending 12/31	—	—	—	20.4	.3	11.2

Distr: Income: Monthly
    Capital Gains: Annually
Minimum: Initial: $2,000
    Subsequent: $100
Portfolio Mgr: William Reynolds—1985

Telephone Exchange: Yes
    With MMF: Yes
Registered In: All states
12b-1: No
Ticker: PRFHX

T. ROWE PRICE TAX-FREE INCOME

T. Rowe Price Associates, Inc.
100 E. Pratt St.
Baltimore, MD 21202
(800) 638-5660/(301) 547-2308

	Years Ending 2/28					
	1983* (2 mos.)	1984	1985	1986	1987	1988
Dividends, Income ($)	.13	.72	.65	.71	.68	.59
Distributions, Cap. Gains ($)	—	—	—	—	—	.54
Net Asset Value ($)	8.85	8.48	8.41	9.73	10.27	8.81
Expense Ratio (%)	.62	.66	.63	.63	.61	.65
Ratio of Net Income to Average Net Assets (%)	9.24	8.25	7.84	8.07	6.94	6.72
Portfolio Turnover Rate (%)	170	221	277	188	237	181
Total Assets (Millions $)	818.5	962.4	937.3	1,325.7	1,558.2	1,094.0
Annual Rate of Return (%) Years Ending 12/31	7.7	7.1	16.9	19.8	(4.2)	7.8

Fiscal year-end changed from 12/31 to 2/28.

Distr: Income: Monthly
    Capital Gains: Annually
Minimum: Initial: $2,000
    Subsequent: $100
Portfolio Mgr: Peter Gordon—1976

Telephone Exchange: Yes
    With MMF: Yes
Registered In: All states
12b-1: No
Ticker: PRTAX

T. ROWE PRICE TAX-FREE SHORT-INTERMEDIATE

T. Rowe Price Associates, Inc.
100 E. Pratt Street
Baltimore, MD 21202
(800) 638-5660/(301) 547-2308

	1983	1984 (2 mos.)	1985	1986	1987	1988
			Years Ending 2/28			
Dividends, Income ($)	—	.06	.32	.32	.29	.27
Distributions, Cap. Gains ($)	—	—	—	—	—	.02
Net Asset Value ($)	—	4.97	5.02	5.20	5.33	5.15
Expense Ratio (%)	—	.90	.90	.90	.73	.74
Ratio of Net Income to Average Net Assets (%)	—	7.11	6.51	6.26	5.60	5.29
Portfolio Turnover Rate (%)	—	111	301	129	120	225
Total Assets (Millions $)	—	23.5	68.0	155.5	404.8	292.0
Annual Rate of Return (%) Years Ending 12/31	—	—	8.9	9.7	2.2	4.9

Distr: Income: Monthly
 Capital Gains: Annually
Minimum: Initial: $2,000
 Subsequent: $100
Portfolio Mgr: Peter Gordon—1983

Telephone Exchange: Yes
 With MMF: Yes
Registered In: All states
12b-1: No
Ticker: PRFSX

RUSHMORE TAX-FREE INVESTORS INTERMEDIATE-TERM

Money Management Associates
4922 Fairmont Avenue
Bethesda, MD 20814
(800) 343-3355/(301) 657-1500

	1983 (4 mos.)	1984	1985	1986	1987	1988
			Years Ending 12/31			
Dividends, Income ($)	.25	.75	.75	.72	.63	.60
Distributions, Cap. Gains ($)	—	—	—	—	—	—
Net Asset Value ($)	9.74	9.78	10.26	10.74	9.99	10.12
Expense Ratio (%)	—	.84	.89	.94	.92	.93
Ratio of Net Income to Average Net Assets (%)	8.45	7.73	7.55	6.87	6.18	5.92
Portfolio Turnover Rate (%)	22	10	67	42	125	78
Total Assets (Millions $)	1.9	3.4	5.7	9.5	8.2	7.8
Annual Rate of Return (%) Years Ending 12/31	—	8.6	13.2	12.1	(1.1)	7.6

Distr: Income: Monthly
 Capital Gains: Annually
Minimum: Initial: $2,500
 Subsequent: None
Portfolio Mgr: Polly Francis—1988

Telephone Exchange: Yes
 With MMF: Yes
Registered In: All states
12b-1: No
Ticker: RSXIX

RUSHMORE TAX-FREE INVESTORS LONG-TERM

Money Management Associates
4922 Fairmont Avenue
Bethesda, MD 20814
(800) 343-3355/(301) 657-1500

	Years Ending 12/31					
	1983 (4 mos.)	1984	1985	1986	1987	1988
Dividends, Income ($)	.29	.82	.85	.80	.73	.70
Distributions, Cap. Gains ($)	—	—	—	—	—	—
Net Asset Value ($)	9.85	9.68	10.33	10.71	10.09	10.34
Expense Ratio (%)	—	.84	.87	.95	.93	.93
Ratio of Net Income to Average Net Assets (%)	9.75	8.60	8.52	7.60	7.04	6.81
Portfolio Turnover Rate (%)	26	28	87	40	84	102
Total Assets (Millions $)	1.6	3.7	6.1	10.0	9.4	9.3
Annual Rate of Return (%) Years Ending 12/31	—	7.1	16.2	11.8	1.1	9.7

Distr: Income: Monthly
    Capital Gains: Annually
Minimum: Initial: $2,500
    Subsequent: None
Portfolio Mgr: Polly Francis—1988

Telephone Exchange: Yes
    With MMF: Yes
Registered In: All states
12b-1: No
Ticker: RSXLX

SAFECO CALIFORNIA TAX-FREE INCOME

Safeco Asset Management Co.
Safeco Plaza
Seattle, WA 98185
(800) 426-6730/(206) 545-5530

	Years Ending 3/31					
	1983	1984 (8 mos.)	1985	1986	1987	1988
Dividends, Income ($)	—	.54	.78	.84	.80	.76
Distributions, Cap. Gains ($)	—	—	—	—	.11	.43
Net Asset Value ($)	—	9.90	9.99	11.68	12.14	10.72
Expense Ratio (%)	—	.90	.77	.76	.70	.72
Ratio of Net Income to Average Net Assets (%)	—	8.09	8.79	7.66	6.71	6.99
Portfolio Turnover Rate (%)	—	44	23	41	45	67
Total Assets (Millions $)	—	8.1	11.5	21.1	34.8	28.8
Annual Rate of Return (%) Years Ending 12/31	—	7.6	21.0	19.7	(2.1)	12.8

Distr: Income: Monthly
    Capital Gains: Apr, Oct
Minimum: Initial: $1,000
    Subsequent: $100
Portfolio Mgr: Stephen Bauer—1983

Telephone Exchange: Yes
    With MMF: Yes
Registered In: CA
12b-1: No
Ticker: SFCAX

SAFECO
MUNICIPAL BOND

SAFECO Asset Management Co.
SAFECO Plaza
Seattle, WA 98185
(800) 426-6730/(206) 545-5530

	Years Ending 3/31					
	1983	**1984**	**1985**	**1986**	**1987**	**1988**
Dividends, Income ($)	1.05	1.05	1.07	1.06	.99	.96
Distributions, Cap. Gains ($)	—	—	—	.02	.21	.40
Net Asset Value ($)	11.87	11.38	11.69	13.74	14.16	12.85
Expense Ratio (%)	.72	.64	.63	.63	.59	.61
Ratio of Net Income to Average Net Assets (%)	9.28	9.17	9.43	8.29	7.20	7.42
Portfolio Turnover Rate (%)	40	92	47	21	23	72
Total Assets (Millions $)	22.6	50.6	84.3	161.0	214.7	183.6
Annual Rate of Return (%) Years Ending 12/31	10.4	10.1	21.4	19.8	.2	13.9

Distr: Income: Monthly
    Capital Gains: Apr, Oct
Minimum: Initial: $1,000
    Subsequent: $100
Portfolio Mgr: Stephen Bauer—1981

Telephone Exchange: Yes
    With MMF: Yes
Registered In: All states except ME, NH, VT
12b-1: No
Ticker: SFCOX

SCUDDER
CALIFORNIA
TAX FREE

Scudder, Stevens & Clark
175 Federal St.
Boston, MA 02110
(800) 225-2470/(617) 439-4640

	Years Ending 3/31					
	1983	**1984** (8 mos.)	**1985**	**1986**	**1987**	**1988**
Dividends, Income ($)	—	.50	.80	.73	.71	.69
Distributions, Cap. Gains ($)	—	—	—	—	.30	.26
Net Asset Value ($)	—	9.61	9.54	10.95	11.18	9.99
Expense Ratio (%)	—	1.00	.99	.88	.84	.88
Ratio of Net Income to Average Net Assets (%)	—	8.26	8.76	7.11	6.55	6.95
Portfolio Turnover Rate (%)	—	92	168	93	68	52
Total Assets (Millions $)	—	38.2	73.1	132.8	194.8	153.0
Annual Rate of Return (%) Years Ending 12/31	—	—	18.4	16.8	(1.7)	11.9

Distr: Income: Monthly
    Capital Gains: May
Minimum: Initial: $1,000
    Subsequent: $100
Portfolio Mgr: David L. Murphy—1987

Telephone Exchange: Yes
    With MMF: Yes
Registered In: All states
12b-1: No
Ticker: SCTFX

SCUDDER HIGH YIELD TAX FREE

Scudder, Stevens & Clark
175 Federal Street
Boston, MA 02110-2267
(800) 225-2470/(617) 439-4640

	Years Ending 12/31					
	1983	1984	1985	1986	1987 (11 mos.)	1988
Dividends, Income ($)	—	—	—	—	.78	.83
Distributions, Cap. Gains ($)	—	—	—	—	—	—
Net Asset Value ($)	—	—	—	—	10.52	11.06
Expense Ratio (%)	—	—	—	—	.40	.67
Ratio of Net Income to Average Net Assets (%)	—	—	—	—	8.45	7.65
Portfolio Turnover Rate (%)	—	—	—	—	124	37
Total Assets (Millions $)	—	—	—	—	36.4	74.1
Annual Rate of Return (%) Years Ending 12/31	—	—	—	—	—	13.5

Distr: Income: Monthly
    Capital Gains: Annually
Minimum: Initial: $1,000
    Subsequent: $100
Portfolio Mgr: Philip G. Condon—1987

Telephone Exchange: Yes
    With MMF: Yes
Registered In: All states
12b-1: No
Ticker: SHYTX

SCUDDER MANAGED MUNICIPAL BONDS

Scudder, Stevens & Clark
175 Federal St.
Boston, MA 02110-2267
(800) 225-2470/(617) 439-4640

	Years Ending 12/31					
	1983	1984	1985	1986	1987	1988
Dividends, Income ($)	.70	.70	.59	.61	.61	.60
Distributions, Cap. Gains ($)	—	—	—	.24	.11	.02
Net Asset Value ($)	7.67	7.69	8.40	8.93	8.24	8.60
Expense Ratio (%)	.65	.61	.58	.58	.63	.61
Ratio of Net Income to Average Net Assets (%)	9.10	9.52	7.27	6.88	7.20	7.13
Portfolio Turnover Rate (%)	83	120	98	78	73	76
Total Assets (Millions $)	479.2	545.1	574.6	662.4	591.8	635.5
Annual Rate of Return (%) Years Ending 12/31	9.1	10.2	17.5	16.8	(0.3)	12.3

Distr: Income: Monthly
    Capital Gains: Annually
Minimum: Initial: $1,000
    Subsequent: $100
Portfolio Mgr: Donald Carleton—1986

Telephone Exchange: Yes
    With MMF: Yes
Registered In: All states
12b-1: No
Ticker: SCMBX

SCUDDER MASSACHUSETTS TAX FREE

Scudder, Stevens & Clark
175 Federal St.
Boston, MA 02110
(800) 225-2470/(617) 439-4640

	Years Ending 3/31					
	1983	1984	1985	1986	1987	1988 (10 mos.)
Dividends, Income ($)	–	–	–	–	–	.62
Distributions, Cap. Gains ($)	–	–	–	–	–	–
Net Asset Value ($)	–	–	–	–	–	12.28
Expense Ratio (%)	–	–	–	–	–	.50
Ratio of Net Income to Average Net Assets (%)	–	–	–	–	–	7.55
Portfolio Turnover Rate (%)	–	–	–	–	–	96
Total Assets (Millions $)	–	–	–	–	–	16.2
Annual Rate of Return (%) Years Ending 12/31	–	–	–	–	–	12.4

Distr: Income: Monthly
    Capital Gains: May
Minimum: Initial: $1,000
    Subsequent: $100
Portfolio Mgr: David Murphy—1987
Ticker: SCMAX

Telephone Exchange: Yes
    With MMF: Yes
Registered In: All states except AK, IA, KY, MI, MN, MO, ND, NE, NM, OH, OK, OR, SC, TN, WA, WI
12b-1: No

SCUDDER NEW YORK TAX FREE

Scudder, Stevens & Clark
175 Federal St.
Boston, MA 02110
(800) 225-2470/(617) 439-4640

	Years Ending 3/31					
	1983	1984 (8 mos.)	1985	1986	1987	1988
Dividends, Income ($)	–	.52	.83	.75	.75	.73
Distributions, Cap. Gains ($)	–	–	–	–	.15	.20
Net Asset Value ($)	–	9.97	10.11	11.19	11.43	10.39
Expense Ratio (%)	–	1.00	1.01	.88	.88	.95
Ratio of Net Income to Average Net Assets (%)	–	8.31	8.42	7.01	6.70	7.05
Portfolio Turnover Rate (%)	–	151	167	40	72	44
Total Assets (Millions $)	–	27.7	61.6	102	153.7	116.1
Annual Rate of Return (%) Years Ending 12/31	–	–	16.0	14.1	(.7)	10.9

Distr: Income: Monthly
    Capital Gains: May
Minimum: Initial: $1,000
    Subsequent: $100
Portfolio Mgr: David L. Murphy—1987

Telephone Exchange: Yes
    With MMF: Yes
Registered In: All states
12b-1: No
Ticker: SCYTX

SCUDDER TAX FREE TARGET 1990

Scudder, Stevens & Clark
175 Federal Street
Boston, MA 02110-2267
(800) 225-2470/(617) 439-4640

	Years Ending 12/31					
	1983 (9 mos.)	1984	1985	1986	1987	1988
Dividends, Income ($)	.45	.73	.68	.62	.54	.54
Distributions, Cap. Gains ($)	—	—	—	.10	.05	—
Net Asset Value ($)	9.65	9.67	10.03	10.34	10.07	10.02
Expense Ratio (%)	1.00	.83	.85	.82	.80	.79
Ratio of Net Income to Average Net Assets (%)	7.03	7.66	6.76	6.00	5.37	5.05
Portfolio Turnover Rate (%)	97	96	132	44	33	31
Total Assets (Millions $)	13.5	30.8	59.1	104.0	125.1	98.6
Annual Rate of Return (%) Years Ending 12/31	—	8.0	11.1	10.5	3.2	4.9

Distr: Income: Monthly
Capital Gains: Annually
Minimum: Initial: $1,000
Subsequent: $100
Portfolio Mgr: Donald Carleton—1983

Telephone Exchange: Yes
With MMF: Yes
Registered In: All states
12b-1: No
Ticker: STFTX

SCUDDER TAX FREE TARGET 1993

Scudder, Stevens & Clark
175 Federal Street
Boston, MA 02110-2267
(800) 225-2470/(617) 439-4640

	Years Ending 12/31					
	1983 (9 mos.)	1984	1985	1986	1987	1988
Dividends, Income ($)	.49	.80	.75	.67	.61	.61
Distributions, Cap. Gains ($)	—	—	—	.23	.14	—
Net Asset Value ($)	9.95	9.95	10.59	11.04	10.57	10.54
Expense Ratio (%)	1.00	.89	.86	.81	.80	.80
Ratio of Net Income to Average Net Assets (%)	7.63	8.15	7.18	6.20	5.76	5.57
Portfolio Turnover Rate (%)	190	78	265	80	64	54
Total Assets (Millions $)	9.5	23.7	55.2	118.8	125.5	104.8
Annual Rate of Return (%) Years Ending 12/31	—	8.3	14.5	13.2	2.6	5.6

Distr: Income: Monthly
Capital Gains: Annually
Minimum: Initial: $1,000
Subsequent: $100
Portfolio Mgr: Donald Carleton—1983

Telephone Exchange: Yes
With MMF: Yes
Registered In: All states
12b-1: No
Ticker: STTFX

SCUDDER TAX FREE TARGET 1996

Scudder, Stevens & Clark
175 Federal Street
Boston, MA 02110
(800) 225-2470/(617) 439-4640

		Years Ending 12/31			
	1983	1984	1985 (8 mos.)	1986	1987	1988
Dividends, Income ($)	—	—	.48	.67	.66	.67
Distributions, Cap. Gains ($)	—	—	—	.02	.08	—
Net Asset Value ($)	—	—	10.35	11.17	10.59	10.70
Expense Ratio (%)	—	—	1.00	1.00	1.06	.98
Ratio of Net Income to Average Net Assets (%)	—	—	6.76	6.07	6.18	6.65
Portfolio Turnover Rate (%)	—	—	102	36	23	76
Total Assets (Millions $)	—	—	7.2	21.6	28.1	32.8
Annual Rate of Return (%) Years Ending 12/31	—	—	—	14.7	1.5	7.5

Distr: Income: Monthly
    Capital Gains: Annually
Minimum: Initial: $1,000
    Subsequent: $100
Portfolio Mgr: Donald Carleton—1983

Telephone Exchange: Yes
    With MMF: Yes
Registered In: All states
12b-1: No
Ticker: STSIX

STEINROE HIGH-YIELD MUNICIPALS

Stein Roe & Farnham
P.O. Box 1143
Chicago, IL 60690
(800) 338-2550/(312) 368-7800

		Years Ending 12/31				6/30
	1983	1984 (10 mos.)	1985	1986	1987	1988* (6 mos.)
Dividends, Income ($)	—	.73	.94	.90	.87	.44
Distributions, Cap. Gains ($)	—	—	—	.15	.11	—
Net Asset Value ($)	—	10.02	11.10	12.06	11.06	11.37
Expense Ratio (%)	—	.80	.80	.76	.73	.76
Ratio of Net Income to Average Net Assets (%)	—	9.60	8.89	7.77	8.20	7.87
Portfolio Turnover Rate (%)	—	68	46	34	110	53
Total Assets (Millions $)	—	32.8	99.8	225.9	181.7	201.2
Annual Rate of Return (%) Years Ending 12/31	—	—	20.9	19.0	(0.3)	13.7

Fiscal year-end changed from 12/31 to 6/30.

Distr: Income: Monthly
    Capital Gains: Annually
Minimum: Initial: $1,000
    Subsequent: $100
Portfolio Mgr: Tom Conlin—1984

Telephone Exchange: Yes
    With MMF: Yes
Registered In: All states
12b-1: No
Ticker: SRMFX

STEINROE INTERMEDIATE MUNICIPALS

Stein Roe & Farnham
P.O. Box 1143
Chicago, IL 60690
(800) 338-2550/(312) 368-7800

			Years Ending 12/31			6/30
	1983	1984	1985 (3 mos.)	1986	1987	1988* (6 mos.)
Dividends, Income ($)	—	—	.12	.58	.57	.29
Distributions, Cap. Gains ($)	—	—	—	—	.01	—
Net Asset Value ($)	—	—	10.14	10.76	10.37	10.43
Expense Ratio (%)	—	—	.80	.80	.80	.80
Ratio of Net Income to Average Net Assets (%)	—	—	5.82	5.45	5.47	5.66
Portfolio Turnover Rate (%)	—	—	—	10	49	22
Total Assets (Millions $)	—	—	23.0	104.7	96.1	97.3
Annual Rate of Return (%) Years Ending 12/31	—	—	—	12.1	1.7	6.1

Fiscal year-end changed from 12/31 to 6/30.

Distr: Income: Monthly
Capital Gains: Annually
Minimum: Initial: $1,000
Subsequent: $100
Portfolio Mgr: Jane McCart—1985

Telephone Exchange: Yes
With MMF: Yes
Registered In: All states
12b-1: No
Ticker: SRIMX

STEINROE MANAGED MUNICIPALS

Stein Roe & Farnham
P.O. Box 1143
Chicago, IL 60690
(800) 338-2550/(312) 368-7800

			Years Ending 12/31			6/30
	1983	1984	1985	1986	1987	1988* (6 mos.)
Dividends, Income ($)	.64	.67	.68	.67	.61	.30
Distributions, Cap. Gains ($)	—	—	.03	.92	.13	—
Net Asset Value ($)	7.71	7.89	8.93	9.22	8.50	8.61
Expense Ratio (%)	.65	.64	.65	.65	.65	.65
Ratio of Net Income to Average Net Assets (%)	8.15	8.74	8.11	7.04	6.99	7.03
Portfolio Turnover Rate (%)	114	190	113	92	113	28
Total Assets (Millions $)	214.9	242.8	357.2	524.0	458.4	467.6
Annual Rate of Return (%) Years Ending 12/31	10.8	11.2	22.8	21.7	0.1	10.9

Fiscal year-end changed from 12/31 to 6/30.

Distr: Income: Monthly
Capital Gains: Annually
Minimum: Initial: $1,000
Subsequent: $100
Portfolio Mgr: David Snowbeck—1977

Telephone Exchange: Yes
With MMF: Yes
Registered In: All states
12b-1: No
Ticker: SRMMX

STRONG MUNICIPAL BOND
(formerly STRONG TAX-FREE INCOME)

Strong/Corneliuson Capital Mgmt.
100 Heritage Reserve
Menomonee Falls, WI 53051
(800) 368-3863/(414) 359-1400

	\multicolumn{6}{c}{Years Ending 12/31}
	1983	1984	1985	1986 (2 mos.)	1987	1988
Dividends, Income ($)	—	—	—	.12	.67	.49
Distributions, Cap. Gains ($)	—	—	—	—	—	—
Net Asset Value ($)	—	—	—	10.01	9.16	9.35
Expense Ratio (%)	—	—	—	.4	1.0	1.3
Ratio of Net Income to Average Net Assets (%)			—	6.4	7.0	5.3
Portfolio Turnover Rate (%)	—	—	—	116	284	344
Total Assets (Millions $)	—	—	—	2.2	19.1	18.3
Annual Rate of Return (%) Years Ending 12/31	—	—	—		(1.4)	7.6

Distr: Income: Monthly
Capital Gains: Annually
Minimum: Initial: $2,500
Subsequent: $200
Portfolio Mgr: William Corneliuson, Richard Strong—1986

Telephone Exchange: Yes
With MMF: Yes
Registered In: All states
12b-1: No
Ticker: SXFIX

20TH CENTURY TAX-EXEMPT INTERMEDIATE TERM

Investors Research Corp.
4500 Main Street
P.O. Box 419200
Kansas City, MO 64141-6200
(800) 345-2021/(816) 531-5575

	\multicolumn{6}{c}{Years Ending 10/31}
	1983	1984	1985	1986	1987 (8 mos.)	1988
Dividends, Income ($)	—	—	—	—	3.00	5.39
Distributions, Cap. Gains ($)	—	—	—	—	—	—
Net Asset Value ($)	—	—	—	—	94.16	97.26
Expense Ratio (%)	—	—	—	—	1.00	1.00
Ratio of Net Income to Average Net Assets (%)				—	4.80	5.57
Portfolio Turnover Rate (%)	—	—	—	—	92	86
Total Assets (Millions $)	—	—	—	—	8.3	14.3
Annual Rate of Return (%) Years Ending 12/31	—	—	—	—	—	6.0

Distr: Income: Monthly
Capital Gains: Dec
Minimum: Initial: None
Subsequent: None
Portfolio Mgr: Charles Duboc—1987

Telephone Exchange: Yes
With MMF: Yes
Registered In: All states
12b-1: No
Ticker: TWTIX

20TH CENTURY TAX-EXEMPT LONG TERM

Investors Research Corp.
4500 Main Street
P.O. Box 419200
Kansas City, MO 64141-6200
(800) 345-2021/(816) 531-5575

	Years Ending 10/31					
	1983	1984	1985	1986	1987 (8 mos.)	1988
Dividends, Income ($)	—	—	—	—	3.70	6.09
Distributions, Cap. Gains ($)	—	—	—	—	—	—
Net Asset Value ($)	—	—	—	—	90.90	97.32
Expense Ratio (%)	—	—	—	—	1.00	1.00
Ratio of Net Income to Average Net Assets (%)	—	—	—	—	6.20	6.43
Portfolio Turnover Rate (%)	—	—	—	—	94	215
Total Assets (Millions $)	—	—	—	—	6.5	12.4
Annual Rate of Return (%) Years Ending 12/31	—	—	—	—	—	10.3

Distr: Income: Monthly
Capital Gains: Dec
Minimum: Initial: None
Subsequent: None
Portfolio Mgr: Charles Duboc—1987

Telephone Exchange: Yes
With MMF: Yes
Registered In: All states
12b-1: No
Ticker: TWTLX

UNIFIED MUNICIPAL— GENERAL SERIES

Unified Management Corp.
429 N. Pennsylvania St.
Indianapolis, IN 46204-1897
(800) 862-7283/(317) 634-3300

	Years Ending 4/30					
	1983	1984	1985 (1 mo.)	1986	1987	1988
Dividends, Income ($)	—	—	—	.58	.65	.64
Distributions, Cap. Gains ($)	—	—	—	.02	.08	.01
Net Asset Value ($)	—	—	7.88	8.77	8.49	8.35
Expense Ratio (%)	—	—	—	1.24	1.06	1.07
Ratio of Net Income to Average Net Assets (%)	—	—	.38	7.40	6.81	7.15
Portfolio Turnover Rate (%)	—	—	—	19	45	29
Total Assets (Millions $)	—	—	4.0	5.4	6.9	5.6
Annual Rate of Return (%) Years Ending 12/31	—	—	—	18.3	(1.0)	10.3

Distr: Income: Apr, Dec
Capital Gains: Apr
Minimum: Initial: $1,000
Subsequent: $25
Portfolio Mgr: Nicholas Kaiser—1985

Telephone Exchange: Yes
With MMF: Yes
Registered In: DC, HI, IN, MI, NJ, WY
12b-1: Yes **Amount:** 0.25%
Ticker: UNMGX

UNIFIED MUNICIPAL— INDIANA SERIES

Unified Management Corp.
429 N. Pennsylvania St.
Indianapolis, IN 46204-1897
(800) 862-7283/(317) 634-3300

	Years Ending 4/30					
	1983	1984	1985 (1 mo.)	1986	1987	1988
Dividends, Income ($)	—	—	—	.49	.60	.61
Distributions, Cap. Gains ($)	—	—	—	—	.08	.01
Net Asset Value ($)	—	—	7.91	8.77	8.62	8.58
Expense Ratio (%)	—	—	—	1.18	1.00	1.00
Ratio of Net Income to Average Net Assets (%)	—	—	.13	7.13	6.63	7.02
Portfolio Turnover Rate (%)	—	—	—	17	37	18
Total Assets (Millions $)	—	—	3.8	8.0	11.5	11.4
Annual Rate of Return (%) Years Ending 12/31	—	—	—	19.0	.2	10.3

Distr: Income: Apr, Dec
Capital Gains: Apr
Minimum: Initial: $1,000
Subsequent: $25
Portfolio Mgr: Nicholas Kaiser—1985

Telephone Exchange: Yes
With MMF: Yes
Registered In: DC, HI, IN, NJ, WY
12b-1: Yes **Amount:** 0.25%
Ticker: UNMIX

USAA TAX EXEMPT HIGH YIELD

USAA Investment Mgmt. Co.
9800 Fredericksburg Rd.
San Antonio, TX 78288
(800) 531-8000/(512) 498-8000

	Years Ending 3/31					
	1983	1984	1985	1986	1987	1988
Dividends, Income ($)	1.40	1.08	1.13	1.13	1.04	.97
Distributions, Cap. Gains ($)	—	—	—	—	.09	.22
Net Asset Value ($)	12.02	11.76	11.88	13.52	13.96	12.44
Expense Ratio (%)	1.09	.68	.56	.50	.49	.51
Ratio of Net Income to Average Net Assets (%)	9.33	9.34	9.78	8.94	7.64	7.75
Portfolio Turnover Rate (%)	18	64	150	122	83	169
Total Assets (Millions $)	50.3	148.2	272.8	648.0	1,039.0	823.5
Annual Rate of Return (%) Years Ending 12/31	11.3	10.2	19.7	17.2	(1.9)	12.5

Distr: Income: Monthly
Capital Gains: Apr
Minimum: Initial: $3,000
Subsequent: $50
Portfolio Mgr: Kenneth Willmann—1982

Telephone Exchange: Yes
With MMF: Yes
Registered In: All states
12b-1: No
Ticker: USTEX

USAA TAX EXEMPT INTERMEDIATE-TERM

USAA Investment Mgmt. Co.
9800 Fredericksburg Rd.
San Antonio, TX 78288
(800) 531-8000/(512) 498-8000

	Years Ending 3/31					
	1983	1984	1985	1986	1987	1988
Dividends, Income ($)	1.25	.98	1.00	.98	.88	.84
Distributions, Cap. Gains ($)	—	—	—	—	—	.02
Net Asset Value ($)	11.39	11.15	11.19	12.27	12.38	11.78
Expense Ratio (%)	1.18	.73	.64	.57	.60	.56
Ratio of Net Income to Average Net Assets (%)	8.84	8.84	9.09	8.36	7.07	7.16
Portfolio Turnover Rate (%)	38	49	127	80	91	139
Total Assets (Millions $)	33.5	70.1	107.3	201.3	402.9	346.0
Annual Rate of Return (%) Years Ending 12/31	9.6	8.8	16.3	13.2	1.0	8.7

Distr: Income: Monthly
    Capital Gains: Apr
Minimum: Initial: $3,000
    Subsequent: $50
Portfolio Mgr: Kenneth Willmann—1982

Telephone Exchange: Yes
    With MMF: Yes
Registered In: All states
12b-1: No
Ticker: USATX

USAA TAX EXEMPT SHORT-TERM

USAA Investment Mgmt. Co.
9800 Fredericksburg Rd.
San Antonio, TX 78288
(800) 531-8000/(512) 498-8000

	Years Ending 3/31					
	1983	1984	1985	1986	1987	1988
Dividends, Income ($)	1.01	.68	.74	.72	.62	.61
Distributions, Cap. Gains ($)	—	—	—	—	—	.04
Net Asset Value ($)	10.35	10.27	10.36	10.66	10.70	10.42
Expense Ratio (%)	1.15	.85	.70	.65	.57	.56
Ratio of Net Income to Average Net Assets (%)	7.56	6.69	7.19	6.85	5.78	5.81
Portfolio Turnover Rate (%)	57	56	159	101	142	148
Total Assets (Millions $)	20.5	62.2	85.2	139.3	287.3	244.6
Annual Rate of Return (%) Years Ending 12/31	6.3	7.6	9.5	8.7	2.8	6.1

Distr: Income: Monthly
    Capital Gains: Apr
Minimum: Initial: $3,000
    Subsequent: $50
Portfolio Mgr: Steven Harrop—1988

Telephone Exchange: Yes
    With MMF: Yes
Registered In: All states
12b-1: No
Ticker: USSTX

US TAX FREE

United Services Advisors
P.O. Box 29467
San Antonio, TX 78229-0467
(800) 873-8637/(512) 696-1234

	1983	1984	1985 (8 mos.)	1986	1987	1988
			Years Ending 6/30			
Dividends, Income ($)	—	—	—	.81	.66	1.10
Distributions, Cap. Gains ($)	—	—	—	—	.12	—
Net Asset Value ($)	—	—	10.48	11.15	10.98	10.75
Expense Ratio (%)	—	—	1.44	.38	.05	—
Ratio of Net Income to Average Net Assets (%)	—	—	5.94	8.57	6.99	7.60
Portfolio Turnover Rate (%)	—	—	67	51	37	121
Total Assets (Millions $)	—	—	1.0	2.3	7.5	7.8
Annual Rate of Return (%) Years Ending 12/31	—	—	11.2	17.0	(.2)	12.0

Distr: Income: Mar, June, Sept, Dec
Capital Gains: Dec
Minimum: Initial: $100
Subsequent: $50
Portfolio Mgr: J. David Edwards—1987

Telephone Exchange: Yes
With MMF: Yes
Registered In: All states
12b-1: No
Ticker: USUTX

UST INTERMEDIATE TAX-EXEMPT BOND

U.S. Trust
One Boston Place
Boston, MA 02108
(800) 233-1136

	1983	1984	1985	1986 (4 mos.)	1987	1988
				Years Ending 3/31		
Dividends, Income ($)	—	—	—	.12	.60	.55
Distributions, Cap. Gains ($)	—	—	—	—	.15	.07
Net Asset Value ($)	—	—	—	8.77	8.87	8.69
Expense Ratio (%)	—	—	—	.62	.81	.70
Ratio of Net Income to Average Net Assets (%)	—	—	—	7.21	6.10	6.44
Portfolio Turnover Rate (%)	—	—	—	85	126	290
Total Assets (Millions $)	—	—	—	6.5	37.7	53.7
Annual Rate of Return (%) Years Ending 12/31	—	—	—	17.3	4.5	7.0

Distr: Income: Monthly
Capital Gains: Annually
Minimum: Initial: $10,000
Subsequent: $1,000
Portfolio Mgr: Ken McAlley—1985

Telephone Exchange: Yes
With MMF: Yes
Registered In: All states
12b-1: No
Ticker: UMITX

VALUE LINE
NEW YORK
TAX EXEMPT TRUST

Value Line, Inc.
711 Third Avenue
New York, NY 10017
(800) 223-0818/(212) 687-3965

			Years Ending 2/28			
	1983	1984	1985	1986	1987	1988 (8 mos.)
Dividends, Income ($)	—	—	—	—	—	.52
Distributions, Cap. Gains ($)	—	—	—	—	—	—
Net Asset Value ($)	—	—	—	—	—	9.93
Expense Ratio (%)	—	—	—	—	—	—
Ratio of Net Income to Average Net Assets (%)	—	—	—	—	—	8.15
Portfolio Turnover Rate (%)	—	—	—	—	—	17
Total Assets (Millions $)	—	—	—	—	—	19.7
Annual Rate of Return (%) Years Ending 12/31	—	—	—	—	—	10.8

Distr: Income: Monthly
    Capital Gains: Annually
Minimum: Initial: $1,000
    Subsequent: $250
Portfolio Mgr: Raymond Cowen—1987

Telephone Exchange: Yes
    With MMF: Yes
Registered In: CT, FL, NJ, NY
12b-1: No
Ticker: VLNYX

VALUE LINE
TAX EXEMPT
HIGH-YIELD

Value Line Securities
711 Third Ave.
New York, NY 10017
(800) 223-0818/(212) 687-3965

			Years Ending 2/28			
	1983	1984	1985 (11 mos.)	1986	1987	1988
Dividends, Income ($)	—	—	.94	.98	.89	.82
Distributions, Cap. Gains ($)	—	—	—	.02	.36	.05
Net Asset Value ($)	—	—	9.97	11.12	11.01	10.31
Expense Ratio (%)	—	—	.17	.66	.68	.64
Ratio of Net Income to Average Net Assets (%)	—	—	10.49	9.36	8.20	7.98
Portfolio Turnover Rate (%)	—	—	187	254	79	76
Total Assets (Millions $)	—	—	36.8	133.9	311.8	259.2
Annual Rate of Return (%) Years Ending 12/31	—	—	19.3	13.4	.5	11.0

Distr: Income: Monthly
    Capital Gains: Annually
Minimum: Initial: $1,000
    Subsequent: $250
Portfolio Mgr: Milton Schlein—1984

Telephone Exchange: Yes
    With MMF: Yes
Registered In: All states
12b-1: No
Ticker: VLTXX

VANGUARD CALIFORNIA TAX-FREE INSURED LONG-TERM

Vanguard Group
Vanguard Financial Center
Valley Forge, PA 19482
(800) 662-7447/(215) 648-6000

	Years Ending 11/30					
	1983	1984	1985	1986 (8 mos.)	1987	1988
Dividends, Income ($)	—	—	—	.41	.67	.66
Distributions, Cap. Gains ($)	—	—	—	.01	—	—
Net Asset Value ($)	—	—	—	10.47	9.26	9.71
Expense Ratio (%)	—	—	—	.33	.31	.30
Ratio of Net Income to Average Net Assets (%)	—	—	—	6.65	6.86	6.83
Portfolio Turnover Rate (%)	—	—	—	12	37	4
Total Assets (Millions $)	—	—	—	76.3	89.3	126.0
Annual Rate of Return (%) Years Ending 12/31	—	—	—	—	(3.9)	12.1

Distr: Income: Monthly
 Capital Gains: Annually
Minimum: Initial: $3,000
 Subsequent: $100
Portfolio Mgr: Ian MacKinnon—1986

Telephone Exchange: Yes
 With MMF: Yes
Registered In: CA
12b-1: No
Ticker: VCITX

VANGUARD HIGH-YIELD MUNICIPAL BOND

Vanguard Group
Vanguard Financial Center
Valley Forge, PA 19482
(800) 662-7447/(215) 648-6000

	Years Ending 8/31					
	1983	1984	1985	1986	1987	1988
Dividends, Income ($)	.85	.87	.87	.85	.78	.75
Distributions, Cap. Gains ($)	—	—	—	.39	—	.20
Net Asset Value ($)	9.03	8.94	9.56	10.55	9.94	9.73
Expense Ratio (%)	.46	.41	.39	.33	.26	.29
Ratio of Net Income to Average Net Assets (%)	9.05	9.69	9.37	8.32	7.55	7.74
Portfolio Turnover Rate (%)	206	90	41	38	83	40
Total Assets (Millions $)	156.2	238.9	451.9	794.1	791.0	690.3
Annual Rate of Return (%) Years Ending 12/31	10.4	9.7	21.7	19.7	(1.6)	13.8

Distr: Income: Monthly
 Capital Gains: Annually
Minimum: Initial: $3,000
 Subsequent: $100
Portfolio Mgr: Ian MacKinnon—1981

Telephone Exchange: Yes
 With MMF: Yes
Registered In: All states
12b-1: No
Ticker: VWAHX

VANGUARD INSURED LONG-TERM MUNICIPAL BOND

Vanguard Group
Vanguard Financial Center
Valley Forge, PA 19482
(800) 662-7447/(215) 648-6000

			Years Ending 8/31			
	1983	1984	1985 (10 mos.)	1986	1987	1988
Dividends, Income ($)	—	—	.83	.90	.85	.83
Distributions, Cap. Gains ($)	—	—	—	.17	—	.10
Net Asset Value ($)	—	—	10.50	11.73	11.24	11.14
Expense Ratio (%)	—	—	.36	.33	.26	.29
Ratio of Net Income to Average Net Assets (%)	—	—	8.70	7.99	7.35	7.50
Portfolio Turnover Rate (%)	—	—	16	20	50	28
Total Assets (Millions $)	—	—	336.0	709.3	793.2	735.3
Annual Rate of Return (%) Years Ending 12/31	—	—	19.3	18.7	0.1	12.8

Distr: Income: Monthly
    Capital Gains: Annually
Minimum: Initial: $3,000
    Subsequent: $100
Portfolio Mgr: Ian MacKinnon—1984

Telephone Exchange: Yes
    With MMF: Yes
Registered In: All states
12b-1: No
Ticker: VILPX

VANGUARD INTERMEDIATE-TERM MUNICIPAL BOND

Vanguard Group
Vanguard Financial Center
Valley Forge, PA 19482
(800) 662-7447/(215) 648-6000

			Years Ending 8/31			
	1983	1984	1985	1986	1987	1988
Dividends, Income ($)	.87	.90	.92	.89	.83	.80
Distributions, Cap. Gains ($)	—	—	—	.02	—	.09
Net Asset Value ($)	10.54	10.44	10.98	12.15	11.79	11.71
Expense Ratio (%)	.46	.41	.39	.33	.26	.29
Ratio of Net Income to Average Net Assets (%)	7.85	8.58	8.53	7.66	6.94	6.88
Portfolio Turnover Rate (%)	117	55	26	13	57	89
Total Assets (Millions $)	150.1	209.1	411.8	811.8	920.0	794.6
Annual Rate of Return (%) Years Ending 12/31	6.5	9.5	17.3	16.2	1.7	10.0

Distr: Income: Monthly
    Capital Gains: Annually
Minimum: Initial: $3,000
    Subsequent: $100
Portfolio Mgr: Ian MacKinnon—1981

Telephone Exchange: Yes
    With MMF: Yes
Registered In: All states
12b-1: No
Ticker: VWITX

VANGUARD LIMITED-TERM MUNICIPAL BOND

Vanguard Group
Vanguard Financial Center
Valley Forge, PA 19482
(800) 662-7447/(215) 648-6000

	Years Ending 8/31					
	1983	1984	1985	1986	1987	1988
Dividends, Income ($)	—	—	—	—	—	.60
Distributions, Cap. Gains ($)	—	—	—	—	—	—
Net Asset Value ($)	—	—	—	—	—	10.10
Expense Ratio (%)	—	—	—	—	—	.29
Ratio of Net Income to Average Net Assets (%)	—	—	—	—	—	5.91
Portfolio Turnover Rate (%)	—	—	—	—	—	122
Total Assets (Millions $)	—	—	—	—	—	162.3
Annual Rate of Return (%) Years Ending 12/31	—	—	—	—	—	6.4

Distr: Income: Monthly
    Capital Gains: Annually
Minimum: Initial: $3,000
    Subsequent: $100
Portfolio Mgr: Ian MacKinnon—1987

Telephone Exchange: Yes
    With MMF: Yes
Registered In: All states
12b-1: No
Ticker: VMLTX

VANGUARD LONG-TERM MUNICIPAL BOND

Vanguard Group
Vanguard Financial Center
Valley Forge, PA 19482
(800) 662-7447/(215) 648-6000

	Years Ending 8/31					
	1983	1984	1985	1986	1987	1988
Dividends, Income ($)	.84	.86	.87	.85	.80	.75
Distributions, Cap. Gains ($)	—	—	—	.19	—	.32
Net Asset Value ($)	9.32	9.17	9.79	10.97	10.38	10.04
Expense Ratio (%)	.46	.41	.39	.33	.26	.29
Ratio of Net Income to Average Net Assets (%)	8.76	9.35	9.13	8.09	7.40	7.48
Portfolio Turnover Rate (%)	211	99	72	32	67	34
Total Assets (Millions $)	230.6	290.0	410.7	627.7	617.3	531.3
Annual Rate of Return (%) Years Ending 12/31	9.5	8.5	20.8	19.4	(1.1)	12.2

Distr: Income: Monthly
    Capital Gains: Annually
Minimum: Initial: $3,000
    Subsequent: $100
Portfolio Mgr: Ian MacKinnon—1981

Telephone Exchange: Yes
    With MMF: Yes
Registered In: All states
12b-1: No
Ticker: VWLTX

VANGUARD NEW YORK INSURED TAX-FREE

Vanguard Group
Vanguard Financial Center
Valley Forge, PA 19482
(800) 662-7447/(215) 648-6000

			Years Ending 11/30			
	1983	1984	1985	1986 (8 mos.)	1987	1988
Dividends, Income ($)	—	—	—	.38	.63	.62
Distributions, Cap. Gains ($)	—	—	—	—	—	—
Net Asset Value ($)	—	—	—	10.08	8.87	9.26
Expense Ratio (%)	—	—	—	.34	.35	.40
Ratio of Net Income to Average Net Assets (%)	—	—	—	6.50	6.80	6.75
Portfolio Turnover Rate (%)	—	—	—	8	31	4
Total Assets (Millions $)	—	—	—	51.6	75.9	103.0
Annual Rate of Return (%) Years Ending 12/31	—	—	—	—	(3.5)	12.0

Distr: Income: Monthly
    Capital Gains: Annually
Minimum: Initial: $3,000
    Subsequent: $100
Portfolio Mgr: Ian MacKinnon—1986

Telephone Exchange: Yes
    With MMF: Yes
Registered In: NY
12b-1: No
Ticker: VNYTX

VANGUARD PENNSYLVANIA TAX-FREE INSURED LONG-TERM
(formerly VANGUARD PENNSYLVANIA INSURED TAX-FREE)

Vanguard Group
Vanguard Financial Center
Valley Forge, PA 19482
(800) 662-7447/(215) 648-6000

			Years Ending 11/30			
	1983	1984	1985	1986 (8 mos.)	1987	1988
Dividends, Income ($)	—	—	—	.41	.68	.67
Distributions, Cap. Gains ($)	—	—	—	—	—	—
Net Asset Value ($)	—	—	—	10.30	9.28	9.70
Expense Ratio (%)	—	—	—	.33	.31	.33
Ratio of Net Income to Average Net Assets (%)	—	—	—	6.65	7.06	6.95
Portfolio Turnover Rate (%)	—	—	—	0	15	3
Total Assets (Millions $)	—	—	—	121.6	193.9	269.7
Annual Rate of Return (%) Years Ending 12/31	—	—	—	—	(1.3)	12.3

Distr: Income: Monthly
    Capital Gains: Annually
Minimum: Initial: $3,000
    Subsequent: $100
Portfolio Mgr: Ian MacKinnon—1986

Telephone Exchange: Yes
    With MMF: Yes
Registered In: PA
12b-1: No
Ticker: VPAIX

VANGUARD
SHORT-TERM
MUNICIPAL BOND

Vanguard Group
Vanguard Financial Center
Valley Forge, PA 19482
(800) 662-7447/(215) 648-6000

	Years Ending 8/31					
	1983	1984	1985	1986	1987	1988
Dividends, Income ($)	.95	.92	.99	.90	.78	.79
Distributions, Cap. Gains ($)	—	—	—	.01	—	.10
Net Asset Value ($)	15.15	15.08	15.24	15.39	15.37	15.21
Expense Ratio (%)	.46	.41	.39	.33	.26	.29
Ratio of Net Income to Average Net Assets (%)	5.99	6.08	6.47	5.81	5.12	5.13
Portfolio Turnover Rate (%)	136	102	55	57	12	113
Total Assets (Millions $)	346.8	353.9	536.3	906.1	1,104.9	841.1
Annual Rate of Return (%) Years Ending 12/31	5.1	6.8	7.0	7.4	4.1	5.6

Distr: Income: Monthly
    Capital Gains: Annually
Minimum: Initial: $3,000
    Subsequent: $100
Portfolio Mgr: Ian MacKinnon—1981

Telephone Exchange: Yes
    With MMF: Yes
Registered In: All states
12b-1: No
Ticker: VWSTX

New Funds

BENHAM GOLD EQUITIES INDEX

Precious Metals

Investment Objectives/Policy: Seeks to achieve a total return that corresponds closely to the total return of the Benham North American Gold Equities Index. The index is exclusively comprised of the equity securities of a group of North American companies engaged in mining, fabricating, processing, or dealing in gold.
Year First Offered: 1988
Distr: Income: Semiannually
    Capital Gains: Annually

Benham Management Corp.
755 Page Mill Road
Palo Alto, CA 94304
(800) 227-8380/(415) 858-3600

12b-1: No
Minimum: Initial: $1,000
    Subsequent: $100
Min IRA: Initial: $100
    Subsequent: $25
Investor Services: IRA, Keogh
Telephone Exchange: Yes
    With MMF: Yes
Registered In: All states
Ticker: BGEIX

COUNSELLORS EMERGING GROWTH

Aggressive Growth

Investment Objectives/Policy: Seeks to achieve maximum capital appreciation. Invests at least 65% of its total assets in common stocks, securities convertible into or exchangeable for common stocks, or warrants of emerging growth companies. May also invest up to 20% of its total assets in Treasury securities and other corporate-grade debt.
Year First Offered: 1988
Distr: Income: Semiannually
    Capital Gains: Annually

Warburg, Pincus Counsellors, Inc.
466 Lexington Avenue
New York, NY 10017-3147
(800) 888-6878/(212) 878-0600

12b-1: No
Minimum: Initial: $25,000
    Subsequent: $5,000
Min IRA: Initial: $10,000
    Subsequent: $2,000
Investor Services: IRA, Keogh, SEP, Withdraw
Telephone Exchange: Yes
    With MMF: Yes
Registered In: All states
Ticker: CUEGX

COUNSELLORS INTERMEDIATE MATURITY GOVERNMENT

Bond

Investment Objectives/Policy: Seeks to achieve as high a level of current income as is consistent with the preservation of capital. Invests at least 65% of its assets in obligations issued or guaranteed by the U.S. government or its agencies or instrumentalities. No government security acquired by the fund will have a remaining maturity of more than 10 years after purchase.
Year First Offered: 1988
Distr: Income: Monthly
    Capital Gains: Dec

Warburg, Pincus Counsellors, Inc.
466 Lexington Avenue
New York, NY 10017-3147
(800) 888-6878/(212) 878-0600

12b-1: No
Minimum: Initial: $25,000
    Subsequent: $5,000
Min IRA: Initial: $10,000
    Subsequent: $2,000
Investor Services: IRA, Keogh, SEP, Withdraw
Telephone Exchange: Yes
    With MMF: Yes
Registered In: All states
Ticker: CUIGX

FIDELITY SHORT-TERM GOVERNMENT

Bond

Fidelity Investments Co.
82 Devonshire Street
Boson, MA 02109
(800) 544-6666/(617) 523-1919

Investment Objectives/Policy: Seeks to achieve as high a level of current income as is consistent with the preservation of capital. Invests exclusively in obligations of the U.S. government or its agencies or instrumentalities, and in repurchase agreements secured by those obligations. The average maturity of the portfolio is three years or less.
Year First Offered: 1988
Distr: Income: Monthly
    Capital Gains: Annually

12b-1: Yes   **Amount:** Pd. by Advisor
Minimum: Initial: $1,000
    Subsequent: $250
Min IRA: Initial: $500
    Subsequent: $250
Investor Services: IRA, Keogh, Corp, SEP, 403(b), Withdraw, Deduct
Telephone Exchange: Yes
    With MMF: Yes
Registered In: All states
Ticker: FSTGX

FLEX MUIRFIELD

Growth

R. Meeder & Associates, Inc.
6000 Memorial Drive
P.O. Box 7177
Dublin, OH 43017
(800) 325-3539/(614) 766-7000

Investment Objectives/Policy: Seeks long-term growth of capital by investing in a diversified portfolio of growth no-load mutual funds. These underlying mutual funds will be investing primarily in common stocks. Tactical asset allocation is used for defensive purposes. May invest in bonds or money market instruments.
Year First Offered: 1988
Distr: Income: Annually
    Capital Gains: Annually
12b-1: Yes   **Amount:** 0.20%

Minimum: Initial: $2,500
    Subsequent: $100
Min IRA: Initial: $500
    Subsequent: $100
Investor Services: IRA, Keogh, Corp, SEP, Withdraw
Telephone Exchange: Yes
    With MMF: Yes
Registered In: AL, AZ, CO, CT, DC, FL, GA, HI, IL, IN, MA, MD, MI, MN, MO, NC, NJ, NY, OH, PA, SC, TN, TX, VA, WA
Ticker: FLMFX

T. ROWE PRICE SMALL-CAP VALUE

Aggressive Growth

T. Rowe Price Associates, Inc.
100 E. Pratt St.
Baltimore, MD 21202
(800) 638-5660/(301) 547-2308

Investment Objectives/Policy: Seeks long-term capital growth by investing primarily in the common stock of companies with relatively small market capitalizations that are believed to be undervalued and have good prospects for capital appreciation. May invest up to 20% of its assets in securities principally traded in markets outside the U.S.
Year First Offered: 1988
Distr: Income: Dec
    Capital Gains: Dec

12b-1: No
Minimum: Initial: $1,000
    Subsequent: $100
Min IRA: Initial: $500
    Subsequent: $50
Investor Services: IRA, Keogh, Corp, SEP, 403(b), Withdraw, Deduct
Telephone Exchange: Yes
    With MMF: Yes
Registered In: All states
Ticker: PRSVX

SBSF CONVERTIBLE SECURITIES

Balanced

Investment Objectives/Policy: Seeks a high level of current income together with long-term capital appreciation. Invests at least 65% of its total assets in convertible securities. May invest up to 10% of its total assets in non-marketable securities.
Year First Offered: 1988
Distr: Income: Mar, June, Sept, Dec
     Capital Gains: Dec

Spears, Benzak, Salomon & Farrell
45 Rockefeller Plaza
New York, NY 10111
(800) 422-7273/(212) 903-1200

12b-1: Yes   **Amount:** 0.25%
Minimum: Initial: None
     Subsequent: None
Min IRA: Initial: $500
     Subsequent: None
Investor Services: IRA, Keogh, Withdraw
Telephone Exchange: Yes
     With MMF: Yes
Registered In: All states except MO, SD
Ticker: SBFCX

SCUDDER GOLD

Precious Metals

Investment Objectives/Policy: Seeks to provide a maximum return. Invests at least 65% of the fund's total assets in: (1) equity securities of U.S. and foreign companies primarily engaged in the exploration, mining, fabrication, processing or distribution of gold; (2) gold bullion; and (3) gold coins. The remaining 35% may be invested in other precious metals and equity securities.
Year First Offered: 1988
Distr: Income: Aug, Dec
    Capital Gains: Aug, Dec

Scudder, Stevens & Clark
175 Federal St.
Boston, MA 02110
(800) 225-2470/(617) 439-4640

12b-1: No
Minimum: Initial: $1,000
     Subsequent: $100
Min IRA: Initial: $500
     Subsequent: $50
Investor Services: IRA, Keogh, Corp, SEP, 403(b), Withdraw, Deduct
Telephone Exchange: Yes
     With MMF: Yes
Registered In: All states
Ticker: SCGDX

20TH CENTURY BALANCED

Balanced

Investment Objectives/Policy: Seeks capital growth and current income. Invests at least 60% of the fund's assets in common stocks that are considered by management to have better-than-average prospects for appreciation, and the balance in bonds and other fixed-income securities. At least 80% of fixed-income assets will be invested in securities that are rated within the three highest categories by Moody's Investors Service or Standard & Poor's.
Year First Offered: 1988
Distr: Income: Mar, June, Sept, Dec
    Capital Gains: Dec

Investors Research Corp.
4500 Main Street
P.O. Box 419200
Kansas City, MO 64141-6200
(800) 345-2021/(816) 531-5575

12b-1: No
Minimum: Initial: None
     Subsequent: None
Min IRA: Initial: None
     Subsequent: None
Investor Services: IRA, Keogh, Corp, 403(b), Withdraw, Deduct
Telephone Exchange: Yes
     With MMF: Yes
Registered In: All states
Ticker: TWBIX

USAA INTERNATIONAL

International

USAA Investment Mgmt. Co.
9800 Fredericksburg Rd.
San Antonio, TX 78288
(800) 531-8000/(512) 498-8000

Investment Objectives/Policy: Primary objective is capital appreciation. Current income is a secondary objective. Invests at least 80% of its assets in equity securities, including those convertible into or carrying the right to buy equity securities of companies organized and operating principally outside the United States.
Year First Offered: 1988
Distr: Income: Annually
    Capital Gains: Annually

12b-1: No
Minimum: Initial: $1,000
    Subsequent: $50
Min IRA: Initial: $1,000
    Subsequent: $25
Investor Services: IRA, Keogh, SEP, 403(b), Withdraw, Deduct
Telephone Exchange: Yes
    With MMF: Yes
Registered In: All states
Ticker: USIFX

VANGUARD ASSET ALLOCATION

Growth & Income

Vanguard Group
Vanguard Financial Center
Valley Forge, PA 19482
(800) 662-7447/(215) 648-6000

Investment Objectives/Policy: Seeks to maximize capital gains plus income while exhibiting less risk than a portfolio consisting entirely of equities. The fund allocates its assets among a common stock portfolio, a bond portfolio, and money market instruments in proportions that reflect the anticipated returns and risks of each asset class.
Year First Offered: 1988
Distr: Income: Semiannually
    Capital Gains: Annually

12b-1: No
Minimum: Initial: $3,000
    Subsequent: $100
Min IRA: Initial: $500
    Subsequent: $100
Investor Services: IRA, Keogh, Corp, SEP, 403(b), Withdraw, Deduct
Telephone Exchange: Yes
    With MMF: Yes
Registered In: All states
Ticker: VAAPX

VANGUARD EQUITY INCOME

Growth & Income

Vanguard Group
Vanguard Financial Center
Valley Forge, PA 19482
(800) 662-7447/(215) 648-6000

Investment Objectives/Policy: Seeks to provide a high level of current income. The fund will also consider the potential for capital appreciation. Invests at least 80% of its assets in income-producing equity securities, including dividend-paying common stocks and securities that are convertible into common stocks. May invest up to 20% of its assets in cash and fixed-income securities.
Year First Offered: 1988
Distr: Income: Quarterly
    Capital Gains: Annually

12b-1: No
Minimum: Initial: $3,000
    Subsequent: $100
Min IRA: Initial: $500
    Subsequent: $100
Investor Services: IRA, Keogh, Corp, SEP, 403(b), Withdraw, Deduct
Telephone Exchange: Yes
    With MMF: Yes
Registered In: All states
Ticker: VEIPX

VANGUARD NEW JERSEY TAX-FREE INSURED LONG-TERM

Tax-Exempt

Vanguard Group
Vanguard Financial Center
Valley Forge, PA 19482
(800) 662-7447/(215) 648-6000

Investment Objectives/Policy: Seeks to provide the highest level of income that is exempt from both federal and New Jersey personal income taxes. Invests at least 80% of its assets in long-term municipal bonds that are covered by insurance guaranteeing the scheduled payment of principal and interest. Up to 20% of the portfolio's assets may be invested in uninsured short-term investments or uninsured bonds rated a minimum of AA by Standard & Poor's.
Year First Offered: 1988
Distr: Income: Monthly
Capital Gains: Annually

12b-1: No
Minimum: Initial: $3,000
Subsequent: $100
Investor Services: Withdraw, Deduct
Telephone Exchange: Yes
With MMF: Yes
Registered In: New Jersey
Ticker: VNJTX

Funds Not Listed In Data Pages

We base our mutual fund guide on the listings that appear in the newspaper; we select only no-load funds. These funds appear in the financial press with an NL (no load) designation in the "offer price" column. The listings, however, are sometimes inaccurate, and some of the funds listed in the newspaper are not true no-loads despite their designation. Others are inappropriate for individuals or are not available to individuals for other reasons. In this section, we list the funds designated as no-loads in the financial press but that are not in the main part of this book, and we state the reasons for their exclusion.

Key to Reasons for Exclusion:

BB: Can be bought only from a bank or broker.

DE: For corporations taking advantage of dividend exclusion tax rules.

I: For institutional or corporate investors only.

L: Limited to certain individuals, such as employees or members of a particular organization.

M: Minimum investment is greater than $25,000.

NS: Information not supplied in time for publication, or insufficient information.

R: Redemption fee does not disappear after 6 months.

SC: Front-end sales charge.

T: Tax-free exchange fund—No longer available for purchase.

L	AMEV Special	I	Federated Cash Mgmt. Trust
L	Bankers System Granit Growth	I	Federated Exchange
T	Chestnut Street Exchange	I	Federated Floating Rate
L	Citibank IRA CIT: Balanced	I	Federated F.T. International
L	Citibank IRA CIT: Equity	I	Federated GNMA Trust
L	Citibank IRA CIT: Income	I	Federated Government Trust
L	Citibank IRA CIT: Short-Term	I	Federated Growth Trust
R	Colonial VIP Diversified Ret.	I	Federated High Yield
R	VIP High Income	I	Federated Income
M	DFA Five Year Govt. Port.	I	Federated Intermediate Gov't.
M	DFA Fixed Income Portfolio	I	Federated Intermediate Muni.
M	Dimensional Cont. Small Comp.	I	Federated Short Inter. Gov't.
M	Dimensional Japan Small Comp.	I	Federated Short Inter. Muni.
M	Dimensional Small Comp.	I	Federated Stock & Bond
M	Dimensional U.K. Small Comp.	I	Federated Stock Trust
L	DIT Capital Growth	I	Federated Vari. Rate Mortgage
L	DIT Current Income	T	Fidelity Congress St.
L	DIT U.S. Gov't. Securities	I	Fidelity CT ARP
NS	Equity Strategies	I	Fidelity Equity Portfolio Inc.
I	Federated Bond Fund	I	Fidelity Fixed Inc. Ltd. Term

I	Fidelity Fixed Inc. Short Gov't.	R	Paine Webber Master Income
I	Fidelity Tax-Exempt Ltd. Term	I	SEI Fds. Bond
I	Fidelity U.S. Equity Index	I	SEI Fds. Equity Index
DE	Flag Investors: Corporate Cash	I	SEI Fds. Inst. Man. Trust Value
DE	Flagship Corporate Cash	I	SEI Fds. Inter. Gov't.
R	Gabelli Asset Fund	I	SEI Fds. Ltd. Volatility Bond
R	Gabelli Growth	I	SEI Fds. Short Term Gov't.
I	Galaxy Bond	I	S-P IFG Diversified
I	Galaxy Equity	I	S-P IFG Intermediate
DE	Geico Qualified Dividend	I	S-P IFG International
BB	General Aggressive Growth	BB	Seagate Inter. Gov't. Oblig.
L	G.E. Elfun Income	NS	Steadman American Industry
L	G.E. Elfun Tax-Exempt	NS	Steadman Associated
L	G.E. Elfun Trust	NS	Steadman Investment
L	G.E. S&S Long-Term Interest	NS	Steadman Ocean., Tech. & Gr.
L	G.E. S&S Program	R	United Services Prospector
BB	General Tax Exempt Bond	T	V.E.—Capital Exch.
M	Gintel Fund	T	V.E.—Depositors of Boston
L	Guardian Bond	T	V.E.—Diversification
L	Guardian Stock	T	V.E.—Exchange Fund
L	Horace Mann Growth Fund	T	V.E.—Exchange of Boston
I	Ivy Institutional	T	V.E.—Fiduciary Exchange
L	Landmark Capital Growth	T	V.E.—Second Fiduciary Exch.
L	Landmark Growth and Income	DE	Vanguard Adj. Rate Pref.
L	Landmark N.Y. Tax Free Inc.	DE	Vanguard Pref. Stock
L	Landmark U.S. Gov't. Income	NS	Viking Equity Index
I	Merrill Lynch Inst. Inter.	L	Wells Fargo IRA: Asset Alloc.
BB	Metlife State Street Gov't. Inc.	L	Wells Fargo IRA: Bond
M	Mutual Beacon	L	Wells Fargo IRA: Corp. Stock
R	Paine Webber Asset Allocation	L	Wells Fargo IRA: Small Comp.
R	Paine Webber Master Growth	I	WPG Growth

Mutual Fund Families

Below we present a list of mutual fund families that are primarily no-load. We have listed all funds within a family, including those with loads and redemption fees that are not included in this book. We do not include families with only 1 non-money market fund, and we do not include families that are primarily loaded.

AMA Advisers, Inc.
5 Sentry Pkwy. W., Suite 120
P.O. Box 1111
Blue Bell, PA 19422
(800) 262-3863/(215) 825-0400

Classic Growth
Classic Income
Emerging Medical Technology
Global Growth
Global Income
Global Short Term
Growth Plus Income
Medical Technology
Money-Prime
Money—Treasury
U.S. Gov't. Income Plus

American Pension Investors, Inc.
2316 Atherholt Road
Lynchburg, VA 24501
(800) 554-6060/(800) 533-4115 (Va.)

Balanced
Investment Grade Securities
Growth
Precious Resources
U.S. Government Intermediate

Avondale Funds
Herbert R. Smith, Inc.
1105 Holliday
Wichita Falls, TX 76301
(817) 761-3777

Avondale Government Securities
Avondale Total Return

Axe-Houghton Management, Inc.
Axe Castle
Tarrytown, NY 10591
(800) 366-0444/(914) 631-8131

Fund B
Income
Money Market
Stock

Babson Funds
Jones & Babson, Inc.
Three Crown Center
2440 Pershing Rd.

Kansas City, MO 64108
(800) 422-2766/(816) 471-5200

Babson-Stewart Ivory Int'l.
Bond Trust—Portfolio L
Bond Trust—Portfolio S
Enterprise
Growth
Money Market—Portfolio F
Money Market—Portfolio P
Shadow Stock
Tax-Free Income Portfolio L
Short Tax-Free Income Portfolio S
Long Tax-Free Income Portfolio MM
UMB Bond
UMB Money Market—Portfolio F
UMB Money Market—Portfolio P
UMB Qualified Dividend
UMB Stock
UMB Tax-Free Money Mkt.
Value

James Baker & Company
1601 Northwest Expressway
20th Floor
Oklahoma City, OK 73118
(405) 842-1400

Baker—Equity Series
Baker—U.S. Government Series

Bartlett & Company
36 E. Fourth St.
Cincinnati, OH 45202
(800) 543-0863/(513) 621-0066

Basic Value
Enhanced Cash Reserves
Fixed Income
Strategic Income

Benham Management Corp.
755 Page Mill Rd.
Palo Alto, CA 94304
(800) 227-8380/(415) 858-3600

California Tax-Free—High Yield
California Tax-Free—Insured
California Tax-Free—Intermediate
California Tax-Free—Long Term
California Tax-Free—Money Market

Capital Preservation
Capital Preservation II
Capital Preservation Treasury Note
GNMA Income
Gold Equities Index
National Tax-Free—Intermediate
National Tax-Free—Long-Term
National Tax-Free—Money Market
Target Maturities Trust Series

Boston Co.
One Boston Place
Boston, MA 02108
(800) 343-6324/(800) 225-5267

Asset Allocation
Blue Chip
Bond Index
Calif. Tax-Free Bond
Calif. Tax-Free Money
Capital Appreciation
Cash Management
Cash Management Plus
Contrarian
Equity Income
Equity Index
GNMA
Government Money
International
Managed Income
Mass. Tax-Free Bond
Mass. Tax-Free Money
N.Y. Tax-Free Bond
N.Y. Tax-Free Money
Small Cap. Equity Index
Special Growth
Tax-Free Bond
Tax-Free Money

Bull & Bear Equity Advisers
11 Hanover Square
New York, NY 10005
(800) 847-4200/(212) 363-1100

Capital Growth
Dollar Reserves
Equity-Income Ltd.
Gold Investors
High Yield
Overseas
Special Equities
Tax-Free Income
U.S. Gov't. Guaranteed Sec.

CCM Partners
44 Montgomery Street, Suite 2200
San Francisco, CA 94104
(800) 826-8166/(415) 398-2727

Calif. Tax-Free Income
Calif. Tax-Free Money Market
Calif. U.S. Government Securities

Columbia Funds Mgmt. Co.
1301 S.W. Fifth Ave.
P.O. Box 1350
Portland, OR 97207-1350
(800) 547-1037/(503) 222-3600

Daily Income
Fixed Income Securities
Growth
Municipal Bond
Special
U.S. Gov't. Guaranteed Sec.

Counsellors
Warburg, Pincus Counsellors, Inc.
466 Lexington Avenue
New York, NY 10017-3147
(800) 888-6878/(212) 878-0600

Capital Appreciation
Cash Reserve
Emerging Growth
Fixed Income
Intermediate Maturity Government
New York Municipal Bond
New York Tax-Exempt

Dividend/Growth Funds
American Investment Managers, Inc.
107 N. Adams St.
Rockville, MD 20850
(800) 638-2042/(301) 251-1002

Dividend Series
Laser Series

Dodge & Cox
One Post St., 35th Fl.
San Francisco, CA 94104
(415) 981-1710

Balanced
Income
Stock

Dreyfus
600 Madison Avenue
New York, NY 10022
(800) 645-6561/(718) 895-1206

A Bonds Plus
Calif. Tax Exempt Bond
Calif. Tax Exempt Money Market
Capital Value
Convertible Securities
Dollar International

Dreyfus Fund
FN Network Tax-Free Money Mkt.
Foreign Investors GNMA
Foreign Investors U.S. Gov't. Bond
General Aggressive Growth
General Calif. Tax Exempt Money
General Government Securities
General Money Market
General N.Y. Tax Ex. Interm. Bond
General N.Y. Tax Exempt Money
General Tax Exempt Bond
General Tax Exempt Money Market
GNMA
Growth Opportunity
Index Fund
Insured Tax Exempt Bond
Intermediate Tax Exempt Bond
Lion Investment
Leverage
Liquid Assets
Mass. Tax Exempt Bond
Money Market Instr.:
    Government Series
    Money Market Series
N. J. Tax Exempt Bond
N. J. Tax Exempt Money Market
New Leaders
N.Y. Insured Tax Exempt Bond
N.Y. Tax Exempt Interm. Bond
N.Y. Tax Exempt Bond
N.Y. Tax Exempt Money Mkt.
Short-Intermediate Government
Short-Intermediate Tax Exempt Bond
Strategic Aggressive Investing
Strategic Income
Strategic Investing
Strategic World Investing
Strategic World Revenues
Tax Exempt
Tax Exempt Money Market
Third Century
U.S. Government Bond
U.S. Gov't. Interm. Securities
U.S. Guaranteed Money Market

Dupree Investment Advisers, Inc.
167 W. Main Street
Lexington, KY 40507
(800) 432-9518/(606) 254-7741

Kentucky Tax-Free Income Series
Kentucky Tax-Free Short to Medium

Evergreen
Saxon Woods Asset Mgmt. Corp.
550 Mamaroneck Ave.
Harrison, NY 10528

(800) 235-0064/(914) 698-5711

Evergreen American Retirement
Evergreen Fund
Evergreen Total Return
Evergreen Value Timing
Money Market
Tax-Exempt Money Mkt.
Tax-Exempt Money Mkt. Calif.

Fidelity
82 Devonshire St.
Boston, MA 02109
(800) 544-6666/(617) 523-1919

Aggressive Tax-Free
Balanced
Blue Chip Growth
CalFree—High Yield Port.
CalFree—Insured Port.
CalFree—Money Market
Canada
Capital Appreciation
Cash Reserves
Congress Street
Conn. Tax-Free
Contrafund
Convertible Securities
Corporate Trust: Adj. Rate Pref.
Daily Income Trust
Daily Money
Daily Tax-Exempt Money
Destiny I
Destiny II
Equity:
    Growth
    Income
Equity-Income
Europe
Exchange
Fidelity Fund
Flexible Bond
Freedom
Ginnie Mae
Global Bond
Growth Company
Growth & Income Port.
High Income
High Yield Municipals
Income
Insured Tax-Free Portfolio
Intermediate Bond
International Growth & Income
Limited Term Municipals
Magellan
Mass. Tax-Free High Yield
Mass. Tax-Free Money Market

Michigan Tax-Free
Minnesota Tax-Free
Money Market Trust:
   Domestic
   U.S. Government
   U.S. Treasury
Mortgage Securities
Municipal Bond
N.J. Tax-Free High Yield
N.J. Tax-Free Money Mkt.
N.Y. Tax-Free High Yield
N.Y. Tax-Free Insured
N.Y. Tax-Free Money Market
Ohio Tax-Free
OTC Portfolio
Overseas
Pacific Basin
Penn. T-F—High Yield Port.
Penn. T-F—Money Market
Puritan
Qualified Dividend
Real Estate Investment
Select Portfolios:
   Air Transportation
   American Gold
   Automation & Machinery
   Automotive
   Biotechnology
   Broadcast and Media
   Brokerage & Investment Cos.
   Capital Goods
   Chemicals
   Computers
   Defense & Aerospace
   Electric Utilities
   Electronics
   Energy
   Energy Services
   Financial Services
   Food & Agriculture
   Health Care
   Housing
   Industrial Materials
   Leisure & Entertainment
   Life Insurance
   Medical Delivery
   Money Markets
   Paper & Forest Products
   Precious Metals & Minerals
   Property & Casualty Insurance
   Regional Banks
   Restaurant Industry
   Retailing
   Savings & Loan
   Software & Computer Services

Technology
Telecommunications
Transportation
Utilities
Short-Term Bond Portfolio
Short-Term Government
Short-Term Tax-Free Portfolio
Special Situations
Tax-Exempt Money Market Trust
Texas Tax-Free
Trend
United Kingdom
U.S. Government Reserves
U.S. Treasury Money Mkt.
Utilities Income
Value

Fiduciary
222 E. Mason St.
Milwaukee, WI 53202
(414) 271-6666

Capital Growth
Income
Money Market
Total Return

Financial Programs
P.O. Box 2040
Denver, CO 80201
(800) 525-8085/(303) 779-1233

Bond Shares:
   High Yield
   Select Income
   U.S. Government
Daily Income Shares
Dynamics
Industrial
Industrial Income
Strategic Portfolios:
   Energy
   European
   Financial Services
   Gold
   Health Sciences
   Leisure
   Pacific Basin
   Technology
   Utilities
Tax-Free Income Shares
Tax-Free Money

Flex-Fund
R. Meeder & Associates
6000 Memorial Dr.
P.O. Box 7177
Dublin, OH 43017

(800) 325-3539/(614) 766-7000

Bond
Growth
Income and Growth
Money Market
Muirfield
Retirement Growth

44 Wall Street
MDB Asset Management Corp.
26 Broadway
New York, NY 10004
(800) 543-2620/(212) 248-8080

44 Wall Street
44 Wall Street Equity

Founders
3033 E. First Avenue
Denver, CO 80206
(800) 525-2440/(303) 394-4404

Blue Chip
Equity Income
Frontier
Government Securities
Growth
Money Market
Special

Fundamental Portfolio Advisors
111 Broadway, Suite 1107
New York, NY 10006
(800) 225-6864/(212) 608-6864

California Muni
Fundamental High Yield
Fundamental Money Market
New York Muni

FundTrust
Furman Selz
230 Park Ave.
New York, NY 10169
(800) 845-8406/(212) 309-8400

Aggressive Growth
Equity Trust
Growth
Growth & Income
Income
International Equity Trust
Money Trust

Furman, Anderson & Co.
19 Rector Street
New York, NY 10006
(212) 509-8532

Insider Reports
Rainbow

Gateway Investment Advisors
P.O. Box 458167
Cincinnati, OH 45245
(800) 354-6339/(513) 248-2700

Government Bond
Growth Plus
Option Index

Gintel
Greenwich Office Park #6
Greenwich, CT 06830
(800) 243-5808/(203) 622-6400

Gintel
Gintel Capital Appreciation
Gintel ERISA
Parkway Money Market

GIT
Bankers Finance Investment Mgmt.
1655 N. Fort Myer Dr.
Arlington, VA 22209
(800) 336-3063/(703) 528-6500

Equity Income
Equity Select
Equity Special Growth
Government Investors
Income:
  A-Rated
  Maximum
Insured Money Market
Tax-Free High Yield
Tax-Free Money Market
Tax-Free Virginia Portfolio

Gradison
The 580 Bldg.
6th & Walnut
Cincinnati, OH 45202-3198
(800) 543-1818/(513) 579-5700

Cash Reserves
Established Growth
Government Income
Opportunity Growth
U.S. Government

Harbor Capital Advisors, Inc.
One SeaGate
Toledo, OH 43666
(800) 422-1050/(419) 247-1940

Bond
Growth
International
Money Market
U.S. Equities
Value

Heine Securities Corporation
51 John F. Kennedy Pkwy.
Short Hills, NJ 07078
(800) 448-3863/(201) 912-2100

Mutual Beacon
Mutual Qualified
Mutual Shares

IAI Funds
Investment Advisers, Inc.
1100 Dain Tower
P.O. Box 357
Minneapolis, MN 55440
(612) 371-2884

Apollo
Bond
International
Regional
Reserve
Stock

Ivy Funds
Ivy Management Inc.
South Shore Park
40 Industrial Park Rd.
Hingham, MA 02043
(800) 235-3322/(617) 749-1416

Money Market
Growth
Institutional Investors
International
U.S. Government Income

Janus
100 Fillmore St., Suite 300
Denver, CO 80206-4923
(800) 525-3713/(303) 333-3863

Janus Flexible Income
Janus Fund
Janus Value
Janus Venture

Kleinwort Benson International
200 Park Ave. 24th Floor
New York, NY 10166
(800) 237-4218/(212) 687-2515

Transatlantic Growth
Transatlantic Income

Legg Mason Fund Adviser
111 South Calvert St.
Baltimore, MD 21203-1476
(800) 822-5544/(301) 539-3400

Cash Reserve
Investment Grade Income

Special Investment Trust
Tax Exempt
Total Return Trust
U.S. Government Intermediate
U.S. Government Money Mkt.
Value Trust

Lexington
P.O. Box 1515
Park 80 W. Plaza 2
Saddle Brook, NJ 07662
(800) 526-0056

GNMA Income
Global
Goldfund
Government Securities Money Mkt.
Growth
Money Market Trust
Research
Tax Exempt Bond Trust
Tax-Free Money
Technical Strategy

Lindner Management Corporation
200 South Bemiston
P.O. Box 11208
St. Louis, MO 63105
(314) 727-5305

Lindner Fund
Lindner Dividend

Loomis-Sayles
P.O. Box 449
Back Bay Annex
Boston, MA 02117
(800) 345-4048/(617) 578-1333

Capital Development
Mutual

Neuberger & Berman Management
342 Madison Ave.
New York, NY 10173
(800) 367-0776/(212) 850-8300

Cash Reserves
Genesis
Government Money
Guardian Mutual
Liberty
Limited Maturity Bond
Manhattan
Money Market Plus
Municipal Money
Municipal Securities
Partners

Selected Sectors Plus Energy

New Beginning Funds
Sit Investment Associates, Inc.
1714 First Bank Place West
Minneapolis, MN 55402
(800) 332-5580/(612) 334-5888

Growth
Income & Growth
Investment Reserve
Tax-Free Income
U.S. Government Securities

Newton Funds
M&I Investment Management Corp.
330 E. Kilbourn Ave.
Two Plaza East, #1150
Milwaukee, WI 53202
(800) 247-7039/(414) 347-1141

Growth
Income
Money

Nicholas
700 N. Water St.
Milwaukee, WI 53202
(414) 272-6133

Nicholas
Nicholas II
Nicholas Income
Nicholas Limited Edition
Nicholas Money Market

Northeast Mgmt. & Research Co.
50 Congress Street
Boston, MA 02109
(617) 523-3588/(800) 225-6704

Northeast Investors Growth
Northeast Investors Trust

100 Funds
Berger Associates
899 Logan St.
Denver, CO 80203
(800) 333-1001/(303) 837-1020

100 Fund
101 Fund

Permanent Portfolio Funds
World Money Managers
7 Fourth Street
Suite 14
Petaluma, CA 94952
(800) 531-5142/(512) 453-7558

Permanent Portfolio
Treasury Bill Portfolio

T. Rowe Price
100 E. Pratt St.
Baltimore, MD 21202
(800) 638-5660/(301) 547-2308

Calif. Tax-Free Bond
Calif. Tax-Free Money
Capital Appreciation
Equity Income
GNMA
Growth & Income
Growth Stock
High Yield
International Bond
International Discovery
International Stock
Maryland Tax-Free Bond
New America Growth
New Era
New Horizons
New Income
New York Tax-Free Bond
New York Tax-Free Money
Prime Reserves
Science and Technology
Short-Term Bond
Small-Cap Value
Tax-Exempt Money
Tax-Free High Yield
Tax-Free Income
Tax-Free Short-Intermediate
U.S. Treasury Money

Reserve Management Co.
810 Seventh Avenue
New York, NY 10019
(800) 421-0261/(212) 977-9675

Equity Trust—Contrarian Portfolio
Equity Trust—Growth Portfolio
Government Portfolio
Tax Exempt:
    Connecticut
    Interstate
    New York
Primary Portfolio

Rushmore
Money Management Associates
4922 Fairmont Avenue
Bethesda, MD 20814
(800) 343-3355/(301) 657-1500

Fund for Government Investors
Fund for Tax-Free Investors:
    Intermediate-Term
    Long-Term
    Money Market

Money Market
Over-the-Counter Index Plus
Stock Market Index Plus
U.S. Gov't. Securities Intermediate
U.S. Gov't. Securities Long-Term

SAFECO Securities
SAFECO Plaza
Seattle, WA 98185
(800) 426-6730/(206) 545-5530

Calif. Tax-Free Income
Equity
Growth
High-Yield Bond
Income
Intermediate-Term Bond
Money Market Mutual
Municipal Bond
Tax-Free Money Market
U.S. Government Securities

SBSF Funds
Spears, Benzak, Salomon & Farrell
45 Rockefeller Plaza
New York, NY 10111
(212) 903-1200

Convertible Securities
Growth
Money Market

Scudder
175 Federal St.
Boston, MA 02110
(800) 225-2470/(617) 439-4640

AARP Capital Growth
AARP General Bond
AARP GNMA & U.S. Treasury
AARP Growth & Income
AARP Insured Tax Free General Bd.
AARP Insured Tax Free Short Term
AARP Money Fund
Calif. Tax Free
Calif. Tax Free Money
Capital Growth
Cash Investment
Development
Equity Income
Global
GNMA
Gold
Government Money
Growth & Income
High Yield Tax Free
Income
International

International Bond
Japan Fund
Managed Municipal Bonds
Mass. Tax Free
N.Y. Tax Free
N.Y. Tax Free Money
Ohio Tax Free
Penn. Tax Free
Target General
Tax Free Money
Tax Free Targets
U.S. Gov't. Zero Coupon

Selected Funds
230 W. Monroe St.
Chicago, IL 60606
(800) 553-5533/(312) 641-7862

American Shares
Government Total Return
Money Market:
    General
    Government
    Tax-Exempt
Special Shares

Stein Roe & Farnham
P.O. Box 1143
Chicago, IL 60690
(800) 338-2550/(312) 368-7800

Capital Opportunities
Cash Reserves
Discovery
Governments Plus
Government Reserves
Growth & Income
High-Yield Bonds
High-Yield Municipals
Intermediate Municipals
International Growth
Managed Bonds
Managed Municipals
Prime Equities
Special
Stock
Tax-Exempt Money
Total Return
Universe

Stratton
Plymouth Meeting Exec. Campus
610 W. Germantown Pike
Suite 361
Plymouth Meeting, PA 19462
(800) 634-5726/(215) 941-0255

Growth
Monthly Dividend Shares

Strong/Corneliuson Capital Mgmt.
100 Heritage Reserve
Menomonee Falls, WI 53051
(800) 368-3863/(414) 359-1400

Advantage
Discovery
Government Securities
Income
Investment
Money Market
Municipal Bond
Municipal Money Mkt.
Opportunity
Short-Term Bond
Total Return

20th Century
Investors Research Corp.
P.O. Box 419200
Kansas City, MO 64141-6200
(800) 345-2021/(816) 531-5575

Balanced
Cash Reserve
Giftrust
Growth
Heritage
Long-Term Bond
Select
Tax-Exempt Intermediate
Tax-Exempt Long Term
Ultra
U.S. Governments
Vista

Unified Management Corporation
429 N. Pennsylvania St.
P.O. Box 6110
Indianapolis, IN 46206-6110
(800) 862-7283/(317) 634-3300

Amana Income
Growth
Income
Liquid Green Trust
Liquid Green Tax-Free Trust
Municipal—General Series
Municipal—Indiana Series
Mutual Shares
P.P.T. Aggressive Growth
P.P.T. Government Sec.
P.P.T. High Yield
P.P.T. International
P.P.T. Timed Equity
P.P.T. Total Return
Tower Bond
Tower Equity

United Services
P.O. Box 29467
San Antonio, TX 78229-0467
(800) 873-8637/(512) 696-1234

Prospector
US GNMA
US Gold Shares
US Good & Bad Times
US Growth
US Income
US LoCap
US New Prospector
US Real Estate
US Tax Free
US Treasury Securities

USAA Funds
9800 Fredericksburg Rd.
USAA Building
San Antonio, TX 78288
(800) 531-8000/(512) 498-8000

Aggressive Growth
Balanced Portfolio
Cornerstone
Gold
Growth
Income
Income Stock
International
Money Market
Tax Exempt Funds:
    High Yield
    Intermediate-Term
    Money Market
    Short-Term

U.S. Boston Investment Mgmt. Corp.
Six New England Executive Park
Burlington, MA 01803
(617) 272-6420

Boston Growth and Income
Boston Foreign Growth and Income

U.S.T. Master
One Boston Place
Boston, MA 02108
(800) 233-1136/(617) 451-1912

Equity
Government Money
Income and Growth
Intermediate Tax-Exempt Bond
International
Long Term Tax Exempt
Managed Income
Money

Short Term Tax-Exempt

Value Line
711 Third Ave.
New York, NY 10017
(800) 223-0818/(212) 687-3965

Aggressive Income
Cash
Convertible
Income
Leveraged Growth
New York Tax-Exempt Trust
Special Situations
Strategic Asset Management Trust
Tax Exempt Funds:
    High-Yield
    Money Market
U.S. Government Securities
Value Line Fund

Vanguard Group
Vanguard Financial Center
Valley Forge, PA 19482
(800) 662-7447/(215) 648-6000

Adjustable Rate Preferred Stock
Asset Allocation
Bond Market
Calif. Tax-Free Insured Long-Term
Calif. Tax-Free Money Market
Convertible Securities
Equity Income
Explorer
Explorer II
Fixed Income Securities:
    GNMA
    High Yield
    Investment Grade
    Short-Term
    Short-Term Government
    U.S. Treasury
High Yield Stock
Index Trust—500
Index Trust—Ext. Market
Money Market Reserves:
    Federal
    Insured
    Prime
Municipal Bond Funds:
    High-Yield
    Insured Long-Term
    Intermediate-Term

Limited-Term
Long-Term
Money Market
Short-Term
Naess & Thomas Special
N.J. Tax-Free Insured Long-Term
N.J. Tax-Free Money Market
N.Y. Insured Tax-Free
Penn. Tax-Free Insured Long-Term
Penn. Tax-Free Money Market
Preferred Stock
Primecap
Quantitative Portfolios
Specialized Portfolios:
    Energy
    Gold & Precious Metals
    Health Care
    Service Economy
    Technology
STAR
Trustees' Commingled—Int'l. Equity
Trustees' Commingled—U.S. Equity
W.L. Morgan Growth
Wellesley Income
Wellington
Windsor
Windsor II
World Fund—International
World Fund—U.S.

Weiss, Peck & Greer Advisers
One New York Plaza
New York, NY 10004
(800) 223-3332/(212) 908-9582

Tudor
WPG Fund
WPG Dividend Income
WPG Government Securities
WPG Growth
WPG Short-Term Income
WPG Tax-Free Money Mkt.

Wood, Struthers & Winthrop
    Management Corp.
140 Broadway
New York, NY 10005
(800) 225-8011/(816) 283-1700

Neuwirth
Pine Street
Winthrop Fixed Income
Winthrop Growth

INDEX